SAXON MATH

Course 2

Stephen Hake

Solutions Manual

SAXON™

A Harcourt Achieve Imprint

www.SaxonPublishers.com

800-531-5015

Solutions Manual

Answers

Solutions

The *Saxon Math Course 2 Solutions Manual* contains answers and solutions that support daily instruction and cumulative assessment in the *Saxon Math Course 2* program.

Daily Power Up

Answers for Power Up facts, Mental Math, and Problem Solving are found in this manual, beginning on page 1. Answers for the optional Power Up facts begin on page 14.

Answers for Power Up facts, Mental Math, and Problem Solving are also located on the corresponding page of the *Saxon Math Course 2 Teacher's Manual.* In addition, the *Teacher's Manual* includes a step-by-step script with a complete solution for every daily Problem Solving exercise. The scripts are found on the interleaf "Power-Up Discussion" page that precedes each lesson.

Daily Lessons and Investigations

Complete solutions for the *Saxon Math Course 2* lessons—Practice Set, Written Practice, and Early Finishers—are located in this manual, beginning on page 90. Answers for these problems are also found on the corresponding *Teacher's Manual* pages and on the *Saxon Math Course 2 Answer Key CD.*

Answers and solutions for the Investigation exercises are located in the same resources—this manual, the *Teacher's Manual*, and the *Saxon Math Course 2 Answer Key CD.* Answers for those Lesson and Investigation Activity Masters that are utilized as worksheets are found in this manual, on page 41.

Course Assessments

Answers and solutions for the Baseline Test, Power-Up Tests, Cumulative Tests, Benchmark Tests, and the End-of-Course Exam are located in this manual. Complete solutions for the Performance Tasks and Performance Activities are also located in this volume, beginning on page 492. Answers for the Placement Test can be found on page 9 of the *Saxon Math Course 2 Course Assessments* book.

Reteaching

Answers for the *Saxon Math Course 2 Reteaching Masters* are located in this manual, beginning on page 42.

Answer Key CD

Answers to Power Up, Mental Math, and Problem Solving, Practice Sets, Written Practice, Early Finishers, and Investigation exercises are located on the *Saxon Math Course 2 Answer Key CD.* This resource provides pdf files of the pages in the *Saxon Math Course 2 Student Edition.* Answers are placed adjacent to each problem. These pages are identical to the reduced student pages located in the *Teacher's Manual.*

Adaptations for Saxon Math

If you are using *Adaptations for Saxon Math Course 2,* the answers for Targeted Practice, Fraction Activities, Facts Practice, and the Quick Tests are located in Volume 2 of the *Adaptations* binder.

Power Up A

Facts	Multiply.

9 × 8 72	8 × 2 16	10 × 10 100	6 × 3 18	4 × 2 8	5 × 5 25	9 × 9 81	6 × 4 24	9 × 6 54	7 × 3 21
9 × 3 27	6 × 5 30	0 × 0 0	7 × 6 42	8 × 8 64	7 × 4 28	5 × 3 15	9 × 7 63	2 × 2 4	8 × 6 48
7 × 7 49	6 × 2 12	4 × 3 12	8 × 5 40	4 × 4 16	3 × 2 6	n × 0 0	8 × 4 32	6 × 6 36	9 × 2 18
8 × 3 24	5 × 4 20	n × 1 n	7 × 2 14	9 × 5 45	8 × 7 56	3 × 3 9	9 × 4 36	5 × 2 10	7 × 5 35

Power Up B

Facts	Solve each equation.

$a + 12 = 20$ $a = 8$	$b - 8 = 10$ $b = 18$	$5c = 40$ $c = 8$	$\dfrac{d}{4} = 12$ $d = 48$	$11 + e = 24$ $e = 13$
$25 - f = 10$ $f = 15$	$10g = 60$ $g = 6$	$\dfrac{24}{h} = 6$ $h = 4$	$15 = j + 8$ $j = 7$	$20 = k - 5$ $k = 25$
$30 = 6m$ $m = 5$	$9 = \dfrac{n}{3}$ $n = 27$	$18 = 6 + p$ $p = 12$	$5 = 15 - q$ $q = 10$	$36 = 4r$ $r = 9$
$2 = \dfrac{16}{s}$ $s = 8$	$t + 8 = 12$ $t = 4$	$u - 15 = 30$ $u = 45$	$8v = 48$ $v = 6$	$\dfrac{w}{3} = 6$ $w = 18$

Power Up C

Facts	Write each improper fraction as a whole number or mixed number.			
$\frac{5}{2} = 2\frac{1}{2}$	$\frac{7}{4} = 1\frac{3}{4}$	$\frac{12}{5} = 2\frac{2}{5}$	$\frac{10}{3} = 3\frac{1}{3}$	$\frac{15}{2} = 7\frac{1}{2}$
$\frac{15}{5} = 3$	$\frac{11}{8} = 1\frac{3}{8}$	$2\frac{3}{2} = 3\frac{1}{2}$	$4\frac{5}{4} = 5\frac{1}{4}$	$3\frac{7}{4} = 4\frac{3}{4}$

Write each mixed number as an improper fraction.

$1\frac{1}{2} = \frac{3}{2}$	$2\frac{2}{3} = \frac{8}{3}$	$3\frac{3}{4} = \frac{15}{4}$	$2\frac{1}{2} = \frac{5}{2}$	$6\frac{2}{3} = \frac{20}{3}$
$2\frac{3}{4} = \frac{11}{4}$	$3\frac{1}{3} = \frac{10}{3}$	$4\frac{1}{2} = \frac{9}{2}$	$1\frac{7}{8} = \frac{15}{8}$	$12\frac{1}{2} = \frac{25}{2}$

Power Up D

Facts	Reduce each fraction to lowest terms.			
$\frac{50}{100} = \frac{1}{2}$	$\frac{4}{16} = \frac{1}{4}$	$\frac{6}{8} = \frac{3}{4}$	$\frac{8}{12} = \frac{2}{3}$	$\frac{10}{100} = \frac{1}{10}$
$\frac{8}{16} = \frac{1}{2}$	$\frac{20}{100} = \frac{1}{5}$	$\frac{3}{12} = \frac{1}{4}$	$\frac{60}{100} = \frac{3}{5}$	$\frac{9}{12} = \frac{3}{4}$
$\frac{6}{9} = \frac{2}{3}$	$\frac{90}{100} = \frac{9}{10}$	$\frac{5}{10} = \frac{1}{2}$	$\frac{12}{16} = \frac{3}{4}$	$\frac{25}{100} = \frac{1}{4}$
$\frac{4}{10} = \frac{2}{5}$	$\frac{4}{6} = \frac{2}{3}$	$\frac{75}{100} = \frac{3}{4}$	$\frac{4}{12} = \frac{1}{3}$	$\frac{6}{10} = \frac{3}{5}$

Power Up E

Facts   Write the word or words to complete each definition.

The distance around a circle is its	Every point on a circle is the same distance from its	The distance across a circle through its center is its	The distance from a circle to its center is its
circumference	center	diameter	radius
Two or more circles with the same center are	A segment between two points on a circle is a	Part of a circumference is an	Part of a circle bounded by an arc and two radii is a
concentric circles	chord	arc	sector
Half a circle is a	An angle whose vertex is the center of a circle is a	An angle whose vertex is on the circle whose sides include chords is an	A polygon whose vertices are on the circle and whose edges are within the circle is an
semicircle	central angle	inscribed angle	inscribed polygon

Power Up F

Facts   Name each figure illustrated.

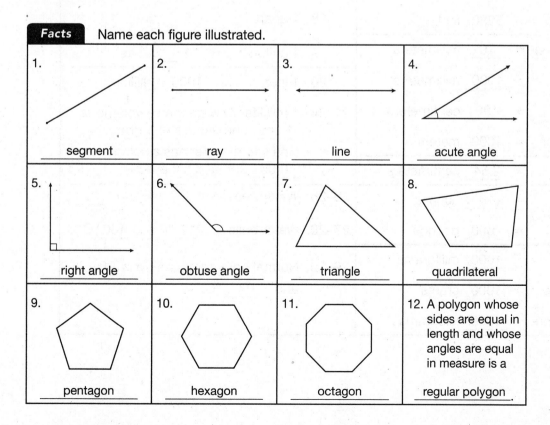

1. segment	2. ray	3. line	4. acute angle
5. right angle	6. obtuse angle	7. triangle	8. quadrilateral
9. pentagon	10. hexagon	11. octagon	12. A polygon whose sides are equal in length and whose angles are equal in measure is a regular polygon

Power Up G

Facts Simplify.			
$\frac{2}{3} + \frac{2}{3} = 1\frac{1}{3}$	$\frac{2}{3} - \frac{1}{3} = \frac{1}{3}$	$\frac{2}{3} \times \frac{2}{3} = \frac{4}{9}$	$\frac{2}{3} \div \frac{2}{3} = 1$
$\frac{3}{4} + \frac{1}{4} = 1$	$\frac{3}{4} - \frac{1}{4} = \frac{1}{2}$	$\frac{3}{4} \times \frac{1}{4} = \frac{3}{16}$	$\frac{3}{4} \div \frac{1}{4} = 3$
$\frac{2}{3} + \frac{1}{2} = 1\frac{1}{6}$	$\frac{2}{3} - \frac{1}{2} = \frac{1}{6}$	$\frac{2}{3} \times \frac{1}{2} = \frac{1}{3}$	$\frac{2}{3} \div \frac{1}{2} = 1\frac{1}{3}$
$\frac{3}{4} + \frac{2}{3} = 1\frac{5}{12}$	$\frac{3}{4} - \frac{2}{3} = \frac{1}{12}$	$\frac{3}{4} \times \frac{2}{3} = \frac{1}{2}$	$\frac{3}{4} \div \frac{2}{3} = 1\frac{1}{8}$

Power Up H

Facts Write the number that completes each equivalent measure.

1. 1 foot = __12__ inches		15. 1 kilogram ≈ __2.2__ pounds	
2. 1 yard = __36__ inches		16. 1 pint = __16__ ounces	
3. 1 yard = __3__ feet		17. 1 pint = __2__ cups	
4. 1 mile = __5280__ feet		18. 1 quart = __2__ pints	
5. 1 centimeter = __10__ millimeters		19. 1 gallon = __4__ quarts	
6. 1 meter = __1000__ millimeters		20. 1 liter = __1000__ milliliters	
7. 1 meter = __100__ centimeters		21–24. 1 milliliter of water has a volume of __1 cm³__ and a mass of __1 gram__.	
8. 1 kilometer = __1000__ meters		One liter of water has a volume of __1000__ cm³ and a mass of __1__ kg.	
9. 1 inch = __2.54__ centimeters			
10. 1 pound = __16__ ounces		25–26. Water freezes at __32__ °F and __0__ °C.	
11. 1 ton = __2000__ pounds		27–28. Water boils at __212__ °F and __100__ °C.	
12. 1 gram = __1000__ milligrams		29–30. Normal body temperature is __98.6__ °F and __37__ °C.	
13. 1 kilogram = __1000__ grams			
14. 1 metric ton = __1000__ kilograms			

4

Power Up I

| Facts | Find the number that completes each proportion. |

$\frac{3}{4} = \frac{a}{12}$	$\frac{3}{4} = \frac{12}{b}$	$\frac{c}{5} = \frac{12}{20}$	$\frac{2}{d} = \frac{12}{24}$	$\frac{8}{12} = \frac{4}{e}$
$a = 9$	$b = 16$	$c = 3$	$d = 4$	$e = 6$
$\frac{f}{10} = \frac{10}{5}$	$\frac{5}{g} = \frac{25}{100}$	$\frac{10}{100} = \frac{5}{h}$	$\frac{8}{4} = \frac{j}{16}$	$\frac{24}{k} = \frac{8}{6}$
$f = 20$	$g = 20$	$h = 50$	$j = 32$	$k = 18$
$\frac{9}{12} = \frac{36}{m}$	$\frac{50}{100} = \frac{w}{30}$	$\frac{3}{9} = \frac{5}{p}$	$\frac{q}{60} = \frac{15}{20}$	$\frac{2}{5} = \frac{r}{100}$
$m = 48$	$w = 15$	$p = 15$	$q = 45$	$r = 40$

Power Up J

| Facts | Simplify. |

$0.8 + 0.4 = 1.2$	$0.8 - 0.4 = 0.4$	$0.8 \times 0.4 = 0.32$	$0.8 \div 0.4 = 2$
$1.2 + 0.4 = 1.6$	$1.2 - 0.4 = 0.8$	$1.2 \times 0.4 = 0.48$	$1.2 \div 0.4 = 3$
$6 + 0.3 = 6.3$	$6 - 0.3 = 5.7$	$6 \times 0.3 = 1.8$	$6 \div 0.3 = 20$
$1.2 + 4 = 5.2$	$0.01 - 0.01 = 0$	$0.3 \times 0.3 = 0.09$	$0.12 \div 4 = 0.03$

Power Up K

| Facts | Simplify each power or root. |

$\sqrt{100} = 10$	$\sqrt{16} = 4$	$\sqrt{81} = 9$	$\sqrt{4} = 2$	$\sqrt{144} = 12$
$\sqrt{64} = 8$	$\sqrt{49} = 7$	$\sqrt{25} = 5$	$\sqrt{9} = 3$	$\sqrt{36} = 6$
$8^2 = 64$	$5^2 = 25$	$3^2 = 9$	$12^2 = 144$	$10^2 = 100$
$7^2 = 49$	$2^3 = 8$	$3^3 = 27$	$10^3 = 1000$	$5^3 = 125$

Power Up L

| Facts | Write the equivalent decimal and percent for each fraction. |

Fraction	Decimal	Percent	Fraction	Decimal	Percent
$\frac{1}{2}$	0.5	50%	$\frac{1}{8}$	0.125	$12\frac{1}{2}\%$
$\frac{1}{3}$	$0.\overline{3}$	$33\frac{1}{3}\%$	$\frac{1}{10}$	0.1	10%
$\frac{2}{3}$	$0.\overline{6}$	$66\frac{2}{3}\%$	$\frac{3}{10}$	0.3	30%
$\frac{1}{4}$	0.25	25%	$\frac{9}{10}$	0.9	90%
$\frac{3}{4}$	0.75	75%	$\frac{1}{100}$	0.01	1%
$\frac{1}{5}$	0.2	20%	$1\frac{1}{2}$	1.5	150%

    6

Power Up M

Facts	Write the number for each conversion or factor.

1. 2 m = __200__ cm

2. 1.5 km = __1500__ m

3. 2.54 cm = __25.4__ mm

4. 125 cm = __1.25__ m

5. 10 km = __10,000__ m

6. 5000 m = __5__ km

7. 50 cm = __0.5__ m

8. 50 cm = __500__ mm

9. 2 L = __2000__ mL

10. 250 mL = __0.25__ L

11. 4 kg = __4000__ g

12. 2.5 g = __2500__ mg

13. 500 mg = __0.5__ g

14. 0.5 kg = __500__ g

15–16. Two liters of water have a volume of __2000__ cm³ and a mass of __2__ kg.

	Prefix	Factor
17.	kilo-	1000
18.	hecto-	100
19.	deka-	10
	(unit)	1
20.	deci-	0.1
21.	centi-	0.01
22.	milli-	0.001

Power Up N

Facts	Simplify. Reduce the answers if possible.

$3 + 1\frac{2}{3} = 4\frac{2}{3}$	$3 - 1\frac{2}{3} = 1\frac{1}{3}$	$3 \times 1\frac{2}{3} = 5$	$3 \div 1\frac{2}{3} = 1\frac{4}{5}$
$1\frac{2}{3} + 1\frac{1}{2} = 3\frac{1}{6}$	$1\frac{2}{3} - 1\frac{1}{2} = \frac{1}{6}$	$1\frac{2}{3} \times 1\frac{1}{2} = 2\frac{1}{2}$	$1\frac{2}{3} \div 1\frac{1}{2} = 1\frac{1}{9}$
$2\frac{1}{2} + 1\frac{2}{3} = 4\frac{1}{6}$	$2\frac{1}{2} - 1\frac{2}{3} = \frac{5}{6}$	$2\frac{1}{2} \times 1\frac{2}{3} = 4\frac{1}{6}$	$2\frac{1}{2} \div 1\frac{2}{3} = 1\frac{1}{2}$
$4\frac{1}{2} + 2\frac{1}{4} = 6\frac{3}{4}$	$4\frac{1}{2} - 2\frac{1}{4} = 2\frac{1}{4}$	$4\frac{1}{2} \times 2\frac{1}{4} = 10\frac{1}{8}$	$4\frac{1}{2} \div 2\frac{1}{4} = 2$

Power Up O

| **Facts** | Select from the words below to describe each figure. |

1.	2.	3.	4.
equilateral triangle			parallelogram
acute triangle	isosceles triangle	scalene triangle	rectangle
isosceles triangle	right triangle	obtuse triangle	rhombus
			square
5.	6.	7.	8.
parallelogram		parallelogram	
rectangle	trapezoid	rhombus	parallelogram

kite	rectangle	isosceles triangle	right triangle
trapezoid	rhombus	scalene triangle	acute triangle
parallelogram	square	equilateral triangle	obtuse triangle

Power Up P

Facts	Simplify.		
$(-8) + (-2) = -10$	$(-8) - (-2) = -6$	$(-8)(-2) = 16$	$\dfrac{-8}{-2} = 4$
$(-9) + (+3) = -6$	$(-9) - (+3) = -12$	$(-9)(+3) = -27$	$\dfrac{-9}{+3} = -3$
$12 + (-2) = 10$	$12 - (-2) = 14$	$(12)(-2) = -24$	$\dfrac{12}{-2} = -6$
$(-4) + (-3) + (-2) = -9$	$(-4) - (-3) - (-2) = 1$	$(-4)(-3)(-2) = -24$	$\dfrac{(-4)(-3)}{(-2)} = -6$

Saxon Math Course 2 **8**

Power Up Q

Facts	Write the equivalent decimal and fraction for each percent.

Percent	Decimal	Fraction	Percent	Decimal	Fraction
10%	0.1	$\frac{1}{10}$	$33\frac{1}{3}$%	$0.\overline{3}$	$\frac{1}{3}$
90%	0.9	$\frac{9}{10}$	20%	0.2	$\frac{1}{5}$
5%	0.05	$\frac{1}{20}$	75%	0.75	$\frac{3}{4}$
$12\frac{1}{2}$%	0.125	$\frac{1}{8}$	$66\frac{2}{3}$%	$0.\overline{6}$	$\frac{2}{3}$
50%	0.5	$\frac{1}{2}$	1%	0.01	$\frac{1}{100}$
25%	0.25	$\frac{1}{4}$	250%	2.5	$2\frac{1}{2}$

Power Up R

Facts	Find the area of each figure. Angles that look like right angles are right angles.

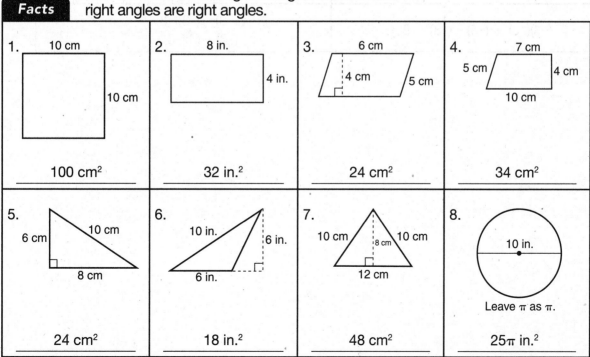

1. 10 cm, 10 cm — 100 cm²
2. 8 in., 4 in. — 32 in.²
3. 6 cm, 4 cm, 5 cm — 24 cm²
4. 7 cm, 5 cm, 4 cm, 10 cm — 34 cm²
5. 6 cm, 10 cm, 8 cm — 24 cm²
6. 10 in., 6 in., 6 in. — 18 in.²
7. 10 cm, 10 cm, 8 cm, 12 cm — 48 cm²
8. 10 in. Leave π as π. — 25π in.²

Answers

Power Up S

Facts	Write each number in scientific notation.	
$186{,}000 = 1.86 \times 10^5$	$0.0005 = 5 \times 10^{-4}$	$30{,}500{,}000 = 3.05 \times 10^7$
2.5 billion $= 2.5 \times 10^9$	12 million $= 1.2 \times 10^7$	$\dfrac{1}{1{,}000{,}000} = 1 \times 10^{-6}$

Write each number in standard form.

$1 \times 10^6 = 1{,}000{,}000$	$1 \times 10^{-6} = 0.000001$	$2.4 \times 10^4 = 24{,}000$
$5 \times 10^{-4} = 0.0005$	$4.75 \times 10^5 = 475{,}000$	$2.5 \times 10^{-3} = 0.0025$

Power Up T

Facts	Simplify.
$6 + 6 \times 6 - 6 \div 6 = 41$	$3^2 + \sqrt{4} + 5(6) - 7 + 8 = 42$
$4 + 2(3 + 5) - 6 \div 2 = 17$	$2 + 2[3 + 4(7 - 5)] = 24$
$\sqrt{1^3 + 2^3 + 3^3} = 6$	$\dfrac{4 + 3(7 - 5)}{6 - (5 - 4)} = 2$
$(-3)(-3) + (-3) - (-3) = 9$	$\dfrac{3(-3) - (-3)(-3)}{(-3) - (3)(-3)} = -3$

Saxon Math Course 2   **10**

Power Up U

Facts	Complete each step to solve each equation.		
$2x + 5 = 45$	$3y + 4 = 22$	$5n - 3 = 12$	$3m - 7 = 14$
$2x = 40$	$3y = 18$	$5n = 15$	$3m = 21$
$x = 20$	$y = 6$	$n = 3$	$m = 7$
$15 = 3a - 6$	$24 = 2w + 6$	$-2x + 9 = 23$	$20 - 3y = 2$
$21 = 3a$	$18 = 2w$	$-2x = 14$	$-3y = -18$
$7 = a$	$9 = w$	$x = -7$	$y = 6$
$\frac{1}{2}m + 6 = 18$	$\frac{3}{4}n - 12 = 12$	$3y + 1.5 = 6$	$0.5w - 1.5 = 4.5$
$\frac{1}{2}m = 12$	$\frac{3}{4}n = 24$	$3y = 4.5$	$0.5w = 6$
$m = 24$	$n = 32$	$y = 1.5$	$w = 12$

Power Up V

Facts	Solve each equation.		
$6x + 2x = 8x$	$6x - 2x = 4x$	$(6x)(2x) = 12x^2$	$\frac{6x}{2x} = 3$
$9xy + 3xy = 12xy$	$9xy - 3xy = 6xy$	$(9xy)(3xy) = 27x^2y^2$	$\frac{9xy}{3xy} = 3$
$x + y + x = 2x + y$	$x + y - x = y$	$(x)(y)(-x) = -x^2y$	$\frac{xy}{x} = y$
$3x + x + 3 = 4x + 3$	$3x - x - 3 = 2x - 3$	$(3x)(-x)(-3) = 9x^2$	$\frac{(2x)(8xy)}{4y} = 4x^2$

11

Power Up W

Facts   Simplify. Write each answer in scientific notation.

$(1 \times 10^6)(1 \times 10^6) =$ 1×10^{12}	$(3 \times 10^3)(3 \times 10^3) =$ 9×10^6	$(4 \times 10^{-5})(2 \times 10^{-6}) =$ 8×10^{-11}
$(5 \times 10^5)(5 \times 10^5) =$ 2.5×10^{11}	$(6 \times 10^{-3})(7 \times 10^{-4}) =$ 4.2×10^{-6}	$(3 \times 10^6)(2 \times 10^{-4}) =$ 6×10^2
$\dfrac{8 \times 10^8}{2 \times 10^2} = 4 \times 10^6$	$\dfrac{5 \times 10^6}{2 \times 10^3} = 2.5 \times 10^3$	$\dfrac{9 \times 10^3}{3 \times 10^8} = 3 \times 10^{-5}$
$\dfrac{2 \times 10^6}{4 \times 10^2} = 5 \times 10^3$	$\dfrac{1 \times 10^{-3}}{4 \times 10^8} = 2.5 \times 10^{-12}$	$\dfrac{8 \times 10^{-8}}{2 \times 10^{-2}} = 4 \times 10^{-6}$

Add.

3 +2 = 5	8 +3 = 11	2 +1 = 3	5 +6 = 11	2 +9 = 11	4 +8 = 12	8 +0 = 8	3 +9 = 12	1 +0 = 1	6 +3 = 9
7 +3 = 10	1 +6 = 7	4 +7 = 11	0 +3 = 3	6 +4 = 10	5 +5 = 10	3 +1 = 4	7 +2 = 9	8 +5 = 13	2 +5 = 7
4 +0 = 4	5 +7 = 12	1 +1 = 2	5 +4 = 9	2 +8 = 10	7 +1 = 8	4 +6 = 10	0 +2 = 2	6 +5 = 11	4 +9 = 13
8 +6 = 14	0 +4 = 4	5 +8 = 13	7 +4 = 11	1 +7 = 8	6 +6 = 12	4 +1 = 5	8 +2 = 10	2 +4 = 6	6 +0 = 6
9 +1 = 10	8 +8 = 16	2 +2 = 4	4 +5 = 9	6 +2 = 8	0 +0 = 0	5 +9 = 14	3 +3 = 6	8 +1 = 9	2 +7 = 9
4 +4 = 8	7 +5 = 12	0 +1 = 1	8 +7 = 15	3 +4 = 7	7 +9 = 16	1 +2 = 3	6 +7 = 13	0 +8 = 8	9 +2 = 11
0 +9 = 9	8 +9 = 17	7 +6 = 13	1 +3 = 4	6 +8 = 14	2 +0 = 2	8 +4 = 12	3 +5 = 8	9 +8 = 17	5 +0 = 5
9 +3 = 12	2 +6 = 8	3 +0 = 3	6 +1 = 7	3 +6 = 9	5 +2 = 7	0 +5 = 5	6 +9 = 15	1 +8 = 9	9 +6 = 15
4 +3 = 7	9 +9 = 18	0 +7 = 7	9 +4 = 13	7 +7 = 14	1 +4 = 5	3 +7 = 10	7 +0 = 7	2 +3 = 5	5 +1 = 6
9 +5 = 14	1 +5 = 6	9 +0 = 9	3 +8 = 11	1 +9 = 10	5 +3 = 8	4 +2 = 6	9 +7 = 16	0 +6 = 6	7 +8 = 15

Subtract.

$16 - 9 = 7$	$7 - 1 = 6$	$18 - 9 = 9$	$11 - 3 = 8$	$13 - 7 = 6$	$8 - 2 = 6$	$11 - 5 = 6$	$5 - 0 = 5$	$17 - 9 = 8$	$6 - 1 = 5$
$10 - 9 = 1$	$6 - 2 = 4$	$13 - 9 = 4$	$4 - 0 = 4$	$10 - 5 = 5$	$5 - 1 = 4$	$10 - 3 = 7$	$12 - 6 = 6$	$10 - 1 = 9$	$6 - 4 = 2$
$7 - 2 = 5$	$14 - 7 = 7$	$8 - 1 = 7$	$11 - 6 = 5$	$3 - 3 = 0$	$16 - 7 = 9$	$5 - 2 = 3$	$12 - 4 = 8$	$3 - 0 = 3$	$11 - 7 = 4$
$17 - 8 = 9$	$6 - 0 = 6$	$10 - 6 = 4$	$4 - 1 = 3$	$9 - 5 = 4$	$9 - 0 = 9$	$5 - 4 = 1$	$12 - 5 = 7$	$4 - 2 = 2$	$9 - 3 = 6$
$12 - 3 = 9$	$16 - 8 = 8$	$9 - 1 = 8$	$15 - 6 = 9$	$11 - 4 = 7$	$13 - 5 = 8$	$1 - 0 = 1$	$8 - 5 = 3$	$9 - 6 = 3$	$11 - 2 = 9$
$7 - 0 = 7$	$10 - 8 = 2$	$6 - 3 = 3$	$14 - 5 = 9$	$3 - 1 = 2$	$8 - 6 = 2$	$4 - 4 = 0$	$11 - 8 = 3$	$3 - 2 = 1$	$15 - 9 = 6$
$13 - 8 = 5$	$7 - 4 = 3$	$10 - 7 = 3$	$0 - 0 = 0$	$12 - 8 = 4$	$5 - 5 = 0$	$4 - 3 = 1$	$8 - 7 = 1$	$7 - 3 = 4$	$7 - 6 = 1$
$5 - 3 = 2$	$7 - 5 = 2$	$2 - 1 = 1$	$6 - 6 = 0$	$8 - 4 = 4$	$2 - 2 = 0$	$13 - 6 = 7$	$15 - 8 = 7$	$2 - 0 = 2$	$13 - 9 = 4$
$1 - 1 = 0$	$11 - 9 = 2$	$10 - 4 = 6$	$9 - 2 = 7$	$14 - 6 = 8$	$8 - 0 = 8$	$9 - 4 = 5$	$10 - 2 = 8$	$6 - 5 = 1$	$8 - 3 = 5$
$7 - 7 = 0$	$14 - 8 = 6$	$12 - 9 = 3$	$9 - 8 = 1$	$12 - 7 = 5$	$9 - 9 = 0$	$15 - 7 = 8$	$8 - 8 = 0$	$14 - 9 = 5$	$9 - 7 = 2$

Multiply.

9 × 9 **81**	3 × 5 **15**	8 × 5 **40**	2 × 6 **12**	4 × 7 **28**	0 × 3 **0**	7 × 2 **14**	1 × 5 **5**	7 × 8 **56**	4 × 0 **0**
3 × 4 **12**	5 × 9 **45**	0 × 2 **0**	7 × 3 **21**	4 × 1 **4**	2 × 7 **14**	6 × 3 **18**	5 × 4 **20**	1 × 0 **0**	9 × 2 **18**
1 × 1 **1**	9 × 0 **0**	2 × 8 **16**	6 × 4 **24**	0 × 7 **0**	8 × 1 **8**	3 × 3 **9**	4 × 8 **32**	9 × 3 **27**	2 × 0 **0**
4 × 9 **36**	7 × 0 **0**	1 × 2 **2**	8 × 4 **32**	6 × 5 **30**	2 × 9 **18**	9 × 4 **36**	0 × 1 **0**	7 × 4 **28**	5 × 8 **40**
0 × 8 **0**	4 × 2 **8**	9 × 8 **72**	3 × 6 **18**	5 × 5 **25**	1 × 6 **6**	5 × 0 **0**	6 × 6 **36**	2 × 1 **2**	7 × 9 **63**
9 × 1 **9**	2 × 2 **4**	5 × 1 **5**	4 × 3 **12**	0 × 0 **0**	8 × 9 **72**	3 × 7 **21**	9 × 7 **63**	1 × 7 **7**	6 × 0 **0**
5 × 6 **30**	7 × 5 **35**	3 × 0 **0**	8 × 8 **64**	1 × 3 **3**	8 × 3 **24**	5 × 2 **10**	0 × 4 **0**	9 × 5 **45**	6 × 7 **42**
2 × 3 **6**	8 × 6 **48**	0 × 5 **0**	6 × 1 **6**	3 × 8 **24**	7 × 6 **42**	1 × 8 **8**	9 × 6 **54**	4 × 4 **16**	5 × 3 **15**
7 × 7 **49**	1 × 4 **4**	6 × 2 **12**	4 × 5 **20**	2 × 4 **8**	8 × 0 **0**	3 × 1 **3**	6 × 8 **48**	0 × 9 **0**	8 × 7 **56**
3 × 2 **6**	4 × 6 **24**	1 × 9 **9**	5 × 7 **35**	8 × 2 **16**	0 × 6 **0**	7 × 1 **7**	2 × 5 **10**	6 × 9 **54**	3 × 9 **27**

Divide.

$\dfrac{3}{7)21}$	$\dfrac{5}{2)10}$	$\dfrac{7}{6)42}$	$\dfrac{3}{1)3}$	$\dfrac{6}{4)24}$	$\dfrac{2}{3)6}$	$\dfrac{6}{9)54}$	$\dfrac{3}{6)18}$	$\dfrac{0}{4)0}$	$\dfrac{6}{5)30}$
$\dfrac{8}{4)32}$	$\dfrac{7}{8)56}$	$\dfrac{0}{1)0}$	$\dfrac{2}{6)12}$	$\dfrac{6}{3)18}$	$\dfrac{8}{9)72}$	$\dfrac{3}{5)15}$	$\dfrac{4}{2)8}$	$\dfrac{6}{7)42}$	$\dfrac{6}{6)36}$
$\dfrac{0}{6)0}$	$\dfrac{2}{5)10}$	$\dfrac{1}{9)9}$	$\dfrac{3}{2)6}$	$\dfrac{9}{7)63}$	$\dfrac{4}{4)16}$	$\dfrac{6}{8)48}$	$\dfrac{2}{1)2}$	$\dfrac{7}{5)35}$	$\dfrac{7}{3)21}$
$\dfrac{9}{2)18}$	$\dfrac{1}{6)6}$	$\dfrac{5}{3)15}$	$\dfrac{5}{8)40}$	$\dfrac{0}{2)0}$	$\dfrac{4}{5)20}$	$\dfrac{3}{9)27}$	$\dfrac{8}{1)8}$	$\dfrac{1}{4)4}$	$\dfrac{5}{7)35}$
$\dfrac{5}{4)20}$	$\dfrac{7}{9)63}$	$\dfrac{4}{1)4}$	$\dfrac{2}{7)14}$	$\dfrac{1}{3)3}$	$\dfrac{3}{8)24}$	$\dfrac{0}{5)0}$	$\dfrac{4}{6)24}$	$\dfrac{1}{8)8}$	$\dfrac{8}{2)16}$
$\dfrac{1}{5)5}$	$\dfrac{8}{8)64}$	$\dfrac{0}{3)0}$	$\dfrac{7}{4)28}$	$\dfrac{7}{7)49}$	$\dfrac{2}{2)4}$	$\dfrac{9}{9)81}$	$\dfrac{4}{3)12}$	$\dfrac{5}{6)30}$	$\dfrac{5}{1)5}$
$\dfrac{4}{8)32}$	$\dfrac{1}{1)1}$	$\dfrac{4}{9)36}$	$\dfrac{9}{3)27}$	$\dfrac{7}{2)14}$	$\dfrac{5}{5)25}$	$\dfrac{8}{6)48}$	$\dfrac{0}{8)0}$	$\dfrac{4}{7)28}$	$\dfrac{9}{4)36}$
$\dfrac{6}{2)12}$	$\dfrac{9}{5)45}$	$\dfrac{7}{1)7}$	$\dfrac{2}{4)8}$	$\dfrac{0}{7)0}$	$\dfrac{2}{8)16}$	$\dfrac{8}{3)24}$	$\dfrac{5}{9)45}$	$\dfrac{9}{1)9}$	$\dfrac{9}{6)54}$
$\dfrac{8}{7)56}$	$\dfrac{0}{9)0}$	$\dfrac{9}{8)72}$	$\dfrac{1}{2)2}$	$\dfrac{8}{5)40}$	$\dfrac{3}{3)9}$	$\dfrac{2}{9)18}$	$\dfrac{6}{1)6}$	$\dfrac{3}{4)12}$	$\dfrac{1}{7)7}$

Mental Math

Lesson 1

a. 60

b. 80

c. 87

d. 6

e. 24

f. 48

g. 1 out of 6, $\frac{1}{6}$

h. 5

Lesson 2

a. 48

b. 18

c. 50

d. 900

e. 6000

f. 600

g. $\frac{1}{2}$

h. 0

Lesson 3

a. 66

b. 30

c. 500

d. 1500

e. 250

f. 900

g. $\frac{1}{2}$

h. 7

Lesson 4

a. 100

b. 120

c. 250

d. 750

e. 2500

f. 40

g. 8 quarts

h. 100

Lesson 5

a. 10

b. 144

c. 1000

d. 275

e. 500

f. 500

g. 2 feet

h. 15

Lesson 6

a. $7.50

b. $15.00

c. $0.55

d. 485

e. 625

f. 75

g. 0

h. 4

17

Answers

Lesson 7

a. −5

b. $25.00

c. 65¢

d. 365

e. 265

f. 48

g. $\frac{1}{3}$

h. 6

Lesson 8

a. −6

b. $2.50

c. 35¢

d. 375

e. 317

f. 2000

g. 120 minutes

h. 11

Lesson 9

a. −2

b. $3.90

c. 71¢

d. 542

e. 540

f. 10

g. 3 quarts

h. 15

Lesson 10

a. −3

b. $12.50

c. 18¢

d. 494

e. 449

f. 10

g. 15 feet

h. 7

Lesson 11

a. $8.25

b. $4.00

c. $4.50

d. 75

e. −750

f. 14

g. 32 ounces

h. 7

Lesson 12

a. $7.10

b. $12.90

c. $7.50

d. 92

e. −1500

f. 32

g. 8 outfits

h. 22

Lesson 13

a. $7.20

b. $2.50

c. $3.25

d. 165

e. −250

f. 43

g. 10 pizzas

h. 9

Lesson 14

a. $6.75

b. $6.30

c. $1.75

d. 144

e. 125

f. 18

g. 6

h. 3

Lesson 15

a. $5.25

b. $0.40

c. $5.02

d. 224

e. 75

f. 26

g. 2 gallons

h. 5

Lesson 16

a. −10

b. $1.50

c. 82¢

d. 92

e. 125

f. $\frac{1}{6}$

g. 6

h. 2

Lesson 17

a. $5.00

b. $0.36

c. $3.60

d. 165

e. 125

f. 16

g. 12

h. 5

Lesson 18

a. $5.50

b. $16.50

c. $7.50

d. 144

e. 125

f. $\frac{1}{8}$

g. 72

h. 7

Answers

Lesson 19

a. $10.00

b. $1.20

c. 24¢

d. 224

e. 375

f. 60

g. 1 yard

h. 12

Lesson 20

a. $7.25

b. $3.60

c. $0.68

d. 215

e. 500

f. $\frac{3}{8}$

g. 42

h. 1

Lesson 21

a. $2.24

b. $0.65

c. $4.25

d. 204

e. 4

f. 12

g. 3 pints

h. 1

Lesson 22

a. $2.53

b. $8.00

c. $2.11

d. 371

e. 5

f. 6

g. a gallon

h. octagon

Lesson 23

a. $4.63

b. $0.25

c. −51

d. 496

e. 4

f. 38

g. $\frac{1}{60}$

h. 5

Lesson 24

a. $6.72

b. $15.00

c. 64¢

d. 260

e. 5

f. 8

g. $\frac{1}{4}$

h. 15

Lesson 25

  a. $4.64

  b. $6.00

  c. $0.76

  d. 252

  e. 6

  f. 9

  g. $\frac{1}{2}$

  h. 7

Lesson 26

  a. $9.54

  b. $30.00

  c. 93¢

  d. 222

  e. $1\frac{1}{3}$

  f. 16

  g. 25

  h. 0

Lesson 27

  a. $5.73

  b. $12.50

  c. 420

  d. 210

  e. $1\frac{1}{2}$

  f. 18

  g. 27

  h. 0

Lesson 28

  a. $9.22

  b. $175.00

  c. $3.71

  d. 424

  e. $1\frac{1}{4}$

  f. 10

  g. 100

  h. $4.00

Lesson 29

  a. $7.30

  b. $1.25

  c. $1.02

  d. 198

  e. $1\frac{2}{3}$

  f. 12

  g. 16

  h. 10

Lesson 30

  a. $3.98

  b. $150.00

  c. 9

  d. 420

  e. $4\frac{1}{3}$

  f. 15

  g. 60

  h. 6

Answers

Lesson 31

a. $3.01

b. $2.45

c. 8

d. $\frac{3}{4}$

e. 19

f. 45

g. 150

h. 3

Lesson 32

a. $2.77

b. $2.00

c. 20

d. $\frac{3}{5}$

e. 25

f. 12

g. 180

h. 2

Lesson 33

a. $1.85

b. $3.30

c. 9

d. $\frac{4}{5}$

e. 20

f. 25

g. 60

h. 12

Lesson 34

a. $5.50

b. $2.40

c. 18

d. $\frac{2}{3}$

e. 42

f. 24

g. 80

h. 3

Lesson 35

a. $5.51

b. $3.20

c. 27

d. $\frac{5}{8}$

e. 14

f. 10

g. 510

h. decade

Lesson 36

a. $14.50

b. $6.00

c. 16

d. $\frac{4}{5}$

e. 3

f. 36

g. 100

h. 9

Lesson 37

a. $4.65

b. $6.25

c. 21

d. $\frac{3}{5}$

e. 2

f. 18

g. 7

h. 30

Lesson 38

a. $6.44

b. $7.50

c. 25

d. $\frac{1}{2}$

e. 60

f. 35

g. 6

h. 6

Lesson 39

a. $2.45

b. $7.20

c. 35

d. $\frac{3}{4}$

e. 16

f. 32

g. Find the difference of the least and the greatest numbers in the list.

h. 0

Lesson 40

a. $18.00

b. $5.00

c. 18

d. $\frac{3}{8}$

e. 23

f. 40

g. Arrange the numbers from least to greatest and find the number that is in the middle of the list.

h. $4.30

Lesson 41

a. 700

b. 15.4

c. 25

d. 9

e. 1200

f. 21

g. Arrange the numbers in order from least to greatest and find the number that appears most in the list.

h. $1\frac{1}{6}, \frac{1}{6}, \frac{1}{3}, 1\frac{1}{3}$

Lesson 42

a. $2.34

b. 40

c. 5

d. 2

e. 6

f. 28

g. Add the numbers in the list and divide the sum by how many numbers that were added.

h. 25

Saxon Math Course 2

23

Answers

Lesson 43

a. $2.88

b. 0.035

c. 7

d. 39

e. $60.00

f. 60

g. 76

h. $\frac{11}{12}, \frac{5}{12}, \frac{1}{6}, 2\frac{2}{3}$

Lesson 44

a. $3.20

b. 0.05

c. 6

d. 60

e. 1

f. 150

g. 50

h. 6

Lesson 45

a. $10.50

b. 125

c. 15

d. 100

e. 12

f. 50

g. 500

h. $1\frac{5}{12}, \frac{1}{12}, \frac{1}{2}, 1\frac{1}{8}$

Lesson 46

a. $7.38

b. 0.036

c. 10

d. 10

e. 12

f. 72

g. 78

h. 24

Lesson 47

a. $41.00

b. 15

c. 6

d. $100.00

e. 32

f. 50

g. 321

h. $\frac{9}{10}, \frac{1}{10}, \frac{1}{5}, 1\frac{1}{4}$

Lesson 48

a. $245.00

b. 1.275

c. 6

d. 4

e. 24

f. 30

g. 70

h. 1

Lesson 49

a. $52.00

b. 257.5

c. 10

d. 6

e. 20

f. 60

g. 67

h. $\frac{14}{15}, \frac{4}{15}, \frac{1}{5}, 1\frac{4}{5}$

Lesson 50

a. $240

b. 1.25

c. 8

d. 15

e. 10

f. 16

g. 46

h. −5

Lesson 51

a. $14.00

b. 450

c. 12

d. 5000 m

e. 200

f. 25

g. 675

h. $1\frac{3}{8}, \frac{3}{8}, \frac{7}{16}, 1\frac{3}{4}$

Lesson 52

a. $4.50

b. 0.045

c. 18

d. 2.5 m

e. 600

f. 180

g. 24

h. 200 km

Lesson 53

a. $10.00

b. 127.5

c. 35

d. 350 mm

e. $\frac{1}{4}$

f. 27

g. 16

h. 121

Lesson 54

a. $18.00

b. 1.275

c. 8

d. 150 cm

e. 3

f. 27

g. 120

h. $1\frac{3}{20}, \frac{7}{20}, \frac{3}{10}, 1\frac{7}{8}$

Answers

Lesson 55

a. $5.00

b. 37.5

c. 40

d. 3 km

e. $\frac{4}{9}$

f. 75

g. $\frac{1}{4}$

h. 75 pages

Lesson 56

a. 75

b. 0.025

c. 12

d. 50 cm

e. 400

f. $35.00

g. $\frac{1}{4}$

h. −3

Lesson 57

a. 128

b. 4200

c. 28

d. 0.5 L

e. 100

f. $10.00

g. 87

h. $2\frac{1}{2}$

Lesson 58

a. 215

b. 0.0042

c. 15

d. 1500 g

e. 10

f. $22.00

g. 78

h. 1.8, 0.6, 0.72, 2

Lesson 59

a. 324

b. 0.5

c. 2

d. 1.85 m

e. 16

f. $35.00

g. 55

h. $60.00

Lesson 60

a. 161

b. 4.35

c. 10

d. 7.5 cm

e. 7

f. 80¢

g. 23

h. 30¢

Lesson 61

a. 230

b. 0.24

c. 30

d. 1500 m

e. 1

f. $2.10

g. equilateral

h. $21.20

Lesson 62

a. 43

b. 0.025

c. 3

d. 2.5 kg

e. 1

f. $16.00

g. square

h. 0

Lesson 63

a. 1230

b. 0.004

c. 6

d. 500 mL

e. 14

f. $9.00

g. isosceles

h. 1400

Lesson 64

a. 180

b. 750

c. 10

d. 200 mm

e. 5

f. $1.00

g. equilateral triangle

h. 0.5

Lesson 65

a. 21

b. 0.125

c. 6

d. 750 mm

e. 25

f. $3.60

g. $3\frac{1}{2}$ ft

h. $21.40

Lesson 66

a. 6.85

b. 0.0012

c. 8

d. 2 meters

e. 20

f. 6

g. 50.24 mm

h. 75

27

Lesson 67

a. 33.6

b. 3850

c. 5

d. 200 dm

e. 100

f. 18

g. $\frac{1}{2}$

h. 720

Lesson 68

a. 1.25

b. $\frac{3}{4}$

c. 9

d. 30

e. 200 cm

f. 8

g. 62.8 mm

h. 7 m; 3 m^2

Lesson 69

a. 2.5

b. 0.075

c. 2

d. 630

e. 2 dm

f. 16

g. 2, 3, 5, 7, 11

h. $3\frac{1}{2}$

Lesson 70

a. 8.1

b. 625

c. 6

d. $240.00

e. 2000 mm

f. 15

g. 2×5

h. 2 m; 0.25 m^2

Lesson 71

a. -15

b. 0.0045

c. 80

d. 30

e. 0.5 m

f. $27

g. $2 \times 2 \times 2 \times 2$

h. $32.40

Lesson 72

a. 7

b. $\frac{4}{9}$

c. 5

d. 3.6

e. 0.5 kg

f. $12

g. $2 \times 2 \times 3 \times 3$

h. $4.50

28

Lesson 73

a. −10

b. 8750

c. 36

d. 63

e. 0.5 L

f. $24

g. $2 \times 2 \times 2 \times 2 \times 3$

h. 6

Lesson 74

a. 4

b. 0.045

c. 7

d. $3.00

e. 0.4 km

f. $20

g. $2 \times 5 \times 5$

h. 1

Lesson 75

a. −35

b. 225

c. 9

d. $60.00

e. 0.25 g

f. $3.50

g. 80

h. 1.8

Lesson 76

a. −12

b. 0.0625

c. 4

d. 18

e. 0.5 cm

f. 8

g. 80

h. $26.50

Lesson 77

a. 30

b. 4,000,000

c. 45

d. $9

e. 0.25 m

f. 16

g. 80

h. 21

Lesson 78

a. 8

b. 2

c. 6

d. $32.00

e. 0.75 kg

f. 72

g. 80

h. $4.50 to $4.80

Answers

Lesson 79

a. −40

b. 3750

c. 250

d. $1.80

e. 1.2 L

f. 25

g. 80

h. 25

Lesson 80

a. −75

b. 1600

c. 8

d. 25

e. 1.5 km

f. 9

g. 60

h. 6 m; 2.25 m^2

Lesson 81

a. +100

b. 0.0012

c. 60

d. $3.60

e. 2.5 cm

f. 36

g. 180 degrees

h. $27

Lesson 82

a. 18

b. $\frac{1}{100}$ or 0.01

c. 9

d. 31.4 ft

e. 1.5 m

f. 32

g. supplementary angles

h. 60

Lesson 83

a. −20

b. 6,750,000

c. 20

d. $18

e. 0.5 g

f. 64

g. adjacent angles

h. 150 mi

Lesson 84

a. 0

b. 625

c. 7

d. 94.2 cm

e. 15 mm

f. 36

g. trapezoid

h. 3

Lesson 85

a. −72

b. 8×10^9

c. 120

d. $48

e. 800 m

f. $3

g. base

h. 10 m; 6.25 m^2

Lesson 86

a. −58

b. 9×10^{-6}

c. 8

d. $2.70

e. 200 mL

f. $90

g. $\frac{5}{11}$

h. $214

Lesson 87

a. −30

b. 8×10^2

c. 40

d. 62.8 ft

e. 0.75 kg

f. $125

g. blue

h. $2\frac{1}{2}$

Lesson 88

a. −75

b. 3×10^9

c. 12

d. $15

e. 25.4 mm

f. $2.50

g. reflection

h. 1250 mi

Lesson 89

a. +20

b. 7.5×10^4

c. 10

d. $0.64

e. 187 cm

f. $2.50

g. right angle

h. 8

Lesson 90

a. −20

b. 8.4×10^{-10}

c. 11

d. $3.60

e. 0.8 kg

f. $1.25

g. obtuse

h. 1000 in.^{3}

Answers

Lesson 91

a. −134

b. 1.44×10^6

c. 60

d. 15

e. 1500 mL

f. $200

g. acute

h. 15

Lesson 92

a. −25

b. 2.25×10^{-10}

c. 16

d. 20

e. 30 cm

f. $60

g. straight angle

h. $36.00

Lesson 93

a. 200

b. 7.5×10^4

c. 250

d. 288 in.^{2}

e. 18

f. 54

g. translation

h. 15 cm

Lesson 94

a. 24

b. 6×10^{-5}

c. 0.6

d. 86°F

e. 16

f. 55

g. rotation

h. 5

Lesson 95

a. −28

b. 6.25×10^{12}

c. 0.9

d. 77°F

e. 22

f. 90

g. $\frac{3}{11}$

h. 10

Lesson 96

a. 23

b. 1×10^{13}

c. 20

d. 59°F

e. 15

f. $100

g. 30 cubic inches

h. $7.50

Lesson 97

  a. -125

  b. 3×10^{12}

  c. 0.9

  d. $41°F$

  e. 65

  f. $60

  g. $\dfrac{1}{2}$

  h. $3\dfrac{1}{2}$

Lesson 98

  a. -45

  b. 1×10^6

  c. $2\dfrac{1}{2}$

  d. 20 g

  e. 15

  f. $80

  g. $\dfrac{1}{100}$

  h. 21 mi

Lesson 99

  a. 3

  b. 3.2×10^{11}

  c. 1

  d. $5°F$

  e. 28

  f. $40

  g. cube

  h. 10

Lesson 100

  a. 6

  b. 2.5×10^{-9}

  c. 24

  d. $-4°F$

  e. 75

  f. $16

  g. sphere

  h. 3

Lesson 101

  a. 16

  b. 3×10^{-10}

  c. 0.06

  d. $-13°F$

  e. $60

  f. $60

  g. $\dfrac{1}{4}$

  h. $4.50

Lesson 102

  a. -1

  b. 6×10^8

  c. $2\dfrac{1}{2}$

  d. 0.5 L

  e. $60

  f. $100

  g. $\dfrac{2}{3}$

  h. 2

Answers

Lesson 103

a. 0.5

b. 1.2×10^{-6}

c. 15

d. $-22°F$

e. $200

f. $400

g. the area of the yard

h. 9×10^6

Lesson 104

a. 0.5

b. 2.5×10^{11}

c. 25

d. 9 sq. ft

e. $50

f. $75

g. 32 ft

h. 9 miles

Lesson 105

a. 16

b. 1.6×10^{-7}

c. 12

d. $-31°F$

e. $100

f. $100

g. proportional

h. 2

Lesson 106

a. -125

b. 4×10^{-1}

c. 1.8

d. 18 sq. ft

e. $30

f. $30

g. the x-axis

h. $6.00

Lesson 107

a. 10

b. 6.25×10^{12}

c. 3

d. $-58°F$

e. $45

f. $105

g. $\frac{1}{4}$

h. 6

Lesson 108

a. 0

b. 1×10^{-7}

c. 8

d. 27 sq. ft

e. $180

f. $180

g. 36

h. 210 mi

Lesson 109

a. $\frac{1}{4}$

b. 1.44×10^{24}

c. 1

d. 1.5 m

e. $10

f. $70

g. 0.33 and $33\frac{1}{3}\%$

h. 40

Lesson 110

a. $\frac{1}{4}$

b. 5.4×10^{16}

c. $\frac{5}{2}$

d. 1500 mL

e. $90

f. $90

g. 0.2 and 20%

h. 10

Lesson 111

a. 0.05

b. 6.4×10^{-7}

c. 60

d. 144 in.^{2}

e. $50

f. $100

g. $\frac{1}{3}$

h. $16.00

Lesson 112

a. −900

b. 2×10^3

c. 10, −10

d. 122°F

e. $500

f. $2500

g. square

h. $2\frac{1}{2}$

Lesson 113

a. −0.25

b. 2×10^{-4}

c. 0.6

d. 288 in.^{2}

e. $1600

f. $800

g. pentagonal

h. $2\frac{1}{2}$ hr

Lesson 114

a. −18

b. 1.6×10^{17}

c. 9

d. 140°F

e. $4500

f. $7500

g. circle

h. 2

Answers

Lesson 115

a. $\frac{1}{100}$

b. 1

c. 1

d. 2.5 m

e. $800

f. $800

g. 19

h. 100¢

Lesson 116

a. $4\frac{1}{4}$

b. 2.5×10^3

c. 0.4

d. 10,000 cm^2

e. $500

f. $500

g. 48

h. $3.60

Lesson 117

a. -60

b. 3.5×10^2

c. 5, -5

d. 212°F

e. $500

f. $3500

g. A

h. -1

Lesson 118

a. $9\frac{1}{9}$

b. 1.5×10^{-3}

c. 22

d. 7.5 kg

e. $6000

f. $10,000

g. 6 ft^2

h. 1 hr 20 min

Lesson 119

a. 1

b. 1×10^{-4}

c. 0

d. 500 mm^2

e. $400

f. $400

g. A

h. $\frac{1}{4}$

Lesson 120

a. 1

b. 2.5×10^{-9}

c. 4, -4

d. 32°F

e. $25

f. $275

g. 30%

h. 1

Problem Solving

Lesson 1   15, 21, 28

Lesson 2   55

Lesson 3   14 unseen dots

Lesson 4   No

Lesson 5   2, 2, 7, and 9 are missing place values in order

Lesson 6   5, 7, and 9

Lesson 7   The pully is not in equilibrium; The right side will be heavier.

Lesson 8   6 permutations; 532 is the greatest.

Lesson 9 $\approx \frac{3}{4}$ in.

Lesson 10   39 seats

Lesson 11   24 glubs

Lesson 12   110

Lesson 13   1 dot and 6 dots

Lesson 14 $2.50; $7.50; $12.50

Lesson 15   8, 2, 4, and 0 are missing place values in order

Lesson 16 $\frac{5}{16}, \frac{3}{8}, \frac{7}{16}, \frac{1}{2}$

Lesson 17   5 dishes

Lesson 18   3 dimes and 4 nickels

Lesson 19   7, 11, and 13

Lesson 20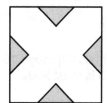

Lesson 21   Yes; To find each sum, multiply the number of terms in the sequence by the next whole number.

Lesson 22   Yin should give 3 tickets to Bobby and 7 tickets to Mary.

Lesson 23   86 dots

Lesson 24   south; 3 paces west of the big tree

Lesson 25
$$\begin{array}{r} 36 \\ \times 15 \\ \hline 180 \\ 36 \\ \hline 540 \end{array}$$

Lesson 26   5 and 12

Lesson 27   8; 2; 20

Lesson 28   6 different routes

Lesson 29   16 pennies

Lesson 30   *See student work.*

Lesson 31   55 blocks; 100 blocks

Lesson 32   Wes

Lesson 33   No; There are only two combinations of faces that total 8. In each combination are numbers which appear on opposite faces of a number cube. Opposite faces total 7, so no adjoining (visible) faces can total 8.

Lesson 34

Lesson 35
$$\begin{array}{r} 116 \\ 8\overline{)928} \\ 8 \\ \hline 12 \\ 8 \\ \hline 48 \\ 48 \\ \hline 0 \end{array}$$

Lesson 36   30

Lesson 37   arp = 2; pom = 5; dar = 12; cob = 7; hilp = 9

Lesson 38   24 permutations

Lesson 39   3 painted faces: 8 blocks; 2 painted faces: 12 blocks; 1 painted face: 6 blocks; no painted faces: 1 block

Answers

Lesson 40	150°	**Lesson 61**	105 m; 3355 m

Lesson 41 0.00000000000002

Lesson 62 Grandfather's method: 50 miles; Grandmother's method: 48 miles.

Lesson 42 No

Lesson 63 6 and 8

Lesson 43 2, 3, and 6; 3, 5, and 6; and 4, 5, and 6

Lesson 64 yellow notebook: school; blue notebook: sketching; red notebook: journal

Lesson 44 the blue face; the purple face; the white face

Lesson 45

$$\begin{array}{r} 16 \\ \times\ 16 \\ \hline 96 \\ 16 \\ \hline 256 \end{array} \quad \text{or} \quad \begin{array}{r} 26 \\ \times\ 11 \\ \hline 26 \\ 26 \\ \hline 286 \end{array}$$

Lesson 65

$$\begin{array}{r} 1231\ R\ 5 \\ 8\overline{)9853} \\ \underline{8} \\ 18 \\ \underline{16} \\ 25 \\ \underline{24} \\ 13 \\ \underline{8} \\ 5 \end{array}$$

Lesson 46 the first box

Lesson 47 1 skilling, 2 ore

Lesson 48 6 combinations; 4 combinations

Lesson 49 18 sq. ft

Lesson 50 *See* Power-Up Discussion *for explanation.*

Lesson 66 The Commutative Property tells us that $1 + 5 = 5 + 1$. By reversing a number's digits we place digits at both ends of the sum that add to the same number.

Lesson 51 204 squares

Lesson 67 70 minutes

Lesson 52 75

Lesson 68 60

Lesson 53 Totals 8 through 18 are possible; 13 is most likely

Lesson 69 56 sq. m

Lesson 70 Yes

Lesson 54 Celia; Marcos

Lesson 71 11 times

Lesson 55

$$\begin{array}{r} 32 \\ 53\overline{)1696} \\ \underline{159} \\ 106 \\ \underline{106} \\ 0 \end{array}$$

Lesson 72 1

Lesson 73 $\dfrac{5}{6}$

Lesson 74 as few as 1 or as many as 10

Lesson 56 $\dfrac{6}{14}$

Lesson 75

$$\begin{array}{r} 982 \\ \times\ \ \ 9 \\ \hline 8838 \end{array}$$

Lesson 57 8 hours

Lesson 58 GGGGBB, BGGGGB, or BBGGGG; GGBGGB, BGGBGG, or GGBBGG

Lesson 76 31

Lesson 77 25 g; $4x + 25 = x + 100$

Lesson 78 12

Lesson 59 One flowerbed is 9 yd by 3 yd; One flowerbed is 7 yd by 5 yd.

Lesson 79 12 sq. units

Lesson 60 8, 8, 2, 2; 8, 4, 4, 4; 3 attempts

Lesson 80   6 in.^{3}

Lesson 81 $\frac{1}{8} + \frac{1}{8} + \frac{1}{8} + \frac{1}{8} + \frac{1}{8} + \frac{1}{8} + \frac{1}{8} = \frac{7}{8}$;

$\frac{1}{4} + \frac{1}{4} + \frac{1}{4} + \frac{1}{8} = \frac{7}{8}$;

$\frac{1}{2} + \frac{1}{4} + \frac{1}{8} = \frac{7}{8}$

Lesson 82   2 in. to the back, and 2 in. to the right.

Lesson 83   10

Lesson 84   To start, turn both timers over at the same time. When the two-minute timers runs out, a game turn begins. At that point there is one minute left in the 3-minute timer. When the 3-minute timer runs out, immediately turn it over. When it runs out again, play stops.

Lesson 85
$$\begin{array}{r} 143 \\ \times \quad 7 \\ \hline 1001 \end{array}$$

Lesson 86   4; 5; 100

Lesson 87   375 g; $m + 1000 = 3m + 250$

Lesson 88   456,976,000 license plates

Lesson 89   2826 feet; more than $\frac{1}{2}$ mile

Lesson 90   5 in.^{3}

Lesson 91   1; 3; 6; $\sqrt{1^3 + 2^3 + 3^3 + 4^3} = 10$; $\sqrt{1^3 + 2^3 + 3^3 + 4^3 + 5^3} = 15$

Lesson 92 $\frac{1}{4}$

Lesson 93 $\frac{1}{5}, \frac{3}{10}, \frac{3}{10}, \frac{2}{3}$

Lesson 94   *Four possible combinations are:* 2 squares, 6 triangles and 12 circles; 3 squares, 8 triangles and 9 circles; 4 squares, 10 triangles and 6 circles; *or* 5 squares, 12 triangles and 3 circles

Lesson 95 367×3; *3 is the only single-digit number greater than 1 by which 1101 is divisible*

Lesson 96   60 guests

Lesson 97 $x = 1.3$ lb

Lesson 98   10 handshakes

Lesson 99 $3600

Lesson 100

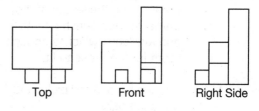

Top   Front   Right Side

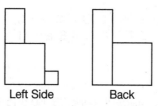

Left Side   Back

Lesson 101   12%

Lesson 102   4 hours and 48 minutes

Lesson 103   0.84448; She knew the approximate value of the product (0.8) and the digit that the product should end with (8) so she was able to quickly identify it on the list.

Lesson 104 $\frac{5}{108}$

Lesson 105
$$\begin{array}{r} 91\frac{1}{2} \\ 10\overline{)915} \\ \underline{90} \\ 15 \\ \underline{10} \\ 5 \end{array}$$

Lesson 106 $15 = 9 + 4 + 1 + 1$; $18 = 9 + 9$; $20 = 16 + 4$

Lesson 107 $x = 125$ g

Lesson 108   456,976,000 license plates

Answers

Lesson 109 $bf = \dfrac{1 \times w \times h}{144}$;

3 in. × 4 in. × 12 in., 4 in. × 6 in. × 6 in., 2 in. × 2 in. × 36 in.; any example with a volume of 144 in.^{3}

Lesson 110   Saturday

Lesson 111   21, 34, 55

Lesson 112   60 cards

Lesson 113   The diagonal of the box is 1 inch greater than the length of the frame, leaving $\frac{1}{2}$-inch on either end available, which is enough room for the frame to fit.

Lesson 114   2 green balls, 3 red balls, and 3 orange balls

Lesson 115   A = 1, B = 2, C = 4, D = 3, E = 5, F = 6, G = 8, and H = 7

Lesson 116 $\dfrac{2}{3}$

Lesson 117   *See student work;* 30, 60 and 90

Lesson 118   8 citizens

Lesson 119   3 cones

Lesson 120   *See* Power-Up Discussion.

Activity Master 10

1. 30°

2. 90°

3. 45°

4. 135°

5. 150°

6. 90°

7. 15°

8. 120°

9. 165°

10. 180°

11. 105°

12. 105°

Activity Master 20

Section B

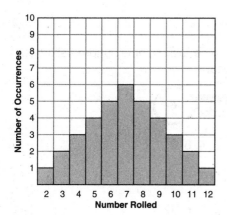

Section C

See student work.

Section D

Student answers will vary, but the most likely reason for any difference between the students' results and the theoretical outcome is the small number of rolls. (Increasing the number of rolls increases the likelihood that actual results will closely conform to the theoretical outcome, as can be demonstrated by totaling the actual results of all of the students.) Less likely reasons for differences may be that the dice were not adequately shaken or that the dice were improperly balanced and were therefore unfair.

Activity Master 24

1. 1

2. −2

3. $-\frac{1}{2}$

4. 2

5. $\frac{1}{3}$

6. $-\frac{2}{3}$

7. $-\frac{4}{3}$

8. $\frac{3}{4}$

41

Answers

1. neither; they are equal.

2. 1918

3. $194.70

4. 247

5. 25

6. 15

7. 100

8. 4

Reteaching 2

1. Commutative Property of addition

2. Commutative Property of multiplication

3. $(2 + 5) + 10 = 2 + (5 + 10)$

4. $(2 \times 5) \times 10 = 2 \times (5 \times 10)$

5. 2

6. 680

7. 0

Reteaching 3

1. 21

2. 8

3. 349

4. 70

5. 14

6. 129

7. 16

8. 12

9. 25

Reteaching 4

1. 81, 243, 729

2. 21, 31, 43

3. >

4. <

5. −184

6. $(2 + 8) > (8 \div 2)$

Reteaching 5

1. $(3 \times 10,000) + (7 \times 1000) + (5 \times 100) + (2 \times 10) + (3 \times 1)$

2. $(4 \times 100,000) + (6 \times 10,000) + (8 \times 1000) + (9 \times 10)$

3. 731,000,000,040

4. 12,601

5. forty-nine million, nine hundred sixty-one thousand

Reteaching 6

1. 1, 2, 3, 4, 6, 8, 12, 24

2. 1, 2, 3, 4, 6, 9, 12, 18, 36

3. 1, 2, 3, 4, 6, 12

4. 12

Reteaching 7

1. angle *A*

2. angle *D*

3. side *CB*

4. side *AD*

5. ray *CD*

6. straight

Reteaching 8

1. $\frac{3}{4}$

2. $\frac{7}{10}$

3. 30%

4. $3\frac{7}{8}$

5. $1\frac{5}{16}$ inch

Reteaching 9

1. 1

2. $\frac{6}{60}$

3. $\frac{4}{7}$

4. $\frac{10}{3}$

5. $\frac{1}{6}$

6. $\frac{5}{9}$

7. $a = \frac{12}{9}$

8. $b = \frac{5}{6}$

9. $c = \frac{1}{12}$

Reteaching 10

1. $4\frac{7}{8}$

2. $3\frac{1}{4}$

3. $7\frac{5}{9}$

4. $1\frac{4}{9}$

5. 9

6. $3\frac{8}{10}$

7. $\frac{51}{4}$

8. $\frac{17}{9}$

9. $\frac{20}{3}$

Reteaching Inv. 1

1. $\frac{1}{6}$

2. $\frac{1}{12}$

3. $\frac{1}{3} + \frac{1}{4} + \frac{1}{6}$

4. 75%

5. $1\frac{3}{4}$

6. 4

7. $\frac{1}{5}, \frac{1}{4}, \frac{1}{3}, \frac{3}{5}, \frac{2}{3}$

Reteaching 11

1. $28.24

2. 18 horses

3. 62 people

4. 4.6 feet

5. 1419 buns

Reteaching 12

1. 45 years

2. 6500 papers

3. 2002

4. 113 birds

5. $1490

Reteaching 13

1. 8 cans

2. 25 pages

3. 325 students

43

Answers

Reteaching 14

1. $\frac{4}{7}$

2. 60%

3. $\frac{1}{5}$

4. 0

Reteaching 15

1. $\frac{1}{3}$

2. $\frac{1}{4}$

3. $6\frac{1}{3}$

4. 24

5. 35

6. 2

7. B. $\frac{12}{5}$

Reteaching 16

1. 36

2. 1

3. $1\frac{1}{2}$

Reteaching 17

1. 23°

2. 40°

3. acute

4. *See student answers.*

Reteaching 18

1. figure B

2. quadrilateral

3. figures A and B; figures C and D

4. figures C and D

Reteaching 19

1. 48 inches

2. 32 inches

3. 46 inches

4. 46 inches

5. 20 feet

6. 40 centimeters

Reteaching 20

1. 300 sq. ft

2. 85

3. $\frac{81}{100}$

4. $3^2 = 9$ and $\sqrt{9} = 3$

Reteaching Inv. 2

1. 2 sectors; each 50% of the area of circle *A*

2. 90°

3. 6

4. 45°

5. 90°

Reteaching 21

1. 4, 6, 8, 9, 10, 12, 14, 15, 16, 18, 20

2. $2 \cdot 3 \cdot 7$

3. $2 \cdot 2 \cdot 2 \cdot 3$

4. $2 \cdot 2 \cdot 3 \cdot 5$

5. $64 = 2^6$; $\sqrt{64} = 2^3$

Reteaching 22

1. 20 children

2. 30 adults

3. $\frac{3}{4}$

4. 3 books

Reteaching 23

1. $3\frac{3}{8}$

2. $\frac{2}{3}$

3. $37\frac{1}{2}\%$

4. $19\frac{2}{6}\% = 19\frac{1}{3}\%$

5. $13\frac{3}{7}$

6. $26\frac{1}{4}\%$

Reteaching 24

1. $\frac{6}{7}$

2. $\frac{11}{30}$

3. $\frac{3}{13}$

4. $\frac{3}{40}$

5. $\frac{1}{2}$

Reteaching 25

1. $1\frac{1}{2}$

2. $\frac{2}{7}$

3. $\frac{8}{9}$

4. 72

5. $1\frac{3}{8}$

6. 1

Reteaching 26

1. $1\frac{1}{2}$

2. $23\frac{3}{4}$

3. $25\frac{1}{2}$

4. $\frac{13}{32}$

5. $3\frac{1}{2}$

6. 25

Reteaching 27

1. 140

2. 231

3. 210

4. 24

5. 120

6. 252

Answers

Reteaching 28

1. 93

2. $2.57

3. 50 miles per hour

4. 350

Reteaching 29

1. 12,000

2. 27,400

3. 1,000

4. 25

Reteaching 30

1. $\frac{20}{35}$ and $\frac{21}{35}$, $1\frac{6}{35}$

2. $10\frac{1}{4}$

3. $2\frac{3}{5}$

4. $\frac{7}{20}$

5. $<$

Reteaching Inv. 3

1. (3, 3)

2. 6 square units

3. 16 units

Reteaching 31

1. 49.13

2. 708.064

3. thirty-eight and four hundred fifty-nine thousandths

4. five hundred and five hundredths

5. 0

Reteaching 32

1. 5 cm 50 mm

2. 10 cm 100 mm

3. 3 cm 30 mm

4. a. 0.5 kg

   b. 500,000 mg

Reteaching 33

1. $>$

2. $<$

3. $<$

4. 16

5. 1154.071

6. 1000

Reteaching 34

1. 407 mm

2. 20.5

3. 2.75

4. a. 70.02

   b. 70.06

   c. 70.13

Reteaching 35

1. 18.144

2. 0.31

3. 26.623

4. 14.74

5. 1.16

6. a. 1.17 square meters

   b. 4.4 meters

Reteaching 36

1. $\frac{2}{5}$

2. $\frac{1}{2}$

3. H1, H2, H3, H4, H5, H6, T1, T2, T3, T4, T5, T6

Reteaching 37

1. 18 square inches

2. 60 square centimeters

3. 105 square feet

Reteaching 38

1. 15,000

2. homeroom 14

3. 73

4. false

Reteaching 39

1. $r = 0.1$

2. $t = 28$

3. $c = 0.15$

4. $a = 14$

5. $b = 27$

6. $w = 20$

Reteaching 40

1. 90° and 30°

2. 35°

3. 85°

4. 95°

5. 85°

Reteaching Inv. 4

1. 37

2. 21

3. 54

4. $46\frac{1}{2}$

Reteaching 41

1. 204

2. $25 + 4a$

3. $6b - 24$

4. $13 + 3p$

5. 24 square inches

6. 7.2 feet

Reteaching 42

1. $5.16\overline{3}$

2. 7.284

3. $0.7\overline{4}$

4. 0.1667

Answers

Reteaching 43

1. $43\frac{3}{4}$
2. $1.8\overline{3}$
3. $\frac{63}{100}$
4. 1.48
5. 0.045
6. $\frac{8}{1}$

Reteaching 44

1. a. 18 R1   b. $18\frac{1}{4}$ c. 18.25
2. 3.267
3. a. 10 rows   b. 11 musicians

Reteaching 45

1. 0.04
2. 1.75
3. 3.02
4. 100
5. 22
6. $x = 59.5$
7. $t = 2.4$

Reteaching 46

1. 250 miles
2. $0.16 per ounce
3. $14.49

Reteaching 47

1. 238
2. 0.01536
3. 8
4. 5
5. $(1 \times 10^3) + (2 \times 10^2) + (9 \times 10^1) + (4 \times 10^0)$

Reteaching 48

1.

Fraction	Decimal	Percent
$\frac{1}{5}$	0.2	20%
$\frac{2}{3}$	$0.\overline{6}$	$66\frac{2}{3}\%$
$\frac{3}{25}$	0.12	12%

2. 40%
3. less

Reteaching 49

1. 8 hours 10 minutes 26 seconds
2. 11 in.
3. 6 yd 5 ft 5 in.
4. 1 lb 14 oz

Reteaching 50

1. 7 kg
2. 180 in.
3. 9.75 lb
4. 75,000 mm
5. 975 ft
6. 1.12 m

Reteaching Inv. 5

Max's Day

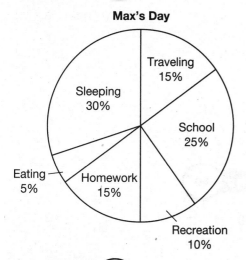

Traveling 15%
Sleeping 30%
School 25%
Eating 5%
Homework 15%
Recreation 10%

Reteaching 51

1. 1.2×10^{10}
2. 2.63×10^5
3. 5,600,000
4. 100,000,000
5. >
6. =

Reteaching 52

1. 34
2. 8.9
3. 3
4. 259
5. 45

Reteaching 53

1. 50 balls
2. 9 eggs
3. 4 musicians

Reteaching 54

1. $1.69
2. $35
3. 45 necklaces

Reteaching 55

1. 96
2. 80 points
3. 4

Reteaching 56

1.

x	y
0	−2
1	1
2	4
3	7

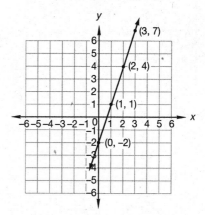

2.

x	y
0	1
1	3
2	5
3	7

Continued on page 50.

Answers

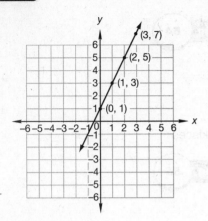

Reteaching 57

1. 9×10^{-5}

2. 7.8×10^{-6}

3. 0.00026

4. 0.00321

Reteaching 58

1.

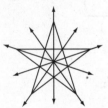

2. (0, −4) and (−4, 0)

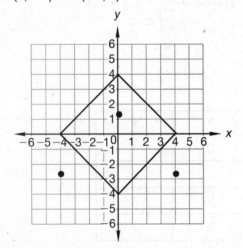

3. D

Reteaching 59

1. −6

2. +1

3. −3

4. 3

5. 1

Reteaching 60

1. $25.56

2. $32

3. 19\frac{1}{4}$

4. 45

Reteaching Inv. 6

1. B

2. D

3. 32 in.

4. trapezium

Reteaching 61

1. $A = 24$ in.^{2}

2. $A = 35$ cm^2

3. $A = 120$ ft^2

4. 125°, 125°, 55°

5. 135°, 45°, 135°

Reteaching 62

1. obtuse

2. right

3. acute

4. scalene

5. isosceles

6. equilateral

7. **a.** △ADC   **b.** △ADC or △ABC

Reteaching 63

1. 396

2. 24

3. 19

4. 5

5. $\frac{1}{10}$

6. $\frac{1}{2}$

Reteaching 64

1. 47

2. −1

3. −40

4. −17

5. −6

6. −22

Reteaching 65

1. 75.36 m

2. 88 in.

3. 5π cm

4. No; The diameter is always about $\frac{1}{3}$ of the circumference, or in this case about 140 inches.

Reteaching 66

1. 360 trucks

2. 480 children

3. 30 tables

Reteaching 67

1. 6 vertices and 9 edges

2. pyramid

3. triangular prism

Reteaching 68

1. 0

2. 6.2

3. −10

4. 6.3

5. −25

6. $6\frac{1}{4}$

Reteaching 69

1. 1.6×10^{-4}

2. 1.6×10^{6}

3. 2.51×10^{-7}

4. 1.5×10^{6}

5. 3.74×10^{2}

6. 5.28×10^{-4}

7. 2.5×10^{-1}

8. 1.53×10^{-3}

9. 1.134×10^{-6}

Answers

Reteaching 70

1. 30 cm³
2. 594 in.³
3. 343 mm³
4. 210 ft³

6 ft   7 ft
   5 ft

Reteaching Inv. 7

1. $x = 6$
2. $y = 3.16$
3. $f = 4\frac{1}{4}$
4. $r = 0.7$
5. $t = 18$
6. $w = 12$

Reteaching 71

1. 20 years old
2. 150 people
3. $30

Reteaching 72

1. 15 pounds
2. 168 customers
3. 50 miles

Reteaching 73

1. 42
2. −24
3. $\frac{1}{3}$
4. −5
5. $-\frac{1}{5}$
6. 0.6
7. −300
8. −120
9. $\frac{1}{5}$

Reteaching 74

1. $64 = \frac{4}{10}x$; $x = 160$
2. $\frac{1}{5}x = 345$; $x = 1725$
3. $\frac{3}{4}x = 300$; $x = 400$

Reteaching 75

1. 14 m²
2. 24 m²
3. 22 m²

Reteaching 76

1. $3\frac{1}{3}$
2. $\frac{1}{8}$
3. 8
4. $\frac{1}{30}$
5. $\frac{1}{6}$
6. $\frac{11}{12}$

Reteaching **77**

1. $33\frac{1}{3}\%$

2. $W_p \times 200 = 56$; 28%

3. 300

4. 60

Reteaching **78**

1.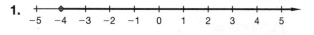

2.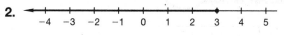

3.

Reteaching **79**

1. about 25 cm^2

2. about 23 cm^2

3. about 21 cm^2

4. about 33 cm^2

Reteaching **80**

1. rotation

2. reflection

3. translation

Reteaching **Inv. 8**

1. $\frac{1}{12}$

2. $\frac{1}{4}$

3. $\frac{1}{2}$

Reteaching **81**

1. 236 plants

2. 1800 customers

3. 108 books

Reteaching **82**

1. 7850 ft^2

2. 616 m^2

3. 3850 cm^2

Reteaching **83**

1. 1.775×10^6

2. 2.492×10^{-7}

3. 3.5×10^2

4. 2.892×10^1

Reteaching **84**

1. $5xy - 6x$

2. $5x - 2y$

3. $17x^2 + y^2 - y$

Reteaching **85**

1. -46

2. -12

3. 1

4. -14

5. 0

6. -1

Reteaching 86

1.

number line with points at −4 and −3

2. number line with points at 1, 2, 3, 4, 5, 6

3. false

4. true

Reteaching 87

1. $12x^2y$

2. $-30s^3t^2$

3. $-28a^2b^4$

4. $30x^2y^4$

5. $-16r^3w^4$

6. $-88b^4c^5$

Reteaching 88

1. 4 yd^2

2. $30,000 \text{ cm}^2$

3. $4,000,000 \text{ cm}^3$

Reteaching 89

1. 5

2. 6

3. $135°$

Reteaching 90

1. $y = 30$

2. $x = -0.06$

3. $a = -6$

4. $b = -5$

5. $w = 0.8$

6. $x = -14$

Reteaching Inv. 9

1.

$y = 2x + 1$	
x	y
0	1
1	3
2	5
3	7

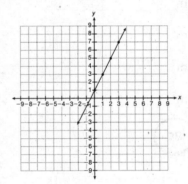

2.

$y = 3x$	
x	y
0	0
1	3
2	6
3	9

Continued on page 55.

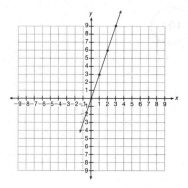

3.

$y = -x - 1$	
x	y
0	−1
1	−2
2	−3
3	−4

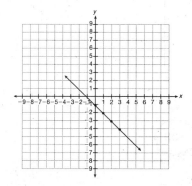

Reteaching 91

1. $y = -10$
2. 10
3. 8
4. −2
5. 26

Reteaching 92

1. $1.40
2. $32,500
3. $45

Reteaching 93

1. $a = 19$
2. $x = 3$
3. $t = 56$
4. $b = 38$
5. $y \le 4$
6. $x > 4$

Reteaching 94

1. $\frac{1}{15}$
2. $\frac{1}{221}$
3. $\frac{1}{6}$

Reteaching 95

1. 360 cm^3
2. 200 cm^3
3. 100.48 cm^3
4. 280 cm^3

Reteaching 96

1. $7x + 7$
2. $-3y + 12$
3. x
4. $5y^2 + 5\frac{2}{3}y$
5. 55°
6. 125°

Answers

Reteaching 97

1. $x = 15$ m

2. $y = 4$ m

3. 60 ft

Reteaching 98

1. 4000 in.

2. 0.4

3. 2.5

Reteaching 99

1. $a = 8$ ft

2. $b = 12$ ft

3. $c = 10$ ft

Reteaching 100

1. $-5, \sqrt{5}, 4, 3^2$

2. $\sqrt{5}$

3. $\sqrt{60}$

Reteaching Inv. 10

1.
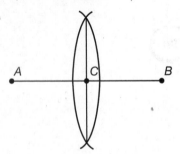

2.
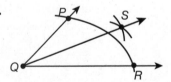

3. *See student work.*

Reteaching 101

1. 20°

2. 10°

3. 60°

4. 98

5. 27

Reteaching 102

1. 80°

2. 80°

3. 100°

4. 100°

5. $y = 9$

6. $a = 5$

Reteaching 103

1. -24

2. 5

3. -288

4. $8x^3y^4$

5. $4a^3bc^2$

6. $2w^2z^3$

Reteaching 104

1. 19.42 m

2. 20.13 m²

3. Area = 4.71 m²; Perimeter = 9.14 m

Answers

Reteaching 105

1. 600 in.^{2}

2. 86 m^2

3. 125π ft^2

Reteaching 106

1. $c = \dfrac{a}{b}$

2. $h = \dfrac{2R}{t}$

3. $y = 13$ and $y = -13$

4. 1

5. -3

Reteaching 107

1.

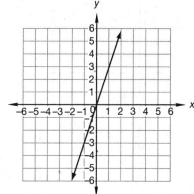

slope = 3

2.

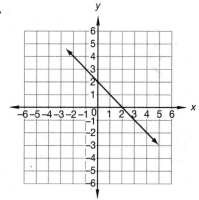

slope = -1

3.

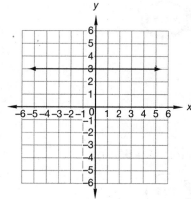

slope = 0

Reteaching 108

1. $w = 5$

2. $s = 25$

3. $C = 5$

4. $g = 5$

Reateaching 109

1. $y = \sqrt{7}, y = -\sqrt{7}$

2. $x = 8, x = -8$

3. $t = 5, t = -5$

4. $x = \sqrt{8}, x = -\sqrt{8}$

5. $x = 10, x = -10$

6. $y = 9, y = -9$

Reteaching 110

1. $249.73

2. $158.40

3. $30.45

Answers

Reteaching Inv. 11

1. 3

2. $\frac{1}{2}$

3. 4

4. s = 384 in.^{2}; V = 512 in.^{3}

Reteaching 111

1. 5×10^{-6}

2. 4×10^{7}

3. 3×10^{-4}

4. 8×10^{11}

5. 6×10^{-3}

6. 9×10^{-9}

Reteaching 112

1. 40 ft

2. 36 in.

3. 14 in.

Reteaching 113

1. 113 in.^{3}

2. 393 in.^{3}

3. 333 in.^{3}

4. 904 in.^{3}

5. 1200 in.^{3}

Reteaching 114

1. 3500 L

2. 35 kg

3. 690 L

4. 200,000 L

Reteaching 115

1. (2)(5)$aaabb$

2. $7xxxxy$

3. (2)(2)(2)(2)$xyzz$

4. $16xy^2(2 - xy)$

5. $ab^3(4a + 5)$

6. $2y^2(x + 2x^2y + y)$

Reteaching 116

1. $y = -2x - 7$

2. $y = 4x - 8$

3.

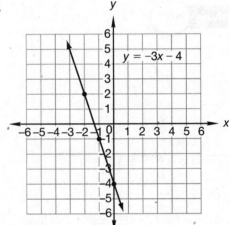

Reteaching 118

1. $x \neq 0$

2. $x \neq -5$

3. $x \neq 0$

4. $x \neq 0$

5. $x \neq 10, -10$

6. $x \neq -5$

7. $0 \div 3 = 0$

Saxon Math Course 2

58

Reteaching **119**

1.

s	A
1	$\frac{1}{4}$
2	1
3	$2\frac{1}{4}$
4	4

2.

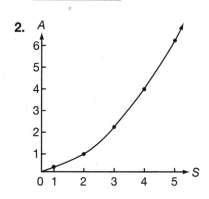

2.

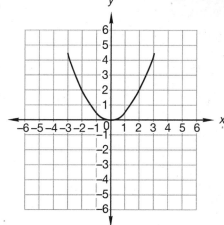

3.

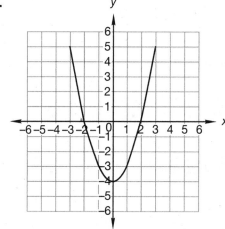

Reteaching **120**

1.

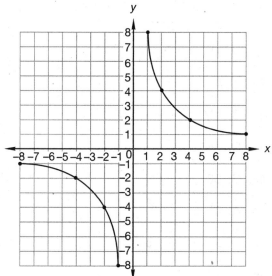

4.

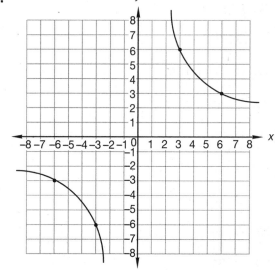

59

Answers

1. C. $304\frac{2}{5}$

2. D. 19.25

3. A. 1.55

4. A. 0.63

5. B. 5.2

6. B. $4\frac{1}{2}$

7. C. $1\frac{9}{10}$

8. C. $2\frac{2}{3}$

9. A. $1\frac{3}{5}$

10. C. $\frac{5}{7}$

11. B. 4

12. A. 2,500,000

13. C. 1200 mm

14. B. 2 m

15. D. 0.04

16. B. 10^7

17. C. 14 and 15

18. E. None correct

19. D. 26

20. C. 0.3, 33%, $\frac{1}{3}$

21. C. 18

22. D. 30

23. D. 31

24. B. 9 in.

25. C. $\frac{1}{2}$

26. B. $3.12

27. C. 13¢/oz

28. C. $27.00

29. B. 84%

30. D. 1000 miles

31. B.

32. A. 52°

33. D. 70 cm

34. B. 62.8 in.

35. B. 54 m^2

36. A. 50 ft^2

37. A. 80 cm^3

38. C.

39. D. $\overline{TS}$

40. A. 5

41. B. −7

42. D. 144

43. C. 36

44. A. $2^3 \cdot 3$

45. D. $6 \cdot 20 + 6 \cdot 5$

46. B. 12

47. A. $\sqrt{9} < 2^2$

48. B. 100

49. D. 13

50. A. (−2, −3)

Power-Up Test

1. 8 kids and 3 cows

2. 43 earrings

3. 32, 16, 8
   32, 8, 16
   16, 32, 8
   16, 8, 32
   8, 32, 16
   8, 16, 32

4. 29 cm

5. 6 nickels + 2 dimes
   1 quarter + 2 dimes + 5 pennies

6. $$\begin{array}{r} 136 \\ \times\ \ \ 7 \\ \hline 952 \end{array}$$

7. 1 cup of milk

8. 8 eggs

9. There is not enough fencing to enclose the dog pen.

10. 60 pages

11. 2 and a half pounds
    about 27 years old

12. 8 more runners
    (11 runners in all)

13. Gaby is correct.

14. 16 boxes

15. Jesse runs 600 ft.

16. 1 cubic yard

17. about 25 square meters

18. 18 games

19. *Answers will vary.*

20. The interior angle of a regular polygon is a factor of 360°.
    equilateral triangle, square
    regular pentagon: no
    regular octagon: no

21. *Answers will vary.*

22. 17 scouts

23. The friend's prediction is incorrect.
    $\frac{1}{4}$

Answers

Cumulative Test 1A

1. 10
2. $4 + 5 = 5 + 4$
3. a. Commutative Property
   b. Associative Property
4. twenty-one million, six hundred thousand, fifty
5. 25, 36, 49
6. $(7 \times 10,000) + (5 \times 1000)$
7. >
8. 45
9. 8,100,060
10. $10.70
11. 15,160
12. $9.25
13. 1348
14. 35
15. 23,440
16. 2376
17. 519
18. 5799
19. 2720
20. $2.95

Cumulative Test 1B

1. 12
2. $5 \cdot 6 = 6 \cdot 5$
3. a. Commutative Property
   b. Associative Property
4. thirty-one million, twenty thousand, thirty
5. 36, 49, 64

6. $(2 \times 100,000) + (5 \times 1000)$
7. >
8. 48
9. 12,300,040
10. $11.60
11. 12,870
12. $7.10
13. 2146
14. 22
15. 2414
16. 1080
17. 447
18. 5145 R 1
19. 2400
20. $7.65

Cumulative Test 2A

1. a. $\frac{3}{10}$ b. 30%
2. $\overline{CB}$ (or $\overline{BC}$)
3. $\frac{4}{3}$
4. $\frac{25}{8}$
5. a. $-3, 0, \frac{1}{3}, 3$ b. $\frac{1}{3}$
6. $(2 + 3) + 5 = 2 + (3 + 5)$
7. a. $\frac{7}{12}$ b. $\frac{5}{12}$
8. forty-two million
9. a. 1, 3, 7, 21

   b. 1, 2, 3, 4, 6, 8, 12, 16, 24, 48

   c. 1, 3

   d. 3

10. Inverse Property

11. 2440

12. $18.30

13. 26

14. $\frac{4}{5}$

15. $\frac{6}{11}$

16. $\frac{12}{35}$

17. 8256 R 5

18. $65.20

19. $\frac{8}{125}$

20. **a.** ray: $\overrightarrow{MC}$

    b. line: $\overleftrightarrow{PM}$ (or $\overleftrightarrow{MP}$)

    c. segment: $\overline{FH}$ (or $\overline{HF}$)

Cumulative Test 2B

1. **a.** $\frac{7}{10}$ **b.** 70%

2. $\angle C$ (or $\angle ACB$ or $\angle BCA$)

3. $\frac{3}{2}$

4. $\frac{20}{3}$

5. **a.** $-2, 0, \frac{1}{2}, 2$ **b.** $\frac{1}{2}$

6. $(2 \cdot 3) \cdot 6 = 2 \cdot (3 \cdot 6)$

7. **a.** $\frac{5}{9}$ **b.** $\frac{4}{9}$

8. fifty-three million

9. **a.** 1, 3, 9, 27

    b. 1, 3, 5, 9, 15, 45

    c. 1, 3, 9

    d. 9

10. Inverse Property

11. 814

12. $17.35

13. 24

14. $\frac{5}{7}$

15. $\frac{4}{9}$

16. $\frac{6}{35}$

17. 9250

18. $70.00

19. $\frac{9}{40}$

20. **a.** segment: $\overline{AB}$ (or $\overline{BA}$)

    b. line: $\overleftrightarrow{CD}$ (or $\overleftrightarrow{DC}$)

    c. ray: $\overrightarrow{GH}$

Cumulative Test 3A

1. 4007

2. 1200 beach balls

3. 47

4. $13.15

5. 26 years

6. 72%

7.

8. **a.** 9   **b.** 8

9. $\frac{1}{6}$

10. **a.** 1, 3, 7, 21

    b. 1, 2, 3, 6, 7, 14, 21, 42

    c. 21

11. $\overline{BC}$ (or $\overline{CB}$), $\overline{AB}$ (or $\overline{BA}$), $\overline{AC}$ (or $\overline{CA}$)

12. $1\frac{6}{7}$

13. $1\frac{1}{11}$

14. $1\frac{1}{6}$

15. 2201 R 2

16. 221

17. 10,290

18. 39

19. 300

20. $11.57

Cumulative Test 3B

1. 3768

2. 900 beach balls

3. 29

4. $12.15

5. 13 years

6. 74%

7.

8. **a.** 10 **b.** 6

9. $\frac{3}{8}$

10. **a.** 1, 3, 5, 15

   b. 1, 2, 3, 5, 6, 10, 15, 30

   c. 15

11. $\overline{XY}$ (or $\overline{YX}$), $\overline{YZ}$ (or $\overline{ZY}$), $\overline{XZ}$ (or $\overline{ZX}$)

12. $4\frac{4}{5}$

13. $1\frac{1}{7}$

14. $1\frac{3}{8}$

15. 2004 R 3

16. 296

17. 8890

18. 44

19. 375

20. $15.17

Cumulative Test 4A

1. 1931

2. 160 bushels

3. 25%

4. $\frac{1}{4}$

5. nine hundred fifty-three million

6. **a.** =

   b. Associative Property of Addition

7. $7 - 9 = -2$

8. **a.** 28 cm **b.** 45 cm^2

9. **a.** $3\frac{2}{3}$ **b.** $\frac{3}{7}$

10. $\frac{5}{6}$

11. **a.** 2 **b.** 16

12.

13. 6768

14. $1.37

15. A. $\frac{11}{3}$

16. $2\frac{1}{4}$

17. $\frac{2}{11}$

18. $\frac{9}{16}$

19. 11

20. 312

Cumulative Test **4B**

1. 1932

2. 140 bushels

3. $33\frac{1}{3}\%$

4. $\frac{1}{3}$

5. nine hundred twenty-six million

6. **a.** =

   b. Associative Property of Addition

7. $7 - 10 = -3$

8. **a.** 24 cm   **b.** 32 cm²

9. **a.** $5\frac{3}{4}$ **b.** $\frac{4}{7}$

10. $\frac{5}{6}$

11. **a.** 30   **b.** 20

12.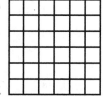

13. 2628

14. $1.34

15. C. $\frac{7}{4}$

16. $1\frac{4}{5}$

17. $\frac{1}{5}$

18. $\frac{4}{9}$

19. 12

20. 288

Cumulative Test **5A**

1. 24 books

2. 1006 years

3. $10.70

4. 126 pages

5. **a.** 24 marbles   **b.** 40 marbles   **c.** $\frac{3}{8}$

6.

7. $2 \cdot 2 \cdot 2 \cdot 2 \cdot 2 \cdot 3 \cdot 5$

8. **a.** $13\frac{1}{2}$ **b.** $9\frac{1}{3}$ **c.** $\frac{2}{15}$

9. B

10. **a.** 30   **b.** 21

11. 350

12. 73

13. 22

14. $5\frac{1}{6}$

15. $12\frac{2}{5}$

16. $3\frac{1}{4}$

17. $\frac{2}{5}$

18. $1\frac{1}{3}$

19. 95

20. **a.** side *AD* (or *DA*)   **b.** 375 mm²

Cumulative Test **5B**

1. 26 books

2. 645 years

Answers

3. $12.70

4. 86 pages

5. a. 16 marbles   **b.** 48 marbles   **c.** $\frac{1}{4}$

6.

7. $2 \cdot 5 \cdot 7 \cdot 7$

8. a. $7\frac{1}{3}$ **b.** $6\frac{2}{3}$ **c.** $\frac{11}{15}$

9. D

10. a. 15   **b.** 10

11. 350

12. 71

13. 23

14. $4\frac{5}{6}$

15. $9\frac{3}{5}$

16. $1\frac{3}{4}$

17. $\frac{2}{7}$

18. $2\frac{2}{3}$

19. 90

20. a. side *BA* (or *AB*)   **b.** 300 mm^2

Cumulative Test 6A

1. 74 in.

2. $3.44

3. 1915 miles

4. a. (1, 4)   **b.** 25 units^2

5. a. 434 mi   **b.** 1736 mi

6. 9 in.

7. $\frac{8}{20} + \frac{15}{20} = \frac{23}{20} = 1\frac{3}{20}$

8. To find the output, multiply the input by 4.

9. 1000

10. $\frac{2}{9}$

11. $<$

12. 24

13. a. $\overline{AB}$ (or $\overline{BA}$)   **b.** $\angle BCA$ (or $\angle ACB$)

14. a. $3 \cdot 3 \cdot 5 \cdot 5$ **b.** 15

15. 12

16. 236

17. 49

18. $\frac{7}{12}$

19. $\frac{1}{12}$

20. $\frac{16}{25}$

Cumulative Test 6B

1. 75 in.

2. $4.54

3. 1472 miles

4. a. (1, 2)   **b.** 16 units^2

5. a. 406 mi   **b.** 1624 mi

6. 15 in.

7. $\frac{12}{20} + \frac{15}{20} = \frac{27}{20} = 1\frac{7}{20}$

8. To find the output, multiply the input by 5.

9. 1000

10. $\frac{4}{9}$

11. $<$

12. 60

13. a. $\overline{PR}$ (or $\overline{RP}$)   **b.** $\angle QMP$ (or $\angle PMQ$)

14. a. $3 \cdot 3 \cdot 7 \cdot 7$ **b.** 21

15. 10

16. 137

17. 39

18. $\frac{5}{12}$

19. $\frac{1}{3}$

20. $1\frac{9}{16}$

Cumulative Test   7A

1. $117.43

2. $2603

3. $0.65

4. 2.5 seconds

5. 20 cm

6. a. 28 fish   **b.** 35 fish

7. 63

8. 15

9. a. $\frac{1}{4}$ **b.** 25%

10. 14.5

11. a. $(-1, 2)$ **b.** 20 units^2

12. 0.34

13. 5

14. one hundred and one hundred thirteen thousandths

15. 2.25

16. 1.25

17. 17.09

18. 39.515

19. $1\frac{1}{10}$

20. $4\frac{3}{10}$

Cumulative Test   7B

1. $112.43

2. $298

3. $0.71

4. 1.6 seconds

5. 12 cm

6. a. 36 fish   **b.** 27 fish

7. 60

8. 18

9. a. $\frac{3}{4}$ **b.** 75%

10. 16.5

11. a. $(-1, -2)$ **b.** 15 units^2

12. 0.57

13. 5

14. one hundred and thirteen hundredths

15. 1.44

16. 0.75

17. 17.18

18. 18.537

19. $1\frac{1}{4}$

20. $\frac{11}{38}$

Cumulative Test   8A

1. $\frac{4}{9}$

2. a. 340 seconds   **b.** 85 seconds

3. 441 miles

Answers

4. **a.** 26 adults   **b.** 78 adults

5. 1.8 m

6. 0.18 m^2

7. 30 mm

8. 4.5 cm

9. {H1, H2, H3, T1, T2, T3}

10. 80°

11. 0.83

12. **a.** 65.03   **b.** $65\frac{3}{100}$

13. 30 cm^2

14. 0.0072

15. 0.024

16. $1\frac{1}{2}$

17. $13\frac{1}{2}$

18. $\frac{7}{9}$

19. 12

20. 0.82

Cumulative Test 8B

1. $\frac{3}{8}$

2. **a.** 380 seconds   **b.** 95 seconds

3. 432 miles

4. **a.** 21 adults   **b.** 84 adults

5. 2.4 m

6. 0.32 m^2

7. 40 mm

8. 2.5 cm

9. {H1, H2, H3, H4, T1, T2, T3, T4}

10. 40°

11. 0.57

12. **a.** 34.07   **b.** $34\frac{7}{100}$

13. 54 cm^2

14. 0.0075

15. 0.018

16. $2\frac{5}{6}$

17. 10

18. $1\frac{2}{7}$

19. 9

20. 1.27

Cumulative Test 9A

1. $\frac{1}{2}$

2. **a.** 91 votes   **b.** 90

3. 1

4. **a.** 2   **b.** $\frac{11}{35}$

5. 10 units^2

6. **a.** $\frac{5}{8}$ were vertiginous.   **b.** $\frac{3}{5}$

7. 22 cm

8. 35°; 145°; 35°

9. 2.25

10. 1.8

11. 52.232

12. $0.4\overline{7}$

13. 0.2

14. 3.86

15. 0.909

16. $8\frac{17}{20}$

17. $2\frac{1}{12}$

18. 72

19. $\frac{3}{8}$

20. 2.4

Cumulative Test **9B**

1. $\frac{1}{3}$

2. a. 90 votes   **b.** 89

3. 0.5

4. a. 6   **b.** $\frac{1}{5}$

5. 12 units^2

6. a. $\frac{5}{9}$ were vertiginous.   **b.** $\frac{4}{5}$

7. 18 cm

8. 50°; 130°; 50°

9. 1.25

10. 1.6

11. 15.545

12. $0.3\overline{7}$

13. 0.6

14. 2.86

15. 0.09

16. $9\frac{13}{20}$

17. $3\frac{5}{12}$

18. 81

19. $2\frac{2}{3}$

20. 1.8

Cumulative Test **10A**

1. 144 miles

2. $2.25

3. 5 to 12 or $\frac{5}{12}$

4. $108.00

5. 0.5

6. a. $\frac{3}{5}$ **b.** 42 buttons

7. 88 cm^2

8. $\frac{6}{25}$

9. $0.4\overline{36}$

10. $\frac{7}{8}$

11. 64 in.^{2}

12. 24

13. 2.8

14. 3.64

15. 37

16. 4 yd 1 ft 3 in.

17. $6\frac{13}{24}$

18. $1\frac{3}{7}$

19. 245

20. 1.255

Cumulative Test **10B**

1. 162 miles

2. $2.55

3. 2 to 5 or $\frac{2}{5}$

4. $106.00

5. 0.5

6. a. $\frac{7}{10}$ **b.** 49 buttons

7. 72 cm^2

8. $\frac{7}{25}$

9. $0.4\overline{45}$

10. $\frac{7}{9}$

69

Answers

11. 49 in.^{2}

12. 33

13. 2.9

14. 3.58

15. 0

16. 4 yd 1 ft 4 in.

17. $4\frac{1}{24}$

18. $2\frac{2}{5}$

19. 425

20. 12.6

Cumulative Test 11A

1. 45 skiffs

2. 128

3. 9¢ per quart

4. 0.6 in.

5. **a.** 12 trucks   **b.** 30%

6. **a.** 4×10^{10} **b.** 18,600,000

7. >

8. 80 cm

9. **a.** $2\frac{1}{2}$ **b.** 2.5   **c.** 0.9   **d.** 90%

10. 6

11. 68 in.^{2}

12. 40 in.

13. 4.36

14. 36

15. 97

16. 19

17. $8\frac{17}{24}$

18. $73\frac{1}{2}$

19. 0.001

20. 300

Cumulative Test 11B

1. 98 dinghies

2. 111

3. 5¢ per liter

4. 0.75 in.

5. **a.** 16 trucks   **b.** 40%

6. **a.** 1.4×10^{10} **b.** 1,500,000

7. >

8. 60 cm

9. **a.** $3\frac{1}{2}$ **b.** 3.5   **c.** 0.7   **d.** 70%

10. 12

11. 36 cm^2

12. 28 cm

13. 3.46

14. 2

15. 43

16. 11

17. $8\frac{19}{24}$

18. 49

19. 0.01

20. 300

Cumulative Test 12A

1. $0.31 per pint

2. $1\frac{1}{3}$ cups

3. 53.4 s

4.

x	y
0	1
1	3
2	5
3	7

5. 13.25

6. a. 60%   **b.** $\frac{2}{3}$

7. a. 2.05×10^{-3} **b.** 0.0000562

8.

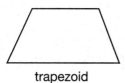

(Sketches may vary.)

trapezoid

9. 5280 ft

10. a. $\frac{3}{25}$ **b.** 0.12   **c.** 0.04   **d.** 4%

11. 15 cm

12. 11 cm^2

13. 6

14. 0.8

15. 109

16. 10,017

17. 12

18. $6\frac{11}{18}$

19. $12\frac{1}{2}$

20. 0.001075

Cumulative Test 12B

1. $0.32 per pint

2. $1\frac{1}{2}$ cups

3. 27.4 s

4.

x	y
0	1
1	4
2	7
3	10

5. $13.50

6. a. 70%   **b.** $\frac{3}{7}$

7. a. 4.05×10^{-3} **b.** 0.0000625

8.

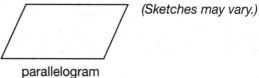

(Sketches may vary.)

parallelogram

9. 3960 ft

10. a. $\frac{4}{25}$ **b.** 0.16   **c.** 0.05   **d.** 5%

11. 13 in.

12. 8 in.^{2}

13. 15

14. 1.9

15. 29

16. 1004

17. 8

18. $7\frac{5}{18}$

19. $2\frac{1}{4}$

20. 0.00055

Cumulative Test 13A

1. $10,750

2. $5.50 per hour

3. 64 girls

4. 3

5. 24

Saxon Math Course 2   **71**

Answers

6. **a.** 25%   **b.** 177 stamps

7. **a.** 8×10^{-5} **b.** 0.00024

8. 110°

9. =

10. 26

11. −7

12. **a.** 0.2   **b.** 20%   **c.** $\frac{3}{25}$ **d.** 12%

13. 180 cm²

14. $\frac{7}{8}$

15. 18

16. 0.05

17. 70

18. $5\frac{1}{12}$

19. 14

20. 0.06

Cumulative Test 13B

1. $10,650

2. $6.50 per hour

3. 100 girls

4. 4

5. 51

6. **a.** 20%   **b.** 188 cards

7. **a.** 6×10^{-4} **b.** 0.0075

8. 60°

9. >

10. 53

11. 4

12. **a.** 0.8   **b.** 80%   **c.** $\frac{3}{20}$ **d.** 15%

13. 140 cm²

14. $\frac{7}{8}$

15. 27

16. 1.5

17. 68

18. $4\frac{7}{12}$

19. 21

20. 0.012

Cumulative Test 14A

1. $24\frac{\text{km}}{\text{hr}}$

2. 147 cats

3. a little too large, because $\pi > 3$

4. **a.** $2.33   **b.** $23.30

5. 0.42

6. **a.** 36 cookies   **b.** 40%

7. **a.** 8 vertices   **b.** 27 ft³

8. **a.** 22π cm   **b.** 880 mm

9. **a.** 1.1×10^{-6} **b.** 1.1×10^{8}

10. 600 mm²

11. 750 mm²

12. 0.1

13. 300

14. **a.** 0.125   **b.** 12.5%

    a. $\frac{9}{50}$ **b.** 0.18

15. 8000 g $\cdot \dfrac{1 \text{ kg}}{1000 \text{ g}}$ = 8 kg

16. 6.6

17. $6\frac{2}{5}$ or 6.4

18. 45.15

19. −12

20. $\frac{4}{21}$

Cumulative Test 14B

1. $16\frac{\text{mi}}{\text{hr}}$

2. 18 cats

3. a little too large, because $\pi > 3$

4. a. $0.41   **b.** $4.10

5. 0.76

6. a. 24 cookies   **b.** 60%

7. a. 12 edges   **b.** 125 in.³

8. a. 16π in.   **b.** 3.14 cm

9. a. 1.2×10^{-5} **b.** 1.2×10^{7}

10. 24 mm²

11. 30 mm²

12. 0.04

13. 180

14. a. 0.375   **b.** 37.5%

   c. $\frac{7}{50}$ **d.** 0.14

15. $9000 \text{ g} \cdot \dfrac{1 \text{ kg}}{1000 \text{ g}} = 9 \text{ kg}$

16. 16.6

17. $5\frac{1}{2}$ or 5.5

18. 14.95

19. −6

20. $\frac{2}{5}$

Cumulative Test 15A

1. 70 pounds

2. 4.8

3. 56 in.

4. 174 in.²

5. 14

6. 250 girls

7. $6.4 \text{ g} \times \dfrac{1000 \text{ mg}}{1 \text{ g}} = 6400 \text{ mg}$

8. a. 60 games   **b.** 36 games

9. 90

10. 2010

11. a. 18   **b.** −54   **c.** 3   **d.** −9

12. 125 cm³

13. a. 132 m   **b.** 40π mm

14. a. $0.1\overline{6}$ **b.** $16\frac{2}{3}$%

   c. $\frac{9}{20}$ **d.** 45%

15. 76

16. 27

17. 3.6

18. $\frac{9}{10}$

19. −6

20. C

Cumulative Test 15B

1. 60 pounds

2. 3.7

3. 38 in.

4. 80 in.²

5. 78

6. 200 girls

7. 4600 mg

8. a. 48 games   **b.** 36 games

9. 96

10. 1200

11. a. 24   **b.** −18   **c.** 4   **d.** −3

12. 27 cm^3

13. a. 62.8 cm   **b.** 30π in.

14. a. 0.08$\overline{3}$ **b.** 8$\frac{1}{3}$%

    c. $\frac{7}{20}$ **d.** 35%

15. 51

16. 16

17. 2.4

18. 1$\frac{1}{8}$

19. −5

20. B

Cumulative Test 16A

1. $\frac{\$6.70}{hr}$

2. 6

3.

4. 15 articles of clothing

5. 960 customers

6. 47 m

7.

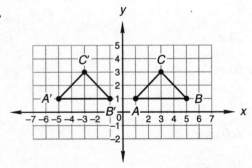

A' (−5, 1)
B' (−1, 1)
C' (−3, 3)

8.

9. 56 in.

10. a. −80   **b.** 1.2   **c.** −300   **d.** −$\frac{1}{6}$

11. a. 0.8$\overline{3}$ **b.** 83$\frac{1}{3}$%   **c.** $\frac{3}{5}$ **d.** 60%

12. 36 m^2

13. 1350

14. 75%

15. 80

16. 1.58

17. $\frac{4}{75}$

18. 5

19. 3$\frac{1}{3}$

20. 5.1

Cumulative Test 16B

1. $\frac{\$6.75}{hr}$

2. 12

3.

4. 10 articles of clothing

5. 720 customers

6. 44 m

7.

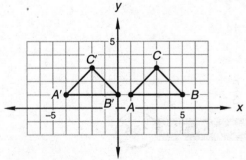

A' (−4, 1)
B' (0, 1)
C' (−2, 3)

8.

```
  ←———●———+———+———+———+———+———→
   -6  -5  -4  -3  -2  -1   0   1
```

9. 64 in.

10. a. −60 **b.** −1.2 **c.** −450 **d.** $\frac{1}{6}$

11. a. $0.\overline{1}$ **b.** $11\frac{1}{9}\%$ **c.** $\frac{4}{5}$ **d.** 80%

12. 22 m^2

13. 1080

14. 80%

15. 75

16. 2.57

17. $\frac{1}{15}$

18. 1

19. $\frac{3}{10}$

20. −0.2

Cumulative Test 17A

1. 6 games

2. a. 77   **b.** 75

  c. 60, 70, 80   **c.** 40

3. 99 dandelions

4. $0.47 \text{ L} \cdot \dfrac{1000 \text{ mL}}{1 \text{ L}} = 470 \text{ mL}$

5.

```
  ←———+———+———+———●———+———+———+———→
   -6  -5  -4  -3  -2  -1   0   1
```

6. $4xy - 3x$

7. 24 miles

8. 180 children

9. a. $50,000   **b.** 10%

10. 24 in.^{3}

11. 113.04 in.^{2}

12. a. 0.35   **b.** 35%

  c. $\frac{3}{50}$ **d.** 0.06

13. 3.25×10^{15}

14. parallelogram; 49 cm

15. 140 cm^2

16. 11

17. $\frac{8}{9}$

18. 12

19. −8

20. $y = 2x + 1$

x	y
0	1
1	3
2	5

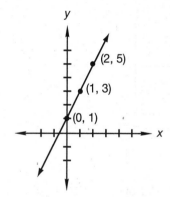

Cumulative Test 17B

1. 15 games

2. a. 67   **b.** 65   **c.** 50, 60, 70   **d.** 40

3. 81 dandelions

4. $0.84 \text{ L} \cdot \dfrac{1000 \text{ mL}}{1 \text{ L}} = 840 \text{ mL}$

5.

```
  ←———+———●———+———+———+———+———+———→
   -4  -3  -2  -1   0   1   2   3
```

6. $5xy - 2x$

Answers

7. 36 miles

8. 200 children

9. **a.** $60,000   **b.** 30%

10. 30 in.³

11. 154 in.²

12. **a.** 0.15   **b.** 15%   **c.** $\frac{2}{25}$ **d.** 0.08

13. 3.6×10^{13}

14. parallelogram; 98 mm

15. 560 mm²

16. 12

17. $\frac{29}{30}$

18. 0

19. −8

20.   **y = 2x − 1**

x	y
0	−1
2	3
3	5

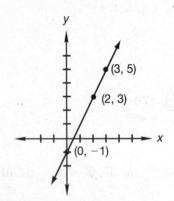

Cumulative Test 18A

1. 8 bears

2. 3000 cm³

3. $\frac{1}{12}$

4. 9 yd²

5.
```
 ←─┼──┼──●──●──┼──┼──┼──┼──→
  −4 −3 −2 −1  0  1  2  3
```

6. 60°

7. **a.** $48   **b.** 75%

8. **a.** 55°   **b.** 55°

9.   3 diagonals

10. 88 in.

11. 400 mm²

12. 7

13. **a.** $\frac{1}{50}$ **b.** 2%

14. 20%

15. 2750 customers

16. 1×10^{-7}

17. 30

18. 6.57

19. $8x^2y$

20. −5

Cumulative Test 18B

1. 18 bears

2. 4500 cm³

3. $\frac{1}{12}$

4. 6 yd²

5.
```
 ←─┼──┼──●──●──●──┼──┼──┼──→
  −5 −4 −3 −2 −1  0  1  2
```

6. 45°

7. **a.** $40   **b.** 80%

8. a. 50°   **b.** 60°

9.   2 diagonals

10. 94.2 in.

11. 500 mm^2

12. 7

13. a. $\frac{1}{25}$ **b.** 4%

14. 40%

15. 1650 customers

16. 1×10^{-8}

17. 45

18. 11.25

19. $-6a^3b^2$

20. -7

Cumulative Test   19A

1. 96

2. $\frac{7}{9}$

3. $8.00

4. $\frac{1}{12}$

5. 40¢ per pound

6. 75%

7. $1000 \text{ cm}^2 \cdot \frac{10 \text{ mm}}{1 \text{ cm}} \cdot \frac{10 \text{ mm}}{1 \text{ cm}} = 100{,}000 \text{ mm}^2$

8. -13

9. 240 cm^3

10. a. 2.5   **b.** 250%

   c. $\frac{1}{40}$ **d.** 0.025

11. a. $5.76   **b.** $101.76

12. 2.8×10^5

13.

-3 -2 -1 0 1 2 3 4

14. 36

15. 33

16. 50

17. $6x^3y^3$

18. $2\frac{5}{6}$

19. $2x + 2y$

20. -13

Cumulative Test   19B

1. 98

2. $\frac{3}{5}$

3. $12.00

4. $\frac{2}{15}$

5. 60¢ per pound

6. 80%

7. $10 \text{ cm}^2 \cdot \frac{10 \text{ mm}}{1 \text{ cm}} \cdot \frac{10 \text{ mm}}{1 \text{ cm}} = 1000 \text{ mm}^2$

8. -9

9. 64 cm^3

10. a. 1.5   **b.** 150%   **c.** $\frac{3}{40}$ **d.** 0.075

11. a. $7.44   **b.** $131.44

12. 1.6×10^8

13.

-1 0 1 2 3 4

14. 18

15. 29

16. 16

17. $-15x^3y^3$

Answers

18. $5\frac{1}{6}$

19. $2x - 2y$

20. -7

Cumulative Test 20A

1. 85.5

2. $9.00 per hour

3. 140%

4. 2,000,000 cm^3

5. **a.** 30 eggs   **b.** $83\frac{1}{3}\%$

6. 5

7. 9 in.^{2}

8. $\frac{1}{9}$

9. 72 cm^3

10. 314 cm^2

11. $381.60

12. $14.00

13. 60°

14. 3.2×10^{-4}

15. 5.5

16. 36

17. 100

18. 4 yd 5 in.

19. $5x + 6$

20. -7

Cumulative Test 20B

1. 86.5

2. $8.00 per hour

3. 130%

4. 3,000,000 cm^3

5. **a.** 18 eggs   **b.** $83\frac{1}{3}\%$

6. 7

7. 36 in.^{2}

8. $\frac{1}{9}$

9. 96 cm^3

10. 616 in.^{2}

11. $342.40

12. $16.00

13. 120°

14. 2.1×10^{-4}

15. 10.5

16. 18

17. 83

18. 3 yd 3 in.

19. $6x + 6$

20. -13

Cumulative Test 21A

1. $3.60

2. $\frac{80 \text{ km}}{\text{hr}}$

3. 576 in. or 48 ft

4. $175

5. $45

6. $51.12

7. 31.7 cm

8. 10 in.

9. 36 in.^{2}

10. 282.6 cm^3

11. .9

12. 36°

13. **a.** $-3, \sqrt{3}, 3, 3^2$ **b.** $\sqrt{3}$

14. 1 to 3

15. B. $\sqrt{79}$

16. 9

17. 1.6

18. $4x$

19. 1

20. 3

Cumulative Test 21B

1. $2.70

2. $\dfrac{600 \text{ mi}}{\text{hr}}$

3. 360 in. or 30 ft

4. $75

5. $65

6. $89.46

7. 29.7 cm

8. 8 in.

9. 144 in.^{2}

10. 251.2 cm^3

11. 15

12. 50°

13. **a.** $-5, \sqrt{5}, 5, 5^2$ **b.** $\sqrt{5}$

14. 1 to 3

15. B. $\sqrt{35}$

16. 12

17. 2.4

18. $8x^3$

19. 12

20. 2

Cumulative Test 22A

1. **a.** 89   **b.** 88.5   **c.** 88   **d.** 11

2. $\dfrac{1}{17}$

3. $140

4. 75 marbles

5. $78 per day

6. 15,700 cm^3

7. 9.01

8.
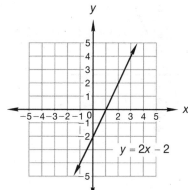
slope = 2

9. $86.00

10. 3500

11. 150 cm^3

12. 75°

13. $\dfrac{d}{r} = t$

14. 20°

15. **a.** 12   **b.** $\dfrac{3}{2}$ or 1.5

16. 36

17. 18

Answers

18. −7

19. 80

20. −2

1. **a.** 94   **b.** 93   **c.** 93   **d.** 10

2. $\frac{1}{17}$

3. $640

4. 462 peanuts

5. $91 per day

6. 18.84 cm³

7. 10.16

8.

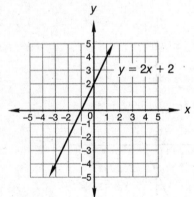

slope = 2

9. $43.00

10. 1750

11. 210 cm³

12. 65°

13. $\frac{d}{t} = r$

14. 40°

15. **a.** 4   **b.** 3

16. 18

17. 18

18. −35

19. 94

20. −2y

1. $14.70

2. $64.75

3. $30

4. 2×10^3

5. 0.94

6. $\frac{2}{3}$

7. $499.20

8. 15%

9. **a.** 3 L   **b.** 3 kg

10. $4 \text{ ft}^2 \cdot \frac{12 \text{ in.}}{1 \text{ ft}} \cdot \frac{12 \text{ in.}}{1 \text{ ft}} = 576 \text{ in.}^2$

11. 40 yd

12. 6000 m³

13.

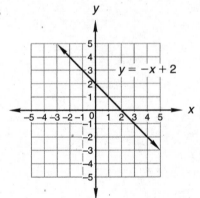

slope = −1

14. 4

15. 60°

16. 25

17. $x < 1$

18. 1

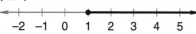

19. $\dfrac{3x}{2}$

20. 2

Cumulative Test **23B**

1. $15.75

2. $71.75

3. $28

4. 4×10^6

5. 1.04

6. $\dfrac{2}{3}$

7. $579.60

8. 25%

9. a. 9 L   **b.** 9 kg

10. 54 ft^2

11. 10 yd

12. 1570 in.^{3}

13.

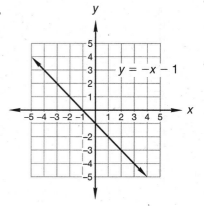

slope $= -1$

14. 8

15. 20°

16. 10

17. $x \geq 1$

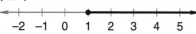

18. 1

19. x

20. 4

Answers

1. B. $24 \cdot 25 = s$

2. A. 156

3. C. $12.65

4. A. $\frac{1}{2}$

5. C. 8

6. C. 21

7. C. $2 \cdot 2 \cdot 2 \cdot 3 \cdot 5 \cdot 5$

8. B. $\frac{4}{5}$

9. B.

10. C. $\frac{63}{72}$

11. B. $\frac{360}{15}$

12. A. $24 + 36$

13. D. $\frac{1}{16}, \frac{1}{8}, \frac{1}{4}, \frac{1}{2}$

14. C. $1\frac{3}{4}$

15. D. $3\frac{1}{10}$ miles

16. C. $2\frac{1}{3}$

17. B. $\frac{1}{2}$

18. C. $\frac{3}{5}$

19. D. 90

20. B. $\overline{DC}$

21. D. 875 mm^2

22. A. Commutative Property

23. D. Inverse Property

24. C. 36

25. D. $36 \cdot 2 = 72$

1. C. 40

2. B. 7 years

3. D. 26

4. B. {HA, HB, HC, TA, TB, TC}

5. D. 36

6. B. 9.3×10^7

7. B. 0.6, 0.65, $0.\overline{6}$

8. A. $12 \text{ yd} \times \frac{3 \text{ ft}}{1 \text{ yd}} = 36 \text{ ft}$

9. C. 0.4, 40%

10. C. 8

11. C. 36 cm

12. A. $A \approx 4 \text{ in.} \times 2 \text{ in.}$

13. D. 4.4

14. B. 8

15. C. 23

16. D. 5

17. B. $5\frac{1}{12}$

18. C. $2\frac{1}{4}$

19. B. 0.1 m^2

20. A. 30

21. D. 0.4

22. C. 6

23. D. 54 cm^2

24. A. $d = 4 \text{ hr} \cdot 55 \text{ mi per hour}$

25. B. Point B

Benchmark Test 3

1. C. 12 days

2. B. $305,000

3. B. 56 mph

4. D. 15.24 cm

5. B. $x < 1$

6. A. $5xy + 3x$

7. D. 6 miles

8. B. 300

9. A. 240

10. C. 360 in.^{3}

11. C. 36π cm^2

12. C. $\frac{4}{5}$, 80%

13. B. 7.5×10^{11}

14. B.

15. A. 96 cm^2

16. B. 12

17. C. $\frac{1}{2}$

18. C. 8

19. A. 0

20. B. $y = 2x$

21. B. 75 inches

22. C. $\frac{1}{9}$

23. B. 55°

24. D. 3

25. C. 88 ft^2

Saxon Math Course 2 **83**

Answers

1. A. 20.8

2. C. 80.44

3. B. 1.98

4. B. 0.021

5. D. 0.002

6. A. 8

7. B. $1\frac{5}{12}$

8. C. $12\frac{1}{2}$

9. A. $2\frac{1}{3}$

10. C. $\frac{3x}{5y}$

11. B. 4

12. D. 3.2×10^8

13. A. 30.48 cm

14. C. 86°F

15. E. None correct

16. B. 2^8

17. C. 4

18. B. 10.02

19. C. 110

20. A. −1, 0, 0.1, 1

21. B. 3.6

22. A. 75

23. A. 92

24. B. 85

25. D. $\frac{1}{36}$

26. C. $205

27. B. 19.3 mpg

28. C. $48.00

29. A. $87\frac{1}{2}$%

30. C. 15 min

31. C.

32. D. 130°

33. A. 13.2 m

34. C. 63 in.

35. C. 54 in.^{2}

36. B. 28.26 in.^{2}

37. B. 240 cm^3

38. A. 15

39. B. 50 mm

40. C. 75°

41. B. −34

42. A. 40

43. D. −12

44. C. $2^2 \cdot 5^3$

45. A. $3x - 9$

46. B. 2

47. C. $2x - 6$

48. D. xy

49. A.

50. C. $y = 2x + 2$

Baseline Test

1.
$$25\overline{)7610} \quad 304\frac{10}{25} = 304\frac{2}{5}$$

$$304\frac{10}{25}$$

$$\begin{array}{r} 75 \\ \hline 11 \\ 0 \\ \hline 110 \\ 100 \\ \hline 10 \end{array}$$

C. $304\frac{2}{5}$

2.
$$\begin{array}{r} 8.75 \\ 6. \\ + 4.5 \\ \hline 19.25 \end{array}$$

D. 19.25

3.
$$\begin{array}{r} 1.80 \\ - 0.25 \\ \hline 1.55 \end{array}$$

A. 1.55

4.
$$\begin{array}{r} 0.15 \\ \times \quad 4.2 \\ \hline 030 \\ 060 \\ \hline 0.630 \end{array}$$

A. 0.63

5.
$$07_{.}\overline{)36_{.}4}$$ with quotient 5.2

$$\begin{array}{r} 35 \\ \hline 1\,4 \\ 1\,4 \\ \hline 0 \end{array}$$

B. 5.2

6. $1\frac{2}{3} + 2\frac{5}{6} = 1\frac{4}{6} + 2\frac{5}{6} = 3\frac{9}{6} = 4\frac{3}{6} = 4\frac{1}{2}$

B. $4\frac{1}{2}$

7. $3\frac{2}{5} - 1\frac{1}{2} = 3\frac{4}{10} - 1\frac{5}{10}$

$$= 2\frac{14}{10} - 1\frac{5}{10} = 1\frac{9}{10}$$

C. $1\frac{9}{10}$

8. $\frac{4}{5} \times 3\frac{1}{3} = \frac{4}{\cancel{5}_1} \times \frac{\cancel{10}^2}{3} = \frac{8}{3} = 2\frac{2}{3}$

C. $2\frac{2}{3}$

9. $2\frac{2}{5} \div 1\frac{1}{2} = \frac{12}{5} \div \frac{3}{2}$

$$= \frac{\cancel{12}^4}{5} \times \frac{2}{\cancel{3}_1} = \frac{8}{5} = 1\frac{3}{5}$$

A. $1\frac{3}{5}$

10. $\frac{60}{84} = \frac{\cancel{2} \cdot \cancel{2} \cdot \cancel{3} \cdot 5}{\cancel{2} \cdot \cancel{2} \cdot \cancel{3} \cdot 7} = \frac{5}{7}$

C. $\frac{5}{7}$

11. B. 4

12. A. 2,500,000

13.
$$1.2 \,\cancel{m} \cdot \left(\frac{1 \text{ km}}{1000 \,\cancel{m}}\right) = 0.0012 \text{ km}$$

$$1.2 \,\cancel{m} \cdot \left(\frac{100 \text{ cm}}{1 \,\cancel{m}}\right) = 120 \text{ cm}$$

$$1.2 \,\cancel{m} \cdot \left(\frac{1000 \text{ mm}}{1 \,\cancel{m}}\right) = 1200 \text{ mm}$$

C. 1200 mm

14. B. 2 m

15.
$$0.4 \times 100\% = 40\%$$
$$\frac{2}{5} \times 100\% = 40\%$$
$$\frac{40}{100} \times 100\% = 40\%$$
$$0.04 \times 100\% = 4\%$$

D. 0.04

16. $10^3 \cdot 10^4 = 10^{3+4} = 10^7$

B. 10^7

17.
$$10 \times 10 = 100 < 199$$
$$14 \times 14 = 196 < 199$$
$$15 \times 15 = 225 > 199$$
$$14 < \sqrt{199} < 15$$

C. 14 and 15

Solutions

18. Twenty-five thousandths = 0.025

E. None correct

19. $17.36 + 8.7 \approx 17 + 9 = 26$

D. 26

20. $33\% = 0.33$

$33\frac{1}{3}\% = 0.\overline{3}$

$\frac{1}{3} = 0.\overline{3}$

C. 0.3, 33%, $\frac{1}{3}$

21. $\frac{8}{12} = \frac{12}{n}$

$8n = (12)(12)$

$8n = 144$

$n = \frac{144}{8}$

$n = 18$

C. 18

22.

	Ratio	Actual Count
Boys	2	B
Girls	3	18
Total	5	T

$\frac{3}{5} = \frac{18}{T}$

$3T = 90$

$T = 30$

D. 30

23. $3(25) = 75$

$75 - 22 - 22 = 75 - 44 = 31$

D. 31

24. The measures, in order, are 6, 8, 8, 8, 9, 9, 10, 11, 12, 16. The number of measures is even, so the median is the average of the two middle values:

$\frac{9 \text{ in.} + 9 \text{ in.}}{2} = \frac{18 \text{ in.}}{2} = 9 \text{ in.}$

B. 9 in.

25. There are 3 favorable outcomes out of 6 possible outcomes.

$\text{Probability} = \frac{\text{Favorable}}{\text{Possible}} = \frac{3}{6} = \frac{1}{2}$

C. $\frac{1}{2}$

26.

$$\begin{array}{r} \$2.89 \\ \times \ \ 0.08 \\ \hline 0.2312 \end{array} \longrightarrow \$0.23 \text{ tax} \qquad \begin{array}{r} \$2.89 \\ + \ \$0.23 \\ \hline \$3.12 \end{array}$$

B. $3.12

27.

$$\begin{array}{r} 0.13 \\ 32\overline{)4.16} \\ \underline{3\ 2} \\ 96 \\ \underline{96} \\ 0 \end{array}$$

C. 13¢/oz

28.

	%	Actual Count
Original	100	$36
Change	25	C
New	75	S

$\frac{100}{75} = \frac{\$36}{S}$

$100S = \$2700$

$S = \$27.00$

C. $27.00

29.

$$\begin{array}{r} 0.84 = 84\% \\ 25\overline{)21.00} \\ \underline{20\ 0} \\ 1\ 00 \\ \underline{1\ 00} \\ 0 \end{array}$$

B. 84%

30. $2\frac{1}{2}\,\text{hours} \times 400\frac{\text{miles}}{\text{hour}} = 1000 \text{ miles}$

D. 1000 miles

31. B.

32. $m\angle x + m\angle y + 90° = 180°$
$m\angle y = 180° - 90° - m\angle x$
$m\angle y = 90° - 38°$
$m\angle y = 52°$

A. 52°

33. Perimeter $= 7\,\text{cm} + 11\,\text{cm} + 8\,\text{cm}$
$+ 9\,\text{cm} + 15\,\text{cm} + 20\,\text{cm} = 70\,\text{cm}$

D. 70 cm

34. Circumference $= 2\pi r \approx 2(3.14)(10\,\text{in.})$
$= 62.8\,\text{in.}$

B. 62.8 in.

35. Area $= \frac{1}{2}bh = \frac{1}{2}(9\,\text{m})(12\,\text{m}) = 54\,\text{m}^2$

B. 54 m²

36. Area $= \pi r^2 = \pi(4\,\text{ft})^2 = 16(3.14)\text{ft}^2$
$= 50.24\,\text{ft}^2$

A. 50 ft²

37. Volume $= lwh = 8\,\text{cm} \times 5\,\text{cm} \times 2\,\text{cm}$
$= 80\,\text{cm}^3$

A. 80 cm³

38. C.

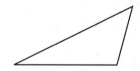

39. D. $\overline{TS}$

40. $3^2 + 4^2 = c^2$
$25 = c^2$
$5 = c$

A. 5

41. $(-6) + (-3) + (+2) = (-9) + (2) = -7$

B. −7

42. $4(3)(12) = 12(12) = 144$

D. 144

43. $3[16 - 2(5 - 3)] = 3[16 - 2(2)]$
$= 3(16 - 4) = 3(12) = 36$

C. 36

44.

$$
\begin{array}{c}
24 \\
2 \quad 12 \\
2 \quad 6 \\
2 \quad 3
\end{array}
\longrightarrow 2^3 \cdot 3 = 24
$$

A. $2^3 \cdot 3$

45. $6(25) = 6(20 + 5) = 6 \cdot 20 + 6 \cdot 5$

D. $6 \cdot 20 + 6 \cdot 5$

46. $3m - 1 = 35$
$3m - 1 + 1 = 35 + 1$
$3m = 36$
$\dfrac{3m}{3} = \dfrac{36}{3}$
$m = 12$

B. 12

47. A. $\sqrt{9} < 2^2$

48. $(-10)(-10) = 100$

B. 100

49. Since $-3 < -2$, x cannot be -3.

D. −3

50.

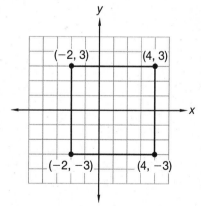

A. $(-2, -3)$

Solutions

a. $0.45 per glass; 45¢ per glass

b. 0

c. Product of 4 and 4 = 16
   Sum of 4 and 4 = 8

$$\begin{array}{r} 2 \\ 8\overline{)16} \\ \underline{16} \\ 0 \end{array}$$

d.
$$\begin{array}{r} \overset{1}{} \$1.75 \\ \$0.60 \\ + \ \$3.00 \\ \hline \$5.35 \end{array}$$

e.
$$\begin{array}{r} \$ \overset{1}{2}. \overset{9}{\cancel{0}}{}^{1}0 \\ - \ \$ 0.4\ 7 \\ \hline \$ 1.5\ 3 \end{array}$$

f.
$$\begin{array}{r} \$0.65 \\ \times \ \ \ \ 5 \\ \hline \$3.25 \end{array}$$

g.
$$\begin{array}{r} 250 \\ \times \ \ 24 \\ \hline 1000 \\ 500 \ \ \\ \hline 6000 \end{array}$$

h.
$$\begin{array}{r} \$4.80 \\ 5\overline{)\$24.00} \\ \underline{20} \ \ \ \ \\ 4\ 0 \\ \underline{4\ 0} \\ 0 \end{array}$$

i.
$$\begin{array}{r} 13 \\ 18\overline{)234} \\ \underline{18} \ \ \\ 54 \\ \underline{54} \\ 0 \end{array}$$

j.
$$\begin{array}{r} 20 \\ + \ \ 4 \\ \hline 24 \end{array}$$

k.
$$\begin{array}{r} 20 \\ - \ \ 4 \\ \hline 16 \end{array}$$

l.
$$\begin{array}{r} 20 \\ \times \ \ 4 \\ \hline 80 \end{array}$$

m.
$$\begin{array}{r} 5 \\ 4\overline{)20} \end{array}$$

n.–s. Answers will vary.

1. Product of 5 and 6 = 30
   Sum of 5 and 6 = 11
   30 − 11 = **19**

2.
$$\begin{array}{r} 8 \\ + \ \ 9 \end{array}$$
   minuend; the minuend is **17**

3.
$$\begin{array}{r} 8 \\ 4\overline{)\text{dividend}} \end{array}$$
   ; the dividend is **32**

4. Product of 6 and 6 = 36
   Sum of 6 and 6 = 12

$$\begin{array}{r} 3 \\ 12\overline{)36} \\ \underline{36} \\ 0 \end{array}$$

5. Addition, subtraction, multiplication, and division

6. **a.** 12 + 4 = **16**

   b. 12 − 4 = **8**

   c. 12 · 4 = **48**

   d. $\dfrac{12}{4} = 3$

7.
$$\begin{array}{r} \$ \overset{3}{\cancel{4}}{}^{1}3. \overset{6}{\cancel{7}}{}^{1}4 \\ - \ \$ 1\ 6.5\ 9 \\ \hline \$ 2\ 7.1\ 5 \end{array}$$

88

8.
```
      64
    × 37
    ─────
     448
     192
    ─────
    2368
```

9.
```
      7
      8
      4
      6
      9
      3
      5
    + 7
    ────
     49
```

10.
```
     ¹²
    364
     52
    867
  +   9
  ──────
   1292
```

11.
```
   ³ ⁹ ⁹
   4̸ 0̸ 0̸ ¹0
 − 3 6 2 5
 ──────────
     3 7 5
```

12.
```
     316
   ×  18
   ──────
    2528
     316
   ──────
    5688
```

13.
```
        $2.18
   20)$43.60
       40
       ──
        36
        20
       ───
       160
       160
       ───
         0
```

14.
```
     300
   ×  40
   ──────
  12,000
```

15.
```
     12          96
   ×  8        ×  0
   ────        ────
     96           0
```

16.
```
       309
   12)3708
      36
      ───
      108
      108
      ───
        0
```

17.
```
     365
   ×  20
   ──────
    7300
```

18.
```
       30 R 17
   25)767
      75
      ──
      17
       0
      ──
      17
```

19.
```
      30
    × 40
    ─────
    1200
```

20.
```
       ⁰ ⁹ ⁹
   $ 1̸ 0̸. 0̸ ¹0
 − $    2. 3 4
 ───────────────
   $    7. 6 6
```

21.
```
     ³ ⁹
   4̸ 0̸ ¹1 7
 − 3 9 5 2
 ──────────
       6 5
```

22.
```
     $2.50
   ×    80
   ────────
   $200.00
```

23.
```
     $2.50
   ×    20
   ────────
    $50.00
```

24.
```
       40
   14)560
      56
      ──
      00
       0
      ──
       0
```

25.
```
       $1.25
   8)$10.00
      8
      ──
      2 0
      1 6
      ───
        40
        40
        ──
         0
```

Solutions

26. Natural numbers

27. $0.25; 25¢

28. All counting numbers are whole numbers.

29. Quotient

30. Minuend − subtrahend = difference

Early Finishers Solutions

a.
$$\begin{array}{r} \$33.50 \\ 4{\overline{\smash{\big)}\,\$134.00}} \end{array}$$

b.
$$\begin{array}{r} 500 \\ -134 \\ \hline 366 \end{array} \qquad \begin{array}{r} 366 \\ +\ 33.50 \\ \hline \$399.50 \end{array}$$

a. The additive identity is zero. The multiplicative identity is 1.

b. Division

c. $(x + y) + z = x + (y + z)$
Numerical answers may vary.

d. Commutative property of multiplication

e. $(5 + 4) + 3 = (9) + 3 = \textbf{12}$

f. $5 + (4 + 3) = 5 + (7) = \textbf{12}$

g. $(10 - 5) - 3 = (5) - 3 = \textbf{2}$

h. $10 - (5 - 3) = 10 - (2) = \textbf{8}$

i. $(6 \cdot 2) \cdot 5 = (12) \cdot 5 = \textbf{60}$

j. $6 \cdot (2 \cdot 5) = 6 \cdot (10) = \textbf{60}$

k. $(12 \div 6) \div 2 = (2) \div 2 = \textbf{1}$

l. $12 \div (6 \div 2) = 12 \div (3) = \textbf{4}$

m.
a. Commutative property of multiplication
b. Associative property of multiplication
c. Multiplied 5 by 2
d. Multiplied 10 by 14

1. Product of 2 and 3 = 6
   Sum of 4 and 5 = 9
   9 − 6 = **3**

2. $0.04; 4¢

3. 75¢ per apple; $0.75 per apple

4. Subtraction

5.
$$\begin{array}{r} 15 \\ 4{\overline{\smash{\big)}\,60}} \\ \underline{4} \\ 20 \\ \underline{20} \\ 0 \end{array}$$

6. $3 \times 5 = 15 \quad 15 \div 5 = 3$
   $5 \times 3 = 15 \quad 15 \div 3 = 5$

7.
a. Commutative property of addition
b. Associative property of addition

8.
$$\begin{array}{r} \$\overset{1}{2}\overset{9}{0}.\overset{9}{0}{}^{1}0 \\ -\ \$14.79 \\ \hline \$5.21 \end{array}$$

9.
$$\begin{array}{r} \$1.54 \\ \times\qquad 7 \\ \hline \$10.78 \end{array}$$

10.
$$\begin{array}{r} \$3.75 \\ 8{\overline{\smash{\big)}\,\$30.00}} \\ \underline{24} \\ 60 \\ \underline{56} \\ 40 \\ \underline{40} \\ 0 \end{array}$$

11.
```
  1 1
$ 4.36
$ 0.75
$12.00
+ $ 0.06
$17.17
```

12.
```
  1 1
$4.89        $ 1̷0. 0̷¹0
+ $0.74      −  $ 5. 6 3
$5.63        $ 4. 3 7
```

13.
```
   8
   5
   4
   6
   5
   4
   3
   7
   2
   4
   1
 + 8
  57
```

14.
```
     207
15)3105
   30
   10
    0
   105
   105
     0
```

15.
```
   40 R 30
40)1630
   160
    30
     0
    30
```

16. 9 ÷ 3 = 3
```
      27
   3)81
     6
     21
     21
      0
```

17.
```
    9
 9)81
   81
    0
```
9 ÷ 3 = **3**

18.
```
   $3.75
 ×   10
 $37.50
```

19.
```
 4̷ 5̷¹0          3̷ 1̷¹6 7
−  7 8         −  3 7 2
  3 7 2          2 7 9 5
```

20.
```
 3̷¹1 6 7         2 7 7̷¹7
−   4 50        −    7 8
  2 7 1 7         2 6 3 9
```

21.
```
       $1.25
16)$20.00
   16
    40
    32
     80
     80
      0
```

22.
```
     70
 ×  800
 56,000
```

23.
```
   1 1 2
   3714
    268
     47
 +    9
   4038
```

24.
```
    5        20        60       120
 ×  4      ×  3      ×  2      ×  1
   20        60       120       120
```

25.
```
  $1.47         $ 2̷0. 0̷¹0
+ $8.00        −  $ 9. 4 7
  $9.47          $ 1 0. 5 3
```

26.
```
   $0.45
 ×     30
 $13.50
```

27. a. **Property of zero for multiplication**

   b. **Identity property of multiplication**

28. a. 18 − 3 = **15**

Solutions

b.
$$\begin{array}{r} 18 \\ \times\ \ 3 \\ \hline 54 \end{array}$$

c. $\dfrac{18}{3} = 6$

d. $18 + 3 = 21$

29. Zero is called the additive identity because when zero is added to another number, the sum is identical to that number.

30. Dividend ÷ divisor = quotient

Practice Set 3

a.
$$\begin{array}{r} \overset{2}{\cancel{3}}{}^{1}1 \\ -\ 1\ 2 \\ \hline 1\ 9 \end{array} \qquad a = 19$$

b.
$$\begin{array}{r} 15 \\ +\ 24 \\ \hline 39 \end{array} \qquad b = 39$$

c.
$$\begin{array}{r} 12 \\ 15\overline{)180} \\ \underline{15} \\ 30 \\ \underline{30} \\ 0 \end{array} \qquad c = 12$$

d.
$$\begin{array}{r} 12 \\ \times\ \ 8 \\ \hline 96 \end{array} \qquad d = 96$$

e.
$$\begin{array}{r} 30 \\ 14\overline{)420} \\ \underline{42} \\ 00 \\ \underline{0} \\ 0 \end{array} \qquad e = 30$$

f.
$$\begin{array}{r} \overset{3}{\cancel{4}}{}^{1}3 \\ -\ 2\ 6 \\ \hline 1\ 7 \end{array} \qquad f = 17$$

g.
$$\begin{array}{r} 51 \\ -\ 20 \\ \hline 31 \end{array} \qquad g = 31$$

h.
$$\begin{array}{r} 52 \\ 7\overline{)364} \\ \underline{35} \\ 14 \\ \underline{14} \\ 0 \end{array} \qquad h = 52$$

i.
$$\begin{array}{r} 6 \\ 4\overline{)24} \\ \underline{24} \\ 0 \end{array} \qquad i = 6$$

j. $3 + 6 + 12 + 5 = 26$
$30 - 26 = 4 \qquad j = 4$

k. Answers will vary.

Written Practice 3

1. Product of 4 and 4 = 16
   Sum of 4 and 4 = 8
   $$\dfrac{16}{8} = 2$$

2. Add the subtrahend and the difference to find the minuend.

3. Associative property of addition

4.
$$\begin{array}{r} \overset{1}{2}{}^{1}1 \\ -\ \ \ 7 \\ \hline 1\ 4 \end{array}$$

5. $3 \cdot 4 = 4 \cdot 3$

6. a. Commutative property
   b. Associative property

7.
$$\begin{array}{r} \overset{0}{\cancel{1}}\ {}^{1}\overset{0}{\cancel{1}}{}^{1}2 \\ -\ \ \ 8\ 3 \\ \hline 2\ 9 \end{array}$$
$x = 29$

8.
$$\begin{array}{r} \overset{8}{\cancel{9}}{}^{1}6 \\ -\ \ 2\ 7 \\ \hline 6\ 9 \end{array}$$
$r = 69$

9.

$$
\begin{array}{r}
17 \\
7\overline{)119} \\
\underline{7} \\
49 \\
\underline{49} \\
0
\end{array}
$$

$k = $ **17**

10.

$$
\begin{array}{r}
\overset{2}{\cancel{3}}\overset{9}{\cancel{0}}{}^{1}0 \\
-\ 1\ 2\ 7 \\
\hline
1\ 7\ 3
\end{array}
$$

$z = $ **173**

11.

$$
\begin{array}{r}
731 \\
+\ 137 \\
\hline
868
\end{array}
$$

$m = $ **868**

12.

$$
\begin{array}{r}
16 \\
25\overline{)400} \\
\underline{25} \\
150 \\
\underline{150} \\
0
\end{array}
$$

$n = $ **16**

13.

$$
\begin{array}{r}
25 \\
25\overline{)625} \\
\underline{50} \\
125 \\
\underline{125} \\
0
\end{array}
$$

$w = $ **25**

14.

$$
\begin{array}{r}
700 \\
\times\ \ \ \ 60 \\
\hline
42{,}000
\end{array}
$$

$x = $ **42,000**

15. **a.** $\dfrac{20}{5} = $ **4**

b. $20 - 5 = $ **15**

c. $20(5) = $ **100**

d. $20 + 5 = $ **25**

16. $16 \div 2 = 8$

$$
\begin{array}{r}
\mathbf{12} \\
8\overline{)96} \\
\underline{8} \\
16 \\
\underline{16} \\
0
\end{array}
$$

17.

$$
\begin{array}{r}
6 \\
16\overline{)96} \\
\underline{96} \\
0
\end{array}
\qquad 6 \div 2 = \mathbf{3}
$$

18.

$$
\begin{array}{r}
\overset{1\ 1}{\ }\overset{1}{\ } \\
\$16.47 \\
\$15.00 \\
+\ \$\ 0.63 \\
\hline
\mathbf{\$32.10}
\end{array}
$$

19.

$$
\begin{array}{r}
\overset{1\ 1}{\ } \\
\$31.75 \\
+\ \$\ 6.48 \\
\hline
\$38.23
\end{array}
\qquad
\begin{array}{r}
\overset{4}{\cancel{5}}\overset{9}{\cancel{0}}.\overset{9}{\cancel{0}}{}^{1}0 \\
-\ \$\ 38.\ 23 \\
\hline
\mathbf{\$\ 1\ 1.\ 7\ 7}
\end{array}
$$

20.

$$
\begin{array}{r}
47 \\
\times\ 39 \\
\hline
423 \\
141 \\
\hline
\mathbf{1833}
\end{array}
$$

21.

$$
\begin{array}{r}
\$8.79 \\
\times\ \ \ \ \ 80 \\
\hline
\mathbf{\$703.20}
\end{array}
$$

22.

$$
\begin{array}{r}
\overset{2}{\cancel{3}}\overset{16}{\cancel{7}}4 \\
-\ \ 87 \\
\hline
2\ 8\ 7
\end{array}
\qquad
\begin{array}{r}
\overset{0}{\cancel{1}}\overset{10}{\cancel{1}}\overset{9}{\cancel{0}}0 \\
-\ 287 \\
\hline
\mathbf{8\ 1\ 3}
\end{array}
$$

23.

$$
\begin{array}{r}
\overset{0}{\cancel{1}}\overset{10}{\cancel{1}}\overset{9}{\cancel{0}}0 \\
-\ \ 374 \\
\hline
7\ 2\ 6
\end{array}
\qquad
\begin{array}{r}
\overset{6}{\cancel{7}}\overset{11}{\cancel{2}}6 \\
-\ \ 87 \\
\hline
\mathbf{6\ 3\ 9}
\end{array}
$$

24.

$$
\begin{array}{r}
\overset{1\ 2\ 2}{\ } \\
4736 \\
271 \\
9 \\
+\ \ 88 \\
\hline
\mathbf{5104}
\end{array}
$$

25.

$$
\begin{array}{r}
\overset{2}{\cancel{3}}\overset{9}{\cancel{0}},\overset{10}{\cancel{1}}\overset{13}{\cancel{4}}5 \\
-\ \ \ 4\ 299 \\
\hline
\mathbf{2\ 5,\ 8\ 4\ 6}
\end{array}
$$

26.

$$
\begin{array}{r}
\mathbf{158} \\
30\overline{)4740} \\
\underline{30} \\
174 \\
\underline{150} \\
240 \\
\underline{240} \\
0
\end{array}
$$

27.
$$32\overline{)\$40.00} = \$1.25$$

```
        $1.25
27. 32)$40.00
        32
        ─────
         8 0
         6 4
        ─────
         1 60
         1 60
        ─────
            0
```

28.
```
        60 R 4
28. 35)2104
       210
       ─────
        04
         0
        ───
         4
```

29.
```
29.    $0.48
     ×    40
     ─────────
      $19.20
```

30. One is the multiplicative identity because when any given number is multiplied by 1, the product is identical to the given number.

Early Finishers Solutions

a. $2(4.50 + 1.25 + x) = \$13.50$
$$5.75 + x = 6.75$$
$$x = \$1.00$$

b. $10 - (4.50 + 1.25 + 1.00) = x$
$$10 - 6.75 = x$$
$$x = \$3.25$$

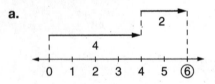

Practice Set 4

a.

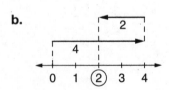

b.

---

c.

d. $-3, -2, -1, 0$

e. $2 + 3 < 2 \times 3$

f. $3 - 4 < 4 - 3$

g. $2 \cdot 2 = 2 + 2$

h. Simplify each expression before comparing them.

i. **0**

j.
```
     5 12
     6 3 10      −194
   − 4 3 6
   ─────────
     1 9 4
```

k. $-2, -3, -4$

l. $k = n \cdot n$
Eighth term: $k = 8 \cdot 8 = \mathbf{64}$
Ninth term: $k = 9 \cdot 9 = \mathbf{81}$
Tenth term: $k = 10 \cdot 10 = \mathbf{100}$

m. Each term in the sequence can be found by doubling the preceding term; **16, 32, 64.**

n. $k = (2n) - 1$
$k = (2 \cdot 1) - 1 = (2) - 1 = 1$
$k = (2 \cdot 2) - 1 = (4) - 1 = 3$
$k = (2 \cdot 3) - 1 = (6) - 1 = 5$
$k = (2 \cdot 4) - 1 = (8) - 1 = 7$
First four terms: **1, 3, 5, 7**

Written Practice 4

1. Sum of 5 and 4 = 9
Product of 3 and 3 = 9
$$9 - 9 = \mathbf{0}$$

2. $27 - 9 = \mathbf{18}$

---

3. **Positive numbers**

4. **a.** $24 - 6 = $ **18**

   b. $6 - 24 = $ **−18**

   c. $\dfrac{24}{6} = $ **4**

   d.
   $$\begin{array}{r} 24 \\ \times\ \ 6 \\ \hline \mathbf{144} \end{array}$$

5. $5 \cdot 2 > 5 + 2$

6. **−2, −1, 0, 1**

7. **Multiply the divisor by the quotient to find the dividend.**

8.

9. $\dfrac{12}{12} = 1$

   $k = \mathbf{1}$

10.
$$\begin{array}{r} 4 \\ 8 \\ +\ 6 \\ \hline 18 \end{array} \qquad \begin{array}{r} \overset{2}{\cancel{3}}{}^{1}0 \\ -\ 1\,8 \\ \hline 1\,2 \end{array}$$

   $n = \mathbf{12}$

11.
$$\begin{array}{r} 654 \\ +\ 123 \\ \hline 777 \end{array}$$

   $z = \mathbf{777}$

12.
$$\begin{array}{r} \overset{0}{\cancel{1}}\overset{9}{\cancel{0}}\overset{9}{\cancel{0}}{}^{1}0 \\ -\ \ \ 1\,0\,1 \\ \hline 8\,9\,9 \end{array}$$

   $m = \mathbf{899}$

13.
$$\begin{array}{r} \$4.95 \\ -\ \$1.45 \\ \hline \$3.50 \end{array}$$

   $p = \mathbf{\$3.50}$

14.
$$\begin{array}{r} 7\ \ \ \\ 32\overline{)224} \\ 224 \\ \hline 0 \end{array}$$

   $k = \mathbf{7}$

15.
$$\begin{array}{r} 24 \\ \times\ \ 8 \\ \hline 192 \end{array}$$

   $r = \mathbf{192}$

16. **a. Commutative property**

    b. Associative property

17. **a.** $3 \cdot 4 = 2(6)$

    b. $-3 < -2$

    c. $3 - 5 < 5 - 3$

    d. $xy = yx$

18.
$$\begin{array}{r} \overset{0}{\cancel{\$1}}\overset{9}{\cancel{0}}\overset{9}{\cancel{0}}.\overset{9}{\cancel{0}}{}^{1}0 \\ -\ \$\ \ 36.49 \\ \hline \$\ \ \mathbf{63.51} \end{array}$$

19.
$$\begin{array}{r} \$0.36 \\ \times\ \ \ \ 48 \\ \hline 288 \\ 144\ \ \\ \hline \mathbf{\$17.28} \end{array}$$

20.
$$\begin{array}{r} 5 \\ \times\ 6 \\ \hline 30 \end{array} \qquad \begin{array}{r} 30 \\ \times\ 7 \\ \hline \mathbf{210} \end{array}$$

21.
$$\begin{array}{r} \mathbf{550}\ \ \ \\ 18\overline{)9900} \\ 90\ \ \ \ \\ \hline 90\ \ \\ 90\ \ \\ \hline 00 \\ 0 \\ \hline 0 \end{array}$$

22.
$$\begin{array}{r} 30 \\ \times\ 20 \\ \hline 600 \end{array} \qquad \begin{array}{r} 600 \\ \times\ \ \ 40 \\ \hline \mathbf{24,000} \end{array}$$

23.
$$\begin{array}{r} \overset{0}{\cancel{1}}\overset{12}{\cancel{3}}{}^{1}0 \\ -\ \ 5\,7 \\ \hline 7\,3 \end{array} \qquad \begin{array}{r} \overset{1}{7}3 \\ +\ 9 \\ \hline \mathbf{82} \end{array}$$

Solutions

24.
$$
\begin{array}{r}
{}^{1}\,{}^{9}\,{}^{10} \\
\cancel{2}\,\cancel{0}\,\cancel{1}{}^{1}4 \\
-\ 1\,9\,8\,7 \\
\hline
2\,7
\end{array}
\qquad -27
$$

25.
$$
\begin{array}{r}
\$9.80 \\
7\overline{)\$68.60} \\
\underline{63} \\
5\,6 \\
\underline{5\,6} \\
00 \\
\underline{0} \\
0
\end{array}
$$

26.
$$
\begin{array}{r}
{}^{1\ 1} \\
\$0.46 \\
+\ \$0.64 \\
\hline
\$1.10
\end{array}
$$

27.
$$
\begin{array}{r}
58 \\
80\overline{)4640} \\
\underline{400} \\
640 \\
\underline{640} \\
0
\end{array}
$$

28.
$$
\begin{array}{r}
\$3.75 \\
\times\quad 30 \\
\hline
\$112.50
\end{array}
$$

29. Answers may vary. One answer is
$(2 \times 3) \times 6 = 2 \times (3 \times 6)$.

30. Each term in the sequence can be found by multiplying the preceding term by ten.
$100(10) = \mathbf{1000}$
$1000(10) = \mathbf{10,000}$

Early Finishers Solutions

a. $150 - (34.73 + 68.98)$
$150 - 103.71 = \$46.29$

b. $2(16.88) + 12.25$
$33.76 + 12.25 = 46.01$
Yes, $\$46.01 < \$46.29$

Practice Set ⑤

a. 3

b. Billions

---

c. $(2 \times 1000) + (5 \times 100)$

d. Thirty-six million, four hundred twenty-seven thousand, five hundred eighty

e. Forty million, three hundred two thousand, ten

f. Commas separate periods in a number. In d and e place a comma after thousands and millions.

g. 25,206,040

h. 50,402,100,000

i. $15,000,000,000

j. $15 million

Written Practice ⑤

1.
$$
\begin{array}{r}
{}^{1\ 1} \\
{}_{1}607 \\
+\ 2393 \\
\hline
3000
\end{array}
$$

2. $101,000 > 1100$

3. Fifty million, five hundred seventy-four thousand, six

4. 2

5. 250,005,070

6. $-12 > -15$
Negative twelve is greater than negative fifteen.

7. $-7, -1, 0, 4, 5, 7$

Saxon Math Course 2

96

8. Draw a number line. Start at the origin and draw an arrow 5 units long to the right. From this point draw an arrow 4 units long to the left. The second arrow ends at 1, showing that 5 − 4 = 1. Circle the number 1.

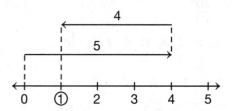

9. (1) $k = 3(1) = 3$
(2) $k = 3(2) = 6$
(3) $k = 3(3) = 9$
(4) $k = 3(4) = 12$

3, 6, 9, 12

10. $2 \cdot 3 = 6$ $6 \cdot 5 = 30$

$$
\begin{array}{r}
32 \\
30{\overline{)960}} \\
90 \\
\hline
60 \\
60 \\
\hline
0
\end{array}
$$

$n = \mathbf{32}$

11.
$$
\begin{array}{r}
2500 \\
+\ 1367 \\
\hline
3867
\end{array}
$$
$a = \mathbf{3867}$

12. $17 + 5 = 22$

$$
\begin{array}{r}
\overset{4}{\cancel{5}}{}^{1}0 \\
-\ 2\,2 \\
\hline
2\,8
\end{array}
$$

$b = \mathbf{28}$

13.
$$
\begin{array}{r}
\$\,\overset{1}{2}\,\overset{14}{\cancel{5}}.{}^{1}0\,0 \\
-\ \$\,1\,8.\,7\,0 \\
\hline
\$\,6.\,3\,0
\end{array}
$$
$k = \mathbf{\$6.30}$

14.
$$
\begin{array}{r}
\overset{0}{\cancel{1}}\,\overset{9}{\cancel{0}},{}^{1}0\,0\,0 \\
-\ \ \ \ 6\,4\,0\,0 \\
\hline
3\,6\,0\,0
\end{array}
$$
$d = \mathbf{3600}$

15.
$$
\begin{array}{r}
18 \\
8{\overline{)144}} \\
8 \\
\hline
64 \\
64 \\
\hline
0
\end{array}
$$
$f = \mathbf{18}$

16. $(7 \times 100{,}000) + (5 \times 10{,}000)$

17.
$$
\begin{array}{r}
{}^{11}\ {}^{11}\\
37{,}428 \\
+\ 59{,}775 \\
\hline
97{,}203
\end{array}
$$

18.
$$
\begin{array}{r}
{}^{2}\ {}^{10}\ \ {}^{9}\ {}^{10}\\
\cancel{3}\,\cancel{1}{,}\,\cancel{0}\,\cancel{1}\,4 \\
-\ 2\,4{,}7\,6\,7 \\
\hline
6\ \ 2\,4\,7
\end{array}
$$

19.
$$
\begin{array}{r}
{}^{2}\\
{}_{1}45 \\
362 \\
7 \\
+\ 4319 \\
\hline
4733
\end{array}
$$

20.
$$
\begin{array}{r}
{}^{11}\ {}^{1}\\
\$\ 64.59 \\
\$124.00 \\
\$\ \ 6.30 \\
+\ \$\ \ 0.37 \\
\hline
\$195.26
\end{array}
$$

21. $12 \div 3 = 4$

$$
\begin{array}{r}
36 \\
4{\overline{)144}} \\
12 \\
\hline
24 \\
24 \\
\hline
0
\end{array}
$$

22.
$$
\begin{array}{r}
12 \\
12{\overline{)144}} \\
12 \\
\hline
24 \\
24 \\
\hline
0
\end{array}
$$
$12 \div 3 = \mathbf{4}$

23.
$$
\begin{array}{r}
40 \\
\times\ 500 \\
\hline
20{,}000
\end{array}
$$

24.
$$\begin{array}{r} 405 \\ 21\overline{)8505} \\ \underline{84} \\ 10 \\ \underline{0} \\ 105 \\ \underline{105} \\ 0 \end{array}$$

25.
$$\begin{array}{r} \overset{5}{\$\,4.\,\cancel{6}^{1}0} \\ -\;\$\,0.\,3\,9 \\ \hline \$\,4.\,2\,1 \end{array} \qquad \begin{array}{r} \overset{0\;\;9\;\;9}{\$\,\cancel{1}\,\cancel{0}.\,\cancel{0}^{1}0} \\ -\;\$\;\;\;\,4.\,2\,1 \\ \hline \$\;\;\;5.\,7\,9 \end{array}$$

26.
$$\begin{array}{r} \$0.29 \\ \times\;\;\;\;\;36 \\ \hline 174 \\ 87 \\ \hline \$10.44 \end{array}$$

27. a. Identity property of multiplication

b. Commutative property of multiplication

28. Each term in the sequence can be found by subtracting two from the preceding term.
$$2 - 2 = \mathbf{0}$$
$$0 - 2 = \mathbf{-2}$$
$$-2 - 2 = \mathbf{-4}$$

29. a. Counting numbers or natural numbers

b. Whole numbers

c. Integers

30. $\{\ldots, -6, -4, -2\}$

Practice Set 6

a. 1, 5, 25

b. 1, 23

c. 1 and 24, 2 and 12, 3 and 8, 4 and 6

---

d. $1 + 2 + 6 + 0 = 9$

$$\begin{array}{r} 15 \\ 4\overline{)60} \\ \underline{4} \\ 20 \\ \underline{20} \\ 0 \end{array} \qquad \begin{array}{r} 32\,R\,4 \\ 8\overline{)260} \\ \underline{24} \\ 20 \\ \underline{16} \\ 4 \end{array} \qquad \begin{array}{r} 180 \\ 7\overline{)1260} \\ \underline{7} \\ 56 \\ \underline{56} \\ 00 \\ \underline{0} \\ 0 \end{array}$$

1, 2, 3, 4, 5, 6, 7, 9, 10

e. $7 + 3 + 5 + 0 + 0 = 15$

$$\begin{array}{r} 62\,R\,4 \\ 8\overline{)500} \\ \underline{48} \\ 20 \\ \underline{16} \\ 4 \end{array} \qquad \begin{array}{r} 10,500 \\ 7\overline{)73,500} \\ \underline{7} \\ 03 \\ \underline{0} \\ 3\,5 \\ \underline{3\,5} \\ 00 \\ \underline{0} \\ 00 \\ \underline{0} \\ 0 \end{array}$$

1, 2, 3, 4, 5, 6, 7, 10

f. $3 + 6 + 0 + 0 = 9$

$$\begin{array}{r} 75 \\ 8\overline{)600} \\ \underline{56} \\ 40 \\ \underline{40} \\ 0 \end{array} \qquad \begin{array}{r} 514\,R\,2 \\ 7\overline{)3600} \\ \underline{35} \\ 10 \\ \underline{7} \\ 30 \\ \underline{28} \\ 2 \end{array}$$

1, 2, 3, 4, 5, 6, 8, 9, 10

g. $1 + 3 + 5 + 6 = 15$

$$\begin{array}{r} 44\,R\,4 \\ 8\overline{)356} \\ \underline{32} \\ 36 \\ \underline{32} \\ 4 \end{array} \qquad \begin{array}{r} 193\,R\,5 \\ 7\overline{)1356} \\ \underline{7} \\ 65 \\ \underline{63} \\ 26 \\ \underline{21} \\ 5 \end{array}$$

1, 2, 3, 4, 6

h. 1, 2, 4, 5, 7, 8

i. Factors of 12: 1, 2, 3, 4, 6, 12
Factors of 20: 1, 2, 4, 5, 10, 20
1, 2, 4

j. Factors of 24: 1, 2, 3, 4, 6, 8, 12, 24
Factors of 40: 1, 2, 4, 5, 8, 10, 20, 40
8

k. **Answers will vary but may include listing the factors of 24 and 40, circling the common factors.**

Written Practice **6**

1. Product of 10 and 20 = 200
Sum of 20 and 30 = 50
$$\frac{200}{50} = 4$$

2. a. Factors of 30: 1, 2, 3, 5, 6, 10, 15, 30
Factors of 40: 1, 2, 4, 5, 8, 10, 20, 40
1, 2, 5, 10

b. 10

3. {. . . , −5, −3, −1}

4. 407,006,962

5. 1 + 2 + 3 + 0 + 0 = 6

$$
\begin{array}{r}
1\,757 \text{ R } 1 \\
7)\overline{12{,}300} \\
\underline{7} \\
5\,3 \\
\underline{4\,9} \\
4\,0 \\
\underline{3\,5} \\
5\,0 \\
\underline{4\,9} \\
1
\end{array}
$$

1, 2, 3, 4, 5, 6, 10

6. −7 > −11
Negative seven is greater than negative eleven.

7.
$$
\begin{array}{r}
14 \\
4)\overline{56} \\
\underline{4} \\
16 \\
\underline{16} \\
0
\end{array}
\qquad
\begin{array}{r}
57 \\
8)\overline{456} \\
\underline{40} \\
56 \\
\underline{56} \\
0
\end{array}
\qquad
\begin{array}{r}
493 \text{ R } 5 \\
7)\overline{3456} \\
\underline{28} \\
65 \\
\underline{63} \\
26 \\
\underline{21} \\
5
\end{array}
$$

3 + 4 + 5 + 6 = 18
1, 2, 3, 4, 6, 8, 9

8.

9. (6 × 1000) + (4 × 100)

10.
$$
\begin{array}{r}
{}^{0\ 9\ 10} \\
\$ \cancel{1}\,0.\,\cancel{0}\,0 \\
-\ \$\ \ \ 4.\,6\,0 \\
\hline
\$\ \ \ 5.\,4\,0
\end{array}
$$

$x =$ **$5.40**

11.
$$
\begin{array}{r}
{}^{1} \\
4500 \\
+\ 3850 \\
\hline
8350
\end{array}
$$

$p =$ **8350**

12.
$$
\begin{array}{r}
\$6.25 \\
8)\overline{\$50.00} \\
\underline{48} \\
2\,0 \\
\underline{1\,6} \\
4\,0 \\
\underline{4\,0} \\
0
\end{array}
$$

$z =$ **$6.25**

13.
$$
\begin{array}{cc}
7 & 60 \\
4 & -\ 51 \\
8 & 9 \\
6 & n = \mathbf{9} \\
2 & \\
1 & \\
6 & \\
8 & \\
+\ 9 & \\
\hline
51 &
\end{array}
$$

14.
$$
\begin{array}{r}
{}^{3\ 11\ 16} \\
1\,\cancel{4}\,\cancel{2}\,6 \\
-\ \ \ 8\,7 \\
\hline
1\,3\,3\,9
\end{array}
$$

$k =$ **1339**

15.
$$
\begin{array}{r}
22 \\
45)\overline{990} \\
\underline{90} \\
90 \\
\underline{90} \\
0
\end{array}
$$

$p =$ **22**

16.
$$\begin{array}{r} 32 \\ \times \quad 8 \\ \hline 256 \end{array}$$
$z = 256$

17.
$$35\overline{)1225}$$
$$\begin{array}{r} 35 \\ \hline 105 \\ \hline 175 \\ 175 \\ \hline 0 \end{array}$$

18.
$$\begin{array}{r} 800 \\ \times \quad 50 \\ \hline 40,000 \end{array}$$

19.
$$\begin{array}{r} {}^{0\,9\,9\,9\,10} \\ \$\,\cancel{1}\,\cancel{0}\,\cancel{0}.\,\cancel{0}\,0 \\ - \$ \quad 4\,8.\,3\,7 \\ \hline \$ \quad 5\,1.\,6\,3 \end{array}$$

20.
$$\begin{array}{r} {}^{1\,1\,\;1\,1} \\ 46,302 \\ + \quad 49,998 \\ \hline 96,300 \end{array}$$

21.
$$20\overline{)\$45.00}$$
$$\begin{array}{r} \$2.25 \\ \hline 40 \\ \hline 5\,0 \\ 4\,0 \\ \hline 1\,00 \\ 1\,00 \\ \hline 0 \end{array}$$

22.
$$\begin{array}{r} 11 \\ \times \quad 7 \\ \hline 77 \end{array} \qquad \begin{array}{r} 77 \\ \times \quad 13 \\ \hline 231 \\ 77 \\ \hline 1001 \end{array}$$

23.
$$9\overline{)43,271}$$
$$\begin{array}{r} 4,807 \; R\,8 \\ \hline 36 \\ \hline 7\,2 \\ 7\,2 \\ \hline 07 \\ 0 \\ \hline 71 \\ 63 \\ \hline 8 \\ 0 \\ \hline 8 \end{array}$$

24.
$$\begin{array}{r} {}^{1} \\ \$ \quad 0.48 \\ \$ \quad 8.49 \\ + \; \$\,{}^{1}14.00 \\ \hline \$ \; 22.97 \end{array}$$

25.
$$\begin{array}{r} {}^{3\,{}^{12}1\,0} \\ \cancel{4}\,\cancel{3}\,\cancel{0} \\ - \quad 5\,8 \\ \hline 3\,7\,2 \end{array} \qquad \begin{array}{r} {}^{0\,9\,9\,10} \\ \cancel{1}\,\cancel{0}\,\cancel{0}\,\cancel{0} \\ - \quad 3\,7\,2 \\ \hline 6\,2\,8 \end{array}$$

26.
$$\begin{array}{r} 140 \\ \times \quad 16 \\ \hline 840 \\ 140 \\ \hline 2240 \end{array}$$

27.
$$\begin{array}{r} \$0.25 \\ \times \quad 24 \\ \hline 1\,00 \\ 5\,0 \\ \hline \$6.00 \end{array}$$

28.
$$10\overline{)\$43.50}$$
$$\begin{array}{r} \$4.35 \\ \hline 40 \\ \hline 3\,5 \\ 3\,0 \\ \hline 50 \\ 50 \\ \hline 0 \end{array}$$

29. Commutative property of multiplication; the order of the factors can be changed without changing the product.

30. a. Associative property
    b. Commutative property
    c. Associative property

Practice Set 7

a. Point *A*

b. $XY = XZ - YZ$
$XY = 10 - 6$
$XY = 4$ cm

c.

d.

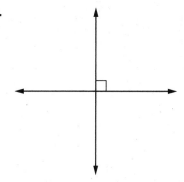

e.

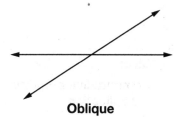

Oblique

f.

g.

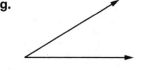

h.

i. **Perpendicular**

j. Possibilities include: **the floor and the ceiling; walls that face each other.**

k. Possibilities include: **the floor and a wall; the ceiling and a wall.**

l. **Line**

m. **c.** skew

n. See student work.

Written Practice 7

1. 7 + 5 = **12**

2. **Identity property of multiplication**

3. **1 and 50, 2 and 25, 5 and 10**

4. **2 − 5 = −3**

5. **90,000,000**

6.
```
   115 R 4        132
8)924          7)924
  8              7
  12             22
   8             21
   44            14
   40            14
    4             0
```
9 + 2 + 4 = 15
1, 2, 3, 4, 5, 6, 7

7. **−10, −7, −2, 0, 5, 8**

8. **This is a sequence of perfect squares.**
11 · 11 = **121**
12 · 12 = **144**
13 · 13 = **169**

9. **Posts**

10. a. Factors of 24: 1, 2, 3, 4, 6, 8, 12, 24
Factors of 32: 1, 2, 4, 8, 16, 32
1, 2, 4, 8

b. **8**

11. **7 units**

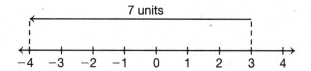

7 units

-4 -3 -2 -1 0 1 2 3 4

Saxon Math Course 2

101

12. $6 \cdot 6 = 36$

$$36\overline{)1224} = 34$$
$$\underline{108}$$
$$144$$
$$\underline{144}$$
$$0$$

$z = \mathbf{34}$

13.
$$\$\overset{0\ 9\ 9\ 9\ 10}{\cancel{1}\cancel{0}\cancel{0}.\cancel{0}\cancel{0}}$$
$$-\ \$\ \ 17.54$$
$$\overline{\$\ \ 82.46}$$

$k = \mathbf{\$82.46}$

14.
$$\overset{1\ 1}{432}$$
$$+\ \ 98$$
$$\overline{530}$$

$w = \mathbf{530}$

15.
$$20\overline{)\$36.00} = \$1.80$$
$$\underline{20}$$
$$16\ 0$$
$$\underline{16\ 0}$$
$$00$$
$$\underline{0}$$
$$0$$

$x = \mathbf{\$1.80}$

16.
$$200$$
$$\times\ \ \ 20$$
$$\overline{4000}$$

$w = \mathbf{4000}$

17.
$$30\overline{)300} = 10$$
$$\underline{30}$$
$$00$$
$$\underline{0}$$
$$0$$

$x = \mathbf{10}$

18. **The quotient does not have a remainder (the remainder is zero). A number is divisible by 9 if the sum of its digits is divisible by 9. The sum of the digits in 4554 is 18, which is divisible by 9.**

19.
$$\overset{1\ 1\ 1}{36{,}475}$$
$$+\ 55{,}984$$
$$\overline{\mathbf{92{,}459}}$$

20.
$$476$$
$$\times\ \ 38$$
$$\overline{3\ 808}$$
$$14\ 28$$
$$\overline{\mathbf{18{,}088}}$$

21.
$$\$\overset{7\ 9\ 9\ 10}{\cancel{8}\cancel{0}.\cancel{0}\cancel{0}}$$
$$-\ \$72.45$$
$$\overline{\$\ \ \ 7.55}$$

22.
$$40\overline{)\$68.00} = \$1.70$$
$$\underline{40}$$
$$28\ 0$$
$$\underline{28\ 0}$$
$$00$$
$$\underline{0}$$
$$0$$

23. One possibility:

$8 \cdot 7 \cdot 5$	**Given**
$7 \cdot 8 \cdot 5$	**Commutative property of multiplication**
$7 \cdot (8 \cdot 5)$	**Associative property of multiplication**
$7 \cdot 40$	$8 \cdot 5 = 40$
280	$7 \cdot 40 = 280$

24. $200 \div 10 = 20$

$$20\overline{)4000} = 200$$
$$\underline{40}$$
$$00$$
$$\underline{0}$$
$$00$$
$$\underline{0}$$
$$0$$

$$200\overline{)4000} = 20 \qquad 20 \div 10 = 2$$
$$\underline{400}$$
$$00$$
$$\underline{0}$$
$$0$$

$200 > 2$

25. **a.** $200(400) = \mathbf{80{,}000}$

b. $200 - 400 = \mathbf{-200}$

c. $\dfrac{400}{200} = \mathbf{2}$

26. **a.** $\angle BMC$ or $\angle CMB$

b. $\angle AMC$ or $\angle CMA$

27. Right angle

28. $\overline{XY}$ (or $\overline{YX}$), $\overline{YZ}$ (or $\overline{ZY}$), $\overline{XZ}$ (or $\overline{ZX}$)

29. Add m$\overline{XY}$ and m$\overline{YZ}$ to find m$\overline{XZ}$.

30.

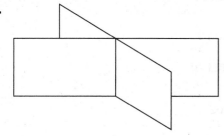

Early Finishers Solutions

a. 64, 62, 66, 60, 68, 63, 61, 66

b. 60, 61, 62, 63, 64, 66, 66, 68

c. 4; 60, 61, 62, 63

Practice Set 8

a. $\dfrac{3}{5}$

b. 100% ÷ 5 = 20%
20% × 3 = **60%**

c. 100% ÷ 2 = **50%**

d.

e.

f.

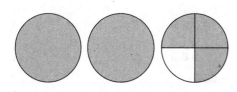

g. $4\dfrac{2}{3}$

h. $13\dfrac{1}{4}$

i. $3\dfrac{5}{16}$ in.

j. $\dfrac{1}{2}$ of $\dfrac{1}{8}$ = $\dfrac{1}{16}$ inch

k. $\dfrac{1}{16}, \dfrac{1}{8}, \dfrac{1}{4}, \dfrac{1}{2}$

Written Practice 8

1. $1\dfrac{3}{4} > 1\dfrac{3}{5}$

2. $XY = 2\dfrac{4}{16} = 2\dfrac{1}{4}$ in.
$YZ = 1\dfrac{1}{16}$ in.

3. Product of 20 and 20 = 400
Sum of 10 and 10 = 20

$$
\begin{array}{r}
20 \\
20\overline{)400} \\
\underline{40} \\
00 \\
\underline{0} \\
0
\end{array}
$$

4.

$$
\begin{array}{r}
85 \\
8\overline{)680} \\
\underline{64} \\
40 \\
\underline{40} \\
0
\end{array}
\qquad
\begin{array}{r}
240 \\
7\overline{)1680} \\
\underline{14} \\
28 \\
\underline{28} \\
00 \\
\underline{0} \\
0
\end{array}
$$

1 + 6 + 8 + 0 = 15
1, 2, 3, 4, 5, 6, 7, 8

5. $3\dfrac{4}{5}$

6. **a.** 3 + 2 = 2 + 3
b. Commutative property of addition

7. Thirty-two billion, five hundred million

8. a. $\dfrac{3}{8}$

    b. $\dfrac{5}{8}$

9. a. $100\% \div 5 = 20\%$
        $20\% \times 1 = \mathbf{20\%}$

    b. $20\% \times 4 = \mathbf{80\%}$

10. Denominator

11.
$$\begin{array}{r} \overset{1}{\$2}.35 \\ + \ \$4.70 \\ \hline \$7.05 \end{array}$$
$a = \mathbf{\$7.05}$

12.
$$\begin{array}{r} \overset{5\ 9\ 9\ 10}{\$\cancel{6}\,\cancel{0}.\cancel{0}\,\cancel{0}} \\ - \ \$25.48 \\ \hline \$34.52 \end{array}$$
$b = \mathbf{\$34.52}$

13.
$$\begin{array}{r} \$7.50 \\ 8\overline{)\$60.00} \\ 56 \\ \hline 4\ 0 \\ 4\ 0 \\ \hline 00 \\ 0 \\ \hline 0 \end{array}$$
$c = \mathbf{\$7.50}$

14.
$$\begin{array}{r} \overset{0\ 9\ 9\ 10}{\cancel{1}\,\cancel{0},\cancel{0}\,\cancel{0}\,0} \\ - \ \ 5,420 \\ \hline 4,580 \end{array}$$
$d = \mathbf{4580}$

15.
$$\begin{array}{r} 15 \\ \times \ 15 \\ \hline 75 \\ 15 \\ \hline 225 \end{array}$$
$e = \mathbf{225}$

16.
$$\begin{array}{r} 14 \\ 14\overline{)196} \\ 14 \\ \hline 56 \\ 56 \\ \hline 0 \end{array}$$
$f = \mathbf{14}$

17. a. **Commutative property**

    b. **Associative property**

18.
$$\begin{array}{r} 400 \\ \times \ \ \ 500 \\ \hline 200,000 \end{array}$$

19.
$$\begin{array}{r} \$0.79 \\ \times \ \ \ \ \ 30 \\ \hline \$23.70 \end{array}$$

20.
$$\begin{array}{r} \overset{1\ 1\ 1}{3625} \\ 431 \\ + \ \ 687 \\ \hline 4743 \end{array}$$

21.
$$\begin{array}{r} 120 \\ 50\overline{)6000} \\ 50 \\ \hline 100 \\ 100 \\ \hline 00 \\ 0 \\ \hline 0 \end{array}$$

22.
$$\begin{array}{r} 20 \\ \times \ 10 \\ \hline 200 \end{array} \qquad \begin{array}{r} 200 \\ \times \ \ \ 5 \\ \hline \mathbf{1000} \end{array}$$

23.
$$\begin{array}{r} \$1.50 \\ 18\overline{)\$27.00} \\ 18 \\ \hline 9\ 0 \\ 9\ 0 \\ \hline 00 \\ 0 \\ \hline 0 \end{array}$$

24.
$$\begin{array}{r} 576 \\ 6\overline{)3456} \\ 30 \\ \hline 45 \\ 42 \\ \hline 36 \\ 36 \\ \hline 0 \end{array}$$

25. a.
$$\begin{array}{r} \overset{0\ 9\ 9\ 10}{\cancel{1}\,\cancel{0}\,\cancel{0}\,0} \\ - \ \ \ \ 11 \\ \hline 989 \end{array}$$

    b. **−989**

26. a. $k = 3(10) - 1$
$k = 30 - 1$
$k = \textbf{29}$

b. add 3

27.

$$\begin{array}{r} \overset{1}{8}6 \\ + \,{}^{1}119 \\ \hline 205 \end{array} \qquad \begin{array}{r} 416 \\ - \,205 \\ \hline 211 \end{array}$$

$$\begin{array}{r} \overset{3}{\cancel{4}}{}^{1}1\,6 \\ - \quad 8\,6 \\ \hline 3\,3\,0 \end{array} \qquad \begin{array}{r} 330 \\ + \,119 \\ \hline 449 \end{array}$$

$211 < 449$

28. Acute: $\angle CBA$ (or $\angle ABC$)
Obtuse: $\angle DAB$ (or $\angle BAD$)
Right: $\angle CDA$ (or $\angle ADC$)
   and $\angle DCB$ (or $\angle BCD$)

29. a. $\overline{CB}$ (or $\overline{BC}$)

b. $\overline{DC}$ (or $\overline{CD}$)

30. $\overline{QR}$ identifies the segment QR, while QR refers to the distance from Q to R. So $\overline{QR}$ is a segment and QR is a length.

Practice Set 9

a. $\dfrac{5}{6} + \dfrac{1}{6} = \dfrac{6}{6} = \textbf{1}$

b. $\dfrac{1}{5}$

c. $\dfrac{3}{5} \times \dfrac{1}{2} = \dfrac{3}{10} \qquad \dfrac{3}{10} \times \dfrac{3}{4} = \dfrac{\textbf{9}}{\textbf{40}}$

d. $\dfrac{8}{3}$

e. $\dfrac{8}{21}$

f. $\dfrac{5}{8} - \dfrac{5}{8} = \dfrac{0}{8} = \textbf{0}$

---

g. $28\dfrac{4}{7}\%$

h. **75%**

i. $\dfrac{5}{4}$

j. $\dfrac{7}{8}$

k. $\dfrac{1}{5}$

l. $\dfrac{8}{5}$

m. $\dfrac{1}{6}$

n. $\dfrac{1}{20}$ of an inch, because $\dfrac{1}{2}$ of $\dfrac{1}{10}$ is $\dfrac{1}{20}$.

o. $\dfrac{3}{2}$

p. $\dfrac{1}{4}$

q. Inverse property of multiplication

Written Practice 9

1. $1 + 2 + 3 = 6 \qquad \dfrac{6}{6} = \textbf{1}$
$1 \cdot 2 \cdot 3 = 6$

2. **99¢ per pound; $0.99 per pound**

3. a. $\dfrac{1}{2} > \dfrac{1}{2} \cdot \dfrac{1}{2}$ One half is greater than one half times one half.

b. $-2 > -4$ Negative two is greater than negative four.

4. $(2 \times 10{,}000) + (6 \times 1000)$

5. a. $\dfrac{10}{100} = \dfrac{1}{10}$

b. $100\% \div 10 = \textbf{10\%}$

Saxon Math Course 2   **105**

Solutions

6. a. $\dfrac{2}{3}$

    b. $\dfrac{1}{3}$

7. It is a segment because it has two endpoints.

8. $LM = 1\dfrac{1}{4}$ in.

    $MN = 1\dfrac{1}{4}$ in.

    $LN = 2\dfrac{1}{2}$ in.

9. a. 1, 2, 3, 6, 9, 18

    b. 1, 2, 3, 4, 6, 8, 12, 24

    c. 1, 2, 3, 6

    d. 6

10. a. $\dfrac{2}{5} + \dfrac{2}{5} = \dfrac{4}{5}$

    b. $\dfrac{2}{5} - \dfrac{2}{5} = \dfrac{0}{5} = 0$

11.
$$
\begin{array}{r}
{}^{1\ 9\ 10}\ \\
2\cancel{0}\cancel{0},000 \\
-\quad 85,000 \\
\hline
115,000
\end{array}
$$

    $b = 115{,}000$

12.
$$
\begin{array}{r}
15 \\
60\overline{)900} \\
\underline{60} \\
300 \\
\underline{300} \\
0
\end{array}
$$

    $c = 15$

13.
$$
\begin{array}{r}
\$20.00 \\
-\ \$5.60 \\
\hline
\$14.40
\end{array}
$$

    $d = \$14.40$

14.
$$
\begin{array}{r}
\$2.50 \\
12\overline{)\$30.00} \\
\underline{24} \\
6\ 0 \\
\underline{6\ 0} \\
00 \\
\underline{0} \\
0
\end{array}
$$

    $e = \$2.50$

15.
$$
\begin{array}{r}
{}^{1\ \ 1}\ \\
\$\ 12.47 \\
+\ \$\ 98.03 \\
\hline
\$110.50
\end{array}
$$

    $f = \$110.50$

16.
$$
\begin{array}{r}
5 \\
7 \\
5 \\
7 \\
6 \\
1 \\
2 \\
3 \\
+\ 4 \\
\hline
40
\end{array}
\qquad
\begin{array}{r}
40 \\
-\ 40 \\
\hline
0
\end{array}
\qquad n = 0
$$

17. $2\dfrac{8}{15}$

18. $2\dfrac{7}{8}$

19. $\dfrac{3}{16}$

20.
$$
\begin{array}{r}
106 \\
17\overline{)1802} \\
\underline{17} \\
10 \\
\underline{0} \\
102 \\
\underline{102} \\
0
\end{array}
$$

21.
$$
\begin{array}{r}
{}^{5\ 9\ \ 9\ 10}\ \\
\$\cancel{6}\cancel{0}.\cancel{0}\cancel{0} \\
-\ \$49.49 \\
\hline
\$10.51
\end{array}
$$

22.
$$
\begin{array}{r}
607 \\
\times\ 78 \\
\hline
4856 \\
4249 \\
\hline
47{,}346
\end{array}
$$

23. $\dfrac{4}{5} \times \dfrac{2}{3} = \dfrac{8}{15} \qquad \dfrac{8}{15} \times \dfrac{1}{3} = \dfrac{8}{45}$

24. $\dfrac{7}{9}$

25. $50 \cdot 36 \cdot 20$

26. Inverse property of multiplication

27. b. Skew

28. a. ∠A and ∠B

    b. $\overline{AC}$ or $\overline{CA}$

29. Each term is half of the preceding term.
    $\frac{1}{8} \times \frac{1}{2} = \frac{1}{16}$

30. $\frac{5}{2}$

Practice Set 10

a. $4\overline{)35}$ → $8\frac{3}{4}$ inches
   $\frac{32}{3}$

b. $7\overline{)100\%}$ → $14\frac{2}{7}\%$
   $\frac{7}{30}$
   $\frac{28}{2}$

c. $5\overline{)12}$ → $2\frac{2}{5}$
   $\frac{10}{2}$

d. $6\overline{)12}$ 2

e. $2\frac{12}{7} = \frac{7 \times 2 + 12}{7} = \frac{26}{7}$
   $7\overline{)26}$ → $3\frac{5}{7}$
   $\frac{21}{5}$

f.

g. $\frac{2}{3} + \frac{2}{3} + \frac{2}{3} = \frac{6}{3} = 2$

h. $\frac{7}{3} \times \frac{2}{3} = \frac{14}{9}$
   $9\overline{)14}$ → $1\frac{5}{9}$
   $\frac{9}{5}$

i. $1\frac{2}{3} + 1\frac{2}{3} = 2\frac{4}{3} = 2 + 1\frac{1}{3} = 3\frac{1}{3}$

j. $1\frac{2}{3} = \frac{3 \times 1 + 2}{3} = \frac{5}{3}$

k. $3\frac{5}{6} = \frac{6 \times 3 + 5}{6} = \frac{23}{6}$

l. $4\frac{3}{4} = \frac{4 \times 4 + 3}{4} = \frac{19}{4}$

m. $5\frac{1}{2} = \frac{2 \times 5 + 1}{2} = \frac{11}{2}$

n. $6\frac{3}{4} = \frac{4 \times 6 + 3}{4} = \frac{27}{4}$

o. $10\frac{2}{5} = \frac{5 \times 10 + 2}{5} = \frac{52}{5}$

p. Answers vary. Sample: $\frac{8}{2}$; $\frac{16}{4}$; $\frac{20}{5}$

Written Practice 10

1. Answers will vary. One answer is $\left(\frac{1}{2} \cdot \frac{1}{3}\right) \cdot \frac{1}{6} = \frac{1}{2} \cdot \left(\frac{1}{3} \cdot \frac{1}{6}\right)$.

2. a. Parallel
   b. Perpendicular

3. $2 + 3 + 4 = 9$
   $2 \times 3 \times 4 = 24$
   $24 - 9 = 15$

4. a. $100\% \div 10 = 10\%$
   $10\% \times 3 = 30\%$
   b. 70%

Saxon Math Course 2   107   © Harcourt Achieve, Inc. and Stephen Hake. All rights reserved.

5. $3\frac{2}{3} = \frac{3 \times 3 + 2}{3} = \frac{11}{3}$

6. **a.** $2 - 2 < 2 \div 2$

   b. $\frac{1}{2} + \frac{1}{2} > \frac{1}{2} \times \frac{1}{2}$

7. $9\frac{5}{6}$

8.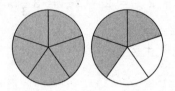

9.
$$\begin{array}{r} 52\,R\,4 \\ 8)\overline{420} \\ \underline{40} \\ 20 \\ \underline{16} \\ 4 \end{array} \qquad \begin{array}{r} 60 \\ 7)\overline{420} \\ \underline{42} \\ 00 \\ 0 \\ \underline{} \\ 0 \end{array}$$

   $4 + 2 + 0 = 6$

   1, 2, 3, 4, 5, 6, 7

10.
$$\begin{array}{r} \overset{5\;\;12}{3\cancel{6},\cancel{2}75} \\ -\;12,500 \\ \hline 23,775 \end{array}$$

   $x = \mathbf{23,775}$

11.
$$\begin{array}{r} 22 \\ 18)\overline{396} \\ \underline{36} \\ 36 \\ \underline{36} \\ 0 \end{array}$$

   $y = \mathbf{22}$

12.
$$\begin{array}{r} \overset{6\;16\;10}{7\,7,\cancel{0}00} \\ -\;39,400 \\ \hline 37,600 \end{array}$$

   $z = \mathbf{37,600}$

13.
$$\begin{array}{r} \$1.25 \\ \times\quad 8 \\ \hline \$10.00 \end{array}$$

   $a = \mathbf{\$10.00}$

14.
$$\begin{array}{r} \$\;8.75 \\ +\;\$16.25 \\ \hline \$25.00 \end{array}$$

   $b = \mathbf{\$25.00}$

15.
$$\begin{array}{r} \overset{6\;14\;10}{\$7\,\cancel{5}.\cancel{0}0} \\ -\;\$37.50 \\ \hline \$37.50 \end{array}$$

   $c = \mathbf{\$37.50}$

16. $\frac{1}{16}, \frac{3}{8}, \frac{1}{2}, \frac{3}{4}$

17. $\frac{5}{2} \times \frac{5}{4} = \frac{25}{8} \qquad \begin{array}{r} 3 \\ 8)\overline{25} \\ \underline{24} \\ 1 \end{array} \longrightarrow \mathbf{3\frac{1}{8}}$

18. $\frac{5}{8} - \frac{5}{8} = \frac{0}{8} = \mathbf{0}$

19. $\frac{11}{20} + \frac{18}{20} = \frac{29}{20} = \frac{20}{20} + \frac{9}{20} = \mathbf{1\frac{9}{20}}$

20.
$$\begin{array}{r} \overset{7\;10}{6\cancel{8}\cancel{0}} \\ -\;59 \\ \hline 621 \end{array} \qquad \begin{array}{r} \overset{1\;9\;9\;10}{\cancel{2}\,\cancel{0}\cancel{0}\cancel{0}} \\ -\;621 \\ \hline \mathbf{1379} \end{array}$$

21.
$$\begin{array}{r} 11 \\ 9)\overline{100\%} \\ \underline{9} \\ 10 \\ \underline{9} \\ 1 \end{array} \longrightarrow \mathbf{11\frac{1}{9}\%}$$

22.
$$\begin{array}{r} \overset{2\;\;2}{\$\;0.89} \\ \$\;0.57 \\ +\;\$15.74 \\ \hline \mathbf{\$17.20} \end{array}$$

23.
$$\begin{array}{r} 800 \\ \times\quad 300 \\ \hline \mathbf{240,000} \end{array}$$

24. $2\frac{2}{3} + 2\frac{2}{3} = 4\frac{4}{3} = 4\frac{1}{3} + \frac{3}{3}$

    $= 4\frac{1}{3} + 1 = \mathbf{5\frac{1}{3}}$

25. $\frac{8}{27}$

26. **a.** Ray; $\overrightarrow{MC}$

    b. Line; $\overleftrightarrow{PM}$ or $\overleftrightarrow{MP}$

    c. Segment; $\overline{FH}$ or $\overline{HF}$

108

27. $\dfrac{9}{5}$

28. $\dfrac{1}{2}$ of $2 = \mathbf{1}$

$\dfrac{1}{2}$ of $1 = \dfrac{1}{2}$

$\dfrac{1}{2}$ of $\dfrac{1}{2} = \dfrac{1}{4}$

29. C. $\dfrac{1}{2}$

30. a. **−5**

b. $\dfrac{1}{3}$

c. **They are reciprocals.**

Investigation 1

Investigating Fractions and Percents with Manipulatives

Note: For questions 1–16, the student chooses one or more manipulative pieces to work out the problem and represent the answer. Possible representations are shown; actual manipulatives may vary.

1.

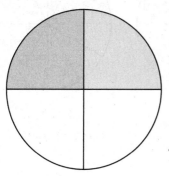

Answer: $\dfrac{1}{4}$

2.

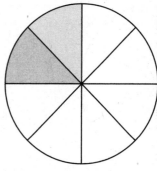

Answer: $\dfrac{1}{8}$

3.

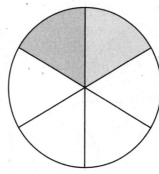

Answer: $\dfrac{1}{6}$

4.

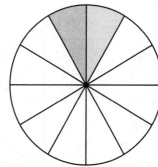

Answer: $\dfrac{1}{12}$

5.

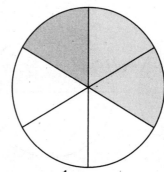

Answer: $\dfrac{1}{6}$

6.

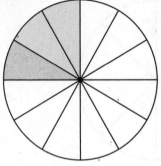

Answer: $\frac{1}{12}$

7.

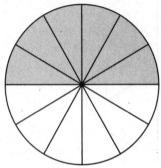

$\frac{6}{12} = \frac{1}{2}$

Answer: **6**

8.

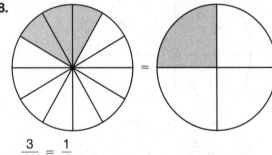

$\frac{3}{12} = \frac{1}{4}$

Answer: $\frac{1}{4}$

9.

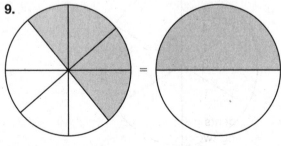

$\frac{4}{8} = \frac{1}{2}$

Answer: $\frac{1}{2}$

10.

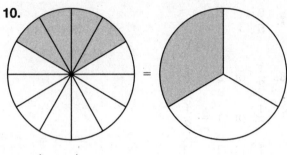

$\frac{4}{12} = \frac{1}{3}$

Answer: $\frac{1}{3}$

11.

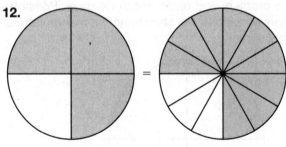

$\frac{2}{3} = \frac{4}{6}$

Answer: **4**

12.

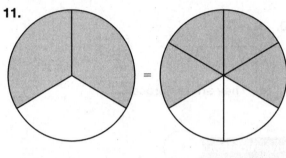

$\frac{3}{4} = \frac{9}{12}$

Answer: **9**

13.

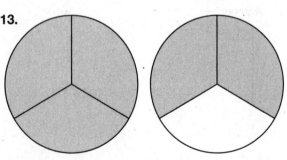

Answer: $5 \times \frac{1}{3} = 1\frac{2}{3}$

110

14.

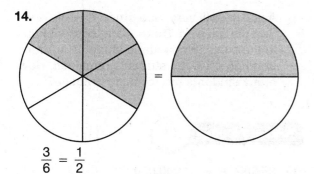

$$\frac{3}{6} = \frac{1}{2}$$

Answer: $\frac{1}{2}$

15.

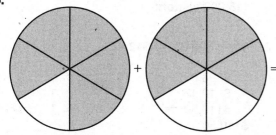

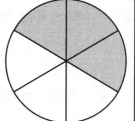

16.

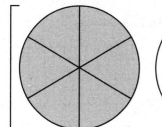

Answer: $\frac{1}{6}$ and $\frac{1}{3}$

17. $\frac{1}{6}$

18. $\frac{1}{12}$

19. $\frac{1}{4}$

20. $\frac{1}{12}$

21. $66\frac{2}{3}\%$

22. 25%

23. $37\frac{1}{2}\%$

24. 50%

25. 33.33%

26.

Answer: $\frac{3}{4}$

27.

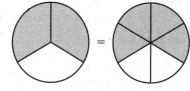

$$2 \times \frac{1}{3} = \frac{4}{6}$$

Answer: $\frac{1}{3}$

28.

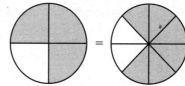

$$3 \times \frac{1}{4} = \frac{3}{4} = \frac{6}{8}$$

Answer: $\frac{1}{4}$

29. Answer: $\frac{1}{3} - \frac{1}{12} = \frac{1}{4}$

OR $\frac{4}{12} - \frac{1}{12} = \frac{3}{12} = \frac{1}{4}$

30. {Students generate possible solutions of adding two manipulatives to equal $\frac{1}{2}$; Their answers depend on what fractions they have, from which to select.}

$$\left[\frac{4}{12} - \frac{1}{12} - \frac{3}{12} = \frac{1}{4} \right]$$

Solutions

Possible answers:

$$\frac{1}{3} + \frac{2}{3} = \frac{1}{2}$$

$$\frac{1}{4} + \frac{1}{4} = \frac{1}{2}$$

$$\frac{1}{6} + \frac{1}{3} = \frac{1}{2}$$

$$\frac{1}{12} + \frac{5}{12} = \frac{1}{2}$$

$$\frac{1}{6} + \frac{1}{6} + \frac{1}{6} = \frac{1}{2} \cdots$$

Practice Set 11

a. $118 + N = 213$

$$\begin{array}{r} \overset{1\ 10\ 13}{2\,\cancel{1}\,\cancel{3}} \\ -\ 118 \\ \hline 95 \end{array} \longrightarrow \begin{array}{r} \overset{1\ 1}{118 \text{ pounds}} \\ +\ \ 95 \text{ pounds} \\ \hline 213 \text{ pounds} \end{array} \quad \text{check}$$

95 pounds

b. $T + 216 = 400$

$$\begin{array}{r} \overset{3\ 9\ 10}{\cancel{4}\,\cancel{0}\,\cancel{0}} \\ -\ 216 \\ \hline 184 \end{array} \longrightarrow \begin{array}{r} \overset{1\ 1}{216 \text{ turns}} \\ +\ 184 \text{ turns} \\ \hline 400 \text{ turns} \end{array} \quad \text{check}$$

184 turns

c. $254 - H = 126$

$$\begin{array}{r} \overset{4\ 14}{2\,\cancel{5}\,\cancel{4}} \\ -\ 126 \\ \hline 128 \end{array} \longrightarrow \begin{array}{r} \overset{1}{126 \text{ horses}} \\ +\ 128 \text{ horses} \\ \hline 254 \text{ horses} \end{array} \quad \text{check}$$

128 horses

d. $P - 36 = 164$

$$\begin{array}{r} \overset{1\ 1}{164} \\ +\ 36 \\ \hline 200 \end{array} \longrightarrow \begin{array}{r} \overset{1\ 9\ 10}{\cancel{2}\,\cancel{0}\,\cancel{0}} \text{ sheets} \\ -\ \ 36 \text{ sheets} \\ \hline 164 \text{ sheets} \end{array} \quad \text{check}$$

200 sheets

e. Answers will vary. See student work. Sample answer: The price on the tag was $15.00, but after tax the total was $16.13. How much was the tax?

f. Answers will vary. See student work. Sample answer: There were 32 students in the class. When some students left for band practice, 25 students remained. How many students left for band practice?

Written Practice 11

1. $85,000 + V = 200,000$

$$\begin{array}{r} \overset{1\ 9\ 10}{2\,\cancel{0}\,\cancel{0}},000 \\ -\ \ 85,000 \\ \hline 115,000 \end{array} \longrightarrow \begin{array}{r} \overset{1\ 1}{115,000} \text{ people} \\ +\ \ 85,000 \text{ people} \\ \hline 200,000 \text{ people} \end{array} \quad \text{check}$$

115,000 visitors

2. $M - \$98.03 = \$12.47$

$$\begin{array}{r} \overset{1\ \ 1}{\$\ 98.03} \\ +\ \$\ 12.47 \\ \hline \$110.50 \end{array} \longrightarrow \begin{array}{r} \overset{0\ 10\ 10\ \ 4\ 10}{\$\,\cancel{1}\,\cancel{1}\,\cancel{0}.\cancel{5}\,\cancel{0}} \\ -\ \$\ \ 98.03 \\ \hline \$\ \ 12.47 \end{array} \quad \text{check}$$

$110.50

3. $17,926 - d = 16,733$

$$\begin{array}{r} \overset{8\,12}{17,\cancel{9}26} \\ -\ 16,733 \\ \hline 1,193 \end{array}$$

$d = $ **1193 runners**

4. a. $\dfrac{7}{8}$

b. $\dfrac{1}{8}$

c. $100\% \div 8 = 12\frac{1}{2}\%$

$12\frac{1}{2}\% \times 1 = \mathbf{12\frac{1}{2}\%}$

5. a. $-2, 0, \dfrac{1}{2}, 1$

b. $\dfrac{1}{2}$

6. $8\overline{)35}$ inches $\longrightarrow$ $4\frac{3}{8}$ inches

$$\begin{array}{r} 4 \\ 8\overline{)35} \\ \underline{32} \\ 3 \end{array}$$

Saxon Math Course 2

112

7. $1 \cdot 2 < 1 + 2$

8.
$$\overset{0\ 9\ 10}{\cancel{1}\cancel{0}\cancel{0}} \text{ million}$$
$$-\ \ \ \ 89 \text{ million}$$
$$\overline{\ \ \ \ 11 \text{ million}}$$
Eleven million

9. a. 1, 2, 4, 8, 16

b. 1, 2, 3, 4, 6, 8, 12, 24

c. 1, 2, 4, 8

d. 8

10. **Answers will vary. See student work. Sample answer: I went to the mall with $20.00. I bought a pair of earrings and a bottle of water. When I got home, I had $12.50. How much money did I spend at the mall?**

$20.00 − k = $12.50

$$\begin{array}{r} \overset{1\ 9\ 10}{\$2\cancel{0}.\cancel{0}0} \\ -\ \$12.50 \\ \hline \$\ \ 7.50 \end{array} \quad \rightarrow \quad \begin{array}{r} \overset{1\ 1}{\$\ 12.50} \\ +\ \$\ \ 7.50 \\ \hline \$\ 20.00 \end{array} \quad \text{check}$$

$7.50

11.

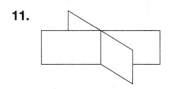

12. $4 \cdot 9 = 36$
$$36\overline{)720}$$
$$\underline{72}$$
$$00$$
$$\underline{0}$$
$$0$$

$n = $ **20**

13.
$$\begin{array}{r} \overset{6\ 15}{\$37\cancel{5}} \\ -\ \$126 \\ \hline \$249 \end{array}$$
$r = $ **$249**

14.
$$\begin{array}{r} 13 \\ 13\overline{)169} \\ \underline{13} \\ 39 \\ \underline{39} \\ 0 \end{array}$$
$s = $ **13**

15.
$$\begin{array}{r} \$25.00 \\ \times\ \ \ \ \ \ 40 \\ \hline \$1000.00 \end{array}$$
$t = $ **$1000.00**

16. $5 \times 20 = 100 \qquad 100 - 100 = 0$

$$100 - 5 = 95 \qquad \begin{array}{r} 95 \\ \times\ \ \ 20 \\ \hline 1900 \end{array}$$

$0 < 1900$
$100 - (5 \times 20) < (100 - 5) \times 20$

17. $1\frac{5}{9} + 1\frac{5}{9} = 2\frac{10}{9} = 2\frac{1}{9} + \frac{9}{9}$
$$= 2\frac{1}{9} + 1 = \mathbf{3\frac{1}{9}}$$

18. $\frac{5}{3} \times \frac{2}{3} = \frac{10}{9} = \frac{9}{9} + \frac{1}{9} = \mathbf{1\frac{1}{9}}$

19.
$$\begin{array}{r} 135 \\ \times\ \ 72 \\ \hline 270 \\ 945 \\ \hline \mathbf{9720} \end{array}$$

20.
$$\begin{array}{r} 25 \\ 40\overline{)1000} \\ \underline{80} \\ 200 \\ \underline{200} \\ 0 \end{array}$$

21.
$$\begin{array}{r} \$1.49 \\ \times\ \ \ \ \ 30 \\ \hline \mathbf{\$44.70} \end{array}$$

22.
$$\begin{array}{r} \mathbf{\$4.02} \\ 35\overline{)\$140.70} \\ \underline{140} \\ 0\ 7 \\ \underline{0} \\ 70 \\ \underline{70} \\ 0 \end{array}$$

23. $\frac{5}{54}$

24. $\frac{5}{8} + \left(\frac{3}{8} - \frac{1}{8}\right) = \frac{5}{8} + \left(\frac{2}{8}\right) = \frac{7}{8}$

25. **a.** $3\frac{3}{4} = \frac{4 \times 3 + 3}{4} = \frac{15}{4}$

  b. $\frac{4}{15}$

  c. $\frac{15}{4} \cdot \frac{4}{15} = \frac{60}{60} = 1$

26. **C. 40%**

27. $\frac{1}{2} + \frac{1}{8} = \frac{4}{8} + \frac{1}{8} = \frac{5}{8}$

$\frac{5}{8} + \frac{1}{8} = \frac{6}{8} = \frac{3}{4}$

$\frac{6}{8} + \frac{1}{8} = \frac{7}{8}$

$\frac{7}{8} + \frac{1}{8} = \frac{8}{8} = 1$

$\frac{5}{8}, \frac{3}{4}, \frac{7}{8}, 1$

28. **a.** $\angle 1, \angle 3$

  b. $\angle 2, \angle 4$

29. $AB = 1\frac{7}{8}$ inches

  $BC = 1\frac{5}{8}$ inches

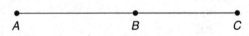

30. $\frac{8}{7}$

Early Finishers Solutions

a. $\frac{30 \times 12}{50} = \frac{360}{50} = 7$ R10; 7 pencils

b. Yes; 10 pencils left over

c. $\frac{10}{360} = \frac{1}{36}$

Practice Set 12

a. $1{,}000{,}000{,}000 - 25{,}000{,}000 = G$

```
                       1 1
  1,000,000,000      975,000,000
-    25,000,000   +   25,000,000
   975,000,000     1,000,000,000  check
975,000,000
```

b. $1791 - 1215 = Y$

```
              1
  1791       1215
- 1215     +  576
   576       1791   check
576 years
```

c. $1960 - B = 43$

```
                5 10
  1960        1 9 6 0
-   43      -  1 9 1 7
  1917            4 3   check
```

John F. Kennedy was born in **1917**.

d. Answers will vary. See student work. Sample answer: Todd is 58 in. tall and Glenda is 55 in. tall. Todd is how many inches taller than Glenda?

e. Answers will vary. See student work. Sample answer: Rosalie turned 14 in 2003. In what year was she born?

Written Practice 12

1. $1{,}870{,}000 - 911{,}000 = d$; **959,000 barrels**

2. $C + 18 = 31$

```
  2 11
  3 1              18 computers
- 1 8           + 13 computers
  1 3              31 computers   check
13 computers
```

3. $1215 - 1066 = Y$

```
               1 1
  1215        1066
- 1066      +  149
   149        1215   check
149 years
```

4. $105{,}000 - 50{,}000 = d$; **55,000 fewer spectators**

5. **Answers will vary. See student work.**
   Sample answer: Marla gave the clerk
   $20.00 to purchase a CD. Marla got back
   $7.13. How much did the CD cost?

6. a. **Identity property of multiplication**

   b. **Inverse property of multiplication**

7. $1{,}000{,}000 - 23{,}000 = D$

   $$
   \begin{array}{r}
   \overset{0\ \ 9\ \ 9\ \ 10}{\cancel{1},\cancel{0}\,\cancel{0}\,\cancel{0},0\,0\,0} \\
   -\quad\ \ 2\,3,0\,0\,0 \\
   \hline
   9\,7\,7,0\,0\,0
   \end{array}
   $$

   Nine hundred seventy-seven thousand

8. a. $2 - 3 = -1$

   b. $\dfrac{1}{2} > \dfrac{1}{3}$

9. $\overline{PQ}$ (or $\overline{QP}$), $\overline{QR}$ (or $\overline{RQ}$), $\overline{PR}$ (or $\overline{RP}$)

10.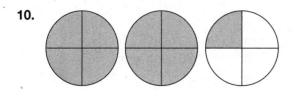

11. a. $\dfrac{3}{4}$

    b. $100\% \div 4 = 25\%$
       $25\% \times 1 = \mathbf{25\%}$

12. **1, 2, 4, 5, 10, 20, 25, 50, 100**

13. $$
    \begin{array}{r}
    42 \\
    15\overline{)630} \\
    \underline{60} \\
    30 \\
    \underline{30} \\
    0
    \end{array}
    $$
    $x = \mathbf{42}$

14. $$
    \begin{array}{r}
    \overset{1}{}3601 \\
    +\ 2714 \\
    \hline
    6315
    \end{array}
    $$
    $y = \mathbf{6315}$

15. $$
    \begin{array}{r}
    \overset{8\ \ 9\ \ 10}{2\,\cancel{9}\,\cancel{0}\,\cancel{0}} \\
    -\quad\ \ 6\,4 \\
    \hline
    2\,8\,3\,6
    \end{array}
    $$
    $p = \mathbf{2836}$

16. $$
    \begin{array}{r}
    \overset{4\ \ 9\ \ 10}{\$\,\cancel{5}.\cancel{0}\,\cancel{0}} \\
    -\ \$\,1.5\,3 \\
    \hline
    \$\,3.\,4\,7
    \end{array}
    $$
    $q = \mathbf{\$3.47}$

17. $$
    \begin{array}{r}
    60 \\
    20\overline{)1200} \\
    \underline{120} \\
    00 \\
    \underline{0} \\
    0
    \end{array}
    $$
    $r = \mathbf{60}$

18. $$
    \begin{array}{r}
    16 \\
    \times\ 14 \\
    \hline
    64 \\
    160 \\
    \hline
    224
    \end{array}
    $$
    $m = \mathbf{224}$

19. $$
    \begin{array}{r}
    \overset{6\ \ 11\ \ 11\ \ 0\ \ 12}{7\,\cancel{2},\cancel{1}\,\cancel{1}\,\cancel{2}} \\
    -\ 6\,4,3\,0\,9 \\
    \hline
    7,8\,0\,3
    \end{array}
    $$

20. $$
    \begin{array}{r}
    \overset{1\,1\,1\ \ 1\,1}{453{,}978} \\
    +\ 386{,}864 \\
    \hline
    840{,}842
    \end{array}
    $$

21. $\dfrac{8}{9} - \left(\dfrac{3}{9} + \dfrac{5}{9}\right) = \dfrac{8}{9} - \left(\dfrac{8}{9}\right) = \mathbf{0}$

22. $\left(\dfrac{8}{9} - \dfrac{3}{9}\right) + \dfrac{5}{9} = \left(\dfrac{5}{9}\right) + \dfrac{5}{9} = \dfrac{10}{9}$

    $$= 1\dfrac{1}{9}$$

23. $\dfrac{9}{2} \times \dfrac{3}{5} = \dfrac{27}{10} = 2\dfrac{7}{10}$

24. $$
    \begin{array}{r}
    \$2.48 \\
    15\overline{)\$37.20} \\
    \underline{30} \\
    7\,2 \\
    \underline{6\,0} \\
    1\,20 \\
    \underline{1\,20} \\
    0
    \end{array}
    $$

25.
$$\begin{array}{r} 4760 \\ 9\overline{)42{,}847} \\ \underline{36} \\ 6\,8 \\ \underline{6\,3} \\ 54 \\ \underline{54} \\ 07 \\ \underline{0} \\ 7 \end{array}$$

$$4760 \frac{7}{9}$$

26. a. **Commutative property**

b. **Associative property**

c. $25 \cdot 4 = 100$

d. $100 \cdot 36 = 3600$

27. $\dfrac{3}{4} + \dfrac{1}{4} = \dfrac{4}{4} = 1$

$\dfrac{4}{4} + \dfrac{1}{4} = \dfrac{5}{4} = 1\dfrac{1}{4}$

$\dfrac{5}{4} + \dfrac{1}{4} = \dfrac{6}{4} = \dfrac{3}{2} = 1\dfrac{1}{2}$

$1,\ 1\dfrac{1}{4},\ 1\dfrac{1}{2}$

28. $\dfrac{3}{2}$

29. $1\dfrac{2}{3} = \dfrac{3 \times 1 + 2}{3} = \dfrac{5}{3}$

$\dfrac{5}{3} \times \dfrac{1}{2} = \dfrac{5}{6}$

30.
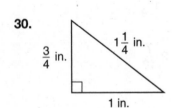

$1\dfrac{1}{4}$ in.

Early Finishers Solutions

4 years, 8 months; Patricia's grandmother was
56 years old in 2004 (2004 − 1948 = 56). So,
her cat was 56 months old. Divide 56 months by
12 months per year to get the number of years:
56 ÷ 12 = 4 R8. The remainder indicates the
number of months.

a. 24×32¢ $= m$

$$\begin{array}{r} \$0.32 \\ \times \quad 24 \\ \hline 128 \\ 64 \\ \hline \$7.68 \end{array} \qquad \textbf{\$7.68}$$

b. $R \times 25 = 375$

$$\begin{array}{r} 15 \\ 25\overline{)375} \\ \underline{25} \\ 125 \\ \underline{125} \\ 0 \end{array} \qquad 15 \times 25 = 375 \qquad \text{check}$$

15 rows

c. $7P = 1225$

$$\begin{array}{r} 175 \\ 7\overline{)1225} \\ \underline{7} \\ 52 \\ \underline{49} \\ 35 \\ \underline{35} \\ 0 \end{array} \qquad 7 \times 175 = 1225 \qquad \text{check}$$

175 push-ups

d. **Answers will vary. See student work.
Sample answer: If a dozen doughnuts cost
$3.00, what is the cost per doughnut?**

1. $24{,}877 - 14{,}619 = d;\ \textbf{10{,}258}$

2. $2\dfrac{1}{2} = \dfrac{2 \times 2 + 1}{2} = \dfrac{5}{2}$

$\dfrac{5}{2} \cdot \dfrac{1}{3} = \dfrac{5}{6}$

3. $1932 - B = 50$

$$\begin{array}{r} {\scriptstyle 8\ 13} \\ 1\,9\,\cancel{3}\,2 \\ - \quad 5\,0 \\ \hline \mathbf{1\,8\,8\,2} \end{array}$$

4. $75 \times 12 = B$

$$
\begin{array}{r}
75 \\
\times\ 12 \\
\hline
150 \\
75 \\
\hline
900
\end{array}
$$

900 beach balls

5. $T \times 8 = 120$

$$
\begin{array}{r}
15 \\
8\overline{)120} \\
8 \\
\hline
40 \\
40 \\
\hline
0
\end{array}
$$

$15 \times 8 = 120$ check

15 truckloads

6. Answers will vary. See student work. Sample answer: Five tickets for the show cost $63.75. If all the tickets were the same price, then what was the cost per ticket?

$$
\begin{array}{r}
\$12.75 \\
5\overline{)\$63.75} \\
5 \\
\hline
13 \\
10 \\
\hline
3\,7 \\
3\,5 \\
\hline
25 \\
25 \\
\hline
0
\end{array}
$$

$5(\$12.75) = \$63.75$ check

$12.75

7. $(5 \times 8) - (5 + 8) = 40 - 13 = \mathbf{27}$

8. a. $\dfrac{3\ \text{quarters}}{4\ \text{quarters}} = \dfrac{3}{4}$

    b. $\dfrac{75¢}{100¢} = \mathbf{75\%}$

9. **10 units**

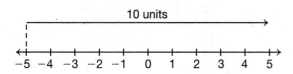

10. a. Line; $\overleftrightarrow{BR}$ (or $\overleftrightarrow{RB}$)

    b. Segment; $\overline{TV}$ (or $\overline{VT}$)

    c. Ray; $\overrightarrow{MW}$

11. a. Factors of 24: 1, 2, 3, 4, 6, 8, 12, 24
Factors of 36: 1, 2, 3, 4, 6, 9, 12, 18, 36
1, 2, 3, 4, 6, 12

    b. **12**

12. a. $A\colon \dfrac{6}{7};\ B\colon 1\dfrac{4}{7}$

    b. $1\dfrac{4}{7} - \dfrac{6}{7} = \dfrac{7 \times 1 + 4}{7} - \dfrac{6}{7}$

$$= \dfrac{11}{7} - \dfrac{6}{7} = \dfrac{5}{7}\ \text{units}$$

13.

$$
\begin{array}{r}
50 \\
36\overline{)1800} \\
180 \\
\hline
00 \\
0 \\
\hline
0
\end{array}
$$

$c = \mathbf{50}$

14.

$$
\begin{array}{r}
\overset{1\ 1}{\$3.77} \\
+\ \$1.64 \\
\hline
\$5.41
\end{array}
$$

$f = \mathbf{\$5.41}$

15.

$$
\begin{array}{r}
28 \\
\times\ 7 \\
\hline
196
\end{array}
$$

$d = \mathbf{196}$

16.

$$
\begin{array}{r}
150 \\
30\overline{)4500} \\
30 \\
\hline
150 \\
150 \\
\hline
00 \\
0 \\
\hline
0
\end{array}
$$

$e = \mathbf{150}$

Solutions

17.

```
    4
    7
    6
    8
    4
    5
    5
    7
    9
    6
  + 8
  ───
   69
```

$$\begin{array}{r} {}^{6}\overset{15}{\cancel{7}\cancel{5}} \\ -\ 69 \\ \hline 6 \end{array}$$

$n = \mathbf{6}$

18.

$$\begin{array}{r} {}^{6}\ {}^{14} \\ 36\,7\cancel{4} \\ -\ 2\,1\,5\,9 \\ \hline 1\,5\,1\,5 \end{array}$$

$a = \mathbf{1515}$

19.

$$\begin{array}{r} {}^{4}\ {}^{11} \\ \cancel{5}\cancel{1}7\,9 \\ -\ 4\,6\,1\,0 \\ \hline 5\,6\,9 \end{array}$$

$b = \mathbf{569}$

20.

$$\begin{array}{r} {}^{2}\ {}^{2} \\ {}_{1}3\,6\,3 \\ 4\,5\,7\,9 \\ 8\,6 \\ +\ 7 \\ \hline 5\,0\,3\,5 \end{array}$$

21. $(5 \cdot 4) \div (3 + 2) = (20) \div (5) = \mathbf{4}$

22. $\dfrac{5}{3} \cdot \dfrac{5}{2} = \dfrac{25}{6} = \mathbf{4\dfrac{1}{6}}$

23. $3\dfrac{4}{5} - \left(\dfrac{2}{5} + 1\dfrac{1}{5}\right)$

$= \dfrac{5 \times 3 + 4}{5} - \left(\dfrac{2}{5} + \dfrac{5 \times 1 + 1}{5}\right)$

$= \dfrac{19}{5} - \left(\dfrac{2}{5} + \dfrac{6}{5}\right) = \dfrac{19}{5} - \left(\dfrac{8}{5}\right)$

$= \dfrac{11}{5} = \mathbf{2\dfrac{1}{5}}$

24.

$$\begin{array}{r} \mathbf{24} \\ 25\overline{)600} \\ \underline{50} \\ 100 \\ \underline{100} \\ 0 \end{array}$$

25.

```
    600
  ×  25
  ─────
   3000
   1200
  ──────
 15,000
```

26. $100 \div 10 = 10,\ 1000 \div 10 = 100$

$1000 \div 100 = 10,\ 10 \div 10 = 1$

$100 > 1$

$1000 \div (100 \div 10) > (1000 \div 100) \div 10$

27. Mr. Lim used 55 eggs; first I multiplied 12 by 6 to find out that Mr. Lim bought 72 eggs; then I used the equation $72 - n = 17$; I found the value of n by subtracting 17 from 72.

28. a. $\dfrac{11}{12} \cdot \dfrac{12}{11} = \mathbf{1}$

b. **Inverse property of multiplication**

29. Obtuse: $\angle D$
Acute: $\angle A$
Right: $\angle B$ and $\angle C$

30. a. $\overline{DC}$ (or $\overline{CD}$)

b. $\overline{CB}$ (or $\overline{BC}$)

Early Finishers Solutions

a.

```
    1.0875
  × 2530
  ───────
   326250
   54375
 + 21750
 ──────────
 2751.3750 = $2751.38
```

b.

```
     455.40
   × 1.0875
   ────────
     227700          2751.38
     318780        +  495.25
     364320        ─────────
  +  455400         $3246.63
   ──────────
   495.247500
```

Practice Set 14

a. 39% + N = 100%

$$
\begin{array}{r}
{\scriptstyle 0\ 9\ 10}\\
\cancel{1}\ \cancel{0}\ \cancel{0}\\
-\quad 3\ 9\\
\hline
6\ 1
\end{array}
$$

61%

b. $\dfrac{2}{5}$ + M = $\dfrac{5}{5}$

$$\dfrac{5}{5} - \dfrac{2}{5} = \dfrac{3}{5}$$

c. Answers will vary. See student work. Sample answer: If 45% of the students were boys, then what percent of the students were girls?

d. Possibilities: 1, 2, 3 = 3
Total possible outcomes: 6
P (number < 4) = $\dfrac{3}{6} = \dfrac{1}{2}$

e. P(3) = $\dfrac{1}{4}$

f. P(5) = $\dfrac{0}{4} = 0$

g. P(number < 6) = $\dfrac{4}{4} = 1$

h. P(A) = $\dfrac{1}{2}$

i. P(A or C) = $\dfrac{1}{2} + \dfrac{1}{4} = \dfrac{2}{4} + \dfrac{1}{4} = \dfrac{3}{4}$

Written Practice 14

1. 63 + C = 85

$$
\begin{array}{r}
85\\
-\ 63\\
\hline
22
\end{array}
\qquad
\begin{array}{r}
63\ \text{grams}\\
+\ 22\ \text{grams}\\
\hline
85\ \text{grams}
\end{array}
\quad \text{check}
$$

22 grams

2. $\dfrac{7}{10}$ + W = $\dfrac{10}{10}$

$$
\begin{array}{r}
\dfrac{10}{10}\\
-\ \dfrac{7}{10}\\
\hline
\dfrac{3}{10}
\end{array}
\quad
\begin{array}{l}
\dfrac{3}{10}\ \text{recruits liked haircut}\\
+\ \dfrac{7}{10}\ \text{recruits did not like haircut}\\
\hline
\dfrac{10}{10}\ \text{total recruits \ check}
\end{array}
$$

$$\dfrac{3}{10}$$

3. 1789 − 1776 = Y

$$
\begin{array}{r}
1789\\
-\ 1776\\
\hline
13
\end{array}
\quad
\begin{array}{r}
1776\\
+\quad 13\\
\hline
1789
\end{array}
\quad \text{check}
$$

13 years

4. Answers will vary. See student work. Sample answer: If a dozen flavored icicles cost $2.40, then what is the cost per flavored icicle?

5. 18% + N_A = 100%
100% − 18% = 82%

18% + 82% = 100%   check

82%

6.

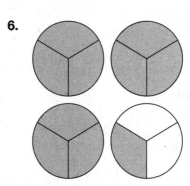

7. 407,042,603

8. Property of zero for multiplication

9. **a.** Factors of 40: 1, 2, 4, 5, 8, 10, 20, 40
Factors of 72: 1, 2, 3, 4, 6, 8, 9, 12, 18, 24, 36, 72
1, 2, 4, 8

b. 8

10. $\overline{XY}$ (or $\overline{YX}$), $\overline{WX}$ (or $\overline{XW}$), $\overline{WY}$ (or $\overline{YW}$)

Solutions

11. Count the number in the group, which is 12. Use this as the denominator. Count the number that are shaded, which is 5. Use this as the numerator $\frac{5}{12}$.

12.
$$\begin{array}{r} \overset{1}{6}23 \\ +\ 407 \\ \hline 1030 \end{array}$$
$b = \mathbf{1030}$

13.
$$\begin{array}{r} \overset{1\ 9\ 9\ 10}{\$2\cancel{0}.\cancel{0}\cancel{0}} \\ -\ \$\ \ 3.47 \\ \hline \$16.53 \end{array}$$
$e = \mathbf{\$16.53}$

14.
$$\begin{array}{r} 202 \\ 35\overline{)7070} \\ 70 \\ \hline 07 \\ 0 \\ \hline 70 \\ 70 \\ \hline 0 \end{array}$$
$f = \mathbf{202}$

15.
$$\begin{array}{r} 25 \\ \times\ 25 \\ \hline 125 \\ 50\ \ \\ \hline 625 \end{array}$$
$m = \mathbf{625}$

16.
$$\begin{array}{l} 5 \\ 8 \\ 7 \\ 6 \\ 5 \\ 9 \\ 4 \\ 3 \\ 6 \\ 4 \\ 7 \\ 8 \\ 5 \\ +\ 6 \\ \hline 83 \end{array} \qquad \begin{array}{r} 89 \\ -\ 83 \\ \hline 6 \end{array} \qquad n = \mathbf{6}$$

17.
$$\begin{array}{r} \overset{0\ 9\ 9\ 10}{\cancel{1}\cancel{0}\cancel{0}\cancel{0}} \\ -\ 295 \\ \hline 705 \end{array}$$
$a = \mathbf{705}$

18. $3\frac{3}{5} + 2\frac{4}{5} = \frac{18}{5} + \frac{14}{5}$
$= \frac{32}{5} = 6\frac{2}{5}$

19. $\frac{5}{2} \cdot \frac{3}{2} = \frac{15}{4} = 3\frac{3}{4}$

20.
$$\begin{array}{r} \overset{2\ 1}{\$3.63} \\ \$0.87 \\ +\ \$0.96 \\ \hline \$5.46 \end{array}$$

21. $5 \cdot 4 \cdot 3 \cdot 2 \cdot 1 = 20 \cdot 3 \cdot 2 \cdot 1$
$= 60 \cdot 2 \cdot 1 = 120 \cdot 1 = \mathbf{120}$

22. $\frac{8}{27}$

23.
$$\begin{array}{r} 45 \\ 20\overline{)900} \\ 80 \\ \hline 100 \\ 100 \\ \hline 0 \end{array}$$

24.
$$\begin{array}{r} 145 \\ \times\ \ 74 \\ \hline 580 \\ 1015\ \ \\ \hline 10,730 \end{array}$$

25.
$$\begin{array}{r} \$0.65 \\ \times\ \ \ 30 \\ \hline \$19.50 \end{array}$$

26. $(5)(5+5) = 5(10) = \mathbf{50}$

27.
$$\begin{array}{r} \overset{0\ 12\ 14}{\cancel{1}\cancel{3},\cancel{4}56} \\ -\ \ 9,714 \\ \hline 3,742 \end{array} \qquad -3742$$

28. a. **Right angle**

    b. **Straight angle**

    c. **Obtuse angle**

29. $\frac{5}{4}$

30. $P(\text{number} > 4) = \frac{2}{6} = \frac{1}{3}$

Practice Set 15

a. $\dfrac{3}{4} \times \dfrac{5}{5} = \dfrac{15}{20}$

$\dfrac{3}{4} \times \dfrac{7}{7} = \dfrac{21}{28}$

$\dfrac{3}{4} \times \dfrac{3}{3} = \dfrac{9}{12}$

b. $\dfrac{3}{4} \times \dfrac{4}{4} = \dfrac{12}{16}$

c. $\dfrac{4}{5} \times \dfrac{4}{4} = \dfrac{16}{20}$

d. $\dfrac{3}{8} \times \dfrac{3}{3} = \dfrac{9}{24}$

e. $\dfrac{3}{5} \times \dfrac{2}{2} = \dfrac{6}{10}$

$-\dfrac{1}{2} \times \dfrac{5}{5} = \dfrac{5}{10}$

$\rule{2cm}{0.4pt}$

$\dfrac{1}{10}$

f. $\dfrac{3}{6} = \dfrac{3 \div 3}{6 \div 3} = \dfrac{1}{2}$

g. $\dfrac{8}{10} = \dfrac{8 \div 2}{10 \div 2} = \dfrac{4}{5}$

h. $\dfrac{8}{16} = \dfrac{8 \div 8}{16 \div 8} = \dfrac{1}{2}$

i. $\dfrac{12}{16} = \dfrac{12 \div 4}{16 \div 4} = \dfrac{3}{4}$

j. $\dfrac{4}{8} = \dfrac{4 \div 4}{8 \div 4} = \dfrac{1}{2}, \ 4\dfrac{4}{8} = 4\dfrac{1}{2}$

k. $\dfrac{9}{12} = \dfrac{9 \div 3}{12 \div 3} = \dfrac{3}{4}, \ 6\dfrac{9}{12} = 6\dfrac{3}{4}$

l. $12\dfrac{8}{15}$

m. $\dfrac{16}{24} = \dfrac{16 \div 8}{24 \div 8} = \dfrac{2}{3}, \ 8\dfrac{16}{24} = 8\dfrac{2}{3}$

n. $\dfrac{5}{12} + \dfrac{5}{12} = \dfrac{10}{12} = \dfrac{10 \div 2}{12 \div 2} = \dfrac{5}{6}$

o. $3\dfrac{7}{10} - 1\dfrac{1}{10} = 2\dfrac{6}{10}$

$\dfrac{6}{10} = \dfrac{6 \div 2}{10 \div 2} = \dfrac{3}{5}, \ 2\dfrac{6}{10} = 2\dfrac{3}{5}$

p. $\dfrac{5}{8} \cdot \dfrac{2}{3} = \dfrac{10}{24} = \dfrac{10 \div 2}{24 \div 2} = \dfrac{5}{12}$

q. $90\% = \dfrac{90}{100}$

$\dfrac{90}{100} \div \dfrac{10}{10} = \dfrac{9}{10}$

r. $75\% = \dfrac{75}{100}$

$\dfrac{75}{100} \div \dfrac{25}{25} = \dfrac{3}{4}$

s. $5\% = \dfrac{5}{100}$

$\dfrac{5}{100} \div \dfrac{5}{5} = \dfrac{1}{20}$

t. $\dfrac{2}{3} \cdot \dfrac{2}{2} = \dfrac{4}{6}$

$\dfrac{4}{6} - \dfrac{1}{6} = \dfrac{3}{6} = \dfrac{3 \div 3}{6 \div 3} = \dfrac{1}{2}$

u. $P(\text{even}) = \dfrac{2 \text{ or } 4 \text{ or } 6}{6} = \dfrac{3 \div 3}{6 \div 3} = \dfrac{1}{2}$

Written Practice 15

1. $1998 - B = 75$

$\begin{array}{r} 1998 \\ - \ 75 \\ \hline 1923 \end{array} \longrightarrow \begin{array}{r} 1923 \\ + \ 75 \\ \hline 1998 \end{array}$ check

$B = 1923$

2. $P(\text{not } 4) = P(1) + P(2) + P(3)$

$P(1) = \dfrac{4}{8}, P(2) = \dfrac{2}{8}, P(3) = \dfrac{1}{8}$

$P(\text{not } 4) = \dfrac{4}{8} + \dfrac{2}{8} + \dfrac{1}{8} = \dfrac{7}{8}$

Solutions

3. $40\% = \dfrac{40}{100}$

$\dfrac{40}{100} \div \dfrac{20}{20} = \dfrac{2}{5}$

4. $60C = 9000$

$$\begin{array}{r} 150 \\ 60\overline{)9000} \\ \underline{60} \\ 300 \\ \underline{300} \\ 00 \\ \underline{0} \\ 0 \end{array}$$

150 bushels

5. $2\dfrac{1}{2}$ in. $- 1\dfrac{7}{8}$ in. $= \dfrac{5}{2}$ in. $- \dfrac{15}{8}$ in.

$= \dfrac{20}{8}$ in. $- \dfrac{15}{8}$ in. $= \dfrac{5}{8}$ **in.**

6. $3 \cdot 5 > 3 + 5$

7. $2 + 1 + 0 + 0 = 3$

$$\begin{array}{r} 12\,\text{R}\,4 \\ 8\overline{)100} \\ \underline{8} \\ 20 \\ \underline{16} \\ 4 \\ \underline{0} \\ 4 \end{array} \qquad \begin{array}{r} 300 \\ 7\overline{)2100} \\ \underline{21} \\ 00 \\ \underline{0} \\ 00 \\ \underline{0} \\ 0 \end{array}$$

1, 2, 3, 4, 5, 6, 7

8. a. $\dfrac{6}{8} = \dfrac{6 \div 2}{8 \div 2} = \dfrac{3}{4}$

b. $\dfrac{6}{10} = \dfrac{6 \div 2}{10 \div 2} = \dfrac{3}{5}$, $2\dfrac{6}{10} = 2\dfrac{3}{5}$

9. $\dfrac{2}{3} \cdot \dfrac{3}{3} = \dfrac{6}{9}$

$\dfrac{2}{3} \cdot \dfrac{5}{5} = \dfrac{10}{15}$

$\dfrac{2}{3} \cdot \dfrac{6}{6} = \dfrac{12}{18}$

Identity property of multiplication

10. a. $\dfrac{3}{5} \cdot \dfrac{4}{4} = \dfrac{12}{20}$

b. $\dfrac{1}{2} \cdot \dfrac{10}{10} = \dfrac{10}{20}$

c. $\dfrac{3}{4} \cdot \dfrac{5}{5} = \dfrac{15}{20}$

11. a. $\overleftrightarrow{QS}$ or $\overleftrightarrow{QR}$ or $\overleftrightarrow{RS}$ (or $\overleftrightarrow{SQ}$ or $\overleftrightarrow{RQ}$ or $\overleftrightarrow{SR}$)

b. $\overrightarrow{RT}, \overrightarrow{RQ}, \overrightarrow{RS}$

c. $\angle TRS$ or $\angle SRT$

12. a. $\dfrac{11}{3} \longrightarrow 3\overline{)11}^{3} \longrightarrow 3\dfrac{2}{3}$
$\phantom{\dfrac{11}{3} \longrightarrow}\underline{9}$
$\phantom{\dfrac{11}{3} \longrightarrow}2$

b. $\dfrac{12}{3} = \dfrac{12 \div 3}{3 \div 3} = \dfrac{4}{1} = 4$

c. $\dfrac{13}{3} \rightarrow 3\overline{)13}^{4} \rightarrow 4\dfrac{1}{3}$
$\phantom{\dfrac{13}{3} \rightarrow}\underline{12}$
$\phantom{\dfrac{13}{3} \rightarrow}1$

13. $11(6 + 7) = 11(13) = 143$
$66 + 77 = 143$
$143 = 143$
$(11)(6 + 7) = 66 + 77$

14. $\begin{array}{r} {}^{4\ 10} \\ \cancel{5}\cancel{0} \\ -\ 39 \\ \hline 11 \end{array}$

$b = 11$

15. $$\begin{array}{r} 50 \\ 6\overline{)300} \\ \underline{30} \\ 00 \\ \underline{0} \\ 0 \end{array}$$

$a = 50$

16. $\begin{array}{r} \$5.00 \\ +\ \$0.05 \\ \hline \$5.05 \end{array}$

$c = \textbf{\$5.05}$

17. $\begin{array}{r} 35 \\ \times\ 35 \\ \hline 175 \\ 105 \\ \hline 1225 \end{array}$

$w = \textbf{1225}$

18. a. $80\% = \dfrac{80}{100}$

$\dfrac{80}{100} \div \dfrac{20}{20} = \dfrac{4}{5}$

b. $35\% = \dfrac{35}{100}$

$\dfrac{35}{100} \div \dfrac{5}{5} = \dfrac{7}{20}$

19. 8

20. a. Commutative property
   b. Associative property
   c. Inverse property of multiplication
   d. Identity property of multiplication

21. $\dfrac{2}{5} + \dfrac{3}{5} + \dfrac{4}{5} = \dfrac{9}{5} = \mathbf{1\dfrac{4}{5}}$

22. $3\dfrac{5}{8} - 1\dfrac{3}{8} = 2\dfrac{2}{8} = \mathbf{2\dfrac{1}{4}}$

23. $\dfrac{4}{3} \cdot \dfrac{3}{4} = \dfrac{12}{12} = \mathbf{1}$

24. $\dfrac{3}{4} + \dfrac{3}{4} = \dfrac{6}{4} = 1\dfrac{2}{4} = \mathbf{1\dfrac{1}{2}}$

25. $\dfrac{7}{5} + \dfrac{8}{5} = \dfrac{15}{5} = \mathbf{3}$

26. $\dfrac{11}{12} - \dfrac{1}{12} = \dfrac{10}{12}$
   $\dfrac{10 \div 2}{12 \div 2} = \dfrac{\mathbf{5}}{\mathbf{6}}$

27. $\dfrac{5}{6} \cdot \dfrac{2}{3} = \dfrac{10}{18}$
   $\dfrac{10 \div 2}{18 \div 2} = \dfrac{\mathbf{5}}{\mathbf{9}}$

28. a. $\dfrac{4}{8} + \dfrac{4}{8} = \dfrac{8}{8} = \mathbf{1}$
   b. $\dfrac{4}{8} - \dfrac{4}{8} = \dfrac{0}{8} = \mathbf{0}$

29. $\dfrac{1}{3} \cdot \dfrac{2}{2} = \dfrac{2}{6}$
   $\dfrac{2}{6} + \dfrac{1}{6} = \dfrac{3}{6} = \dfrac{\mathbf{1}}{\mathbf{2}}$

30. $2\dfrac{2}{3} = \dfrac{8}{3}$
   $\dfrac{8}{3} \cdot \dfrac{1}{4} = \dfrac{8}{12}$
   $\dfrac{8 \div 4}{12 \div 4} = \dfrac{\mathbf{2}}{\mathbf{3}}$

Practice Set 16

a. **Nearly 7 feet**

b. **2 quarts**

c. **8 lb**

d. 1 cup = 8 ounces
   8 ounces · 2 cups = **16 ounces**

e. $\begin{array}{r} {\scriptstyle 1\ 9\ 10} \\ \cancel{2}\cancel{0}\cancel{0}\,° \\ -\ 1\ 7\ 2\,° \\ \hline \mathbf{2\ 8}\,°F \end{array}$

f. $\dfrac{3}{8}$ in. $+ \dfrac{5}{8}$ in. $= \dfrac{8}{8}$ in. $= \mathbf{1\ in.}$

g. $\begin{array}{r} 32°\ F \\ +\ 180°\ F \\ \hline \mathbf{212°\ F} \end{array}$

h. 2(3 ft + 4 ft) = 2(7 ft) = **14 ft**

i. 1 ton = 2000 pounds
   $\begin{array}{r} 2000\ \text{pounds} \\ -\ 1000\ \text{pounds} \\ \hline \mathbf{1000\ pounds} \end{array}$

j. 1 foot = 12 inches
   2 feet = 24 inches
   3 feet = 36 inches
   4 feet = **48 inches**
   To find the number of inches, multiply the number of feet by 12.

Written Practice 16

1. $44 + r = 193$; 149 flags

Solutions

2. $18C = 4500$

$$18\overline{)4500}$$
$$\underset{}{250}$$

250 cartons

$$\begin{array}{r} 250 \\ 18\overline{)4500} \\ 36 \\ \hline 90 \\ 90 \\ \hline 00 \\ 0 \\ \hline 0 \end{array}$$

$250 \cdot 18 = 4500$

check

3.

Cartons	Eggs
1	18
2	36
3	54
4	72
5	90

4. The outcomes are equally likely. The probability of each is $\frac{1}{2}$.

5. a. $\dfrac{8}{10} = \dfrac{4}{5}$

b. $\dfrac{8}{5} = 1\dfrac{3}{5}$

$\dfrac{8}{5} > 1\dfrac{2}{5}$

6. AB is $1\frac{3}{8}$ in.; CB is $1\frac{3}{8}$ in.; CA is $2\frac{3}{4}$ in.

7. a. $\dfrac{8}{12} = \dfrac{8 \div 4}{12 \div 4} = \dfrac{2}{3}$

b. $40\% = \dfrac{40}{100}$

$\dfrac{40}{100} \div \dfrac{20}{20} = \dfrac{2}{5}$

c. $\dfrac{10}{12} = \dfrac{10 \div 2}{12 \div 2} = \dfrac{5}{6}, \; 6\dfrac{10}{12} = 6\dfrac{5}{6}$

8. a. $\dfrac{5}{6} \cdot \dfrac{4}{4} = \dfrac{20}{24}$

b. $\dfrac{3}{8} \cdot \dfrac{3}{3} = \dfrac{9}{24}$

c. $\dfrac{1}{4} \cdot \dfrac{6}{6} = \dfrac{6}{24}$

9. $\dfrac{5}{8}, \dfrac{3}{4}, \dfrac{5}{6}$

10. a. $100\% \div 3 = 33\dfrac{1}{3}\%$

b. $\dfrac{1 \text{ quart}}{4 \text{ quarts}} = \dfrac{1}{4}$

11.
$$\begin{array}{r} 90 \\ 7\overline{)630} \\ 63 \\ \hline 00 \\ 0 \\ \hline 0 \end{array}$$
1, ×2, 3, 5, 6, 7, 9
$6 + 3 + 0 = 9$

$$\begin{array}{r} 78 \text{ R } 6 \\ 8\overline{)630} \\ 56 \\ \hline 70 \\ 64 \\ \hline 6 \end{array}$$

12. a. $2\dfrac{2}{7}$

b. $3\dfrac{16}{8} = 3\dfrac{2}{1} = \dfrac{5}{1} = 5$

c. $2\dfrac{16}{9} = \dfrac{34}{9} = 3\dfrac{7}{9}$

13. a. Identity property of multiplication

b. Inverse property of multiplication

14.
$$\begin{array}{r} \overset{11}{1776} \\ +87 \\ \hline 1863 \end{array}$$
$m = 1863$

15.
$$\begin{array}{r} \$16.25 \\ -\$10.15 \\ \hline \$6.10 \end{array}$$
$b = \$6.10$

16.
$$\begin{array}{r} 77 \\ 13\overline{)1001} \\ 91 \\ \hline 91 \\ 91 \\ \hline 0 \end{array}$$
$n = 77$

17.
$$\begin{array}{r} 42 \\ 42\overline{)1764} \\ 168 \\ \hline 84 \\ 84 \\ \hline 0 \end{array}$$
$d = 42$

18. $3\frac{3}{4} - 1\frac{1}{4} = 2\frac{2}{4} = \mathbf{2\frac{1}{2}}$

19. $\frac{3}{10}$ in. $+ \frac{8}{10}$ in. $= \frac{11}{10}$ in. $= \mathbf{1\frac{1}{10}}$ **in.**

20. $\frac{3}{4} \times \frac{1}{3} = \frac{3}{12} = \frac{3 \div 3}{12 \div 3} = \mathbf{\frac{1}{4}}$

21. $\frac{4}{3} \cdot \frac{3}{2} = \frac{12}{6} = \mathbf{2}$

22.
$$
\begin{array}{r}
625 \\
16\overline{)10{,}000} \\
\underline{9\,6} \\
40 \\
\underline{32} \\
80 \\
\underline{80} \\
0
\end{array}
$$

23. $\frac{100\%}{8} = \frac{100\% \div 4}{8 \div 4} = \frac{25\%}{2}$

    $= \mathbf{12\frac{1}{2}\%}$

24.
$$
\begin{array}{r}
7\,777 \\
9\overline{)70{,}000} \\
\underline{63} \\
7\,0 \\
\underline{6\,3} \\
70 \\
\underline{63} \\
70 \\
\underline{63} \\
7
\end{array}
$$
$\longrightarrow$ $\mathbf{7777\frac{7}{9}}$

25.
$$
\begin{array}{r}
45 \\
\times\ 45 \\
\hline
225 \\
180 \\
\hline
\mathbf{2025}
\end{array}
$$

26. **Each term can be found by adding $\frac{1}{16}$ to the preceding term (or K $= \frac{1}{16}$ n).**

    $\frac{3}{16} + \frac{1}{16} = \frac{4}{16} = \frac{1}{4}$

    $\frac{4}{16} + \frac{1}{16} = \frac{5}{16}$

    $\frac{5}{16} + \frac{1}{16} = \frac{6}{16},\ \frac{6 \div 2}{16 \div 2} = \frac{3}{8}$

    $\mathbf{\frac{1}{4}, \frac{5}{16}, \frac{3}{8}}$

27. **Acute angle, obtuse angle**

28. **B. Line**

29. $\frac{2}{3} \cdot \frac{2}{2} = \frac{4}{6}$

    $\frac{4}{6} + \frac{1}{6} = \frac{5}{6}$

30. $\frac{8}{3}$

Early Finishers Solutions

a.
$$
\begin{array}{r}
600 \\
25\overline{)15000}
\end{array}
$$
gallons

b.
$$
\begin{array}{r}
\$2.39 \\
\times\ 600 \\
\hline
\$1434.00
\end{array}
$$

Practice Set **17**

a. **90°**

b. **50°**

c. **115°**

d. **65°**

e. **130°**

f. **23°**

g.
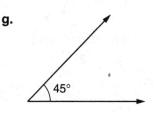

h.
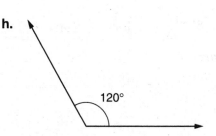

Solutions

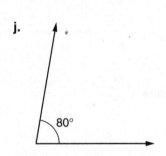

i.

100°

j.

80°

k. $\frac{1}{2}$ degree

Written Practice 17

1. $2420 + 5090 = T$

$$\overset{1}{}2420 \text{ soldiers}$$
$$+\ 5090 \text{ soldiers}$$
$$\overline{7510 \text{ soldiers}}$$

2. a. $\frac{1}{6}$

   b. $\frac{5}{6}$

3. $15S = 210$

$$15\overline{)210} \quad \textbf{14 students}$$
$$\frac{14}{15\overline{)210}}$$
$$\frac{15}{60}$$
$$\frac{60}{0}$$

$$\begin{array}{r} 15 \\ \times\ 14 \\ \hline 60 \\ 15 \\ \hline 210 \ \text{check} \end{array}$$

4. $1620 - 1492 = D$

$$\begin{array}{r} \overset{5\ 11\ 10}{1\cancel{6}\cancel{2}\cancel{0}} \\ -\ 1\ 4\ 9\ 2 \\ \hline 1\ 2\ 8 \end{array} \longrightarrow \begin{array}{r} 1492 \\ +\ \ 128 \\ \hline 1620 \quad \text{check} \end{array}$$

128 years

5. A. $\frac{4}{3} = 1\frac{1}{3}$

   B. $1\frac{2}{6} = 1\frac{2 \div 2}{6 \div 2} = 1\frac{1}{3}$

   C. $\frac{5}{3} = 1\frac{2}{3}$

   D. $1\frac{4}{12} = 1\frac{4 \div 4}{12 \div 4} = 1\frac{1}{3}$

   $\frac{5}{3}$ **is not equal to** $1\frac{1}{3}$.

6. a. $\overleftrightarrow{QR}$ (or $\overleftrightarrow{RQ}$)

   b. $\overleftrightarrow{RT}$ (or $\overleftrightarrow{TR}$)

   c. **90°**

7. a. $\frac{12 \div 4}{16 \div 4} = \frac{3}{4}$

   b. $\frac{12 \div 6}{18 \div 6} = \frac{2}{3},\ 3\frac{12}{18} = 3\frac{2}{3}$

   c. $\frac{25}{100} \div \frac{25}{25} = \frac{1}{4}$

8. $2\text{ lb} = 2\ (16\text{ oz}) = 32\text{ oz}$
   $32\text{ oz} + 8\text{ oz} = \textbf{40 oz}$

9. a. $\frac{2}{9} \cdot \frac{2}{2} = \frac{4}{18}$

   b. $\frac{1}{3} \cdot \frac{6}{6} = \frac{6}{18}$

   c. $\frac{5}{6} \cdot \frac{3}{3} = \frac{15}{18}$

10.
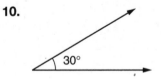

30°

11. a. Factors of 20: 1, 2, 4, 5, 10, 20
       Factors of 50: 1, 2, 5, 10, 25, 50
       1, 2, 5, 10

    b. **10**

12.

T

R $1\frac{3}{4}$ in. S

13. a. $\dfrac{8}{4} - \dfrac{4}{8} = \dfrac{8}{4} - \dfrac{4 \div 2}{8 \div 2}$

$= \dfrac{8}{4} - \dfrac{2}{4} = \dfrac{6}{4} = \mathbf{\dfrac{3}{2}}$ or $\mathbf{1\dfrac{1}{2}}$

b. $4 - \dfrac{4}{8} = \dfrac{4}{1} - \dfrac{4}{8}$

$= \dfrac{4}{1} \cdot \dfrac{8}{8} - \dfrac{4}{8} = \dfrac{32}{8} - \dfrac{4}{8}$

$= \dfrac{28}{8} = \dfrac{28 \div 4}{8 \div 4} = \mathbf{\dfrac{7}{2}}$ or $\mathbf{3\dfrac{1}{2}}$

14.
$$\begin{array}{r} 141 \\ + \ 231 \\ \hline 372 \end{array}$$
$x = \mathbf{372}$

15.
$$\begin{array}{r} \overset{1\ 14\ 10}{\$2\cancel{5}.\cancel{0}\,0} \\ - \ \$\ \ 6.3\,0 \\ \hline \$1\,8.7\,0 \end{array}$$
$y = \mathbf{\$18.70}$

16.
$$\begin{array}{r} \$3.75 \\ 8\overline{)\$30.00} \\ \underline{24} \\ 60 \\ \underline{56} \\ 40 \\ \underline{40} \\ 0 \end{array}$$
$w = \mathbf{\$3.75}$

17.
$$\begin{array}{r} 5 \\ 20\%\overline{)100\%} \\ \underline{100} \\ 0 \end{array}$$
$m = \mathbf{5}$

18. $3\dfrac{5}{6} - 1\dfrac{1}{6} = 2\dfrac{4}{6}$

$\dfrac{4 \div 2}{6 \div 2} = \dfrac{2}{3}$

$2\dfrac{4}{6} = \mathbf{2\dfrac{2}{3}}$

19. $\dfrac{1}{2} \cdot \dfrac{2}{3} = \dfrac{2}{6} = \mathbf{\dfrac{1}{3}}$

20.
$$\begin{array}{r} \$2.50 \\ 40\overline{)\$100.00} \\ \underline{80} \\ 200 \\ \underline{200} \\ 00 \\ \underline{0} \\ 0 \end{array}$$

21.
$$\begin{array}{r} 55 \\ \times \ 55 \\ \hline 275 \\ 275 \\ \hline 3025 \end{array}$$

22. $2(8 \text{ in.} + 6 \text{ in.}) = 2(14 \text{ in.})$
$\qquad\qquad\qquad\quad = \mathbf{28\ in.}$

23. $\dfrac{3}{4} \text{ in} + \dfrac{3}{4} \text{ in.} = \dfrac{6}{4} \text{ in.}$

$= \dfrac{3}{2} \text{ in.} = \mathbf{1\dfrac{1}{2}\ in.}$

24. $\dfrac{15}{16} \text{ in.} - \dfrac{3}{16} \text{ in.} = \dfrac{12 \div 4}{16 \div 4} \text{ in.}$

$= \mathbf{\dfrac{3}{4}\ in.}$

25. $\dfrac{1}{2} \cdot \dfrac{4}{3} \cdot \dfrac{9}{2} = \dfrac{4}{6} \cdot \dfrac{9}{2}$

$= \dfrac{36}{12} = \mathbf{3}$

26.
$$\begin{array}{r} \overset{1\ 10\quad 1\ 15}{\$2\cancel{0}.\cancel{2}\cancel{5}} \\ - \ \$1\,5.1\,7 \\ \hline \$\ \ 5.0\,8 \end{array}$$
\$5 bill, 1 nickel, 3 pennies

27. a. $\left(\dfrac{1}{2} \cdot \dfrac{3}{4}\right) \cdot \dfrac{2}{3} = \left(\dfrac{3}{8}\right) \cdot \dfrac{2}{3}$

$= \dfrac{6 \div 6}{24 \div 6}$

$= \dfrac{1}{4}$

$\dfrac{1}{2} \cdot \left(\dfrac{3}{4} \cdot \dfrac{2}{3}\right) = \dfrac{1}{2} \cdot \left(\dfrac{6}{12}\right)$

$= \dfrac{6}{24} = \dfrac{1}{4}, \ \dfrac{1}{4} = \dfrac{1}{4}$

$\left(\dfrac{1}{2} \cdot \dfrac{3}{4}\right) \cdot \dfrac{2}{3} = \dfrac{1}{2}\left(\dfrac{3}{4} \cdot \dfrac{2}{3}\right)$

b. Associative property of multiplication

28. Answers will vary. See student work.
Sample answer: If 85% of Shyla's answers were correct, then what percent were not correct?

29. $3\dfrac{3}{4} = \dfrac{4 \times 3 + 3}{4} = \dfrac{15}{4}$

$\text{reciprocal} = \dfrac{4}{15}$

30. $\frac{3}{4} \cdot \frac{2}{2} = \frac{6}{8}$

$\frac{6}{8} + \frac{5}{8} = \frac{11}{8} = 1\frac{3}{8}$

Practice Set 18

a. Octagon

b. Square

c. Acute angle

d. Yes

e. No

f. Check sketches for 5, 6, and 7 sides, respectively.

g. $\angle B$

h. Equal in measure; each angle is a right angle with a measure of 90°.

i.
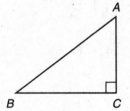

j. Answer B is not a polygon because it is not closed.

Written Practice 18

1. $6d = 2825$; about 471 miles

2. a.

Quarts	Gallons
1	$\frac{1}{4}$
2	$\frac{1}{2}$
3	$\frac{3}{4}$
4	1
5	$1\frac{1}{4}$
6	$1\frac{1}{2}$
7	$1\frac{3}{4}$
8	2

b. Multiply by $\frac{1}{4}$ (or divide by 4); One gallon equals 4 quarts, so 1 quart is $\frac{1}{4}$ gallon. Thus $5 \times \frac{1}{4} = \frac{5}{4} = 1\frac{1}{4}$.

3. $3977 + W = 5000$

$$\begin{array}{r} \overset{4\ 9\ 9\ 10}{\cancel{5}\,\cancel{0}\,\cancel{0}\,\cancel{0}} \text{ meters} \\ -\ 3\ 9\ 7\ 7 \text{ meters} \\ \hline 1\ 0\ 2\ 3 \text{ meters} \end{array}$$

4. $1,000,000,000 - 10,000,000 = D$

$$\begin{array}{r} \overset{0\ 9\ 10}{\cancel{1},\cancel{0}\,\cancel{0}\,0,0\,0\,0,0\,0\,0} \\ -\quad\ \ 10,0\,0\,0,0\,0\,0 \\ \hline 9\,9\,0,0\,0\,0,0\,0\,0 \end{array}$$

Nine hundred ninety million

5. a. $-1, 0, \frac{3}{4}, 1, \frac{5}{3}$

b. $-1, 0$

6. Side *AD* (or side *DA*)

7. a. -2

b. 4

8. a. $2\% = \frac{2}{100} = \frac{2}{100} \div \frac{2}{2} = \frac{1}{50}$

b. $\frac{12 \div 4}{20 \div 4} = \frac{3}{5}$

c. $\frac{15 \div 5}{20 \div 5} = \frac{3}{4}, \ 6\frac{15}{20} = 6\frac{3}{4}$

9. a. $\dfrac{4}{5} \cdot \dfrac{6}{6} = \dfrac{24}{30}$

   b. $\dfrac{2}{3} \cdot \dfrac{10}{10} = \dfrac{20}{30}$

   c. $\dfrac{1}{6} \cdot \dfrac{5}{5} = \dfrac{5}{30}$

10. a. A. Octagon; B. Pentagon; C. Circle

   b. C, the circle, is not a polygon because it does not have sides that are segments.

11. a.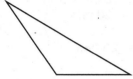

   b. Acute angles

12. a. $\dfrac{2}{8} = \dfrac{2 \div 2}{8 \div 2} = \dfrac{1}{4}$

   b. $\dfrac{6}{8} = \dfrac{6 \div 2}{8 \div 2} = \dfrac{3}{4}$

13. a. Identity property of multiplication

   b. Inverse property of multiplication

14. $\dfrac{5}{8} + \dfrac{3}{8} = \dfrac{8}{8}$

   $x = \dfrac{8}{8}$ or **1**

15. $\dfrac{7}{10} - \dfrac{3}{10} = \dfrac{4}{10}$

   $y = \dfrac{4}{10}$ or $\dfrac{2}{5}$

16. $\dfrac{5}{6} - \dfrac{1}{6} = \dfrac{4}{6}$

   $m = \dfrac{4}{6}$ or $\dfrac{2}{3}$

17. $1 \div \dfrac{3}{4} = \dfrac{4}{3}$

   $x = \dfrac{4}{3}$

18. $5\dfrac{7}{10} - \dfrac{3}{10} = 5\dfrac{4}{10} = 5\dfrac{2}{5}$

19. $\dfrac{3}{2} \cdot \dfrac{2}{4} = \dfrac{6}{8} = \dfrac{3}{4}$

20.
```
          45
   45)2025
      180
      ‾‾‾‾
      225
      225
      ‾‾‾‾
        0
```

21.
```
     750
  ×   80
  ‾‾‾‾‾‾‾
  60,000
```

22.
```
      21
  ×   21
  ‾‾‾‾‾
      21
      42
  ‾‾‾‾‾
     441
```

23.

$\dfrac{5}{8} \cdot \dfrac{4}{9} \cdot \dfrac{8}{5}$	Given
$\dfrac{5}{8} \cdot \dfrac{8}{5} \cdot \dfrac{4}{9}$	Commutative property
$\left(\dfrac{5}{8} \cdot \dfrac{8}{5}\right) \cdot \dfrac{4}{9}$	Associative property
$1 \cdot \dfrac{4}{9}$	Inverse property
$\dfrac{4}{9}$	Identity property

24. $\dfrac{8}{16} = \dfrac{1}{2} = \dfrac{50}{100} = \mathbf{50\%}$

25. a. $360° \div 4 = \mathbf{90°}$

   b. $360° \div 6 = \mathbf{60°}$

26. a.

b. $180° - 135° = \mathbf{45°}$

27. a. $\triangle SQR$

   b. $\triangle XYZ$

   c. $\angle F$

    129

Solutions

28.
$$\frac{1}{2} \cdot \frac{3}{3} = \frac{3}{6}$$
$$\frac{1}{3} \cdot \frac{2}{2} = \frac{2}{6}$$
$$\frac{3}{6} + \frac{2}{6} = \frac{5}{6}$$

29. $2\frac{1}{4} = \frac{9}{4}$

$$\frac{9}{4} \cdot \frac{4}{3} = \frac{36}{12} = 3$$

30.

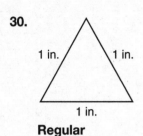

1 in.   1 in.

1 in.

Regular

Early Finishers Solutions

a. $12\frac{1}{2}$ ft needed; Sample: $10 \times 1\frac{1}{4}$ ft =
$$\frac{10}{1} \times \frac{5}{4} = \frac{50}{4} = 12\frac{1}{2}$$

b. One 6-foot board and one 8-foot board;
Sample: The 6-foot board would give:
$6 \div 1\frac{1}{4} = \frac{6}{1} \div \frac{5}{4} = \frac{6}{1} \times \frac{4}{5} = \frac{24}{5} = 4\frac{4}{5}$,
which is 4 pieces with 1 ft of board left over.

The 8-foot long board would give:
$8 \div 1\frac{1}{4} = \frac{8}{1} \div \frac{5}{4} = \frac{8}{1} \times \frac{4}{5} = \frac{32}{5} = 6\frac{2}{5}$,
which is 6 pieces with $\frac{1}{2}$ ft of board left over.
$1 + \frac{1}{2} = 1\frac{1}{2}$ ft of wood left over.

Other combinations will give these results.
Three 6-ft boards: Board 1 and Board 2,
8 pieces plus $1 \times 2 = 2$ ft left. Board 3,
2 pieces plus $6 - 2(1\frac{1}{4}) = 3\frac{1}{2}$ ft left.

$2 + 3\frac{1}{2} > 1\frac{1}{2}$

Two 8-ft boards:
Board 1, 6 pieces with $\frac{1}{2}$ ft left
Board 2, 4 pieces plus $8 - 4(1\frac{1}{4}) = 3$ ft left
$\frac{1}{2} + 3 > 1\frac{1}{2}$

---

a. Perimeter = 3 in. + 3 in. + 2 in. + 5 in.
= **13 in.**

b. Perimeter = 5(5 cm) = **25 cm**

c. Perimeter = 8(12 in.) = **96 in.**

d. Missing length = 10 in. − 4 in. = 6 in.
Missing height = 5 in. − 2 in. = 3 in.
Perimeter = 10 in. + 2 in. + 6 in.
+ 3 in. + 4 in. + 5 in.
= **30 in.**

e. 100 feet ÷ 4 = **25 feet**

f.

$\frac{3}{4}$ in.

$\frac{3}{4}$ in.

Perimeter = $4\left(\frac{3}{4}\text{ in.}\right)$
$= \frac{4}{1} \cdot \frac{3}{4}$ in. $= \frac{12}{4}$ in.
= **3 in.**

g. **P = a + b + c + d**

Written Practice 19

1. $\frac{1}{8} + N_L = \frac{8}{8}$

$$\frac{8}{8}$$
$$-\frac{1}{8}$$
$$\overline{\frac{7}{8}}$$ **not left-handed**

2. $F - 76 = 124$

$\overset{1\ 1}{124}$ people
$+\ \ 76$ people
200 people

3. $84 \times 6 = T$

$$84$$
$$\times\ \ 6$$
$$\overline{504}$$
504 legs

4.

Side Length	Perimeter
1	4
2	6
3	12
4	16
5	20

5. **a.** Eighteen million, seven hundred thousand

b. $(8 \times 100) + (7 \times 10) + (4 \times 1)$

6. $3 - 7 = -4$

7. Water freezes at 32°F. Water boils at 212°F.

8. $P = 2l + 2w$ or $P = 2(l + w)$
Perimeter = 6 cm + 6 cm + 8 cm + 8 cm
= **28 cm**

9. **a.** $3\frac{16}{24} = 3\frac{16 \div 8}{24 \div 8} = 3\frac{2}{3}$

b. $\frac{15 \div 3}{24 \div 3} = \frac{5}{8}$

c. $4\% = \frac{4}{100} = \frac{4 \div 4}{100 \div 4} = \frac{1}{25}$

10. **a.** $\frac{3}{4} \cdot \frac{9}{9} = \frac{27}{36}$

b. $\frac{4}{9} \cdot \frac{4}{4} = \frac{16}{36}$

11. Figure A is not a polygon because it is not a plane (2-dimensional) figure.

12. Octagon

13. **a.** **90°**

b. $4(90°) = $ **360°**

14. $k = \frac{1}{8} \cdot 8 = \frac{1}{8} \cdot \frac{8}{1} = \frac{8}{8} = 1$

15.
```
  8998
- 1547
------
  7451
```
$a = $ **7451**

16.
```
        $1.37
30)$41.10
     30
     ---
     111
      90
     ---
     210
     210
     ---
       0
```
$b = $ **$1.37**

17.
```
            23
$0.32)$7.36
        6 4
        ---
         96
         96
        ---
          0
```
$c = $ **23**

18.
```
      2 9 10 10
    $ 3 0. 1 0
  - $ 2 6. 5 7
  -----------
    $  3. 5 3
```
$d = $ **$3.53**

19. $\frac{2}{3} + \frac{2}{3} + \frac{2}{3} = \frac{6}{3} = $ **2**

20. $3\frac{7}{8} - \frac{5}{8} = 3\frac{2}{8} = $ **$3\frac{1}{4}$**

21. $\frac{2}{3} \cdot \frac{3}{7} = \frac{6}{21} = $ **$\frac{2}{7}$**

22. $3\frac{7}{8} + \frac{5}{8} = 3\frac{12}{8} = 4\frac{4}{8} = $ **$4\frac{1}{2}$**

23.
```
     50
×    50
-------
   2500
```

24.
```
      9,100
11)100,100
    99
    --
     1 1
     1 1
     ---
       00
        0
       --
       00
        0
       --
        0
```

25. **a.** **2**

b. $2 \cdot 5 = $ **10**

Solutions

26.

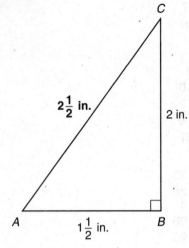

27. $3\frac{1}{3} = \frac{10}{3}$

$\frac{10}{3} \cdot \frac{3}{2} = \frac{30}{6} = \mathbf{5}$

28. $\frac{1}{2} \cdot \frac{5}{5} = \frac{5}{10}$

$\frac{9}{10} - \frac{5}{10} = \frac{4}{10} = \mathbf{\frac{2}{5}}$

29. $100\% \div 3 = \mathbf{33\frac{1}{3}\%}$

30. Missing length = 10 in. − 6 in. = 4 in.
Missing height = 7 in. − 4 in. = 3 in.
  Perimeter = 10 in. + 4 in. + 6 in.
  + 3 in. + 4 in. + 7 in.
  = **34 in.**

Early Finishers Solutions

a. No, Magali will need 2 packets; Sample: there are 4 quarts in a gallon. So the cooler holds $5 \times 4 = 20$ quarts. Since one packet makes 10 quarts, 2 packets are needed.

b. $\$12 \div 8 = \$1.50$; $\$1.50 \times 2 = \$3.00$

a. Four cubed
  $4 \cdot 4 \cdot 4 = \mathbf{64}$

b. One half squared
  $\frac{1}{2} \cdot \frac{1}{2} = \mathbf{\frac{1}{4}}$

c. Ten to the sixth power
  $10 \cdot 10 \cdot 10 \cdot 10 \cdot 10 \cdot 10 = \mathbf{1,000,000}$

d. Base is 10; exponent is 3

e. $2^3 \cdot 2^2 = 2 \cdot 2 \cdot 2 \cdot 2 \cdot 2$
  $= 2^5$

f. $\frac{2^6}{2^2} = \frac{2 \cdot 2 \cdot 2 \cdot 2 \cdot 2 \cdot 2}{2 \cdot 2}$
  $= \frac{64}{4} = 16 = 2 \cdot 2 \cdot 2 \cdot 2 = 2^4$

g. 10

h. 20

i. 15

j. Area = 15 m × 10 m
  = **150 m²**

k. Area = 2 in. × 5 in.
  = **10 in.²**

l. Area = 4 cm × 4 cm
  = **16 cm²**

m. 20 cm ÷ 4 = 5 cm
  Area = 5 cm × 5 cm = **25 cm²**

n. Area = 100 yards × 100 yards
  = **10,000 square yards**

o. $4^2 = 16$
  $\sqrt{16} = 4$

Written Practice 20

1. $4D = 628$

$$4\overline{)628}$$

157 students

$$\begin{array}{r} 157 \\ 4\overline{)628} \\ \underline{4} \\ 22 \\ \underline{20} \\ 28 \\ \underline{28} \\ 0 \end{array}$$

2. $P - 36 = 39$

$$\begin{array}{r} 39 \text{ counties} \\ + \ 36 \text{ counties} \\ \hline 75 \text{ counties} \end{array}$$

3.

Side Length (units)	Area (units²)
1	1
2	4
3	9
4	16
5	25

4. **C.** $A = s^2$

5. $k = 2^6 = 2 \cdot 2 \cdot 2 \cdot 2 \cdot 2 \cdot 2$
  $= \mathbf{64}$

6. **a.** $-2, -\frac{1}{2}, 0, \frac{1}{3}, 1$ **b.** See Student work.

  c. $\frac{1}{3}, -\frac{1}{2}$

7. **B.** $33\frac{1}{3}\%$

8. **Side *DC* (or side *CD*) and side *AB* (or side *BA*)**

9. **a.** $\left(\frac{1}{3}\right)^3 = \frac{1}{3} \cdot \frac{1}{3} \cdot \frac{1}{3} = \frac{1}{27}$

  b. $10^4 = 10 \cdot 10 \cdot 10 \cdot 10$
    $= \mathbf{10{,}000}$

  c. $\sqrt{12^2} = \sqrt{144} = \mathbf{12}$

10. **a.** $\frac{2}{9} \cdot \frac{4}{4} = \frac{8}{36}$

  b. $\frac{3}{4} \cdot \frac{9}{9} = \frac{27}{36}$

  c. Answers will vary but should include adding, subtracting, or comparing fractions.

11. **a. 1, 2, 5, 10**

  b. 1, 7

  c. 1

12. 2 feet $=$ 24 inches
  24 inches $\div$ 4 $=$ **6 inches**

13. $6^2 = 36$
  $\sqrt{36} = 6$

14. $P(\text{even}) = \frac{3}{6} = \frac{1}{2}$

15. $\begin{array}{r} 12 \\ 5\overline{)60} \\ \underline{5} \\ 10 \\ \underline{10} \\ 0 \end{array}$
  $x = \mathbf{12}$

16. $\begin{array}{r} {\scriptstyle 0\ 9\ 10} \\ \cancel{1}\cancel{0}\cancel{0} \\ -\ \ 6\ 4 \\ \hline 3\ 6 \end{array}$
  $m = \mathbf{36}$

17. $5^4 \cdot 5^2 = 5 \cdot 5 \cdot 5 \cdot 5 \cdot 5 \cdot 5 = 5^6$
  $n = \mathbf{6}$

18. $\begin{array}{r} 15 \\ 4\overline{)60} \\ \underline{4} \\ 20 \\ \underline{20} \\ 0 \end{array}$
  $y = \mathbf{15}$

19. $1\frac{8}{9} + 1\frac{7}{9} = 2\frac{15}{9} = 3\frac{6}{9} = 3\frac{2}{3}$

20. $\frac{5}{2} \cdot \frac{5}{6} = \frac{25}{12} = 2\frac{1}{12}$

21. $\begin{array}{r} 705 \\ 9\overline{)6345} \\ \underline{63} \\ 04 \\ \underline{0} \\ 45 \\ \underline{45} \\ 0 \end{array}$

Solutions

22.
$$\begin{array}{r} 360 \\ \times\ 25 \\ \hline 1800 \\ 720 \\ \hline 9000 \end{array}$$

23. $\dfrac{3}{4} - \left(\dfrac{1}{4} + \dfrac{2}{4}\right) = \dfrac{3}{4} - \left(\dfrac{3}{4}\right) = \mathbf{0}$

24. $\left(\dfrac{3}{4} - \dfrac{1}{4}\right) + \dfrac{2}{4} = \dfrac{2}{4} + \dfrac{2}{4}$

$\qquad\qquad = \dfrac{4}{4} = \mathbf{1}$

25. a. $\dfrac{3}{10} + \dfrac{3}{10} = \dfrac{6}{10} = \dfrac{\mathbf{3}}{\mathbf{5}}$

b. $\dfrac{3}{10} \cdot \dfrac{3}{10} = \dfrac{\mathbf{9}}{\mathbf{100}}$

26. $\dfrac{1}{2} \cdot \dfrac{5}{5} = \dfrac{5}{10}$

$\dfrac{5}{10} + \dfrac{3}{10} = \dfrac{8}{10} = \dfrac{\mathbf{4}}{\mathbf{5}}$

27. $1\dfrac{4}{5} = \dfrac{9}{5}$

$\dfrac{9}{5} \cdot \dfrac{1}{3} = \dfrac{9}{15} = \dfrac{\mathbf{3}}{\mathbf{5}}$

28. a. Inverse property of multiplication

b. Identity property of multiplication

29. a. Perimeter = 12 in. + 12 in. + 12 in.
+ 12 in. = **48 in. or 4 ft**

b. Area = 12 in. × 12 in. = **144 in.² or 1 ft²**

30. Missing length = 10 in. − 5 in. = 5 in.
Missing height = 8 in. − 4 in. = 4 in.
Perimeter = 10 in. + 4 in. + 5 in.
+ 4 in.+ 5 in. + 8 in.
= **36 in.**

Early Finishers Solutions

a. 2(12 + 12 + 10 + 12 + 24 + 10
+ 6 + 8 + 15 + 10 + 12 + 11)
2(24 + 22 + 34 + 14 + 25 + 23)
2(142) = 284 ft

b. 36 sections; $8\overline{)284.0}^{\,35.5} \approx 36$

Investigation 2

Using a Compass and Straightedge, Part 1

1. {Students draw concentric circles as shown in the textbook.}

2. {Students use tools to inscribe a regular hexagon in a circle as shown in the textbook.}

3. {Students use tools to inscribe regular triangle in a circle as shown in the textbook.}

4. **120°**

5. **180°**

6. Acceptable answers: Either a **hexagon** OR a **triangle.**

7. {Students use tools to draw a circle, and then to divide it into thirds as shown in the textbook.}

8. {Students manually measure central angles.}

9. $33\frac{1}{3}\%$

10. **60°**

11. $16\frac{2}{3}\%$

12. **Circumference**

13. **Diameter**

14. Acceptable answers: **Radius** OR **area**

15. **Arc**

16. **Sector**

17. **Concentric circles**

18. **Chord**

19. **Inscribed**

20. **Semicircle**

21. **Central angle**

22. **Radius**

23. **Center**

24. **Inscribed**

---

a. 2, 3, 5, 7, 11, 13, 17, 19, 23, 29

b. Composite number

c.

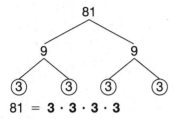

$81 = 3 \cdot 3 \cdot 3 \cdot 3$

d. $360 = 2 \cdot 2 \cdot 2 \cdot 3 \cdot 3 \cdot 5$

$$
\begin{array}{r}
1 \\
5\overline{)5} \\
3\overline{)15} \\
3\overline{)45} \\
2\overline{)90} \\
2\overline{)180} \\
2\overline{)360}
\end{array}
$$

e.

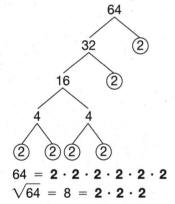

$64 = 2 \cdot 2 \cdot 2 \cdot 2 \cdot 2 \cdot 2$
$\sqrt{64} = 8 = 2 \cdot 2 \cdot 2$

f.

18   81 $18 = 2 \cdot 3 \cdot 3$
9 2   9   9 $81 = 3 \cdot 3 \cdot 3 \cdot 3$
3 3   3 3 3 3   **The greatest common factor is $3 \cdot 3 = 9$.**

1. $\dfrac{2}{3} + N_G = \dfrac{3}{3}$

$\dfrac{3}{3} - \dfrac{2}{3} = \dfrac{1}{3}$

2. **7Q = 343**

$$
\begin{array}{r}
49 \\
7\overline{)343} \\
28 \\
\overline{63} \\
63 \\
\overline{0}
\end{array}
$$
49 quills

3. **A.** $P = 2l + 2w$

4. $5^2 = 25$
$\sqrt{25} = 5$

5. a. $3\dfrac{12 \div 3}{21 \div 3} = 3\dfrac{4}{7}$

b. $\dfrac{12 \div 12}{48 \div 12} = \dfrac{1}{4}$

c. $12\% = \dfrac{12}{100} \div \dfrac{4}{4} = \dfrac{3}{25}$

6. 53, 59

7. a. $50 = 2 \cdot 5 \cdot 5$

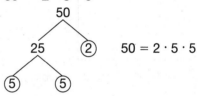

$50 = 2 \cdot 5 \cdot 5$

b. $60 = 2 \cdot 2 \cdot 3 \cdot 5$

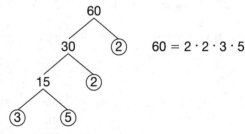

$60 = 2 \cdot 2 \cdot 3 \cdot 5$

c. $300 = 2 \cdot 2 \cdot 3 \cdot 5 \cdot 5$

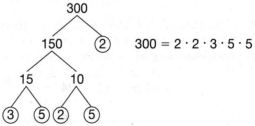

$300 = 2 \cdot 2 \cdot 3 \cdot 5 \cdot 5$

Solutions

8. Point *C*; The tick mark between points *B* and *C* is halfway between 1000 and 2000, which is 1500, so points *A* and *B* are eliminated. Point *C* is closer to 1500 than 2000, so *C* is the best choice. Point *D* is too close to 2000 to represent 1610.

9. a. $\frac{2}{3} \cdot \frac{5}{5} = \frac{10}{15}$

   b. $\frac{3}{5} \cdot \frac{3}{3} = \frac{9}{15}$

   c. $\frac{8 \div 4}{12 \div 4} = \frac{2}{3}$

   d. Identity property of multiplication

10. a. **3**

   b. $3 \cdot 3 = \textbf{9}$

11. 12 inches $\div$ 4 = 3 inches
Area = 3 inches $\times$ 3 inches
      = **9 square inches**

12.

(rectangle: $\frac{3}{4}$ in. on the right side, $1\frac{1}{2}$ in. on the bottom)

   a. $2 \times \frac{3}{4}$ in. $= \frac{6}{4}$ in. $= \textbf{1}\frac{\textbf{1}}{\textbf{2}}$ **in.**

   b. Perimeter $= \frac{3}{4}$ in. $+ \frac{3}{4}$ in. $+ 1\frac{1}{2}$ in.
         $+ 1\frac{1}{2}$ in. $= \frac{6}{4}$ in. $+ 2\frac{2}{2}$ in.
         $= \frac{6}{4}$ in. $+ \frac{6}{2}$ in. $= \frac{6}{4}$ in.
         $+ \frac{12}{4}$ in. $= \frac{18}{4}$ in. $= \textbf{4}\frac{\textbf{1}}{\textbf{2}}$ **in.**

13. Missing length = 3 in. + 12 in. = 15 in.
Missing height = 8 in. $-$ 5 in. = 3 in.
Perimeter = 8 in. + 15 in. + 5 in.
        + 12 in. + 3 in. + 3 in.
        = **46 in.**

14. P(odd number > 5) $= \frac{0}{6} = \textbf{0}$

15. $1 - \frac{3}{5} = \frac{5}{5} - \frac{3}{5} = \frac{2}{5}$
   $p = \frac{\textbf{2}}{\textbf{5}}$

16. $1 \cdot \frac{5}{3}$
   $q = \frac{\textbf{5}}{\textbf{3}}$

17. $\begin{array}{r} 25 \\ \times\ 50 \\ \hline 1250 \end{array}$
   $w = \textbf{1250}$

18. $\frac{5}{6} - \frac{1}{6} = \frac{4}{6}$
   $f = \frac{\textbf{4}}{\textbf{6}}$ or $\frac{\textbf{2}}{\textbf{3}}$

19. $1\frac{2}{3} + 3\frac{2}{3} = 4\frac{4}{3} = 5\frac{1}{3}$
   $m = \textbf{5}\frac{\textbf{1}}{\textbf{3}}$

20. $\begin{array}{r} 17 \\ 3\overline{)51} \\ \underline{3} \\ 21 \\ \underline{21} \\ 0 \end{array}$
   $c = \textbf{17}$

21. $\frac{2}{3} + \frac{2}{3} + \frac{2}{3} = \frac{6}{3} = \textbf{2}$

22. $\left(\frac{2}{3}\right)^3 = \frac{2}{3} \cdot \frac{2}{3} \cdot \frac{2}{3} = \frac{\textbf{8}}{\textbf{27}}$

23. a. $225 = \textbf{3} \cdot \textbf{3} \cdot \textbf{5} \cdot \textbf{5}$

   b. $\sqrt{225} = 15$
       $15 = \textbf{3} \cdot \textbf{5}$

24. If we divide the numerator and the denominator of a fraction by their GCF, we reduce the fraction to lowest terms in one step.

25.

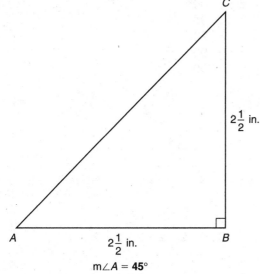

$2\frac{1}{2}$ in.

$2\frac{1}{2}$ in.

$m\angle A = 45°$

26. $1\frac{3}{4} = \frac{7}{4}$

$\frac{7}{4} \times \frac{3}{2} = \frac{21}{8} = 2\frac{5}{8}$

27. a. $\overline{CB}$ (or $\overline{BC}$)

b. $\overline{AB}$ (or $\overline{BA}$)

c. $\overline{MC}$ and $\overline{MB}$

d. $\angle ABC$ (or $\angle CBA$)

28. $\frac{1 \text{ quart}}{4 \text{ quarts}} = \frac{1}{4}, \frac{1}{4} \cdot \frac{25}{25} = \frac{25}{100} = \mathbf{25\%}$

29. a. $a + b = b + a$

b. Commutative property of addition

30. a. $\triangle KLJ$

b. $\triangle DEF$

c. $\angle S$

Practice Set **22**

a.–b.

$\frac{1}{4}$ were not red.

$\frac{3}{4}$ were red.

60 marbles
| 15 marbles |
| 15 marbles |
| 15 marbles |
| 15 marbles |

a. 3×15 marbles = **45 marbles**

b. 15 marbles

c.–d.

$\frac{3}{5}$ were green.

$\frac{2}{5}$ were not green.

20 tomatoes
| 4 tomatoes |
| 4 tomatoes |
| 4 tomatoes |
| 4 tomatoes |
| 4 tomatoes |

c. $100\% - 60\% = 40\%$

$40\% = \frac{40}{100} \div \frac{20}{20} = \frac{2}{5}$

d. 3×4 tomatoes = **12 tomatoes**

e. See student work.

Written Practice **22**

1. $28 + 30 + 23 = T$

$\begin{array}{r} 1 \\ 28 \text{ students} \\ 30 \text{ students} \\ + 23 \text{ students} \\ \hline \mathbf{81 \text{ students}} \end{array}$

2. $3R = 81$

$\begin{array}{r} 27 \\ 3\overline{)81} \\ 6 \\ \hline 21 \\ 21 \\ \hline 0 \end{array}$ **27 students**

3. $663,000 - 1500 = A$; **about 661,500 square miles more.**

4. a. $P = 4s$

b. 96 feet

5.

$\frac{5}{9}$ were happy.

$\frac{4}{9}$ were not happy.

36 spectators
| 4 spectators |
| 4 spectators |
| 4 spectators |
| 4 spectators |
| 4 spectators |
| 4 spectators |
| 4 spectators |
| 4 spectators |
| 4 spectators |

Saxon Math Course 2

a. 5×4 spectators = **20 spectators**

b. 4×4 spectators = **16 spectators**

6.

36 eggs	
$\frac{3}{4}$ were not cracked.	9 eggs
	9 eggs
	9 eggs
$\frac{1}{4}$ were cracked.	9 eggs

$25\% = \dfrac{25}{100} \div \dfrac{25}{25}$

$= \dfrac{1}{4}$

a. $\dfrac{4}{4} - \dfrac{1}{4} = \dfrac{3}{4}$

b. 3×9 eggs = **27 plants**

7. a. $\dfrac{4 \div 2}{10 \div 2} = \dfrac{2}{5}$

b. $\dfrac{6}{10} = \dfrac{6}{10} \times \dfrac{10}{10} = \dfrac{60}{100} =$ **60%**

8. a. 4

b. $4 \times 3 =$ **12**

9. a. 0

b. Property of zero for multiplication

10. $\dfrac{3}{3} - \left(\dfrac{1}{3} \cdot \dfrac{3}{1}\right) = \dfrac{3}{3} - \left(\dfrac{3}{3}\right) = 0$

$\left(\dfrac{3}{3} - \dfrac{1}{3}\right) \cdot \dfrac{3}{1} = \left(\dfrac{2}{3}\right) \cdot \dfrac{3}{1} = \dfrac{6}{3} = 2$

0 < 2

11.

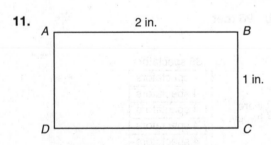

a. Perimeter = 2 in. + 2 in.
+ 1 in. + 1 in. = **6 in.**

b. Area = 2 in. × 1 in. = **2 in.²**

c.
$$\begin{array}{r} 90° \\ 90° \\ 90° \\ + \ 90° \\ \hline \mathbf{360°} \end{array}$$

12. a.

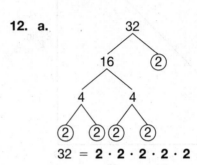

$32 = \mathbf{2 \cdot 2 \cdot 2 \cdot 2 \cdot 2}$

b.

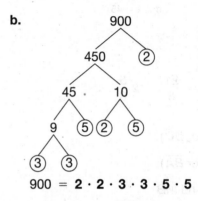

$900 = \mathbf{2 \cdot 2 \cdot 3 \cdot 3 \cdot 5 \cdot 5}$

c. $\sqrt{900} = 30$

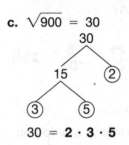

$30 = \mathbf{2 \cdot 3 \cdot 5}$

13. a. $\dfrac{5}{6} \cdot \dfrac{10}{10} = \dfrac{\mathbf{50}}{\mathbf{60}}$

b. $\dfrac{3}{5} \cdot \dfrac{12}{12} = \dfrac{\mathbf{36}}{\mathbf{60}}$

c. $\dfrac{7}{12} \cdot \dfrac{5}{5} = \dfrac{\mathbf{35}}{\mathbf{60}}$

14. $\dfrac{50}{60} + \dfrac{36}{60} + \dfrac{35}{60} = \dfrac{121}{60} = 2\dfrac{1}{60}$

15. a. $-2, \ -\dfrac{2}{3}, \ 0, \ 1, \ \dfrac{3}{2}$

b. $1, \ \dfrac{3}{2}$

138

16. 52 cards in a deck; 13 cards are hearts

$$\frac{13 \div 13}{52 \div 13} = \frac{1}{4}$$

17. $\frac{11}{12} - \frac{5}{12} = \frac{6}{12}$

$a = \frac{6}{12}$ or $\frac{1}{2}$

18. $11\overline{)121}$
$\quad \frac{11}{\ \ 11}$
$\quad \ \ \frac{11}{\ \ \ 0}$

$x = 11$

19. $2\frac{2}{3} + 1\frac{1}{3} = 3\frac{3}{3} = 4$

$y = 4$

20. $10^2 \cdot 10^5 =$
$10 \cdot 10 \cdot 10 \cdot 10 \cdot 10 \cdot 10 \cdot 10$
$\qquad\qquad = 10^7$

$n = 7$

21. $\frac{5}{6} + \frac{5}{6} + \frac{5}{6} = \frac{15}{6} = 2\frac{3}{6} = 2\frac{1}{2}$

22. $\frac{15}{2} \cdot \frac{10}{3} = \frac{150}{6} = 25$

23. $\left(\frac{5}{6}\right)^2 = \frac{5}{6} \cdot \frac{5}{6} = \frac{25}{36}$

24. $\sqrt{30^2} = \sqrt{900} = 30$

25. $\frac{3}{1} \times \frac{2}{3} \times \frac{1}{3}$ **Given**

$\frac{3}{1} \times \frac{1}{3} \times \frac{2}{3}$ **Commutative property**

$\left(\frac{3}{1} \times \frac{1}{3}\right) \times \frac{2}{3}$ **Associative property**

$1 \times \frac{2}{3}$ **Inverse property**

$\frac{2}{3}$ **Identity property**

26. $1\frac{1}{2} = \frac{3}{2}, 1\frac{2}{3} = \frac{5}{3}$

$\frac{3}{2} \times \frac{5}{3} = \frac{15}{6} = 2\frac{3}{6} = 2\frac{1}{2}$

27. 1 lb = 16 oz

16 oz + 5 oz = **21 oz**

28.

29. $\frac{1}{10} \times \frac{1}{10} = \frac{1}{100}$

30. -1

Early Finishers Solutions

a. Perimeter = $2(360 + 160)$
$\qquad\qquad = 2(520)$
$\qquad\qquad = 1040$ ft
$\quad$ Area = 360×160
$\qquad\qquad = 57600$ ft^2

b. 6 quarts; $200\overline{)1040.0}$ (quotient 5.2); So 6 quarts must be purchased

c. $\frac{26 \text{ sec}}{800 \text{ ft}^2} = \frac{t}{57600 \text{ ft}^2}$

$\quad t = \frac{(25 \text{ sec})(57600 \text{ ft}^2)}{800 \text{ ft}^2}$

$\quad t = (25 \text{ sec}) \times 72 = 1800 \text{ sec}$

$\frac{\overset{30}{\cancel{1800} \text{ sec}}}{1} \times \frac{1 \text{ min}}{\cancel{60 \text{ sec}}} = 30 \text{ min}$

Practice Set 23

a.
$$7 \longrightarrow 6\frac{3}{3}$$
$$\underline{-\ 2\frac{1}{3}} \qquad \underline{-\ 2\frac{1}{3}}$$
$$\qquad\qquad 4\frac{2}{3}$$

b.
$$6\frac{2}{5} \xrightarrow{\ 5 + \frac{5}{5} + \frac{2}{5}\ } 5\frac{7}{5}$$
$$\underline{-\ 1\frac{4}{5}} \qquad\qquad \underline{-\ 1\frac{4}{5}}$$
$$\qquad\qquad\qquad\qquad 4\frac{3}{5}$$

Solutions

c. $5\frac{1}{6}$ $\xrightarrow{4\,+\,\frac{6}{6}\,+\,\frac{1}{6}}$ $4\frac{7}{6}$
$-\,1\frac{5}{6}$ $\qquad\qquad$ $-\,1\frac{5}{6}$
$\qquad\qquad\qquad\qquad\qquad$ $3\frac{2}{6}$

$3\frac{2}{6} = \mathbf{3\frac{1}{3}}$

d. 100% $\longrightarrow$ $99\frac{2}{2}\%$
$-\quad 12\frac{1}{2}\%$ $\qquad\quad$ $-\;12\frac{1}{2}\%$
$\qquad\qquad\qquad\qquad\qquad$ $\mathbf{87\frac{1}{2}\%}$

e. $83\frac{1}{3}\%$ $\xrightarrow{\left(82\,+\,\frac{3}{3}\,+\,\frac{1}{3}\right)\%}$
$-\;16\frac{2}{3}\%$ $\qquad\qquad$ $82\frac{4}{3}\%$
$\qquad\qquad\qquad\qquad\qquad$ $-\;16\frac{2}{3}\%$
$\qquad\qquad\qquad\qquad\qquad$ $\mathbf{66\frac{2}{3}\%}$

Written Practice 23

1. $18 \times 36 = E$

$\quad\;18$
$\underline{\times\;36}$ $\qquad$ **648 exposures**
$\;108$
$\;\underline{54}$
$\;648$

2.

Yards²	Feet²
1	9
2	18
3	27
4	36
5	45

3. a. $A = lw$

   b. **4700 square feet**

4. $16P = \$14.24$

$\qquad\;\;\$\,0.89$
$16\overline{)\$14.24}$ $\qquad$ **89¢ per pound**
$\quad\;\underline{12\;8}$
$\qquad 1\;44$
$\qquad \underline{1\;44}$
$\qquad\qquad 0$

5.

$\frac{3}{8}$ were closed.
$\frac{5}{8}$ were open.

56 restaurants
- 7 restaurants
- 7 restaurants
- 7 restaurants
- 7 restaurants
- 7 restaurants
- 7 restaurants
- 7 restaurants
- 7 restaurants

   a. 3×7 restaurants = **21 restaurants**

   b. 5×7 restaurants = **35 restaurants**

6. $40\% = \dfrac{40}{100} \div \dfrac{20}{20} = \dfrac{\mathbf{2}}{\mathbf{5}}$

$\frac{3}{5}$ were girls.
$\frac{2}{5}$ were boys.

30 students
- 6 students
- 6 students
- 6 students
- 6 students
- 6 students

   a. 2×6 students = 12 students; **12 boys**.

   b. $\dfrac{5}{5} - \dfrac{2}{5} = \dfrac{3}{5}$
   3×6 students = 18 students; **18 girls**

7. 1 yard = 36 inches

$\qquad\quad 115$ $\qquad$ **115 yards**
$36\overline{)4140}$
$\quad\;\underline{36}$
$\quad\;\;54$
$\quad\;\;\underline{36}$
$\qquad 180$
$\qquad \underline{180}$
$\qquad\quad 0$

8. a. **5**

   b. $5 \times 3 = \mathbf{15}$

   c. Multiply $5 \times 3 = \mathbf{15}$

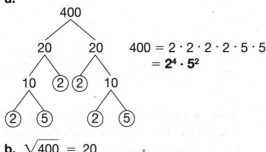

9. Express the mixed number as an improper fraction. Then switch the numerator and the denominator of the improper fraction.

10. **a.** $\dfrac{2}{3} \cdot \dfrac{3}{2} = \dfrac{6}{6} = 1; \dfrac{5}{5} = 1$

$\dfrac{2}{3} \cdot \dfrac{3}{2} = \dfrac{5}{5}$

b. $\dfrac{12 \div 12}{36 \div 12} = \dfrac{1}{3}$

$\dfrac{12 \div 12}{24 \div 12} = \dfrac{1}{2}$

$\dfrac{1}{3} < \dfrac{1}{2}$

$\dfrac{12}{36} < \dfrac{12}{24}$

11. $2\dfrac{1}{4} = \dfrac{9}{4}, 3\dfrac{1}{3} = \dfrac{10}{3}$

$\dfrac{9}{4} \times \dfrac{10}{3} = \dfrac{90}{12} = \dfrac{15}{2} = \mathbf{7\dfrac{1}{2}}$

12. **a.** $\dfrac{3}{4} \cdot \dfrac{10}{10} = \dfrac{\mathbf{30}}{\mathbf{40}}$

b. $\dfrac{2}{5} \cdot \dfrac{8}{8} = \dfrac{\mathbf{16}}{40}$

c. $\dfrac{15 \div 5}{40 \div 5} = \dfrac{\mathbf{3}}{\mathbf{8}}$

13. **a.**

```
          400
         /   \
       20     20      400 = 2 · 2 · 2 · 2 · 5 · 5
      /  \   /  \          = 2⁴ · 5²
    10  (2)(2) 10
   / \        / \
 (2)(5)     (2) (5)
```

b. $\sqrt{400} = 20$

```
       20
      /  \
    10   (2)     20 = 2 · 2 · 5
   / \              = 2² · 5
 (5) (2)
```

14. **a.** Acute angle

b. Right angle

c. Obtuse angle

d. $\overrightarrow{DC}$

15. $\dfrac{3}{4} \cdot \dfrac{3}{3} = \dfrac{9}{12}$

$\dfrac{2}{3} \cdot \dfrac{4}{4} = \dfrac{8}{12}$

$\dfrac{9}{12} - \dfrac{8}{12} = \dfrac{\mathbf{1}}{\mathbf{12}}$

16.
```
      15
   7)105
      7
     ___
      35
      35
     ___
       0
```
$w = \mathbf{15}$

17. $2x = 100, 100 \div 2 = 50$

$x = \mathbf{50}$

18. $6\dfrac{3}{4} - 1\dfrac{1}{4} = 5\dfrac{2}{4}$

$x = \mathbf{5\dfrac{2}{4}}$ or $\mathbf{5\dfrac{1}{2}}$

19. $1\dfrac{5}{8} + 4\dfrac{1}{8} = 5\dfrac{6}{8}$

$x = \mathbf{5\dfrac{6}{8}}$ or $\mathbf{5\dfrac{3}{4}}$

20.
$$5 \longrightarrow 4\dfrac{3}{3}$$
$$-3\dfrac{1}{3} \qquad -3\dfrac{1}{3}$$
$$\qquad\qquad \mathbf{1\dfrac{2}{3}} \text{ yards}$$

21.
$$83\dfrac{1}{3}\% \xrightarrow{\left(82 + \dfrac{3}{3} + \dfrac{1}{3}\right)\%} $$
$$-66\dfrac{2}{3}\% \qquad\qquad 82\dfrac{4}{3}\%$$
$$\qquad\qquad\qquad -66\dfrac{2}{3}\%$$
$$\qquad\qquad\qquad \mathbf{16\dfrac{2}{3}\%}$$

22. $\dfrac{7}{12} + \left(\dfrac{1}{4} \cdot \dfrac{1}{3}\right) = \dfrac{7}{12} + \left(\dfrac{1}{12}\right)$

$= \dfrac{8}{12} = \dfrac{\mathbf{2}}{\mathbf{3}}$

23. $\dfrac{7}{8} - \left(\dfrac{3}{4} \cdot \dfrac{1}{2}\right) = \dfrac{7}{8} - \left(\dfrac{3}{8}\right) = \dfrac{4}{8} = \dfrac{\mathbf{1}}{\mathbf{2}}$

24.

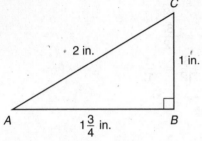

$\overline{AC}$ is about 2 inches long.

Perimeter = 2 in. + 1 in. + $1\frac{3}{4}$ in.

$= 4\frac{3}{4}$ in.

The perimeter is about $4\frac{3}{4}$ inches.

25. About 30°

26. Perimeter = 14 ft + 14 ft + 12 ft + 12 ft
$= \textbf{52 ft}$

27. $\frac{3}{4} \times \frac{1}{3} = \frac{3}{12} = \frac{1}{4}$

28. Check polygon for eight sides; one possibility:

29. a. $4^3, 5^3$

b. $4^3 = 4 \cdot 4 \cdot 4 = 64$
$5^3 = 5 \cdot 5 \cdot 5 = 125$
64, 125

30. a. $\overline{AB}$ (or $\overline{BA}$)

b. $\angle CMB$ (or $\angle BMC$)

c. $\angle ACB$ (or $\angle BCA$)

Early Finishers Solutions

a. $\frac{3}{5} \cdot 30 = 18$

b. $\frac{\overset{1}{\cancel{2}}}{\cancel{5}} \cdot \frac{1}{\cancel{2}} \cdot \overset{6}{\cancel{30}} = 6$

c. $\frac{1}{\cancel{2}} \cdot \frac{\overset{1}{\cancel{2}}}{5} = \frac{1}{5}$

Practice Set 24

a. $\frac{48}{144} = \frac{\overset{1}{\cancel{2}} \cdot \overset{1}{\cancel{2}} \cdot \overset{1}{\cancel{2}} \cdot \overset{1}{\cancel{2}} \cdot \overset{1}{\cancel{3}}}{\underset{1}{\cancel{2}} \cdot \underset{1}{\cancel{2}} \cdot \underset{1}{\cancel{2}} \cdot \underset{1}{\cancel{2}} \cdot \underset{1}{\cancel{3}} \cdot 3} = \frac{1}{3}$

b. $\frac{90}{324} = \frac{\overset{1}{\cancel{2}} \cdot \overset{1}{\cancel{3}} \cdot \overset{1}{\cancel{3}} \cdot 5}{\underset{1}{\cancel{2}} \cdot 2 \cdot \underset{1}{\cancel{3}} \cdot \underset{1}{\cancel{3}} \cdot 3 \cdot 3} = \frac{5}{18}$

c. $90 = 2 \cdot 3 \cdot 3 \cdot 5$
$324 = 2 \cdot 2 \cdot 3 \cdot 3 \cdot 3 \cdot 3$
$GCF = 2 \cdot 3 \cdot 3 = \textbf{18}$

d. $\frac{\overset{1}{\cancel{5}}}{8} \cdot \frac{3}{\underset{2}{\cancel{10}}} = \frac{3}{16}$

e. $\frac{\overset{1}{\cancel{\overset{2}{\cancel{8}}}}}{\underset{\underset{1}{\cancel{3}}}{\cancel{15}}} \cdot \frac{\overset{1}{\cancel{5}}}{\underset{\underset{1}{\cancel{3}}}{\cancel{12}}} \cdot \frac{\overset{\overset{1}{\cancel{3}}}{\cancel{9}}}{\underset{5}{\cancel{10}}} = \frac{1}{5}$

f. $\frac{\overset{1}{\cancel{8}}}{\underset{1}{\cancel{3}}} \cdot \frac{\overset{\overset{1}{\cancel{2}}}{\cancel{6}}}{7} \cdot \frac{5}{\underset{\underset{1}{\cancel{2}}}{\cancel{16}}} = \frac{5}{7}$

g. $\frac{\overset{1}{\cancel{2}} \cdot \overset{1}{\cancel{2}} \cdot \overset{1}{\cancel{3}} \cdot \overset{1}{\cancel{3}}}{\underset{1}{\cancel{3}} \cdot \underset{1}{\cancel{3}} \cdot \underset{1}{\cancel{5}}} \cdot \frac{\overset{1}{\cancel{5}} \cdot 5}{\underset{1}{\cancel{2}} \cdot \underset{1}{\cancel{2}} \cdot 2 \cdot 3} = \frac{5}{6}$

h. $\frac{324}{900} = \frac{\overset{1}{\cancel{2}} \cdot \overset{1}{\cancel{2}} \cdot \overset{1}{\cancel{3}} \cdot \overset{1}{\cancel{3}} \cdot 3 \cdot 3}{\underset{1}{\cancel{2}} \cdot \underset{1}{\cancel{2}} \cdot \underset{1}{\cancel{3}} \cdot \underset{1}{\cancel{3}} \cdot 5 \cdot 5} = \frac{9}{25}$

i. Sample answer: Write any fraction and its reciprocal. Pair the numerator of each fraction with the denominator of the other fraction. They will always reduce to 1.

Written Practice 24

1. $3026 - 2895 = D$

$\overset{2\ \ 9\ 12}{\cancel{3}\cancel{0}\cancel{2}6}$ miles
$-\ \ 2\ 8\ 9\ 5$ miles
$\overline{\hphantom{00}\textbf{1 3 1 miles}}$

---

2. $15 \times 24 = M$

$$
\begin{array}{r}
15 \\
\times\ 24 \\
\hline
60 \\
30 \\
\hline
360
\end{array}
$$

360 microprocessors

3. $75\% = \dfrac{75}{100} \div \dfrac{25}{25} = \dfrac{3}{4}$

	$30.00
$\frac{1}{4}$ not spent	$ 7.50
	$ 7.50
$\frac{3}{4}$ spent	$ 7.50
	$ 7.50

a. $\dfrac{3}{4}$

b.
$$
\begin{array}{r}
\$7.50 \\
\times\ \ \ 3 \\
\hline
\$22.50
\end{array}
$$

4. a. Diameter $= 2 \times$ radius
1 yard $= 36$ inches
36 inches $= 2 \times$ radius
Radius $= 36$ inches $\div 2$
$= $ **18 inches**

b. **Sample answer: I know a radius is half the length of a diameter and that one yard equals 36 inches. Therefore the radius is half of 36 inches, or 18 inches.**

5. 30 steps $\div 3 = 10$ steps
10 steps $\times 2 = $ **20 steps**

6. a. 8

b. $8 \times 3 = $ **24**

7. a. $\dfrac{1}{3}$

b. $\dfrac{1}{3}$

8. a. $\dfrac{540}{600} = \dfrac{\cancel{2} \cdot \cancel{2} \cdot \cancel{3} \cdot 3 \cdot 3 \cdot \cancel{5}}{\cancel{2} \cdot \cancel{2} \cdot 2 \cdot \cancel{3} \cdot \cancel{5} \cdot 5} = \dfrac{9}{10}$

b. $2 \cdot 2 \cdot 3 \cdot 5 = $ **60**

9. a. Acute angle

b. Right angle

c. Obtuse angle

10. Equivalent fractions are formed by multiplying or dividing a fraction by a fraction equal to 1. To change from fifths to thirtieths, multiply $\frac{3}{5}$ by $\frac{6}{6}$. We use the identity property of multiplication.

11. a.
$$10{,}000 = 1000 \cdot 10$$
$$1000 = 2 \cdot 2 \cdot 2 \cdot 5 \cdot 5 \cdot 5$$
$$10 = 2 \cdot 5$$
$$1000 \cdot 10 = 2 \cdot 2 \cdot 2 \cdot 5 \cdot 5 \cdot 5 \cdot 2 \cdot 5$$
$$= 2^4 \cdot 5^4$$

b. $\sqrt{10{,}000} = 100$
$$100 = 2 \cdot 2 \cdot 5 \cdot 5 = 2^2 \cdot 5^2$$

12. a.

b. Right angles

13. a.
$$1 \text{ yard} = 36 \text{ inches}$$
$$36 \text{ inches} \div 4 = \textbf{9 inches}$$

b. Area $= 9$ inches $\times 9$ inches
$= $ **81 square inches**

14. Commutative property

15. A. Parallel

16. Answers will vary. See student work. Sample answer: Twelve cans of juice cost $3.36. What is the cost of each can?

$12p = \$3.36$

$$
\begin{array}{r}
\$0.28 \\
12\overline{)\$3.36} \\
2\ 4 \\
\hline
96 \\
96 \\
\hline
0
\end{array}
$$

$0.28

17. $4\dfrac{7}{12} - 1\dfrac{1}{12} = 3\dfrac{6}{12} = 3\dfrac{1}{2}$

$x = 3\dfrac{1}{2}$

Solutions

18. $2\frac{3}{4} + 3\frac{3}{4} = 5\frac{6}{4} = 6\frac{1}{2}$

$w = 6\frac{1}{2}$

19. $\dfrac{10^5}{10^2} = \dfrac{\cancel{10} \cdot \cancel{10} \cdot 10 \cdot 10 \cdot 10}{\cancel{10} \cdot \cancel{10}}$

$= 10 \cdot 10 \cdot 10 = \mathbf{10^3}$ or **1000**

20. $\sqrt{9} - \sqrt{4^2} = 3 - 4 = \mathbf{-1}$

21.
$$\begin{array}{r} 100\% \\ -\ 66\frac{2}{3}\% \\ \hline \end{array} \longrightarrow \begin{array}{r} 99\frac{3}{3}\% \\ -\ 66\frac{2}{3}\% \\ \hline 33\frac{1}{3}\% \end{array}$$

22.
$$\begin{array}{r} 5\frac{1}{8} \\ -\ 1\frac{7}{8} \\ \hline \end{array} \xrightarrow{\ 4 + \frac{8}{8} + \frac{1}{8}\ } \begin{array}{r} 4\frac{9}{8} \\ -\ 1\frac{7}{8} \\ \hline 3\frac{2}{8} \end{array}$$

$3\frac{2}{8} = \mathbf{3\frac{1}{4}}$

23. $\left(\dfrac{5}{6}\right)^2 = \dfrac{5}{6} \cdot \dfrac{5}{6} = \mathbf{\dfrac{25}{36}}$

24. $\dfrac{\cancel{3}}{\cancel{4}} \cdot \dfrac{1}{\cancel{2}} \cdot \dfrac{\cancel{8}}{\cancel{9}} = \mathbf{\dfrac{1}{3}}$

25. **Heptagon**

26. **a.** $10 \cdot 100 = \mathbf{1000}$

b. $10 - 100 = \mathbf{-90}$

c. $\dfrac{10}{100} = \mathbf{\dfrac{1}{10}}$

27. **a.** Missing length = 10 yards + 10 yards
                 = 20 yards
    Missing height = 25 yards − 20 yards
                 = 5 yards
        Perimeter = 25 yards + 10 yards
            + 5 yards + 10 yards
            + 20 yards + 20 yards
            = **90 yards**

b. Sample: To find the missing measure
of the bottom of the figure I added the

measures of the opposite side 10 + 10
= 20, so the missing measure was 20
yards. To find the missing measure of
the top part I subtracted the right
side's measure from the left side's
measure: 25 − 20 = 5 yards.

28. $\dfrac{1}{4} \cdot \dfrac{3}{3} = \dfrac{3}{12}, \dfrac{1}{6} \cdot \dfrac{2}{2} = \dfrac{2}{12}$

$\dfrac{3}{12} + \dfrac{2}{12} = \mathbf{\dfrac{5}{12}}$

29. $\angle DAC$ and $\angle BCA$ (or $\angle CAD$ and $\angle ACB$);
$\angle DCA$ and $\angle BAC$ (or $\angle ACD$ and $\angle CAB$)

30. **a.** $-1, -\dfrac{1}{2}, 0, \dfrac{1}{2}, 1$

b. $1 + \dfrac{1}{2} = 1\dfrac{1}{2}$

$1\dfrac{1}{2} + \dfrac{1}{2} = 1\dfrac{2}{2} = 2$

$2 + \dfrac{1}{2} = 2\dfrac{1}{2}$

$\mathbf{1\dfrac{1}{2}, 2, 2\dfrac{1}{2}}$

Practice Set 25

a. $1 \div \dfrac{2}{3} = \dfrac{3}{2}$

$\dfrac{3}{4} \div \dfrac{2}{3} = \dfrac{3}{4} \times \dfrac{3}{2} = \dfrac{9}{8} = \mathbf{1\dfrac{1}{8}}$

b. $1 \div \dfrac{3}{4} = \dfrac{4}{3}$

$3 \div \dfrac{3}{4} = 3 \times \dfrac{4}{3} = \dfrac{12}{3} = \mathbf{4}$

c. Step 1: There are four quarters in
one dollar.
Step 2: There are 6 × 4 = 24 quarters in
six dollars.

d. Instead of dividing by the divisor, multiply
by the reciprocal of the divisor.

e. Pressing this key changes the number
previously entered to its reciprocal
(in decimal form).

f. $1 \div \dfrac{2}{3} = \dfrac{3}{2}$

$\dfrac{3}{5} \div \dfrac{2}{3} = \dfrac{3}{5} \times \dfrac{3}{2} = \mathbf{\dfrac{9}{10}}$

g. $1 \div \frac{1}{4} = \frac{4}{1}$

$\frac{7}{8} \div \frac{1}{4} = \frac{7}{\overset{}{\underset{2}{8}}} \times \frac{\overset{1}{\cancel{4}}}{1} = \frac{7}{2} = 3\frac{1}{2}$

h. $1 \div \frac{2}{3} = \frac{3}{2}$

$\frac{5}{6} \div \frac{2}{3} = \frac{5}{\overset{}{\underset{2}{6}}} \times \frac{\overset{1}{\cancel{3}}}{2} = \frac{5}{4} = 1\frac{1}{4}$

i. $\dfrac{\text{part}}{\text{whole}}$ $\begin{array}{c}\frac{1}{2}\\\frac{3}{4}\end{array}$ "One half divided by three-fourths."

$\frac{1}{2} \div \frac{3}{4}$

$1 \div \frac{3}{4} = \frac{4}{3}$

$\frac{1}{2} \div \frac{3}{4} = \frac{1}{\overset{}{\underset{1}{2}}} \cdot \frac{\overset{2}{\cancel{4}}}{3} = \frac{2}{3}$

Amanda used $\frac{2}{3}$ of the ribbon.

Written Practice 25

1. **$6P = 324$**

$\begin{array}{r} 54 \\ 6\overline{)324} \\ \underline{30} \\ 24 \\ \underline{24} \\ 0 \end{array}$ **54 boxes**

2.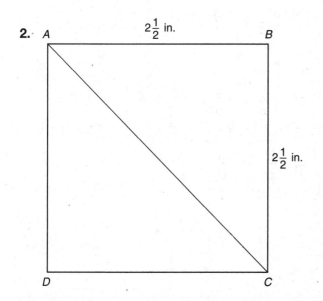

a. Perimeter $= 2\frac{1}{2}$ in. $+ 2\frac{1}{2}$ in.

$+ 2\frac{1}{2}$ in. $+ 2\frac{1}{2}$ in.

$= 8\frac{4}{2}$ in. $=$ **10 in.**

b. **90°**

c. $180° - 90° = 90°$
    $90° \div 2 =$ **45°**

d. $90° + 45° + 45° =$ **180°**

3. a. 56 relatives $\div 2 =$ **28 relatives**

b. $\begin{array}{r} 28 \text{ players} \\ - 10 \text{ players} \\ \hline \textbf{18 players} \end{array}$

c. 28 players $\div 2 =$ **14 players**

4.

Radius	Diameter
$\frac{1}{4}$	$\frac{1}{2}$
$\frac{1}{2}$	1
$\frac{3}{4}$	$1\frac{1}{2}$
1	2

5. $72 = 2 \cdot 2 \cdot 2 \cdot 3 \cdot 3$
    $54 = 2 \cdot 3 \cdot 3 \cdot 3$
    GCF $= 2 \cdot 3 \cdot 3 =$ **18**

6. $75\% = \frac{75}{100} \div \frac{25}{25} = \frac{3}{4}$

$\begin{array}{l} \frac{3}{4} \text{ read.} \\ \\ \frac{1}{4} \text{ not read.} \end{array} \left\{ \begin{array}{|c|} \hline 80 \text{ pages} \\ \hline 80 \text{ pages} \\ \hline 80 \text{ pages} \\ \hline 80 \text{ pages} \\ \hline \end{array} \right.$ 320 pages

a. 3×80 pages $=$ **240 pages**

b. 1×80 pages $=$ **80 pages**

7. a. $1 \div \frac{3}{4} = \frac{4}{3}$

b. $\frac{7}{8} \div \frac{3}{4} = \frac{7}{\overset{}{\underset{2}{8}}} \times \frac{\overset{1}{\cancel{4}}}{3} = \frac{7}{6} = 1\frac{1}{6}$

8. **C.** $\frac{2}{5}$

A little less than half is shaded. We eliminate $\frac{2}{3}$, which is more than $\frac{1}{2}$. Since $\frac{2}{4}$ equals $\frac{1}{2}$, and $\frac{2}{5}$ is a little less than $\frac{1}{2}$, we choose $\frac{2}{5}$.

9. **a.** $84 = 2 \cdot 2 \cdot 3 \cdot 7$
$210 = 2 \cdot 3 \cdot 5 \cdot 7$

$$\frac{\overset{1}{\cancel{2}} \cdot 2 \cdot \overset{1}{\cancel{3}} \cdot \overset{1}{\cancel{7}}}{\underset{1}{\cancel{2}} \cdot \underset{1}{\cancel{3}} \cdot 5 \cdot \underset{1}{\cancel{7}}} = \frac{2}{5}$$

b. $GCF = 2 \cdot 3 \cdot 7 = \mathbf{42}$

10. **a.** $\frac{10}{9}$

b. $\frac{1}{8}$

c. $2\frac{3}{8} = \frac{19}{8}, \frac{8}{19}$

d. $2\frac{3}{8} = \frac{19}{8}$

$$\frac{\overset{1}{\cancel{19}}}{\underset{1}{\cancel{8}}} \cdot \frac{\overset{1}{\cancel{8}}}{\underset{1}{\cancel{19}}} = 1$$

11. $\frac{3}{4} \cdot \frac{5}{5} = \frac{15}{20}, \frac{4}{5} \cdot \frac{4}{4} = \frac{16}{20}$

$\frac{15}{20} + \frac{16}{20} = \frac{31}{20} = 1\frac{11}{20}$

12. $640 = 40 \cdot 16 = 2^3 \cdot 5 \cdot 16$
$\quad = 2 \cdot 2 \cdot 2 \cdot 5 \cdot 2 \cdot 2 \cdot 2 \cdot 2$
$\quad = \mathbf{2^7 \cdot 5}$

13. $2\frac{2}{3} = \frac{8}{3}, 2\frac{1}{4} = \frac{9}{4}$

$$\frac{\overset{2}{\cancel{8}}}{\underset{1}{\cancel{3}}} \times \frac{\overset{3}{\cancel{9}}}{\underset{1}{\cancel{4}}} = 6$$

14. **a.** $A: 4\frac{4}{6} = 4\frac{2}{3}$
$\quad\quad B: 5\frac{3}{6} = 5\frac{1}{2}$

b. $\begin{array}{c} 5\frac{3}{6} \\ - 4\frac{4}{6} \\ \hline \end{array} \xrightarrow{4 + \frac{6}{6} + \frac{3}{6}} \begin{array}{c} 4\frac{9}{6} \\ - 4\frac{4}{6} \\ \hline \frac{5}{6} \end{array}$

15. **a.**

b. Acute angle

16. $\begin{array}{c} 3 \\ - 1\frac{7}{12} \\ \hline \end{array} \longrightarrow \begin{array}{c} 2\frac{12}{12} \\ - 1\frac{7}{12} \\ \hline y = 1\frac{5}{12} \end{array}$

17. $5\frac{7}{8} + 4\frac{5}{8} = 9\frac{12}{8} = 10\frac{4}{8} = 10\frac{1}{2}$

$x = \mathbf{10\frac{1}{2}}$

18. $\begin{array}{r} 45° \\ 8\overline{)360°} \\ \underline{32} \\ 40 \\ \underline{40} \\ 0 \end{array}$

$n = \mathbf{45°}$

19. $1^3 \cdot \frac{3}{4} = 1 \cdot 1 \cdot 1 \cdot \frac{3}{4} = \frac{3}{4}$

$m = \frac{3}{4}$

20. $6\frac{1}{6} + 1\frac{5}{6} = 7\frac{6}{6} = 8$

21. $\frac{\overset{1}{\cancel{3}}}{\underset{1}{\cancel{4}}} \cdot \frac{\overset{1}{\cancel{5}}}{\underset{3}{\cancel{9}}} \cdot \frac{\overset{2}{\cancel{8}}}{\underset{3}{\cancel{15}}} = \frac{2}{9}$

22. $1 \div \frac{2}{1} = \frac{1}{2}$

$\frac{4}{5} \div \frac{2}{1} = \frac{\overset{2}{\cancel{4}}}{5} \times \frac{1}{\underset{1}{\cancel{2}}} = \frac{2}{5}$

23. $1 \div \frac{6}{5} = \frac{5}{6}$

$\frac{8}{5} \div \frac{6}{5} = \frac{\overset{4}{\cancel{8}}}{\cancel{5}} \times \frac{\overset{1}{\cancel{5}}}{\underset{3}{\cancel{6}}} = \frac{4}{3} = \mathbf{1\frac{1}{3}}$

24. $1 \div \frac{5}{6} = \frac{6}{5}$

$\frac{3}{7} \div \frac{5}{6} = \frac{3}{7} \times \frac{6}{5} = \frac{\mathbf{18}}{\mathbf{35}}$

25.

$$8)\overline{100}$$
$$\underline{8}$$
$$20$$
$$\underline{16}$$
$$4$$
$$\underline{0}$$
$$4$$

with quotient 12

$12\frac{4}{8}\% = \mathbf{12\frac{1}{2}\%}$

26. $\frac{5}{3}$

27. a. $2^2 \cdot 2^3 = 4 \cdot 8$
$\mathbf{4 \cdot 8 = 8 \cdot 4}$ or
$\mathbf{32 = 32}$

b. 2

28. Perimeter = 6 inches + 6 inches
 + 6 inches + 6 inches
 + 6 inches + 6 inches
 = 36 inches
36 inches ÷ 12 = **3 feet**

29. Perimeter = 4 in. + 2 in. + 2 in.
 + 2 in. + 2 in. + 4 in.
 = **16 in.**

30. Third prime number = 5, **−5**

a.

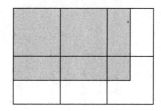

Area $= 2 \text{ in.}^2 + \frac{3}{2} \text{ in.}^2 + \frac{1}{4} \text{ in.}^2$

$ = 2 \text{ in.}^2 + \frac{6}{4} \text{ in.}^2 + \frac{1}{4} \text{ in.}^2$

$ = 2\frac{7}{4} \text{ in.}^2 = \mathbf{3\frac{3}{4} \text{ in.}^2}$

check: $\quad 1\frac{1}{2} \text{ in.} \times 2\frac{1}{2} \text{ in.}$

$ = \frac{3}{2} \text{ in.} \times \frac{5}{2} \text{ in.} = \frac{15}{4} \text{ in.}^2$

$ = 3\frac{3}{4} \text{ in.}^2$

Explanation: There are two whole squares, three half squares, and one quarter square in the rectangle. Two of the half squares equal a whole square, and the remaining one half square and one quarter square equal $\frac{3}{4}$ square. So $3\frac{3}{4}$ are in the rectangle.

b. $6\frac{2}{3} \times \frac{3}{5} = \frac{\overset{4}{\cancel{20}}}{\underset{1}{\cancel{3}}} \times \frac{\overset{1}{\cancel{3}}}{\underset{1}{\cancel{5}}} = \mathbf{4}$

c. $2\frac{1}{3} \times 3\frac{1}{2} = \frac{7}{3} \times \frac{7}{2} = \frac{49}{6} = \mathbf{8\frac{1}{6}}$

d. $3 \times 3\frac{3}{4} = \frac{3}{1} \times \frac{15}{4} = \frac{45}{4} = \mathbf{11\frac{1}{4}}$

e. $1\frac{2}{3} \div 3 = 1\frac{2}{3} \times \frac{1}{3} = \frac{5}{3} \times \frac{1}{3} = \mathbf{\frac{5}{9}}$

f. $2\frac{1}{2} \div 3\frac{1}{3} = \frac{5}{2} \div \frac{10}{3}$

$ = \frac{\overset{1}{\cancel{5}}}{2} \times \frac{3}{\underset{2}{\cancel{10}}} = \mathbf{\frac{3}{4}}$

g. $5 \div \frac{2}{3} = \frac{5}{1} \times \frac{3}{2} = \frac{15}{2} = \mathbf{7\frac{1}{2}}$

Solutions

h. $2\frac{2}{3} \div 1\frac{1}{3} = \frac{8}{3} \div \frac{4}{3}$

$= \frac{\overset{2}{\cancel{8}}}{\underset{1}{\cancel{3}}} \times \frac{\overset{1}{\cancel{3}}}{\underset{1}{\cancel{4}}} = \mathbf{2}$

i. $1\frac{1}{3} \div 2\frac{2}{3} = \frac{4}{3} \div \frac{8}{3} = \frac{\overset{1}{\cancel{4}}}{\underset{1}{\cancel{3}}} \times \frac{\overset{1}{\cancel{3}}}{\underset{2}{\cancel{8}}} = \mathbf{\frac{1}{2}}$

j. $4\frac{1}{2} \times 1\frac{2}{3} = \frac{\overset{3}{\cancel{9}}}{2} \times \frac{5}{\underset{1}{\cancel{3}}} = \frac{15}{2} = \mathbf{7\frac{1}{2}}$

Written Practice 26

1. $23 + M = 61$

$$\overset{5\;11}{\cancel{6}\cancel{1}} \text{ millimeters}$$
$$- \;\;2\,3 \text{ millimeters}$$
$$\overline{\;\;3\,8 \text{ millimeters}}$$

2. $26 \times 85¢ = T$

$$\begin{array}{r} \$0.85 \\ \times \;\;\;\; 26 \\ \hline 510 \\ 170 \\ \hline \mathbf{\$22.10} \end{array}$$

3. $1453 - 330 = B$

$$\begin{array}{r} 1453 \\ - \;\;330 \\ \hline 1123 \end{array} \quad \textbf{1123 years}$$

4. $\$20.00 - S = \$10.25$

$$\begin{array}{r} \overset{1\;9\;9\;10}{\$2\,0.\,\cancel{0}\,\cancel{0}} \\ - \$1\,0.\,2\,5 \\ \hline \$ \;\;9.\,7\,5 \end{array}$$

5. $12 \times 12 = P$

$$\begin{array}{r} 12 \\ \times \;\; 12 \\ \hline 24 \\ 12 \\ \hline 144 \end{array}$$
144 pencils

6.

	60 marbles
$\frac{2}{5}$ were blue.	12 marbles
	12 marbles
	12 marbles
$\frac{3}{5}$ were not blue.	12 marbles
	12 marbles

$40\% = \frac{40}{100} \div \frac{20}{20} = \mathbf{\frac{2}{5}}$

a. 2×12 marbles = **24 marbles**

b. 3×12 marbles = **36 marbles**

7. a. 1 ton = 2000 pounds

$$\frac{\overset{500}{\cancel{2000}} \text{ pounds}}{\underset{1}{\cancel{4}}} = \textbf{500 pounds}$$

b. Sample answer: I know that a ton is 2000 pounds, so a quarter of ton is $2000 \times \frac{1}{4} = \textbf{500 pounds}$

8. a. $\frac{7}{10} \cdot \frac{7}{10} = \mathbf{\frac{49}{100}}$

$100 - 49 = 51$

b. $\frac{51}{100} = \mathbf{51\%}$

9. a. $210 = 2 \cdot 3 \cdot 5 \cdot 7$
$252 = 2 \cdot 2 \cdot 3 \cdot 3 \cdot 7$

$$\frac{\overset{1}{\cancel{2}} \cdot \overset{1}{\cancel{3}} \cdot 5 \cdot \overset{1}{\cancel{7}}}{\underset{1}{\cancel{2}} \cdot 2 \cdot \underset{1}{\cancel{3}} \cdot 3 \cdot \underset{1}{\cancel{7}}} = \mathbf{\frac{5}{6}}$$

b. GCF = $2 \cdot 3 \cdot 7 = \mathbf{42}$

10. a. $\mathbf{\frac{9}{5}}$

b. $\mathbf{\frac{4}{23}}$

c. $\mathbf{\frac{1}{7}}$

11. a. $\frac{5}{8} \cdot \frac{3}{3} = \mathbf{\frac{15}{24}}$

b. $\frac{5}{12} \cdot \frac{2}{2} = \mathbf{\frac{10}{24}}$

c. $\frac{15}{24} + \frac{10}{24} = \frac{25}{24} = \mathbf{1\frac{1}{24}}$

Saxon Math Course 2 **148**

12.

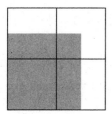

Area $= 1$ in.$^2 + \dfrac{1}{2}$ in.$^2 + \dfrac{1}{2}$ in.$^2 + \dfrac{1}{4}$ in.^{2}

$= 1$ in.$^2 + 1$ in.$^2 + \dfrac{1}{4}$ in.^{2}

$= \mathbf{2\dfrac{1}{4}}$ **in.^{2}**

Explanation: One whole square, two half squares, and one quarter square total $2\frac{1}{4}$ squares.

13.

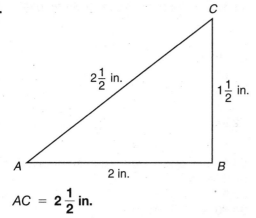

$AC = \mathbf{2\dfrac{1}{2}}$ **in.**

14. a. $-3,\ 0,\ \dfrac{5}{6},\ 1,\ \dfrac{4}{3}$

   b. 0, 1

15. $6\dfrac{5}{12} + 8\dfrac{11}{12} = 14\dfrac{16}{12} = 15\dfrac{4}{12}$

$x = \mathbf{15\dfrac{1}{3}}$

16.
$$\begin{array}{r}
1\overset{7}{\cancel{8}}\,\overset{10}{\cancel{0}} \\
-\ \ 7\,5 \\
\hline
1\,0\,5
\end{array}$$
$y = \mathbf{105}$

17.
$$\begin{array}{r}
30° \\
12\overline{)360°} \\
\underline{36}\ \ \\
00 \\
\underline{\ 0} \\
0
\end{array}$$
$w = \mathbf{30°}$

18.
$$\begin{array}{rcl}
100 & \longrightarrow & 99\dfrac{3}{3} \\
-\ 58\dfrac{1}{3} & & -\ 58\dfrac{1}{3} \\
\hline
& & w = \mathbf{41\dfrac{2}{3}}
\end{array}$$

19. a. Area $= 10$ in. $\times$ 10 in.
   $= \mathbf{100}$ **in.^{2}**

   b. $\dfrac{100\text{ in.}^2}{2} = \mathbf{50}$ **in.^{2}**

20.
$$\begin{array}{rcl}
9\dfrac{1}{9} & \xrightarrow{\ 8\ +\ \frac{9}{9}\ +\ \frac{1}{9}\ } & 8\dfrac{10}{9} \\
-\ 4\dfrac{4}{9} & & -\ 4\dfrac{4}{9} \\
\hline
& & 4\dfrac{6}{9}
\end{array}$$

$4\dfrac{6}{9} = \mathbf{4\dfrac{2}{3}}$

21. $\dfrac{\overset{1}{\cancel{5}}}{8} \cdot \dfrac{\overset{1}{\cancel{3}}}{\underset{2}{\cancel{10}}} \cdot \dfrac{1}{\underset{2}{\cancel{6}}} = \mathbf{\dfrac{1}{32}}$

22. $\left(2\dfrac{1}{2}\right)^2 = 2\dfrac{1}{2} \times 2\dfrac{1}{2}$

$= \dfrac{5}{2} \times \dfrac{5}{2} = \dfrac{25}{4} = \mathbf{6\dfrac{1}{4}}$

23. $1\dfrac{3}{5} \div 2\dfrac{2}{3}$

$= \dfrac{8}{5} \div \dfrac{8}{3} = \dfrac{\overset{1}{\cancel{8}}}{5} \times \dfrac{3}{\underset{1}{\cancel{8}}} = \mathbf{\dfrac{3}{5}}$

24. $3\dfrac{1}{3} \div 4 = \dfrac{10}{3} \div \dfrac{4}{1}$

$= \dfrac{\overset{5}{\cancel{10}}}{3} \times \dfrac{1}{\underset{2}{\cancel{4}}} = \mathbf{\dfrac{5}{6}}$

25. $5 \cdot 1\dfrac{3}{4} = \dfrac{5}{1} \times \dfrac{7}{4} = \dfrac{35}{4}$

$= \mathbf{8\dfrac{3}{4}}$

26. a. Associative property
   b. Inverse property of multiplication
   c. Identity property of multiplication

Solutions

27. $P(7) = \dfrac{\text{possible outcomes}}{\text{total outcomes}} = \dfrac{1}{10}$

28. a. $3 - \dfrac{6}{3} = 3 - 2 = \mathbf{1}$

b. $\dfrac{3 \cdot \cancel{6}^{\,1}}{\cancel{6}_{\,1}} = \mathbf{3}$

c. $\dfrac{\cancel{3}^{\,1}}{\cancel{6}_{\,1}} \cdot \dfrac{\cancel{6}^{\,1}}{\cancel{3}_{\,1}} = \mathbf{1}$

d. Inverse property of multiplication

29. $k = 3(9) - 2 = 27 - 2 = \mathbf{25}$

30. $\dfrac{1}{2} \times 90° = \dfrac{90°}{2} = \mathbf{45°}$

Early Finishers Solutions

$9\dfrac{3}{5} \times 8\dfrac{1}{3} = \dfrac{48}{5} \times \dfrac{25}{3} = 80 \text{ ft}^2 \times 4 = 320 \text{ ft}^2$

$39 \times 8\dfrac{1}{3} = \dfrac{39}{1} \times \dfrac{25}{3} = 325 \text{ ft}^2 \times 2 = \dfrac{650 \text{ ft}^2}{970 \text{ ft}^2}$

Practice Set   27

a. 8, 16, 24, 32, ⃝40 , 48, …
10, 20, 30, ⃝40 , 50, …
LCM (8, 10) = **40**

b.
$4 = 2 \cdot 2$
$6 = 2 \cdot 3$
$10 = 2 \cdot 5$
LCM (4, 6, 10) $= 2 \cdot 2 \cdot 3 \cdot 5 = 4 \cdot 15$
$= \mathbf{60}$

c.
$24 = 2 \cdot 2 \cdot 2 \cdot 3$
$40 = 2 \cdot 2 \cdot 2 \cdot 5$
LCM (24, 40) $= 2 \cdot 2 \cdot 2 \cdot 3 \cdot 5$
$= 24 \cdot 5 = \mathbf{120}$

d.
$30 = 2 \cdot 3 \cdot 5$
$75 = 3 \cdot 5 \cdot 5$
LCM (30, 75) $= 2 \cdot 3 \cdot 5 \cdot 5$
$= \mathbf{150}$

e. $\left(7\dfrac{1}{2}\right)2 = 15;\ \left(1\dfrac{1}{2}\right)2 = 3$
$15 \div 3 = \mathbf{5}$

f.–h. See student work. Sample answers:

f. $240 \div 4 = \mathbf{60}$

g. $\dfrac{\$6.00 \div 6}{12 \div 6} = \dfrac{\$1.00}{2} = \mathbf{50¢}$

h. $280 \div 10 = \mathbf{28}$

Written Practice   27

1. $11{,}123 + 7416 + 8449 = P;\ \mathbf{26{,}988}$

2. $6 \cdot 12 = I$
$\begin{array}{r} 12 \\ \times\ 6 \\ \hline 72 \end{array}$
72 inches

3. **\$0.15 per egg; Some equivalent division problems:**
$\$0.90 \div 6 = \$0.15$
$\$0.60 \div 4 = \$0.15$
$\$0.45 \div 3 = \$0.15$
$\$0.30 \div 2 = \$0.15$

4. **C. 10^9**

5. a. $3 \times 89 \text{ students} = \mathbf{267 \text{ students}}$
b. $5 \times 89 \text{ students} = \mathbf{445 \text{ students}}$

6. a. $30 \text{ in.} - 6 \text{ in.} - 6 \text{ in.}$
$= 18 \text{ in.}$
$18 \text{ in.} \div 2 = \mathbf{9 \text{ in.}}$

b. Area $= 6 \text{ in.} \times 9 \text{ in.} = \mathbf{54 \text{ in.}^2}$

7.
$25 = 5 \cdot 5$
$45 = 3 \cdot 3 \cdot 5$
LCM(25, 45) $= 3 \cdot 3 \cdot 5 \cdot 5$
$= \mathbf{225}$

8. **3500**

9. a. $\dfrac{24}{100} \div \dfrac{4}{4} = \dfrac{6}{25}$

b. $36 = 2 \cdot 2 \cdot 3 \cdot 3$
$180 = 2 \cdot 2 \cdot 3 \cdot 3 \cdot 5$

$\dfrac{\overset{1}{\cancel{2}} \cdot \overset{1}{\cancel{2}} \cdot \overset{1}{\cancel{3}} \cdot \overset{1}{\cancel{3}}}{\underset{1}{\cancel{2}} \cdot \underset{1}{\cancel{2}} \cdot \underset{1}{\cancel{3}} \cdot \underset{1}{\cancel{3}} \cdot 5} = \dfrac{1}{5}$

10. a.
$\begin{array}{r} 102° \text{F} \\ - \ 32° \text{F} \\ \hline \mathbf{70° \ F} \end{array}$

b.
$\begin{array}{r} 212° \text{F} \\ - \ 102° \text{F} \\ \hline \mathbf{110° \ F} \end{array}$

c. We needed to know the freezing point (32°F) and boiling point (212°F) of water.

11. a. $\dfrac{5}{12} \cdot \dfrac{3}{3} = \dfrac{15}{36}$

b. $\dfrac{1}{6} \cdot \dfrac{6}{6} = \dfrac{6}{36}$

c. $\dfrac{7}{9} \cdot \dfrac{4}{4} = \dfrac{28}{36}$

d. Identity property of multiplication

12. a.

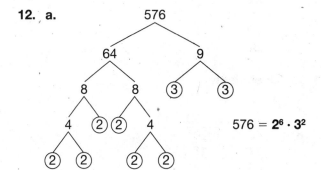

576

$576 = \mathbf{2^6 \cdot 3^2}$

b. 24

13. $5\dfrac{5}{6} \times 6\dfrac{6}{7} = \dfrac{35}{\cancel{6}} \times \dfrac{\overset{8}{\cancel{48}}}{7} = \mathbf{40}$

14. a. Obtuse angle

b. $\overline{AB}$ (or $\overline{BA}$) and $\overline{ED}$ (or $\overline{DE}$)

15. a. $\dfrac{1}{2}$

b. $\dfrac{1}{2}$

c. $\dfrac{1}{2}$

16. a. Perimeter $= 3\,\text{ft} + 3\,\text{ft} + 6\,\text{ft} + 6\,\text{ft}$
$= \mathbf{18\ ft}$

b. Area $= 3\,\text{ft} \times 6\,\text{ft} = \mathbf{18\ ft^2}$

17.
$\begin{array}{r} 36° \\ 10\overline{)360°} \\ \underline{30} \\ 60 \\ \underline{60} \\ 0 \end{array}$
$y = \mathbf{36°}$

18. $12^2 - 2^4 = 144 - 16 = 128$
$p = \mathbf{128}$

19.
$5\dfrac{1}{8} \xrightarrow{\ 4 + \frac{8}{8} + \frac{1}{8}\ } 4\dfrac{9}{8}$
$- 1\dfrac{3}{8} \qquad\qquad\qquad - 1\dfrac{3}{8}$
$\qquad\qquad\qquad\qquad\qquad \overline{\ 3\dfrac{6}{8}\ }$

$n = 3\dfrac{6}{8} = \mathbf{3\dfrac{3}{4}}$

20. $4\dfrac{1}{3} + 6\dfrac{2}{3} = 10\dfrac{3}{3} = 11$
$m = \mathbf{11}$

21.
$10 \longrightarrow 9\dfrac{5}{5}$
$- 1\dfrac{3}{5} \qquad\quad - 1\dfrac{3}{5}$
$\qquad\qquad\qquad\quad \overline{\ 8\dfrac{2}{5}\ }$

22. $5\dfrac{1}{3} \cdot 1\dfrac{1}{2} = \dfrac{\overset{8}{\cancel{16}}}{\underset{1}{\cancel{3}}} \cdot \dfrac{\overset{1}{\cancel{3}}}{\underset{1}{\cancel{2}}} = \mathbf{8}$

23. $3\dfrac{1}{3} \div \dfrac{5}{6} = \dfrac{10}{3} \div \dfrac{5}{6}$

$= \dfrac{\overset{2}{\cancel{10}}}{\underset{1}{\cancel{3}}} \times \dfrac{\overset{2}{\cancel{6}}}{\underset{1}{\cancel{5}}} = \mathbf{4}$

24. $5\dfrac{1}{4} \div 3 = \dfrac{21}{4} \div \dfrac{3}{1}$

$= \dfrac{\overset{7}{\cancel{21}}}{4} \times \dfrac{1}{\underset{1}{\cancel{3}}} = \dfrac{7}{4} = \mathbf{1\dfrac{3}{4}}$

151

Solutions

25. $\dfrac{\overset{1}{\cancel{5}}}{4} \cdot \dfrac{\overset{3}{\cancel{9}}}{\underset{2}{\cancel{8}}} \cdot \dfrac{\overset{1}{\cancel{4}}}{\underset{1}{\cancel{15}}} = \dfrac{3}{8}$

26. $\dfrac{8}{9} - \left(\dfrac{7}{9} - \dfrac{5}{9} \right) = \dfrac{8}{9} - \left(\dfrac{2}{9} \right) = \dfrac{6}{9} = \dfrac{2}{3}$

27. 1 yard = 36 inches

$\dfrac{36 \text{ inches}}{2} = 18$ inches

radius $= \dfrac{18 \text{ inches}}{2} =$ **9 inches**

28.
$$
\begin{array}{r}
\$\,0.75 \\
16)\overline{\$12.00} \\
11\,2 \\
\overline{80} \\
80 \\
\overline{0}
\end{array}
$$

Example: $\$1.50 \div 2 =$ **75¢**

29. a. Missing length = 5 in. − 3 in.
= 2 in.
Missing height = 5 in. − 3 in.
= 2 in.
Perimeter = 5 in. + 5 in.
+ 2 in.
+ 3 in. + 3 in. + 2 in.
= **20 in.**

b. Area of large square = 5 in. × 5 in.
= 25 in.²
Area of small square = 3 in. × 3 in.
= 9 in.²
Area remaining = 25 in.² − 9 in.²
= **16 in.²**

30. a. $\overline{CB}$ (or $\overline{BC}$)

b. $\overline{AB}$ (or $\overline{BA}$)

c. ∠*AMC* (or ∠*CMA*)

d. ∠*ABC* (or ∠*CBA* or ∠*ABM* or ∠*MBA*)
and ∠*BAM* (or ∠*MAB*)

e. $\overline{MA}$ (or $\overline{AM}$) and $\overline{MB}$ (or $\overline{BM}$)

Practice Set 28

a.
$$
\begin{array}{r}
\overset{1\ 9\ 9\ 10}{\$\,2\cancel{0}.\cancel{0}\cancel{0}} \\
- \ \$\ \ 5.3\,6 \\
\hline
\$\,1\,4.6\,4
\end{array}
$$

$$
\begin{array}{r}
\$4.88 \\
3)\overline{\$14.64} \\
12 \\
\overline{2\,6} \\
2\,4 \\
\overline{24} \\
24 \\
\overline{0}
\end{array}
$$
$4.88

b. 32 wild ducks ÷ 8 = 4 wild ducks
5 × 4 wild ducks = 20 wild ducks
20 mallards

c.
$$
\begin{array}{r}
\overset{2}{28} \text{ students} \\
29 \text{ students} \\
30 \text{ students} \\
+ \ 25 \text{ students} \\
\hline
112 \text{ students}
\end{array}
$$

$$
\begin{array}{r}
28 \\
4)\overline{112} \\
8 \\
\overline{3\,2} \\
32 \\
\overline{0}
\end{array}
$$
28 students

d.
$$
\begin{array}{r}
\overset{3}{46} \\
37 \\
34 \\
31 \\
29 \\
+ \ 24 \\
\hline
201
\end{array}
\qquad
\begin{array}{r}
33 \\
6)\overline{201} \\
18 \\
\overline{2\,1} \\
18 \\
\overline{3}
\end{array}
$$

$33\dfrac{3}{6} =$ **$33\dfrac{1}{2}$**

e.
$$
\begin{array}{r}
40 \\
+ \ 70 \\
\hline
110
\end{array}
\qquad
\begin{array}{r}
55 \\
2)\overline{110} \\
10 \\
\overline{1\,0} \\
10 \\
\overline{0}
\end{array}
$$
55; 55

f. **B. 84; The average score must fall
between the highest and lowest scores.**

1.
$$
\begin{array}{r}
\overset{2\,3}{242} \text{ bottles} \\
236 \text{ bottles} \\
248 \text{ bottles} \\
268 \text{ bottles} \\
+\ 226 \text{ bottles} \\
\hline
1220 \text{ bottles}
\end{array}
$$

$$
\begin{array}{r}
244 \\
5\overline{)1220} \\
\underline{10} \\
22 \\
\underline{20} \\
20 \\
\underline{20} \\
0
\end{array}
$$

244 bottles

2. 5 minutes $= 5 \times 60$ seconds
$\qquad\qquad = 300$ seconds

$$
\begin{array}{r}
300 \text{ seconds} \\
+\ 14 \text{ seconds} \\
\hline
314 \text{ seconds}
\end{array}
$$

3.
$$
\begin{array}{r}
\$15.99 \\
\times \qquad 3 \\
\hline
\$47.97
\end{array}
$$

$$
\begin{array}{r}
\overset{1\ 1\ 1}{\$47.97} \\
+\ \$24.95 \\
\hline
\mathbf{\$72.92}
\end{array}
$$

4.
$$
\begin{array}{r}
1492 \\
-\quad 41 \\
\hline
\mathbf{1451}
\end{array}
$$

5. $75\% = \dfrac{75}{100} = \dfrac{3}{4}$

5000 meters		
Salma led $\frac{3}{4}$.	1250 meters	
	1250 meters	
	1250 meters	
Salma did not lead $\frac{1}{4}$.	1250 meters	

a.
$$
\begin{array}{r}
1250 \\
\times \qquad 3 \\
\hline
3750
\end{array}
$$
3750 meters

b. **1250 meters**

6. a. Width $= 8$ in. $\div 2 = 4$ in.
Perimeter $= 4$ in. $+ 4$ in. $+ 8$ in.
$\qquad\qquad\quad + 8$ in. $= $ **24 in.**

b. Area $= 4$ in. $\times 8$ in. $= $ **32 in.²**

7. a. 3, 6, 9, 12, 15, 18

b. 4, 8, 12, 16, 20, 24

c. 12

d.
$$
\begin{aligned}
27 &= 3 \cdot 3 \cdot 3 \\
36 &= 2 \cdot 2 \cdot 3 \cdot 3 \\
\text{LCM}(27, 36) &= 2 \cdot 2 \cdot 3 \cdot 3 \cdot 3 \\
&= \mathbf{108}
\end{aligned}
$$

8. a. 280

b. 300

9.
$$
\begin{aligned}
56 &= 2 \cdot 2 \cdot 2 \cdot 7 \\
240 &= 2 \cdot 2 \cdot 2 \cdot 2 \cdot 3 \cdot 5
\end{aligned}
$$
$$
\frac{\cancel{2} \cdot \cancel{2} \cdot \cancel{2} \cdot 7}{\cancel{2} \cdot \cancel{2} \cdot \cancel{2} \cdot 2 \cdot 3 \cdot 5} = \frac{7}{30}
$$

10.
$$
\begin{array}{r}
1760 \\
3\overline{)5280} \\
\underline{3} \\
22 \\
\underline{21} \\
18 \\
\underline{18} \\
00 \\
\underline{0} \\
0
\end{array}
$$
1760 yards

11. a. $\dfrac{7}{8} \cdot \dfrac{3}{3} = \dfrac{21}{24}$

b. $\dfrac{11}{12} \cdot \dfrac{2}{2} = \dfrac{22}{24}$

c. **Identity property of multiplication**

12. a.

$3600 = \mathbf{2^4 \cdot 3^2 \cdot 5^2}$

b. $\sqrt{3600} = \sqrt{60^2} = \mathbf{60}$

13. **Add the six numbers. Then divide the sum by 6.**

Solutions

14. a.

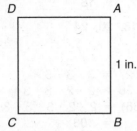

Area = 1 in. × 1 in.
  = **1 square inch**

b. – c.

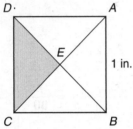

d. 25%

15. a. $-1,\ 0,\ \dfrac{1}{10},\ 1,\ \dfrac{11}{10}$

b. $-1,\ 1$

16.

$$12\overline{)360°}$$

with work:
$$\begin{array}{r} 30° \\ 12\overline{)360°} \\ 36 \\ \overline{00} \\ 0 \\ \overline{0} \end{array}$$

$y = \mathbf{30°}$

17. $10^2 - 8^2 = 100 - 64 = 36$
$m = \mathbf{36}$

18.

$$\begin{array}{r} 3 \\ 60\overline{)180} \\ 180 \\ \overline{0} \end{array}$$

$w = \mathbf{3}$

19. $4\dfrac{5}{12} - 1\dfrac{1}{12} = 3\dfrac{4}{12} = \mathbf{3\dfrac{1}{3}}$

20. $8\dfrac{7}{8} + 3\dfrac{3}{8} = 11\dfrac{10}{8} = 12\dfrac{2}{8} = \mathbf{12\dfrac{1}{4}}$

21.

$$\begin{array}{ccc} 12 & \longrightarrow & 11\dfrac{8}{8} \\ -\ 8\dfrac{1}{8} & & -\ 8\dfrac{1}{8} \\ & & \overline{\ \ 3\dfrac{7}{8}} \end{array}$$

22. $6\dfrac{2}{3} \cdot 1\dfrac{1}{5} = \dfrac{\overset{4}{\cancel{20}}}{\underset{1}{\cancel{3}}} \cdot \dfrac{\overset{2}{\cancel{6}}}{\underset{1}{\cancel{5}}} = \mathbf{8}$

23. $\left(1\dfrac{1}{2}\right)^2 \div 7\dfrac{1}{2} = \left(\dfrac{3}{2}\right)^2 \div \dfrac{15}{2}$

$= \left(\dfrac{3}{2} \cdot \dfrac{3}{2}\right) \div \dfrac{15}{2} = \dfrac{9}{4} \div \dfrac{15}{2}$

$= \dfrac{\overset{3}{\cancel{9}}}{\underset{2}{\cancel{4}}} \times \dfrac{\overset{1}{\cancel{2}}}{\underset{5}{\cancel{15}}} = \mathbf{\dfrac{3}{10}}$

24. $8 \div 2\dfrac{2}{3} = \dfrac{8}{1} \div \dfrac{8}{3} = \dfrac{\overset{1}{\cancel{8}}}{1} \times \dfrac{3}{\underset{1}{\cancel{8}}} = \mathbf{3}$

25.

$$\begin{array}{r} 125 \\ 80\overline{)10{,}000} \\ 80 \\ \overline{2\ 00} \\ 1\ 60 \\ \overline{400} \\ 400 \\ \overline{0} \end{array}$$

26. $\dfrac{3}{4} - \left(\dfrac{1}{2} \div \dfrac{2}{3}\right)$

$= \dfrac{3}{4} - \left(\dfrac{1}{2} \times \dfrac{3}{2}\right) = \dfrac{3}{4} - \left(\dfrac{3}{4}\right) = \mathbf{0}$

27. a. $3^4 = 3 \cdot 3 \cdot 3 \cdot 3 = 9 \cdot 9 = \mathbf{81}$

b. $3^2 + 4^2 = 9 + 16 = \mathbf{25}$

28. To find the output, double the input and add 1.

29. a. $\angle ACD$

b. $\overline{CB}$

c. Area $= 2\left(7\dfrac{1}{2}\ \text{in.}^2\right)$

$= 2 \times \dfrac{15}{2}\ \text{in.}^2 = \mathbf{15\ in.^2}$

154

30.

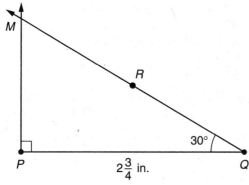

∠*PMQ* measures 60°.

Early Finishers Solutions

a. $\dfrac{80 + 75 + 77 + 66 + 61 + 73 + 65}{7}$

$= \dfrac{497}{7} = \mathbf{71}$

b. Yes, 71 is between 60 and 80.

Practice Set 29

a. 17⑥0 ⟶ **1800**

b. 5④89 ⟶ **5000**

c. 186,②82 ⟶ **186,000**

d. 7986 − 3074
 ↓   ↓
8000 − 3000 = **5000**

e. 297 ⟶ 300
31 ⟶ 30
$\begin{array}{r} 300 \\ \times\ 30 \\ \hline \mathbf{9000} \end{array}$

f. $\dfrac{5860}{19}$ ⟶ $\dfrac{6000}{20}$ = **300**

g. $12\dfrac{1}{4} \div 3\dfrac{7}{8}$
  ↓   ↓
12 ÷ 4 = **3**

h. Area $= 1\dfrac{7}{8}$ in. $\times\ 1\dfrac{1}{8}$ in.

$= \dfrac{15}{8}$ in. $\times\ \dfrac{9}{8}$ in. $= \dfrac{135}{64}$ in.²

$= \mathbf{2\dfrac{7}{64}}$ **in.²**

The answer is reasonable because the estimated area is 2 in. × 1 in. = 2 in.².

Written Practice 29

1. 7 feet = 7(12 inches)
$\begin{array}{r} 12 \\ \times\ 7 \\ \hline 84 \end{array}$ inches
84 inches + 10 inches = **94 inches**

2. **The cost per pound is $0.69. To find the cost per pound, divide $5.52 by 8.**

3.
$\begin{array}{r} {}^{1}\ \\ 75 \\ 70 \\ 80 \\ 80 \\ 85 \\ +\ 90 \\ \hline 480 \end{array}$
$\begin{array}{r} 80 \\ 6\overline{)480} \\ 48 \\ \hline 00 \\ 0 \\ \hline 0 \end{array}$

4. P(prime number)

$= \dfrac{\text{possible outcomes (2, 3, or 5)}}{\text{total outcomes (6)}} = \dfrac{3}{6} = \mathbf{\dfrac{1}{2}}$

5. $40\% = \dfrac{40}{100} \div \dfrac{20}{20} = \dfrac{2}{5}$

80 birds

$\dfrac{2}{5}$ were robins. $\left\{ \begin{array}{|c|} \hline \text{16 birds} \\ \hline \text{16 birds} \\ \hline \end{array} \right.$

$\dfrac{3}{5}$ were not robins. $\left\{ \begin{array}{|c|} \hline \text{16 birds} \\ \hline \text{16 birds} \\ \hline \text{16 birds} \\ \hline \end{array} \right.$

a. 2 × 16 chips = **32 birds**

b. 3 × 16 chips = **48 birds**

Solutions

6. a.

$$4 = 2 \cdot 2$$
$$6 = 2 \cdot 3$$
$$8 = 2 \cdot 2 \cdot 2$$
$$\text{LCM}(4, 6, 8) = 2 \cdot 2 \cdot 2 \cdot 3 = \mathbf{24}$$

b.

$$16 = 2 \cdot 2 \cdot 2 \cdot 2$$
$$36 = 2 \cdot 2 \cdot 3 \cdot 3$$
$$\text{LCM}(16, 36) = 2 \cdot 2 \cdot 2 \cdot 2 \cdot 3 \cdot 3$$
$$= \mathbf{144}$$

7. a. Perimeter $= \frac{3}{4}$ in. $+ \frac{3}{4}$ in. $+ \frac{3}{4}$ in.
$+ \frac{3}{4}$ in. $= \frac{12}{4}$ in.
$= \mathbf{3 \text{ in.}}$

b. Area $= \frac{3}{4}$ in. $\times \frac{3}{4}$ in. $= \mathbf{\frac{9}{16} \text{ in.}^2}$

8. a. $3\underline{\textcircled{6}}6 \longrightarrow \mathbf{400}$

b. $36\underline{\textcircled{6}} \longrightarrow \mathbf{370}$

9. $6143 + 4952$
$\quad\downarrow \qquad\quad \downarrow$
$6000 + 5000 = \mathbf{11{,}000}$

10. a. $\frac{3}{4} \cdot 5\frac{1}{3} \cdot 1\frac{1}{8}$
$\quad\downarrow \qquad \downarrow \qquad \downarrow$
$\quad 1 \;\cdot\; 5 \;\cdot\; 1 \;=\; \mathbf{5}$

b. $\frac{3}{4} \cdot 5\frac{1}{3} \cdot 1\frac{1}{8}$

$= \frac{\overset{1}{\cancel{3}}}{\underset{2}{\cancel{4}}} \cdot \frac{\overset{2}{\cancel{16}}}{\underset{1}{\cancel{3}}} \cdot \frac{9}{\underset{1}{\cancel{8}}} = \frac{9}{2} = \mathbf{4\frac{1}{2}}$

11. a. $\frac{2}{3} \cdot \frac{10}{10} = \mathbf{\frac{20}{30}}$

b. $\frac{25 \div 5}{30 \div 5} = \mathbf{\frac{5}{6}}$

12. $1{,}000{,}000{,}000 =$
$1{,}000{,}000 \cdot 1000 =$
$1000 \cdot 1000 \cdot 1000 =$
$2 \cdot 2 \cdot 2 \cdot 5 \cdot 5 \cdot 5 \cdot 2 \cdot 2 \cdot 2 \cdot 5 \cdot 5 \cdot 5$
$\cdot 2 \cdot 2 \cdot 2 \cdot 5 \cdot 5 \cdot 5$
$= \mathbf{2^9 \cdot 5^9}$

13. a. 50%

b. 50%

c. 50%

14. $BC = 2$ in. $+ 2$ in. $= 4$ in.
$AC = 2$ in. $+ 4$ in. $= 6$ in.
$AF + CD = AC = 6$ in.
$AF = 3$ in.
$CD = 3$ in.

a. Perimeter $= 3$ in. $+ 3$ in. $+ 2$ in.
$+ 2$ in. $= \mathbf{10 \text{ in.}}$

b. Area $= 4$ in. $\times 3$ in. $= \mathbf{12 \text{ in.}^2}$

15. a. $\angle AFB$

b. 90°

16. $8^2 = 64$
$$\begin{array}{r} 16 \\ 4\overline{)64} \\ \underline{4} \\ 24 \\ \underline{24} \\ 0 \end{array}$$
$m = \mathbf{16}$

17.
$$\begin{array}{cc} 15 & \longrightarrow \quad 14\frac{9}{9} \\ -\;4\frac{4}{9} & \quad\quad\; -\;4\frac{4}{9} \\ \hline & x = \mathbf{10\frac{5}{9}} \end{array}$$

18. $3\frac{5}{9} + 4\frac{7}{9} = 7\frac{12}{9} = 8\frac{3}{9} = 8\frac{1}{3}$
$n = \mathbf{8\frac{1}{3}}$

19.
$$\begin{array}{cc} 6\frac{1}{3} & \xrightarrow{\; 5 + \frac{3}{3} + \frac{1}{3}\;} \quad 5\frac{4}{3} \\ -\;5\frac{2}{3} & \quad\quad\quad\quad\quad -\;5\frac{2}{3} \\ \hline & \quad\quad\quad\quad\quad\quad \frac{2}{3} \end{array}$$

20. $6\frac{2}{3} \div 5 = \frac{20}{3} \div 5 = \frac{\overset{4}{\cancel{20}}}{3} \times \frac{1}{\underset{1}{\cancel{5}}} = \frac{4}{3}$

$= \mathbf{1\frac{1}{3}}$

21. $1\frac{2}{3} \div 3\frac{1}{2} = \frac{5}{3} \div \frac{7}{2}$

$= \frac{5}{3} \times \frac{2}{7} = \frac{10}{21}$

22.
$$
\begin{array}{r}
\$7.49 \\
\times \quad 24 \\
\hline
2996 \\
1498 \\
\hline
\$179.76
\end{array}
$$

23. Round $5\frac{1}{3}$ to 5 and round $4\frac{7}{8}$ to 5. Then multiply the rounded numbers. The product of the mixed numbers is about **25**.

24. a. $10^3 \cdot 10^3 = 10 \cdot 10 \cdot 10 \cdot 10 \cdot 10 \cdot 10$
$= 10^6$
$m = \mathbf{6}$

b. $\frac{10^6}{10^3} = \frac{\overset{1}{\cancel{10}} \cdot \overset{1}{\cancel{10}} \cdot \overset{1}{\cancel{10}} \cdot 10 \cdot 10 \cdot 10}{\underset{1}{\cancel{10}} \cdot \underset{1}{\cancel{10}} \cdot \underset{1}{\cancel{10}}}$
$= 10 \cdot 10 \cdot 10 = 10^3$
$n = \mathbf{3}$

25. $k = 2^5 + 1 = 2 \cdot 2 \cdot 2 \cdot 2 \cdot 2 + 1$
$= 32 + 1 = \mathbf{33}$

26. a. Diameter $= 2$ (1 inch)
$= \mathbf{2\ inches}$

b. Perimeter $= 6$ (1 inch)
$= \mathbf{6\ inches}$

27. a. Acute angle

b. Obtuse angle

c. Straight angle

28. $\frac{2}{3} \cdot \frac{2}{2} = \frac{4}{6}; \frac{1}{2} \cdot \frac{3}{3} = \frac{3}{6}$
$\frac{4}{6} - \frac{3}{6} = \mathbf{\frac{1}{6}}$

29. 1 quart $= 4$ cups $= 32$ ounces
2 cups $= 16$ ounces
32 ounces $- 16$ ounces $= \mathbf{16\ ounces}$

30. a. $4\frac{1}{8}$ in. $\rightarrow$ 4 in.; $3\frac{1}{4}$ in. $\rightarrow$ 3 in.
Estimated area $= 4$ in. $\times$ 3 in. $= \mathbf{12\ in.^2}$

b. The actual area is greater than the estimated area because the actual length and width are greater than the numbers used to estimate the area.

Early Finishers Solutions

a. 58,000,000; 108,000,000; 150,000,000; 228,000,000; 778,000,000; 1,427,000,000; 2,871,000,000; 4,497,000,000; 5,914,000,000

b. Venus; 150,000,000 − 108,000,000 = 42,000,000 km from Earth to Venus; 228,000,000 − 150,000,000 = 78,000,000 km from Earth to Mars. Venus is closer to Earth.

Practice Set 30

a. $\frac{3}{5} \cdot \frac{2}{2} = \frac{6}{10}$
$\frac{6}{10} < \frac{7}{10}$

b. $\frac{5}{12} \cdot \frac{5}{5} = \frac{25}{60}, \frac{7}{15} \cdot \frac{4}{4} = \frac{28}{60}$
$\frac{25}{60} < \frac{28}{60}$

c. $\frac{1}{2} \cdot \frac{5}{5} = \frac{5}{10}, \frac{2}{5} \cdot \frac{2}{2} = \frac{4}{10}$
$\frac{3}{10}, \frac{4}{10}, \frac{5}{10} \rightarrow \mathbf{\frac{3}{10}, \frac{2}{5}, \frac{1}{2}}$

d.
$$
\begin{aligned}
\frac{3}{4} \cdot \frac{6}{6} &= \frac{18}{24} \\
\frac{5}{6} \cdot \frac{4}{4} &= \frac{20}{24} \\
+ \frac{3}{8} \cdot \frac{3}{3} &= \frac{9}{24} \\
\hline
&\quad \frac{47}{24}
\end{aligned}
$$
$\frac{47}{24} = \mathbf{1\frac{23}{24}}$

Solutions

e.
$$7\frac{5}{6} = 7\frac{5}{6}$$
$$-\ 2\frac{1}{2} = 2\frac{3}{6}$$
$$5\frac{2}{6} = \mathbf{5\frac{1}{3}}$$

f.
$$4\frac{3}{4} = 4\frac{6}{8}$$
$$+\ 5\frac{5}{8} = 5\frac{5}{8}$$
$$9\frac{11}{8} = \mathbf{10\frac{3}{8}}$$

g.
$$4\frac{1}{6} \cdot \frac{3}{3} = 4\frac{3}{18}$$
$$2\frac{5}{9} \cdot \frac{2}{2} = 2\frac{10}{18}$$

$$4\frac{3}{18} \xrightarrow{\ 3 + \frac{18}{18} + \frac{3}{18}\ } 3\frac{21}{18}$$
$$-\ 2\frac{10}{18} \qquad\qquad -\ 2\frac{10}{18}$$
$$\mathbf{1\frac{11}{18}}$$

h. $\dfrac{25}{36} = \dfrac{25}{2 \cdot 2 \cdot 3 \cdot 3}, \dfrac{5}{60} = \dfrac{5}{2 \cdot 2 \cdot 3 \cdot 5}$

$2 \cdot 2 \cdot 3 \cdot 3 \cdot 5 = 180$

$\dfrac{25}{36} \cdot \dfrac{5}{5} = \dfrac{125}{180}, \dfrac{5}{60} \cdot \dfrac{3}{3} = \dfrac{15}{180}$

$\dfrac{125}{180} + \dfrac{15}{180} = \dfrac{140}{180}$

$\dfrac{140}{180} \div \dfrac{20}{20} = \mathbf{\dfrac{7}{9}}$

i. $\dfrac{3}{25} = \dfrac{3}{5 \cdot 5}, \dfrac{2}{45} = \dfrac{2}{3 \cdot 3 \cdot 5}$

$3 \cdot 3 \cdot 5 \cdot 5 = 225$

$\dfrac{3}{25} \cdot \dfrac{9}{9} = \dfrac{27}{225}$

$-\ \dfrac{2}{45} \cdot \dfrac{5}{5} = \dfrac{10}{225}$

$\mathbf{\dfrac{17}{225}}$

j. **Answers will vary based on the exercise each student chose.**

1.
```
   3
  76 inches
  77 inches
  77 inches
  78 inches
+ 82 inches
 390 inches
```
$$\begin{array}{r} 78 \\ 5\overline{)390} \\ \underline{35} \\ 40 \\ \underline{40} \\ 0 \end{array}$$ **78 inches**

2.
$$\begin{array}{r} \$0.87 \\ \times\ \ \ \ 6 \\ \hline \$5.22 \end{array} \qquad \begin{array}{r} {}^{0\ 9\ 9\ 10} \\ \$\cancel{1}0.\cancel{0}\cancel{0} \\ -\ \$\ 5.22 \\ \hline \$\ \ 4.78 \end{array}$$

3.
$$17 \to 20$$
$$8 \to 10$$
$$20 \times 10 = 200$$

Her father is correct. By estimating, we know the total is closer to 200 pounds than 2000 pounds.

4.
$$\begin{array}{r} 260 \\ -\ 140 \\ \hline 120 \end{array} \qquad \dfrac{120 \div 10}{260 \div 10} = \dfrac{12}{26} = \mathbf{\dfrac{6}{13}}$$

5. $30\% = \dfrac{30}{100} \div \dfrac{10}{10} = \dfrac{3}{10}$

$2140 \div 10 = 214$

a. 3×214 miles = **642 miles**

b. 7×214 miles = **1498 miles**

6. 5 feet = 5(12 inches) = 60 inches

60 inches $\div$ 4 = **15 inches**

7.
$$18 = 2 \cdot 3 \cdot 3$$
$$30 = 2 \cdot 3 \cdot 5$$
$$2 \cdot 3 \cdot 3 \cdot 5 = 90$$

$$\dfrac{1}{18} \cdot \dfrac{5}{5} = \dfrac{5}{90}$$
$$-\ \dfrac{1}{30} \cdot \dfrac{3}{3} = \dfrac{3}{90}$$
$$\dfrac{2}{90} = \mathbf{\dfrac{1}{45}}$$

8. **a.** **14,000 ft**

b. **14,500 ft**

Saxon Math Course 2 **158**

9. Martin did not enter the problem correctly.

$28,910 \rightarrow 30,000$

$49 \rightarrow 50$

$\dfrac{30,000}{50} = 600$

By estimating, we find that the answer should be near 600.

10. **a.** $\dfrac{32}{100} \div \dfrac{4}{4} = \dfrac{8}{25}$

b. $\dfrac{48}{72} = \dfrac{\overset{1}{\cancel{2}} \cdot \overset{1}{\cancel{2}} \cdot \overset{1}{\cancel{2}} \cdot 2 \cdot \overset{1}{\cancel{3}}}{\underset{1}{\cancel{2}} \cdot \underset{1}{\cancel{2}} \cdot \underset{1}{\cancel{2}} \cdot \underset{1}{\cancel{3}} \cdot 3}$

$= \dfrac{2}{3}$

11. $\dfrac{5}{6} \cdot \dfrac{4}{4} = \dfrac{20}{24}, \quad \dfrac{7}{8} \cdot \dfrac{3}{3} = \dfrac{21}{24}$

$\dfrac{20}{24} < \dfrac{21}{24}$

12. **a.** Area $= 3$ in. $\times$ 3 in. $= $ **9 in.²**

b. Area $= 4$ in. $\times$ 4 in. $= $ **16 in.²**

c. 16 in.² $+ 9$ in.² $= $ **25 in.²**

13. **a.** Perimeter $= 3$ in. $+ 3$ in.
$+ 1$ in. $+ 4$ in. $+ 4$ in.
$+ 4$ in. $+ 3$ in. $= $ **22 in.**

b. Perimeter $= 4(3$ in.$) + 4(4$ in.$) = 28$ in.
28 in. $- 22$ in. $= 6$ in.

The perimeter of the hexagon is 6 in. less than the perimeter of the two squares.

c. **The perimeter of the hexagon is 6 in. less than the combined perimeter of the squares because a 3 in. side of the smaller square and the adjoining 3 in. portion of a side of the larger square are not part of the perimeter of the hexagon.**

14. **a.**

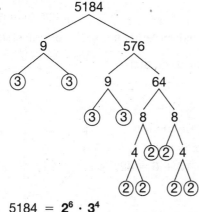

$5184 = $ **$2^6 \cdot 3^4$**

b. $\sqrt{5184} = \sqrt{2^6 \cdot 2^4}$
$= 2^3 \cdot 3^2 = $ **72**

15.

$$\begin{array}{r} 16 \\ 5 10)\overline{160} \\ 7 10 \\ 9 \overline{60} \\ 11 60 \\ 12 \overline{0} \\ 13 \\ 24 \\ 25 \\ 26 \\ + 28 \\ \hline 160 \end{array}$$

16. $5 + 6 + 7 + 0 = 18$

$$\begin{array}{r} 810 \\ 7)\overline{5670} \\ 56 \\ \hline 07 \\ 7 \\ \hline 00 \\ 0 \\ \hline 0 \end{array} \qquad \begin{array}{r} 708 \\ 8)\overline{5670} \to 708\ R6 \\ 56 \\ \hline 07 \\ 0 \\ \hline 70 \\ 64 \\ \hline 6 \end{array}$$

1, 2, 3, 5, 6, 7, 9

17. $3\dfrac{2}{3} + 1\dfrac{5}{6}$

$\downarrow \qquad \downarrow$

$4 \ + \ 2 = $ **6**

$3\dfrac{2}{3} = 3\dfrac{4}{6}$

$+ \ 1\dfrac{5}{6} = 1\dfrac{5}{6}$

$\overline{}$

$4\dfrac{9}{6} = $ **$5\dfrac{1}{2}$**

18. $5\dfrac{1}{8} - 1\dfrac{3}{4}$

$\downarrow \qquad \downarrow$

$5 \ - \ 2 = $ **3**

$1\dfrac{3}{4} \cdot \dfrac{2}{2} = 1\dfrac{6}{8}$

$\begin{array}{r} 5\dfrac{1}{8} \\ - 1\dfrac{6}{8} \\ \hline \end{array}$ $\xrightarrow{\ 4 + \dfrac{8}{8} + \dfrac{1}{8}\ }$ $\begin{array}{r} 4\dfrac{9}{8} \\ - 1\dfrac{6}{8} \\ \hline 3\dfrac{3}{8} \end{array}$

159

Solutions

19. Answers will vary. See student work.
Sample answer: I bought 36 packs of
trading cards for a total of $45.00. What is
the price of one pack of trading cards?

$$
\begin{array}{r}
\$1.25 \\
36\overline{)\$45.00} \\
\underline{36} \\
9\,0 \\
\underline{7\,2} \\
1\,80 \\
\underline{1\,80} \\
0
\end{array}
$$

$x = \mathbf{\$1.25}$

20.

Cars Washed	Dollars Earned
1	**6**
3	**18**
5	**30**
10	**60**
20	**120**

21.
$$
\begin{aligned}
\frac{1}{2} \cdot \frac{3}{3} &= \frac{3}{6} \\
+ \frac{1}{3} \cdot \frac{2}{2} &= \frac{2}{6} \\
\hline
&\quad \frac{5}{6}
\end{aligned}
$$

22.
$$
\begin{aligned}
\frac{3}{4} \cdot \frac{3}{3} &= \frac{9}{12} \\
- \frac{1}{3} \cdot \frac{4}{4} &= \frac{4}{12} \\
\hline
&\quad \frac{5}{12}
\end{aligned}
$$

23.
$$
\begin{aligned}
2\frac{5}{6} &= 2\frac{5}{6} \\
- 1\frac{1}{2} &= 1\frac{3}{6} \\
\hline
&\quad 1\frac{2}{6}
\end{aligned}
$$

$1\frac{2}{6} = \mathbf{1\frac{1}{3}}$

24. $\dfrac{4}{5} \cdot 1\dfrac{2}{3} \cdot 1\dfrac{1}{8}$

$= \dfrac{\cancel{4}}{\cancel{5}} \cdot \dfrac{\cancel{5}}{\cancel{3}} \cdot \dfrac{\cancel{9}}{\cancel{8}} = \dfrac{3}{2} = \mathbf{1\frac{1}{2}}$

25. $1\dfrac{3}{4} \div 2\dfrac{2}{3} = \dfrac{7}{4} \div \dfrac{8}{3}$

$= \dfrac{7}{4} \times \dfrac{3}{8} = \dfrac{21}{32}$

26. $3 \div 1\dfrac{7}{8} = \dfrac{3}{1} \div \dfrac{15}{8}$

$= \dfrac{\cancel{3}}{1} \times \dfrac{8}{\cancel{15}} = \dfrac{8}{5} = \mathbf{1\frac{3}{5}}$

27. $6^3 = 6 \cdot 6 \cdot 6 = 36 \cdot 6 = 216$

$$
\begin{array}{r}
36 \\
6\overline{)216} \\
\underline{18} \\
36 \\
\underline{36} \\
0
\end{array}
$$

$w = \mathbf{36}$

28. $90° + 30° = 120°$
$180° - 120° = 60°$
$a = \mathbf{60°}$

29.

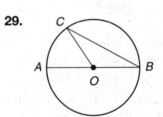

See student work. One possibility is shown.

30. a. $\overline{AB}$ (or $\overline{BA}$)

b. $\overline{OA}, \overline{OB}, \overline{OC}$

c. $\angle BOC$ (or $\angle COB$)

Early Finishers Solutions

$\frac{1}{2} + \frac{1}{8} + \frac{1}{4} = \frac{4}{8} + \frac{1}{8} + \frac{2}{8} = \frac{7}{8}$, this means the
other 6 children represent $\frac{1}{8}$ of the total children.

If $\frac{1}{8} = 6$ children, then
$\frac{1}{4} = 2(\frac{1}{8}) = 12$ children
and $\frac{1}{2} = 4(\frac{1}{8}) = 24$
children. So the total
number of children is
$24 + 6 + 12 + 6 = 48$.

160

Investigation 3

Coordinate Plane

1.

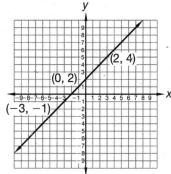

(−1, 1) is a point on the line in the second quadrant.

2. (−2, −2)

3. Perimeter = 16; Area = 15 sq. units

4. Area = 8 sq. units

5.

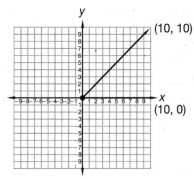

Angle measures 45°

6. a. Quadrant III

   b. Quadrant I

   c. Quadrant IV

   d. Quadrant II

7.

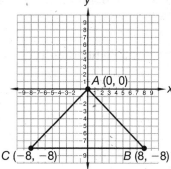

{Students use a protractor to find the measure of each angle in the triangle.}

∠ABC = 45°

∠ACB = 45°

∠CAB = 90°

8.

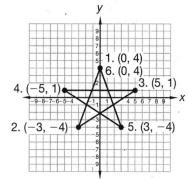

9. {Students create a straight-segment drawing on graph paper. Then, they write directions according to instructions in the textbook.}

10. {Students graph a dot-to-dot drawing created by a classmate.}

Practice Set 31

a. $\frac{3}{100}$; 0.03

b. $\frac{3}{10}$; 0.3

c. 3

d. 4

Saxon Math Course 2   **161**

e. Twenty-five and one hundred thirty-four thousandths

f. One hundred and one hundredth

g. 102.3

h. 0.0125

i. 300.075

j. and

Written Practice **31**

1.
$26.47
+ $32.54
———
$59.01

$89.89
− $59.01
———
$30.88

2.
326 pages
288 pages
349 pages
+ 401 pages
————
1364 pages

341 pages
4)1364

3.
$1.33
12)$15.96
12
——
3 9
3 6
——
36
36
——
0

4.
1607
− 1492
————
115 years

5. Divide the perimeter of the square by 4 to find the length of a side. Then multiply the length of a side by 6 to find the perimeter of the hexagon.

6. $80\% = \dfrac{80}{100} = \dfrac{4}{5}$

20 stamps
$\dfrac{4}{5}$ used {
4 stamps
4 stamps
4 stamps
4 stamps
$\dfrac{1}{5}$ left {
4 stamps

a. 4×4 stamps = **16 stamps**

b. **4 stamps**

7. a. **500,000**

b. **481,000**

8. $50,000 - 20,000 = $ **30,000**

9. a. $\dfrac{7}{100}$

b. **0.07**

c. $\dfrac{7}{100} = $ **7%**

10. **7**

11. a. $\dfrac{3}{10} = 0.3$

b. $\dfrac{3}{100} < 0.3$

12.

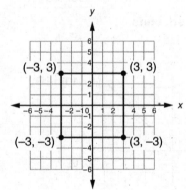

a. Perimeter = 4(6 units) = **24 units**

b. Area = (6 units)(6 units)
= **36 units²**

13. a. $\dfrac{15 \div 3}{24 \div 3} = \dfrac{5}{8}$

b. $\dfrac{7}{12} \cdot \dfrac{2}{2} = \dfrac{14}{24}$

c. $\dfrac{4 \div 4}{24 \div 4} = \dfrac{1}{6}$

14. a.

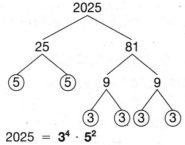

$$2025 = 3^4 \cdot 5^2$$

b. $\sqrt{2025} = \sqrt{3^4 \cdot 5^2}$
$$= 3^2 \cdot 5 = 45$$

15. One possibility:

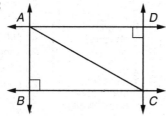

a. Rectangle

b. $\angle BCA$ (or $\angle ACB$)

16. $P(\text{not red}) = \dfrac{\text{possible outcomes }(15)}{\text{total outcomes }(12 + 15)} =$
$$\dfrac{15 \div 3}{27 \div 3} = \dfrac{5}{9}$$

17. a. Associative property
   b. Inverse property of multiplication
   c. Identity property of multiplication

18. $\dfrac{\overset{2}{\cancel{6}} \cdot \overset{4}{\cancel{12}}}{\underset{1}{\cancel{\underset{3}{9}}}} = 8 \qquad n = 8$

19.
$$\begin{array}{r} 90° \\ + \ 45° \\ \hline 135° \end{array} \qquad \begin{array}{r} 180° \\ - \ 135° \\ \hline 45° \end{array}$$
$$b = 45°$$

20.
$$\begin{array}{r} \dfrac{1}{2} \cdot \dfrac{3}{3} = \dfrac{3}{6} \\ + \ \dfrac{2}{3} \cdot \dfrac{2}{2} = \dfrac{4}{6} \\ \hline \dfrac{7}{6} = 1\dfrac{1}{6} \end{array}$$

21. $\dfrac{\overset{1}{\cancel{3}}}{\underset{2}{\cancel{4}}} \cdot \dfrac{\overset{1}{\cancel{2}}}{\underset{1}{\cancel{3}}} = \dfrac{1}{2}$

$$\dfrac{1}{2} - \dfrac{1}{2} = 0$$

22.
$$\begin{array}{r} 3\dfrac{5}{6} = 3\dfrac{5}{6} \\ - \ \dfrac{1}{3} \cdot \dfrac{2}{2} = \dfrac{2}{6} \\ \hline 3\dfrac{3}{6} = 3\dfrac{1}{2} \end{array}$$

23. $\dfrac{5}{8} \cdot 2\dfrac{2}{5} \cdot \dfrac{4}{9}$

$$= \dfrac{\overset{1}{\cancel{5}}}{\underset{2}{\cancel{8}}} \cdot \dfrac{\overset{\overset{1}{\cancel{3}}}{\cancel{12}}}{\underset{1}{\cancel{5}}} \cdot \dfrac{4}{\underset{3}{\cancel{9}}} = \dfrac{4}{6} = \dfrac{2}{3}$$

24. $2\dfrac{2}{3} \div 1\dfrac{3}{4}$
$$= \dfrac{8}{3} \div \dfrac{7}{4} = \dfrac{8}{3} \times \dfrac{4}{7}$$
$$= \dfrac{32}{21} = 1\dfrac{11}{21}$$

25. $1\dfrac{7}{8} \div 3 = \dfrac{15}{8} \div \dfrac{3}{1}$
$$= \dfrac{\overset{5}{\cancel{15}}}{8} \times \dfrac{1}{\underset{1}{\cancel{3}}} = \dfrac{5}{8}$$

26.
$$\begin{array}{r} 3\dfrac{1}{2} = 3\dfrac{3}{6} \\ + \ 1\dfrac{5}{6} = 1\dfrac{5}{6} \\ \hline 4\dfrac{8}{6} = 5\dfrac{2}{6} = 5\dfrac{1}{3} \end{array}$$

27.
$$\begin{array}{r} 5\dfrac{1}{4} = 5\dfrac{2}{8} \\ - \ 1\dfrac{5}{8} = 1\dfrac{5}{8} \end{array} \qquad \begin{array}{r} 4\dfrac{8}{8} + \dfrac{2}{8} \end{array} \qquad \begin{array}{r} 4\dfrac{10}{8} \\ - \ 1\dfrac{5}{8} \\ \hline 3\dfrac{5}{8} \end{array}$$

28.
$$\begin{array}{r} \dfrac{4}{3} = \dfrac{16}{12} \\ + \ \dfrac{3}{4} = \dfrac{9}{12} \\ \hline \dfrac{25}{12} = 2\dfrac{1}{12} \end{array}$$

29. $k = 10^6 = 10 \cdot 10 \cdot 10 \cdot 10 \cdot 10 \cdot 10$
$$= 1{,}000{,}000$$
One million

30. a. 180°

   b. 90°

   c. 45°

Practice Set (**32**)

a. 2 meters = 2(100 centimeters)
          = **200 centimeters**

b. A 1-gallon jug can hold a little less than four liters. (Have students check the label on a gallon bottle; 3.78 liters.)

c. **1000 × 2.2 pounds is about 2200 pounds.**

d. A 100°C difference is equivalent to a difference of 180°F. Divide both by 10°. A 10°C difference is equivalent to a difference of 18°F.
                       18°F

e. 3 kilometers = 3000 meters

$$\begin{array}{r} 3000 \text{ meters} \\ -\ 800 \text{ meters} \\ \hline \mathbf{2200 \text{ meters}} \end{array}$$

f. 30 cm = 300 mm

$$\begin{array}{r} 300 \text{ mm} \\ -\ 120 \text{ mm} \\ \hline \mathbf{180 \text{ mm}} \end{array}$$

g. **12 inches**

Written Practice (**32**)

1.
$$\begin{array}{r} 4248 \\ 3584 \\ +\ 9418 \\ \hline 17{,}250 \end{array}$$

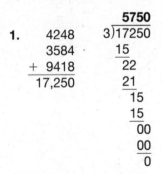

$$\begin{array}{r} 5750 \\ 3\overline{)17250} \\ \underline{15} \\ 22 \\ \underline{21} \\ 15 \\ \underline{15} \\ 00 \\ \underline{00} \\ 0 \end{array}$$

2.
$$\begin{array}{r} 3 \\ 60\overline{)206} \\ \underline{180} \\ 26 \end{array} \rightarrow 3 \text{ R } 26$$

3 hours, 26 minutes

3. $\dfrac{440}{1760}$ mile = $\dfrac{22}{88}$ mile = $\dfrac{1}{4}$ **mile**

4. 20 cm ÷ 4 = 5 cm
Perimeter = (5)(5 cm) = **25 cm**

5. a. <u>3</u>,(1)97,270 → **3,000,000**

   b. 3,<u>1</u>(9)7,270 → **3,200,000**

6. 313 → 300, 489 → 500
   300 × 500 = **150,000**

7.

$\dfrac{5}{8}$ were about love and chivalry.

$\dfrac{3}{8}$ were not about love and chivalry.

200 songs
25 songs
25 songs
25 songs
25 songs
25 songs
25 songs
25 songs
25 songs

   a. 5(25 songs) = **125 songs**

   b. 3(25 songs) = **75 songs**

8. a. $\dfrac{9}{10}$

   b. **0.9**

   c. $\dfrac{9}{10} = \dfrac{90}{100} =$ **90%**

9. **Three and twenty-five thousandths**

10. **7.40 meters**

11. $15.00 × 2 = $30.00; $2\dfrac{1}{2} × 2 = 5$
    $30.00 ÷ 5 = $6.00

12. a. **(2 × 1000) + (5 × 100)**

   b.

2500
25   100
⑤ ⑤ 10 10
②⑤②⑤

2500 = **2² · 5⁴**

   c. $\sqrt{2500} = \sqrt{2^2 \cdot 5^4}$
              $= 2 \cdot 5^2 = \mathbf{50}$

13.

$$35\overline{)\begin{array}{r}\$\,0.80 \\ \$28.00\end{array}}$$

$\underline{28\ 0}$

00

$\underline{0}$

0

$0.80 per liter

14.

15. a. Area = (6 cm)(6 cm) = **36 cm²**

   b. Area = (8 cm)(8 cm) = **64 cm²**

   c. Area = 36 cm² + 64 cm² = **100 cm²**

16. Perimeter = 6 cm + 6 cm + 6 cm

   + 2 cm + 8 cm + 8 cm + 8 cm

   = **44 cm**

17. $\dfrac{\overset{5}{\cancel{10}}\cdot\overset{3}{\cancel{6}}}{\underset{1}{\underset{2}{\cancel{\underset{4}{\cancel{4}}}}}} = 15$ $w = \mathbf{15}$

18.

$1\,\overset{7}{\cancel{8}}\,\overset{10}{\cancel{0}}°$

$\underline{-\ \ 6\,5°}$

$1\,1\,5°$

$s = \mathbf{115°}$

19.

$\dfrac{1}{4} = \dfrac{2}{8}$

$\dfrac{3}{8} = \dfrac{3}{8}$

$+\ \dfrac{1}{2} = \dfrac{4}{8}$

$\phantom{+\ \dfrac{1}{2} =\ }\dfrac{9}{8} = 1\dfrac{1}{8}$

20.

$\dfrac{5}{6} = \dfrac{10}{12}$

$-\ \dfrac{3}{4} = \dfrac{9}{12}$

$\phantom{-\ \dfrac{3}{4} =\ }\dfrac{1}{12}$

21.

$\dfrac{5}{16} = \dfrac{25}{80}$

$-\ \dfrac{3}{20} = \dfrac{12}{80}$

$\phantom{-\ \dfrac{3}{20} =\ }\dfrac{13}{80}$

22. $\dfrac{8}{9}\cdot 1\dfrac{1}{5}\cdot 10 = \dfrac{8}{\underset{3}{\cancel{9}}}\cdot \dfrac{\overset{2}{\cancel{6}}}{\underset{1}{\cancel{5}}}\cdot \dfrac{\overset{2}{\cancel{10}}}{1}$

$\phantom{\dfrac{8}{9}\cdot 1\dfrac{1}{5}\cdot 10\ } = \dfrac{32}{3} = \mathbf{10\dfrac{2}{3}}$

23.

$\begin{array}{l}6\dfrac{1}{6} = 6\dfrac{1}{6} \\ -\ 2\dfrac{1}{2} = 2\dfrac{3}{6}\end{array}$ $\begin{array}{l}5\dfrac{6}{6}+\dfrac{1}{6} \\ \hline\end{array}$ $\begin{array}{l}5\dfrac{7}{6} \\ -\ 2\dfrac{3}{6} \\ \hline 3\dfrac{4}{6}\end{array}$

$3\dfrac{4}{6} = \mathbf{3\dfrac{2}{3}}$

24.

$4\dfrac{5}{8} = 4\dfrac{5}{8}$

$+\ 1\dfrac{1}{2} = 1\dfrac{4}{8}$

$\phantom{+\ 1\dfrac{1}{2} =\ }5\dfrac{9}{8} = \mathbf{6\dfrac{1}{8}}$

25. $\dfrac{2}{3}\div\dfrac{1}{2} = \dfrac{2}{3}\cdot\dfrac{2}{1} = \dfrac{4}{3}$

$\dfrac{2}{3}+\dfrac{4}{3} = \dfrac{6}{3} = \mathbf{2}$

26. $\dfrac{\overset{1}{\cancel{25}}}{\underset{1}{\cancel{\underset{4}{36}}}}\cdot\dfrac{\overset{1}{\cancel{9}}}{\underset{2}{\cancel{10}}}\cdot\dfrac{\overset{1}{\cancel{\overset{2}{8}}}}{\underset{3}{\cancel{15}}} = \mathbf{\dfrac{1}{3}}$

27. $5\dfrac{2}{5}\div\dfrac{9}{10}$

$\phantom{5\dfrac{2}{5}}\downarrow\ \ \downarrow$

$\phantom{5\dfrac{2}{5}}5\ \div\ 1 = \mathbf{5}$

$5\dfrac{2}{5}\div\dfrac{9}{10} = \dfrac{\overset{3}{\cancel{27}}}{\underset{1}{\cancel{5}}}\times\dfrac{\overset{2}{\cancel{10}}}{\underset{1}{\cancel{9}}} = \mathbf{6}$

165

28. $7\frac{3}{4} + 1\frac{7}{8}$

$\downarrow \qquad \downarrow$

$8 \ + \ 2 = \mathbf{10}$

$7\frac{3}{4} = 7\frac{6}{8}$

$+ \ 1\frac{7}{8} = 1\frac{7}{8}$

$8\frac{13}{8} = \mathbf{9\frac{5}{8}}$

29.

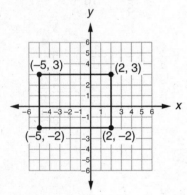

a. **(2, 3)**

b. Area $= (5 \text{ units})(7 \text{ units}) = \mathbf{35 \ units^2}$

30. a. $\overline{BC}$ (or $\overline{CB}$)

b. $\angle AOC$ (or $\angle COA$) or
$\angle BOC$ (or $\angle COB$)

c. $\angle ABC$ (or $\angle CBA$) or
$\angle BCO$ (or $\angle OCB$)

Early Finishers Solutions

$1\frac{3}{4} + 2\frac{3}{5} + 2\frac{3}{5} + 1\frac{3}{4} = 2\frac{6}{4} + 4\frac{6}{5}$

$= 3\frac{1}{2} + 5\frac{1}{5} = \mathbf{8\frac{7}{10}}$ mi

Practice Set **33**

a. $10.30 = \mathbf{10.3}$

b. $5.06 \ \mathbf{<} \ 5.60$

c. $1.1 \ \mathbf{>} \ 1.099$

d. $3.1415\underline{\textcircled{9}} \ \rightarrow \ \mathbf{3.1416}$

e. $3\underline{\textcircled{6}}5.2418 \ \longrightarrow \ 400.\cancel{0000} \ \longrightarrow \ \mathbf{400}$

f. $57.\textcircled{4}32 \ \longrightarrow \ 57.\cancel{000} \ \longrightarrow \ \mathbf{57}$

g. $10.2\cancel{000} \ \longrightarrow \ \mathbf{10.2}$

h. $8.\textcircled{6}5 \ \longrightarrow \ 9$
$\overline{2}1.\textcircled{7} \ \longrightarrow \ 22$
$1\overline{1}.\textcircled{0}38 \ \longrightarrow \ 11$

9
22
$+ \ 11$
$\overline{\mathbf{42}}$

Written Practice **33**

1. **Multiply 12 inches by 5 to find the number of inches in 5 feet. Then add 8 inches to find the total number of inches in 5 feet 8 inches.**

2.
	$\overset{46°}{7\overline{)322°}}$
42°F	
43°F	28
38°F	$\overline{42}$
47°F	42
51°F	$\overline{0}$
52°F	
+ 49°F	
$\overline{322°F}$	

3. $\overset{0 \ 11 \ 10 \ 2 \ 10 \ 10}{\cancel{1} \ \cancel{2} \ \cancel{0}, \cancel{3} \ \cancel{1} \ \cancel{0}}$ people
$- \quad \ 8 \ 7, 1 \ 9 \ 6$ people
$\overline{\quad 3 \ 3, 1 \ 1 \ 4}$ **people**

86,719 people

4.
Centimeters	Millimeters
1	10
3	30
5	50

Answers will vary. See student work.
Sample answer: 10, 100.

5. a. 24 cm ÷ 6 = 4 cm
Perimeter = (4 cm) 8 = **32 cm**

b. **A regular hexagon has 6 sides of equal length, so I divided 24 by 6 and got 4. Then I multiplied 4 by 8 because a regular octagon has 8 equal sides. I found that the octagon has a perimeter of 32 cm.**

6.

60 fish	
$\frac{2}{3}$ were not goldfish.	20 fish
	20 fish
$\frac{1}{3}$ were goldfish.	20 fish

a. **20 fish**

b. 2 × 20 fish
= **40 fish**

c. $\frac{100\%}{3}$ = **33$\frac{1}{3}$%**

7.

Area = (5 units)(5 units) = **25 units²**

8. a. 15.73⑤91 ⟶ **15.74**

b. 15.⑦3591 ⟶ 16
$\underline{3.①4} ⟶ 3$
16 × 3 = **48**

9. a. **One hundred fifty and thirty-five thousandths**

b. **Fifteen ten-thousandths**

10. a. **0.125**

b. **100.025**

11. a. 0.128 < 0.14

b. 0.03 > 0.0015

12. a. **4 cm**

b. **40 mm**

13.

14. $n \cdot 0 = \mathbf{0}$

15. $\frac{5}{27} = \frac{5}{3 \cdot 3 \cdot 3}, \frac{5}{36} = \frac{5}{2 \cdot 2 \cdot 3 \cdot 3}$
LCD = $2 \cdot 2 \cdot 3 \cdot 3 \cdot 3$ = **108**

16. $\frac{\overset{1}{\cancel{4}} \cdot \overset{9}{\cancel{18}}}{\underset{\underset{1}{2}}{\cancel{8}}} = 9$
$m = \mathbf{9}$

17. $\overset{7\ 10}{1\,\cancel{8}\,\cancel{0}}°$
$\underline{-\ 1\ 3\ 5°}$
$4\ 5°$
$a = \mathbf{45°}$

18. $\frac{3}{4} = \frac{6}{8}$
$\frac{5}{8} = \frac{5}{8}$
$\underline{+\ \frac{1}{2} = \frac{4}{8}}$
$\frac{15}{8} = \mathbf{1\frac{7}{8}}$

19. $\frac{3}{4} = \frac{9}{12}$
$\underline{-\ \frac{1}{6} = \frac{2}{12}}$
$\frac{7}{12}$

20. $4\frac{1}{2} = 4\frac{4}{8}$
$\underline{-\ \frac{3}{8} = \frac{3}{8}}$
$4\frac{1}{8}$

Saxon Math Course 2

167

Solutions

21. $\dfrac{3}{8} \cdot 2\dfrac{2}{5} \cdot 3\dfrac{1}{3}$

$= \dfrac{\overset{1}{\cancel{3}}}{\underset{2}{\underset{1}{\cancel{8}}}} \cdot \dfrac{\overset{3}{\cancel{12}}}{\underset{1}{\cancel{5}}} \cdot \dfrac{\overset{\overset{1}{\cancel{2}}}{\cancel{10}}}{\underset{1}{\cancel{3}}} = \mathbf{3}$

22. $2\dfrac{7}{10} \div 5\dfrac{2}{5} = \dfrac{27}{10} \div \dfrac{27}{5}$

$= \dfrac{27}{\underset{2}{\cancel{10}}} \times \dfrac{\overset{1}{\cancel{5}}}{\underset{1}{\cancel{27}}} = \mathbf{\dfrac{1}{2}}$

23. $5 \div 4\dfrac{1}{6} = \dfrac{5}{1} \div \dfrac{25}{6}$

$= \dfrac{\overset{1}{\cancel{5}}}{1} \times \dfrac{6}{\underset{5}{\cancel{25}}} = \dfrac{6}{5} = \mathbf{1\dfrac{1}{5}}$

24.

$\begin{array}{r} 6\dfrac{1}{2} = 6\dfrac{3}{6} \\ -\ 2\dfrac{5}{6} = 2\dfrac{5}{6} \\ \hline \end{array}$ $\quad \begin{array}{r} 5\dfrac{6}{6} + \dfrac{3}{6} \\ \hline \end{array}$ $\quad \begin{array}{r} 5\dfrac{9}{6} \\ -\ 2\dfrac{5}{6} \\ \hline 3\dfrac{4}{6} \end{array}$

$3\dfrac{4}{6} = \mathbf{3\dfrac{2}{3}}$

25. $\dfrac{1}{2} \div \dfrac{2}{3} = \dfrac{1}{2} \times \dfrac{3}{2} = \dfrac{3}{4}$

$\qquad \dfrac{3}{4} + \dfrac{3}{4} = \dfrac{6}{4} = \mathbf{1\dfrac{1}{2}}$

26. P(not ace)

$= \dfrac{\text{possible outcomes } (52 - 4 = 48)}{\text{total outcomes } (52)}$

$= \dfrac{48 \div 4}{52 \div 4} = \mathbf{\dfrac{12}{13}}$

27. a. $54 - 54 = 0$
$\qquad\qquad y = \mathbf{0}$

b. Identity property of addition

28. The quotient will be greater than 1 because a larger number is divided by a smaller number.

29. The mixed numbers are greater than 8 and 5, so the sum is greater than 13. The mixed numbers are less than 9 and 6, so the sum is less than 15.

30.

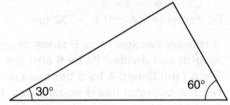

Practice Set   34

a. 1.6 cm

b. 16 mm

c. $\dfrac{1}{2}$ **mm or 0.5 mm**

d. $\dfrac{75\text{ cm}}{100\text{ cm}} =$ **0.75 meter**

e. 1.57 m $\times$ 100 cm = **157 centimeters**

f. 2.65

g. 10.01

**h. Estimates will vary. See student work.
5 cm**

i. 4.6 > 4.45

j. 2.5 cm = 25 mm

Written Practice   34

1.
$\begin{array}{r} 188\text{ raisins} \\ 212\text{ raisins} \\ +\ 203\text{ raisins} \\ \hline 603\text{ raisins} \end{array}$ $\qquad \begin{array}{r} \mathbf{201}\text{ raisins} \\ 3\overline{)603} \end{array}$

2.
$\begin{array}{r} 1698\text{ parts per cubic meter} \\ -\ 1024\text{ parts per cubic meter} \\ \hline \mathbf{674}\text{ parts per cubic meter} \end{array}$

3.
$\begin{array}{r} \$12.55 \\ +\ \ \$3.95 \\ \hline \mathbf{\$16.50} \end{array}$

4.
$$1903$$
$$+ \quad 66$$
$$\overline{1969}$$

5. Perimeter $= 6(6 \text{ inches})$
$\qquad\qquad\quad = 36 \text{ inches}$

$\dfrac{36 \text{ inches}}{4} = \textbf{9 inches}$

6. $40\% = \dfrac{40}{100} = \dfrac{\textbf{2}}{\textbf{5}}$

	$12.00
$\frac{2}{5}$ is saved.	$2.40
	$2.40
	$2.40
$\frac{3}{5}$ is not saved.	$2.40
	$2.40

a.
$$\$2.40$$
$$\times \quad 2$$
$$\overline{\$4.80}$$

b.
$$\$2.40$$
$$\times \quad 3$$
$$\overline{\$7.20}$$

7. Round the length to 22 inches and the width to 16 inches. Then multiply 22 in. × 16 in. The estimated area is 352 in.².

8. $7.493\underline{\textcircled{6}}2 \longrightarrow \textbf{7.494}$

9. a. Two hundred and two hundredths

b. One thousand, six hundred twenty-five millionths

10. a. 0.000175

b. 3030.03

11. a. $6.174 < 6.17401$

b. $14.276 > 1.4276$

12. a. 2.7 cm

b. 27 mm

13. 8.25

14.

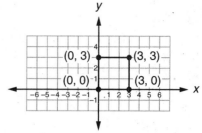

a. (3, 0)

b. Area $= (3 \text{ units})(3 \text{ units})$
$\qquad\quad = \textbf{9 units}^2$

15. a. 7.5

b. 0.75

16. $\dfrac{\overset{5}{\cancel{15}} \cdot \overset{\overset{5}{\cancel{10}}}{\cancel{20}}}{\underset{\underset{\underset{1}{2}}{\cancel{6}}}{\cancel{12}}} = 25$

$y = \textbf{25}$

17.
$$1\,\overset{7}{\cancel{8}}\,\overset{10}{\cancel{0}}^\circ$$
$$- \quad 7\,4^\circ$$
$$\overline{10\,6^\circ}$$

$c = \textbf{106}°$

18.
$$\frac{5}{6} = \frac{5}{6}$$
$$\frac{2}{3} = \frac{4}{6}$$
$$+ \; \frac{1}{2} = \frac{3}{6}$$
$$\overline{\qquad \frac{12}{6} = \textbf{2}}$$

19.
$$\frac{5}{36} = \frac{10}{72}$$
$$- \; \frac{1}{24} = \frac{3}{72}$$
$$\overline{\qquad\quad \frac{7}{72}}$$

20. $\quad 5\frac{1}{6} = 5\frac{1}{6} \qquad 4\frac{6}{6} + \frac{1}{6} \qquad 4\frac{7}{6}$

$\quad - 1\frac{2}{3} = 1\frac{4}{6} \qquad\qquad\qquad\qquad - 1\frac{4}{6}$

$\qquad\qquad\qquad\qquad\qquad\qquad\qquad\qquad \overline{3\frac{3}{6}}$

$3\frac{3}{6} = \textbf{3}\frac{\textbf{1}}{\textbf{2}}$

Solutions

21. $\frac{1}{10} \cdot 2\frac{2}{3} \cdot 3\frac{3}{4}$

$$= \frac{1}{\cancel{10}_{\cancel{5}_1}} \cdot \frac{\cancel{8}^{\;\;2}_{\;\cancel{3}_1}}{\cancel{3}_1} \cdot \frac{\cancel{15}^{\;\;5}}{\cancel{4}_1} = 1$$

22. $5\frac{1}{4} \div 1\frac{2}{3} = \frac{21}{4} \div \frac{5}{3}$

$$= \frac{21}{4} \times \frac{3}{5} = \frac{63}{20} = 3\frac{3}{20}$$

23. $3\frac{1}{5} \div 4 = \frac{16}{5} \div \frac{4}{1}$

$$= \frac{\cancel{16}^{\;4}}{5} \times \frac{1}{\cancel{4}_1} = \frac{4}{5}$$

24.
$$6\frac{7}{8} = 6\frac{7}{8}$$
$$+ 4\frac{1}{4} = 4\frac{2}{8}$$
$$\overline{\qquad\qquad 10\frac{9}{8} = 11\frac{1}{8}}$$

25. $\frac{5}{\cancel{6}_2} \cdot \frac{\cancel{3}^{\;1}}{4} = \frac{5}{8}$

$$\frac{1}{8} + \frac{5}{8} = \frac{6}{8} = \frac{3}{4}$$

26. a. $3.6\text{ cm} - 2.4\text{ cm} = \mathbf{1.2\text{ cm}}$

　　b. $36\text{ mm} - 24\text{ mm} = \mathbf{12\text{ mm}}$

27. $2^2 \cdot 2^3 = 2 \cdot 2 \cdot 2 \cdot 2 \cdot 2 = 2^5$

　　A. 2^5

28. **0.3575, 0.36, 0.365**

29. $\frac{10}{5} - 5 = 2 - 5 = \mathbf{-3}$

30.
　　　3 red marbles
　　　4 white marbles
　　$+\;$ 5 blue marbles
　　$\overline{\qquad\text{12 total}}$

　　a. $\dfrac{\text{red marbles}}{\text{total marbles}} = \dfrac{3}{12} = \dfrac{1}{4}$

　　b. $\dfrac{\text{white marbles}}{\text{total marbles}} = \dfrac{4}{12} = \dfrac{1}{3}$

c. $\dfrac{\text{blue marbles}}{\text{total marbles}} = \dfrac{5}{12}$

d. $\dfrac{\text{green marbles}}{\text{total marbles}} = \dfrac{0}{12} = \mathbf{0}$

Early Finishers Solutions

a.

5.00 m　　　5.10 m　　　5.20 m

b. Answers will vary. Some possible answers are:

- The range was $5.22 - 4.99 = 0.23$ m.
- The median jump length was 5.12 m.
- Most of James' jumps were between 5.09 m and 5.17 m.

Practice Set 35

a.
$$\begin{array}{r} \overset{1}{}1.2 \\ 3.45 \\ +\;23.6 \\ \hline \mathbf{28.25} \end{array}$$

b.
$$\begin{array}{r} \overset{1}{}4.5 \\ 0.51 \\ \overset{1}{}6 \\ +\;12.4 \\ \hline \mathbf{23.41} \end{array}$$

c. Perimeter $= 0.6\text{ m} + 0.6\text{ m} + 0.4\text{ m} + 0.4\text{ m} =$
$$\begin{array}{r} \overset{2}{}0.6 \\ 0.6 \\ 0.4 \\ +\;0.4 \\ \hline 2.0 = \mathbf{2\text{ meters}} \end{array}$$

d.
$$\begin{array}{r} 8.\overset{4}{\cancel{5}}\overset{12}{\cancel{2}}\text{ seconds} \\ -\;8.4\;6\text{ seconds} \\ \hline \mathbf{0.0\;6\text{ seconds}} \end{array}$$

e.
$$\begin{array}{r} 1\overset{5}{\cancel{6}}.\overset{16}{\cancel{7}}\;\overset{9}{\cancel{0}}{}^1 0 \\ -\;\;\;\;1.9\;3\;6 \\ \hline \mathbf{1\,4.7\;6\;4} \end{array}$$

f.

$$\begin{array}{r} {\scriptstyle 1\ \ 9\ \ 9} \\ 1\ 2.\ \cancel{0}\ \cancel{0}^{1}0 \\ -\ \ \ 0.\ 8\ 7\ 5 \\ \hline 1\ 1.\ 1\ 2\ 5 \end{array}$$

g.

$$\begin{array}{r} 4.20 \\ \times\ 0.24 \\ \hline 1680 \\ 840 \\ \hline 1.0080\ =\ \textbf{1.008} \end{array}$$

h.

$$\begin{array}{r} 0.06 \\ \times\ 0.06 \\ \hline \textbf{0.0036} \end{array}$$

i. 1 in. = 2.54 cm

$$\begin{array}{r} 2.54 \\ \times\ \ \ \ 6 \\ \hline 15.24 \end{array}\qquad \textbf{15.24 cm}$$

j. $3 \times 2 \times 1 = 6$

$0\underset{\curvearrowleft}{.}6 \longrightarrow \textbf{0.006}$

k.

$$\begin{array}{r} 0.04 \\ \times\ \ \ 10 \\ \hline 00 \\ 04 \\ \hline 0.40 \longrightarrow\ \textbf{0.4} \end{array}$$

l. Area = 1.2 cm × 0.8 cm = **0.96 cm²**

$$\begin{array}{r} 1.2 \\ \times\ 0.8 \\ \hline 0.96 \end{array}$$

m.

$$\begin{array}{r} \textbf{2.4} \\ 6\overline{)14.4} \\ \underline{12} \\ 2\ 4 \\ \underline{2\ 4} \\ 0 \end{array}$$

n.

$$\begin{array}{r} \textbf{0.006} \\ 8\overline{)0.048} \\ \underline{48} \\ 0 \end{array}$$

o.

$$\begin{array}{r} \textbf{0.68} \\ 5\overline{)3.40} \\ \underline{3\ 0} \\ 40 \\ \underline{40} \\ 0 \end{array}$$

p.

$$\begin{array}{r} \textbf{0.05} \\ 6\overline{)0.30} \\ \underline{30} \\ 0 \end{array}$$

q. Length of side = 0.6 m ÷ 4 = **0.15 meters**

$$\begin{array}{r} 0.15 \\ 4\overline{)0.60} \\ \underline{4} \\ 20 \\ \underline{20} \\ 0 \end{array}$$

Written Practice 35

1. Add all the bills together and divide by 6.

2.

$$\begin{array}{r} 2\frac{1}{2} = 2\frac{2}{4} \\ -\ 1\frac{3}{4} = 1\frac{3}{4} \end{array} \longrightarrow \begin{array}{r} 1\frac{6}{4} \\ -\ 1\frac{3}{4} \\ \hline \frac{3}{4}\ \text{gallon} \end{array}$$

3.

$$\begin{array}{r} \$1.30 \\ 12\overline{)\$15.60} \\ \underline{12} \\ 3\ 6 \\ \underline{3\ 6} \\ 00 \\ \underline{00} \\ 0 \end{array} \qquad \begin{array}{r} \$1.75 \\ -\ \$1.30 \\ \hline \textbf{\$0.45} \end{array}$$

4. 1 minute = 60 seconds
60 seconds + 22 seconds = 82 seconds
82 seconds − 27 seconds = **55 seconds**

5. Perimeter = 5(16 cm) = 80 cm

$$\frac{80\ \text{cm}}{4} = \textbf{20 cm}$$

6. a. $\frac{1}{11} \times 110 = \frac{110}{11} = \textbf{10}$

b. 110 − 10 = **100**

7. a. Area $= (10 \text{ cm})(10 \text{ cm}) = $ **100 cm²**

   b. Area $= (6 \text{ cm})(6 \text{ cm}) = $ **36 cm²**

   c. Area $= 100 \text{ cm}^2 - 36 \text{ cm}^2$
             $= $ **64 cm²**

8. a. $\dfrac{99}{100}$

   b. **0.99**

   c. $\dfrac{99}{100} = $ **99%**

9.

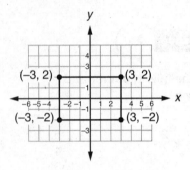

   a. **(3, 2)**

   b. Area $= (4 \text{ units})(6 \text{ units})$
             $= $ **24 units²**

10. a. **One hundred and seventy-five thousandths**

    b. **0.00025**

11. a. **3.5 centimeters**

    b. **35 millimeters**

12. a. 10.38 gallons → 10 gallons

        $\$2.28 \dfrac{9}{10} \rightarrow \$2.30$

           2.30
          $\times$ 10
       $\overline{}$
       $23.00

    b. **No. They give their prices this way so they seem 1¢ cheaper than they really are.**

13. 3.37

14. 0.5 × 0.7 = 0.35

15. a. Perimeter $= 0.4 \text{ m} + 0.4 \text{ m}$
                      $+ 0.2 \text{ m} + 0.2 \text{ m}$
                 $= $ **1.2 meters**

    b. Area $= 0.4 \text{ m} \times 0.2 \text{ m} = $ **0.08 meters²**

16. $\dfrac{\overset{3}{\cancel{9}} \cdot \overset{2}{\cancel{10}}}{\underset{\underset{1}{\cancel{3}}}{15}} = 6 \qquad x = $ **6**

17. $\begin{array}{r} 5.83 \\ -\ 4.6 \\ \hline 1.23 \end{array}$
     $f = $ **1.23**

18. $\begin{array}{r} 5.8 \\ 8\overline{)46.4} \\ 40 \\ \hline 6\ 4 \\ 6\ 4 \\ \hline 0 \end{array}$
     $y = $ **5.8**

19. $\begin{array}{r} 12 \\ +\ 3.4 \\ \hline 15.4 \end{array}$
     $w = $ **15.4**

20. $\begin{array}{r} \overset{1}{3}.65 \\ 0.9 \\ \overset{1}{8} \\ +\ 15.23 \\ \hline 27.78 \end{array}$

21. $\begin{array}{r} 1\frac{1}{2} = 1\frac{6}{12} \\ 2\frac{2}{3} = 2\frac{8}{12} \\ +\ 3\frac{3}{4} = 3\frac{9}{12} \\ \hline 6\frac{23}{12} = 7\frac{11}{12} \end{array}$

22. $1\dfrac{1}{2} \cdot 2\dfrac{2}{3} \cdot 3\dfrac{3}{4} = \dfrac{\overset{1}{\cancel{3}}}{\underset{1}{\cancel{2}}} \cdot \dfrac{\overset{\overset{2}{\cancel{\cancel{8}}}}{}}{\underset{1}{\cancel{3}}} \cdot \dfrac{15}{\underset{1}{\cancel{4}}} = $ **15**

23.

$$\frac{1}{2} = \frac{3}{6}$$
$$+ \frac{1}{3} = \frac{2}{6}$$
$$\frac{5}{6}$$

$$1\frac{1}{6} \longrightarrow \frac{7}{6}$$
$$- \frac{5}{6} \qquad - \frac{5}{6}$$
$$\frac{2}{6} = \frac{1}{3}$$

24.

$$3\frac{1}{12} = 3\frac{1}{12} \longrightarrow 2\frac{13}{12}$$
$$- 1\frac{3}{4} = 1\frac{9}{12} \qquad - 1\frac{9}{12}$$
$$1\frac{4}{12}$$

$$1\frac{4}{12} = 1\frac{1}{3}$$

25.

$$\begin{array}{r} 0.12 \\ 10\overline{)1.20} \\ \underline{1\ 0} \\ 20 \\ \underline{20} \\ 0 \end{array}$$

26. $3 \times 4 \times 5 = 60$
$0.60 \longrightarrow \textbf{0.06}$

27. Identity property of multiplication

28. a.

Inches	Centimeters
1	2.54
2	5.08
3	7.62
4	10.16

For every 1 inch there are 2.54 cm

b. Multiply the number in the left (Inches) column by 2.54 to get the number in the right column.

29. a. $36.45 - 4.912$
$$\downarrow \qquad \qquad \downarrow$$
$$36 \quad - \quad 5 = \textbf{31}$$

$$\begin{array}{r} 3\overset{5}{\cancel{6}}.\overset{1}{4}\overset{4}{\cancel{5}}{}^{1}0 \\ - \quad 4.9\,1\,2 \\ \hline 3\,1.5\,3\,8 \end{array}$$

b. 4.2×0.9
$$\downarrow \qquad \qquad \downarrow$$
$$4 \quad \times \quad 1 = \textbf{4}$$
$$\begin{array}{r} 4.2 \\ \times\ 0.9 \\ \hline \textbf{3.78} \end{array}$$

30.

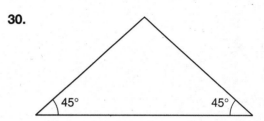

Early Finishers Solutions

a. $3 + 3 + 4 + 1 + 1 = \$12$

b. $2.99 + 3.09 + 3.89 + 1.23 + 1.29 = \$12.49$;
Her estimate is under by \$0.49.

She could round each price up to make sure the total is an overestimate.

Practice Set 36

a. $\dfrac{\text{big fish}}{\text{little fish}} = \dfrac{90}{240} = \dfrac{3}{8}$

b.
$$\begin{array}{l} \text{14 girls} \\ + \text{? boys} \\ \hline \text{30 total} \end{array} \longrightarrow \begin{array}{l} \text{14 girls} \\ + \text{16 boys} \\ \hline \text{30 total} \end{array}$$

$$\frac{\text{boys}}{\text{girls}} = \frac{16}{14} = \frac{8}{7}$$

c.
$$\begin{array}{l} \text{3 won} \\ + \text{? lost} \\ \hline \text{8 total} \end{array} \longrightarrow \begin{array}{l} \text{3 won} \\ + \text{5 lost} \\ \hline \text{8 total} \end{array}$$

$$\frac{\text{won}}{\text{lost}} = \frac{3}{5}$$

d.
$$\begin{array}{l} \text{5 red marbles} \\ + \text{3 blue marbles} \\ \hline \text{8 total} \end{array}$$

$$\frac{\text{blue marbles}}{\text{total marbles}} = \frac{3}{8}$$

e. Sample space

Solutions

f.

```
      Penny   Nickel
              H
        H  <
              T
              H
        T  <
              T
```

Sample space = **{HH, HT, TH, TT}**

g.

```
           1
      H  < 2
           3

           1
      T  < 2
           3
```

Sample space = **{H1, H2, H3, T1, T2, T3}**

h. $P(T1, T2) = \dfrac{2}{6} = \dfrac{1}{3}$

i. Sample space 2 is better than sample space 1 because sample space 2 shows all 36 equally likely outcomes.

$P(7) = \dfrac{6}{36} = \dfrac{1}{6}$

Written Practice   36

1. $\dfrac{|\{\text{Mobile, San Francisco, Portland, San Juan}\}|}{|\{\text{Honolulu, Salt Lake City}\}|}$

$= \dfrac{4}{2} = \dfrac{2}{1}$ (or 2 to 1)

2. $\dfrac{66.3 + 20.1 + 18.3 + 45.8 + 50.8 + 16.5}{6}$

$= \dfrac{217.8}{6} = $ **36.3 inches**

3.
```
   35 pages
 ×  7
  245 pages
```

4.
```
   59.48 seconds
 − 56.24 seconds
    3.24 seconds
```

5. $40\% = \dfrac{40}{100} = \dfrac{2}{5}$

```
                      30 players
  2/5 had never    ┌ 6 players
      played       │ 6 players
      rugby.       ┤ 6 players
  3/5 had          │ 6 players
      played       └ 6 players
      rugby.
```

a. 2×6 players = **12 players**

b. $\dfrac{\text{had played}}{\text{had not played}} = \dfrac{3}{2}$

6. One way to find *BC* in millimeters is to first convert *AB* to 40 mm and *AC* to 95 mm. Then subtract 40 mm from 95 mm.

7. Length = 8 cm + 5 cm = 13 cm

a. Area = (8 cm)(13 cm) = **104 cm²**

b. Perimeter = 8 cm + 8 cm + 13 cm + 13 cm = **42 cm**

8. 1014 mm → 1000 mm
936 mm → 900 mm
390 mm → 400 mm
Perimeter = 1000 mm + 900 mm + 400 mm = **2300 mm**

9. a. 6.857_①42 ⟶ **6.857**

b. 6.8571420 ⟶ 7
1.9870 ⟶ 2
7 × 2 = **14**

10. a. **12,000,000**

b. **0.000012**

11.

```
           1
           2
      H  < 3
           4
           5
           6

           1
           2
      T  < 3
           4
           5
           6
```

Sample space = {H1, H2, H3, H4, H5, H6, T1, T2, T3, T4, T5, T6}

$P(H, \text{even}) = \dfrac{3}{12} = \dfrac{1}{4}$

12. a. 4.2 cm

   b. 42 mm

13. 13.56

14. a. $85\% = \dfrac{85}{100} = \dfrac{\mathbf{17}}{\mathbf{20}}$

   b. $\dfrac{144}{600} = \dfrac{\overset{1}{\cancel{2}} \cdot \overset{1}{\cancel{2}} \cdot \overset{1}{\cancel{2}} \cdot 2 \cdot \overset{1}{\cancel{3}} \cdot 3}{\underset{1}{\cancel{2}} \cdot \underset{1}{\cancel{2}} \cdot \underset{1}{\cancel{2}} \cdot \underset{1}{\cancel{3}} \cdot 5 \cdot 5} = \dfrac{\mathbf{6}}{\mathbf{25}}$

15. Estimate: $6\dfrac{3}{4}$ **hr** or **7 hr**
   $11 per hour
   $11 × 7 hr = $77
   She earned a little less than $77.

16. a. $\angle MPN$ (or $\angle NPM$)

   b. $\angle LPM$ (or $\angle MPL$)

   c. $\angle LPN$ (or $\angle NPL$)

17. $8y = 12^2$

   $8y = 144$

   $y = \mathbf{18}$

$$\begin{array}{r} 18 \\ 8\overline{)144} \\ \underline{8} \\ 64 \\ \underline{64} \\ 0 \end{array}$$

18.
$$\begin{array}{r} 1.2 \\ \times\quad 4 \\ \hline 4.8 \end{array}$$
   $w = \mathbf{4.8}$

19. $4.27 + 16.3 + 10$
   $\downarrow \qquad \downarrow \qquad \downarrow$
   $4 \;+\; 16 + 10 = \mathbf{30}$

$$\begin{array}{r} {}_{1}4.27 \\ 16.3 \\ +\,10. \\ \hline \mathbf{30.57} \end{array}$$

20. $4.2 - 0.42$
   $\downarrow \qquad \downarrow$
   $4 \;-\; 0 = \mathbf{4}$

$$\begin{array}{r} \overset{3}{\cancel{4}}.\,\overset{1}{2}{}^{1}0 \\ -\,0.\,4\,2 \\ \hline \mathbf{3.\,7\,8} \end{array}$$

21.
$$\begin{aligned} 3\tfrac{1}{2} &= 3\tfrac{6}{12} \\ 1\tfrac{1}{3} &= 1\tfrac{4}{12} \\ +\,2\tfrac{1}{4} &= 2\tfrac{3}{12} \\ \hline 6\tfrac{13}{12} &= \mathbf{7\tfrac{1}{12}} \end{aligned}$$

22. $3\tfrac{1}{2} \cdot 1\tfrac{1}{3} \cdot 2\tfrac{1}{4}$

$= \dfrac{7}{2} \cdot \dfrac{\overset{1}{\cancel{4}}}{\underset{1}{\cancel{3}}} \cdot \dfrac{\overset{3}{\cancel{9}}}{\underset{1}{\cancel{4}}} = \dfrac{21}{2} = \mathbf{10\tfrac{1}{2}}$

23.
$$\begin{aligned} \tfrac{2}{3} &= \tfrac{4}{6} \\ -\,\tfrac{1}{2} &= \tfrac{3}{6} \\ \hline &\tfrac{1}{6} \end{aligned}$$

   $3\tfrac{5}{6} - \tfrac{1}{6} = 3\tfrac{4}{6} = \mathbf{3\tfrac{2}{3}}$

24.
$$\begin{aligned} 8\tfrac{5}{12} &= 8\tfrac{5}{12} \longrightarrow \quad 7\tfrac{17}{12} \\ -\,3\tfrac{2}{3} &= 3\tfrac{8}{12} \qquad\qquad -\,3\tfrac{8}{12} \\ \hline &\qquad\qquad\qquad\quad 4\tfrac{9}{12} = \mathbf{4\tfrac{3}{4}} \end{aligned}$$

25. $2\tfrac{3}{4} \div 4\tfrac{1}{2} = \dfrac{11}{4} \div \dfrac{9}{2}$

$= \dfrac{11}{\underset{2}{\cancel{4}}} \times \dfrac{\overset{1}{\cancel{2}}}{9} = \dfrac{\mathbf{11}}{\mathbf{18}}$

26. $\dfrac{2}{3} \div \dfrac{1}{2} = \dfrac{2}{3} \times \dfrac{2}{1} = \dfrac{4}{3} = 1\tfrac{1}{3}$

$$\begin{aligned} 5 &\longrightarrow \quad 4\tfrac{3}{3} \\ -\,1\tfrac{1}{3} &\qquad\quad -\,1\tfrac{1}{3} \\ \hline &\qquad\qquad\quad \mathbf{3\tfrac{2}{3}} \end{aligned}$$

27.
$$\begin{array}{r} \mathbf{0.175} \\ 8\overline{)1.400} \\ \underline{8} \\ 60 \\ \underline{56} \\ 40 \\ \underline{40} \\ 0 \end{array}$$

Solutions

28. $2 \times 3 \times 4 = 24$

$0.\underset{\frown}{24} \longrightarrow$ **0.024**

29. a.
$$\begin{array}{r} 12.25 \\ \times \quad 10 \\ \hline 122.50 \end{array} = \textbf{122.5}$$

b.
$$10)\overline{12.250} \quad \textbf{1.225}$$
$$\underline{10}$$
$$2\,2$$
$$\underline{2\,0}$$
$$25$$
$$\underline{20}$$
$$50$$
$$\underline{50}$$
$$0$$

30. Answers may vary. See student work.
Sample answer:

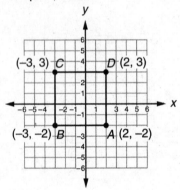

Coordinates: **A (2, −2), B (−3, −2),
C (−3, 3), D (2, 3)**

Early Finishers Solutions

a. $\dfrac{4}{3} = \dfrac{12}{9}$; There are 12 girls.

b. The eight students she asked.

c. 12 girls + 9 boys = 21 students.

Practice Set (37)

a. Area $= \dfrac{5 \text{ cm} \cdot 12 \text{ cm}}{2} = \dfrac{60 \text{ cm}^2}{2}$

   $= \textbf{30 cm}^2$

b. Area $= \dfrac{12 \text{ cm} \cdot 8 \text{ cm}}{2} = \dfrac{96 \text{ cm}^2}{2}$

   $= \textbf{48 cm}^2$

c. Area $= \dfrac{6 \text{ cm} \cdot 6 \text{ cm}}{2} = \dfrac{36 \text{ cm}^2}{2}$

   $= \textbf{18 cm}^2$

d.

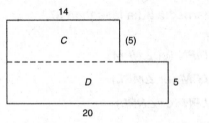

Area $A = 14 \text{ m} \times 10 \text{ m} = 140 \text{ m}^2$
$+ \text{ Area } B = \quad 6 \text{ m} \times \quad 5 \text{ m} = \quad 30 \text{ m}^2$
$\overline{\qquad\qquad\qquad\qquad \text{Total} = \textbf{170 m}^2}$

or

Area $C = 14 \text{ m} \times 5 \text{ m} = \quad 70 \text{ m}^2$
$+ \text{ Area } D = 20 \text{ m} \times 5 \text{ m} = 100 \text{ m}^2$
$\overline{\qquad\qquad\qquad\qquad \text{Total} = \textbf{170 m}^2}$

e. Area of rectangle $= 10 \text{ in.} \times 12 \text{ in.}$

   $= 120 \text{ in.}^2$

Area of square $= 4 \text{ in.} \times 4 \text{ in.} = 16 \text{ in.}^2$

Area of hexagon $= 120 \text{ in.}^2 - 16 \text{ in.}^2$

   $= \textbf{104 in.}^2$

f.

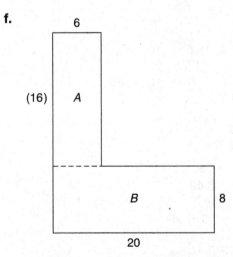

Area $A = 16 \text{ in.} \times 6 \text{ in.} = \quad 96 \text{ in.}^2$
$+ \text{ Area } B = 20 \text{ in.} \times 8 \text{ in.} = 160 \text{ in.}^2$
$\overline{\qquad\qquad\qquad\qquad \text{Total} = \textbf{256 in.}^2}$

or

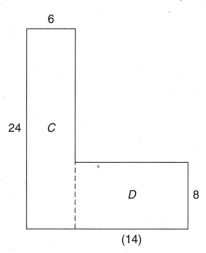

(14)

$$Area\ C\ =\ 24\ \text{in.}\ \times\ 6\ \text{in.}\ =\ 144\ \text{in.}^2$$
$$+\ Area\ D\ =\ 14\ \text{in.}\ \times\ 8\ \text{in.}\ =\ 112\ \text{in.}^2$$
$$Total\ =\ \textbf{256 in.}^2$$

g. Answers will vary but should describe either the addition method used in new concepts, example 3, or the subtraction method used in example 4.

h. $A = \frac{1}{2}bh$; $A = \frac{bh}{2}$

Written Practice 37

1.
$$\begin{array}{ccc} 2\ \text{won} & & 2\ \text{won} \\ +\ ?\ \text{lost} & \longrightarrow & +\ 1\ \text{lost} \\ \hline 3\ \text{total} & & 3\ \text{total} \end{array}$$
$$\frac{\text{won}}{\text{lost}} = \frac{2}{1}$$

2.
$$\begin{array}{r} \overset{3}{47} \\ 53 \\ 62 \\ 56 \\ 46 \\ +\ 48 \\ \hline 312\ \text{cars} \end{array} \qquad \begin{array}{r} \textbf{52 cars} \\ 6\overline{)312\ \text{cars}} \\ \underline{30} \\ 12 \\ \underline{12} \\ 0 \end{array}$$

3.
$$\begin{array}{r} \overset{2}{11.6}\ \text{seconds} \\ 11.3\ \text{seconds} \\ 11.2\ \text{seconds} \\ +\ 10.9\ \text{seconds} \\ \hline 45.0\ \text{seconds}\ =\ \textbf{45 seconds} \end{array}$$

4. Subtract $1.30 from $10 to find how much the 3 gallons of milk cost. Then divide that number by 3 to find how much each gallon cost.

5.
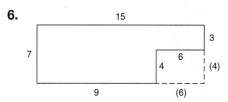

$\frac{2}{3}$ were sold.

$\frac{1}{3}$ were not sold.

a. 2×6 muffins = **12 muffins**

b. **6 muffins**

6.

Perimeter $= 15\ \text{in.}\ +\ 7\ \text{in.}\ +\ 9\ \text{in.}\ +\ 4\ \text{in.}$
$+\ 6\ \text{in.}\ +\ 3\ \text{in.}\ =\ \textbf{44 in.}$

7.
$$\begin{aligned} Area\ of\ large\ rectangle\ &=\ 7\ \text{in.}\ \times\ 15\ \text{in.} \\ &=\ 105\ \text{in.}^2 \\ -\ Area\ of\ small\ rectangle\ &=\ 6\ \text{in.}\ \times\ 4\ \text{in.} \\ &=\ 24\ \text{in.}^2 \\ \hline Area\ of\ figure\ &=\ \textbf{81 in.}^2 \end{aligned}$$

8. a. $\frac{5}{6} \cdot \frac{3}{3} = \frac{15}{18}$

b. $\frac{9 \div 3}{24 \div 3} = \frac{3}{8}$

c. $\frac{3}{4} \cdot \frac{5}{5} = \frac{15}{20}$

9. a. **0.49**

b. **0.51**

c. $\frac{51}{100} = \textbf{51%}$

10. a. $3184.56\textcircled{4}1 \longrightarrow$
3184.56

b. $31\textcircled{8}4.5641 \longrightarrow$
$3200.\cancel{0000}$
$\longrightarrow$ **3200**

11. a. **Twenty-five hundred-thousandths**

b. **60.07**

12. a. $2\% = \dfrac{2}{100} = \dfrac{1}{50}$

b. $\dfrac{720}{1080} = \dfrac{\overset{1}{\cancel{2}} \cdot \overset{1}{\cancel{2}} \cdot \overset{1}{\cancel{2}} \cdot 2 \cdot \overset{1}{\cancel{3}} \cdot \overset{1}{\cancel{3}} \cdot 5}{\underset{1}{\cancel{2}} \cdot \underset{1}{\cancel{2}} \cdot \underset{1}{\cancel{2}} \cdot \underset{1}{\cancel{3}} \cdot \underset{1}{\cancel{3}} \cdot 3 \cdot \underset{1}{\cancel{5}}} = \dfrac{2}{3}$

13. $\overline{BC} = \overline{AC} - \overline{AB}$

$\overline{AC} = 2\dfrac{7}{8}$ in., $\overline{AB} = 1\dfrac{3}{4}$ in.

$$2\dfrac{7}{8} \rightarrow 2\dfrac{7}{8}$$
$$-1\dfrac{3}{4} \rightarrow 1\dfrac{6}{8}$$
$$\overline{\qquad\qquad 1\dfrac{1}{8} \text{ in.}}$$

14. One possibility:

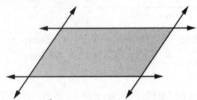

15. a. Perimeter $= 15\,\text{cm} + 15\,\text{cm} + 18\,\text{cm}$
$= \textbf{48 cm}$

b. Area $= \dfrac{18\,\text{cm} \cdot 12\,\text{cm}}{2} = \textbf{108 cm}^2$

16.

0.2	0.2
+ 0.3	× 0.3
0.5	0.06

0.5 > 0.06

17.
A ⟨ A B C

B ⟨ A B C

C ⟨ A B C

a. Sample space = {AA, AB, AC, BA, BB, BC, CA, CB, CC}

b. P(A at least once) $= \dfrac{5}{9}$

18. $\dfrac{7 \cdot \overset{2}{\cancel{8}}}{\underset{1}{\cancel{4}}} = 14 \qquad x = \textbf{14}$

19.
$$\begin{array}{r} \overset{3}{\cancel{4}}.^{1}2 \\ -\ 1.7 \\ \hline \textbf{2.5} \end{array}$$

20.
$$\begin{array}{r} 0.45 \\ +\ 3.6 \\ \hline \textbf{4.05} \end{array}$$

21.
$$\begin{array}{r} 1.5 \\ 3\overline{)4.5} \\ \underline{3} \\ 1\,5 \\ \underline{1\,5} \\ 0 \end{array}$$

22. $\dfrac{3}{5} \cdot 12 \cdot 4\dfrac{1}{6} = \dfrac{3}{\underset{1}{\cancel{5}}} \cdot \dfrac{\overset{2}{\cancel{12}}}{1} \cdot \dfrac{\overset{5}{\cancel{25}}}{\underset{1}{\cancel{6}}}$

$= \textbf{30}$

23.
$$\dfrac{5}{6} = \dfrac{10}{12}$$
$$1\dfrac{3}{4} = 1\dfrac{9}{12}$$
$$+\ 2\dfrac{1}{2} = 2\dfrac{6}{12}$$
$$\overline{\qquad 3\dfrac{25}{12} = 5\dfrac{1}{12}}$$

24.
$$\dfrac{5}{8} = \dfrac{5}{8}$$
$$\dfrac{1}{2} = \dfrac{4}{8}$$
$$+\ \dfrac{3}{8} = \dfrac{3}{8}$$
$$\overline{\qquad \dfrac{12}{8} = 1\dfrac{1}{2}}$$

25.
$$3\dfrac{9}{20} = 3\dfrac{27}{60}$$
$$-\ 1\dfrac{5}{12} = 1\dfrac{25}{60}$$
$$\overline{\qquad 2\dfrac{2}{60} = 2\dfrac{1}{30}}$$

26. $\dfrac{a}{b} = a \div b = 3\dfrac{1}{3} \div 5$

$= \dfrac{10}{3} \div \dfrac{5}{1} = \dfrac{\overset{2}{\cancel{10}}}{3} \times \dfrac{1}{\underset{1}{\cancel{5}}} = \dfrac{2}{3}$

27. $2 \cdot 2 \cdot 2 \cdot 2 \cdot 2 \cdot 2 = 2^6$

28. **a.**
$$\begin{array}{r} 0.25 \\ \times \quad 10 \\ \hline 2.50 \end{array} = \mathbf{2.5}$$

b.
$$\begin{array}{r} \mathbf{0.025} \\ 10\overline{)0.250} \\ \underline{20} \\ 50 \\ \underline{50} \\ 0 \end{array}$$

29. **Fourth quadrant**

30. **About 50 miles**

Practice Set 38

a. January: 4×100 tires $= 400$ tires
February: 6×100 tires $= 600$ tires
$$\begin{array}{r} 600 \text{ tires} \\ - \quad 400 \text{ tires} \\ \hline \mathbf{200 \text{ tires}} \end{array}$$

b.
$$\begin{array}{r} 5000 \text{ cans} \\ 8000 \text{ cans} \\ 9000 \text{ cans} \\ + \quad 4000 \text{ cans} \\ \hline \mathbf{26,000 \text{ cans}} \end{array}$$

c. **Game 4**

d. $\dfrac{4}{24} = \dfrac{\mathbf{1}}{\mathbf{6}}$

e. **Circle graph**

f. **Line graph**

g. **Bar graph**

Written Practice 38

1.
$$\begin{array}{r} 7 \text{ joggers} \\ + \quad 3 \text{ walkers} \\ \hline 10 \text{ total} \end{array}$$
$$\dfrac{\text{walkers}}{\text{total}} = \dfrac{\mathbf{3}}{\mathbf{10}}$$

2.
$$\begin{array}{r} \mathbf{115 \text{ pages}} \\ 3\overline{)345} \text{ pages} \\ \underline{3} \\ 04 \\ \underline{3} \\ 15 \\ \underline{15} \\ 0 \end{array}$$

3. 5 minutes $= 5(60 \text{ seconds})$
$= 300$ seconds
$$\begin{array}{r} 300 \text{ seconds} \\ + \quad 52 \text{ seconds} \\ \hline \mathbf{352 \text{ seconds}} \end{array}$$

4.
$$\begin{array}{r} 9000 \text{ cans} \\ - \quad 4000 \text{ cans} \\ \hline \mathbf{5000 \text{ cans}} \end{array}$$

5.
$$\begin{array}{r} 60 \\ 70 \\ 75 \\ 70 \\ 80 \\ 85 \\ + \quad 85 \\ \hline 525 \end{array} \qquad \begin{array}{r} \mathbf{75} \\ 7\overline{)525} \\ \underline{49} \\ 35 \\ \underline{35} \\ 0 \end{array}$$

175

6. **Answers will vary. See student work. Sample answer: By how many points did Paul improve from Test 1 to Test 6?**

7.

384 pages	
Mira read $\dfrac{3}{8}$	48 pages
	48 pages
	48 pages
Mira did not read $\dfrac{5}{8}$	48 pages
	48 pages
	48 pages
	48 pages
	48 pages

a. 3×48 pages $= \mathbf{144 \text{ pages}}$

b. Half $= \dfrac{4}{8}$, Already read $= \dfrac{3}{8}$

$\dfrac{4}{8} - \dfrac{3}{8} = \dfrac{1}{8}$ left to read $\rightarrow$ **48 pages**

Solutions

8.

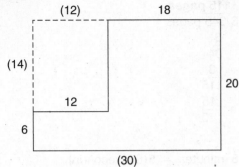

a. Area of large rectangle = 30 in. × 20 in.
$$= 600 \text{ in}^2$$
Area of small rectangle = 12 in. × 14 in.
$$= 168 \text{ in.}^2$$
Area of figure = 600 in.² − 168 in.²
$$= \textbf{432 in.}^2$$

b. Perimeter = 18 in. + 20 in. + 30 in.
+ 6 in. + 12 in. + 14 in.
$$= \textbf{100 in.}$$

9. a. $\dfrac{7}{9} \cdot \dfrac{2}{2} = \dfrac{\mathbf{14}}{\mathbf{18}}$

b. $\dfrac{20}{36} \div \dfrac{4}{4} = \dfrac{\mathbf{5}}{\mathbf{9}}$

c. $\dfrac{4}{5} \cdot \dfrac{6}{6} = \dfrac{\mathbf{24}}{\mathbf{30}}$

d. **Identity property of multiplication**

10. a. 2⑨86.34157 $\longrightarrow$
3000.00000 $\longrightarrow$ **3000**

b. 2986.341⑤7 $\longrightarrow$ **2986.342**

11. Probability of stopping on

$1 = \dfrac{3}{8}$

$2 = \dfrac{2}{8} = \dfrac{1}{4}$

$3 = \dfrac{2}{8} = \dfrac{1}{4}$

$4 = \dfrac{1}{8}$

a. **1**

b. **4**

c. **Sample space 2 is better because it lists the outcomes that are equally likely.**

12. a. **1.2 cm**

b. **12 mm**

13. 10 mm = 1 cm
Perimeter = 1.2 cm + 1 cm + 1.2 cm
+ 1 cm = **4.4 cm**

14. The number 3.4 is about halfway between 3 and 4. Point *B* is too close to 3 to represent 3.4. So the best choice is point *C.*

15. a. $\overline{AC}$ (or $\overline{CA}$)

b. $\overline{BC}$ (or $\overline{CB}$)

16. a. Area = $\dfrac{6 \text{ cm} \cdot 6 \text{ cm}}{2} = \textbf{18 cm}^2$

b. Area = $\dfrac{6 \text{ cm} \cdot 6 \text{ cm}}{2} = \textbf{18 cm}^2$

c. Area = 18 cm² + 18 cm² = **36 cm²**

17.
$$\begin{array}{r} 6.7 \\ -\ 4.3 \\ \hline 2.4 \end{array}$$
$a = \textbf{2.4}$

18.
$$\begin{array}{r} \overset{1}{4.7} \\ +\ 3.6 \\ \hline 8.3 \end{array}$$
$m = \textbf{8.3}$

19.
$$\begin{array}{r} 0.45 \\ 10\overline{)4.50} \\ \underline{4\,0} \\ 50 \\ \underline{50} \\ 0 \end{array}$$
$w = \textbf{0.45}$

20.
$$\begin{array}{r} 2.5 \\ \times\ 2.5 \\ \hline 125 \\ 50\ \ \\ \hline 6.25 \end{array}$$
$x = \textbf{6.25}$

21.
$$\begin{array}{r} {}_1^{}5.37 \\ 27.7 \\ +\ \ 4. \\ \hline 37.07 \end{array}$$

22.
$$\begin{array}{r} 0.25 \\ 5\overline{)1.25} \\ \underline{10} \\ 25 \\ \underline{25} \\ 0 \end{array}$$

23. $\frac{5}{9} \cdot 6 \cdot 2\frac{1}{10}$

$$\frac{\overset{1}{\cancel{5}}}{\underset{1}{\cancel{9}}} \cdot \frac{\overset{2}{\cancel{6}}}{1} \cdot \frac{\overset{7}{\cancel{21}}}{\underset{1}{\cancel{10}}} = \mathbf{7}$$

24.
$$\begin{array}{r} \frac{5}{8} = \frac{5}{8} \\ \frac{3}{4} = \frac{6}{8} \\ +\frac{1}{2} = \frac{4}{8} \\ \hline \frac{15}{8} = \mathbf{1\frac{7}{8}} \end{array}$$

25. $5 \div 3\frac{1}{3} = \frac{5}{1} \div \frac{10}{3} = \frac{\overset{1}{\cancel{5}}}{1} \times \frac{3}{\underset{2}{\cancel{10}}}$

$$= \frac{3}{2} = \mathbf{1\frac{1}{2}}$$

26.
$$\begin{array}{r} \frac{1}{2} = \frac{5}{10} \\ -\frac{1}{5} = \frac{2}{10} \\ \hline \frac{3}{10} \end{array}$$

$$\frac{3}{10} - \frac{3}{10} = \mathbf{0}$$

27. A. $4 \cdot 4^2$

28. a. 125 mL

b.
$$\begin{array}{r} 1000 \text{ mL} \\ - 125 \text{ mL} \\ \hline \mathbf{875 \text{ mL}} \end{array}$$

29. Switch 916.42 and 916.37

30.

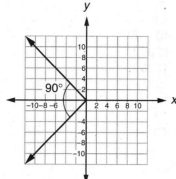

a. $\frac{a}{12} = \frac{6}{8}$

$$8 \cdot a = 12 \cdot 6$$
$$8a = 72$$
$$a = \frac{72}{8}$$
$$a = \mathbf{9}$$
$$\frac{9}{12} = \frac{6}{8}$$

b. $\frac{30}{b} = \frac{20}{16}$

$$20 \cdot b = 30 \cdot 16$$
$$20b = 480$$
$$b = \frac{480}{20}$$
$$b = \mathbf{24}$$
$$\frac{30}{24} = \frac{20}{16}$$

c. $\frac{14}{21} = \frac{c}{15}$

$$21 \cdot c = 15 \cdot 14$$
$$21c = 210$$
$$c = \frac{210}{21}$$
$$c = \mathbf{10}$$
$$\frac{14}{21} = \frac{10}{15}$$

d. $\frac{30}{25} = \frac{2.4}{d}$

$$30 \cdot d = 2.4 \cdot 25$$
$$30d = 60$$
$$d = \frac{60}{30}$$
$$d = \mathbf{2}$$
$$\frac{30}{25} = \frac{2.4}{2}$$

181

Solutions

e.
$$\frac{30}{100} = \frac{n}{40}$$
$$100 \cdot n = 40 \cdot 30$$
$$100n = 1200$$
$$n = \frac{1200}{100}$$
$$n = \mathbf{12}$$
$$\frac{30}{100} = \frac{12}{40}$$

f.
$$\frac{m}{100} = \frac{9}{12}$$
$$12 \cdot m = 100 \cdot 9$$
$$12m = 900$$
$$m = \frac{900}{12}$$
$$m = \mathbf{75}$$
$$\frac{75}{100} = \frac{9}{12}$$

Written Practice   39

1.
```
  78 pounds
- 64 pounds
  14 pounds
```

2. Between the 9th and 10th months.

3. $\dfrac{\text{trumpet players}}{\text{flute players}} = \dfrac{12}{16} = \mathbf{\dfrac{3}{4}}$

4.
```
   497        464 miles
   513      4)1856
   436        16
 + 410        25
  1856 miles  24
              16
              16
               0
```

5.

Weeks	Dollars Received
1	4.50
2	9.00
3	13.50
5	22.50
8	36.00

6.
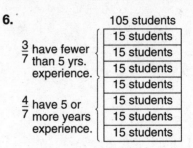

105 students

$\frac{3}{7}$ have fewer than 5 yrs. experience.

$\frac{4}{7}$ have 5 or more years experience.

a. 3×15 students $= $ **45 students**

b. 4×15 students $= $ **60 students**

7.
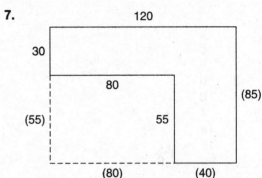

Area of large rectangle $= 85 \text{ mm} \times 120 \text{ mm}$
$$= 10{,}200 \text{ mm}^2$$

Area of small rectangle $= 55 \text{ mm} \times 80 \text{ mm}$
$$= 4400 \text{ mm}^2$$

Area of figure $= 10{,}200 \text{ mm}^2 - 4400 \text{ mm}^2$
$$= \mathbf{5800 \text{ mm}^2}$$

8. Perimeter $= 120 \text{ mm} + 85 \text{ mm} + 40 \text{ mm}$
$+ 55 \text{ mm} + 80 \text{ mm} + 30 \text{ mm}$
$$= \mathbf{410 \text{ mm}}$$

9. a. 2.5

b. $2\dfrac{5}{10} = \mathbf{2\dfrac{1}{2}}$

10. a. $0.91\underline{\textcircled{6}}6666 \longrightarrow$ **0.92**

b. $0.91666\underline{\textcircled{6}}6 \longrightarrow$ **0.91667**

11. $9.16 \longrightarrow 9$
$\$1.99\dfrac{9}{10} \longrightarrow \$2.00$
```
  $2.00
×     9
 $18.00
```

12. a. 100.075

b. 0.175

182

13. a. $\angle RPS$ (or $\angle SPR$)

   b. $\angle QPR$ (or $\angle RPQ$)

   c. $\angle QPS$ (or $\angle SPQ$)

14. **Each term can be found by dividing the previous term by 10.**

$0.1 \div 10 = 0.01$

$0.01 \div 10 = 0.001$

$0.001 \div 10 = 0.0001$

0.01, 0.001, 0.0001

15.
$$\frac{8}{12} = \frac{6}{x}$$
$$8 \cdot x = 6 \cdot 12$$
$$8x = 72$$
$$x = \frac{72}{8}$$
$$x = \mathbf{9}$$

16.
$$\frac{16}{y} = \frac{2}{3}$$
$$2 \cdot y = 16 \cdot 3$$
$$2y = 48$$
$$y = \frac{48}{2}$$
$$y = \mathbf{24}$$

17.
$$\frac{21}{14} = \frac{n}{4}$$
$$14 \cdot n = 4 \cdot 21$$
$$14n = 84$$
$$n = \frac{84}{14}$$
$$n = \mathbf{6}$$

18.
$$0.\overset{6}{\cancel{7}}5$$
$$-\ 0.36$$
$$\overline{0.39}$$
$$m = \mathbf{0.39}$$

19.
$$\overset{0}{\cancel{1}}.\overset{1}{}4$$
$$-\ 0.8$$
$$\overline{0.6}$$
$$w = \mathbf{0.6}$$

20.
$$8\overline{)7.2}\ \ ^{0.9}$$
$$\underline{72}$$
$$0$$
$$x = \mathbf{0.9}$$

21.
$$\begin{array}{r} 1.2 \\ \times\ 0.4 \\ \hline 0.48 \end{array}$$
$$y = \mathbf{0.48}$$

22. $9.6 + 12 + 8.59$

     $\downarrow$ $\downarrow$ $\downarrow$

   $10 + 12 + 9 = \mathbf{31}$

$$\begin{array}{r} \overset{1}{\underset{2}{}}9.6 \\ 12. \\ +\ 8.59 \\ \hline 30.19 \end{array}$$

23. $3.15 - (2.1 - 0.06)$

     $\downarrow$ $\downarrow$ $\downarrow$

   $3 - (2 - 0) = \mathbf{1}$

$$\begin{array}{r} 2.\overset{0}{\cancel{1}}{}^{1}0 \\ -\ 0.06 \\ \hline 2.04 \end{array} \qquad \begin{array}{r} 3.15 \\ -\ 2.04 \\ \hline \mathbf{1.11} \end{array}$$

24.
$$\begin{array}{r} 4\dfrac{5}{12} = 4\dfrac{10}{24} \\ +\ 6\dfrac{5}{8} = 6\dfrac{15}{24} \\ \hline 10\dfrac{25}{24} = \mathbf{11\dfrac{1}{24}} \end{array}$$

25.
$$\begin{array}{r} 4\dfrac{1}{4} = 4\dfrac{5}{20} \longrightarrow 3\dfrac{25}{20} \\ -\ 1\dfrac{3}{5} = 1\dfrac{12}{20} \qquad\quad -\ 1\dfrac{12}{20} \\ \hline \mathbf{2\dfrac{13}{20}} \end{array}$$

26. $8\dfrac{1}{3} \cdot 1\dfrac{4}{5} = \dfrac{\overset{5}{\cancel{25}}}{\cancel{3}_1} \cdot \dfrac{\overset{3}{\cancel{9}}}{\cancel{5}_1} = \mathbf{15}$

27. $5\dfrac{5}{6} \div 7 = \dfrac{35}{6} \div \dfrac{7}{1}$

$$= \dfrac{\overset{5}{\cancel{35}}}{6} \times \dfrac{1}{\cancel{7}_1} = \mathbf{\dfrac{5}{6}}$$

28. a. Perimeter $= 15\text{ mm} + 15\text{ mm} + 18\text{ mm}$
$$= \mathbf{48\text{ mm}}$$

    b. Area $= \dfrac{18\text{ mm} \cdot 12\text{ mm}}{2} = \mathbf{108\text{ mm}^2}$

29. $P(\text{odd prime}) = \dfrac{\text{favorable outcomes } (3, 5)}{\text{total outcomes } (6)}$

$$= \dfrac{2}{6} = \dfrac{1}{3}$$

30. $\dfrac{2}{3} = \dfrac{8}{12}$

$\dfrac{1}{2} = \dfrac{6}{12}$

$\dfrac{5}{6} = \dfrac{10}{12}$

$\dfrac{1}{2}, \dfrac{7}{12}, \dfrac{2}{3}, \dfrac{5}{6}$

Practice Set 40

a. Each angle measures 60° because the angles equally share 180°.
$$\dfrac{180°}{3} = 60°$$

b. 20°. Angle *ACB* and ∠*ACD* are complementary:
90° − 70° = 20°

c. Angle *CAB* measures 70° because it is the third angle of a triangle whose other angles measure 90° and 20°:
180° − (90° + 20°) = 180° − 110° = 70°

d. They are not vertical angles. Their angles are equal in measure, but they are not nonadjacent angles formed by two intersecting lines.

e. Angle *x* is the third angle of a triangle:
m∠*x* = 180° − (40° + 80°)
    = 180° − 120° = 60°
Angle *x* and ∠*y* are supplementary angles:
m∠*y* = 180° − 60° = 120°

Angles *z* and *x* are vertical angles:
m∠*z* = 60°

Written Practice 40

1. a.
$$
\begin{array}{r}
3 \text{ red marbles} \\
+ \ 2 \text{ white marbles} \\
\hline
5 \text{ total marbles}
\end{array}
$$
$\dfrac{\text{white marbles}}{\text{total marbles}} = \dfrac{2}{5}$

b. $\dfrac{2}{5}$

2. a.   6 minutes = 6(60 seconds)
        = 360 seconds
360 seconds + 20 seconds
        = **380 seconds**

b. $\dfrac{380 \text{ seconds}}{4} = $ **95 seconds**

3.
$$
\begin{array}{r}
18 \\
\times \ 24 \text{ miles} \\
\hline
72 \\
36 \ \\
\hline
432 \text{ miles}
\end{array}
$$

4. a.
$$
\begin{array}{r}
212°F \\
- \ 202°F \\
\hline
10°F
\end{array}
$$
10°F

b.
$$
\begin{array}{r}
{\overset{1\ \ 10\ 12}{2\!\!\not1\ \not2°F}} \\
- 1\ 8\ 3°F \\
\hline
2\ 9°F
\end{array}
\rightarrow
\begin{array}{r}
550 \\
\times \ 29 \\
\hline
4950 \\
1100 \ \\
\hline
15,950
\end{array}
$$

15,950 feet above sea level

5. length = 2 × width
70 mm = 2 × width
$\dfrac{70}{2} = $ width
width = 35 mm

a. Perimeter = 35 mm + 35 mm + 70 mm
        + 70 mm = **210 mm**

b. Area = 35 mm × 70 mm = **2450 mm²**

6.

200 sheep	
$\frac{5}{8}$ grazed.	25 sheep
	25 sheep
	25 sheep
	25 sheep
	25 sheep
$\frac{3}{8}$ drank.	25 sheep
	25 sheep
	25 sheep

a. 5 · 25 sheep = **125 sheep**

b. 3 · 25 sheep = **75 sheep**

7. *BC* = *AD* − (*AB* + *CD*)
BC = 100 mm − (30 mm + 45 mm)
    = 100 mm − 75 mm = 25 mm
25 mm = **2.5 cm**

8. a. 0.083③33 ⟶ **0.083**

b. 0.0⑧3333 ⟶ **0.1**

9. a. Twelve and fifty-four thousandths

   b. Ten and eleven hundredths

10.

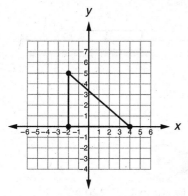

$$\text{Area} = \frac{6 \text{ units} \cdot 5 \text{ units}}{2} = \textbf{15 units}^2$$

11. **0.76**

12. a. $\angle ACB = 180° - (70° + 75°)$
    $= 180° - 145° = \textbf{35°}$

   b. $\angle ACD = 180° - 35° = \textbf{145°}$

   c. $\angle DCE = \textbf{35°}$

13. $\angle$ **BCE** (or $\angle ECB$)

14. a. **Identity property of multiplication**

   b.
$$
\begin{array}{r}
24 \\
5)\overline{120} \\
\underline{10} \\
20 \\
\underline{20} \\
0
\end{array}
$$

15. $10w = 25 \cdot 8$
    $w = \dfrac{25 \cdot 8}{10} = \dfrac{200}{10}$
    $w = \textbf{20}$

16. $9n = 1.5 \cdot 6$
    $n = \dfrac{(1.5)(6)}{9} = \dfrac{9}{9}$
    $n = \textbf{1}$

17. $9m = 12 \cdot 15$
    $m = \dfrac{12 \cdot 15}{9} = \dfrac{180}{9}$
    $m = \textbf{20}$

18.
$$
\begin{array}{r}
\overset{3}{\cancel{4}}.{}^{1}0 \\
-\ 1.8 \\
\hline
2.2
\end{array}
$$
    $a = \textbf{2.2}$

19.
$$
\begin{array}{r}
{}^{1} \\
3.9 \\
+\ 0.39 \\
\hline
4.29
\end{array}
$$
    $t = \textbf{4.29}$

20. 12 cm = 0.12 m
$$
\begin{array}{r}
1.{}^{1}2{}^{1}0 \text{ m} \\
-\ 0.12 \text{ m} \\
\hline
\textbf{1.08 m}
\end{array}
$$

21.
$$
\begin{array}{r}
0.15 \\
\times\ 0.05 \\
\hline
\textbf{0.0075}
\end{array}
$$

22.
$$
\begin{array}{r}
15 \\
\times\ 1.5 \\
\hline
75 \\
15 \\
\hline
\textbf{22.5}
\end{array}
$$

23.
$$
\begin{array}{r}
1.2 \\
12)\overline{14.4} \\
\underline{12} \\
24 \\
\underline{24} \\
0
\end{array}
$$

24.
$$
\begin{array}{r}
\overset{3}{\cancel{4}}.\overset{9}{\cancel{0}}{}^{1}0 \\
-\ 1.25 \\
\hline
2.75
\end{array}
\qquad
\begin{array}{r}
\overset{4}{\cancel{5}}.\overset{15}{\cancel{6}}{}^{1}0 \\
-\ 2.75 \\
\hline
\textbf{2.85}
\end{array}
$$

25.
$$
\begin{array}{r}
3.14 \\
+\ 1.20 \\
\hline
4.34
\end{array}
\qquad
\begin{array}{r}
\overset{4}{\cancel{5}}.\overset{9}{\cancel{0}}{}^{1}0 \\
-\ 4.34 \\
\hline
\textbf{0.66}
\end{array}
$$

26. $6\dfrac{1}{4} \cdot 1\dfrac{3}{5} = \dfrac{\overset{5}{\cancel{25}}}{\underset{1}{\cancel{4}}} \cdot \dfrac{\overset{2}{\cancel{8}}}{\underset{1}{\cancel{5}}} = \dfrac{10}{1} = \textbf{10}$

27. $7 \div 5\dfrac{5}{6} = \dfrac{7}{1} \div \dfrac{35}{6} = \dfrac{7}{1} \cdot \dfrac{6}{\underset{5}{\cancel{35}}}{}^{1}$
    $= \dfrac{6}{5} = \textbf{1}\dfrac{1}{5}$

28.
$$
\begin{array}{r}
\dfrac{8}{15} = \dfrac{40}{75} \\[2mm]
+\ \dfrac{12}{25} = \dfrac{36}{75} \\[1mm]
\hline
\dfrac{76}{75} = 1\dfrac{1}{75}
\end{array}
$$

Saxon Math Course 2   **185**

Solutions

29.
$$4\frac{2}{5} = 4\frac{8}{20} \longrightarrow 3\frac{28}{20}$$
$$-1\frac{3}{4} = -1\frac{15}{20} \qquad -1\frac{15}{20}$$
$$\qquad\qquad\qquad\qquad\quad 2\frac{13}{20}$$

30. Perimeter $= 15.84\,\text{m} \rightarrow 16\,\text{m}$
$16\,\text{m} \div 4 = 4\,\text{m}$
Area $= 4\,\text{m} \times 4\,\text{m} = \textbf{16 m}^2$

Early Finishers Solutions

$180° - 90° - 36° = 54°$

Stem-and-Leaf Plots, Box-and-Whisker Plots

1. 41

2. 37

3. 40

4. First quartile = **32**
Third quartile = **47**

5.
1	5							
2	6	6	7	8	9	9		
3	0	2	3	5	6	8	8 8 8	
4	0	1	2	3	5	5	6 7	7 8
5	0	2	4	5	7	8		

6. Lower quartile = **31**
Median = **39**
Upper quartile = **47**

7. 38

8. 58, 15

9. 43

10. 16

11. {Students are asked to create a box-and-whisker plot for a given set of test scores. Their plots may be more detailed, including marker labels.}

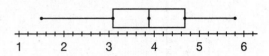

12. 15

a. $A = (15\text{ in.})(8\text{ in.}) = \textbf{120 in.}^2$

b. $\dfrac{(6\text{ ft})(8\text{ ft})}{2} = \textbf{24 ft}^2$

c. One possibility: $x(y + z) = xy + xz$

d. $6(15) = 90$
$(6 \cdot 20) - (6 \cdot 5) = 120 - 30 = 90$

e. $p = 2(l + w)$
$p = 2l + 2w$

f. One way is to add 6 and 4. Then multiply the sum by 2. Another way is to multiply 6 by 2 and 4 by 2. Then add the products.

g.
$2(n + 5)$	**Given**
$2n + 2 \cdot 5$	**Distributive property**
$2n + 10$	$2 \cdot 5 = 10$

1. $\dfrac{\text{gazelles}}{\text{wildebeests}} = \dfrac{150}{200} = \dfrac{3}{4}$

2.
$$\begin{array}{r} \overset{1\,2}{105}\text{ points} \\ 112\text{ points} \\ 98\text{ points} \\ 113\text{ points} \\ +\ 107\text{ points} \\ \hline 535\text{ points} \end{array}$$

$$\begin{array}{r} 107 \\ 5\overline{)535} \\ \underline{5} \\ 03 \\ \underline{0} \\ 35 \\ \underline{35} \\ 0 \end{array}$$
$\rightarrow$ **107 points**

3. 19 feet 6 inches = 19 (12 inches) + 6 inches
$$= 228 \text{ inches} + 6 \text{ inches}$$
$$= \textbf{234 inches}$$

4. **a. Associative property of addition**

   b. Associative property of multiplication

   c. Distributive property

5.

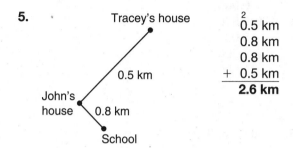

Tracey's house

$$\begin{array}{r} \overset{2}{0.5} \text{ km} \\ 0.8 \text{ km} \\ 0.8 \text{ km} \\ + \ 0.5 \text{ km} \\ \hline \textbf{2.6 km} \end{array}$$

6. **a.** $100\% - 70\% = 30\%$
$$30\% = \frac{30}{100} = \frac{\mathbf{3}}{\mathbf{10}}$$

   b. $\dfrac{\text{water area}}{\text{land area}} = \dfrac{70\%}{30\%} = \dfrac{\mathbf{7}}{\mathbf{3}}$

7. **a.** For 20 scores, the median is the average of the 10th and 11th scores.
$(10^{th} \text{ score} + 11^{th} \text{ score}) \div 2 = (30 + 30)$
$\div 2 = 60 \div 2 = $ **30 correct answers**

   b. For 20 scores, the first quartile is the average of the 5th and 6th scores.
$(5^{th} \text{ score} + 6^{th} \text{ score}) \div 2 = (26 + 26)$
$\div 2 = 52 \div 2 = $ **26 correct answers**

   c. For 20 scores, the third quartile is the average of the 15th and 16th scores.
$(15^{th} \text{ score} + 16^{th} \text{ score}) \div 2 = (33 + 35)$
$\div 2 = 68 \div 2 = $ **34 correct answers**

   d. Outliers are distant from the other numbers in the set. **11 correct answers** is an outlier.

8.

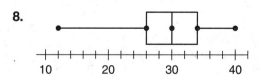

9.

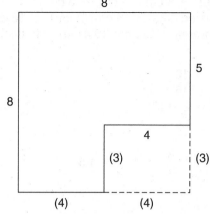

   a. Area of large rectangle $= (8 \text{ ft}) (8 \text{ ft})$
$$= 64 \text{ ft}^2$$
   Area of small rectangle $= (3 \text{ ft}) (4 \text{ ft})$
$$= 12 \text{ ft}^2$$
   Area of figure $= 64 \text{ ft}^2 - 12 \text{ ft}^2$
$$= \textbf{52 ft}^2$$

   b. Perimeter $= 8 \text{ ft} + 5 \text{ ft} + 4 \text{ ft} + 3 \text{ ft}$
$+ \ 4 \text{ ft} + 8 \text{ ft} = $ **32 ft**

10. **a. 3.6**

   b. $3 \dfrac{6}{10} = \mathbf{3 \dfrac{3}{5}}$

11. $2 + 3 + 5 + 7 = \mathbf{17}$

12. **a.** Perimeter $= 13 \text{ mm} + 15 \text{ mm}$
$+ \ 14 \text{ mm} = $ **42 mm**

   b. Area $= \dfrac{(14 \text{ mm})(12 \text{ mm})}{2} = $ **84 mm²**

13. **a. 0.00067**

   b. 100.023

14. $2\pi r = 2(3.14)(10)$
$$= 2(31.4) = \mathbf{62.8}$$

15. $\dfrac{3}{5} \cdot \dfrac{14}{14} = \dfrac{42}{70}$
$\dfrac{1}{2} \cdot \dfrac{35}{35} = \dfrac{35}{70}$
$\dfrac{5}{7} \cdot \dfrac{10}{10} = \dfrac{50}{70}$
$\dfrac{\mathbf{35}}{\mathbf{70}}, \dfrac{\mathbf{42}}{\mathbf{70}}, \dfrac{\mathbf{50}}{\mathbf{70}}$

Solutions

16. 5.6 cm → 6 cm, 3.4 cm → 3 cm

Estimated area = (6 cm)(3 cm) = **18 cm²**

Actual area = (5.6 cm)(3.4 cm) = **19.04 cm²**

17.
$$\frac{x}{2.4} = \frac{10}{16}$$
$$16x = 2.4(10)$$
$$x = \frac{24}{16}$$
$$x = 1\frac{8}{16} = 1\frac{1}{2} = \textbf{1.5}$$

18.
$$\frac{18}{8} = \frac{m}{20}$$
$$8m = 18 \cdot 20$$
$$m = \frac{360}{8}$$
$$m = \textbf{45}$$

19.
$$\begin{array}{r} 7.\overset{5}{\cancel{6}}{}^{1}0 \\ -\ 3.45 \\ \hline 4.15 \end{array}$$
$$a = \textbf{4.15}$$

20.
$$\begin{array}{r} 0.048 \\ 3)\overline{0.144} \\ \underline{12} \\ 24 \\ \underline{24} \\ 0 \end{array}$$
$$y = \textbf{0.048}$$

21.
$$\begin{array}{r} 0.925 \\ 8)\overline{7.400} \\ \underline{7\,2} \\ 20 \\ \underline{16} \\ 40 \\ \underline{40} \\ 0 \end{array}$$

22.
$$\begin{array}{r} 0.4 \\ \times\ 0.6 \\ \hline 0.24 \end{array} \qquad \begin{array}{r} 0.24 \\ \times\ 0.02 \\ \hline \textbf{0.0048} \end{array}$$

23.
$$\begin{array}{r} 0.863 \\ 5)\overline{4.315} \\ \underline{4\,0} \\ 31 \\ \underline{30} \\ 15 \\ \underline{15} \\ 0 \end{array}$$

24.
$$\begin{array}{r} 0.065 \\ 100)\overline{6.500} \\ \underline{6\,00} \\ 500 \\ \underline{500} \\ 0 \end{array}$$

25.
$$3\frac{1}{3} = 3\frac{4}{12}$$
$$1\frac{5}{6} = 1\frac{10}{12}$$
$$+\ \frac{7}{12} = \frac{7}{12}$$
$$4\frac{21}{12} = 5\frac{9}{12} = \textbf{5}\frac{\textbf{3}}{\textbf{4}}$$

26.
$$\begin{array}{ccc} 4 & \longrightarrow & 3\frac{4}{4} \\ -\ 1\frac{1}{4} & & -\ 1\frac{1}{4} \\ \hline & & 2\frac{3}{4} \end{array}$$

$$\begin{array}{ccc} 4\frac{1}{6} = 4\frac{2}{12} & \longrightarrow & 3\frac{14}{12} \\ -\ 2\frac{3}{4} = 2\frac{9}{12} & & -\ 2\frac{9}{12} \\ \hline & & \textbf{1}\frac{\textbf{5}}{\textbf{12}} \end{array}$$

27. $3\frac{1}{5} \cdot 2\frac{5}{8} \cdot 1\frac{3}{7}$

$$= \frac{\overset{2}{\cancel{16}}}{\underset{1}{\cancel{5}}} \cdot \frac{\overset{3}{\cancel{21}}}{\underset{1}{\cancel{8}}} \cdot \frac{\overset{2}{\cancel{10}}}{\underset{1}{\cancel{7}}} = \textbf{12}$$

28. $4\frac{1}{2} \div 6 = \frac{9}{2} \div \frac{6}{1} = \frac{\overset{3}{\cancel{9}}}{2} \times \frac{1}{\underset{2}{\cancel{6}}} = \frac{\textbf{3}}{\textbf{4}}$

29. a. $(12 \cdot 7) + (12 \cdot 13)$
   $= 84 + 156 = 240$
   or
   $12(7 + 13) = 12 \cdot 20 = 240$
   $(12 \cdot 7) + (12 \cdot 13) = 12(7 + 13)$

   b. **Distributive property**

30. $m\angle x = 180° - (90° + 42°)$
   $= 180° - 132° = \mathbf{48°}$
   $m\angle y = 180° - 48° = \mathbf{132°}$
   $m\angle z = m\angle x = \mathbf{48°}$

Early Finishers Solutions

Line Plot; A line plot is the most appropriate display because it shows individual data points. Every bid except one begins with the digit 2, so a stem-and-leaf plot would not be a good choice.

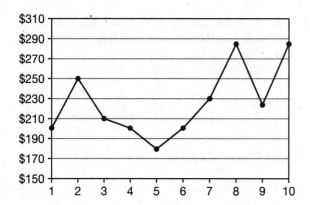

Practice Set 42

a. $2.\overline{72}$

b. $0.81\overline{6}$

c. $0.\overline{6} = 0.6666\ldots$
   $0.666\textcircled{6}\ldots \longrightarrow \mathbf{0.667}$

d. $5.3\overline{81} = 5.38181\ldots$
   $5.381\underline{\textcircled{8}}1\ldots \longrightarrow \mathbf{5.382}$

e. $0.6 < 0.6666\ldots$

f. $1.3, 1.\overline{3}, 1.35$

g.
```
      0.141666 ...
12)1.7000000 ...
   12
   ──
    50
    48
    ──
     20
     12
     ──
      80
      72
      ──
       80
       72
       ──
        80
```
0.141̄6

h. $0.1416\textcircled{6}6\ldots \longrightarrow \mathbf{0.1417}$

Written Practice 42

1. 2 boys   2 boys
   $\underline{+ \text{? girls}} \longrightarrow \underline{+ \text{ 3 girls}}$
   5 total   5 total

   $\dfrac{\text{boys}}{\text{girls}} = \dfrac{2}{3}$

2.   **27 students**
```
   16)432
      32
      ──
      112
      112
      ───
        0
```

3.   33 miles
    $\underline{\times \quad 7}$
   231 miles

4.
```
                450 students
           ┌──────────────┐
           │ 50 students  │
           │ 50 students  │
           │ 50 students  │
   7        │ 50 students  │
   ─ were   │ 50 students  │
   9 entertained.│ 50 students │
           │ 50 students  │
           │ 50 students  │
   2        │ 50 students  │
   ─ were not │ 50 students │
   9 entertained.└──────────────┘
```

   a. 7(50 students) = **350 students**

   b. 2(50 students) = **100 students**

5. a. $5.1\overline{6} = 5.16666\ldots$
   $5.1666\textcircled{6}\ldots \longrightarrow \mathbf{5.1667}$

   b. $5.\overline{27} = 5.272727\ldots$
   $5.2727\underline{\textcircled{2}}7\ldots \longrightarrow \mathbf{5.2727}$

Solutions

6. a. **30 Students**

    b. **8 Students**

    c. $\dfrac{1}{3}$

    d. $\dfrac{3}{10}$

7. Area $= \dfrac{(6 \text{ units}) (6 \text{ units})}{2} = $ **18 units²**

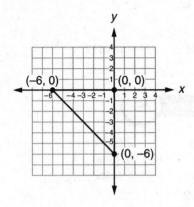

8. a. Perimeter $=$ 10 in. $+$ 8 in. $+$ 10 in.
        $+$ 20 in. $+$ 20 in. $+$ 12 in.
        $=$ **80 in.**

    b.
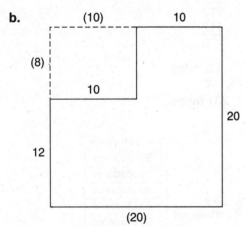

    Area of large rectangle $=$ 20 in. $\times$ 20 in.
    $=$ 400 in.²
    Area of small rectangle $=$ 10 in. $\times$ 8 in.
    $=$ 80 in.²
    Area of figure $=$ 400 in.² $-$ 80 in.²
    $=$ **320 in.²**

9.
```
        0.15454 ...
   11)1.700000 ...
      11
      ──
       60
       55
       ──
        50
        44
        ──
         60
         55
         ──
          50
          44
          ──
           60
```

    a. **0.15̄4̄**

    b. 0.154⑤4 ... ⟶ **0.155**

    c. **thousandths**

10.
```
     1
    0.027
  + 0.58
    ─────
    0.607
```

11. a. **Sample space $=$ {A1, A2, A3, A4, B1,
        B2, B3, B4, C1, C2, C3, C4}**

    b. Consonants $=$ B and C,
        Composite number $=$ 4
        $P(\text{B4 or C4}) = \dfrac{2}{12} = \dfrac{1}{6}$

12. a. One possibility:
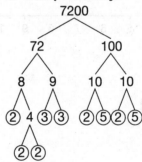

    b. **$2^5 \cdot 3^2 \cdot 5^2$**

13.
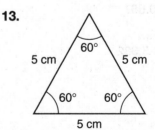

Saxon Math Course 2   190

14. $12 = 2 \cdot 2 \cdot 3$
$15 = 3 \cdot 5$
$\text{LCM}(12, 15) = 2 \cdot 2 \cdot 3 \cdot 5 = \mathbf{60}$

15. $\dfrac{21}{24} = \dfrac{w}{40}$
$24w = 21 \cdot 40$
$w = \dfrac{840}{24}$
$w = \mathbf{35}$

16. $\dfrac{1.2}{x} = \dfrac{9}{6}$
$9x = (1.2)6$
$x = \dfrac{7.2}{9}$
$x = \mathbf{0.8}$

17.
$$\begin{array}{r} \cancel{1}\overset{0}{}\,\cancel{4}\overset{1}{}.\overset{1}{}0 \\ -\ \ 9.\,6 \\ \hline 4.\,4 \end{array}$$
$m = \mathbf{4.4}$

18.
$$\begin{array}{r} 1.63 \\ +\ 4.2 \\ \hline 5.83 \end{array}$$
$n = \mathbf{5.83}$

19. $\dfrac{1}{2}(12)(10) = \dfrac{1}{2}(120) = \mathbf{60}$

20. $4(11) = \mathbf{44}$
or
$(4 \cdot 5) + (4 \cdot 6) = 20 + 24 = \mathbf{44}$

21. a. Distributive property

b. Inverse property of multiplication

22.
$$\begin{array}{r} \$4.56 \\ \times\ 0.08 \\ \hline \$0.3648 \end{array} \longrightarrow \mathbf{\$0.36}$$

23. $24 \div 6 = \mathbf{4}$

24. a. Diameter

b. Radius

25.
$$\begin{array}{r} \mathbf{1.775} \\ 4\overline{)7.100} \\ \underline{4\ \ \ \ } \\ 3\,1 \\ \underline{2\,8} \\ 30 \\ \underline{28} \\ 20 \\ \underline{20} \\ 0 \end{array}$$

26.
$$\begin{array}{r} 6\dfrac{1}{4} = 6\dfrac{3}{12} \\ 5\dfrac{5}{12} = 5\dfrac{5}{12} \\ +\ \dfrac{2}{3} = \dfrac{8}{12} \\ \hline 11\dfrac{16}{12} = 12\dfrac{4}{12} = \mathbf{12\dfrac{1}{3}} \end{array}$$

27.
$$4\dfrac{1}{6} = 4\dfrac{2}{12} \longrightarrow 3\dfrac{14}{12}$$
$$-\ 1\dfrac{1}{4} = 1\dfrac{3}{12} \qquad -\ 1\dfrac{3}{12}$$
$$\overline{\qquad\qquad\qquad\quad 2\dfrac{11}{12}}$$

$$4 \longrightarrow 3\dfrac{12}{12}$$
$$-\ 2\dfrac{11}{12} \qquad -\ 2\dfrac{11}{12}$$
$$\overline{\qquad\qquad\quad 1\dfrac{1}{12}}$$

28. $6\dfrac{2}{5} \cdot 2\dfrac{5}{8} \cdot 2\dfrac{6}{7}$

$= \dfrac{\overset{4}{\cancel{32}}}{\underset{1}{\cancel{5}}} \cdot \dfrac{\overset{3}{\cancel{21}}}{\underset{1}{\cancel{8}}} \cdot \dfrac{\overset{4}{\cancel{20}}}{\underset{1}{7}} = \mathbf{48}$

29. The quotient is greater than 1 because the dividend is greater than the divisor.

$6 \div 4\dfrac{1}{2} = \dfrac{6}{1} \div \dfrac{9}{2} = \dfrac{\overset{2}{\cancel{6}}}{1} \times \dfrac{2}{\underset{3}{\cancel{9}}} = \dfrac{4}{3}$

$= \mathbf{1\dfrac{1}{3}}$

30. $m\angle a = 180° - 40° = \mathbf{140°}$
$m\angle b = 180° - (90° + 40°)$
$\qquad = 180° - 130° = \mathbf{50°}$
$m\angle c = 180° - 50° = \mathbf{130°}$

Early Finishers Solutions

a. $\dfrac{\$77.52}{\$135.66} = \dfrac{4}{7}$

b. $135.66 - 77.52 = 58.14 \cdot \dfrac{1}{3} = 19.38$

$58.14 - 19.38 = \$38.76$ remaining

Practice Set 43

a. $0.24 = \dfrac{24}{100} = \dfrac{6}{25}$

b. $45.6 = 45\dfrac{6}{10} = \mathbf{45\dfrac{3}{5}}$

c. $2.375 = 2\dfrac{375}{1000} = \mathbf{2\dfrac{3}{8}}$

d.
```
    5.75
 4)23.00
   20
    3 0
    2 8
      20
      20
       0
```

e. $4\dfrac{3}{5} = \dfrac{23}{5}$
```
    4.6
 5)23.0
   20
    3 0
    3 0
      0
```

f.
```
    0.625
 8)5.000
   4 8
     20
     16
      40
      40
       0
```

g.
```
    0.8333 ...
 6)5.0000 ...
   4 8
     20
     18
      20
      18
       20
```
$0.8\overline{3}$

h. $8\% = \dfrac{8}{100} = \mathbf{0.08}$

i. $12.5\% = \dfrac{12.5}{100} = \mathbf{0.125}$

j. $150\% = \dfrac{150}{100} = \mathbf{1.50}$

k. $6\dfrac{1}{2}\% = 6.5\% = \dfrac{6.5}{100} = \mathbf{0.065}$

l. $200\% = \dfrac{200}{100} = \mathbf{2}$

Written Practice 43

1. $\dfrac{\text{Celtic soldiers}}{\text{total soldiers}} = \dfrac{2}{7}$

2. a. 11 minutes 44 seconds =
11(60 seconds) + 44 seconds =
704 seconds

b.
```
    88 seconds
 8)704 seconds
   64
   64
   64
    0
```

3. $G + 13.3 = 21.0$
```
  1 10
 2 1.0 gallons
-1 3.3 gallons
  7.7 gallons
```

4.
```
   9 9 10
 1,0 0 0,200,000 people
- 7 2 5,000,000 people
  2 7 5,200,000 people
```

5.

	15 games
$\dfrac{2}{3}$ dry.	5 games
	5 games
$\dfrac{1}{3}$ rain.	5 games

a. $2(5 \text{ games}) = \mathbf{10 \text{ games}}$

b. $\dfrac{\text{dry}}{\text{rain}} = \dfrac{2}{1}$

6. **a.** For 15 finish times, the median is the 8th finish time. 8th finish time = **13.5 seconds**

   b. For 15 finish times, the lower quartile is the 4th finish time.
   4th finish time = **12.8 seconds**

   c. For the 15 finish times, the upper quartile is the 12th finish time.
   12th finish time = **14.7 seconds**

7.
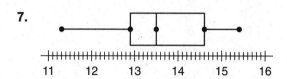

8. $\dfrac{120 \text{ mm}}{6} = 20 \text{ mm}$

   Perimeter = $(4)(20 \text{ mm}) = $ **80 mm**

9. **a.** $0.375 = \dfrac{375}{1000} = \dfrac{3}{8}$

   b. $5.55 = 5\dfrac{55}{100} = 5\dfrac{11}{20}$

   c. $250\% = \dfrac{250}{100} = 2\dfrac{1}{2}$

10. **a.** $2\dfrac{2}{5} = \dfrac{12}{5}$

$$
\begin{array}{r}
2.4 \\
5)\overline{12.0} \\
\underline{10} \\
2\,0 \\
\underline{2\,0} \\
0
\end{array}
$$

   b.
$$
\begin{array}{r}
0.125 \\
8)\overline{1.000} \\
\underline{8} \\
20 \\
\underline{16} \\
40 \\
\underline{40} \\
0
\end{array}
$$

   c. $250\% = \dfrac{250}{100}$

$$
\begin{array}{r}
2.5 \\
100)\overline{250.0} \\
\underline{200} \\
500 \\
\underline{500} \\
0
\end{array}
$$

11. **a.** $0.\overline{45} = 0.4545\ldots$
   $0.454\text{⑤}\ldots \longrightarrow$ **0.455**

   b. $3.\overline{142857} =$
   $3.142857142857\ldots$
   $3.142\text{⑧}57142857 \longrightarrow$ **3.143**

12.
$$
\begin{array}{r}
0.15833\ldots \\
12)\overline{1.90000\ldots} \\
\underline{12} \\
70 \\
\underline{60} \\
100 \\
\underline{96} \\
40 \\
\underline{36} \\
40 \\
\underline{36} \\
40
\end{array}
$$

   a. **0.158$\overline{3}$**

   b. $0.158\text{③}\ldots \longrightarrow$ **0.158**

13.
$$
\begin{array}{r}
\overset{3}{\cancel{4}}.\,\overset{9}{\cancel{0}}\,\overset{14}{\cancel{5}}\!0 \\
-\ 0.\,1\,6\,7 \\
\hline
3.\,8\,8\,3
\end{array}
$$

14.

C at top, $\dfrac{3}{4}$ in. on left side, $1\dfrac{1}{4}$ in. on hypotenuse, right angle at A, 1 in. from A to B.

   $BC = $ **$1\dfrac{1}{4}$ inches**

15. $\dfrac{26}{52} = \dfrac{1}{2}$

   $\dfrac{1}{2} \times \dfrac{5}{5} = \dfrac{5}{10} = $ **0.5**

16. **a.** **One possibility:**

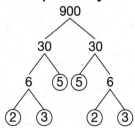

   b. $2^2 \cdot 3^2 \cdot 5^2$

   c. $\sqrt{900} = 30 = $ **2 · 3 · 5**

17. 1 liter = 1000 milliliters

$$\frac{1000 \text{ milliliters}}{2 \text{ milliliters}} = 500$$

500 eyedroppers

18. a. $8\% = \frac{8}{100} = \mathbf{0.08}$

b.
$$\begin{array}{r} \$8.90 \\ \times\ 0.08 \\ \hline \$0.7120 \end{array} \longrightarrow \mathbf{\$0.71}$$

19. a. Perimeter = 0.6 m + 1 m + 0.8 m
= **2.4 m**

b. Area = $\dfrac{(0.8 \text{ m})(0.6 \text{ m})}{2} = \mathbf{0.24\ m^2}$

20. $\dfrac{32}{2} = \dfrac{320}{20}$

The division problems are equivalent problems because the quotients are equal.

21. 2(3 + 4) = 2(7) = **14**

or

2(3 + 4) = 2 · 3 + 2 · 4 = 6 + 8 = **14**

22. $\dfrac{10}{18} = \dfrac{c}{4.5}$

$18c = 10 \cdot 4.5$

$c = \dfrac{45}{18}$

$c = 2\dfrac{1}{2}$ or **2.5**

23.
$$\begin{array}{r} 1.\overset{8}{\cancel{9}}{}^{1}0 \\ -\ 0.4\ 2 \\ \hline 1.4\ 8 \end{array}$$
$w = \mathbf{1.48}$

24.
$$\begin{array}{r} \mathbf{1.625} \\ 4\overline{)6.500} \\ \underline{4} \\ 2\ 5 \\ \underline{2\ 4} \\ 10 \\ \underline{8} \\ 20 \\ \underline{20} \\ 0 \end{array}$$

25.
$$3\dfrac{3}{10} = 3\dfrac{9}{30} \longrightarrow 2\dfrac{39}{30}$$
$$-\ 1\dfrac{11}{15} = 1\dfrac{22}{30} \qquad -\ 1\dfrac{22}{30}$$
$$\rule{2cm}{0.4pt} \qquad \qquad \overline{1\dfrac{17}{30}}$$

26.
$$5\dfrac{1}{2} = 5\dfrac{5}{10}$$
$$6\dfrac{3}{10} = 6\dfrac{3}{10}$$
$$+\ \dfrac{4}{5} = \dfrac{8}{10}$$
$$\overline{11\dfrac{16}{10} = 12\dfrac{6}{10} = \mathbf{12\dfrac{3}{5}}}$$

27. $7\dfrac{1}{2} \cdot 3\dfrac{1}{3} \cdot \dfrac{4}{5} = \dfrac{\overset{5}{\cancel{15}}}{\cancel{2}_{1}} \cdot \dfrac{\overset{\overset{1}{\cancel{2}}}{\cancel{10}}}{\cancel{3}_{1}} \cdot \dfrac{4}{\cancel{5}_{1}} = 20$

20 ÷ 5 = **4**

28. **(5, 10)**

29. m∠a = 180° − 110° = **70°**
m∠b = 180° − (70° + 50°)
= 180° − 120° = **60°**
m∠c = 180° − 60° = **120°**

30. a. **180°**

b. **90°**

c. **45°**

Practice Set **44**

a.
$$\begin{array}{r} \mathbf{13\ R\ 3} \\ 4\overline{)55} \\ \underline{4} \\ 15 \\ \underline{12} \\ 3 \end{array}$$

b.
$$\begin{array}{r} \mathbf{13\dfrac{3}{4}} \\ 4\overline{)55} \\ \underline{4} \\ 15 \\ \underline{12} \\ 3 \end{array}$$

c.

$$
\begin{array}{r}
13.75 \\
4\overline{)55.00} \\
\underline{4} \\
15 \\
\underline{12} \\
3\,0 \\
\underline{2\,8} \\
20 \\
\underline{20} \\
0
\end{array}
$$

d.

$$
\begin{array}{r}
1.8333\ldots \\
3\overline{)5.5000\ldots} \\
\underline{3} \\
2\,5 \\
\underline{2\,4} \\
10 \\
\underline{9} \\
10 \\
\underline{9} \\
10
\end{array}
$$

$1.833\underline{③}\ldots \longrightarrow$ **1.833**

e.

$$
\begin{array}{r}
23 \text{ R } 1 \\
4\overline{)93} \\
\underline{8} \\
13 \\
\underline{12} \\
1
\end{array}
$$

23 students are in three classrooms, and 24 students are in the fourth classroom.
23, 23, 23, and 24 students

f.

$$
\begin{array}{r}
\$0.6666\ldots \\
3\overline{)\$2.0000\ldots} \\
\underline{1\,8} \\
20 \\
\underline{18} \\
20 \\
\underline{18} \\
20
\end{array}
$$

$\$0.6666\ldots = $ **\$0.67**

\$0.67; Divide \$2.00 by 3 to find the cost per pound. The answer is \$0.6666 . . . Round up to the next cent, which is \$0.67.

g. **13 pages.**
Sample: I divided 74 by 6 to find the number of pages. The quotient is 12 R 2. That means 12 pages have six photos. There are 2 photos left, and they are on the 13th page.

1. $\dfrac{\text{length}}{\text{width}} = \dfrac{24}{18} = \dfrac{4}{3}$

2.

$$
\begin{array}{r}
\overset{2}{90} \\
95 \\
90 \\
85 \\
80 \\
85 \\
90 \\
80 \\
\overset{7}{95} \\
+\ 100 \\
\hline
890
\end{array}
\qquad
\begin{array}{r}
89 \\
10\overline{)890} \\
\underline{80} \\
90 \\
\underline{90} \\
0
\end{array}
$$

3. **A bar graph is a better way to display the scores than a circle graph. A bar graph shows comparisons. A circle graph shows parts of a whole.**

4.

$$
\begin{array}{r}
\$\ 0.37 \\
\times\quad 50 \\
\hline
\$18.50
\end{array}
$$

$$
\begin{array}{r}
\overset{1\ 9\ 10}{\$2\cancel{0}.\cancel{0}\,0} \\
-\ \$18.50 \\
\hline
\$\ \ 1.50
\end{array}
$$

5.

$$
\begin{array}{r}
\overset{8\ ^{1}7}{2.\cancel{9}\,\cancel{8}\,0} \\
-\ 0.097 \\
\hline
2.883
\end{array}
$$

Two and eight hundred eighty-three thousandths

6. a. $\dfrac{5}{6} \cdot 30 = \dfrac{5 \cdot 30}{6} = \dfrac{150}{6} = 25$

$30 - 25 = $ **5 motorcycles**

b. $\dfrac{\text{new motorcycles}}{\text{used motorcycles}} = \dfrac{25}{5} = \dfrac{5}{1}$

Solutions

7.

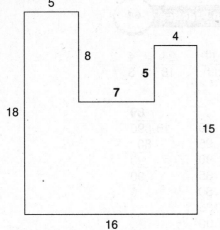

Perimeter = 18m + 5m + 8m + 7m
+ 5m + 4m + 15m + 16m
= **78 m**

8. a. $0.75 = \dfrac{75}{100} = \dfrac{3}{4}$

b.
$$\begin{array}{r} 0.625 \\ 8\overline{)5.000} \\ \underline{4\ 8} \\ 20 \\ \underline{16} \\ 40 \\ \underline{40} \\ 0 \end{array}$$

c. $125\% = \dfrac{125}{100} = \mathbf{1.25}$

9. $\dfrac{\text{hearts}}{\text{total cards}} = \dfrac{13}{52} = \dfrac{1}{4}$

$\dfrac{1}{4} \times \dfrac{25}{25} = \dfrac{25}{100} = \mathbf{0.25}$

10. B. $(2 \cdot 3) + (2 \cdot 4)$

11. a.

15   21

b. $n = 10$

$\left(\dfrac{n^2 + n}{2}\right) = \dfrac{10^2 + 10}{2}$

$= \dfrac{100 + 10}{2} = \dfrac{110}{2} = \mathbf{55}$

12.
$$\begin{array}{r} 0.49090\ldots \\ 11\overline{)5.40000\ldots} \\ \underline{4\ 4} \\ 1\ 00 \\ \underline{99} \\ 10 \\ \underline{0} \\ 100 \\ \underline{99} \\ 10 \\ \underline{0} \\ 10 \end{array}$$

a. $\mathbf{0.4\overline{90}}$

b. $0.490\textcircled{9}0\ldots \longrightarrow \mathbf{0.491}$

13. $2 \times 3 \times 5 \times 7 = \mathbf{210}$

14. a. $-12, 0, 0.12, \dfrac{1}{2}, 1.2, 1.\overline{2}$

b. $-12, 0$

15. a. $12\left(1\dfrac{1}{2} \text{ inches}\right)$

$= 12\left(\dfrac{3}{2} \text{ inches}\right) = 6 \times 3 \text{ inches}$

$= \mathbf{18\ inches}$

b. 1 yard = 36 inches

$36 \text{ inches} \div 1\dfrac{1}{2} = \dfrac{36}{1} \div \dfrac{3}{2}$

$= \dfrac{\overset{12}{\cancel{36}}}{1} \times \dfrac{2}{\underset{1}{\cancel{3}}} = \mathbf{24\ books}$

16.
$$\begin{array}{r} \overset{1\ 1}{2.46} \\ + \ 2.54 \\ \hline 5.00 = \mathbf{5} \end{array}$$

17. $3 \times 10 \text{ meters} = \mathbf{30\ meters}$

18. Answers will vary. See student work.

a. Area = $(2.5 \text{ cm})(2.5 \text{ cm}) = \mathbf{6.25\ cm^2}$

b. Perimeter = $4(2.5 \text{ cm}) = \mathbf{10\ cm}$

19.

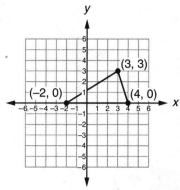

$$\text{Area} = \frac{(6 \text{ units})(3 \text{ units})}{2} = \textbf{9 units}^2$$

20. $\dfrac{25}{15} = \dfrac{n}{1.2}$

$15n = 25 \cdot 1.2$

$n = \dfrac{30}{15}$

$n = \textbf{2}$

21. $\dfrac{p}{90} = \dfrac{4}{18}$

$18p = 90 \cdot 4$

$p = \dfrac{360}{18}$

$p = \textbf{20}$

22.
$$\begin{array}{r} \overset{3}{\cancel{4}}.\overset{9}{\cancel{1}}\overset{}{\cancel{0}}0 \\ -\ 3.\ 1\ 4 \\ \hline 0.\ 8\ 6 \end{array}$$
$x = \textbf{0.86}$

23.
$$\begin{array}{r} \overset{0}{\cancel{1}}\,{}^{1}0 \\ -\ 0.\ 1 \\ \hline 0.\ 9 \end{array}$$
$z = \textbf{0.9}$

24.
$$\begin{array}{r} 2.0525 \\ 8\overline{)16.4200} \\ \underline{16} \\ 0\ 4 \\ \underline{\ 0} \\ 4\,2 \\ \underline{4\,0} \\ 2\,0 \\ \underline{1\,6} \\ 4\,0 \\ \underline{4\,0} \\ 0 \end{array}$$

25.
$$\begin{array}{r} 0.017 \\ 9\overline{)0.153} \\ \underline{9} \\ 63 \\ \underline{63} \\ 0 \end{array}$$

26.
$$\begin{array}{r} 5\dfrac{3}{4} = 5\dfrac{9}{12} \\ \dfrac{5}{6} = \dfrac{10}{12} \\ +\ 2\dfrac{1}{2} = 2\dfrac{6}{12} \\ \hline 7\dfrac{25}{12} = \textbf{9}\dfrac{\textbf{1}}{\textbf{12}} \end{array}$$

27.
$$\begin{array}{ccc} 5 & 4\dfrac{6}{6} & 3\dfrac{1}{3} = 3\dfrac{2}{6} \\ -\ 1\dfrac{5}{6} & \longrightarrow \quad -\ 1\dfrac{5}{6} & -\ 3\dfrac{1}{6} = 3\dfrac{1}{6} \\ \hline & 3\dfrac{1}{6} & \dfrac{\textbf{1}}{\textbf{6}} \end{array}$$

28. $3\dfrac{3}{4} \cdot 3\dfrac{1}{3} \cdot 8 = \dfrac{\overset{5}{\cancel{15}}}{\underset{1}{\cancel{4}}} \cdot \dfrac{10}{\underset{1}{\cancel{3}}} \cdot \dfrac{\overset{2}{\cancel{8}}}{1} = \textbf{100}$

29. $7 \div 10\dfrac{1}{2} = \dfrac{7}{1} \div \dfrac{21}{2} = \dfrac{\overset{1}{\cancel{7}}}{1} \times \dfrac{2}{\underset{3}{\cancel{21}}} = \dfrac{\textbf{2}}{\textbf{3}}$

30. **a.** $m\angle ABD = 180° - (35° + 90°)$
$= 180° - 125° = \textbf{55°}$

b. $m\angle CBD = 90° - 55° = \textbf{35°}$

c. $m\angle BDC = 90° - 35° = \textbf{55°}$

a. The other two angles of $\triangle ABD$ measure 35° and 90°. For the sum to be 180°, $m\angle ABD$ must be 55°.

b. Since the figure is a rectangle, $m\angle ABC$ is 90°. We found that $m\angle ABC$ is 55°; $\angle CBD$ is the complement of $\angle ABD$, so $m\angle CBD$ is 35°.

c. Angle *BDC* is the complement of a 35° angle. Also, $\angle BCD$ is the third angle of a triangle whose other two angles measure 35° and 90°.

Solutions

a.
$$
\begin{array}{r}
8.6 \\
06.\overline{)51.6} \\
48 \\
\overline{36} \\
36 \\
\overline{0}
\end{array}
$$

b.
$$
\begin{array}{r}
1.6 \\
\$09.\overline{)14.4} \\
9 \\
\overline{54} \\
54 \\
\overline{0}
\end{array}
$$

c.
$$
\begin{array}{r}
340. \\
007.\overline{)2380} \\
21 \\
\overline{28} \\
28 \\
\overline{00} \\
0 \\
\overline{0}
\end{array}
$$

d.
$$
\begin{array}{r}
300. \\
008.\overline{)2400} \\
24 \\
\overline{00} \\
0 \\
\overline{00} \\
0 \\
\overline{0}
\end{array}
$$

e.
$$
\begin{array}{r}
16 \text{ pens} \\
\$075.\overline{)\$1200} \\
75 \\
\overline{450} \\
450 \\
\overline{0}
\end{array}
$$

f. If we multiply $\frac{0.25}{0.5}$ by $\frac{10}{10}$, the result is $\frac{2.5}{5}$. Since $\frac{10}{10}$ equals 1, we have not changed the value by multiplying—we have only changed the form.

g.
$$
\frac{x}{4} = \frac{3}{0.8}
$$
$$
0.8x = 3 \cdot 4
$$
$$
0.8x = 12
$$
$$
x = \frac{12}{0.8}
$$
$$
x = 15
$$
$$
\frac{15}{4} = \frac{3}{0.8}
$$

$$
\begin{array}{r}
15. \\
08.\overline{)120} \\
8 \\
\overline{40} \\
40 \\
\overline{0}
\end{array}
$$

1.
$$
\begin{array}{c}
5 \text{ nuts} \\
+\ ?\ \text{raisins} \\
\hline
8 \text{ total}
\end{array}
\rightarrow
\begin{array}{c}
5 \text{ nuts} \\
+\ 3\ \text{raisins} \\
\hline
8 \text{ total}
\end{array}
$$
$$
\frac{\text{raisins}}{\text{nuts}} = \frac{3}{5}
$$

2. $2 \text{ miles} \div \frac{1}{4} \text{ mile} = \frac{2}{1} \div \frac{1}{4} = \frac{2}{1} \times \frac{4}{1} = 8$

$\$1 + \$0.80(8) = \$1 + \$6.40 = \mathbf{\$7.40}$

3.
$$
\begin{array}{r}
54.05 \\
-\ 50.04 \\
\hline
4.01
\end{array}
$$
Four and one-hundredth

4. a.
$$
\begin{array}{r}
22 \text{ votes} \\
-\ 18 \text{ votes} \\
\hline
\mathbf{4 \text{ votes}}
\end{array}
$$

b. $\dfrac{\text{Carlos's votes}}{\text{total votes}} = \dfrac{14}{70} = \dfrac{1}{5}$

5.

Riders on the Giant Gyro

$\frac{4}{7}$ were euphoric.	$\frac{1}{7}$ of riders
	$\frac{1}{7}$ of riders
	$\frac{1}{7}$ of riders
	$\frac{1}{7}$ of riders
	$\frac{1}{7}$ of riders
$\frac{3}{7}$ were vertiginous.	$\frac{1}{7}$ of riders
	$\frac{1}{7}$ of riders

a. $\dfrac{3}{7}$

b. $\dfrac{\text{euphoric riders}}{\text{vertiginous riders}} = \dfrac{4}{3}$

6. **a.** **Distributive property**

    b. **Inverse property of multiplication**

7. $5^2 \times 10^2 = 5 \cdot 5 \cdot 10 \cdot 10$
               $= 25 \cdot 100 = \mathbf{2500}$

8. **a.** $56 \text{ cm} - 20 \text{ cm} = 36 \text{ cm}$
            $\dfrac{36 \text{ cm}}{2} = \mathbf{18 \text{ cm}}$

    b. Area $= (10 \text{ cm})(18 \text{ cm})$
                $= \mathbf{180 \text{ cm}^2}$

9. **a.** $62\dfrac{1}{2}$

    b. **0.09**

    c. $7.5\% = \dfrac{7.5}{100} = \mathbf{0.075}$

10. **a.** $23.54545\underline{4}5\ldots \longrightarrow \mathbf{23.54545}$

    b. $0.91666\underline{6}\ldots \longrightarrow \mathbf{0.91667}$

11. 2 kilograms $= 2(1000 \text{ grams})$
                  $= \mathbf{2000 \text{ grams}}$

12.
$$\begin{array}{r} 0.065 \\ \times \quad \$5.00 \\ \hline \$0.32500 \longrightarrow \mathbf{\$0.33} \end{array}$$

13.
$$\begin{array}{r} 0.566\ldots \\ 9\overline{)5.100\ldots} \\ \underline{4\,5} \\ 60 \\ \underline{54} \\ 60 \\ \underline{54} \\ 6 \end{array}$$

    a. $0.566\underline{6}\ldots \longrightarrow \mathbf{0.567}$

    b. $\mathbf{0.5\overline{6}}$

14. $\dfrac{1}{26}$, **0.04**

15.

$XZ = \mathbf{2.5 \text{ cm}}$

16. **a.** Perimeter $= 2.5 \text{ cm} + 1.5 \text{ cm} + 2 \text{ cm}$
                       $= \mathbf{6 \text{ cm}}$

    b. Area $= \dfrac{(1.5 \text{ cm})(2 \text{ cm})}{2}$
               $= \mathbf{1.5 \text{ cm}^2}$

17. $\dfrac{3}{w} = \dfrac{25}{100}$
    $25w = 3 \cdot 100$
      $w = \dfrac{300}{25}$
      $w = \mathbf{12}$

18. $\dfrac{1.2}{4.4} = \dfrac{3}{a}$
    $1.2a = 3 \cdot 4.4$
      $a = \dfrac{13.2}{1.2}$
      $a = \mathbf{11}$

19.
$$\begin{array}{r} {}^{0}\ \ {}^{1}1 \\ \cancel{1}.\,\cancel{2}\,0 \\ -\ 0.\,2\,3 \\ \hline 0.\,9\,7 \end{array}$$
    $m = \mathbf{0.97}$

20.
$$\begin{array}{r} {}^{1}\ {}^{1} \\ 0.65 \\ +\ 1.97 \\ \hline 2.62 \end{array}$$
    $r = \mathbf{2.62}$

21.
$$\begin{array}{r} 0.15 \\ \times\ 0.15 \\ \hline 75 \\ 15 \\ \hline \mathbf{0.0225} \end{array}$$

22.
$$\begin{array}{r} 1.2 \\ \times\ 2.5 \\ \hline 6\,0 \\ 2\,4 \\ \hline 3.00 = 3 \end{array}$$
    $3 \times 4 = \mathbf{12}$

23.
$$
\begin{array}{r}
2.828 \\
5\overline{)14.140} \\
\underline{10} \\
4\,1 \\
\underline{4\,0} \\
14 \\
\underline{10} \\
40 \\
\underline{40} \\
0 \\
\end{array}
$$

24.
$$
\begin{array}{r}
0.8 \\
012.\overline{)009.6} \\
\underline{96} \\
0 \\
\end{array}
$$

25.
$$
\begin{array}{r}
\dfrac{5}{8} = \dfrac{15}{24} \\[4pt]
\dfrac{5}{6} = \dfrac{20}{24} \\[4pt]
+\ \dfrac{5}{12} = \dfrac{10}{24} \\[4pt]
\hline
\dfrac{45}{24} = 1\dfrac{21}{24} = \mathbf{1\dfrac{7}{8}}
\end{array}
$$

26.
$$
\begin{array}{r}
2\dfrac{1}{3} = 2\dfrac{4}{12} \\[4pt]
-\ 1\dfrac{1}{4} = 1\dfrac{3}{12} \\[4pt]
\hline
1\dfrac{1}{12}
\end{array}
$$

$$
\begin{array}{r}
4\dfrac{1}{2} = 4\dfrac{6}{12} \\[4pt]
-\ 1\dfrac{1}{12} = 1\dfrac{1}{12} \\[4pt]
\hline
3\dfrac{5}{12}
\end{array}
$$

27. $\dfrac{7}{15} \cdot 10 \cdot 2\dfrac{1}{7} = \dfrac{7}{\cancel{15}} \cdot \dfrac{\cancel{10}}{1} \cdot \dfrac{\cancel{15}}{\cancel{7}} = \mathbf{10}$

28. $6\dfrac{3}{5} \div 1\dfrac{1}{10} = \dfrac{33}{5} \div \dfrac{11}{10}$

$= \dfrac{\cancel{33}^{3}}{\cancel{5}} \times \dfrac{\cancel{10}^{2}}{\cancel{11}} = \mathbf{6}$

29.
$$
\begin{array}{r}
33\dfrac{1}{3} \\
\$021.\overline{)\$700.} \\
\underline{63} \\
70 \\
\underline{63} \\
7 \\
\end{array}
$$

33 pencils

30. a. **Answers will vary. See student work.**

   b. **The sum of the angle measures of a triangle is 180°.**

Practice Set 46

a. $\dfrac{416 \text{ miles}}{8 \text{ hours}} = \dfrac{52 \text{ miles}}{1 \text{ hour}}$

   52 mi/hr or **52 mph**

b. $\dfrac{416 \text{ miles}}{16 \text{ gallons}} = \dfrac{26 \text{ miles}}{1 \text{ gallon}}$

   26 mi/gal or **26 mpg**

c. $\dfrac{\$170.00}{20 \text{ hours}} = \dfrac{\$8.50}{1 \text{ hour}}$

   \$8.50 per hour

d.
$$
\begin{array}{r}
\$\ 9.25 \\
\times\quad 30 \text{ hours} \\
\hline
\$277.50 \\
\end{array}
$$

e.
$$
\begin{array}{r}
45 \text{ mpg} \\
\times\ 8 \text{ gal} \\
\hline
360 \text{ miles} \\
\end{array}
$$

f. $\dfrac{\$3.84}{24 \text{ ounces}} = \dfrac{\$0.16}{1 \text{ ounce}}$

   16¢ per ounce

g. $d = rt$

   $d = \dfrac{14 \text{ miles}}{1 \text{ hour}} \cdot 6 \text{ hours} = \mathbf{84 \text{ miles}}$

200

Written Practice (**46**)

1. $\dfrac{\$2.40}{16 \text{ ounces}} = \dfrac{\$0.15}{1 \text{ ounce}}$

$0.15/ounce

2. $\dfrac{702 \text{ kilometers}}{6 \text{ hours}} = 117 \dfrac{\text{kilometers}}{\text{hour}}$

117 kilometers per hour

3.

Penny	Nickel	Dime

Sample space = {HHH, HHT, HTH, HTT, THH, THT, TTH, TTT}

4.

```
              $2.94
$2.86      4)$11.76
$2.83        8
$2.98        3 7
+ $3.09      3 6
$11.76        16
              16
               0
```

5.
$$
\begin{array}{r}
3.\overset{1}{\cancel{2}}0 \\
-\,2.0\,3 \\
\hline
1.\,1\,7
\end{array}
$$

One and seventeen hundredths

6. 2 feet = 24 inches

24 inches ÷ $1\dfrac{1}{2}$ = $\dfrac{24 \text{ inches}}{1}$ ÷ $\dfrac{3}{2}$

$= \dfrac{\overset{8}{\cancel{24}}}{1} \times \dfrac{2}{\underset{1}{\cancel{3}}}$

= 16 books

7.

$\dfrac{3}{8}$ were red.

$\dfrac{5}{8}$ were not red.

48 roses
6 roses
6 roses
6 roses
6 roses
6 roses
6 roses
6 roses
6 roses

a. 3(6 roses) = **18 roses**

b. $\dfrac{\text{red roses}}{\text{not red roses}} = \dfrac{3}{5}$

c. $\dfrac{\text{not red roses}}{\text{total roses}} = \dfrac{30}{48} = \dfrac{5}{8}$

8. a. $3.0303 < 3.303$

b. $0.\overline{6} > 0.600$

9. 100 yards = 100(3 feet)
= **300 feet**

10. a. $0.080 = \dfrac{8}{100} = \dfrac{2}{25}$

b. $37\dfrac{1}{2}\% = 37.5\%$

$= \dfrac{37.5}{100} = \mathbf{0.375}$

c.
```
        0.0909 ...
    11)1.0000 ...
       99
       10
        0
       100
        99
         1
```
$0.\overline{09}$

11.
```
    $9.50
  ×   8 hours
  $76.00
```

Solutions

12.

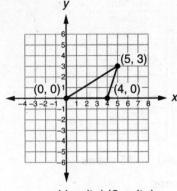

$$\text{Area} = \frac{(4 \text{ units})(3 \text{ units})}{2}$$
$$= \textbf{6 units}^2$$

13. $\dfrac{\text{face cards}}{\text{total cards}} = \dfrac{12}{52} = \dfrac{\textbf{3}}{\textbf{13}}$

14.
$$\begin{array}{r} 2 \\ 3 \\ 5 \\ 7 \\ + \ 11 \\ \hline 28 \end{array} \qquad \begin{array}{r} 5.6 \\ 5\overline{)28.0} \\ 25 \\ \hline 3\ 0 \\ 3\ 0 \\ \hline 0 \end{array}$$

15. $0.3(0.4 + 0.5) = 0.3(0.9) = \textbf{0.27}$
or
$0.3(0.4 + 0.5) = 0.12 + 0.15 = \textbf{0.27}$

16. a. Perimeter $= 3 \text{ in.} + 5 \text{ in.} + 4 \text{ in.}$
$+ \ 3 \text{ in.} + 11 \text{ in.} + 3 \text{ in.}$
$+ \ 4 \text{ in.} + 5 \text{ in.} = \textbf{38 in.}$

b.

```
          11
  ┌──────────────────┐
3 │         A        │
  └────┐        ┌────┘
 (4)   │        │   (4)
     5 │   B    │
       └────────┘
           3
```

$$\begin{array}{rl} \text{Area } A = & (11 \text{ in.})(3 \text{ in.}) = 33 \text{ in.}^2 \\ + \ \text{Area } B = & (5 \text{ in.})(3 \text{ in.}) = 15 \text{ in.}^2 \\ \hline & \text{Area of figure} = \textbf{48 in.}^2 \end{array}$$

17. a. $\textbf{180}°$

b. $\dfrac{360°}{3} = \textbf{120}°$

c. $\dfrac{360°}{6} = \textbf{60}°$

18. $\dfrac{10}{12} = \dfrac{2.5}{a}$
$10a = 2.5 \cdot 12$
$a = \dfrac{30}{10}$
$a = \textbf{3}$

19. $\dfrac{6}{8} = \dfrac{b}{100}$
$8b = 100 \cdot 6$
$b = \dfrac{600}{8}$
$b = \textbf{75}$

20.
$$\begin{array}{r} 4.7 \\ - \ 1.2 \\ \hline 3.5 \end{array}$$
$w = \textbf{3.5}$

21. $\dfrac{10^2}{10} = \dfrac{100}{10} = 10$
$x = \textbf{10}$

22. $1\dfrac{11}{18} + 2\dfrac{11}{24}$
$\downarrow \qquad \downarrow$
$2 \ + \ 2 = \textbf{4}$

$$\begin{array}{r} 1\dfrac{11}{18} = 1\dfrac{44}{72} \\ + \ 2\dfrac{11}{24} = 2\dfrac{33}{72} \\ \hline 3\dfrac{77}{72} = \textbf{4}\dfrac{\textbf{5}}{\textbf{72}} \end{array}$$

23. $5\dfrac{5}{6} - \left(3 - 1\dfrac{1}{3}\right)$
$\downarrow \qquad \downarrow \qquad \downarrow$
$6 \ - \ (3 - 1) = 6 - 2 = \textbf{4}$

$$\begin{array}{r} 3 = 2\dfrac{3}{3} \\ - \ 1\dfrac{1}{3} = 1\dfrac{1}{3} \\ \hline 1\dfrac{2}{3} \end{array}$$

$$\begin{array}{r} 5\dfrac{5}{6} = 5\dfrac{5}{6} \\ - \ 1\dfrac{2}{3} = 1\dfrac{4}{6} \\ \hline = \textbf{4}\dfrac{\textbf{1}}{\textbf{6}} \end{array}$$

24. $\frac{2}{3} \times 4 \times 1\frac{1}{8} = \frac{\cancel{2}}{\cancel{3}} \times \frac{\cancel{4}}{1} \times \frac{\cancel{9}}{\cancel{8}} = 3$

25. $6\frac{2}{3} \div 4 = \frac{20}{3} \div \frac{4}{1} = \frac{\overset{5}{\cancel{20}}}{3} \times \frac{1}{\cancel{4}}$

$= \frac{5}{3} = 1\frac{2}{3}$

26.

```
  4 1
  5. 2¹0        3.45
 − 0.5 7        6
  ───────     + 4.63
  4. 6 3       ───────
               14.08
```

27.

```
          150.
  0016. )2400.
         16
         ───
          80
          80
          ───
          00
           0
          ───
           0
```

28. Round the length to 7 inches and the width to 4 inches. Then multiply the rounded measures. (The estimated area is 28 in.²)

29. a. $\angle CAB$

b. $\overline{BA}$

30. a. $m\angle B = m\angle ADC = 60°$

b. $m\angle CAB = 180° - (60° + 45°)$
$= 180° - 105° = 75°$

c. $m\angle CAD = m\angle ACB = 45°$

Early Finishers Solutions

a. 39 min ÷ 4 = 9.75 min = $9\frac{3}{4}$ min
= 9 minutes 45 seconds.

b. 5 mi ÷ 4 = 1.25 mi = $1\frac{1}{4}$ mi

Practice Set 47

a. 400 + 50 + 6
$(4 \times 10^2) + (5 \times 10^1) + (6 \times 10^0)$

b. 24.25×10^3
$= 24.25 \times 1000$
$= \mathbf{24,250}$

c. $25 \times 10^6 = 25 \times 1,000,000$
$= \mathbf{25,000,000}$

d. $12.5 \div 10^3$
$= 12.5 \div 1000$
$= \mathbf{0.0125}$

e. $4.8 \div 10^4 = 4.8 \div 10,000$
$= \mathbf{0.00048}$

f. $10^3 \cdot 10^4 = \mathbf{10^7}$

g. $10^8 \div 10^2 = \mathbf{10^6}$

h. $(10^4)^2 = \mathbf{10^8}$

i. $n^3 \cdot n^4 = \mathbf{n^7}$

j. 2,500,000

k. 15,000,000,000

l. 1,600,000,000,000

Written Practice 47

1. a. True

b. True

2. $\frac{walk}{ride\ in\ bus} = \frac{10}{12} = \frac{5}{6}$

3. $\frac{ride\ in\ bus}{total} = \frac{12}{33} = \frac{4}{11}$

Solutions

4.
```
  1
  1.2      1.56
  1.4    5)7.80
  1.5      5
  1.7      ‾‾
+ 2       2 8
‾‾‾        2 5
  7.8      ‾‾‾
            30
            30
            ‾‾
             0
```

5. **134,800,000 viewers**

6. a. $\dfrac{1}{8} \cdot 40 = \dfrac{40}{8} =$ **5 paintings**

b. $40 - 5 =$ **35 paintings**

7. a.
```
      10 2/3
  12)128
     12
     ‾‾
     08
      0
      ‾
      8
```
10 glasses

b. 11 glasses

8. a. Answers may vary.

b. Answers may vary.

9. a. $0.375 = \dfrac{375}{1000} = \dfrac{3}{8}$

b. $62\dfrac{1}{2}\% = 62.5\% = \dfrac{62.5}{100} =$ **0.625**

10. a.

Minutes	Miles
10	$\dfrac{1}{2}$
20	1
30	$1\dfrac{1}{2}$
40	2
50	$2\dfrac{1}{2}$
60	3

b. 2 hours = 2(60 minutes) = 120 minutes
$d = rt$

$d = \dfrac{1 \text{ mile}}{20 \text{ minutes}} \cdot \overset{6}{\cancel{120 \text{ minutes}}} =$ **6 miles**

11. a. 53,714.545④ . . .
⟶ **53,714.545**

b. 53,⑦14.5454 . . .
⟶ **54,000**

12. a. $10^5 \cdot 10^2 = 10^7$

b. $10^8 \div 10^4 = 10^4$

13. 3.03

14. $BC = 6$ cm, $AF = 6$ cm
$AB = 6$ cm, $FE = 9$ cm
$ED = 12$ cm
Perimeter = 6 cm + 6 cm + 6 cm
　　　　　　+ 3 cm + 12 cm + 9 cm
　　　　　= **42 cm**

15.

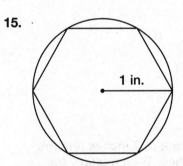

a. Diameter = 2(1 inch) = **2 inches**

b. Perimeter = 6(1 inch) = **6 inches**

16. $\dfrac{6}{10} = \dfrac{w}{100}$
$10w = 6 \cdot 100$
$w = \dfrac{600}{10}$
$w =$ **60**

17. $\dfrac{3.6}{x} = \dfrac{16}{24}$
$16x = (3.6)(24)$
$x = \dfrac{86.4}{16}$
$x =$ **5.4**

18.
```
    1.5
 ×  1.5
 ‾‾‾‾‾
    7 5
   15
   ‾‾‾‾
   2.25
```
$a =$ **2.25**

19.
$$\overset{\overset{8}{\cancel{9}}.^{1}8}{\underline{-\ 8.9}}$$
$$0.9$$
$$x = \mathbf{0.9}$$

20. $4\dfrac{1}{5} + 5\dfrac{1}{3} + \dfrac{1}{2}$

$\qquad \downarrow \qquad \downarrow \qquad \downarrow$

$\qquad 4\ +\ \ 5\ +\ 1 = \mathbf{10}$

$\qquad 4\dfrac{1}{5} = 4\dfrac{6}{30}$

$\qquad 5\dfrac{1}{3} = 5\dfrac{10}{30}$

$+\ \dfrac{1}{2} = \dfrac{15}{30}$

$\qquad\qquad 9\dfrac{31}{30} = \mathbf{10\dfrac{1}{30}}$

21. $6\dfrac{1}{8} - \left(5 - 1\dfrac{2}{3}\right)$

$\qquad \downarrow \qquad \downarrow \qquad \downarrow$

$\qquad 6\ -\ (5\ -\ 2) = 6 - 3 = \mathbf{3}$

$\qquad 5 \longrightarrow 4\dfrac{3}{3}$

$\qquad \underline{-\ 1\dfrac{2}{3}} \qquad \underline{-\ 1\dfrac{2}{3}}$

$\qquad\qquad\qquad\qquad 3\dfrac{1}{3}$

$6\dfrac{1}{8} = 6\dfrac{3}{24} \longrightarrow 5\dfrac{27}{24}$

$\underline{-\ 3\dfrac{1}{3} = 3\dfrac{8}{24}} \qquad \underline{-\ 3\dfrac{8}{24}}$

$\qquad\qquad\qquad\qquad\qquad \mathbf{2\dfrac{19}{24}}$

22. $\sqrt{16 \cdot 25} = \sqrt{400} = \mathbf{20}$

23. 3.6×10^3
$= 3.6 \times 1000$
$= \mathbf{3600}$

24. $8\dfrac{1}{3} \times 3\dfrac{3}{5} \times \dfrac{1}{3}$

$= \dfrac{\overset{5}{\cancel{25}}}{\underset{1}{\cancel{3}}} \times \dfrac{\overset{\overset{2}{\cancel{6}}}{\cancel{18}}}{\underset{1}{\cancel{5}}} \times \dfrac{1}{\underset{1}{\cancel{3}}}$

$= \mathbf{10}$

25. $3\dfrac{1}{8} \div 6\dfrac{1}{4} = \dfrac{25}{8} \div \dfrac{25}{4}$

$\qquad = \dfrac{\overset{1}{\cancel{25}}}{\underset{2}{\cancel{8}}} \times \dfrac{\overset{1}{\cancel{4}}}{\underset{1}{\cancel{25}}} = \mathbf{\dfrac{1}{2}}$

26.
$$\begin{array}{r} \overset{2\ 1}{26.7} \\ 3.45 \\ 0.036 \\ 12 \\ +\ 8.7 \\ \hline \mathbf{50.886} \end{array}$$

27. a. Perimeter $= 15$ in. $+ 13$ in. $+ 14$ in.
$\qquad\qquad\qquad = \mathbf{42\ in.}$

b. Area $= \dfrac{(14\ \text{in.})(12\ \text{in.})}{2}$
$\qquad\quad = \mathbf{84\ in.^2}$

28. $\quad 125 \div 10^2 = 125 \div 100 = 1.25$
$\quad 0.125 \times 10^2 = 0.125 \times 100 = 12.5$
$\qquad\qquad \mathbf{1.25 < 12.5}$

29. $\dfrac{2}{3} = \dfrac{8}{12}$

$\dfrac{1}{2} = \dfrac{6}{12} \qquad \mathbf{\dfrac{1}{2},\ \dfrac{7}{12},\ \dfrac{2}{3},\ \dfrac{5}{6}}$

$\dfrac{5}{6} = \dfrac{10}{12}$

30. a. $\angle a = 180° - 130° = \mathbf{50°}$

b. $\angle b = 180° - (65° + 50°)$
$\qquad = 180° - 115° = \mathbf{65°}$

c. Together, $\angle b$ and $\angle c$ form a straight angle that measures 180°. To find the measure of $\angle c$, we subtract the measure of $\angle b$ from 180°.

Practice Set (**48**)

a.
$$\begin{array}{r} 0.66\ldots \\ 3\overline{)2.00\ldots} \\ \underline{1\ 8} \\ 20 \\ \underline{18} \\ 2 \end{array} \qquad \mathbf{0.\overline{6}}$$

b. $\frac{2}{3} \times 100\% = \frac{200\%}{3} = 66\frac{2}{3}\%$

c. $1.1 = 1\frac{1}{10}$

d. $1.1 \times 100\% = \mathbf{110\%}$

e. $4\% = \frac{4}{100} = \frac{1}{25}$

f. $4\% = \frac{4}{100} = \mathbf{0.04}$

g. 3 or $\frac{3}{1}$

h. $3 \times 100\% = \mathbf{300\%}$

Written Practice 48

1. $\frac{195 \text{ kilometers}}{3.9 \text{ hours}} = 50 \frac{\textbf{kilometers}}{\textbf{hour}}$

2. $\frac{1008}{1323} = \frac{2 \cdot 2 \cdot 2 \cdot 2 \cdot \overset{1}{\cancel{3}} \cdot \overset{1}{\cancel{3}} \cdot \overset{1}{\cancel{7}}}{\underset{1}{\cancel{3}} \cdot \underset{1}{\cancel{3}} \cdot 3 \cdot \underset{1}{\cancel{7}} \cdot 7}$

$= \frac{\mathbf{16}}{\mathbf{21}}$

3. $\begin{array}{r} 1867 \\ -\ 1803 \\ \hline \mathbf{64 \text{ years}} \end{array}$

4. a. $\frac{\text{blue marbles}}{\text{total marbles}} = \frac{\mathbf{7}}{\mathbf{12}}$

b. $\frac{\text{red marbles}}{\text{blue marbles}} = \frac{\mathbf{5}}{\mathbf{7}}$

c. $P(\text{red}) = \frac{\mathbf{5}}{\mathbf{12}}, \mathbf{0.42}$

$$12\overline{)5.0000\ldots} \quad 0.4\,1\,6\,\overline{6} \to 0.42$$
$$\begin{array}{r} 0.4166\ldots \\ \underline{4\ 8} \\ 20 \\ \underline{12} \\ 80 \\ \underline{72} \\ 80 \\ \underline{72} \\ 8 \end{array}$$

5. $\frac{\$1.26}{9 \text{ ounces}} = \frac{\$0.14}{1 \text{ ounce}}$

$0.14 per ounce

6. $\begin{array}{r} 2550 \\ +\ 2900 \\ \hline 5450 \end{array}$

$$\begin{array}{r} \mathbf{2725} \\ 2\overline{)5450} \\ \underline{4} \\ 14 \\ \underline{14} \\ 5 \\ \underline{4} \\ 10 \\ \underline{10} \\ 0 \end{array}$$

7.

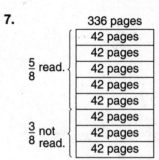

336 pages

$\frac{5}{8}$ read.
| 42 pages |
| 42 pages |
| 42 pages |
| 42 pages |
| 42 pages |

$\frac{3}{8}$ not read.
| 42 pages |
| 42 pages |
| 42 pages |

a. $5(42 \text{ pages}) = \mathbf{210 \text{ pages}}$

b. $3(42 \text{ pages}) = \mathbf{126 \text{ pages}}$

8.

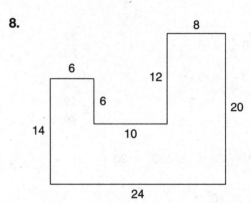

Perimeter $= 24 \text{ cm} + 14 \text{ cm} + 6 \text{ cm} + 6 \text{ cm}$
$+ 10 \text{ cm} + 12 \text{ cm} + 8 \text{ cm} + 20 \text{ cm}$
$= \mathbf{100 \text{ cm}}$

9. a. $100\% - (10\% + 12\% + 20\% + 25\%$
$+ 20\%) = 100\% - 87\% = \mathbf{13\%}$

b. $20\% = \frac{20}{100} = \frac{\mathbf{1}}{\mathbf{5}}$

c. $2(\$3200) = \mathbf{\$6400}$

10. $0.545\text{④}\ldots \longrightarrow \mathbf{0.545}$

Left column

11. **a.** See student answers.

    b. 5 centimeters

12. **a.** The exponent is 3 and the base is 5.

    b. $10^4 \cdot 10^4 = 10^8$

13.   1 foot = 12 inches

$$\frac{12 \text{ inches}}{6} = 2 \text{ inches}$$

14. **a.** $2\overline{)1.0}$ $\rightarrow 0.5$

    b. $\frac{1}{2} \times 100\% = \frac{100\%}{2} = 50\%$

    c. $0.1 = \frac{1}{10}$

    d. $0.1 \times 100\% = 10\%$

    e. $25\% = \frac{25}{100} = \frac{1}{4}$

    f. $25\% = \frac{25}{100} = 0.25$

    g. $1\overline{)4}$ $\rightarrow 4$

    h. $4 \times 100\% = 400\%$

15. $\dfrac{78 \text{ miles}}{1.2 \text{ gallons}} = 65 \dfrac{\text{miles}}{\text{gallon}}$

    65 mpg

16. $\dfrac{6}{100} = \dfrac{15}{w}$

$6w = 100 \cdot 15$

$w = \dfrac{1500}{6}$

$w = 250$

17. $\dfrac{20}{x} = \dfrac{15}{12}$

$15x = 20 \cdot 12$

$x = \dfrac{240}{15}$

$x = 16$

18. $6\overline{)1.44}$ $\rightarrow 0.24$

    $\underline{1\ 2}$
     24
    $\underline{24}$
      0

$m = 0.24$

Right column

19.
$$\frac{1}{2} = \frac{3}{6}$$
$$-\ \frac{1}{3} = \frac{2}{6}$$
$$f = \frac{1}{6}$$

20. $2^5 + 1^4 + 3^3$
$= 2 \cdot 2 \cdot 2 \cdot 2 \cdot 2 + 1 + 3 \cdot 3 \cdot 3$
$= 32 + 1 + 27 = 60$

21. $\sqrt{10^2 \cdot 6^2} = \sqrt{100 \cdot 36} = \sqrt{3600}$
$= 60$

22.
$$1\frac{1}{4} = 1\frac{3}{12}$$
$$+\ 1\frac{1}{6} = 1\frac{2}{12}$$
$$2\frac{5}{12}$$

$$3\frac{5}{6} = 3\frac{10}{12}$$
$$-\ 2\frac{5}{12} = 2\frac{5}{12}$$
$$1\frac{5}{12}$$

23.
$$4 \longrightarrow 3\frac{3}{3}$$
$$-\ \frac{2}{3} \qquad\quad -\ \frac{2}{3}$$
$$3\frac{1}{3}$$

$$8\frac{3}{4} = 8\frac{9}{12}$$
$$+\ 3\frac{1}{3} = 3\frac{4}{12}$$
$$11\frac{13}{12} = 12\frac{1}{12}$$

24. $\dfrac{15}{16} \cdot \dfrac{24}{25} \cdot 1\dfrac{1}{9}$

$$= \frac{\overset{3}{\cancel{15}}}{\underset{2}{\cancel{16}}} \cdot \frac{\overset{3}{\cancel{24}}}{\underset{5}{\cancel{25}}} \cdot \frac{\overset{2}{\cancel{10}}}{\underset{3}{\cancel{9}}} = 1$$

25. $2\dfrac{2}{3} \div 4 = \dfrac{8}{3} \div \dfrac{4}{1}$

$$= \frac{\overset{2}{\cancel{8}}}{3} \times \frac{1}{\underset{1}{\cancel{4}}} = \frac{2}{3}$$

$1\dfrac{1}{3} \div \dfrac{2}{3} = \dfrac{4}{3} \div \dfrac{2}{3} = \dfrac{\overset{2}{\cancel{4}}}{\underset{1}{\cancel{3}}} \times \dfrac{\overset{1}{\cancel{3}}}{\underset{1}{\cancel{2}}}$

$= 2$

26. $\dfrac{a}{b} = \dfrac{\$13.93}{0.07}$

$$
\begin{array}{r}
\$199. \\
0\,07\overline{\big)\,\$1393.} \\
\underline{7} \\
69 \\
\underline{63} \\
63 \\
\underline{63} \\
0
\end{array}
$$

$199.00

27.

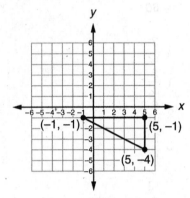

Area $= \dfrac{(6 \text{ units})(3 \text{ units})}{2} = \textbf{9 sq. units}$

28. $\dfrac{\text{students with more than one sibling}}{\text{total students}}$

$= \dfrac{8}{20} = \dfrac{\textbf{2}}{\textbf{5}}$

29. Answers will vary. See student work. Sample answer:

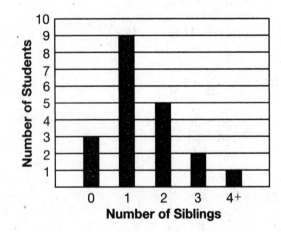

30. $m\angle a = 180° - (50° + 90°)$
$\quad\quad = 180° - 140° = \textbf{40°}$
$m\angle b = \textbf{50°}$
$m\angle c = 180° - 50° = \textbf{130°}$

Practice Set 49

a. $12\overline{)70}$ $\dfrac{5}{}$ **5 feet 10 in.**
$\quad\quad \underline{60}$
$\quad\quad 10$

b. 6 feet $= 6(12 \text{ inches})$
$\quad\quad\quad = 72 \text{ inches}$
72 inches $+$ 3 inches
$\quad\quad\quad = \textbf{75 inches}$

c. 20 in. $=$ 1 ft 8 in.
    1 ft 8 in.
$\underline{+ \text{ 5 ft}}$
    6 ft 8 in.

d.
$$
\begin{array}{llll}
& 2 \text{ yd} & 1 \text{ ft} & 8 \text{ in.} \\
+ & 1 \text{ yd} & 2 \text{ ft} & 9 \text{ in.} \\
\hline
& 3 \text{ yd} & 3 \text{ ft} & 17 \text{ in.}
\end{array}
$$

17 in. $=$ 1 ft 5 in.
    1 ft 5 in.
$\underline{+ \text{ 3 ft}}$
    4 ft 5 in. $\longrightarrow$ 3 yd 4 ft 5 in.

4 ft $=$ 1 yd 1 ft
    1 yd 1 ft
$\underline{+ \text{ 3 yd}}$
    4 yd 1 ft $\longrightarrow$ **4 yd 1 ft 5 in.**

e.
$$
\begin{array}{llll}
& 5 \text{ hr} & 42 \text{ min} & 53 \text{ s} \\
+ & 6 \text{ hr} & 17 \text{ min} & 27 \text{ s} \\
\hline
& 11 \text{ hr} & 59 \text{ min} & 80 \text{ s}
\end{array}
$$

80 s $=$ 1 min 20 s
    1 min 20 s
$\underline{+ \text{ 59 min}}$
    60 min 20 s $\longrightarrow$ 11 hr 60 min 20 s

60 min $=$ 1 hr
11 hr $+$ 1 hr $=$ 12 hr
12 hr 20 s

f.

$$\overset{2}{\cancel{3}}\text{ hr} \qquad\qquad 3\text{ s} \quad\nearrow(60\text{ min})$$
$$-\ 1\text{ hr}\quad 15\text{ min}\quad 55\text{ s}\ \longrightarrow$$

$$\overset{2}{\cancel{3}}\text{ hr}\quad \overset{59}{\cancel{60}}\text{ min}\quad \overset{63}{\cancel{3}}\text{ s}$$
$$-\ 1\text{ hr}\quad 15\text{ min}\quad 55\text{ s}$$
$$\overline{\ \ 1\textbf{ hr}\quad 44\textbf{ min}\quad 8\textbf{ s}}$$

g.

$$8\text{ yd}\quad \overset{0}{\cancel{1}}\text{ ft}\quad 5\text{ in.}\quad\nearrow(12\text{ in.})$$
$$-\ 3\text{ yd}\quad 2\text{ ft}\quad 7\text{ in.}\ \longrightarrow$$

$$\overset{7}{\cancel{8}}\text{ yd}\quad \overset{0}{\cancel{1}}\text{ ft}\quad \overset{17}{\cancel{5}}\text{ in.}\quad\nearrow(3\text{ ft})$$
$$-\ 3\text{ yd}\quad 2\text{ ft}\quad 7\text{ in.}\ \longrightarrow$$
$$\overline{\qquad\qquad\qquad\qquad 10\text{ in.}}$$

$$\overset{7}{\cancel{8}}\text{ yd}\quad \overset{3}{\overset{\cancel{0}}{\cancel{1}}}\text{ ft}\quad \overset{17}{\cancel{5}}\text{ in.}$$
$$-\ 3\text{ yd}\quad 2\text{ ft}\quad 7\text{ in.}$$
$$\overline{\ \ 4\textbf{ yd}\quad 1\textbf{ ft}\quad 10\textbf{ in.}}$$

h.

$$2\text{ days}\quad \overset{2}{\cancel{3}}\text{ hr}\quad 30\text{ min}\quad\nearrow(60\text{ min})$$
$$-\ 1\text{ day}\quad 8\text{ hr}\quad 45\text{ min}\ \longrightarrow$$

$$\overset{1}{\cancel{2}}\text{ days}\quad \overset{2}{\cancel{3}}\text{ hr}\quad \overset{90}{\cancel{30}}\text{ min}\quad\nearrow(24\text{ hr})$$
$$-\ 1\text{ day}\quad 8\text{ hr}\quad 45\text{ min}\ \longrightarrow$$
$$\overline{\qquad\qquad\qquad\qquad 45\text{ min}}$$

$$\overset{1}{\cancel{2}}\text{ days}\quad \overset{26}{\overset{\cancel{2}}{\cancel{3}}}\text{ hr}\quad \overset{90}{\cancel{30}}\text{ min}$$
$$-\ 1\text{ day}\quad 8\text{ hr}\quad 45\text{ min}$$
$$\overline{\qquad\qquad 18\textbf{ hr}\quad 45\textbf{ min}}$$

i. Add 18 hr, 45 min + 1 day, 8 hr, 45 min to see if the sum is 2 days, 3 hr, 30 min.

Written Practice 49

1.

$$\begin{array}{r}0.2\\+\ 0.05\\\hline 0.25\end{array}\qquad \begin{array}{r}0.05\\\times\ \ 0.2\\\hline 0.010\end{array}\longrightarrow 0.01$$

$$001\overline{)025.}\quad\begin{array}{r}25\\\hline 2\ \ \\\hline 05\\5\\\hline 0\end{array}$$

2.
$$\begin{array}{r}9.2\text{ yards}\\20\overline{)184.0}\\180\\\hline 4\ 0\\4\ 0\\\hline 0\end{array}$$

3.
$$\begin{array}{r}\$0.25\\24\overline{)\$6.00}\\48\\\hline 1\ 20\\1\ 20\\\hline 0\end{array}$$

25¢ per pen

4. 3(8 sides) + 2(6 sides) + 5 sides
  + 2(4 sides)
  = 24 sides + 12 sides + 5 sides + 8 sides
  = **49 sides**

5.
$$\begin{array}{r}\overset{2\ 1}{6.21}\\4.38\\7.5\\6.3\\5.91\\+\ 8.04\\\hline 38.34\end{array}\qquad \begin{array}{r}6.39\\6\overline{)38.34}\\36\\\hline 2\ 3\\1\ 8\\\hline 54\\54\\\hline 0\end{array}$$

6.

72 billy goats
$\frac{2}{9}$ were gruff. { 8 billy goats / 8 billy goats
$\frac{7}{9}$ were cordial. { 8 billy goats (×7)

a. 7(8 billy goats) = **56 billy goats**

b. $\dfrac{\text{gruff billy goats}}{\text{cordial billy goats}} = \dfrac{2}{7}$

7. 0.5, 0.5$\overline{4}$, 0.$\overline{5}$

8. a. Answers may vary.

b. $2\dfrac{5}{8}$ inches

Solutions

9. a. $0.9 \times 100\% = \mathbf{90\%}$

b. $1\frac{3}{5} \times 100\%$

$$= \frac{8}{5} \times 100\% = \frac{800\%}{5}$$

$$= \mathbf{160\%}$$

c. $\frac{5}{6} \times 100\% = \frac{500\%}{6}$

$$\frac{250\%}{3} = \mathbf{83\frac{1}{3}\%}$$

10. a. $75\% = \frac{75}{100} = \frac{3}{4}$

b. $75\% = \frac{75}{100} = \mathbf{0.75}$

c. $5\% = \frac{5}{100} = \frac{1}{20}$

d. $5\% = \frac{5}{100} = \mathbf{0.05}$

11.
$$\begin{array}{r} 62 \\ \times\ \ 60 \\ \hline \mathbf{3720\ times} \end{array}$$

12. even primes: 2

$$\frac{\text{even primes}}{\text{total}} = \frac{1}{6}$$

$$\begin{array}{r} 0.166\ldots \\ 6\overline{)1.000\ldots} \\ 6 \\ \hline 40 \\ 36 \\ \hline 40 \\ 36 \\ \hline 4 \end{array} \quad 0.16\overline{6} \to \mathbf{0.17}$$

13. a. Area = $(1\text{ in.})(1\text{ in.}) = \mathbf{1\ in.^2}$

b. Area = $\left(\frac{1}{2}\text{ in.}\right)\left(\frac{1}{2}\text{ in.}\right) = \mathbf{\frac{1}{4}\ in.^2}$

c. Area = $1\text{ in.}^2 - \frac{1}{4}\text{ in.}^2$

$$= \frac{4}{4}\text{ in.}^2 - \frac{1}{4}\text{ in.}^2 = \mathbf{\frac{3}{4}\ in.^2}$$

14. Perimeter = $\frac{1}{2}$ in. + 1 in. + 1 in.

$$+ \frac{1}{2}\text{ in.} + \frac{1}{2}\text{ in.} + \frac{1}{2}\text{ in.}$$

$$= 2\text{ in.} + \frac{4}{2}\text{ in.} = 2\text{ in.} + 2\text{ in.}$$

$$= \mathbf{4\ in.}$$

15. a. 8 cm

b. 6 cm

c. When the base is 6 cm and the height is 8 cm, the area is:

$$\frac{(6\text{ cm})(8\text{ cm})}{2} = \frac{48\text{ cm}^2}{2} = 24\text{ cm}^2$$

So, when the base is 10 cm, we can find the height:

$$\frac{1}{2}(10\text{ cm})(h) = 24\text{ cm}^2$$

$$(5\text{ cm})(h) = 24\text{ cm}^2$$

$$h = \frac{24\text{ cm}^2}{5\text{ cm}} = \mathbf{4.8\ cm}$$

16. $\frac{y}{100} = \frac{18}{45}$

$$45y = 100 \cdot 18$$

$$y = \frac{1800}{45}$$

$$y = \mathbf{40}$$

17. $\frac{35}{40} = \frac{1.4}{m}$

$$35m = (1.4)(40)$$

$$m = \frac{56}{35}$$

$$m = 1\frac{21}{35} = 1\frac{3}{5} = \mathbf{1.6}$$

18.
$$\begin{array}{r} \frac{1}{2} = \frac{3}{6} \\ -\frac{1}{6} = \frac{1}{6} \\ \hline \frac{2}{6} = \frac{1}{3} \end{array}$$

$$n = \mathbf{\frac{1}{3}}$$

19.
$$\begin{array}{r} 0.29 \\ 9\overline{)2.61} \\ 1\,8 \\ \hline 81 \\ 81 \\ \hline 0 \end{array}$$

$$d = \mathbf{0.29}$$

20. $\sqrt{100} + 4^3 = 10 + 4 \cdot 4 \cdot 4$

$$= 10 + 64 = \mathbf{74}$$

21. $3.14 \times 10^4 = 3.14 \times 10,000 = \mathbf{31,400}$

22.

$$4\frac{1}{6} = 4\frac{1}{6} \longrightarrow 3\frac{7}{6}$$
$$-\ 2\frac{1}{2} = 2\frac{3}{6} \qquad -\ 2\frac{3}{6}$$
$$\overline{\qquad\qquad} \qquad \overline{1\frac{4}{6} = 1\frac{2}{3}}$$

$$3\frac{3}{4} = 3\frac{9}{12}$$
$$+\ 1\frac{2}{3} = 1\frac{8}{12}$$
$$\overline{\qquad\qquad}$$
$$4\frac{17}{12} = 5\frac{5}{12}$$

23. $3\frac{3}{4} \div 1\frac{1}{2} = \frac{15}{4} \div \frac{3}{2} = \frac{\overset{5}{\cancel{15}}}{\underset{2}{\cancel{4}}} \times \frac{\overset{1}{\cancel{2}}}{\underset{1}{\cancel{3}}} = \frac{5}{2}$

$6\frac{2}{3} \cdot \frac{5}{2} = \frac{\overset{10}{\cancel{20}}}{3} \cdot \frac{5}{\underset{1}{\cancel{2}}} = \frac{50}{3} = \mathbf{16\frac{2}{3}}$

24.
```
    3 days   8 hr  15 min
  + 2 days  15 hr  45 min
  ───────────────────────
    5 days  23 hr  60 min
```
60 min = 1 hr; 23 hr + 1 hr = 24 hr
24 hr = 1 day
5 days + 1 day = **6 days**

25.
$$\overset{3}{\cancel{4}}\ yd\ \overset{\overset{3}{\cancel{0}}}{\cancel{1}}\ ft\ \overset{15}{\cancel{3}}\ in.$$
$$-\ 2\ yd\ \ 1\ ft\ \ 9\ in.$$
$$\overline{\mathbf{1\ yd\ \ 2\ ft\ \ 6\ in.}}$$

26.
```
          $300.
  006. )$1800.
         18
         ──
         00
          0
          ──
          00
           0
           ─
           0
```
$300.00

27. Round 35.675 to 36. Round $2\frac{7}{8}$ to 3. Then divide 36 by 3.

28. Jorge's sample space is better because it lists the equally-likely outcomes.

29. $LWH = (0.5)(0.2)(0.1)$

```
    0.5                0.1
  × 0.2              × 0.1
  ───── ⟶ 0.1      ───────
  0.10               0.01
```

30. $m\angle a = \mathbf{32°}$
$m\angle b = 180° - (90° + 32°)$
$\qquad = 180° - 122° = \mathbf{58°}$
$m\angle c = 180° - 58° = \mathbf{122°}$

Practice Set 50

a. $\dfrac{\mathbf{1\ yd}}{\mathbf{36\ in.}}$ and $\dfrac{\mathbf{36\ in.}}{\mathbf{1\ yd}}$

b. $\dfrac{\mathbf{100\ cm}}{\mathbf{1\ m}}$ and $\dfrac{\mathbf{1\ m}}{\mathbf{100\ cm}}$

c. $\dfrac{\mathbf{16\ oz}}{\mathbf{1\ lb}}$ and $\dfrac{\mathbf{1\ lb}}{\mathbf{16\ oz}}$

d. $10\ \cancel{yards} \cdot \dfrac{36\ inches}{1\ \cancel{yard}}$
$= \mathbf{360\ inches}$

e. $24\ \cancel{ft} \cdot \dfrac{1\ yd}{3\ \cancel{ft}}$
$= \mathbf{8\ yd}$

f. $20\ \cancel{in.} \times \dfrac{2.54\ cm}{1\ \cancel{in.}} = 50.8\ cm$

$50.8\ cm > 50\ cm$

$20\ in. > 50\ cm$

g. $\dfrac{\overset{5}{\cancel{20}}\ miles}{\cancel{gallon}} \times \dfrac{1\ \cancel{gallon}}{\underset{1}{\cancel{4}}\ quarts} = \mathbf{5\ miles\ per\ quart}$

h. $\dfrac{60\ beats}{\cancel{minute}} \times \dfrac{60\ \cancel{minutes}}{1\ hour} = \mathbf{3600\ beats\ per\ hour}$

Written Practice 50

1.
```
    3.5                    3.5
  × 0.4                  + 0.4
  ──────              ────────
  1.40 ⟶ 1.4             3.9
```
```
    3.9
  − 1.4
  ──────
    2.5
```

2. a. $\dfrac{\text{parts with 1}}{\text{total parts}} = \dfrac{4}{10} = \dfrac{2}{5}$

b. $\dfrac{3}{5} \times 100\% = \dfrac{300\%}{5} = \textbf{60\%}$

c. $P(\text{number} > 2) = \dfrac{\text{numbers} > 2}{\text{total}}$

$= \dfrac{3}{10} = \textbf{0.3}$

3. $\dfrac{\$1.44}{18 \text{ ounces}} = \dfrac{\$0.08}{1 \text{ ounce}}$

8¢ per ounce

4. $\dfrac{20 \text{ miles}}{2.5 \text{ hours}} = 8 \dfrac{\textbf{miles}}{\textbf{hour}}$

5. First hour costs $2, 50¢ for each additional half hour or part thereof 3 hours 20 minutes 2 + hour = 2 hours 20 minutes → 5 half hours
$\$2 + \$0.50(5)$
$= \$2 + \$2.50 = \textbf{\$4.50}$

6. $\dfrac{1 \text{ mile}}{\cancel{6} \text{ minutes}_1} \times \dfrac{\cancel{60}^{10} \text{ minutes}}{1 \text{ hour}} =$

10 miles per hour

7. a. $2(6 \text{ members})$
$= \textbf{12 members}$

b. $\dfrac{3}{5} \times 100\% = \dfrac{300\%}{5} = \textbf{60\%}$

8. B. 40%

9.
$$\begin{array}{r} 0.8333\ldots \\ 6\overline{)5.0000\ldots} \\ \underline{4\,8} \\ 20 \\ \underline{18} \\ 20 \\ \underline{18} \\ 20 \\ \underline{18} \\ 2 \end{array}$$
3.8333

10. 7,500,000
$= 7,000,000 + 500,000$
$= \textbf{(7} \times \textbf{10}^6\textbf{)} + \textbf{(5} \times \textbf{10}^5\textbf{)}$

11. a. $0.6 \times 100\% = \textbf{60\%}$

b. $\dfrac{1}{6} \times 100\% = \dfrac{100\%}{6}$
$= \textbf{16}\dfrac{\textbf{2}}{\textbf{3}}\textbf{\%}$

c. $1\dfrac{1}{2} \times 100\% = \dfrac{3}{2} \times 100\%$
$= \dfrac{300\%}{2} = \textbf{150\%}$

12. a. $30\% = \dfrac{30}{100} = \dfrac{\textbf{3}}{\textbf{10}}$

b.
$$\begin{array}{r} 0.3 \\ 10\overline{)3.0} \\ \underline{3\,0} \\ 0 \end{array}$$
0.3

c. $250\% = \dfrac{250}{100} = \dfrac{25}{10} = \dfrac{5}{2} = \textbf{2}\dfrac{\textbf{1}}{\textbf{2}}$

d. $250\% = 2\dfrac{1}{2} = \textbf{2.5}$

e. 5 or $\dfrac{\textbf{5}}{\textbf{1}}$

f. $5 \times 100\% = \textbf{500\%}$

13. 97

14. a. Area $= (8 \text{ cm})(12 \text{ cm})$
$= \textbf{96 cm}^2$

b. Area $= \dfrac{(6 \text{ cm})(8 \text{ cm})}{2} = \textbf{24 cm}^2$

c. Area $= 96 \text{ cm}^2 + 24 \text{ cm}^2$
$= \textbf{120 cm}^2$

15.

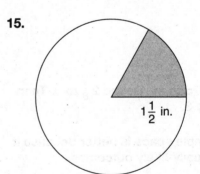

$1\dfrac{1}{2}$ in.

212

16. $\dfrac{10}{x} = \dfrac{7}{42}$

$7x = 10 \cdot 42$

$x = \dfrac{420}{7}$

$x = \mathbf{60}$

17. $\dfrac{1.5}{1} = \dfrac{w}{4}$

$1w = (1.5)4$

$w = \dfrac{6}{1}$

$w = \mathbf{6}$

18.
$$\begin{array}{r} 5.\overset{5}{\cancel{6}}{}^{1}0 \\ -\;3.56 \\ \hline 2.04 \end{array}$$
$y = \mathbf{2.04}$

19.
$$\begin{array}{rcl} \dfrac{3}{20} &=& \dfrac{9}{60} \\ -\dfrac{1}{15} &=& \dfrac{4}{60} \\ \hline & & \dfrac{5}{60} = \dfrac{1}{12} \end{array}$$

$w = \mathbf{\dfrac{1}{12}}$

20. **a.** Distributive property

b. Commutative property of addition

c. Identity property of multiplication

21. **B.** 10^4

22.

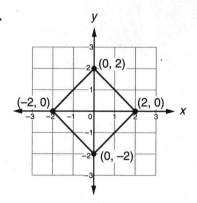

a. **(0, 2)**

b. Area $= 4(1\text{ sq. units}) + 8\left(\dfrac{1}{2}\text{ sq. units}\right)$

$= 4\text{ sq. units} + 4\text{ sq. units}$

$= \mathbf{8\text{ sq. units}}$

23. $\begin{array}{r} 2\frac{1}{2}\text{ muffins} \\ 4\overline{)10} \\ \underline{8} \\ 2 \end{array}$

24. **a.** $20 - 6 = \mathbf{14}$

b. **15**

c. **See student work.**

25. $\dfrac{10\text{ mm}}{1\text{ cm}},\ \dfrac{1\text{ cm}}{10\text{ mm}}$

$\overset{16}{\cancel{160}}\text{ mm} \cdot \dfrac{1\text{ cm}}{\underset{1}{\cancel{10}}\text{ mm}} = \mathbf{16\text{ cm}}$

26.
$$\begin{array}{r} 4\text{ yd}\quad 2\text{ ft}\quad 7\text{ in.} \\ +\;3\text{ yd}\qquad\quad\; 5\text{ in.} \\ \hline 7\text{ yd}\quad 2\text{ ft}\quad 12\text{ in.} \end{array}$$
$12\text{ in.} = 1\text{ ft},\ 1\text{ ft} + 2\text{ ft} = 3\text{ ft}$

$3\text{ ft} = 1\text{ yd},\ 7\text{ yd} + 1\text{ yd} = \mathbf{8\text{ yd}}$

27. $1\dfrac{3}{4} \div 2\dfrac{1}{3} = \dfrac{7}{4} \div \dfrac{7}{3}$

$= \dfrac{\overset{1}{\cancel{7}}}{4} \times \dfrac{3}{\underset{1}{\cancel{7}}} = \dfrac{3}{4}$

$$\begin{array}{rcl} 5\dfrac{1}{6} &=& 5\dfrac{2}{12} \longrightarrow\quad 4\dfrac{14}{12} \\ -\dfrac{3}{4} &=& \dfrac{9}{12}\qquad\qquad -\dfrac{9}{12} \\ \hline & & \qquad\qquad\qquad 4\dfrac{5}{12} \end{array}$$

28. $3\dfrac{1}{8} \cdot 2\dfrac{2}{5} = \dfrac{\overset{5}{\cancel{25}}}{\underset{2}{\cancel{8}}} \cdot \dfrac{\overset{3}{\cancel{12}}}{\underset{1}{\cancel{5}}} = \dfrac{15}{2}$

$$\begin{array}{rcl} 3\dfrac{5}{7} &=& 3\dfrac{10}{14} \\ +\dfrac{15}{2} &=& \dfrac{105}{14} \\ \hline & & 3\dfrac{115}{14} = \mathbf{11\dfrac{3}{14}} \end{array}$$

29. **a.** $m\angle BAC = m\angle CDB = \mathbf{60°}$

b. $m\angle BCA = 180° - (70° + 60°)$

$= 180° - 130° = \mathbf{50°}$

c. $m\angle CBD = m\angle BCA = \mathbf{50°}$

30. **a.** 4(5 − 3) or 4(5 − 3)
       4(2)   20 − 12
        8   8

   b. Yes

   c. Distributive property

Early Finishers Solutions

a. $31.50 × 0.08 = $2.52

b. $31.50 + $2.52 = $34.02

$$\frac{$34.02}{2} = $17.01$$

Creating Graphs

1. {Students use data from Investigation 4 to draw a histogram.}

2. **Left (first); Range and interval of "Units Sold" (y-axis) were decreased.**

3. {Students create a bar graph using data from the bar graph in the Investigation. Check whether students alter the x-axis interval/scale.} **One possibility is shown.**

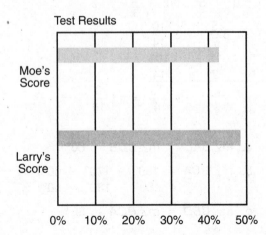

4. {Students create a double-line graph using information in a provided table. Check whether a) students have labeled axes; b) chosen appropriate scales; and, c) provided a legend to distinguish between graphed lines.} **One possibility is shown.**

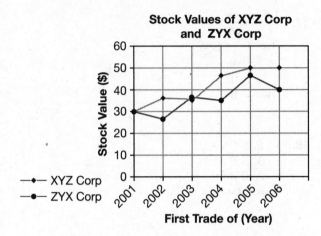

5. {Students use a compass, straightedge and protractor to draw a circle graph (pie chart) with accurate proportional measurements, given percentages for each category of data. They have to convert percentages to correct angles and then draw appropriately sized sectors.} **An approximation is shown.**

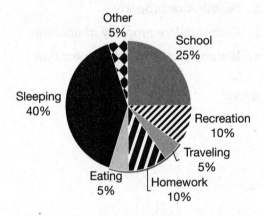

Practice Set 51

a. $1{,}5000000 \longrightarrow \mathbf{1.5 \times 10^7}$

b. $4{,}00000000000 \longrightarrow \mathbf{4 \times 10^{11}}$

c. $5{,}090000 \longrightarrow \mathbf{5.09 \times 10^6}$

d. $2{,}50000000000 \longrightarrow \mathbf{2.5 \times 10^{11}}$

e. $\mathbf{2.4 \times 10^5}$

f. $34000000{.} \longrightarrow \mathbf{3{,}400{,}000}$

g. $100000{.} \longrightarrow \mathbf{100{,}000}$

h. $150000{.} \longrightarrow 150{,}000$
$\quad 1500000{.} \longrightarrow 1{,}500{,}000$
$\qquad 1.5 \times 10^5 < 1.5 \times 10^6$

i. $1000000{.} \longrightarrow 1{,}000{,}000$
$\quad 1{,}000{,}000 = 1{,}000{,}000$
$\quad \text{one million} = 1 \times 10^6$

j. **Nine point three times ten to the seventh**

Written Practice 51

1. **3 tests**

2.
$$\begin{array}{r} 70 \\ 80 \\ 75 \\ 85 \\ + \ 90 \\ \hline 400 \end{array} \qquad \begin{array}{r} \mathbf{80} \\ 5\overline{)400} \end{array}$$

3. $\dfrac{9 \text{ in.}}{6} = \dfrac{3}{2} \text{ in.}$

$5\left(\dfrac{3}{2} \text{ in.}\right) = \dfrac{15}{2} \text{ in.} = \mathbf{7\dfrac{1}{2} \text{ in.}}$

4.
$$\begin{array}{r} \$ 0.65 \\ \times \ \ 6 \\ \hline \$ 3.90 \end{array} \longrightarrow \begin{array}{r} \$ 3.90 \\ - \ \$ 3.36 \\ \hline \$ 0.54 \end{array}$$

$$\begin{array}{r} \$ 0.09 \\ 6\overline{)\$ 0.54} \\ \underline{54} \\ 0 \end{array}$$

9¢ per can

5. a. $\dfrac{\text{unconvinced people}}{\text{total people}} = \dfrac{2}{7}$

   b. $\dfrac{\text{convinced people}}{\text{unconvinced people}} = \dfrac{5}{2}$

6. a. $1{,}2000000 \longrightarrow \mathbf{1.2 \times 10^7}$

   b. $1{,}7600 \longrightarrow \mathbf{1.76 \times 10^4}$

7. a. $12000{.} \longrightarrow \mathbf{12{,}000}$

   b. $5000000{.} \longrightarrow \mathbf{5{,}000{,}000}$

8. a.
$$\begin{array}{r} 0.125 \\ 8\overline{)1.000} \\ \underline{8} \\ 20 \\ \underline{16} \\ 40 \\ \underline{40} \\ 0 \end{array}$$

   b. $87\dfrac{1}{2}\% = \dfrac{87.5}{100} = \mathbf{0.875}$

9. $176 \ \cancel{\text{pounds}} \times \dfrac{1 \text{ kilogram}}{2.2 \ \cancel{\text{pounds}}} = \mathbf{80 \text{ kilograms}}$

10. a. $40\% = \dfrac{40}{100} = \dfrac{2}{5}$

    b. $40\% = \dfrac{40}{100} = \dfrac{4}{10} = \mathbf{0.4}$

    c. $4\% = \dfrac{4}{100} = \dfrac{1}{25}$

    d. $4\% = \dfrac{4}{100} = \mathbf{0.04}$

11. a. $0.5 \times 360° = \mathbf{180°}$

    b. $0.25 \times 360° = \mathbf{90°}$

    c. $0.125 \times 360° = \mathbf{45°}$

    d. $0.125 \times 360° = \mathbf{45°}$

12. a.

Sales	Tax
$1	$0.06
$2	$0.12
$3	$0.18
$4	$0.24
$5	$0.30

   b. $\$15 \times \$0.06 = \mathbf{\$0.90}$

13. a. {2, 4, 6, 8}

    b. P(7) = **0**

14. a. $\angle Z$

    b. $\overline{DC}$

15. 19 ft 10 in. → 20 ft

    30 ft 4 in. → 30 ft

    24 ft 10 in. → 25 ft

    20 ft 2 in. → 20 ft

    Missing length: 30 ft − 20 ft = 10 ft

    Missing width: 25 ft − 20 ft = 5 ft

    Estimated perimeter

      = 20 ft + 30 ft + 25 ft

      + 20 ft + 5 ft + 10 ft = **110 ft**

16.

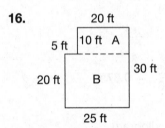

    Estimated area A = (10 ft)(20 ft) = 200 ft²

  + Estimated area B = (20 ft)(25 ft) = 500 ft²

                   Total estimated area = **700 ft²**

17. $\dfrac{24}{x} = \dfrac{60}{40}$

    $60x = 24 \cdot 40$

    $x = \dfrac{960}{60}$

    $x = \mathbf{16}$

18. $\dfrac{6}{4.2} = \dfrac{n}{7}$

    $4.2n = 6 \cdot 7$

    $n = \dfrac{42}{4.2}$

    $n = \mathbf{10}$

19.
```
    1.68
 5)8.40
    5
    3 4
    3 0
      40
      40
       0
```
    $m = \mathbf{1.68}$

20.
```
    4 10
  6.5̸ Ø̸
 −5.0 6
  1.4 4
```
    $y = \mathbf{1.44}$

21. $5^2 + 3^3 + \sqrt{64}$

    $= 25 + 27 + 8 = \mathbf{60}$

22. $16 \, \cancel{cm} \cdot \dfrac{10 \text{ mm}}{1 \, \cancel{cm}} = \mathbf{160 \text{ mm}}$

23.
```
     7       26      75
     8̸ days   3̸ hr   1̸5̸ min
  −  5 days  18 hr  50 min
     2 days   8 hr  25 min
```

24.
```
    3 yd  2 ft   5 in.
  + 1 yd        9 in.
    4 yd  2 ft  14 in.
```
    14 in. = 1 ft 2 in.
```
    1 ft  2 in.
  + 2 ft
    3 ft  2 in.
```
    3 ft = 1 yd; 1 yd + 4 yd = 5 yd

    5 yd 2 in.

25.
$$5\tfrac{1}{4} = 5\tfrac{2}{8} \longrightarrow 4\tfrac{10}{8}$$
$$-\,3\tfrac{7}{8} = 3\tfrac{7}{8} \qquad\quad -\,3\tfrac{7}{8}$$
$$\qquad\qquad\qquad\qquad\qquad 1\tfrac{3}{8}$$

$$6\tfrac{2}{3} = 6\tfrac{16}{24}$$
$$+\,1\tfrac{3}{8} = 1\tfrac{9}{24}$$
$$\qquad\quad 7\tfrac{25}{24} = \mathbf{8\tfrac{1}{24}}$$

26. $2\tfrac{2}{3} \div 1\tfrac{1}{2} = \dfrac{8}{3} \div \dfrac{3}{2}$

             $= \dfrac{8}{3} \times \dfrac{2}{3} = \dfrac{16}{9}$

    $3\tfrac{1}{3} \times \dfrac{16}{9} = \dfrac{10}{3} \times \dfrac{16}{9} = \dfrac{160}{27}$

                $= \mathbf{5\tfrac{25}{27}}$

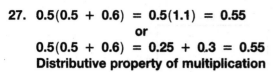

27. $0.5(0.5 + 0.6) = 0.5(1.1) = 0.55$
$$\text{or}$$
$0.5(0.5 + 0.6) = 0.25 + 0.3 = 0.55$
Distributive property of multiplication

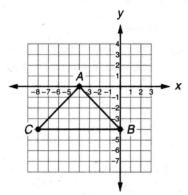

28. $m\angle A = 90°; m\angle B = 45°;$
$m\angle C = 45°$

29. Area $= \dfrac{(8 \text{ units})(4 \text{ units})}{2}$
$= \textbf{16 sq. units}$

30. 180°F

Practice Set   52

a. $5 + 5 \cdot 5 - 5 \div 5$
$5 + 25 - 1$
$30 - 1$
29

b. $50 - 8 \cdot 5 + 6 \div 3$
$50 - 40 + 2$
$10 + 2$
12

c. $24 - 8 - 6 \cdot 2 \div 4$
$24 - 8 - 12 \div 4$
$24 - 8 - 3$
$16 - 3$
13

d. $\dfrac{2^3 + 3^2 + 2 \cdot 5}{3}$
$\dfrac{8 + 9 + 2 \cdot 5}{3}$
$\dfrac{8 + 9 + 10}{3}$
$\dfrac{17 + 10}{3}$
$\dfrac{27}{3}$
9

e. $(5)(3) - (3)(4)$
$\dfrac{15 - 12}{3}$

f. $(6)(4) + \dfrac{(6)}{(2)}$
$24 + 3$
27

g. $\left(\dfrac{2}{3}\right) - \left(\dfrac{2}{3}\right)\left(\dfrac{3}{4}\right)$
$\dfrac{2}{3} - \dfrac{1}{2}$
$\dfrac{4}{6} - \dfrac{3}{6}$
$\dfrac{1}{6}$

Written Practice   52

1. $(2 \cdot 3 \cdot 5) \div (2 + 3 + 5)$
$= 30 \div 10 = \textbf{3}$

2. $40 \text{ in.} \times \dfrac{2.54 \text{ cm}}{1 \text{ in.}} = 101.6 \text{ cm}$

$101.6 \text{ cm} > 100 \text{ cm}$
$40 \text{ in.} > 100 \text{ cm}$

3. $\begin{array}{r} {\scriptstyle 1\ 9\ 11\ \ 10\ 1\ 10} \\ 2\,0\,2\,.\,0\,2\,0 \\ -\ \ 2\,5\,.\,2\,1\,7 \\ \hline 1\,7\,6\,.\,8\,0\,3 \end{array}$

4. $0.89 per CD

5. a. 140 pages

   b. 190 pages

   c. No. We did not need to know the time when Ginger started reading.

6. $75\% = \dfrac{75}{100} = \dfrac{3}{4}$

60 passengers

$\dfrac{3}{4}$ disembarked. $\left\{\begin{array}{l} \boxed{15 \text{ passengers}} \\ \boxed{15 \text{ passengers}} \\ \boxed{15 \text{ passengers}} \end{array}\right.$

$\dfrac{1}{4}$ did not disembark. $\left\{\begin{array}{l} \boxed{15 \text{ passengers}} \end{array}\right.$

a. $3 \times 15 = \textbf{45 passengers}$

b. $\dfrac{1}{4} \times \dfrac{25}{25} = \dfrac{25}{100} = \textbf{25\%}$

7. a. 2.7563×10^9 mi

  b. four billion, five hundred thirty-nine million, six hundred thousand miles

8. a. $16,000,000,000

  b. two hundred forty million dollars

9. a.
$$
\begin{array}{r}
0.375 \\
8\overline{)3.000} \\
\underline{2\,4} \\
60 \\
\underline{56} \\
40 \\
\underline{40} \\
0
\end{array}
$$

  b. $6.5\% = \dfrac{6.5}{100} = \mathbf{0.065}$

10. $3.\overline{27} = 3.2727\ldots$
  3.273

11. a. $250\% = \dfrac{250}{100} = \dfrac{5}{2} = \mathbf{2\dfrac{1}{2}}$

  b. $250\% = 2\dfrac{1}{2} = \mathbf{2.5}$

  c. $25\% = \dfrac{25}{100} = \mathbf{\dfrac{1}{4}}$

  d. $25\% = \dfrac{25}{100} = \mathbf{0.25}$

12. a.
$$
\begin{array}{r}
7\frac{7}{9} \\
9\overline{)70} \\
\underline{63} \\
7
\end{array}
$$

  b.
$$
\begin{array}{r}
7.77\ldots \\
9\overline{)70.00}\ldots \quad \mathbf{7.\overline{7}} \\
\underline{63} \\
7\,0 \\
\underline{6\,3} \\
70 \\
\underline{63} \\
7
\end{array}
$$

13. 0.99

14.

3 cm

2 cm

  a. Perimeter $= 2(30\text{ mm}) + 2(20\text{ mm})$
    $= 60\text{ mm} + 40\text{ mm} = \mathbf{100\text{ mm}}$

  b. Area $= (2\text{ cm})(3\text{ cm}) = \mathbf{6\text{ cm}^2}$

15. a. Area $= \dfrac{(12\text{ cm})(6\text{ cm})}{2} = \mathbf{36\text{ cm}^2}$

  b. Area $= \dfrac{(8\text{ cm})(6\text{ cm})}{2} = \mathbf{24\text{ cm}^2}$

  c. Area $= 36\text{ cm}^2 + 24\text{ cm}^2 = \mathbf{60\text{ cm}^2}$

16.
$$
\begin{aligned}
\frac{8}{f} &= \frac{56}{105} \\
56f &= 105 \cdot 8 \\
f &= \frac{840}{56} \\
f &= \mathbf{15}
\end{aligned}
$$

17.
$$
\begin{aligned}
\frac{12}{15} &= \frac{w}{2.5} \\
15w &= 12 \cdot 2.5 \\
w &= \frac{30}{15} \\
w &= \mathbf{2}
\end{aligned}
$$

18.
$$
\begin{array}{r}
\overset{1\ \ 9\ \ 10}{2\cancel{0}.\cancel{0}} \\
-\ \ 6.8 \\
\hline
1\,3.2
\end{array}
$$
  $p = \mathbf{13.2}$

19.
$$
\begin{array}{r}
\overset{1}{6.4} \\
+\ 3.6 \\
\hline
10.0 = 10
\end{array}
$$
  $q = \mathbf{10}$

20. $5^3 - 10^2 - \sqrt{25}$
  $= 125 - 100 - 5 = \mathbf{20}$

21. $4 + 4 \cdot 4 - 4 \div 4$
  $4 + 16 - 1$
  $20 - 1$
  19

22. $\dfrac{4.8 - 0.24}{(0.2)(0.6)}$

$= \dfrac{4.8 - 0.24}{0.12}$

$= \dfrac{4.56}{0.12} = \mathbf{38}$

23.
```
    5 hr   45 min   30 s
 +  2 hr   53 min   55 s
 ───────────────────────
    7 hr   98 min   85 s
          85 s = 1 min   25 s
                 1 min   25 s
 +               98 min
 ───────────────────────
                 99 min   25 s
          99 min = 1 hr   39 min
                   1 hr   39 min   25 s
 +                 7 hr
 ───────────────────────
    8 hr   39 min   25 s
```

24. $5\dfrac{1}{3} \cdot 2\dfrac{1}{2} = \dfrac{\overset{8}{\cancel{16}}}{3} \cdot \dfrac{5}{\underset{1}{\cancel{2}}}$

$\qquad = \dfrac{40}{3} = 13\dfrac{1}{3}$

$\qquad 6\dfrac{3}{4} = 6\dfrac{9}{12}$

$\qquad + 13\dfrac{1}{3} = 13\dfrac{4}{12}$

$\qquad\qquad\quad 19\dfrac{13}{12} = \mathbf{20\dfrac{1}{12}}$

25. $3\dfrac{3}{4} \div 2 = \dfrac{15}{4} \div \dfrac{2}{1}$

$\qquad = \dfrac{15}{4} \times \dfrac{1}{2} = \dfrac{15}{8} = 1\dfrac{7}{8}$

$\qquad 5\dfrac{1}{2} = 5\dfrac{4}{8} \longrightarrow \quad 4\dfrac{12}{8}$

$\qquad - 1\dfrac{7}{8} = 1\dfrac{7}{8} \qquad\quad - 1\dfrac{7}{8}$

$\qquad\qquad\qquad\qquad\qquad\qquad \mathbf{3\dfrac{5}{8}}$

26. 8.575 + 12.625 + 8.4 + 70.4

$\qquad \downarrow \qquad\quad \downarrow \qquad \downarrow \qquad \downarrow$

$\quad$ 9 $\;+\;$ 13 $\;+\;$ 8 $\;+\;$ 70 $\;=\;$ **100**

```
    8.575
   12.625
    8.4
 + 70.4
 ─────────
  100.000  = 100
```

27.
```
    1.25
 ×  0.8
 ─────────
  1.000  = 1
```
$1 \times 10^6 = \mathbf{1{,}000{,}000}$

28. $(4)(0.5) + \dfrac{(4)}{(0.5)}$

$\qquad 2 + 8$

$\qquad \mathbf{10}$

29. $1.4 \,\cancel{\text{meters}} \cdot \dfrac{100 \text{ centimeters}}{1 \,\cancel{\text{meter}}}$

$\qquad\qquad = \mathbf{140 \text{ centimeters}}$

30. $P(\text{basketball}) = \dfrac{10}{30} = \dfrac{1}{3}, \mathbf{0.33}$

$$\begin{array}{r} 0.3333\ldots \\ 3\overline{)1.0000\ldots} \\ \underline{9} \\ 10 \\ \underline{9} \\ 10 \\ \underline{9} \\ 10 \end{array}$$

$0.33\overset{\leftarrow}{33}\ldots \to 0.33$

Early Finishers Solutions

a. $1.390 \times 10^6 \,\cancel{\text{km}} \cdot \dfrac{1 \text{ mi}}{1.6 \,\cancel{\text{km}}} = \dfrac{1.390}{1.6} \times 10^6$

$\qquad = 0.86875 \times 10^6 \text{ mi} = 868{,}750 \text{ mi or}$

$\qquad$ about 870,000 mi.

b. $870{,}000 \times 3.14 = 2{,}731{,}800$ mi or
about 2,700,000 mi.

Practice Set 53

a.

	Ratio	Actual Count
Girls	9	63
Boys	7	B

$\dfrac{9}{7} = \dfrac{63}{B}$

$9B = 441$

$B = \mathbf{49 \text{ boys}}$

b.

	Ratio	Actual Count
Sparrows	5	S
Blue jays	3	15

$\dfrac{5}{3} = \dfrac{S}{15}$

$3S = 75$

$S = \mathbf{25 \text{ sparrows}}$

c.

	Ratio	Actual Count
Tagged fish	2	90
Untagged fish	9	U

$$\frac{2}{9} = \frac{90}{U}$$
$$2U = 810$$
$$U = \textbf{405 untagged fish}$$

d. **See student work. If desired, have students form other ratios that use the classroom environment (e.g., lefthanders to righthanders, windows to doors, students to computers).**

Written Practice   53

1. **a.** $3 + 5 + 4 + 4 = $ **16 boys**

   b. $2 + 6 + 5 + 3 = $ **16 girls**

2. $\dfrac{\text{January through June birthdays}}{\text{total birthdays}}$

$$= \frac{16}{32} = \frac{1}{2}$$
$$\frac{1}{2} \times 100\% = \frac{100\%}{2} = \textbf{50\%}$$

3. $\dfrac{\text{April through June boys' birthdays}}{\text{total boys' birthdays}} = \dfrac{\textbf{5}}{\textbf{16}}$

4. **a.**
$$\begin{array}{r} \$3.95 \\ \$4.47 \\ \$4.95 \\ \$4.95 \\ \hline \$18.32 \end{array}$$

$$\begin{array}{r} \textbf{\$4.58 per book} \\ 4\overline{)\$18.32} \\ \underline{16} \\ 2\,3 \\ \underline{2\,0} \\ 32 \\ \underline{32} \\ 0 \end{array}$$

   b. **Decrease, because the four books average price was $4.58 and this book is less than the average, so it would bring the average price down.**

5. **a.** $\dfrac{12}{12} - \dfrac{7}{12} = \dfrac{\textbf{5}}{\textbf{12}}$ **were not hiding**

   b. $\dfrac{5}{\cancel{12}} \times \overset{70}{\cancel{840}} = $ **350 students**

6. **a.** $1\underset{\frown}{,}000000000000 \longrightarrow 1 \times 10^{12}$

   b. $4\underset{\frown}{.}75000 \longrightarrow 4.75 \times 10^{5}$

7. **a.** $700\underset{\frown}{,} \longrightarrow 700$

   b. $2500000\underset{\frown}{,} \longrightarrow 2,500,000$
   $250000\underset{\frown}{,} \longrightarrow 250,000$
   $2.5 \times 10^{6} > 2.5 \times 10^{5}$

8. **a.** $35 \text{ yd} \cdot \dfrac{3 \text{ ft}}{1 \text{ yd}} = \textbf{105 ft}$

   b. $\overset{20}{\cancel{2000}} \text{ cm} \cdot \dfrac{1 \text{ m}}{\underset{1}{\cancel{100}} \text{ cm}} = \textbf{20 m}$

9.
$$54 = 2 \cdot 3 \cdot 3 \cdot 3$$
$$36 = 2 \cdot 2 \cdot 3 \cdot 3$$
$$\text{LCM } (54, 36) = 2 \cdot 2 \cdot 3 \cdot 3 \cdot 3$$
$$= \textbf{108}$$

10. $\dfrac{62 \text{ miles}}{\text{hour}} \times \dfrac{1 \text{ kilometer}}{0.62 \text{ miles}} \approx \textbf{100 km/hr}$

11. **a.** $150\% = \dfrac{150}{100} = \dfrac{3}{2} = 1\dfrac{1}{2}$

   b. $150\% = \dfrac{3}{2} = 1\dfrac{1}{2} = \textbf{1.5}$

   c. $15\% = \dfrac{15}{100} = \dfrac{\textbf{3}}{\textbf{20}}$

   d. $15\% = \dfrac{15}{100} = \textbf{0.15}$

12. **a.** $\dfrac{4}{5} \times 100\% = \dfrac{400\%}{5} = \textbf{80\%}$

   b. $0.06 = \dfrac{6}{100} = \textbf{6\%}$

13. $2 \text{ m} = 200 \text{ cm}$
$$\begin{array}{r} \overset{1\ 9\ 10}{2\,\cancel{0}\,\cancel{0}} \text{ cm} \\ -\ 1\ 6\ 5 \text{ cm} \\ \hline 3\ 5 \text{ cm} \end{array}$$

14.

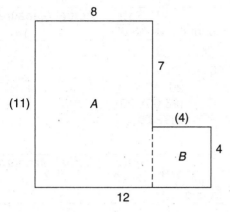

a. Area $A = (11 \text{ ft})(8 \text{ ft}) = 88 \text{ ft}^2$
+ Area $B = (4 \text{ ft})(4 \text{ ft}) = 16 \text{ ft}^2$
Area of figure = **104 ft²**

b. Perimeter = $8 \text{ ft} + 7 \text{ ft} + 4 \text{ ft} + 4 \text{ ft}$
$+ 12 \text{ ft} + 11 \text{ ft} = $ **46 ft**

15. **15 trumpet players**

16. $\dfrac{18}{100} = \dfrac{90}{p}$
$18p = 100 \cdot 90$
$p = \dfrac{9000}{18}$
$p = $ **500**

17. $\dfrac{6}{9} = \dfrac{t}{1.5}$
$9t = 6 \cdot 1.5$
$t = \dfrac{9}{9}$
$t = $ **1**

18.
$\begin{array}{r} \overset{7\,\,\,9\,\,10}{\cancel{8}.\cancel{0}\,\cancel{0}} \\ -\,7.25 \\ \hline 0.75 \end{array}$
$m = $ **0.75**

19. $\dfrac{1.5}{10} = 0.15$
$n = $ **0.15**

20. $\sqrt{81} + 9^2 - 2^5$
$= 9 + 81 - 32 = $ **58**

21. $16 \div 4 \div 2 + 3 \times 4$
$4 \div 2 + 12$
$2 + 12$
14

22.
$\begin{array}{lll} & 3 \text{ yd} & 1 \text{ ft} & 7\frac{1}{2} \text{ in.} \\ + & & 2 \text{ ft} & 6\frac{1}{2} \text{ in.} \\ \hline & 3 \text{ yd} & 3 \text{ ft} & 14 \text{ in.} \end{array}$
14 in. = 1 ft 2 in.
$\begin{array}{ll} & 1 \text{ ft} & 2 \text{ in.} \\ + & 3 \text{ ft} \\ \hline & 4 \text{ ft} & 2 \text{ in.} \end{array}$
4 ft = 1 yd 1 ft
$\begin{array}{lll} & 1 \text{ yd} & 1 \text{ ft} & 2 \text{ in.} \\ + & 3 \text{ yd} \\ \hline & \textbf{4 yd} & \textbf{1 ft} & \textbf{2 in.} \end{array}$

23. $5\dfrac{5}{6} \div 2\dfrac{1}{3} = \dfrac{35}{6} \div \dfrac{7}{3}$
$= \dfrac{\overset{5}{\cancel{35}}}{\underset{2}{\cancel{6}}} \times \dfrac{\overset{1}{\cancel{3}}}{\underset{1}{\cancel{7}}} = \dfrac{5}{2} = 2\dfrac{1}{2}$

$\begin{array}{r} 12\dfrac{2}{3} = 12\dfrac{4}{6} \\ + \,\, 2\dfrac{1}{2} = \,\, 2\dfrac{3}{6} \\ \hline 14\dfrac{7}{6} = \mathbf{15\dfrac{1}{6}} \end{array}$

24. $1\dfrac{1}{2} \cdot 3\dfrac{1}{5} = \dfrac{3}{\underset{1}{\cancel{2}}} \cdot \dfrac{\overset{8}{\cancel{16}}}{5} = \dfrac{24}{5} = 4\dfrac{4}{5}$

$\begin{array}{r} 8\dfrac{3}{5} \longrightarrow 7\dfrac{8}{5} \\ -\,4\dfrac{4}{5} \qquad -\,4\dfrac{4}{5} \\ \hline 3\dfrac{4}{5} \end{array}$

25. $3.875 \times 10^1 \longrightarrow 38.75$
$\begin{array}{r} 10.6 \\ 4.2 \\ 16.4 \\ +\,38.75 \\ \hline \mathbf{69.95} \end{array}$

26. $7 \times 4 = $ **28**

27. $\dfrac{(6)(0.9)}{(0.9)(5)}$
$\dfrac{5.4}{4.5}$
1.2

28. $30\overline{)1000}^{\,33\frac{1}{3}}$

33 flats

29. $\dfrac{\text{guessing wrong answer}}{\text{all answers}} = \dfrac{4}{5} = 0.8$

30. $m\angle a = 180° - 130° = \mathbf{50°}$
$m\angle b = 180° - (90° + 50°)$
$\quad = 180° - 140° = \mathbf{40°}$
$m\angle c = 180° - (40° + 60°)$
$\quad = 180° - 100° = \mathbf{80°}$

Early Finishers Solutions

a. $\dfrac{6}{9} = \dfrac{2}{3}$ or $2:3$

b. $\dfrac{12}{12} = \dfrac{1}{1}$ or $1:1$

c. The number of boys increased by six while the number of girls stayed the same.

Practice Set 54

a.

	Rate	Actual Measure
Miles	50	600
Hour	1	H

$\dfrac{50}{1} = \dfrac{600}{H}$
$50H = 600$
$H = \mathbf{12\ hours}$

b.

	Rate	Actual Measure
Miles	30	600
Gallon	1	G

$\dfrac{30}{1} = \dfrac{600}{G}$
$30G = 600$
$G = \mathbf{20\ gallons}$

c.

	Rate	Actual Measure
Amount ($)	R	$68.80
Hour	1	8

$\dfrac{R}{1} = \dfrac{\$68.80}{8}$
$8R = \$68.80$
$R = \mathbf{\$8.60}$

d.

	Rate	Actual Measure
Amount ($)	$8.60	P
Hour	1	20

$\dfrac{\$8.60}{1} = \dfrac{P}{20}$
$P = (\$8.60)(20)$
$P = \mathbf{\$172.00}$

e.

	Rate	Actual Measure
Amount ($)	$2.60	A
Pound	1	2.5

$\dfrac{\$2.60}{1} = \dfrac{A}{2.5}$
$A = (\$2.60)(2.5)$
$A = \mathbf{\$6.50}$

f. Sample: We could multiply $2.60 by $\frac{1}{2}$.

Written Practice 54

1. $1776 + 50 = 1826$

$\begin{array}{r} 1826 \\ -\ 1743 \\ \hline \mathbf{83\ years} \end{array}$

2. $\begin{array}{r} 190\ \text{cm} \\ 195\ \text{cm} \\ 197\ \text{cm} \\ 201\ \text{cm} \\ +\ 203\ \text{cm} \\ \hline 986\ \text{cm} \end{array}$ $\qquad 5\overline{)986}^{\,197.2}$

197 cm

3.

	Ratio	Actual Count
Women	5	1200
Men	4	L

$\dfrac{5}{4} = \dfrac{1200}{L}$
$5L = 4800$
$L = \mathbf{960\ men}$

4.  2.6 ~~pounds~~ $\dfrac{\$6.75}{1\ \text{pound}}$
$= \mathbf{\$17.55}$

222

5. $4 = 2 \cdot 2$
$6 = 2 \cdot 3$
$LCM\,(4, 6) = 2 \cdot 2 \cdot 3 = 12$
$GCF\,(4, 6) = 2$
$\dfrac{12}{2} = \mathbf{6}$

6.

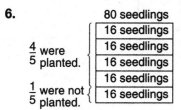

$\dfrac{4}{5}$ were planted.

$\dfrac{1}{5}$ were not planted.

80 seedlings

| 16 seedlings |
| 16 seedlings |
| 16 seedlings |
| 16 seedlings |
| 16 seedlings |

 a. 64 seedlings

 b. 16 seedlings

7. **a.** 4.05000 $\longrightarrow$ **4.05 × 10⁵**

 b. 004000. $\longrightarrow$ **4000**

8. **a.** 10^8

 b. 10^4

9. **a.** $\overset{1760}{\cancel{5280}}\ \cancel{ft} \cdot \dfrac{1\ yd}{\underset{1}{\cancel{3}\ \cancel{ft}}} = \mathbf{1760\ yd}$

 b. $300\ \cancel{cm} \cdot \dfrac{10\ mm}{1\ \cancel{cm}} = \mathbf{3000\ mm}$

10. $3.141\underset{\uparrow}{5}926 \to \mathbf{3.1416}$

11. **a.** $4\ \cancel{hours} \cdot \dfrac{60\ miles}{1\ \cancel{hour}} = \mathbf{240\ miles}$

 b. $\overset{5}{\cancel{300}}\ \cancel{miles} \cdot \dfrac{1\ hour}{\underset{1}{\cancel{60}\ \cancel{miles}}} = \mathbf{5\ hours}$

12. **a.** $0.4 \times 360° = \mathbf{144°}$

 b. $0.3 \times 360° = \mathbf{108°}$

 c. $0.2 \times 360° = \mathbf{72°}$

 d. $0.1 \times 360° = \mathbf{36°}$

13. **B.** 2^4

14. Perimeter $= 5\ cm + 8\ cm + 3\ cm$
$+\ 5\ cm + 6\ cm + 9\ cm$
$+\ 2\ cm + 4\ cm = \mathbf{42\ cm}$

15.

Area $A = (4\ cm)(5\ cm) = 20\ cm^2$
Area $B = (4\ cm)(3\ cm) = 12\ cm^2$
$+$ Area $C = (5\ cm)(6\ cm) = 30\ cm^2$
Area of figure $= \mathbf{62\ cm^2}$

16. **a. Identity property of addition**

 b. Distributive property

 c. Associative property of addition

 d. Inverse property of multiplication

17. 0.5 in.

0.5 in.

 a. Perimeter $= 4(0.5\ in.) = \mathbf{2\ inches}$

 b. Area $= (0.5\ in.)(0.5\ in.)$
 $= \mathbf{0.25\ square\ inch}$

18. The average score is likely to be below the median score. The mean "balances" low scores with high scores. The scores above the median are not far enough above the median to allow the balance point for all the scores to be at or above the median.

19. $\begin{array}{r} 6.2 \\ -\ 4.1 \\ \hline 2.1 \end{array}$
$x = \mathbf{2.1}$

20. $\begin{array}{r} 1.2 \\ +\ 0.21 \\ \hline 1.41 \end{array}$
$y = \mathbf{1.41}$

21. $\dfrac{24}{r} = \dfrac{36}{27}$
$36r = 24 \cdot 27$
$r = \dfrac{648}{36}$
$r = \mathbf{18}$

22.
$$\begin{array}{r} 6.25 \\ \times\ 0.16 \\ \hline 3750 \\ 625 \\ \hline 1.0000 = 1 \end{array}$$
$w = \mathbf{1}$

23. $11^2 + 1^3 - \sqrt{121}$
$= 121 + 1 - 11 = \mathbf{111}$

24. $24 - 4 \times 5 \div 2 + 5$
$\qquad 24 - 20 \div 2 + 5$
$\qquad\quad 24 - 10 + 5$
$\qquad\qquad 14 + 5$
$\qquad\qquad\quad \mathbf{19}$

25. $\dfrac{(2.5)^2}{2(2.5)} = \dfrac{6.25}{5} = \mathbf{1.25}$

26.
$$\begin{array}{rll} & 1\ \text{week} & 5\ \text{days} & 14\ \text{hr} \\ + & 2\ \text{weeks} & 6\ \text{days} & 10\ \text{hr} \\ \hline & 3\ \text{weeks} & 11\ \text{days} & 24\ \text{hr} \end{array}$$
$24\ \text{hr} = 1\ \text{day}$
$11\ \text{days} + 1\ \text{day} = 12\ \text{days}$
$12\ \text{days} = 1\ \text{week}\ 5\ \text{days}$

$$\begin{array}{rll} & 1\ \text{week} & 5\ \text{days} \\ + & 3\ \text{weeks} & \\ \hline & \mathbf{4\ weeks} & \mathbf{5\ days} \end{array}$$

27.
$$9\tfrac{1}{2} = 9\tfrac{3}{6} \longrightarrow 8\tfrac{9}{6}$$
$$-\ 6\tfrac{2}{3} = 6\tfrac{4}{6} \qquad\quad -\ 6\tfrac{4}{6}$$
$$\rule{3cm}{0.4pt} \qquad\qquad \rule{2cm}{0.4pt}$$
$$\qquad\qquad\qquad\qquad\quad 2\tfrac{5}{6}$$

$$3\tfrac{5}{10} = 3\tfrac{15}{30}$$
$$+\ 2\tfrac{5}{6} = 2\tfrac{25}{30}$$
$$\rule{3cm}{0.4pt}$$
$$\qquad 5\tfrac{40}{30} = 6\tfrac{10}{30} = \mathbf{6\tfrac{1}{3}}$$

28. $6 \div 3\tfrac{2}{3} = \dfrac{6}{1} \div \dfrac{11}{3}$
$$= \dfrac{6}{1} \times \dfrac{3}{11} = \dfrac{18}{11}$$
$$7\tfrac{1}{3} \cdot \dfrac{18}{11} = \dfrac{\overset{2}{\cancel{22}}}{\underset{1}{\cancel{3}}} \cdot \dfrac{\overset{6}{\cancel{18}}}{\underset{1}{\cancel{11}}}$$
$$= \mathbf{12}$$

29.

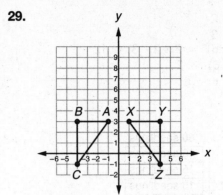

30. a. Yes

b. Yes

c. $\angle C$

Early Finishers Solutions

a. Ngo $\quad 0.875;\ 87.5\%;\ \tfrac{7}{8}$

Marley $\quad 0.2;\ 20\%;\ \tfrac{1}{5}$

Vega $\quad 0.546;\ 54.6\%;\ \tfrac{273}{500}$

b. Ngo and Vega both won because they received the majority (over 50%) of the votes. Marley probably lost because she received less than half of the total votes.

Practice Set 55

a. $5(18\ \text{points}) = \mathbf{90\ points}$

b.
$$4(45) = 180$$
$$24 + 36 + 52 + n = 180$$
$$112 + n = 180$$
$$n = 180 - 112$$
$$n = \mathbf{68}$$

c.
$$5(91) = 455$$
$$6(89) = 534$$
$$\begin{array}{r} 534 \\ -\ 455 \\ \hline \mathbf{79} \end{array}$$

d. $4 \times \$20 = \$80$
$\$18 + \$22 + \$15 = \$55$
$\$80 - \$55 = \mathbf{\$25}$

e. Cheddar cheese: $\dfrac{\$3.60}{10\ oz} = \mathbf{\$0.36/oz}$

$\dfrac{1}{2}$ lb $= 8$ oz

American cheese: $\dfrac{\$3.04}{8\ oz} = \mathbf{\$0.38/oz}$

$\$0.36 < \$0.38$

Cheddar cheese is the better buy at $0.36/oz.

f. To Austin: $\dfrac{180\ miles}{3\ hours} = \mathbf{60\ mph}$

Return trip: $\dfrac{180\ miles}{4\ hours} = \mathbf{45\ mph}$

Round trip: $\dfrac{360\ miles}{7\ hours} = 51.42\ mph = \mathbf{51\ mph}$

Practice Set 55

1. **52 white keys**

2.
$$4(85) = 340$$
$$76 + 78 + 81 + n = 340$$
$$235 + n = 340$$
$$n = 340 - 235$$
$$n = \mathbf{105}$$

3.

$$\begin{array}{r} \$\ 2.38 \\ 12\overline{)\$28.56} \\ \underline{24} \\ 45 \\ \underline{36} \\ 96 \\ \underline{96} \\ 0 \end{array}$$

$$\begin{array}{r} \$2.89 \\ -\$2.38 \\ \hline \$0.51 \end{array}$$

$0.51 per container

4. $BC - AB = 2\dfrac{2}{8}$ in. $- 1\dfrac{6}{8}$ in.

$2\dfrac{2}{8}$ in. $\longrightarrow$ $1\dfrac{10}{8}$ in.

$-1\dfrac{6}{8}$ in. $\qquad -1\dfrac{6}{8}$ in.

$\qquad\qquad\qquad \dfrac{4}{8}$ in. $= \dfrac{1}{2}$ **in.**

5.

30 students

$\dfrac{3}{10}$ earned an A. $\left\{\begin{array}{l}\text{3 students}\\ \text{3 students}\\ \text{3 students}\end{array}\right.$

$\left.\begin{array}{l}\text{3 students}\\ \text{3 students}\\ \text{3 students}\\ \text{3 students}\\ \text{3 students}\\ \text{3 students}\\ \text{3 students}\end{array}\right\}$ $\dfrac{7}{10}$ did not earn an A.

a. 9 students

b. $\dfrac{3}{10} \times 100\% = \mathbf{30\%}$

6. a. $6.75000000 \longrightarrow \mathbf{6.75 \times 10^8}$

b. $186000. \longrightarrow \mathbf{186{,}000}$

7. a. 10^{10}

b. 10^6

8. a. $24\ \text{feet} \cdot \dfrac{12\ inches}{1\ foot} = \mathbf{288\ inches}$

b. $\dfrac{\overset{1}{60}\ miles}{1\ hour} \times \dfrac{1\ hour}{\underset{1}{60}\ minutes}$

$= \mathbf{1\ mile/minute}$

9. $0.02 \cdot 0.025 = \mathbf{0.0005}$

10. a. $\$35 + 4(\$7) = \mathbf{\$63.00}$

b. $\dfrac{\$63.00}{7\ hours} = \mathbf{\$9.00}$

11. a.
$$\begin{array}{r} 0.2 \\ 5\overline{)1.0} \end{array}$$

b. $\dfrac{1}{5} \times 100\% = \dfrac{100\%}{5} = \mathbf{20\%}$

c. $0.1 = \dfrac{1}{10}$

d. $0.1 \times 100\% = \mathbf{10\%}$

e. $75\% = \dfrac{75}{100} = \dfrac{3}{4}$

f. $75\% = \dfrac{75}{100} = \mathbf{0.75}$

12. a. $\overline{AD}$ (or $\overline{DA}$)

b. $\overline{DC}$ (or $\overline{CD}$) and $\overline{AH}$ (or $\overline{HA}$)

c. $\angle DAB$ (or $\angle BAD$)

13. a. Area $= (6\ cm)(8\ cm) = \mathbf{48\ cm^2}$

b. Area $= \dfrac{(4\ cm)(8\ cm)}{2} = \mathbf{16\ cm^2}$

c. Area $= 48\ cm^2 + 16\ cm^2 = \mathbf{64\ cm^2}$

14. 6 feet 2 inches $= 6(12 \text{ inches}) + 2 \text{ inches}$
$= 74 \text{ inches}$

$$
\begin{array}{r}
74 \text{ inches} \\
- \ 68 \text{ inches} \\
\hline
\mathbf{6 \text{ inches}}
\end{array}
$$

15. a. $\overset{5}{\cancel{20}} \text{ min} \cdot \dfrac{5 \text{ laps}}{\underset{1}{\cancel{4}} \text{ min}} = \textbf{25 laps}$

   b. $\overset{4}{\cancel{20}} \text{ laps} \cdot \dfrac{4 \text{ min}}{\underset{1}{\cancel{5}} \text{ laps}} = \textbf{16 minutes}$

16. $\dfrac{1}{2}\left(\dfrac{1}{4} + \dfrac{1}{2}\right)$ or $\dfrac{1}{2}\left(\dfrac{1}{4} + \dfrac{1}{2}\right)$

   $\dfrac{1}{2}\left(\dfrac{3}{4}\right) \qquad\qquad \dfrac{1}{8} + \dfrac{1}{4}$

   $\quad\dfrac{\mathbf{3}}{\mathbf{8}} \qquad\qquad\qquad \dfrac{\mathbf{3}}{\mathbf{8}}$

17. $\dfrac{30}{70} = \dfrac{21}{x}$

   $30x = 21 \cdot 70$

   $x = \dfrac{1470}{30}$

   $x = \mathbf{49}$

18. $25\overline{)10000}^{\,400}$

   $w = \mathbf{400}$

19. $2 + 7 + 5 = \mathbf{14}$

$$
\begin{array}{r}
2\dfrac{5}{12} = 2\dfrac{10}{24} \\[4pt]
6\dfrac{5}{6} = 6\dfrac{20}{24} \\[4pt]
+ \ 4\dfrac{7}{8} = 4\dfrac{21}{24} \\
\hline
\end{array}
$$

   $12\dfrac{51}{24} = 14\dfrac{3}{24} = \mathbf{14\dfrac{1}{8}}$

20. $6 - (7 - 5) = 6 - 2 = \mathbf{4}$

$$
\begin{array}{rcr}
7\dfrac{1}{3} = 7\dfrac{5}{15} & \longrightarrow & 6\dfrac{20}{15} \\[4pt]
- \ 4\dfrac{4}{5} = 4\dfrac{12}{15} & & - \ 4\dfrac{12}{15} \\
\hline
& & 2\dfrac{8}{15}
\end{array}
$$

$$
\begin{array}{rcr}
6 & \longrightarrow & 5\dfrac{15}{15} \\[4pt]
- \ 2\dfrac{8}{15} & & - \ 2\dfrac{8}{15} \\
\hline
& & 3\dfrac{7}{15}
\end{array}
$$

21. $10 \ \cancel{\text{yd}} \cdot \dfrac{36 \text{ in.}}{1 \ \cancel{\text{yd}}} = \textbf{360 in.}$

22.
$$
\begin{array}{r}
8 \text{ yd} \ 2 \text{ ft} \ \ 7 \text{ in.} \\
+ \qquad\qquad 5 \text{ in.} \\
\hline
8 \text{ yd} \ 2 \text{ ft} \ 12 \text{ in.}
\end{array}
$$
12 in. = 1 ft
   2 ft + 1 ft = 3 ft
3 ft = 1 yd
   8 yd + 1 yd = 9 yd
9 yd

23. $12^2 - 4^3 - 2^4 - \sqrt{144}$
$= 144 - 64 - 16 - 12 = \mathbf{52}$

24. $50 + 30 \div 5 \cdot 2 - 6$
   $50 + 6 \cdot 2 - 6$
      $50 + 12 - 6$
         $62 - 6$
         $\mathbf{56}$

25. $6\dfrac{2}{3} \cdot 5\dfrac{1}{4} \cdot 2\dfrac{1}{10}$

   $= \dfrac{\overset{1}{\underset{\underset{1}{\cancel{3}}}{\cancel{20}}}\overset{2}{}}{} \cdot \dfrac{\overset{7}{\cancel{21}}}{\underset{2}{\cancel{4}}} \cdot \dfrac{21}{\underset{1}{\cancel{10}}} = \dfrac{147}{2} = \mathbf{73\dfrac{1}{2}}$

26. $3\dfrac{1}{3} \div 3 \div 2\dfrac{1}{2}$

   $= \dfrac{10}{3} \div \dfrac{3}{1} \div \dfrac{5}{2}$

   $= \left(\dfrac{10}{3} \times \dfrac{1}{3}\right) \div \dfrac{5}{2} = \dfrac{10}{9} \div \dfrac{5}{2}$

   $= \dfrac{\overset{2}{\cancel{10}}}{9} \times \dfrac{2}{\underset{1}{\cancel{5}}} = \mathbf{\dfrac{4}{9}}$

27.
$$
\begin{array}{rr}
6.000 & 3.47 \\
- \ 1.359 & + \ 4.641 \\
\hline
4.641 & \mathbf{8.111}
\end{array}
$$

28. $75\overline{)\$1500.00}^{\ \$20.00}$

29. a. Commutative property

   b. Inverse property

   c. Identity property

30. $m\angle a = 180° - (90° + 52°)$
$\qquad = 180° - 142° = \textbf{38°}$
$m\angle b = 90° - 38° = \textbf{52°}$
$m\angle c = 90° - 52° = \textbf{38°}$

Early Finishers Solutions

a. $\dfrac{\text{head}}{\text{body}} = \dfrac{1}{7} = \dfrac{9.5 \text{ in.}}{x}$;
$9.5 \times 7 = x = 66.5 \text{ in.}$

b. $66.5 \div 12 = 5 \text{ ft } 6\frac{1}{2} \text{ inches}$

Practice Set 56

a. To find the number of hours, multiply the number of days by 24.

b. $10 \times 24 = \textbf{240}$

c. $h = 24d$

d. Answers may vary. See student work. Sample answer:

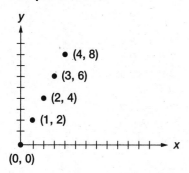

(4, 8)
(3, 6)
(2, 4)
(1, 2)
(0, 0)

e. Answers may vary. See student work. Sample answer:

$y = 3x$

x	y
0	0
1	3
2	6
3	9

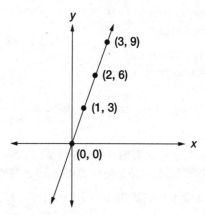

(3, 9)
(2, 6)
(1, 3)
(0, 0)

f. $y = 4x$; Any (x, y) pair in which y is four times x is correct, such as (4, 16) and $\left(\dfrac{1}{4}, 1\right)$.

g. (1, 4); One way: The point (1, 4) is on the line. Another way: The rule for the function is $y = 4x$. Substituting we get, $4 = 4(1)$.

Written Practice 56

1. a. Sample space = {H1, H2, H3, H4, H5, H6, T1, T2, T3, T4, T5, T6}

b. $P(\text{H2 or H3 or H5}) = \dfrac{3}{12} = \dfrac{1}{4}, \textbf{0.25}$

2.

	Ratio	Actual Count
Length	4	12 feet
Width	3	W

a. $\dfrac{4}{3} = \dfrac{12 \text{ feet}}{W}$
$4W = 3(12 \text{ feet})$
$W = \textbf{9 feet}$

b. Perimeter $= 2(12 \text{ feet}) + 2(9 \text{ feet})$
$\qquad = 24 \text{ feet} + 18 \text{ feet} = \textbf{42 feet}$

3. $\$2 + \$0.50(4) = \$2 + \$2 = \textbf{\$4}$

4. $\quad 4(45) = 180$
$180 + 60 = 240$
$\dfrac{240}{5} = 48$

48 minutes

5. $\dfrac{\$1.50}{12 \text{ ounces}} = \dfrac{\$0.125}{1 \text{ ounce}}$

$\dfrac{\$1.92}{16 \text{ ounces}} = \dfrac{\$0.12}{1 \text{ ounce}}$

Brand X $= \textbf{12.5¢ per ounce}$
Brand Y $= \textbf{12¢ per ounce}$
Brand Y is the better buy.

Solutions

6. a. $\dfrac{\text{igneous rocks}}{\text{total rocks}} = \dfrac{3}{8}$

b. $\dfrac{\text{igneous rocks}}{\text{metamorphic rocks}} = \dfrac{3}{5}$

c. $\dfrac{5}{8} \times 100\% = \dfrac{500\%}{8} = \mathbf{62\dfrac{1}{2}\%}$

7. a. $\angle QPR$ and $\angle TPS$ (or $\angle RPQ$ and $\angle SPT$)
$\angle RPS$ and $\angle QPT$ (or $\angle SPR$ and $\angle TPQ$)

b. $\angle RPQ$ (or $\angle QPR$) and $\angle SPT$ (or $\angle TPS$)

8. a. $6.\underaccent{\frown}{10000} \longrightarrow \mathbf{6.1 \times 10^5}$

b. $1\underaccent{\frown}{5000}. \longrightarrow \mathbf{15{,}000}$

9. $100 \cancel{\text{yd}} \times \dfrac{1 \text{ m}}{1.1 \cancel{\text{yd}}} \approx \mathbf{91 \text{ m}}$

10. a.
$$
\begin{array}{r}
0.166\ldots \\
6\overline{)1.000\ldots} \\
\underline{6} \\
40 \\
\underline{36} \\
40 \\
\underline{36} \\
4
\end{array}
$$

0.17

b. $\dfrac{1}{6} \times 100\% = \dfrac{100\%}{6} = \mathbf{16\dfrac{2}{3}\%}$

11. $1{,}000{,}000 \cancel{\text{dollars}} \cdot \dfrac{100 \text{ pennies}}{1 \cancel{\text{dollar}}}$
$= 100{,}000{,}000 \text{ pennies} = \mathbf{1 \times 10^8 \text{ pennies}}$

12. $1.\underaccent{\frown}{1000000} \longrightarrow \mathbf{1.1 \times 10^7}$
11 million $> 1.1 \times 10^6$

13. 5, 10, 15, 20, 25, 30, 35, 40, 45, 50, 55, 60, 65, **70**, 75, 80 ...
7, 14, 21, 28, 35, 42, 49, 56, 63, **70**, 77, 84 ...
70

14. $47\dfrac{1}{2}$ in. $\rightarrow 48 \cancel{\text{in.}} \times \dfrac{1 \text{ ft}}{12 \cancel{\text{in.}}} = 4$ ft

$35\dfrac{1}{2}$ in. $\rightarrow 36 \cancel{\text{in.}} \times \dfrac{1 \text{ ft}}{12 \cancel{\text{in.}}} = 3$ ft

Estimated perimeter $= 4 \text{ ft} + 4 \text{ ft} + 3 \text{ ft}$
$+ 3 \text{ ft} = \mathbf{14 \text{ ft}}$

15. Estimated area $= (4 \text{ ft})(3 \text{ ft}) = \mathbf{12 \text{ ft}^2}$

16. $\dfrac{100°}{180°} = \dfrac{10°}{F}$

$F(100°) = (180°)(10°)$
$= \mathbf{18° \ F}$

17. $\dfrac{3}{2.5} = \dfrac{48}{c}$
$3c = 48(2.5)$
$c = \dfrac{120}{3}$
$c = \mathbf{40}$

18.
$$
\begin{array}{r}
0.75 \\
+\ 0.75 \\
\hline
1.50 = 1.5
\end{array}
$$
$k = \mathbf{1.5}$

19. $15^2 - 5^3 - \sqrt{100} = 225 - 125 - 10$
$= 100 - 10 = \mathbf{90}$

20. $6 + 12 \div 3 \cdot 2 - 3 \cdot 4$
$6 + 4 \cdot 2 - 12$
$6 + 8 - 12$
$14 - 12$
$\mathbf{2}$

21.
$$
\begin{array}{rrr}
5 \text{ yd} & 2 \text{ ft} & 3 \text{ in.} \\
+\ 2 \text{ yd} & 2 \text{ ft} & 9 \text{ in.} \\
\hline
7 \text{ yd} & 4 \text{ ft} & 12 \text{ in.}
\end{array}
$$
12 in. = 1 ft
4 ft + 1 ft = 5 ft
5 ft = 1 yd 2 ft
$$
\begin{array}{rr}
1 \text{ yd} & 2 \text{ ft} \\
+\ 7 \text{ yd} & \\
\hline
\mathbf{8 \text{ yd}} & \mathbf{2 \text{ ft}}
\end{array}
$$

22.
$$
\begin{array}{rrr}
 & \overset{1}{\nearrow}(12 \text{ in.}) & \\
5 \text{ yd} & 2 \text{ ft} & 3 \text{ in.} \\
-\ 2 \text{ yd} & 2 \text{ ft} & 9 \text{ in.} \longrightarrow
\end{array}
$$
$$
\begin{array}{rrr}
 & \nearrow(3 \text{ ft}) & \\
\overset{4}{\cancel{5}} \text{ yd} & \overset{1}{2} \text{ ft} & \overset{15}{\cancel{3}} \text{ in.} \\
-\ 2 \text{ yd} & 2 \text{ ft} & 9 \text{ in.} \longrightarrow \\
\hline
 & & 6 \text{ in.}
\end{array}
$$
$$
\begin{array}{rrr}
\overset{4}{\cancel{5}} \text{ yd} & \overset{4}{\cancel{2}} \text{ ft} & \overset{15}{\cancel{3}} \text{ in.} \\
-\ 2 \text{ yd} & 2 \text{ ft} & 9 \text{ in.} \\
\hline
\mathbf{2 \text{ yd}} & \mathbf{2 \text{ ft}} & \mathbf{6 \text{ in.}}
\end{array}
$$

23. $\dfrac{\overset{1}{\cancel{18}}}{\underset{1}{\cancel{19}}} \cdot \dfrac{\overset{1}{\cancel{19}}}{\underset{1}{\cancel{18}}} = \mathbf{1}$

24.

$$5\frac{1}{6} = 5\frac{2}{12} \longrightarrow 4\frac{14}{12}$$

$$- 1\frac{1}{4} = 1\frac{3}{12} \qquad - 1\frac{3}{12}$$

$$\qquad\qquad\qquad\qquad\qquad 3\frac{11}{12}$$

$$2\frac{3}{4} = 2\frac{9}{12}$$

$$+ 3\frac{11}{12} = 3\frac{11}{12}$$

$$5\frac{20}{12} = 6\frac{8}{12} = \mathbf{6\frac{2}{3}}$$

25. $3\frac{3}{4} \cdot 2\frac{1}{2} \div 3\frac{1}{8}$

$$= \left(\frac{15}{4} \cdot \frac{5}{2}\right) \div \frac{25}{8}$$

$$= \frac{75}{8} \div \frac{25}{8} = \frac{\overset{3}{\cancel{75}}}{\cancel{8}} \times \frac{\overset{1}{\cancel{8}}}{\cancel{25}} = \mathbf{3}$$

26. $3\frac{3}{4} \div 2\frac{1}{2} \cdot 3\frac{1}{8}$

$$= \left(\frac{15}{4} \div \frac{5}{2}\right) \cdot \frac{25}{8} = \left(\frac{\overset{3}{\cancel{15}}}{\underset{2}{\cancel{4}}} \times \frac{\overset{1}{\cancel{2}}}{\cancel{5}}\right) \cdot \frac{25}{8}$$

$$= \frac{3}{2} \cdot \frac{25}{8} = \frac{75}{16} = \mathbf{4\frac{11}{16}}$$

27. The first five numbers in the sequence are the squares of the first five counting numbers. So the 99th number in the sequence is 99^2.

28. See student work. If the triangle is drawn and measured accurately, the longest side is twice the length of the shortest side.

29. 0.5 meter = 50 centimeters

$$\text{radius} = \frac{50 \text{ centimeters}}{2}$$

$$= \mathbf{25 \text{ centimeters}}$$

30. $\boldsymbol{d = 2r}$

r	d
1	2
2	4
3	6

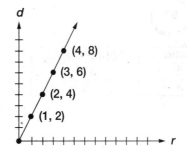

We place an arrowhead at the end of the line in the first quadrant to indicate that it continues.

Practice Set 57

a. $5^{-2} = \frac{1}{5^2} = \mathbf{\frac{1}{25}}$

b. $3^0 = \mathbf{1}$

c. $10^{-4} = \frac{1}{10^4} = \frac{1}{\mathbf{10,000}}$ or **0.0001**

d. $\underset{\smile}{0000002}.5 \longrightarrow \mathbf{2.5 \times 10^{-7}}$

e. $\underset{\smile}{000000001}. \longrightarrow \mathbf{1 \times 10^{-9}}$

f. $\underset{\smile}{0001}.05 \longrightarrow \mathbf{1.05 \times 10^{-4}}$

g. $\underset{\smile}{.00000045} \longrightarrow \mathbf{0.00000045}$

h. $\underset{\smile}{.001} \longrightarrow \mathbf{0.001}$

i. $\underset{\smile}{.0000125} \longrightarrow \mathbf{0.0000125}$

j. g: I shifted the decimal point seven places to the left. h: I shifted the decimal point three places to the left. i: I shifted the decimal point five places to the left.

k. $1 \times 10^{-3} = 0.001$
$1 \times 10^2 = 100$
$\mathbf{1 \times 10^{-3} < 1 \times 10^2}$

l. $2.5 \times 10^{-2} = 0.025$
$2.5 \times 10^{-3} = 0.0025$
$\mathbf{2.5 \times 10^{-2} > 2.5 \times 10^{-3}}$

m. $\mathbf{3.5 \times 10^{-8}}$

Saxon Math Course 2

1.

	Ratio	Actual Count
Walkers	5	315
Riders	3	R

$$\frac{5}{3} = \frac{315}{R}$$
$$5R = 3(315)$$
$$R = \mathbf{189 \ riders}$$

2. $5(88) = 440$
$6(90) = 540$

$$\begin{array}{r} 540 \\ - \ 440 \\ \hline \mathbf{100} \end{array}$$

3. $\$0.39 + 3(\$0.25) = \$1.14$
$\qquad\qquad 2(\$1.14) = \mathbf{\$2.28}$

4. 1 pint = 2 cups

$$\begin{array}{r} \mathbf{\$0.26} \ \textbf{per cup} \\ 2\overline{)\$0.52} \\ 4 \\ \hline .12 \\ 12 \\ \hline 0 \end{array}$$

5. a. $\dfrac{2}{\cancel{5}} \times \overset{12}{\cancel{60}}$ minutes = **24 minutes**
    $\quad{}_{1}$

b. $\dfrac{2}{5} \times 100\% = \dfrac{200\%}{5} = \mathbf{40\%}$

c. There are 60 minutes in 1 hour.

6. a. $1.86000 \longrightarrow \mathbf{1.86 \times 10^5}$

b. $000004. \longrightarrow \mathbf{4 \times 10^{-5}}$

7. a. $32.5 \longrightarrow \mathbf{32.5}$

b. $000001.5 \longrightarrow \mathbf{0.0000015}$

8. a. $2^{-3} = \dfrac{1}{2^3} = \dfrac{1}{8}$

b. $5^0 = \mathbf{1}$

c. $10^{-2} = \dfrac{1}{10^2} = \dfrac{1}{100}$ or **0.01**

9. a. $2\overset{2}{\cancel{000}} \ \cancel{\text{milliliters}} \cdot \dfrac{1 \ \text{liter}}{\cancel{1000} \ \cancel{\text{milliliters}}}$
    $\qquad\qquad\qquad\qquad\quad {}_{1}$
    $= \mathbf{2 \ liters}$

b. $10 \ \cancel{L} \cdot \dfrac{1.06 \ qt}{1 \ \cancel{L}} = \mathbf{10.6 \ qt}$

10. $P(4 \ \text{or} \ 6) = \dfrac{2}{6} = \mathbf{\dfrac{1}{3}, 0.33}$

$$\begin{array}{r} 0.333 \ldots \\ 3\overline{)1.000 \ldots} \\ 9 \\ \hline 10 \\ 9 \\ \hline 10 \end{array} \rightarrow 0.33$$

11.
$$\begin{array}{r} \mathbf{\$27.50} \\ 12\overline{)\$330.00} \\ 24 \\ \hline 90 \\ 84 \\ \hline 60 \\ 60 \\ \hline 00 \\ 00 \\ \hline 0 \end{array}$$

12.

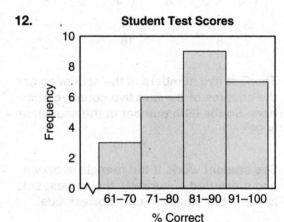

Student Test Scores

13. a. $2.5 \times 10^{-2} = 0.025$
$\quad 2.5 \div 10^2 = \dfrac{2.5}{100} = 0.025$
$\quad 2.5 \times 10^{-2} = 2.5 \div 10^2$

b. $1 \times 10^{-6} \quad = 0.000001$
$\quad$ one millionth $= 1 \times 10^{-6}$

c. $3^0 = 1, \ 2^0 = 1$
$\quad 3^0 = 2^0$

14. Perimeter $=$ 4 yd $+$ 3 yd $+$ 1 yd
$\qquad\qquad\qquad + \ $ 1 yd $+$ 1.5 yd $+$ 2 yd
$\qquad\qquad\qquad + \ $ 1.5 yd $+$ 4 yd $= \mathbf{18 \ yd}$

15.

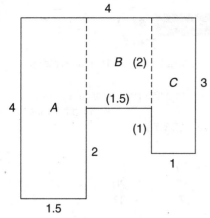

Area A = $(1.5\text{ yd})(4\text{ yd})$ = 6 yd^2
Area B = $(1.5\text{ yd})(2\text{ yd})$ = 3 yd^2
+ Area C = $(1\text{ yd})(3\text{ yd})$ = 3 yd^2
Area of figure = **12 yd²**

16. $4(5)(0.5) = 20(0.5) =$ **10**

17. $\$20.00 \div 4 =$ **\$5.00**

18.

x	y
0	5
1	8
2	11
3	14

$y = 3x + 5$
$y = 3(0) + 5 = 5$
$y = 3(1) + 5 = 8$
$y = 3(2) + 5 = 11$
$y = 3(3) + 5 = 14$

19. $20^2 + 10^3 - \sqrt{36}$
$= 400 + 1000 - 6 =$ **1394**

20. $48 \div 12 \div 2 + 2(3)$
$4 \div 2 + 6$
$2 + 6$
8

21.

$\overset{1}{\phantom{3\text{ yd }}} \!\!\!\!\!\!\!\!\! \overset{\nearrow(12\text{ in.})}{}$
$3\text{ yd} \quad \overset{1}{\cancel{2}}\text{ ft} \quad 1\text{ in.} \longrightarrow$
$-1\text{ yd} \quad 2\text{ ft} \quad 3\text{ in.} \longrightarrow$

$\overset{\nearrow(3\text{ ft})}{}$
$\overset{2}{\cancel{3}}\text{ yd} \quad \overset{1}{\cancel{2}}\text{ ft} \quad \overset{13}{\cancel{1}}\text{ in.} \longrightarrow$
$-1\text{ yd} \quad 2\text{ ft} \quad 3\text{ in.} \longrightarrow$
$\underline{}$
10 in.

$\overset{2}{\cancel{3}}\text{ yd} \quad \overset{4}{\cancel{\overset{1}{\cancel{2}}}}\text{ft} \quad \overset{13}{\cancel{1}}\text{ in.}$
$-\ 1\text{ yd} \quad 2\text{ ft} \quad 3\text{ in.}$
$\mathbf{1\text{ yd} \quad 2\text{ ft} \quad 10\text{ in.}}$

22.

$\ 4\text{ gal} \quad 3\text{ qt} \quad 1\text{ pt} \quad 6\text{ oz}$
$+\ 1\text{ gal} \quad 2\text{ qt} \quad 1\text{ pt} \quad 5\text{ oz}$
$\ 5\text{ gal} \quad 5\text{ qt} \quad 2\text{ pt} \quad 11\text{ oz}$

$2\text{ pt} = 1\text{ qt}$
$\ 1\text{ qt} \quad 11\text{ oz}$
$\underline{+\ 5\text{ qt}}$
$\ 6\text{ qt} \quad 11\text{ oz}$

$6\text{ qt} = 1\text{ gal} \quad 2\text{ qt}$
$\ 1\text{ gal} \quad 2\text{ qt} \quad 11\text{ oz}$
$\underline{+\ 5\text{ gal}}$
$\ \mathbf{6\text{ gal} \quad 2\text{ qt} \quad 11\text{ oz}}$

23. $\overset{3}{\cancel{48}}\text{ oz} \cdot \dfrac{1\text{ pt}}{\underset{1}{\cancel{16}\text{ oz}}} =$ **3 pt**

24. $7 \div 1\dfrac{3}{4} = \dfrac{7}{1} \div \dfrac{7}{4} =$
$\dfrac{\overset{1}{\cancel{7}}}{1} \times \dfrac{4}{\underset{1}{\cancel{7}}} = 4$
$5\dfrac{1}{3} \cdot 4 = \dfrac{16}{3} \cdot \dfrac{4}{1} = \dfrac{64}{3} = \mathbf{21\dfrac{1}{3}}$

25.
$5\dfrac{1}{6} = 5\dfrac{4}{24}$
$3\dfrac{5}{8} = 3\dfrac{15}{24}$
$\underline{+\ 2\dfrac{7}{12} = 2\dfrac{14}{24}}$
$10\dfrac{33}{24} = 11\dfrac{9}{24} = \mathbf{11\dfrac{3}{8}}$

26.
$\ \dfrac{1}{20} = \dfrac{9}{180}$
$\underline{-\ \dfrac{1}{36} = \dfrac{5}{180}}$
$\dfrac{4}{180} = \dfrac{1}{\mathbf{45}}$

27. $4.6 \times 10^{-2} = 0.046$
$\ 0.46$
$\underline{+\ 0.046}$
$\ \mathbf{0.506}$

28.
$\ 2.300 10.000$
$\underline{-\ 0.575} \underline{-\ 1.725}$
$\ 1.725 \mathbf{8.275}$

Solutions

29.

$$\begin{array}{r} 0.24 \\ \times\ 0.15 \\ \hline 1\,20 \\ 2\,4 \\ \hline 0.03\,60 \end{array} = 0.036$$

$$\begin{array}{r} 0.036 \\ \times\ 0.05 \\ \hline 0.00180 \end{array} = \mathbf{0.0018}$$

30. $70\overline{)0.140}^{\ 0.002}$ $\qquad 0\underset{\curvearrowright}{002}\overline{)10000}^{\ 5000}$

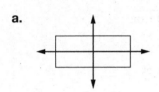

Practice Set 58

a.

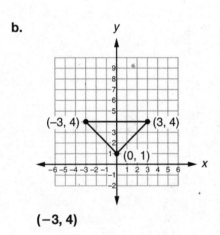

b.

y

(−3, 4) ● ── ● (3, 4)

(0, 1)

x

(−3, 4)

c. Only X has rotational symmetry. All four letters have reflective symmetry.

d. A triangle has rotational symmetry only if all sides are the same length. All examples of the other three polygons have rotational symmetry.

Example:

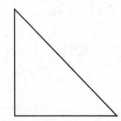

Written Practice 58

1. 10(1.4 kilometers) = **14 kilometers**

2. 10:45 am to 1:05 pm = 2 hr 20 min
  → 5 half hours
  5($0.75) = **$3.75**

3. $17n = 340$ $\qquad$ 17
  $n = \dfrac{340}{17}$ $\qquad \dfrac{+\ 20}{37}$
  $n = 20$

4. a. $\dfrac{\text{won}}{\text{lost}} = \dfrac{3}{9} = \dfrac{1}{3}$

  b. $\dfrac{\text{lost}}{\text{total games}} = \dfrac{9}{12} = \dfrac{3}{4}$

  c. $\dfrac{1}{4} \times 100\% = \dfrac{100\%}{4} = \mathbf{25\%}$

5. $5(120) = 600$ $\qquad\qquad 8\overline{)984}^{\ 123}$

$$\begin{array}{r} 600 \\ 118 \\ 124 \\ +\ 142 \\ \hline 984 \end{array} = \text{total score for 8 games}$$

$$\begin{array}{r} 8 \\ \hline 18 \\ 16 \\ \hline 24 \\ 24 \\ \hline 0 \end{array}$$

Average score = **123**

6.

60 questions	
$\frac{3}{5}$ were multiple-choice.	12 questions
	12 questions
	12 questions
$\frac{2}{5}$ were not multiple-choice	12 questions
	12 questions

  a. **36 questions**

  b. $\dfrac{2}{5} \times 100\% = \dfrac{200\%}{5} = \mathbf{40\%}$

7. a. $\overline{OA}, \overline{OB}, \overline{OC}$

  b. $\overline{AC}$ (or $\overline{CA}$), $\overline{BC}$ (or $\overline{CB}$)

  c. **60°**

  d. **30°**

Saxon Math Course 2 © Harcourt Achieve, Inc. and Stephen Hake. All rights reserved.

8. a. 15000000. ⟶ **15,000,000**

   b. .00025 ⟶ **0.00025**

   c. $10^{-1} = \dfrac{1}{10}$ or **0.1**

   d. **1**

9. $2 \cancel{\text{gal}} \times \dfrac{4 \text{ qt}}{1 \cancel{\text{gal}}} = 8 \text{ qt}$

   $8 \cancel{\text{L}} \times \dfrac{1.06 \text{ qt}}{1 \cancel{\text{L}}} \approx 8.48 \text{ qt}$

   $8 \text{ qt} < 8.48 \text{ qt}$

   $2 \text{ gal} < 8 \text{ L}$

10.
$$\begin{array}{r} 19.16\ldots \\ 18\overline{)345.00\ldots} \\ \underline{18} \\ 165 \\ \underline{162} \\ 3\,0 \\ \underline{1\,8} \\ 1\,20 \\ \underline{1\,08} \\ 12 \end{array}$$

    19

11. **5, 0, −5**

12. a.
$$\begin{array}{r} 0.16\overline{6}\ldots \\ 6\overline{)1.000\ldots} \end{array} \qquad \mathbf{0.1\overline{6}}$$

    b. $\dfrac{1}{6} \times 100\% = \dfrac{100\%}{6} = \mathbf{16\dfrac{2}{3}\%}$

    c. $16\% = \dfrac{16}{100} = \mathbf{\dfrac{4}{25}}$

    d. $16\% = \dfrac{16}{100} = \mathbf{0.16}$

13. a. **To find _y_, multiply _x_ by 4.**
    b. $y = 4(2) = \mathbf{8}$
    c. $\mathbf{y = 4x}$

14. a. $m\angle ACB = 180° - (90° + 35°)$
    $= 180° - 125° = \mathbf{55°}$

    b. $\angle ACD = 180° - 55° = \mathbf{125°}$

    c. $\angle CAD = 180° - (35° + 125°)$
    $= 180° - 160° = \mathbf{20°}$

15.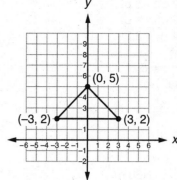

    a. **(3, 2)**

    b. $\text{Area} = \dfrac{(6 \text{ units})(3 \text{ units})}{2}$
    $= \mathbf{9 \text{ units}^2}$

16. a. **5 lines**
    b. **Yes, of order 5**

17. a. $\overset{7}{2\cancel{10}} \ \cancel{\text{miles}} \cdot \dfrac{1 \text{ hr}}{\underset{2}{\cancel{60}} \ \cancel{\text{miles}}}$

    $= \dfrac{7}{2} \text{ hr} = \mathbf{3\dfrac{1}{2} \text{ hr}}$

    b. $\overset{3}{2\cancel{10}} \ \cancel{\text{miles}} \cdot \dfrac{1 \text{ hr}}{\underset{1}{\cancel{70}} \ \cancel{\text{miles}}}$

    $= \mathbf{3 \text{ hr}}$

18. $\dfrac{1.5}{2} = \dfrac{7.5}{w}$
    $1.5w = 2(7.5)$
    $w = \dfrac{15}{1.5}$
    $w = \mathbf{10}$

19.
$$\begin{array}{r} 1.70 \\ -\ 0.17 \\ \hline 1.53 \end{array}$$
    $y = \mathbf{1.53}$

20. $10^3 - 10^2 + 10^1 - 10^0$
    $1000 - 100 + 10 - 1$
    $900 + 10 - 1$
    $910 - 1$
    909

21. $6 + 3(2) - 4 - (5 + 3)$
    $6 + 6 - 4 - 8$
    $12 - 4 - 8$
    $8 - 8$
    0

233

22.
$$\begin{array}{r} 1 \text{ gal} \quad 2 \text{ qt} \quad 1 \text{ pt} \\ + \; 1 \text{ gal} \quad 2 \text{ qt} \quad 1 \text{ pt} \\ \hline 2 \text{ gal} \quad 4 \text{ qt} \quad 2 \text{ pt} \end{array}$$

2 pt = 1 qt
4 qt + 1 qt = 5 qt
5 qt = 1 gal 1 qt

$$\begin{array}{r} 1 \text{ gal} \quad 1 \text{ qt} \\ + \; 2 \text{ gal} \\ \hline \textbf{3 gal} \quad \textbf{1 qt} \end{array}$$

23.

$$\begin{array}{r} \overset{2}{} \quad \overset{\rightarrow (60 \text{ min})}{} \\ 1 \text{ day} \quad \cancel{3} \text{ hr} \quad 15 \text{ min} \\ - \qquad\qquad 8 \text{ hr} \quad 30 \text{ min} \end{array} \longrightarrow$$

$$\begin{array}{r} \overset{\rightarrow (24 \text{ hr})}{} \\ \overset{0}{\cancel{1}} \text{ day} \quad \overset{2}{\cancel{3}} \text{ hr} \quad \overset{75}{\cancel{15}} \text{ min} \\ - \qquad\qquad 8 \text{ hr} \quad 30 \text{ min} \\ \hline \qquad\qquad\qquad\qquad 45 \text{ min} \end{array} \longrightarrow$$

$$\begin{array}{r} \overset{0}{\cancel{1}} \text{ day} \quad \overset{26}{\overset{\cancel{2}}{\cancel{3}}} \text{ hr} \quad \overset{75}{\cancel{15}} \text{ min} \\ - \qquad\qquad 8 \text{ hr} \quad 30 \text{ min} \\ \hline \textbf{18 hr} \quad \textbf{45 min} \end{array}$$

24. $2 \cancel{\text{mi}} \cdot \dfrac{5280 \text{ ft}}{1 \cancel{\text{mi}}} = \textbf{10,560 ft}$

25.
$$\begin{array}{r} 5\dfrac{3}{4} = 5\dfrac{9}{12} \longrightarrow 4\dfrac{21}{12} \\ - \; 1\dfrac{5}{6} = 1\dfrac{10}{12} \qquad - \; 1\dfrac{10}{12} \\ \hline \qquad\qquad\qquad\qquad 3\dfrac{11}{12} \end{array}$$

$$\begin{array}{r} 10 \longrightarrow 9\dfrac{12}{12} \\ - \; 3\dfrac{11}{12} \qquad - \; 3\dfrac{11}{12} \\ \hline \qquad\qquad \textbf{6}\dfrac{\textbf{1}}{\textbf{12}} \end{array}$$

26.
$$\begin{array}{r} 2\dfrac{1}{5} = 2\dfrac{2}{10} \\ + \; 5\dfrac{1}{2} = 5\dfrac{5}{10} \\ \hline 7\dfrac{7}{10} \end{array}$$

$$7\dfrac{7}{10} \div 2\dfrac{1}{5} = \dfrac{77}{10} \div \dfrac{11}{5}$$

$$= \dfrac{\overset{7}{\cancel{77}}}{\underset{2}{\cancel{10}}} \times \dfrac{\overset{1}{\cancel{5}}}{\underset{1}{\cancel{11}}} = \dfrac{7}{2} = \textbf{3}\dfrac{\textbf{1}}{\textbf{2}}$$

27. $6 \div 4\dfrac{1}{2} = \dfrac{6}{1} \div \dfrac{9}{2} =$

$$\dfrac{\overset{2}{\cancel{6}}}{1} \times \dfrac{2}{\underset{3}{\cancel{9}}} = \dfrac{4}{3}$$

$$3\dfrac{3}{4} \cdot \dfrac{4}{3} = \dfrac{\overset{5}{\cancel{15}}}{\underset{1}{\cancel{4}}} \cdot \dfrac{\overset{1}{\cancel{4}}}{\underset{1}{\cancel{3}}} = \textbf{5}$$

28. $(6)^2 - 4(3.6)(2.5)$
$$= 36 - 36 = \textbf{0}$$

29. a. $2.5, \; 2, \; \dfrac{3}{2}, \; 0.\bar{2}, \; 0, \; -\dfrac{1}{2}, \; -1$

   b. $-1, 0, 2$

30. Lindsey could double both numbers before dividing, forming the equivalent division problem $70 \div 5$. She could also double both of these numbers to form $140 \div 10$.

Early Finishers Solutions

a. electron

b. neutron

Practice Set 59

a.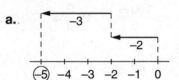

b.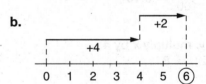

c.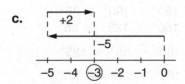

d.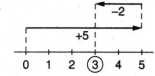

e.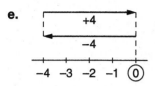

f.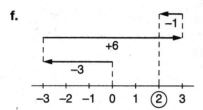

g. $\dfrac{1}{4}$

h. **11**

i. **0.05**

j. $|-3| + |3| = 3 + 3 = \mathbf{6}$

k. $|3 - 3| = |0| = \mathbf{0}$

l. $|5 - 3| = |2| = \mathbf{2}$

m.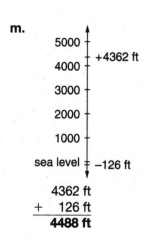

```
  4362 ft
+  126 ft
  4488 ft
```

n.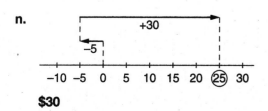

$30

Written Practice (59)

1. $2(\$2.35) + \$0.60(6)$
$= \$4.70 + \$3.60$
$= \mathbf{\$8.30}$

2.
```
   90°F
−  85°F
    5°F
```

3.
```
82°F        86°F
84°F    7)602°F
86°F
88°F
84°F
90°F
+ 88°F
602°F
```

4.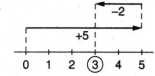

16°F

5.

	Ratio	Actual Count
red	7	r
green	4	56

$\dfrac{7}{4} = \dfrac{r}{56}$

$4r = 392$

$r = 98$

98 red apples

6.
20 games
$\dfrac{3}{4}$ won.
```
5 games
5 games
5 games
```
$\dfrac{1}{4}$ failed to win.
```
5 games
```

a. **15 games**

b. $\dfrac{1}{4} \times 100\% = \dfrac{100\%}{4} = \mathbf{25\%}$

7. $|-3| = 3, |3| = 3$
$\quad 3 = 3$
$|-3| = |3|$

8. a. $4.000000000000 \longrightarrow \mathbf{4 \times 10^{12}}$

b. $3670000000.$ miles $\longrightarrow$
3,670,000,000 miles

9. a. $.000001$ meter $\longrightarrow$ **0.000001 meter**

b. 1 millimeter $= 0.001$ meter
1×10^{-3} meter $= 0.001$ meter
1 millimeter $= 1 \times 10^{-3}$ meter

Saxon Math Course 2

10. $\overset{3}{\cancel{300}}\text{ mm} \cdot \dfrac{1\text{ m}}{\underset{10}{\cancel{1000}}\text{ mm}} = \dfrac{3}{10}\text{ m} = \textbf{0.3 m}$

11. a. $12\% = \dfrac{12}{100} = \dfrac{\textbf{3}}{\textbf{25}}$

b. $12\% = \dfrac{12}{100} = \textbf{0.12}$

c. $3\overline{)1.00\ldots}\ \dfrac{0.33\ldots}{}\quad \textbf{0.}\overline{\textbf{3}}$

d. $\dfrac{1}{3} \times 100\% = \dfrac{100\%}{3} = \textbf{33}\dfrac{\textbf{1}}{\textbf{3}}\textbf{\%}$

12. a.
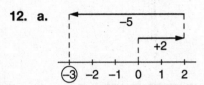

b.
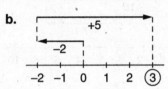

13. a. **To find *y*, add 12 to *x*.**

b. $y = 12 + 12 = \textbf{24}$

c. $\boldsymbol{y = x + 12}$

14. Perimeter $= 50\text{ mm} + 60\text{ mm} + 35\text{ mm}$
$+ 15\text{ mm} + 15\text{ mm} + 25\text{ mm}$
$+ 30\text{ mm} + 20\text{ mm}$
$= \textbf{250 mm}$

15.
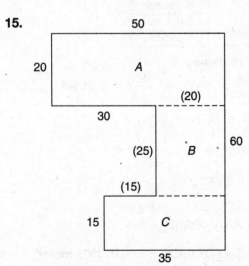

Area $A = (50\text{ mm})(20\text{ mm}) = 1000\text{ mm}^2$
Area $B = (20\text{ mm})(25\text{ mm}) = 500\text{ mm}^2$
$+$ Area $C = (35\text{ mm})(15\text{ mm}) = 525\text{ mm}^2$
Area of figure $= \textbf{2025 mm}^2$

16. $8\overline{)4.40}\ \overset{0.55}{}$
$w = \textbf{0.55}$

17. $\dfrac{0.8}{1} = \dfrac{x}{1.5}$
$1x = (0.8)(1.5)$
$x = \textbf{1.2}$

18. $\dfrac{17}{30} = \dfrac{34}{60}$
$-\ \dfrac{11}{20} = \dfrac{33}{60}$
$n = \dfrac{\textbf{1}}{\textbf{60}}$

19. $7\overline{)0.364}\ \overset{0.052}{}$
$\dfrac{35}{14}$
$\dfrac{14}{0}$
$m = \textbf{0.052}$

20. $2^{-1} + 2^{-1} = \dfrac{1}{2} + \dfrac{1}{2}$
$= \dfrac{2}{2} = \textbf{1}$

21. $\sqrt{64} - 2^3 + 4^0 = 8 - 8 + 1$
$= \textbf{1}$

22.
$3\text{ yd}\quad 2\text{ ft}\quad 7\dfrac{1}{2}\text{ in.}$
$+\ 1\text{ yd}\qquad\qquad 5\dfrac{1}{2}\text{ in.}$
$\overline{\ 4\text{ yd}\quad 2\text{ ft}\quad 13\text{ in.}\ }$
13 in. $=$ 1 ft 1 in.
1 ft 1 in.
$\dfrac{2\text{ ft}}{3\text{ ft 1 in.}}$
3 ft $=$ 1 yd
$\quad$ 1 yd 1 in.
$+\ 4\text{ yd}$
$\overline{\ \textbf{5 yd\ \ 1 in.}\ }$

236

23.

$$\overset{0}{\cancel{1}}\text{ qt}\quad\overset{\longrightarrow(2\text{ pt})}{1\text{ pt}}\quad 6\text{ oz}\longrightarrow$$
$$-\qquad\quad 1\text{ pt}\quad 12\text{ oz}\longrightarrow$$

$$\overset{0}{\cancel{1}}\text{ qt}\quad\overset{\overset{2}{\cancel{3}}\longrightarrow(16\text{ oz})}{\cancel{1}\text{ pt}}\quad 6\text{ oz}\longrightarrow$$
$$-\qquad\quad 1\text{ pt}\quad 12\text{ oz}\longrightarrow$$

$$\overset{0}{\cancel{1}}\text{ qt}\quad\overset{\overset{2}{\cancel{3}}}{\cancel{1}}\text{ pt}\quad\overset{22}{\cancel{6}}\text{ oz}$$
$$-\qquad\quad 1\text{ pt}\quad 12\text{ oz}$$
$$\overline{\qquad\qquad\mathbf{1\text{ pt}\quad 10\text{ oz}}}$$

24. $2\frac{1}{2}\ \cancel{\text{hr}}\cdot\dfrac{50\text{ mi}}{1\ \cancel{\text{hr}}}=\mathbf{125\text{ mi}}$

25. $\dfrac{5}{9}\cdot 12=\dfrac{5}{\underset{3}{\cancel{9}}}\cdot\dfrac{\overset{4}{\cancel{12}}}{1}=\dfrac{20}{3}$

$$\dfrac{20}{3}\div 6\dfrac{2}{3}=\dfrac{20}{3}\div\dfrac{20}{3}$$

$$=\dfrac{\overset{1}{\cancel{20}}}{\underset{1}{\cancel{3}}}\times\dfrac{\overset{1}{\cancel{3}}}{\underset{1}{\cancel{20}}}=\mathbf{1}$$

26. $4-(4-1)=4-3=\mathbf{1}$

$$4\longrightarrow 3\dfrac{9}{9}$$
$$-\ 1\dfrac{1}{9}\qquad -\ 1\dfrac{1}{9}$$
$$\overline{\qquad\qquad\quad 2\dfrac{8}{9}}$$

$$3\dfrac{5}{6}=3\dfrac{15}{18}\longrightarrow 2\dfrac{33}{18}$$
$$-\ 2\dfrac{8}{9}=2\dfrac{16}{18}\qquad -\ 2\dfrac{16}{18}$$
$$\overline{\qquad\qquad\qquad\qquad\mathbf{\dfrac{17}{18}}}$$

27. $(6+6)\div 6=12\div 6=\mathbf{2}$

$$5\dfrac{5}{8}=5\dfrac{5}{8}$$
$$+\ 6\dfrac{1}{4}=6\dfrac{2}{8}$$
$$\overline{\qquad\quad 11\dfrac{7}{8}}$$

$$11\dfrac{7}{8}\div 6\dfrac{1}{4}=\dfrac{95}{8}\div\dfrac{25}{4}$$

$$=\dfrac{\overset{19}{\cancel{95}}}{\underset{2}{\cancel{8}}}\times\dfrac{\overset{1}{\cancel{4}}}{\underset{5}{\cancel{25}}}=\dfrac{19}{10}=\mathbf{1\dfrac{9}{10}}$$

28. $(0.1)-(0.2)(0.3)$
$$=0.1-0.06=\mathbf{0.04}$$

29. (a) To the lake: $\dfrac{30\text{ miles}}{2\text{ hours}}=\mathbf{15\text{ mph}}$

(b) Return trip: $\dfrac{30\text{ miles}}{3\text{ hours}}=\mathbf{10\text{ mph}}$

(c) Round trip: $\dfrac{60\text{ miles}}{5\text{ hours}}=\mathbf{12\text{ mph}}$

30. $P(\text{Lam})=\dfrac{10}{25}=\dfrac{2}{5},\mathbf{0.4}\qquad 5\overline{)2.0}^{\,0.4}$

Early Finishers Solutions

See student work. Sample polygons include: triangle, regular pentagon, regular hexagon, etc. (any regular polygon), and any parallelogram.

Practice Set 60

a. $W_N=\dfrac{4}{5}\times 71$
$$W_N=\dfrac{284}{5}$$
$$W_N=\mathbf{56\dfrac{4}{5}}$$

b. $0.75\times 14.4=W_N$
$\mathbf{10.8}=W_N$

c. $W_N=0.5\times 150$
$W_N=\mathbf{75}$

d. $0.03\times\$39=M$
$\mathbf{\$1.17}=M$

e. $W_N=0.25\times 64$
$W_N=\mathbf{16}$

f. $0.12\times\$250{,}000=C$
$\mathbf{\$30{,}000}=C$

g.
$$\begin{array}{r}\$36.89\\ \times\quad 0.07\\ \hline \$2.5823\end{array}\rightarrow\mathbf{\$2.58}$$

h.
$36.89
+ $ 2.58
—————
$39.47

i.
$ 6.95
$ 0.95
+ $ 2.45
—————
$10.35

$ 10.35
× 0.06
—————
$ 0.6210 → $0.62

$10.35
+ $ 0.62
—————
$10.97

Written Practice **60**

1.
$$\overset{6\ \ \ 9\ \ 9\ \ 12}{7.\cancel{0}\cancel{0}\cancel{2}1}$$
$$-\ 5.7840$$
$$\overline{1.2181}$$

2. $0.20x = \$10.00$
$x = 50$
$2(50) = 100$
100 magazines

3. a. $d = \$0.20b$

b. **Answers may vary. See student work.**
Sample answer:

Boards	Dollars
10	2.00
20	4.00
30	6.00
40	8.00

4. a. $\frac{1}{5} \times 100\% =$ **20%**

b. $\dfrac{\text{students who passed}}{\text{students who did not pass}} = \dfrac{4}{1}$

5. $5(77 \text{ inches}) = 385 \text{ inches}$
71 inches
74 inches   385 inches
78 inches   − 301 inches
+ 78 inches   ————————
————————   **84 inches**
301 inches

6. a. 8×10^{-8}

b. 6.75×10^{10}

7.
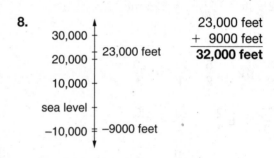
$\frac{2}{3}$ approved.
$\frac{1}{3}$ did not approve.

a. **64 members**

b. $\frac{1}{3} \times 100\% =$ **33$\frac{1}{3}$%**

8.

23,000 feet
+ 9000 feet
——————————
32,000 feet

9. $W_N = \frac{3}{4} \times 17$

$W_N = \frac{51}{4}$

$W_N = 12\frac{3}{4}$

10. $0.4 \times \$65 = P$
$26 $= P$

11. a. $3\overline{)1.00\ldots} \quad \frac{1}{3} > 0.33$
$0.33\ldots$

b. $|5 - 3| = |2| = 2$
$|3 - 5| = |-2| = 2$
$|5 - 3| = |3 - 5|$

12. a. $8\overline{)1.000} \quad$ **0.125**

b. $\frac{1}{8} \times 100\% =$ **12$\frac{1}{2}$%**

c. $125\% = \frac{125}{100} = 1\frac{1}{4}$

d. $125\% = \frac{125}{100} =$ **1.25**

238

13. (a)

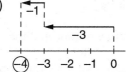

(b)

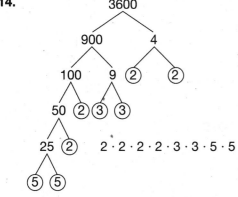

14.

```
                3600
              /      \
           900        4
          /    \     / \
       100      9  (2) (2)
      /   \    /|\
    50  (2)(2)(3)(3)
    / \
  25 (2)   2·2·2·2·3·3·5·5
  / \
(5) (5)
```

   a. $2^4 \cdot 3^2 \cdot 5^2$

   b. $\sqrt{3600} = 60 = 2^2 \cdot 3 \cdot 5$

15. **a.** $360° \times \dfrac{1}{2} = \dfrac{360°}{2} = \mathbf{180°}$

   b. $360° \times \dfrac{1}{3} = \dfrac{360°}{3} = \mathbf{120°}$

   c. $360° \times \dfrac{1}{6} = \dfrac{360°}{6} = \mathbf{60°}$

16. **a.** $\triangle$**CDB**

   b. $\triangle$**CEA**

17. **a.** Area $= \dfrac{(6\text{ ft})(8\text{ ft})}{2} = \mathbf{24\text{ ft}^2}$

   b. Area $= \dfrac{(12\text{ ft})(16\text{ ft})}{2} = \mathbf{96\text{ ft}^2}$

18. Area($\triangle DEF$) $= \dfrac{(6\text{ ft})(8\text{ ft})}{2} = 24\text{ ft}^2$

   $96\text{ ft}^2 - 24\text{ ft}^2 - 24\text{ ft}^2 = \mathbf{48\text{ ft}^2}$

19.
$$\begin{aligned} \dfrac{1}{20} &= \dfrac{3}{60} \\ + \dfrac{1}{30} &= \dfrac{2}{60} \\ \hline \dfrac{5}{60} &= \dfrac{1}{12} \end{aligned}$$

$$p = \mathbf{\dfrac{1}{12}}$$

20.
$$9\overline{)0.117} \quad \dfrac{0.013}{}$$
$$\begin{aligned} &\underline{9} \\ &27 \\ &\underline{27} \\ &\ \ 0 \end{aligned}$$

$m = \mathbf{0.013}$

21. $3^2 + 4(3 + 2) - 2^3 \cdot 2^{-2} + \sqrt{36}$

   $9 + 4(3 + 2) - 8 \cdot \dfrac{1}{4} + 6$

      $9 + 4(5) - 2 + 6$

       $9 + 20 - 2 + 6$

         $29 - 2 + 6$

           $27 + 6$

             33

22. **a.** $\dfrac{3}{4}\left(\dfrac{4}{9} + \dfrac{2}{3}\right) = \dfrac{3}{4}\left(\dfrac{4}{9} + \dfrac{6}{9}\right) = \dfrac{\overset{1}{\cancel{3}}}{\underset{2}{\cancel{4}}}\left(\dfrac{\overset{5}{\cancel{10}}}{\underset{3}{\cancel{9}}}\right) = \dfrac{5}{6}$

      $\dfrac{\overset{1}{\cancel{3}}}{\underset{1}{\cancel{4}}} \cdot \dfrac{\overset{1}{\cancel{4}}}{\underset{3}{\cancel{9}}} + \dfrac{\overset{1}{\cancel{3}}}{\underset{2}{\cancel{4}}} \cdot \dfrac{\overset{1}{\cancel{2}}}{\underset{1}{\cancel{3}}} = \dfrac{1}{3} + \dfrac{1}{2} = \dfrac{2}{6} + \dfrac{3}{6} = \dfrac{5}{6}$

      $\dfrac{5}{6} = \dfrac{5}{6}$

      $\dfrac{3}{4}\left(\dfrac{4}{9} + \dfrac{2}{3}\right) = \dfrac{3}{4} \cdot \dfrac{4}{9} + \dfrac{3}{4} \cdot \dfrac{2}{3}$

   b. **Distributive property**

23. **a.** **Sample space = {AA, Ab, AC, BA, BB, BC, CA, CB, CC}**

   b. P(A in either spin) $= \dfrac{5}{9}$

Solutions

24. $\frac{5}{6} \cdot 4 = \frac{5}{\overset{3}{\cancel{6}}} \cdot \frac{\overset{2}{\cancel{4}}}{1} = \frac{10}{3} = 3\frac{1}{3}$

$$3\frac{3}{5} = 3\frac{9}{15}$$
$$-3\frac{1}{3} = 3\frac{5}{15}$$
$$\overline{\frac{4}{15}}$$

25. $1\frac{1}{4} \div \frac{5}{12} = \frac{5}{4} \div \frac{5}{12}$

$= \frac{\overset{1}{\cancel{5}}}{\underset{1}{\cancel{4}}} \times \frac{\overset{3}{\cancel{12}}}{\underset{1}{\cancel{5}}} = 3$

$3 \div 24 = \frac{3}{24} = \frac{1}{8}$ or **0.125**

26. $0.\overset{5\,\,^14\,\,10}{\cancel{6}\cancel{5}\cancel{0}}$ $\overset{5\quad\,^14\,\,9\,\,10}{\cancel{6}.\cancel{5}\cancel{0}\cancel{0}}$
   $-\,0.065$ $-\,0.585$
   $\overline{\,\,0.585}$ $\overline{\,\,5.915}$

27. $3 \div 0.03 = 100$
  $0.3 \div 100 = \textbf{0.003}$

28. $3.5 \text{ centimeters} \cdot \frac{1 \text{ meter}}{100 \text{ centimeters}}$

$= \frac{3.5}{100} \text{ meter} = \textbf{0.035 meter}$

29. The first division problem can be multiplied by $\frac{100}{100}$ to form the second division problem. Since $\frac{100}{100}$ equals 1, the quotients are the same.
One possibility: $\frac{\$1.50}{\$0.25} = \frac{150¢}{25¢}$

30.

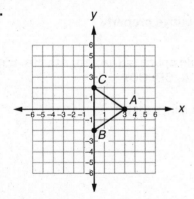

a. **(0, 2)**
b. **No**

Early Finishers Solutions

a. $16.11; See student work for method justification.

b. 4 weeks; See student work for method justification.

Investigation 6

Classifying Quadrilaterals

1. **A, C**

2. **C, D**

3. **A, B, C, D**

4. **E**

5. **F, G**

6. **A, B, C, D**
{Figures C and D have two equal-length sides, or two pair of two equal-length sides.}

7. **A, B, C, D**

8. **E**

9. **F, G**

10. **C, D**

11. **A, C**

12. {Students draw a Venn diagram as shown in the textbook, and then place figures A–E in the correct area of the diagram. Figure E should be outside the parallelogram category.}

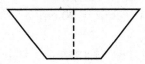**Solutions**

13. No

14. Yes

15. Yes

16. Yes

17. F

18. Perimeter = 10 ft.

19. One possibility shown.

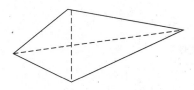

20. One possibility shown.

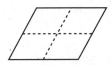

21. One possibility shown.

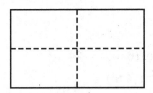

22. {Student's figure must be a square.}

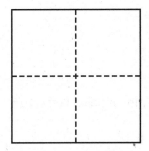

23. One possibility shown.

24. {Students find point of symmetry using cut-out parallelograms.}

25. A. Parallelogram, B. rectangle, C. rhombus, D. square

26. True

27. True

28. False

29. True

30.

Quadrilaterals
Trapezoids
Parallelograms

Practice Set 61

a. Perimeter = 10 cm + 12 cm + 10 cm
 + 12 cm = **44 cm**
 Area = (12 cm)(8 cm) = **96 cm²**

b. Perimeter = 10 cm + 13 cm + 10 cm
 + 13 cm = **46 cm**
 Area = (10 cm)(12 cm) = **120 cm²**

Solutions

c. Perimeter = 10 cm + 10 cm + 10 cm
 + 10 cm = **40 cm**
 Area = (10 cm)(9 cm) = **90 cm²**

d. $m\angle d = 180° - 75° = $ **105°**

e. $m\angle e = 180° - 105° = $ **75°**

f. $m\angle f = m\angle d = $ **105°**

g. $m\angle g = m\angle e = $ **75°**

h. $m\angle A = m\angle C = $ **60°**

i. $m\angle ADB = 180° - (90° + 60°)$
 $= 180° - 150° = $ **30°**

j. $m\angle ABC = 180° - 60° = $ **120°**

k. **A = bh**

l. The perimeter of the frame did not change; the boards were the same length. The area did change (from 2400 in.² to 2250 in.²). As the frame shifts, the area decreases. If the frame is flattened, the area becomes zero.

Written Practice 61

1. $\frac{1}{2}$ gallon = 2 quarts = 4 pints

$$4\overline{)\$1.12}^{\ \$0.28\ \text{per pint}}$$

2.

	Ratio	Actual Count
Oatmeal	2	3 cups
Brown sugar	1	B

$\frac{2}{1} = \frac{3\text{ cups}}{B}$

$2B = 1(3\text{ cups})$

$B = \frac{3}{2}$ cups $= 1\frac{1}{2}$ **cups**

3. 3(55.0 seconds) = 165 seconds
 54.3 seconds + 56.1 seconds + n
 = 165 seconds
 n = 165 seconds − 110.4 seconds
 n = **54.6 seconds**

4. $\frac{9\text{ miles}}{60\text{ minutes}} = \frac{9\text{ miles}}{1\text{ hour}} = $ **9 miles per hour**

5. $\begin{array}{r} 63{,}100{,}000 \\ -\ \ 7{,}060{,}000 \\ \hline 56{,}040{,}000 \end{array}$

56,040,000 = **5.604 × 10⁷**

6. a. $\frac{7}{10} \times 100\% = \frac{700\%}{10} = $ **70%**

b. $\frac{\text{news area}}{\text{advertisement area}} = \frac{3}{7}$

c. $\frac{\text{advertisement area}}{\text{total area}} = \frac{7}{10}$

7. a. **1.05 × 10⁻³**

b. **302,000**

8. a. $\frac{128}{192} = \frac{\overset{1}{\cancel{2}} \cdot \overset{1}{\cancel{2}} \cdot \overset{1}{\cancel{2}} \cdot \overset{1}{\cancel{2}} \cdot \overset{1}{\cancel{2}} \cdot \overset{1}{\cancel{2}} \cdot 2}{\underset{1}{\cancel{2}} \cdot \underset{1}{\cancel{2}} \cdot \underset{1}{\cancel{2}} \cdot \underset{1}{\cancel{2}} \cdot \underset{1}{\cancel{2}} \cdot \underset{1}{\cancel{2}} \cdot 3} = \frac{2}{3}$

b. $2 \cdot 2 \cdot 2 \cdot 2 \cdot 2 \cdot 2 = $ **64**

9. $1760\ \cancel{\text{yards}} \cdot \frac{3\text{ feet}}{1\ \cancel{\text{yard}}} = $ **5280 feet**

10. a. Parallelogram

b. Trapezoid

11. a. Area = (4 m)(6 m) = **24 m²**

b. Area $= \frac{(2\text{ m})(4\text{ m})}{2} = $ **4 m²**

c. Area = 24 m² + 4 m² = **28 m²**

12. a. Obtuse angle

b. Right angle

c. Acute angle

13. a. For 19 scores, the median is the 10th score.
 10th score = **8**

b. For 19 scores, the lower quartile is the 5th score.
 5th score = **6**

c. For 19 scores, the upper quartile is the 15th score.

15th score = **9**

d. Outliers = **2**

14. a. Perimeter = 120 m + 100 m + 120 m + 100 m = **560 m**

b. Area = (160 m)(100 m) = **16,000 m²**

c. Yes, order 2

15. a. m∠a = 180° − (59° + 61°)
= 180° − 120° = **60°**

b. m∠b = **61°**

c. m∠c = **59°**

d. m∠d = m∠a = **60°**

16. 2 ~~centimeters~~ · $\dfrac{1 \text{ meter}}{100 \text{ } \sout{centimeters}}$

$= \dfrac{2}{100}$ meter = **0.02 meter**

17.

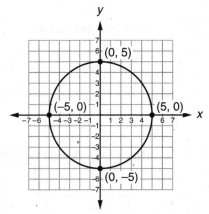

a. (0, 5), (0, −5)

b. 10 units

18. The scale is balanced so the 3 items on the left have a total mass of 50 g. The labeled masses total 15 g, so the cube must be 35 g because 35 g + 15 g = 50 g.

19.

$\begin{array}{r} 164 \text{ feet} \\ + \quad 27 \text{ feet} \\ \hline \textbf{191 feet} \end{array}$

+164 feet

−27 feet

20. 10 + 10 × 10 − 10 ÷ 10
10 + 100 − 1
110 − 1
109

21. $2^0 - 2^{-3} = 1 - \dfrac{1}{2^3}$

$= 1 - \dfrac{1}{8} = \dfrac{8}{8} - \dfrac{1}{8} = \dfrac{7}{8}$

22. 70 cm = 0.7 m

$\begin{array}{r} 4.5 \text{ m} \\ + \quad 0.7 \text{ m} \\ \hline \textbf{5.2 m} \end{array}$

23. $2.75 \, \cancel{L} \cdot \dfrac{1000 \text{ mL}}{1 \, \cancel{L}} = \textbf{2750 mL}$

24.

$\begin{array}{l} 3\dfrac{1}{3} = 3\dfrac{2}{6} \\ -\ 1\dfrac{1}{2} = 1\dfrac{3}{6} \end{array} \longrightarrow \begin{array}{l} 2\dfrac{8}{6} \\ -\ 1\dfrac{3}{6} \\ \hline 1\dfrac{5}{6} \end{array}$

$\begin{array}{l} 5\dfrac{7}{8} = 5\dfrac{21}{24} \\ +\ 1\dfrac{5}{6} = 1\dfrac{20}{24} \\ \hline \qquad 6\dfrac{41}{24} = 7\dfrac{17}{24} \end{array}$

25. $4\dfrac{4}{5} \cdot 1\dfrac{1}{9} \cdot 1\dfrac{7}{8}$

$= \dfrac{\overset{\overset{1}{\cancel{3}}}{\cancel{24}}}{\cancel{5}} \cdot \dfrac{10}{\underset{\underset{1}{\cancel{3}}}{\cancel{9}}} \cdot \dfrac{\overset{\overset{1}{\cancel{3}}}{\cancel{15}}}{\underset{1}{\cancel{8}}} = \textbf{10}$

243

Solutions

26. $3\frac{1}{5} \div 8 = \frac{16}{5} \div \frac{8}{1} = \frac{\overset{2}{\cancel{16}}}{5} \times \frac{1}{\underset{1}{\cancel{8}}} = \frac{2}{5}$

$6\frac{2}{3} \div \frac{2}{5} = \frac{20}{3} \div \frac{2}{5} = \frac{\overset{10}{\cancel{20}}}{3} \times \frac{5}{\underset{1}{\cancel{2}}} = \frac{50}{3}$

$= 16\frac{2}{3}$

27.

$$\begin{array}{r} 0.8 \\ + \ 0.97 \\ \hline 1.77 \end{array} \qquad \begin{array}{r} \overset{1\ \ 9\ 10}{1\cancel{2}.\cancel{0}\cancel{0}} \\ - \quad 1.77 \\ \hline \mathbf{10.23} \end{array}$$

28.

$$\begin{array}{r} 0.05 \\ \times \quad 2.4 \\ \hline 0.12 \end{array} \qquad \begin{array}{r} 0.005 \\ \times \quad 0.12 \\ \hline \mathbf{0.0006} \end{array}$$

29. $4 \times 10^2 = 4 \times 100 = 400$
$0.2 \div 400 = \mathbf{0.0005}$

30. $4 \div 0.25 = 16$
$0.36 \div 16 = \mathbf{0.0225}$

Early Finishers Solutions

mean $= \dfrac{\$9 + \$28 + \$8 + \$11 + \$9 + \$7}{6}$
$= \$12$
median $= \$7, \$8, \boxed{\$9, \$9}, \$11, \$28 = \$9$
mode $= \$9$
range $= \$28 - \$7 = \$21$

The median or mode gives the best description because most of the meals are between \$7 and \$9.

Practice Set 62

a. Right triangle

b. Obtuse triangle

c. Acute triangle

d. Scalene triangle

e. Equilateral triangle

f. Isosceles triangle

g. 11 cm; Since the triangle is isosceles, two sides are the same length, either 3-3-4 or 3-4-4. Since the perimeter is not 10 cm (3-3-4), the perimeter must be 11 cm (3-4-4).

h. The triangle is acute because all the angles are acute. The triangle is scalene because the three angles are different measures so the three sides are different lengths.

i. $\angle L, \angle N, \angle M$

Written Practice 62

1. $4(15 \text{ minutes}) = 60 \text{ minutes}$
$60 \text{ minutes} + 10 \text{ minutes} = 70 \text{ minutes}$
$= 1 \text{ hour } 10 \text{ minutes}$
2:40 p.m.

2.
$$\begin{array}{r} 40,060 \text{ miles} \\ - \ 39,872 \text{ miles} \\ \hline \mathbf{188 \text{ miles}} \end{array}$$

3. $\dfrac{188 \text{ miles}}{8 \text{ gallons}} = \mathbf{23.5 \text{ miles per gallon}}$

4. $24 \cdot w = 288$
$w = 12$
$24 \div 12 = \mathbf{2}$

5.

	Ratio	Actual Count
Bolsheviks	9	144
Czarists	8	C

$\dfrac{9}{8} = \dfrac{144}{C}$
$9C = 1152$
$C = \mathbf{128 \text{ czarists}}$

6. a. $\dfrac{7}{10} \times 100\% = \dfrac{700\%}{10} = \mathbf{70\%}$

b. $\dfrac{3}{10}$

7. $W_N = \frac{5}{6} \times 3\frac{1}{3}$

$W_N = \frac{5}{\underset{3}{\cancel{6}}} \times \frac{\overset{5}{\cancel{10}}}{3} = \frac{25}{9} = 2\frac{7}{9}$

8.
$$\begin{array}{r} \$10{,}000 \\ \times \quad 0.085 \\ \hline 50\ 000 \\ 800\ 00 \\ \hline \$850.000 = \$850 \end{array}$$
$\$10{,}000 + \$850 = \mathbf{\$10{,}850}$

9. **186,000; one hundred eighty-six thousand**

10. 1 quart $\boxed{<}$ 1 liter

11.

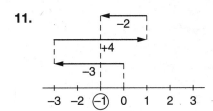

12. a. $8\overline{)5.000}$ → **0.625**

b. $\frac{5}{8} \times 100\% = \frac{500\%}{8} = \mathbf{62\frac{1}{2}\%}$

c. $275\% = \frac{275}{100} = \frac{11}{4} = \mathbf{2\frac{3}{4}}$

d. $275\% = \frac{275}{100} = \mathbf{2.75}$

13. $(12) + \frac{(12)}{(3)} - 3 =$

$12 + 4 - 3 = 16 - 3 = \mathbf{13}$

14. a. 2^8

b. 2^2

c. 2^0

d. 2^{-2}

15. a. $\triangle \mathbf{ZWY}$

b. $\triangle \mathbf{WYX}$

c. $\triangle \mathbf{ZWX}$

16.

a. Perimeter $= 4\frac{1}{2}$ in. $+$ 4 in. $+$ $2\frac{1}{2}$ in.
$+$ 2 in. $+$ 2 in. $+$ 6 in.
$= \mathbf{21\ in.}$

b.
$$\begin{array}{l} \text{Area } A = (2\text{ in.})(2\text{ in.}) = 4\text{ in.}^2 \\ + \text{ Area } B = (4\frac{1}{2}\text{ in.})(4\text{ in.}) = 18\text{ in.}^2 \\ \hline \text{Area of figure} = \mathbf{22\ in.^2} \end{array}$$

17. a. Isosceles triangle

b. $\frac{180° - 90°}{2} = \frac{90°}{2} = \mathbf{45°}$

c. Area $= \frac{(6\text{ cm})(6\text{ cm})}{2} = \mathbf{18\ cm^2}$

d. $\angle \mathbf{C}$

18. $7\overline{)1.428}$ → **0.204**

19. $\frac{30}{70} = \frac{w}{\$2.10}$
$70w = 30(\$2.10)$
$w = \frac{\$63.00}{70}$
$w = \mathbf{\$0.90}$

20. $5^2 + 2^5 - \sqrt{49} = 25 + 32 - 7 = \mathbf{50}$

21. $3(8) - (5)(2) + 10 \div 2$
$24 - 10 + 5$
$14 + 5$
$\mathbf{19}$

22.
$$\begin{array}{llll} & 1\text{ yd} & 2\text{ ft} & 3\frac{3}{4}\text{ in.} \\ + & & 2\text{ ft} & 6\frac{1}{2}\text{ in.} \\ \hline & 1\text{ yd} & 4\text{ ft} & 10\frac{1}{4}\text{ in.} \end{array}$$

4 ft = 1 yd 1 ft

$$\begin{array}{llll} & 1\text{ yd} & 1\text{ ft} & 10\frac{1}{4}\text{ in.} \\ + & 1\text{ yd} & & \\ \hline & \mathbf{2\ yd} & \mathbf{1\ ft} & \mathbf{10\frac{1}{4}\ in.} \end{array}$$

Solutions

23. 1 L = 1000 mL,
1000 mL − 50 mL = **950 mL**

24. $\dfrac{\overset{1}{\cancel{60}} \text{ mi}}{1 \cancel{\text{hr}}} \cdot \dfrac{1 \cancel{\text{hr}}}{\underset{1}{\cancel{60}} \text{ min}} = \mathbf{1 \dfrac{\text{mi}}{\text{min}}}$

25.
$$
\begin{aligned}
2\tfrac{7}{24} &= 2\tfrac{28}{96}\\
+\ 3\tfrac{9}{32} &= 3\tfrac{27}{96}\\
\hline
&\ \ 5\tfrac{55}{96}
\end{aligned}
$$

26. $4\dfrac{1}{5} \div 1\dfrac{3}{4} = \dfrac{21}{5} \div \dfrac{7}{4} = \dfrac{\overset{3}{\cancel{21}}}{5} \times \dfrac{4}{\underset{1}{\cancel{7}}} = \dfrac{12}{5}$

$2\dfrac{2}{5} \div \dfrac{12}{5} = \dfrac{12}{5} \div \dfrac{12}{5} = \dfrac{\overset{1}{\cancel{12}}}{\underset{1}{\cancel{5}}} \times \dfrac{\overset{1}{\cancel{5}}}{\underset{1}{\cancel{12}}} = \mathbf{1}$

27. $7\dfrac{1}{2} \div \dfrac{2}{3} = \dfrac{15}{2} \div \dfrac{2}{3}$

$= \dfrac{15}{2} \times \dfrac{3}{2} = \dfrac{45}{4} = 11\dfrac{1}{4}$

$$
\begin{array}{rcl}
20 & \longrightarrow & 19\tfrac{4}{4}\\
-\ 11\tfrac{1}{4} & & -\ 11\tfrac{1}{4}\\
\hline
& & \ \ 8\tfrac{3}{4}
\end{array}
$$

28. a.

b. Yes, order 3

29. $|3 - 4| = |-1| = \mathbf{1}$

30.
$$
\begin{aligned}
&\ \ 1000 \text{ g}\\
-&\ \ \ \ 250 \text{ g}\\
\hline
&\ \ \ \ \mathbf{750 \text{ g}}
\end{aligned}
$$

Early Finishers Solutions

Yes, she is correct.

$\dfrac{1}{2} \cdot 41 + \dfrac{1}{2} \cdot 35 + \dfrac{1}{2} \cdot 24 =$

$\quad \dfrac{1}{2}(41 + 35 + 24) = $ Distributive
Property

$\quad\quad \dfrac{1}{2}(100) = 50$

$\dfrac{1}{4} \cdot 20.5 + \dfrac{1}{4} \cdot 3.5 + \dfrac{1}{4} + 5.25 + \dfrac{3}{4} =$

$\quad \dfrac{1}{4}(20.5 + 3.5) + \dfrac{1}{4} + 5.25 + \dfrac{3}{4} = $ Distributive
Property

$\quad\quad \dfrac{1}{4}(24) + \dfrac{1}{4} + \dfrac{3}{4} + 5.25 =$

$\quad\quad\quad 6 + 1 + 5.25 = 12.25$

Practice Set 63

a. $30 - [40 - (10 - 2)]$
$\quad 30 - [40 - (8)]$
$\quad\quad 30 - [32]$
$\quad\quad\quad \mathbf{-2}$

b. $100 - 3[2(6 - 2)]$
$\quad 100 - 3[2(4)]$
$\quad\quad 100 - 3[8]$
$\quad\quad 100 - 24$
$\quad\quad\quad \mathbf{76}$

c. $\dfrac{10 + 9 \cdot 8 - 7}{6 \cdot 5 - 4 - 3 + 2}$
$\quad \dfrac{10 + 72 - 7}{30 - 4 - 3 + 2}$
$\quad\quad \dfrac{75}{25}$
$\quad\quad\quad \mathbf{3}$

d. $\dfrac{1 + 2(3 + 4) - 5}{10 - 9(8 - 7)}$
$\quad \dfrac{1 + 14 - 5}{10 - 9}$
$\quad\quad \dfrac{10}{1}$
$\quad\quad\quad \mathbf{10}$

e. $12 + 3(8 - |-2|)$
$\quad 12 + 3(8 - 2)$
$\quad\quad 12 + 3(6)$
$\quad\quad 12 + 18$
$\quad\quad\quad \mathbf{30}$

Written Practice 63

1. $\$11(3) + \$11(2\frac{1}{2}) = \$33 + \$27.50 = \textbf{\$60.50}$

2. $30 \text{ min} \cdot \dfrac{70 \text{ times}}{1 \text{ min}} = 2100 \text{ times}$

$30 \text{ min} \cdot \dfrac{150 \text{ times}}{1 \text{ min}} = 4500 \text{ times}$

$\ 4500 \text{ times}$
$\underline{-\ 2100 \text{ times}}$
$\ \textbf{2400 times}$

3.

	Ratio	Actual Count
Brachiopods	2	B
Trilobites	9	720

$\dfrac{2}{9} = \dfrac{B}{720}$

$9B = 2 \cdot 720$

$B = \textbf{160 brachiopods}$

4. $5 \text{ days} \cdot \dfrac{18 \text{ miles}}{1 \text{ day}} = 90 \text{ miles}$

$\ 90 \text{ miles}$
$\ 16 \text{ miles}$
$\underline{+\ 21 \text{ miles}}$
$\ 127 \text{ miles}$

$\ 1017 \text{ miles}$
$\underline{- 127 \text{ miles}}$
$\ \textbf{890 miles}$

5.

$\ 2850 \text{ feet}$
$\underline{+ 160 \text{ feet}}$
$\ \textbf{3010 feet}$

6. **One hundred forty-nine million, six hundred thousand kilometers**

7. a. $\dfrac{12}{40} \div \dfrac{4}{4} = \dfrac{3}{10}$

b. $\dfrac{7}{10} \times 100\% = \dfrac{700\%}{10} = \textbf{70\%}$

8. **Two thousandths mile per hour**

9. $1.5 \cancel{\text{ km}} \cdot \dfrac{1000 \text{ m}}{1 \cancel{\text{ km}}} = \textbf{1500 m}$

10.

$$12\overline{)4360.0\ldots}\quad \begin{array}{r} 363.3\ldots \\ \end{array} \qquad \textbf{363.}\overline{\textbf{3}}$$

$\begin{array}{r} 36 \\ \hline 76 \\ 72 \\ \hline 40 \\ 36 \\ \hline 4\ 0 \\ 3\ 6 \\ \hline 4 \end{array}$

11.

12. a. $33\% = \dfrac{33}{100}$

b. $33\% = \dfrac{33}{100} = \textbf{0.33}$

c. $3\overline{)1.0}\quad \begin{array}{c} 0.\overline{3} \end{array}$

d. $\dfrac{1}{3} \times 100\% = \dfrac{100\%}{3} = \textbf{33}\dfrac{\textbf{1}}{\textbf{3}}\textbf{\%}$

13. **Divide the "in" number by 3 to find the "out" number.**

$y = \dfrac{1}{3}x$ or $y = \dfrac{x}{3}.$

14. $\dfrac{\text{red face card}}{\text{total cards}} = \dfrac{6}{52} = \dfrac{3}{26}$

15. a. Isosceles triangle

b. Perimeter $= 5 \text{ cm} + 5 \text{ cm} + 5 \text{ cm}$
$= \textbf{15 cm}$

c. $\triangle \textbf{ABC}$

16. a. $m\angle BAC = \dfrac{180°}{3} = \textbf{60°}$

b. $m\angle ADB = \dfrac{180°}{3} = \textbf{60°}$

Solutions

c. $m\angle BDC = 180° - 60° = \textbf{120°}$

d. $m\angle DBA = \dfrac{180°}{3} = \textbf{60°}$

e. $m\angle DBC = \dfrac{180° - 120°}{2} = \dfrac{60°}{2} = \textbf{30°}$

f. $m\angle DCB = m\angle DBC = \textbf{30°}$

17. $\dfrac{\text{length of shortest side}}{\text{length of longest side}} = \dfrac{5}{10} = \dfrac{\textbf{1}}{\textbf{2}}$

18.
$$\dfrac{5}{18} = \dfrac{10}{36}$$
$$-\dfrac{1}{12} = \dfrac{3}{36}$$
$$\dfrac{7}{36}$$

19. $2 \div 0.4 = \textbf{5}$

20. $3[24 - (8 + 3 \cdot 2)] - \dfrac{6 + 4}{|-2|}$

$3[24 - (8 + 6)] - \dfrac{6 + 4}{2}$

$3[24 - (14)] - \dfrac{10}{2}$

$3[10] - 5$

$30 - 5$

$\textbf{25}$

21. $3^3 - \sqrt{3^2 + 4^2}$

$27 - \sqrt{9 + 16}$

$27 - \sqrt{25}$

$27 - 5$

$\textbf{22}$

22.

0 → (7 days)
1̸ week 2 days 7 hr
−   5 days 9 hr →

0 8 9 → (24 hr)
1̸ week 2̸ days 7 hr
−   5 days 9 hr →

0   8   31
1̸ week 2̸ days 7̸ hr
−   5 days 9 hr
3 days 22 hr

23. $\dfrac{20 \text{ mi}}{1 \text{ gal}} \cdot \dfrac{1 \text{ gal}}{4 \text{ qt}} = \textbf{5} \dfrac{\textbf{mi}}{\textbf{qt}}$

24.
$$4\dfrac{2}{3} = 4\dfrac{12}{18}$$
$$3\dfrac{5}{6} = 3\dfrac{15}{18}$$
$$+ 2\dfrac{5}{9} = 2\dfrac{10}{18}$$
$$9\dfrac{37}{18} = 11\dfrac{1}{18}$$

25. $12\dfrac{1}{2} \cdot 4\dfrac{4}{5} \cdot 3\dfrac{1}{3}$

$= \dfrac{\overset{5}{\cancel{25}}}{\underset{1}{\cancel{2}}} \cdot \dfrac{\overset{8}{\cancel{24}}}{\underset{1}{\cancel{5}}} \cdot \dfrac{\overset{5}{\cancel{10}}}{\underset{1}{\cancel{3}}} = \textbf{200}$

26. $1\dfrac{2}{3} \div 3 = \dfrac{5}{3} \div \dfrac{3}{1}$

$= \dfrac{5}{3} \times \dfrac{1}{3} = \dfrac{5}{9}$

$6\dfrac{1}{3} = 6\dfrac{3}{9} \longrightarrow 5\dfrac{12}{9}$

$-\dfrac{5}{9} = \dfrac{5}{9} \qquad\qquad -\dfrac{5}{9}$

$5\dfrac{7}{9}$

27. $(3)^2 + 2(3)(4) + (4)^2$
$= 9 + 24 + 16 = \textbf{49}$

28.

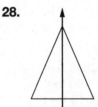

29. a.

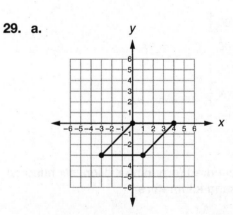

b. Area $= (20 \text{ ft})(15 \text{ ft}) = \textbf{300 ft}^2$

30. $3\overline{)750 \text{ g}}$ → $\dfrac{250 \text{ g}}{}$

Early Finishers Solutions

a. $\dfrac{70}{100} = \dfrac{x}{79}; x = \$55.30$

b. $0.85 \times \$55.30 = \$47.01$

c. Dexter paid 85% of 70% = 59.5%. Dexter saved 100% − 59.5% = 40.5%. After rounding, the answer is either 40% or 41%.

Practice Set 64

a. $(-56) + (+96) = \mathbf{+40}$

$$\begin{array}{r} 96 \\ -\ 56 \\ \hline 40 \end{array}$$

b. $(-28) + (-145) = \mathbf{-173}$

$$\begin{array}{r} 145 \\ +\ 28 \\ \hline 173 \end{array}$$

c. $(-5) + (+7) + (+9) + (-3)$
$(+2) + (+9) + (-3)$
$(+11) + (-3)$
$\mathbf{+8}$

d. $(-3) + (-8) + (+15)$
$(-11) + (+15)$
$\mathbf{+4}$

e. $(-12) + (-9) + (+16)$
$(-21) + (+16)$
$\mathbf{-5}$

f. $(+12) + (-18) + (+6)$
$(-6) + (+6)$
$\mathbf{0}$

g. $\left(-3\dfrac{5}{6}\right) + \left(+5\dfrac{1}{3}\right)$

$\left(-3\dfrac{5}{6}\right) + \left(+5\dfrac{2}{6}\right)$

$\left(-3\dfrac{5}{6}\right) + \left(+4\dfrac{8}{6}\right)$

$1\dfrac{3}{6} = \mathbf{1\dfrac{1}{2}}$

h. $(-1.6) + (-11.47)$
$\mathbf{-13.07}$

$$\begin{array}{r} 11.47 \\ +\ 1.60 \\ \hline 13.07 \end{array}$$

i. $(+\$250) + (-\$300) + (+\$525)$; The net result was a gain of \$475.

Written Practice 64

1.
$$\begin{array}{r} 2{,}000{,}000{,}000{,}000 \\ -\ \ \ 750{,}000{,}000{,}000 \\ \hline 1{,}250{,}000{,}000{,}000 \end{array}$$
$\mathbf{1.25 \times 10^{12}}$

2. $\$2.25 + \$0.15(42)$
$\quad = \$2.25 + \$6.30 = \$8.55$
$\$10 - \$8.55 = \mathbf{\$1.45}$

3. $5(\$0.25) + 3(\$0.10) + 2(\$0.05)$
$\quad = \$1.25 + \$0.30 + \$0.10$
$\quad = \$1.65$

$$\begin{array}{r} 4.71 \\ 35{\overline{)165.00}} \end{array}$$
4 packages

4. $53 + 59 = \mathbf{112}$

5.
$$\begin{array}{r} 1.74 \\ 2.8 \\ 3.4 \\ 0.96 \\ 2 \\ +\ 1.22 \\ \hline 12.12 \end{array}$$
$12.12 \div 6 = \mathbf{2.02}$

6.

	1200 serfs
$\dfrac{2}{5}$ were conscripted.	240 serfs
	240 serfs
$\dfrac{3}{5}$ were not conscripted.	240 serfs
	240 serfs
	240 serfs

a. **480 serfs**

b. $\dfrac{3}{5} \times 100\% = \dfrac{300\%}{5} = \mathbf{60\%}$

7. $W_N = \dfrac{5}{9} \times 100$

$W_N = \dfrac{500}{9}$

$W_N = \mathbf{55\dfrac{5}{9}}$

Solutions

8. **a.** Sixteen million degrees Celsius

    b. Seven millionths meter

9. **a.** $1.6 \times 10^7 \enspace \textcircled{>} \enspace 7 \times 10^{-6}$

    b. $7 \times 10^{-6} \enspace \textcircled{>} \enspace 0$

    c. $2^{-3} \enspace \textcircled{<} \enspace 2^{-2}$

10.
$$
\begin{array}{r}
16.285\ldots \\
28)\overline{456.000\ldots} \\
\underline{28} \\
176 \\
\underline{168} \\
8\,0 \\
\underline{5\,6} \\
2\,40 \\
\underline{2\,24} \\
160 \\
\underline{140} \\
20
\end{array}
$$

    a. $16\frac{2}{7}$

    b. **16.29**

    c. **16**

11. **a.** $(-63) + (-14) = \mathbf{-77}$

    b. $(-16) + (+20) + (-32) = \mathbf{-28}$

    c. $\left(-\frac{1}{2}\right) + \left(-\frac{1}{2}\right) = \mathbf{-1}$

12. $(-\$327) + (+\$280) = -\$47;$ **a loss of \$47**

13. **a.** **60°**

    b. **The chords are $\overline{AB}$ (or $\overline{BA}$), $\overline{BC}$ (or $\overline{CB}$), and $\overline{CA}$ (or $\overline{AC}$). Each chord is shorter than the diameter, which is the longest chord of a circle.**

14. $\left(\dfrac{2}{3}\right) + \left(\dfrac{2}{3}\right)\left(\dfrac{3}{4}\right)$

$$= \frac{2}{3} + \frac{1}{2} = \frac{4}{6} + \frac{3}{6} = \frac{7}{6} = \mathbf{1\frac{1}{6}}$$

15.

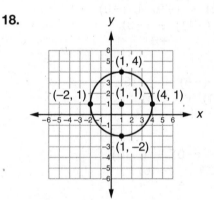

Perimeter $= 0.7\,\text{m} + 0.4\,\text{m} + 0.3\,\text{m}$
$+ \ 0.6\,\text{m} + 0.4\,\text{m} + 1\,\text{m} = \mathbf{3.4\,m}$

16.
$$
\begin{array}{ll}
\text{Area } A = (0.7\,\text{m})(0.4\,\text{m}) = 0.28\,\text{m}^2 \\
+\ \text{Area } B = (0.6\,\text{m})(0.4\,\text{m}) = 0.24\,\text{m}^2 \\
\hline
\text{Area of figure} \qquad\qquad\qquad = \mathbf{0.52\,m^2}
\end{array}
$$

17. Sample space = {2, 3, 3, 4, 4, 4, 5, 5, 5, 5, 6, 6, 6, 6, 6, 7, 7, 7, 7, 7, 7, 7, 8, 8, 8, 8, 8, 9, 9, 9, 9, 10, 10, 10, 11, 11, 12}

$$P(10) = \frac{3}{36} = \mathbf{\frac{1}{12}}$$

18.

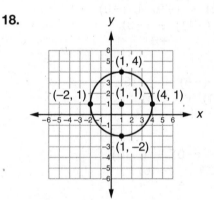

B. (−2, 1)

19. $\dfrac{4}{9} + \dfrac{2}{9} = \dfrac{6}{9} = \mathbf{\dfrac{2}{3}}$

20. $\dfrac{10}{25} = \mathbf{\dfrac{2}{5}}$ or **0.4**

21. $\dfrac{3^2 + 4^2}{\sqrt{3^2 + 4^2}} = \dfrac{9 + 16}{\sqrt{9 + 16}} = \dfrac{25}{\sqrt{25}} = \dfrac{25}{5}$

$$= \mathbf{5}$$

22. $6 \div 2\frac{1}{2} = \frac{6}{1} \div \frac{5}{2}$

$= \frac{6}{1} \times \frac{2}{5} = \frac{12}{5} = 2\frac{2}{5}$

$2\frac{4}{5} \div 2\frac{2}{5} = \frac{14}{5} \div \frac{12}{5}$

$= \frac{\overset{7}{\cancel{14}}}{\cancel{5}} \times \frac{\overset{1}{\cancel{5}}}{\cancel{12}_{6}} = \frac{7}{6} = \mathbf{1\frac{1}{6}}$

23. $100 - [20 + 5(4) + 3(2 + 4^0)]$
$100 - [20 + 20 + 3(2 + 1)]$
$100 - [20 + 20 + 9]$
$100 - [49]$
$\mathbf{51}$

24.
```
    5 gal  2 qt  1 pt   7 oz
+   1 gal  1 qt  1 pt   9 oz
    6 gal  3 qt  2 pt  16 oz
```
16 oz = 1 pt, 2 pt + 1 pt = 3 pt
3 pt = 1 qt 1 pt
```
    1 qt   1 pt
+   3 qt
    4 qt   1 pt
```
4 qt = 1 gal, 6 gal + 1 gal = 7 gal, **7 gal 1 pt**

25. $\left(1\frac{1}{2}\right)^2 - \left(4 - 2\frac{1}{3}\right)$

$= \frac{9}{4} - \left(4 - 2\frac{1}{3}\right)$

$= 2\frac{1}{4} - \left(4 - 2\frac{1}{3}\right)$

$\begin{array}{ccc} 4 & \longrightarrow & 3\frac{3}{3} \\ -\,2\frac{1}{3} & & -\,2\frac{1}{3} \\ \hline & & 1\frac{2}{3} \end{array}$

$\begin{array}{ccc} 2\frac{1}{4} = 2\frac{3}{12} & \longrightarrow & 1\frac{15}{12} \\ -\,1\frac{2}{3} = 1\frac{8}{12} & & -\,1\frac{8}{12} \\ \hline & & \frac{7}{12} \end{array}$

26.
```
   0.010        0.100
-  0.001     -  0.009
   0.009        0.091
```

27. $y = 2x$; any x, y pair in which y is twice x satisfies the function, such as (4, 8) and $(-1, -2)$.

28. $5\overline{)1.0}$ with 0.2 above

```
   4.375
-  3.200
   1.175
```

29. $\dfrac{\text{even primes}}{\text{total}} = \dfrac{1}{6}$

30. **a.** $m\angle B = 180° - 58° = \mathbf{122°}$

b. $m\angle BCD = m\angle A = \mathbf{58°}$

c. $m\angle BCM = 180° - 58° = \mathbf{122°}$

Practice Set 65

a. $C = \pi d$
$C \approx 3.14(8 \text{ in.})$
$C \approx \mathbf{25.12 \text{ in.}}$

b. $C = \pi d$
$C \approx \frac{22}{7}(42 \text{ mm})$
$C \approx \mathbf{132 \text{ mm}}$

c. $C = \pi d$
$C = \pi(4 \text{ ft})$
$C = \mathbf{4\pi \text{ ft}}$

d. $C = \pi d$
$C \approx 3.14(6 \text{ inches})$
$C \approx \mathbf{18.84 \text{ inches}}$

Written Practice 65

1. a. $\dfrac{\$2.40}{5 \text{ pounds}} = \dfrac{\$0.48}{1 \text{ pound}}$
$0.48 per pound

b.
```
    $0.48
×       8
    $3.84
```

2. a. $(0.3)(0.4) + (0.3)(0.5) = 0.12 + 0.15$
$= 0.27$
$0.3(0.4 + 0.5) = 0.3(0.9) = 0.27$
$\mathbf{0.27 = 0.27}$

b. Distributive property

Solutions

3. a. $C = \pi d$
 $C = \pi(16\text{ ft})$
 $C = \textbf{16}\boldsymbol{\pi}\textbf{ ft}$

b. $C = \pi d$
 $C \approx 3.14(10\text{ cm})$
 $C \approx \textbf{31.4 cm}$

c. $C = \pi d$
 $C \approx \dfrac{22}{7}(14\text{ in.})$
 $C \approx \textbf{44 in.}$

4. $\dfrac{350\text{ miles}}{15\text{ gallons}} = 23.\overline{3}\,\dfrac{\text{miles}}{\text{gallon}}$

$\textbf{23.3}\,\dfrac{\textbf{miles}}{\textbf{gallon}}$

5. $\dfrac{1}{2} + \dfrac{1}{4} = \dfrac{2}{4} + \dfrac{1}{4} = \dfrac{3}{4}$

$\dfrac{3}{4} \div 2 = \dfrac{3}{4} \times \dfrac{1}{2} = \dfrac{\textbf{3}}{\textbf{8}}$

6. $\textbf{1.2} \times \textbf{10}^{\textbf{10}}$

7.

	60 eggs
$\frac{1}{6}$ were cracked.	10 eggs
	10 eggs
$\frac{5}{6}$ were not cracked.	10 eggs
	10 eggs
	10 eggs
	10 eggs

a. 50 eggs

b. $\dfrac{\text{cracked eggs}}{\text{uncracked eggs}} = \dfrac{1}{5}$

c. $\dfrac{1}{6} \times 100\% = \textbf{16}\dfrac{\textbf{2}}{\textbf{3}}\%$

8. a. One possibility:

b. Trapezoid

9. a. $\text{Area} = \dfrac{(6\text{ cm})(4\text{ cm})}{2} = \textbf{12 cm}^2$

b. $\text{Area} = \dfrac{(6\text{ cm})(4\text{ cm})}{2} = \textbf{12 cm}^2$

c. $\text{Area} = \dfrac{(6\text{ cm})(4\text{ cm})}{2} = \textbf{12 cm}^2$

10.
$$\begin{array}{r} 0.76 \\ +\ 0.88 \\ \hline 1.64 \end{array} \qquad \begin{array}{r} 0.82 \\ 2\overline{)1.64} \end{array}$$

11. $W_N = 0.75 \times 64$
 $W_N = \textbf{48}$

12. $t = 0.08 \times \$7.40$
 $t = \textbf{\$0.59}$

13. a. $(-3) + (-8) = \textbf{-11}$

b. $(+3) + (-8) = \textbf{-5}$

c. $(-0.3) + (+0.8) + (-0.5) = \textbf{0}$

14.

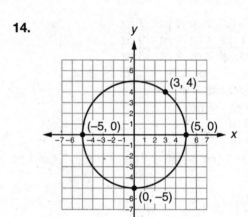

a. $\textbf{(5, 0), (-5, 0)}$

b. 10 units

15. $0.95\text{ liters} \cdot \dfrac{1000\text{ milliliters}}{1\text{ liter}}$
 $= \textbf{950 milliliters}$

16. $(5)(0.2) + 5 + \dfrac{5}{0.2}$
 $= 1 + 5 + 25 = \textbf{31}$

17. 27 blocks

18. a. $\angle COD$ or $\angle DOC$

b. $\angle AOB$ or $\angle BOA$

19. $20 \times 5 = \textbf{100}$

20. a. $m\angle A = 180° - (62° + 59°)$
$= 180° - 121° = \textbf{59°}$

b. $\overline{AB}$ or $\overline{BA}$

c. Isosceles triangle

d. *C*

21. a. Arrange the numbers in order, and look for the middle number. Since there is an even number of scores, there are two middle numbers. So the median is the mean of the two middle numbers.

b. $14, 15, 15, 16, 16, \underline{16, 17}, 17, 18, 18, 19, 20$
$16 + 17 = 33$
$33 \div 2 = \textbf{16.5}$

22. a. False

b. True

23. 2.20 meters
$-$ 2.15 meters
0.05 meters $= \textbf{5 centimeters}$

24. $\dfrac{10^3 \cdot 10^3}{10^2} = \dfrac{10^6}{10^2} = \textbf{10}^4$ **or 10,000**

25.

$\begin{array}{c} 3 \quad \overset{28}{\cancel{4}} \quad \overset{75}{\cancel{15}} \\ \cancel{4}\text{ days} \quad \cancel{5}\text{ hr} \quad \cancel{15}\text{ min} \\ -\ 1\text{ day} \quad 7\text{ hr} \quad 50\text{ min} \\ \hline \textbf{2 days} \quad \textbf{21 hr} \quad \textbf{25 min} \end{array}$

26. $4.5 \div (0.4 + 0.5) = 4.5 \div 0.9 = \textbf{5}$

27. $\dfrac{3 + 0.6}{3 - 0.6} = \dfrac{3.6}{2.4} = \textbf{1.5}$

28. $1\dfrac{1}{6} \cdot 3 = \dfrac{7}{\cancel{6}} \cdot \dfrac{\cancel{3}}{1} = \dfrac{7}{2} = 3\dfrac{1}{2}$

$4\dfrac{1}{5} \div 3\dfrac{1}{2} = \dfrac{21}{5} \div \dfrac{7}{2}$

$= \dfrac{\overset{3}{\cancel{21}}}{5} \times \dfrac{2}{\cancel{7}} = \dfrac{6}{5} = \textbf{1}\dfrac{\textbf{1}}{\textbf{5}}$

29. $3^2 + \sqrt{4 \cdot 7 - 3}$
$= 9 + \sqrt{28 - 3}$
$= 9 + \sqrt{25} = 9 + 5 = \textbf{14}$

30. $|-3| + 4[(5 - 2)(3 + 1)]$
$3 + 4[(3)(4)]$
$3 + 4[12]$
$3 + 48$
51

Early Finishers Solutions

a. $(0.8\text{ km})(l) = 3.41\text{ km}^2$
$l = 4.2625\text{ km} = 4{,}262.5\text{ m} \cong 4{,}623\text{ m}$

b. $\dfrac{3.41\text{ km}^2}{1} \times \dfrac{247\text{ acres}}{1\text{ km}^2} = 842.27$
$\cong \textbf{842 acres}$

Practice Set 66

a.

	Ratio	Actual Count
Acrobats	3	A
Clowns	5	C
Total	8	72

$\dfrac{5}{8} = \dfrac{C}{72}$
$8C = 360$
$C = \textbf{45 clowns}$

b.

	Ratio	Actual Count
Young men	8	240
Young women	9	W
Total	17	T

$\dfrac{8}{17} = \dfrac{240}{T}$
$8T = 4080$
$T = \textbf{510 young people}$

c.

	Ratio	Actual Count
Big fish	4	B
Little fish	11	L
Total	15	1320

$\dfrac{4}{15} = \dfrac{B}{1320}$
$15B = 5280$
$B = \textbf{352 big fish}$

Written Practice 66

1. a. $100\% - (42\% + 25\%) =$ **33%**

b.
$$\begin{array}{r} \$25{,}000 \\ \times\ \ \ \ 0.25 \\ \hline \$6250 \end{array}$$

2. $10\left(1\dfrac{1}{4}\text{ miles}\right) = \dfrac{25}{2}\text{ miles} = \mathbf{12\dfrac{1}{2}}$ **miles**

3. $(1.9)(2.2) - (1.9 + 2.2) = 4.18 - 4.1$
$\qquad\qquad\qquad\qquad = \mathbf{0.08}$

4.

	Ratio	Actual Count
Dimes	5	D
Quarters	8	Q
Total	13	520

$\dfrac{5}{13} = \dfrac{D}{520}$
$13D = 2600$
$\quad D = \mathbf{200\ dimes}$

5. 9×10^8 **miles**

6.

$\dfrac{3}{10}$ were planted with alfalfa.

$\dfrac{7}{10}$ were not planted with alfalfa.

400 acres

40 acres (×10)

a. $\dfrac{3}{10} \times 100\% = \dfrac{300\%}{10} = \mathbf{30\%}$

b. **280 acres**

7. a. $\dfrac{12}{30} = \dfrac{2}{5}$

b. $\dfrac{2}{5} \times 100\% = \dfrac{200\%}{5} = \mathbf{40\%}$

c. **It is more likely that the grade on a randomly selected test is not an A, because less than half the tests have A's.**

8. a. $C = \pi d$
$C \approx 3.14(21\text{ in.})$
$C \approx \mathbf{65.94\ in.}$

b. $C = \pi d$
$C \approx \dfrac{22}{7}(21\text{ in.})$
$C \approx \mathbf{66\ in.}$

9. a. Area $= (14\text{ cm})(24\text{ cm}) = \mathbf{336\ cm^2}$

b. Area $= \dfrac{(14\text{ cm})(24\text{ cm})}{2} = \mathbf{168\ cm^2}$

c. Perimeter $= 25\text{ cm} + 14\text{ cm} + 25\text{ cm}$
$\qquad\qquad = \mathbf{64\ cm}$

10. $\mathbf{3.25 \times 10^{10}}$

11. $W_N = 0.9 \times 3500$
$W_N = \mathbf{3150}$

12. $W_N = \dfrac{5}{6} \times 2\dfrac{2}{5}$
$W_N = \dfrac{\overset{1}{\cancel{5}}}{\underset{1}{\cancel{6}}} \times \dfrac{\overset{2}{\cancel{12}}}{\underset{1}{\cancel{5}}}$
$W_N = \mathbf{2}$

13. a. $0.45 = \dfrac{45}{100} = \mathbf{\dfrac{9}{20}}$

b. $0.45 = \dfrac{45}{100} = \mathbf{45\%}$

c. $7.5\% = \dfrac{7.5}{100} = \mathbf{\dfrac{3}{40}}$

d. $7.5\% = \dfrac{7.5}{100} = \mathbf{0.075}$

14. a. $(5) + (-4) + (6) + (-1)$
$\quad = 1 + (6) + (-1)$
$\quad = 7 + (-1) = \mathbf{6}$

b. $3 + (-5) + (+4) + (-2)$
$\quad = -2 + (+4) + (-2)$
$\quad = 2 + (-2) = \mathbf{0}$

c. $(-0.3) + (-0.5) = \mathbf{-0.8}$

15. $1.4\ \cancel{\text{kilograms}} \cdot \dfrac{1000\text{ grams}}{1\ \cancel{\text{kilogram}}} = \mathbf{1400\ grams}$

16. a. $m\angle a = 180° - (90° + 35°)$
$= 180° - 125° = \mathbf{55°}$

b. $m\angle b = m\angle a = \mathbf{55°}$

c. $m\angle c = 180° - 55° = \mathbf{125°}$

d. $m\angle d = m\angle b = \mathbf{55°}$

e. $m\angle e = m\angle c = \mathbf{125°}$

17. $(3000)(500)(20) = \mathbf{30{,}000{,}000}$

18.

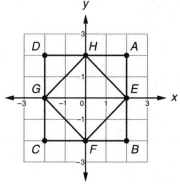

a. Area $= (4 \text{ units})(4 \text{ units}) = \mathbf{16 \ units^2}$

b. 4 units

c. Area $= 4(1 \text{ unit}^2) + 8\left(\dfrac{1}{2} \text{ unit}^2\right)$
$= 4 \text{ units}^2 + 4 \text{ units}^2 = \mathbf{8 \ units^2}$

d. $\sqrt{8}$ **units**

19. $\dfrac{0.9}{1.5} = \dfrac{12}{n}$
$0.9n = 1.5(12)$
$n = \dfrac{18}{0.9}$
$n = \mathbf{20}$

20. $\dfrac{11}{12} = \dfrac{22}{24}$
$-\dfrac{11}{24} = \dfrac{11}{24}$
$\dfrac{11}{24}$

21. $2^1 - 2^0 - 2^{-1} = 2 - 1 - \dfrac{1}{2}$
$= 1 - \dfrac{1}{2} = \dfrac{2}{2} - \dfrac{1}{2} = \mathbf{\dfrac{1}{2}}$

22.
```
   4 lb   12 oz
 + 1 lb    7 oz
   5 lb   19 oz
```
$19 \text{ oz} = 1 \text{ lb } 3 \text{ oz}$
```
   1 lb   3 oz
 + 5 lb
   6 lb   3 oz
```

23. $\dfrac{3 \ ft}{1 \ yd} \cdot \dfrac{12 \ in.}{1 \ ft} = \mathbf{36} \ \dfrac{in.}{yd}$

24. $16 \div (0.8 \div 0.04) = 16 \div 20 = \mathbf{0.8}$

25. $0.4[0.5 - (0.6)(0.7)]$
$0.4[0.5 - 0.42]$
$0.4[0.08]$
$\mathbf{0.032}$

26. $\dfrac{3}{8} \cdot 1\dfrac{2}{3} \cdot 4 \div 1\dfrac{2}{3}$

$= \left(\dfrac{\overset{1}{\cancel{3}}}{8} \cdot \dfrac{5}{\underset{1}{\cancel{3}}}\right) \cdot \dfrac{4}{1} \div \dfrac{5}{3}$

$= \dfrac{5}{\underset{2}{\cancel{8}}} \cdot \dfrac{\overset{1}{\cancel{4}}}{1} \div \dfrac{5}{3} = \dfrac{5}{2} \div \dfrac{5}{3}$

$= \dfrac{\cancel{5}}{2} \times \dfrac{3}{\underset{1}{\cancel{5}}} = \dfrac{3}{2} = \mathbf{1\dfrac{1}{2}}$

27. $30 - 5[4 + (3)(2) - 5]$
$30 - 5[4 + 6 - 5]$
$30 - 5[10 - 5]$
$30 - 5[5]$
$30 - 25$
$\mathbf{5}$

28. One possibility: If a dozen flavored icicles cost $2.88, what is the price of each flavored icicle?

29. $\dfrac{9 \text{ ounces}}{2} = \mathbf{4\dfrac{1}{2} \ ounces}$

30. a. $\overline{AB}$ or $\overline{BA}$,
$\overline{BC}$ or $\overline{CB}$

b. Isosceles triangle

c. 90°

255

Solutions

Early Finishers Solutions

a. $2 \times \$712$; $14 \times 30 + 65$

b. $\$500 + (2 \times \$712) - (14 \times \$30 + \$65)$
$\$500 + \$1424 - (\$420 + \$65)$
$\$1924 - \$485 = \$1439$

Practice Set 67

a. **Triangular prism**

b. **Cone**

c. **Rectangular prism**

d. **5 faces**

e. **9 edges**

f. **6 vertices**

g.

h.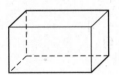

i.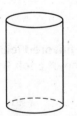

j. **Triangular prism**

k. $3 \text{ cm} \times 3 \text{ cm} = 9 \text{ cm}^2$
$6 \times 9 \text{ cm}^2 = \mathbf{54 \text{ cm}^2}$

l. **Triangular prism**

m. **The bottom face**

Written Practice 67

1. a. $\dfrac{\text{red marbles}}{\text{blue marbles}} = \dfrac{20}{40} = \mathbf{\dfrac{1}{2}}$

   b. $\dfrac{\text{white marbles}}{\text{red marbles}} = \dfrac{30}{20} = \mathbf{\dfrac{3}{2}}$

   c. $\dfrac{\text{not white marbles}}{\text{total marbles}} = \dfrac{60}{90} = \mathbf{\dfrac{2}{3}}$

2. $\left(\dfrac{1}{3} + \dfrac{1}{2}\right) - \left(\dfrac{1}{3} \times \dfrac{1}{2}\right)$
$= \left(\dfrac{2}{6} + \dfrac{3}{6}\right) - \left(\dfrac{1}{6}\right)$
$= \dfrac{5}{6} - \dfrac{1}{6} = \dfrac{4}{6} = \mathbf{\dfrac{2}{3}}$

3. $180 \text{ pounds} - 165\dfrac{1}{2} \text{ pounds} = \mathbf{14\dfrac{1}{2} \text{ pounds}}$

4. a.
$$\begin{array}{r} 94 \text{ points} \\ 85 \text{ points} \\ +\ 85 \text{ points} \\ \hline 264 \text{ points} \end{array}$$
$$3\overline{)264} = \mathbf{88 \text{ points}}$$

   b. $5(92 \text{ points}) = 460 \text{ points}$
   $460 \text{ points} + 264 \text{ points} = 724 \text{ points}$
   $$8\overline{)724.0} = \mathbf{90.5 \text{ points}}$$

5.

	Ratio	Actual Count
Diamonds	5	D
Rubies	2	R
Total	7	210

$\dfrac{5}{7} = \dfrac{D}{210}$
$7D = 1050$
$D = \mathbf{150 \text{ diamonds}}$

6.

360 dolls

$\dfrac{4}{5}$ were sold.	72 dolls
	72 dolls
	72 dolls
	72 dolls
$\dfrac{1}{5}$ were not sold.	72 dolls

a. **288 dolls**

b. $\dfrac{1}{5} \times 100\% = \dfrac{100\%}{5} = \mathbf{20\%}$

7. **a.** 12 edges

b. 6 faces

c. 8 vertices

8. **a.** Area $= \dfrac{(12\,m)(9\,m)}{2} =$ **54 m²**

b. Perimeter $= 5\,m + 5\,m + 6\,m$
$= $ **16 m**

c. $90° - 37° =$ **53°**

d. The right triangle is not symmetrical.

9.
$$\begin{array}{r} 7.65 \\ +\ 7.83 \\ \hline 15.48 \end{array}$$

$$\begin{array}{r} \textbf{7.74} \\ 2\overline{)15.48} \end{array}$$

10. 2.5×10^{-3}

11. $W_N = 0.24 \times 75$
$W_N = $ **18**

12. $W_N = 1.2 \times 12$
$W_N = $ **14.4**

13. **a.** $\left(-\dfrac{1}{4}\right) + \left(+\dfrac{1}{4}\right) =$ **0**

b. $(+2) + (-3) + (+4) =$ **3**

14. **a.** $4\% = \dfrac{4}{100} = \dfrac{1}{25}$

b. $4\% = \dfrac{4}{100} =$ **0.04**

c. $\begin{array}{r} \textbf{0.875} \\ 8\overline{)7.000} \end{array}$

d. $\dfrac{7}{8} \times 100\% = \dfrac{700\%}{8}$

$= $ **87.5%** or $87\dfrac{1}{2}\%$

15. $\overset{70}{\cancel{700}}\ \text{mm} \cdot \dfrac{1\ \text{cm}}{\underset{1}{\cancel{10}\ \text{mm}}} =$ **70 cm**

16. $(-\$560) + (+\$850) + (-\$280) = +\$10$
A gain of \$10

17. Multiply the "in" number by 7 to find the "out" number.

$$y = 7x$$

x Input	y Output
7	49
0	0
11	77
1	7

18. **a.** 7856.43

b. 7900

19. $C = \pi d$
$C \approx 3.14(24\ \text{inches})$
$C \approx 75.36\ \text{inches} \approx$ **75 inches**

20. **a.** $\angle A$ and $\angle B$

b. $\angle B$ and $\angle D$

21. **a.** $2(5\ \text{ft} + 3\ \text{ft})$
$2(8\ \text{ft})$
16 ft
or
$2(5\ \text{ft}) + 2(3\ \text{ft})$
$10\ \text{ft} + 6\ \text{ft}$
16 ft

b. Distributive property

22. $\dfrac{2.5}{w} = \dfrac{15}{12}$
$15w = 2.5(12)$
$w = \dfrac{30}{15}$
$w = $ **2**

23. $9 + 8\{7 \cdot 6 - 5[4 + (3 - 2 \cdot 1)]\}$
$9 + 8\{7 \cdot 6 - 5[4 + (1)]\}$
$9 + 8\{7 \cdot 6 - 5[5]\}$
$9 + 8\{7 \cdot 6 - 25\}$
$9 + 8\{42 - 25\}$
$9 + 8\{17\}$
$9 + 136$
145

257

Solutions

24.

$$\overset{0}{\cancel{1}} \text{ yd (3 ft)}$$
$$- \qquad\quad 1 \text{ ft} \quad 3 \text{ in.} \longrightarrow$$

$$\overset{0}{\cancel{1}} \text{ yd} \quad \overset{2}{\cancel{3}} \text{ ft (12 in.)}$$
$$- \qquad\qquad 1 \text{ ft} \qquad 3 \text{ in.} \longrightarrow$$

$$\overset{0}{\cancel{1}} \text{ yd} \quad \overset{2}{\cancel{3}} \text{ ft} \quad 12 \text{ in.}$$
$$- \qquad\qquad\quad 1 \text{ ft} \quad 3 \text{ in.}$$
$$\qquad\qquad\qquad \mathbf{1 \text{ ft}} \quad \mathbf{9 \text{ in.}}$$

25. $6.4 - (0.6 - 0.04)$
$$= 6.4 - 0.56 = \mathbf{5.84}$$

26. $\dfrac{3 + 0.6}{3(0.6)} = \dfrac{3.6}{1.8} = \mathbf{2}$

27.
$$1\frac{2}{3} = 1\frac{8}{12}$$
$$+ 3\frac{1}{4} = 3\frac{3}{12}$$
$$\overline{\qquad\qquad 4\frac{11}{12}}$$

$$4\frac{11}{12} = 4\frac{11}{12}$$
$$- 1\frac{5}{6} = 1\frac{10}{12}$$
$$\overline{\qquad\qquad 3\frac{1}{12}}$$

28. $\dfrac{3}{5} \div 3\frac{1}{5} \cdot 5\frac{1}{3} \cdot |-1|$

$$= \left(\frac{3}{5} \div \frac{16}{5} \right) \cdot \frac{16}{3} \cdot 1$$

$$= \left(\frac{3}{\cancel{5}} \times \frac{\cancel{5}}{16} \right) \cdot \frac{16}{3} \cdot 1$$

$$= \frac{\overset{1}{\cancel{3}}}{\underset{1}{\cancel{16}}} \cdot \frac{\overset{1}{\cancel{16}}}{\underset{1}{\cancel{3}}} \cdot 1 = \mathbf{1}$$

29. $3 \div 1\frac{2}{3} = \dfrac{3}{1} \div \dfrac{5}{3}$

$$= \frac{3}{1} \times \frac{3}{5} = \frac{9}{5} = 1\frac{4}{5}$$

$$3\frac{3}{4} \div 1\frac{4}{5} = \frac{15}{4} \div \frac{9}{5}$$

$$= \frac{\overset{5}{\cancel{15}}}{4} \times \frac{5}{\underset{3}{\cancel{9}}} = \frac{25}{12} = \mathbf{2\frac{1}{12}}$$

30. $5^2 - \sqrt{4^2} + 2^{-2}$
$$= 25 - 4 + \frac{1}{4} = \mathbf{21\frac{1}{4}}$$

Early Finishers Solutions

a.

Ratio	Points
5	$\frac{1216}{8} \times 5 = 760$
2	$\frac{1216}{8} \times 2 = 304$
1	$\frac{1216}{8} \times 1 = 152$
8 (total)	1216

b. $\dfrac{760}{1216} = 0.625 = 62.5\%$

$\dfrac{304}{1216} = 0.25 = 25\%$

$\dfrac{152}{1216} = 0.125 = 12.5\%$

$62.5\% + 25\% + 12.5\% = 100\%$

Practice Set 68

a. $(-3) - (+2)$
$(-3) + [-(+2)]$
$(-3) + [-2] = \mathbf{-5}$

b. $(-3) - (-2)$
$(-3) + [-(-2)]$
$(-3) + [2] = \mathbf{-1}$

c. $(+3) - (2)$
$(+3) + [-(+2)]$
$(+3) + [-2] = \mathbf{1}$

d. $(-3) - (+2) - (-4)$
$(-3) + [-(+2)] + [-(-4)]$
$(-3) + [-2] + [4] = \mathbf{-1}$

e. $(-8) + (-3) - (+2)$
$(-8) + (-3) + [-(+2)]$
$(-8) + (-3) + [-2] = \mathbf{-13}$

f. $(-8) - (+3) + (-2)$
$(-8) + [-(+3)] + (-2)$
$(-8) + [-3] + (-2) = \mathbf{-13}$

g. $\left(-\dfrac{3}{5}\right) - \left(-\dfrac{1}{5}\right)$

$\left(-\dfrac{3}{5}\right) + \left[-\left(-\dfrac{1}{5}\right)\right]$

$\left(-\dfrac{3}{5}\right) + \left[\dfrac{1}{5}\right] = -\dfrac{2}{5}$

h. $(-0.2) - (+0.3)$
$(-0.2) + [-(+0.3)]$
$(-0.2) + [-0.3] = \mathbf{-0.5}$

Written Practice 68

1.
$$\begin{array}{r} 1037 \text{ g} \\ -\ \ 350 \text{ g} \\ \hline \mathbf{687\ g} \end{array}$$

2.

	Ratio	Actual Count
Pentagons	3	12
Hexagons	5	H

$\dfrac{3}{5} = \dfrac{12}{H}$

$3H = 60$

$H = \mathbf{20\ hexagons}$

3. $\left(\dfrac{1}{4} + \dfrac{1}{2}\right) \div \left(\dfrac{1}{4} \times \dfrac{1}{2}\right)$

$= \left(\dfrac{2}{8} + \dfrac{4}{8}\right) \div \left(\dfrac{1}{8}\right)$

$= \dfrac{6}{8} \div \dfrac{1}{8} = \dfrac{6}{\cancel{8}_1} \times \dfrac{\cancel{8}^1}{1} = \mathbf{6}$

4. a. $\overset{\$0.31 \text{ per pen}}{4)\overline{\$1.24}}$

b. $100(\$0.31) = \mathbf{\$31.00}$

5. a. $\dfrac{60 \text{ miles}}{5 \text{ hours}} = 12 \dfrac{\text{miles}}{\text{hr}}$, **12 miles per hour**

b. $\dfrac{5 \text{ hours}}{60 \text{ miles}} = \dfrac{300 \text{ minutes}}{60 \text{ miles}}$

$= \dfrac{5 \text{ minutes}}{1 \text{ mile}}$, **5 minutes per mile**

6. $1000 \text{ meters} \cdot \dfrac{1 \text{ second}}{331 \text{ meters}} = \dfrac{1000}{331} \text{ seconds}$
About 3 seconds

7. a. 88

b. 72, 76, 80, <u>84</u>, 88, 88, 100
84

c.
$$\begin{array}{r} 72 \\ 80 \\ 84 \\ 88 \\ 100 \\ 88 \\ +\ \ 76 \\ \hline 588 \end{array} \qquad \overset{\mathbf{84}}{7)\overline{588}}$$

8.
$$\begin{array}{r} 8.4 \\ +\ 9.8 \\ \hline 18.2 \end{array} \qquad \overset{\mathbf{9.1}}{2)\overline{18.2}}$$

9. a. 12 cubes

b. Rectangular prism

10. a. $C = \pi d$
$C \approx 3.14(40 \text{ cm})$
$C \approx \mathbf{125.6\ cm}$

b. $C = \pi d$
$C = \pi(40 \text{ cm})$
$C = \mathbf{40\pi\ cm}$

11.

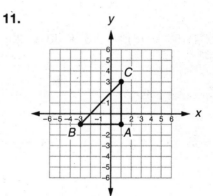

a. Right triangle

b. Isosceles triangle

c. A

d. $m\angle B = \dfrac{90°}{2} = \mathbf{45°}$

e. Area $= \dfrac{(4 \text{ units})(4 \text{ units})}{2} = \mathbf{8\ sq.\ units}$

12. $20{,}000 \times 30{,}000 = 600{,}000{,}000$
$= \mathbf{6 \times 10^8}$

Solutions

13. $W_N = 0.75 \times 400$
$W_N = 300$

14. a. $(-4) - (-6)$
$(-4) + [-(-6)]$
$(-4) + [6] = \mathbf{2}$

b. $(-4) - (+6)$
$(-4) + [-(+6)]$
$(-4) + [-6] = \mathbf{-10}$

c. $(-6) - (-4)$
$(-6) + [-(-4)]$
$(-6) + [4] = \mathbf{-2}$

d. $(+6) - (-4)$
$(+6) + [-(-4)]$
$(+6) + [4] = \mathbf{10}$

15. $(4 \text{ in.})(4 \text{ in.}) = 16 \text{ in.}^2$
$6(16 \text{ in.}^2) = \mathbf{96 \text{ in.}^2}$

16. a. $25\overline{)3.00}$ quotient $\mathbf{0.12}$

b. $\dfrac{3}{25} \times 100\% = \dfrac{300\%}{25} = \mathbf{12\%}$

c. $120\% = \dfrac{120}{100} = \dfrac{6}{5} = \mathbf{1\dfrac{1}{5}}$

d. $120\% = \dfrac{120}{100} = \mathbf{1.2}$

17. $(4)^2 + 2(4)(5) + (5)^2 = 16 + 40 + 25$
$= \mathbf{81}$

18. a. Rectangular prism

b. Cone

c. Cylinder

19. Cone

20. a. $m\angle DCA = \dfrac{90°}{2} = \mathbf{45°}$

b. $m\angle DAC = 120° - 45° = \mathbf{75°}$

c. $m\angle CAB = m\angle DCA = \mathbf{45°}$

d. $m\angle ABC = m\angle CDA = \mathbf{60°}$

e. $m\angle BCA = 120° - 45° = \mathbf{75°}$

f. $m\angle BCD = 180° - 60° = \mathbf{120°}$

21. One possibility: How many $0.25 pens can you buy with $3.00?

22. $\dfrac{4}{c} = \dfrac{3}{7\frac{1}{2}}$

$3c = 4\left(7\dfrac{1}{2}\right)$

$3c = 4\left(\dfrac{15}{2}\right)$

$c = \dfrac{30}{3}$

$c = \mathbf{10}$

23. $\dfrac{(1.5)^2}{15} = \dfrac{2.25}{15} = \mathbf{0.15}$

24.

$\begin{array}{llll} \overset{0}{\cancel{1}}\text{ gal} & (4\text{ qt}) & & \\ - & 1\text{ qt} & 1\text{ pt} & 1\text{ oz} \end{array} \longrightarrow$

$\begin{array}{llll} \overset{0}{\cancel{1}}\text{ gal} & \overset{3}{\cancel{4}}\text{ qt} & (2\text{ pt}) & \\ - & 1\text{ qt} & 1\text{ pt} & 1\text{ oz} \end{array} \longrightarrow$

$\begin{array}{llll} \overset{0}{\cancel{1}}\text{ gal} & \overset{3}{\cancel{4}}\text{ qt} & \overset{1}{\cancel{2}}\text{ pt} & (16\text{ oz}) \\ - & 1\text{ qt} & 1\text{ pt} & 1\text{ oz} \end{array} \longrightarrow$

$\begin{array}{llll} \overset{0}{\cancel{1}}\text{ gal} & \overset{3}{\cancel{4}}\text{ qt} & \overset{1}{\cancel{2}}\text{ pt} & 16\text{ oz} \\ - & 1\text{ qt} & 1\text{ pt} & 1\text{ oz} \\ \hline & \mathbf{2\text{ qt}} & & \mathbf{15\text{ oz}} \end{array}$

25. $16 \div (0.04 \div 0.8) = 16 \div 0.05 = \mathbf{320}$

26. $10 - [0.1 - (0.01)(0.1)]$
$10 - [0.1 - 0.001]$
$10 - 0.099$
$\mathbf{9.901}$

27. $\dfrac{5}{8} + \dfrac{2}{3} \cdot \dfrac{3}{4} - \dfrac{3}{4}$

$= \dfrac{5}{8} + \dfrac{1}{2} \div \dfrac{3}{4} = \dfrac{5}{8} + \dfrac{4}{8} - \dfrac{6}{8}$

$= \dfrac{9}{8} - \dfrac{6}{8} = \mathbf{\dfrac{3}{8}}$

28. $4\dfrac{1}{2} \cdot 3\dfrac{3}{4} \div 1\dfrac{2}{3}$

$= \left(\dfrac{9}{2} \cdot \dfrac{15}{4}\right) \div \dfrac{5}{3} = \dfrac{135}{8} \div \dfrac{5}{3}$

$= \dfrac{\overset{27}{\cancel{135}}}{8} \times \dfrac{3}{\underset{1}{\cancel{5}}} = \dfrac{81}{8} = \mathbf{10\dfrac{1}{8}}$

29. $\sqrt{5^2 - 2^4} = \sqrt{25 - 16} = \sqrt{9} = \mathbf{3}$

30. $3 + 6[10 - (3 \cdot 4 - 5)]$
$3 + 6[10 - (7)]$
$3 + 6[3]$
$3 + 18$
21

Practice Set 69

a. $0.16 \times 10^6 = 1.6 \times 10^{-1} \times 10^6$
$\qquad = \mathbf{1.6 \times 10^5}$

b. $24 \times 10^{-7} = 2.4 \times 10^1 \times 10^{-7}$
$\qquad = \mathbf{2.4 \times 10^{-6}}$

c. $30 \times 10^5 = 3 \times 10^1 \times 10^5$
$\qquad = \mathbf{3 \times 10^6}$

d. $0.75 \times 10^{-8} = 7.5 \times 10^{-1} \times 10^{-8}$
$\qquad = \mathbf{7.5 \times 10^{-9}}$

e. $14.4 \times 10^8 = 1.44 \times 10^1 \times 10^8$
$\qquad = \mathbf{1.44 \times 10^9}$

f. $12.4 \times 10^{-5} = 1.24 \times 10^1 \times 10^{-5}$
$\qquad = \mathbf{1.24 \times 10^{-4}}$

Written Practice 69

1. a. 6.5

b.

6.0	6.5	6.5	**6.5**	7.0	7.0	7.4

6.5

c.

$$7)\overline{46.9} \quad \frac{6.7}{}$$

$\quad\;\; 7.0$
$\quad\;\; 6.5$
$\quad\;\; 6.5$
$\quad\;\; 7.4$
$\quad\;\; 7.0$
$\quad\;\; 6.5$
$\underline{+\;\; 6.0}$
$\quad\; 46.9$

d. $7.4 - 6.0 = \mathbf{1.4}$

2.

	Ratio	Actual Count
Won	5	15
Lost	3	L
Total	8	T

$\dfrac{5}{8} = \dfrac{15}{T}$
$5T = 120$
$T = \mathbf{24\ games}$

3. $\overset{5}{\cancel{10}}$ laps $\cdot \dfrac{\overset{3}{\cancel{6}}\ minutes}{\underset{\underset{1}{2}}{\cancel{4}}\ laps} = \mathbf{15\ minutes}$

4. a. $15 \times 10^5 = 1.5 \times 10^1 \times 10^5$
$\qquad\qquad = \mathbf{1.5 \times 10^6}$

b. $0.15 \times 10^5 = 1.5 \times 10^{-1} \times 10^5$
$\qquad\qquad = \mathbf{1.5 \times 10^4}$

5. a. $\dfrac{do\ not\ believe\ in\ giants}{total\ Lilliputians} = \dfrac{3}{5}$

b. $\dfrac{2}{5} = \dfrac{L}{60}$
$5L = 120$
$L = \mathbf{24\ Lilliputians}$

c. $\dfrac{2}{5}$

6. $C = \pi d$
$C \approx 3.14(40\ cm)$
$C \approx 125.6\ cm \approx \mathbf{126\ cm}$

7. a. Sphere
b. Cylinder
c. Cone

8. a. Perimeter $= \dfrac{10}{16}$ in. $+ \dfrac{10}{16}$ in. $+ \dfrac{10}{16}$ in.
$\qquad\qquad\quad = \dfrac{30}{16}$ in. $= \dfrac{15}{8}$ in. $= \mathbf{1\dfrac{7}{8}\ in.}$

b. 60°

c.

261

Solutions

9. a. $(-4) + (-5) - (-6)$
$(-4) + (-5) + [-(-6)]$
$(-4) + (-5) + [6]$
$\quad\quad\quad -3$

b. $(-2) + (-3) - (-4) - (+5)$
$(-2) + (-3) + [-(-4)] + [-(+5)]$
$(-2) + (-3) + [4] + [-5]$
$\quad\quad\quad\quad -6$

c. $(-0.3) - (-0.3)$
$(-0.3) + [-(-0.3)]$
$(-0.3) + [0.3] = \mathbf{0}$

10. a. $C = \pi d$
$C \approx 3.14(7\text{ cm})$
$C \approx \mathbf{21.98\ cm}$

b. $C = \pi d$
$C \approx \dfrac{22}{7}(7\text{ cm})$
$C \approx \mathbf{22\ cm}$

11.

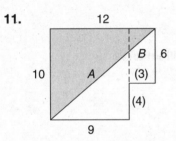

a.   Area A = $(9\text{ mm})(10\text{ mm})$ = 90 mm^2
+ Area B = $(3\text{ mm})(6\text{ mm})$ = 18 mm^2
 Area of figure = $\mathbf{108\ mm^2}$

b. Area = $\dfrac{(12\text{ mm})(10\text{ mm})}{2}$ = $\mathbf{60\ mm^2}$

c. $\dfrac{60}{108} = \mathbf{\dfrac{5}{9}}$

12. $W_N = \dfrac{1}{2} \times 200$
$W_N = \mathbf{100}$

13. $W_N = 2.5 \times 4.2$
$W_N = \mathbf{10.5}$

14. a. $20\overline{)3.00}$ (quotient 0.15)

b. $\dfrac{3}{20} \times 100\% = \dfrac{300\%}{20} = \mathbf{15\%}$

c. $150\% = \dfrac{150}{100} = \mathbf{1\dfrac{1}{2}}$

d. $150\% = \dfrac{150}{100} = \mathbf{1.5}$

15. a. $\angle \mathbf{\mathit{TPQ}}$ or $\angle \mathbf{\mathit{QPT}}$

b. $\angle \mathbf{\mathit{SPR}}$ or $\angle \mathbf{\mathit{RPS}}$

c. $m\angle QPT = 360° - (125° + 90°)$
$ = 360° - 215° = \mathbf{145°}$

16. $(4)^2 - \sqrt{(4)} + (4)(0.5) - (4)^0$
$ = 16 - 2 + 2 - 1 = \mathbf{15}$

17. Multiply the "in" number by 2, then subtract 1 to find the "out" number.

$y = 2x - 1$

x Input	y Output
8	15
6	11
10	19
4	**7**

$4 \times 2 - 1 = 8 - 1 = \mathbf{7}$

18.

```
        13.0909 . . .
  11)144.0000 . . .
     11
     ──
     34
     33
     ──
      1 0
        0
      ───
      1 00
        99
      ───
        10
         0
       ───
        100
```

a. $\mathbf{13.\overline{09}}$

b. $\mathbf{13}$

19. $1.8(20°C) + 32 = \mathbf{68°F}$

20. **Sphere**

21.
$$\dfrac{15}{16} = \dfrac{15}{16}$$
$$-\dfrac{5}{8} = \dfrac{10}{16}$$
$$\overline{\dfrac{5}{16}}$$

22.

$$\frac{a}{8} = \frac{3\frac{1}{2}}{2}$$

$$2a = 3\frac{1}{2}(8)$$

$$2a = \frac{7}{2}(8)$$

$$2a = 28$$

$$a = \mathbf{14}$$

23. $(4 \div 2) \cdot 3 = 2 \cdot 3 = \mathbf{6}$

$$3\frac{3}{4} \div 1\frac{2}{3} = \frac{15}{4} \div \frac{5}{3}$$

$$= \frac{\overset{3}{\cancel{15}}}{4} \times \frac{3}{\underset{1}{\cancel{5}}} = \frac{9}{4}$$

$$3 \cdot \frac{9}{4} = \frac{27}{4} = \mathbf{6\frac{3}{4}}$$

24. $4 + (5 \div 1) = 4 + 5 = \mathbf{9}$
or
$5 + (5 \div 1) = 5 + 5 = \mathbf{10}$

$$5\frac{1}{6} \div 1\frac{1}{3} = \frac{31}{6} \div \frac{4}{3}$$

$$= \frac{31}{\underset{2}{\cancel{6}}} \times \frac{\overset{1}{\cancel{3}}}{4} = \frac{31}{8} = 3\frac{7}{8}$$

$$4\frac{1}{2} = 4\frac{4}{8}$$
$$+ \ 3\frac{7}{8} = 3\frac{7}{8}$$
$$\overline{\qquad\qquad 7\frac{11}{8} = 8\frac{3}{8}}$$

25.
$$\begin{array}{r} 5 \text{ ft} \quad 7 \text{ in.} \\ + \ 6 \text{ ft} \quad 8 \text{ in.} \\ \hline 11 \text{ ft} \quad 15 \text{ in.} \end{array}$$

15 in. = 1 ft 3 in.
$$\begin{array}{r} 1 \text{ ft} \quad 3 \text{ in.} \\ + \ 11 \text{ ft} \\ \hline \mathbf{12 \text{ ft} \quad 3 \text{ in.}} \end{array}$$

26. $\dfrac{350 \ \cancel{m}}{1 \ \cancel{s}} \cdot \dfrac{60 \ \cancel{s}}{1 \min} \cdot \dfrac{1 \text{ km}}{1000 \ \cancel{m}}$

$$= \frac{21{,}000 \text{ km}}{1000 \min} = \mathbf{21 \ \frac{km}{min}}$$

27. $6 - (0.5 \div 4) = 6 - 0.125$
$$= \mathbf{5.875}$$

28. $\begin{array}{r}\mathbf{\$100.00}\\ 75)\overline{\$7500}\end{array}$

29. $\dfrac{432}{675} = \dfrac{2 \cdot 2 \cdot 2 \cdot 2 \cdot \overset{1}{\cancel{3}} \cdot \overset{1}{\cancel{3}} \cdot \overset{1}{\cancel{3}}}{\underset{1}{\cancel{3}} \cdot \underset{1}{\cancel{3}} \cdot \underset{1}{\cancel{3}} \cdot 5 \cdot 5}$

$$= \mathbf{\frac{16}{25}}$$

30. a. $2\frac{1}{4} = 2.25, \quad 2.25 + 0.15 = \mathbf{2.4}$

b.
$$6.5 = 6\frac{1}{2}$$
$$6\frac{1}{2} = 6\frac{3}{6}$$
$$+ \quad \frac{5}{6} = \frac{5}{6}$$
$$\overline{\qquad 6\frac{8}{6} = 7\frac{2}{6} = \mathbf{7\frac{1}{3}}}$$

Early Finishers Solutions

a. Fig. A: cone

b. Fig. B: sphere

Practice Set 70

a. (6 sugar cubes)(3 sugar cubes)
= 18 sugar cubes

$$\frac{18 \text{ sugar cubes}}{\cancel{\text{layer}}} \times 4 \ \cancel{\text{layers}}$$
= **72 sugar cubes**

b. (10 1-cm cubes)(10 1-cm cubes)
= 100 1-cm cubes,

$$\frac{100 \text{ 1-cm cubes}}{1 \ \cancel{\text{layer}}} \times 10 \ \cancel{\text{layers}}$$
= **1000 1-cm cubes**

c. (10 cubes)(4 cubes) = 40 cubes
$$\frac{40 \text{ cubes}}{1 \ \cancel{\text{layer}}} \times 6 \ \cancel{\text{layers}} = 240 \text{ cubes}$$
240 ft³

d. Answers may vary. See student work.

e. $V = lwh$

Solutions

f.

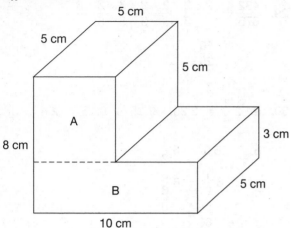

Volume A = (5 cm) (5 cm)(5 cm) = 125 cm³
Volume B = (10 cm)(5 cm)(3 cm) = 150 cm³
_____
                        Total Volume = **275 cm³**

Written Practice 70

1. $\dfrac{2(38 \text{ kilometers})}{4 \text{ hours}}$ = **19 kilometers per hour**

2.

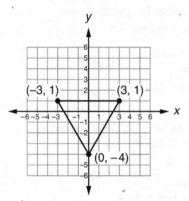

a. **(−3, 1)**

b. Area = $\dfrac{(6 \text{ units}) (5 \text{ units})}{2}$ = **15 sq. units**

3. A little too large. The actual value of π is greater than 3. Dividing the circumference, 600 cm, by π results in a measurement less than 200 cm.

4. a. $\dfrac{\$1.29}{3 \text{ pounds}} = \dfrac{\$0.43}{1 \text{ pound}}$
$0.43 per pound

b. 10($0.43) = **$4.30**

5. (0.7 + 0.6) − (0.9 × 0.8)
    = 1.3 − 0.72 = **0.58**

6. a. $\dfrac{3}{4}$ (188 hits) = **141 hits**

b. $\dfrac{1}{4}$ × 100% = $\dfrac{100\%}{4}$ = **25%**

7. $\left(1\dfrac{1}{2} \text{ in.} + 3 \text{ in.}\right) \div 2$

$\left(\dfrac{3}{2} \text{ in.} + \dfrac{6}{2} \text{ in.}\right) \div 2$

$\left(\dfrac{9}{2} \text{ in.}\right) \div \dfrac{2}{1}$

$\left(\dfrac{9}{2} \text{ in.}\right) \times \dfrac{1}{2} = \dfrac{9}{4}$ in. = $2\dfrac{1}{4}$**-in. mark**

8. (5 1-cm cubes) (5 1-cm cubes)
    = 25 1-cm cubes,

$\dfrac{25 \text{ 1-cm cubes}}{1 \text{ layer}}$ × 3 layers

= **75 1-cm cubes**

9. a. C = πd
      C = π(2 in.)
      C = **2π in.**

b. C = πd
      C ≈ 3.14(1 in.)
      C ≈ **3.14 in.**

10. a. $12 \times 10^{-6} = 1.2 \times 10^{1} \times 10^{-6}$
        $= \mathbf{1.2 \times 10^{-5}}$

b. $0.12 \times 10^{-6} = 1.2 \times 10^{-1} \times 10^{-6}$
        $= \mathbf{1.2 \times 10^{-7}}$

11.
$$3\overline{)2.55} = 0.85$$
    0.74
    0.83
  + 0.98
  _____
    2.55

12. 1.25 kilograms · $\dfrac{1000 \text{ grams}}{1 \text{ kilogram}}$
    = **1250 grams**

13. a. 2^9

b. 2^3

c. 2^{-3}

d. 2^0

14. $W_N = \dfrac{1}{6} \times 100$

$W_N = \dfrac{100}{6}$

$W_N = \mathbf{16\dfrac{2}{3}}$

15. a. $14\% = \dfrac{14}{100} = \dfrac{\mathbf{7}}{\mathbf{50}}$

b. $14\% = \dfrac{14}{100} = \mathbf{0.14}$

c. $6\overline{)5.00\ldots}\ \ 0.8\overline{3}$

d. $\dfrac{5}{6} \times 100\% = \dfrac{500\%}{6} = \mathbf{83\dfrac{1}{3}\%}$

16. a. $(-6) - (-4) + (+2)$
$(-6) + [-(-4)] + (+2)$
$(-6) + [4] + (+2) = \mathbf{0}$

b. $(-5) + (-2) - (-7) - (+9)$
$(-5) + (-2) + [-(-7)] + [-(+9)]$
$(-5) + (-2) + [7] + [-9]$
$\mathbf{-9}$

c. $\left(-\dfrac{1}{2}\right) - \left(-\dfrac{1}{4}\right)$
$\left(-\dfrac{2}{4}\right) + \left[-\left(-\dfrac{1}{4}\right)\right]$
$\left(-\dfrac{2}{4}\right) + \left[\dfrac{1}{4}\right] = \mathbf{-\dfrac{1}{4}}$

17. $(0.4)(0.3) - (0.4 - 0.3)$
$= 0.12 - 0.1 = \mathbf{0.02}$

18. 29,375

19. $6 \times 8 = \mathbf{48}$

20. Pyramid;

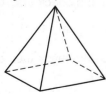

21. $2\text{ ft} \times 2\text{ ft} = 4\text{ ft}^2,$
$6(4\text{ ft}^2) = \mathbf{24\text{ ft}^2}$

22.
$\begin{array}{r} 4.3 \\ +\ 0.8 \\ \hline \mathbf{5.1} \end{array}$

23. $\dfrac{2}{d} = \dfrac{1.2}{1.5}$
$1.2d = 2(1.5)$
$d = \dfrac{3}{1.2}$
$d = \mathbf{2.5}$

24.
$\begin{array}{r} \overset{9}{\cancel{10}}\text{ lb }(16\text{ oz}) \\ -\ 6\text{ lb }\ \ 7\text{ oz} \\ \hline \end{array}$
$\begin{array}{r} \overset{9}{\cancel{10}}\text{ lb }\ 16\text{ oz} \\ -\ 6\text{ lb }\ \ 7\text{ oz} \\ \hline \mathbf{3\text{ lb }\ \ 9\text{ oz}} \end{array}$

25. $\dfrac{\$5.25}{1\text{ hr}} \cdot \dfrac{8\text{ hr}}{1\text{ day}} \cdot \dfrac{5\text{ days}}{1\text{ week}}$
$= \dfrac{\mathbf{\$210.00}}{\mathbf{week}}$

26. $1\dfrac{2}{3} \cdot 3 = \dfrac{5}{\cancel{3}} \cdot \dfrac{\cancel{3}}{1} = 5$

$3\dfrac{3}{4} \div 5 = \dfrac{15}{4} \div \dfrac{5}{1}$
$= \dfrac{\overset{3}{\cancel{15}}}{4} \times \dfrac{1}{\cancel{5}} = \dfrac{\mathbf{3}}{\mathbf{4}}$

27. $4\dfrac{1}{2} + 5\dfrac{1}{6} - 1\dfrac{1}{3}$
$= 4\dfrac{3}{6} + 5\dfrac{1}{6} - 1\dfrac{2}{6} = 8\dfrac{2}{6} = \mathbf{8\dfrac{1}{3}}$

28. $(0.06 \div 5) \div 0.004$
$= (0.012) \div 0.004$
$= \mathbf{3}$

29. $9\dfrac{1}{2} = 9.5, \quad 9.5 \times 9.2 = \mathbf{87.4}$

30. a. Sample space = {HA, HB, HC, HD, TA, TB, TC, TD}

b. P(heads & consonant) $= \dfrac{\mathbf{3}}{\mathbf{8}}$

Solutions

Early Finishers Solutions

a. 1.86×10^5 miles per second

b. $1 \text{ year} \cdot \dfrac{365 \text{ days}}{1 \text{ year}} \cdot \dfrac{24 \text{ hours}}{1 \text{ day}} \cdot \dfrac{60 \text{ minutes}}{1 \text{ hour}}$
$\cdot \dfrac{60 \text{ seconds}}{1 \text{ minute}} = 3.1536 \times 10^7$
seconds per year

c. $(1.86 \times 10^5) \times (3.1536 \times 10^7)$
$= 5.865696 \times 10^{12}$ miles

d. 6×10^{12} miles, six trillion miles

Investigation 7

Balanced Equations

1. **To isolate x, subtract 18**

2. **Subtract 18 from both sides**

3. **27 will remain on the left; x will remain on the right**

4. **Yes (balanced); $x + 18 = 45$**

5. **{Students draw a balance-scale model to represent the given equation.}**

   $\underline{3x \mid 132}$

6. **To isolate x, divide by 3**

7. **Divide both sides by 3**

8. **{Students draw a balance-scale model to represent the given equation.}**

   $\underline{x \mid 44}$

9. $3x = 132$
   $\dfrac{3x}{3} = \dfrac{132}{3}$
   $x = 44$

10. $3(44) = 132$

11. **Multiply by $\frac{4}{3}$**

12. **Multiply both sides by the reciprocal of $\frac{3}{4}$**

13. $\dfrac{3}{4}x = \dfrac{9}{10}$
    $\dfrac{4}{3}\left(\dfrac{3}{4}x\right) = \left(\dfrac{4}{3}\right)\left(\dfrac{9}{10}\right)$
    $x = \dfrac{36}{30}$
    $x = 1\dfrac{1}{5},$ or $\dfrac{6}{5}$

14. $\dfrac{3}{4}x = \dfrac{9}{10}$
    $\dfrac{3}{4}\left(\dfrac{6}{5}\right) = \dfrac{9}{10}$
    $\dfrac{18}{20} = \dfrac{9}{10}$
    $\dfrac{9}{10} = \dfrac{9}{10}$

{For questions 15–20, students are asked to state the operation, explain how to keep the equation balanced, solve the equation and provide a solution. In the answers here, the first two steps are combined and the solution is given.}

15. **Subtract 2.5 from each side; $x = 4.5$**

16. **Subtract 2 from each side;**
    $y = 1.6$

17. **Divide both sides by 4 or multiply both sides by $\frac{1}{4}$;**
    $w = 33$

18. **Divide both sides by 1.2;**
    $m = 1.1$

19. **Subtract $\frac{3}{4}$ from each side;**
    $x = \dfrac{1}{12}$

20. **Multiply both sides by $\frac{4}{3}$;**
    $x = \dfrac{20}{18}$, which reduces to $\dfrac{10}{9}$

21. {Students create, solve and check their own addition equations.}

22. {Students create, solve and check their own multiplication equations.}

Practice Set (71)

a.

_ students	
$\frac{3}{5}$ were boys (15).	5 students
	5 students
	5 students
$\frac{2}{5}$ were girls.	5 students
	5 students

$15 \div 3 = 5$

$5 \times 5 \text{ students} = \textbf{25 students}$

b.

_ clowns
5 clowns
5 clowns
5 clowns
5 clowns
5 clowns
5 clowns
5 clowns
5 clowns

$\frac{5}{8}$ had happy faces.

$\frac{3}{8}$ did not have happy faces (15).

$15 \div 3 = 5$

$5 \times 8 \text{ clowns} = \textbf{40 clowns}$

c.

_ questions
4 questions
4 questions
4 questions
4 questions

$\frac{3}{4}$ had been answered (12).

$\frac{1}{4}$ will be answered.

$12 \div 3 = 4$

$4 \times 4 \text{ questions} = \textbf{16 questions}$

d. $\frac{3}{4}H = 12$

$\frac{4}{3} \cdot \frac{3}{4}H = \frac{4}{3} \cdot 12$

$1H = \frac{48}{3}$

$H = \textbf{16}$

e. Students create and solve their own equations.

Written Practice (71)

1. $9 \text{ seconds} \cdot \frac{331 \text{ meters}}{1 \text{ second}}$

$= 2979 \text{ meters}; \textbf{about 3 kilometers}$

2.
$$
\begin{array}{r}
3.33 \\
3.45 \\
+\ 3.51 \\
\hline
10.29
\end{array}
\qquad
\begin{array}{r}
3.43 \\
3\overline{)10.29}
\end{array}
$$

3. $2(80 \text{ percent}) + 3(90 \text{ percent})$

$160 + 270 = 430 \text{ percent}$

$\dfrac{430 \text{ percent}}{5} = \textbf{86 percent}$

4.
$$
\begin{array}{r}
20,000,000,000 \\
-\ 9,000,000,000 \\
\hline
11,000,000,000
\end{array}
$$

$\textbf{1.1} \times \textbf{10}^{\textbf{10}}$

5.
$$
\begin{array}{r}
2 \\
3 \\
5 \\
7 \\
+\ 11 \\
\hline
\textbf{28}
\end{array}
$$

6.

	Ratio	Actual Count
New ones	4	N
Used ones	7	U
Total	11	242

$\dfrac{4}{11} = \dfrac{N}{242}$

$11N = 968$

$N = \textbf{88 new ones}$

7.

_ pages
26 pages
26 pages
26 pages
26 pages
26 pages

$\frac{3}{5}$ read (78)

$\frac{2}{5}$ not read

a. $78 \div 3 = 26$

$5 \times 26 = \textbf{130 pages}$

b. $2 \times 26 = \textbf{52 pages}$

8. $(4 \text{ 1-inch cubes})(4 \text{ 1-inch cubes})$

$= 16 \text{ 1-inch cubes}$

$\dfrac{16 \text{ 1-inch cubes}}{1 \text{ layer}} \cdot 4 \text{ layers}$

$= \textbf{64 1-inch cubes}$

9. $(4 \text{ in.})(4 \text{ in.}) = 16 \text{ in.}^2$

$6(16 \text{ in.}^2) = \textbf{96 in.}^2$

10. a. $C \approx 3.14(28 \text{ cm})$
    $C \approx \textbf{87.92 cm}$

b. $C \approx \dfrac{22}{7}(28 \text{ cm})$
    $C \approx \textbf{88 cm}$

11. a. $\textbf{2.5} \times \textbf{10}^{7}$

b. $\textbf{2.5} \times \textbf{10}^{-5}$

12. a. $0.1 = \dfrac{1}{10}$

b. $0.1 = \dfrac{1}{10} = \dfrac{10}{100} = \textbf{10\%}$

c. $0.5\% = \dfrac{0.5}{100} = \dfrac{\textbf{1}}{\textbf{200}}$

d. $0.5\% = \dfrac{0.5}{100} = \textbf{0.005}$

13. a. $W_N = 0.35 \times 80$
    $W_N = \textbf{28}$

b. $\dfrac{3}{\overset{1}{\cancel{4}}} \times \overset{6}{\cancel{24}} = W_N$

    $3(6) = W_N$
    $\textbf{18} = W_N$

14. Add 7 to x to find y.

$$y = x + 7$$

x	y
3	10
0	7
5	12
7	**14**

15.

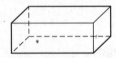

8 vertices

16. a. Perimeter $= 10 \text{ cm} + 12 \text{ cm}$
        $+ 8 \text{ cm} + 6 \text{ cm} = \textbf{36 cm}$

b. Area $= \dfrac{(6 \text{ cm})(8 \text{ cm})}{2} = \textbf{24 cm}^2$

c. Area $= \dfrac{(12 \text{ cm})(8 \text{ cm})}{2} = \textbf{48 cm}^2$

d. Area $= 24 \text{ cm}^2 + 48 \text{ cm}^2 = \textbf{72 cm}^2$

17.

$$\begin{array}{r} \$16.50 \\ \times \quad 0.15 \\ \hline \$2.475 \end{array}$$

About \$2.50

18.

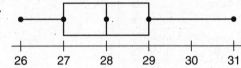

19.

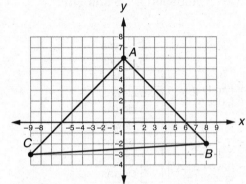

$m\angle A = \textbf{90}°$
$m\angle B = \textbf{48}°$
$m\angle C = \textbf{42}°$

20. $(0.01) - (0.1)(0.01)$
    $= 0.01 - 0.001 = \textbf{0.009}$

21.
$$m + 5.75 = 26.4$$
$$m + 5.75 - 5.75 = 26.4 - 5.75$$
$$m = \textbf{20.65}$$

Subtraction property of equality
check: $20.65 + 5.75 = 26.4$
                $26.4 = 26.4$

22.
$$\dfrac{3}{4}x = 48$$

$$\left(\dfrac{\overset{1}{\cancel{4}}}{\underset{1}{\cancel{3}}}\right)\dfrac{\overset{1}{\cancel{3}}}{\underset{1}{\cancel{4}}}x = \left(\dfrac{4}{3}\right)\overset{16}{\cancel{48}}$$

$$x = \textbf{64}$$

Multiplication property of equality

check: $\dfrac{3}{\underset{1}{\cancel{4}}}(\overset{16}{\cancel{64}}) = 48$

        $3(16) = 48$
            $48 = 48$

23. Rhombus

24.

$$\frac{4^2 + \{20 - 2[6 - (5 - 2)]\}}{\sqrt{36}}$$

$$\frac{16 + \{20 - 2[6 - (3)]\}}{6}$$

$$\frac{16 + \{20 - 2[3]\}}{6}$$

$$\frac{16 + \{20 - 6\}}{6}$$

$$\frac{16 + \{14\}}{6}$$

$$\frac{30}{6}$$

$$5$$

25.

$$\overset{0}{\cancel{1}} \text{ yd } (\overset{2}{\cancel{3}} \text{ ft}) \text{ (12 in.)}$$
$$- \qquad 1 \text{ ft} \quad 1 \text{ in.}$$
$$\overline{\qquad\qquad \mathbf{1 \text{ ft} \quad 11 \text{ in.}}}$$

26. $3.5 \, \cancel{hr} \cdot \dfrac{60 \, \cancel{min}}{1 \, \cancel{hr}} \cdot \dfrac{60 \, s}{1 \, \cancel{min}} = \mathbf{12{,}600 \, s}$

27. $4\dfrac{1}{2} \cdot 2\dfrac{2}{3} = \dfrac{\overset{3}{\cancel{9}}}{\underset{1}{\cancel{2}}} \cdot \dfrac{\overset{4}{\cancel{8}}}{\underset{1}{\cancel{3}}} = 12$

$6\dfrac{2}{3} \div 12 = \dfrac{20}{3} \div \dfrac{12}{1}$

$\qquad\qquad = \dfrac{\overset{5}{\cancel{20}}}{3} \times \dfrac{1}{\underset{3}{\cancel{12}}} = \mathbf{\dfrac{5}{9}}$

28.

$$7\dfrac{1}{2} = 7\dfrac{3}{6}$$
$$- \, 5\dfrac{1}{6} = 5\dfrac{1}{6}$$
$$\overline{\qquad\qquad 2\dfrac{2}{6} = 2\dfrac{1}{3}}$$

$$2\dfrac{1}{3}$$
$$+ \, 1\dfrac{1}{3}$$
$$\overline{\quad \mathbf{3\dfrac{2}{3}}}$$

29. a.

$$(-5) + (-6) - |-7|$$
$$(-5) + (-6) + [-|-7|]$$
$$(-5) + (-6) + [-7]$$
$$\mathbf{-18}$$

b.

$$(-15) - (-24) - (+8)$$
$$(-15) + [-(-24)] + [-(+8)]$$
$$(-15) + [24] + [-8]$$
$$\mathbf{1}$$

c.

$$\left(-\dfrac{4}{5}\right) - \left(-\dfrac{1}{5}\right)$$
$$\left(-\dfrac{4}{5}\right) + \left[-\left(-\dfrac{1}{5}\right)\right]$$
$$\left(-\dfrac{4}{5}\right) + \left[\dfrac{1}{5}\right] = \mathbf{-\dfrac{3}{5}}$$

30.

$$1.5 = 1\dfrac{1}{2}$$
$$2\dfrac{2}{3} = 2\dfrac{4}{6}$$
$$- \, 1\dfrac{1}{2} = 1\dfrac{3}{6}$$
$$\overline{\qquad\qquad \mathbf{1\dfrac{1}{6}}}$$

Practice Set 72

a. Between 4 and 6 hours

	Case 1	Case 2
km	30	75
Hours	2	h

$$\dfrac{30}{2} = \dfrac{75}{h}$$
$$30h = 2(75)$$
$$30h = 150$$
$$h = \dfrac{\overset{5}{\cancel{150}}}{\underset{1}{\cancel{30}}}$$
$$h = \mathbf{5 \text{ hours}}$$

b.

	Case 1	Case 2
Head of cattle	40	50
Bales	6	b

$$\dfrac{40}{6} = \dfrac{50}{b}$$
$$40b = 6(50)$$
$$40b = 300$$
$$b = \dfrac{\overset{\overset{15}{\cancel{30}}}{\cancel{300}}}{\underset{\underset{2}{\cancel{4}}}{\cancel{40}}}$$
$$b = \dfrac{15}{2} \text{ bales} = \mathbf{7\dfrac{1}{2} \text{ bales}}$$

Solutions

c.

	Case 1	Case 2
First number	5	9
Second number	15	n

$$\frac{5}{15} = \frac{9}{n}$$

$$5n = 15(9)$$

$$5n = 135$$

$$n = \frac{\overset{27}{\cancel{135}}}{\underset{1}{\cancel{5}}}$$

$$n = \textbf{27}$$

Written Practice   72

1.
$$\begin{array}{r} 1821 \\ -\ 1769 \\ \hline \textbf{52 years} \end{array}$$

2. 4(4 points) + 6(9 points)
$$= 16 \text{ points} + 54 \text{ points}$$
$$= 70 \text{ points}$$
$$\frac{70 \text{ points}}{10} = \textbf{7 points}$$

3. 2.5 liters $\cdot \dfrac{\textbf{1000 milliliters}}{\textbf{1 liter}}$
$$= \textbf{2500 milliliters}$$

4. $\left(\dfrac{1}{2} + \dfrac{2}{5}\right) - \left(\dfrac{1}{2} \cdot \dfrac{2}{5}\right)$

$$= \left(\frac{5}{10} + \frac{4}{10}\right) - \left(\frac{1}{5}\right)$$

$$= \frac{9}{10} - \frac{1}{5} = \frac{9}{10} - \frac{2}{10} = \frac{\textbf{7}}{\textbf{10}}$$

5.

	Ratio	Actual Count
Carnivores	2	126
Herbivores	7	H

$$\frac{2}{7} = \frac{126}{H}$$
$$2H = 882$$
$$H = \textbf{441 herbivores}$$

6.

	Case 1	Case 2
Books	4	14
Pounds	9	P

$$\frac{4}{9} = \frac{14}{p}$$
$$4p = 9(14)$$
$$4p = 126$$
$$p = \frac{\overset{63}{\cancel{126}}}{\underset{2}{\cancel{4}}}$$
$$p = \textbf{31}\frac{\textbf{1}}{\textbf{2}} \textbf{ pounds}$$

7. a. $\dfrac{2}{\underset{1}{\cancel{5}}} \times \overset{12}{\cancel{60}} = W_N$

$$24 = W_N$$

b. $M = 0.75 \times \$24$
$$M = \textbf{\$18}$$

8. $C \approx \pi d$
$$C \approx 3.14\,(20 \text{ in.})$$
$$C \approx 62.8 \text{ in.} \approx \textbf{63 in.}$$

9.

	225 voters
$\dfrac{2}{3}$ for Kayla (150)	75 voters
	75 voters
$\dfrac{1}{3}$ not for Kayla	75 voters

a. $\dfrac{150 \text{ votes}}{2} = 75 \text{ votes}$

$3(75 \text{ votes}) = \textbf{225 votes}$

b. $1(75 \text{ votes}) = \textbf{75 votes}$

10. (10 ice cubes)(8 ice cubes)
$$= 80 \text{ ice cubes}$$
$$\frac{80 \text{ ice cubes}}{1 \text{ layer}} \cdot 6 \text{ layers}$$
$$= \textbf{480 ice cubes}$$

11. (10 in.)(8 in.) = 80 in.^{2}
(6 in.)(10 in.) = 60 in.^{2}
(6 in.)(8 in.) = 48 in.^{2}
2(80 in.^{2}) + 2(60 in.^{2}) + 2(48 in.^{2})
$$= 160 \text{ in.}^2 + 120 \text{ in.}^2 + 96 \text{ in.}^2$$
$$= \textbf{376 in.}^2$$

12. a. 6×10^5

b. 6×10^{-7}

13.
$$3\overline{)4.38} = 1.46$$

$$\begin{array}{r} 1.35 \\ 1.44 \\ +\ 1.59 \\ \hline 4.38 \end{array}$$

14. **a.** $3\overline{)5.0} = 0.6$

b. $\dfrac{3}{5} \times 100\% = \dfrac{300\%}{5} = \mathbf{60\%}$

c. $2.5\% = \dfrac{2.5}{100} = \dfrac{\mathbf{1}}{\mathbf{40}}$

d. $2.5\% = \dfrac{2.5}{100} = \mathbf{0.025}$

15. **a.** $\mathbf{2^2 \cdot 3^4 \cdot 5^2}$

b. **90**

16. **a.** Area $= (8\text{ in.})(6\text{ in.}) = \mathbf{48\text{ in.}^2}$

b. Area $= \dfrac{(8\text{ in.})(6\text{ in.})}{2} = \mathbf{24\text{ in.}^2}$

c. $180° - 72° = \mathbf{108°}$

17. **a.** **Sphere**

b. **Triangular prism**

c. **Cylinder**

Only the triangular prism is a polyhedron, because it is the only figure whose faces are polygons.

18. **Cylinder**

19. **a.** $C = \pi(60\text{ mm})$
$C = \mathbf{60\pi\text{ mm}}$

b. $C \approx 3.14(60\text{ mm})$
$C \approx \mathbf{188.4\text{ mm}}$

20. $\dfrac{2}{3}$ $\lessgtr$ 0.667

21. **a.** $(5)^2 - (4)^2 = 25 - 16 = \mathbf{9}$

b. $(5)^0 - (4)^{-1} = 1 - \dfrac{1}{4}$
$= \dfrac{4}{4} - \dfrac{1}{4} = \dfrac{\mathbf{3}}{\mathbf{4}}$

22.
$$m - \dfrac{2}{3} = 1\dfrac{3}{4}$$
$$m - \dfrac{2}{3} + \dfrac{2}{3} = 1\dfrac{3}{4} + \dfrac{2}{3}$$
$$m = 1\dfrac{9}{12} + \dfrac{8}{12}$$
$$m = 1\dfrac{17}{12} = \mathbf{2\dfrac{5}{12}}$$

check:
$$2\dfrac{5}{12} - \dfrac{2}{3} = 1\dfrac{3}{4}$$
$$2\dfrac{5}{12} - \dfrac{8}{12} = 1\dfrac{3}{4}$$
$$1\dfrac{17}{12} - \dfrac{8}{12} = 1\dfrac{3}{4}$$
$$1\dfrac{9}{12} = 1\dfrac{3}{4}$$
$$1\dfrac{3}{4} = 1\dfrac{3}{4}$$

23.
$$\dfrac{2}{3}w = 24$$
$$\left(\dfrac{\cancel{3}^{1}}{\cancel{2}_{1}}\right)\dfrac{\cancel{2}^{1}}{\cancel{3}_{1}}w = \left(\dfrac{3}{\cancel{2}_{1}}\right)\cancel{24}^{12}$$
$$w = 3(12)$$
$$w = \mathbf{36}$$

check:
$$\left(\dfrac{2}{\cancel{3}_{1}}\right)\cancel{36}^{12} = 24$$
$$2(12) = 24$$
$$24 = 24$$

24.
$$\dfrac{[30 - 4(5 - 2)] + 5(3^3 - 5^2)}{\sqrt{9} + \sqrt{16}}$$
$$\dfrac{[30 - 12] + 5(27 - 25)}{3 + 4}$$
$$\dfrac{18 + 5(2)}{7}$$
$$\dfrac{18 + 10}{7}$$
$$\dfrac{28}{7}$$
$$\mathbf{4}$$

25.
$$\begin{array}{r} \overset{1}{\cancel{2}}\text{ gal}\ \ \overset{(4\text{ qt})}{1\text{ qt}} \\ -\ 1\text{ gal}\ \ 1\text{ qt}\ \ 1\text{ pt} \end{array} \longrightarrow$$

$$\begin{array}{r} \overset{1}{\cancel{2}}\text{ gal}\ \ \overset{\overset{4}{\cancel{5}}}{\cancel{1}}\text{ qt}\ \ (2\text{ pt}) \\ -\ 1\text{ gal}\ \ 1\text{ qt}\ \ 1\text{ pt} \end{array} \longrightarrow$$

$$\begin{array}{r} \overset{1}{\cancel{2}}\text{ gal}\ \ \overset{\overset{4}{\cancel{5}}}{\cancel{1}}\text{ qt}\ \ 2\text{ pt} \\ -\ 1\text{ gal}\ \ 1\text{ qt}\ \ 1\text{ pt} \\ \hline \mathbf{3\text{ qt}\ \ 1\text{ pt}} \end{array}$$

Solutions

26. $\frac{1}{\cancel{2}_{1}}\,\cancel{mi} \cdot \dfrac{\overset{880}{\cancel{5280}}\,ft}{1\,\cancel{mi}} \cdot \dfrac{1\,yd}{\cancel{3}\,\cancel{ft}_{1}}$

$= \textbf{880 yd}$

27. $4\dfrac{1}{2} \cdot 6\dfrac{2}{3} = \dfrac{\overset{3}{\cancel{9}}}{\underset{1}{\cancel{2}}} \cdot \dfrac{\overset{10}{\cancel{20}}}{\underset{1}{\cancel{3}}} = 30$

$\left(2\dfrac{1}{2}\right)^{2} \div 30 = \left(\dfrac{5}{2}\right)^{2} \div 30$

$= \dfrac{25}{4} \div \dfrac{30}{1} = \dfrac{\overset{5}{\cancel{25}}}{4} \times \dfrac{1}{\underset{6}{\cancel{30}}}$

$= \dfrac{5}{24}$

28.
$$5\dfrac{1}{6} = 5\dfrac{1}{6}$$
$$+\ 1\dfrac{1}{3} = 1\dfrac{2}{6}$$
$$\overline{\qquad\qquad 6\dfrac{3}{6} = 6\dfrac{1}{2}}$$

$$7\dfrac{1}{2}$$
$$-\ 6\dfrac{1}{2}$$
$$\overline{\qquad\ 1}$$

29. a. $(-7) + |+5| + (-9)$
$\qquad = (-7) + 5 + (-9) = \textbf{-11}$

  b. $(16) + (-24) - (-18)$
  $(16) + (-24) + [-(-18)]$
  $(16) + (-24) + [18]$
  $\qquad\qquad\textbf{10}$

  c. $(-0.2) + (-0.3) - (-0.4)$
  $(-0.2) + (-0.3) + [-(-0.4)]$
  $(-0.2) + (-0.3) + [0.4]$
  $\qquad\qquad\textbf{-0.1}$

30. $5\dfrac{1}{4} = 5.25$

$$5.25$$
$$+\ 1.9$$
$$\overline{\ \ 7.15}$$

Early Finishers Solutions

  a. Volume $= lwh$

  $= (10\ ft)(40\ ft)(4\ ft) = 1600\ ft^2$

  b. $0.95 \times 1600\ ft^2 = 1520\ ft^2$

c. $1520\ ft^2 \cdot \dfrac{7.48\ \text{gallons}}{1ft^2} = 11369.6\ \text{gallons}$

d. No, because 20 gal./min. for 12 hours is 14,400 gallons. This is greater than the 11369.6 gallon limit and greater than the maximum capacity of the pool.

Practice Set 73

a. $(-7)(3) = \textbf{-21}$

b. $(+4)(-8) = \textbf{-32}$

c. $(8)(+5) = \textbf{40}$

d. $(-8)(-3) = \textbf{24}$

e. $\dfrac{25}{-5} = \textbf{-5}$

f. $\dfrac{-27}{-3} = \textbf{9}$

g. $\dfrac{-28}{4} = \textbf{-7}$

h. $\dfrac{+30}{6} = \textbf{5}$

i. $\dfrac{+45}{-3} = \textbf{-15}$

j. $\left(-\dfrac{1}{2}\right)\left(\dfrac{1}{4}\right) = \textbf{-}\dfrac{\textbf{1}}{\textbf{8}}$

k. $\dfrac{-1.2}{0.3} = \textbf{-4}$

l. $(-1.2)(-2) = \textbf{2.4}$

m.

$3(-2) = \textbf{-6}$

n. $\dfrac{-8}{2} = \textbf{4},\ \dfrac{-8}{-4} = \textbf{2}$

Written Practice 73

b. $W_N = 0.8 \times 760$
$W_N = 608$

1.

	Case 1	Case 2
Packages	12	p
Minutes	5	60

$\frac{12}{5} = \frac{p}{60}$

$5p = 12(60)$

$p = \frac{720}{5}$

$p = \textbf{144 packages}$

2. $5(30 \text{ minutes}) + 3(46 \text{ minutes})$
$= 150 \text{ minutes} + 138 \text{ minutes}$
$= 288 \text{ minutes}$

$\frac{288 \text{ minutes}}{8} = \textbf{36 minutes}$

3. $\frac{(0.2 + 0.5)}{(0.2)(0.5)} = \frac{0.7}{0.1} = \textbf{7}$

4. $23 \text{ cm} \cdot \frac{10 \text{ mm}}{1 \text{ cm}} = \textbf{230 mm}$

5.

	Ratio	Actual Count
Paperback books	3	P
Hardback books	11	9240
Total	14	T

$\frac{11}{14} = \frac{9240}{T}$

$11T = 14(9240)$

$T = \frac{129,360}{11}$

$T = \textbf{11,760 books}$

6. **a.** $\textbf{2.4} \times \textbf{10}^{-4}$

b. $\textbf{2.4} \times \textbf{10}^{8}$

7.

$\frac{1}{4}$ were true-false.

$\frac{3}{4}$ were not true-false.

120 questions
- 30 questions
- 30 questions
- 30 questions
- 30 questions

a. $4(30 \text{ questions}) = \textbf{120 questions}$

b. $3(30 \text{ questions}) = \textbf{90 questions}$

8. **a.** $\frac{5}{\cancel{9}_1} \times \cancel{45}^5 = W_N$

$25 = W_N$

9. **a.** $\frac{-36}{9} = \textbf{-4}$

b. $\frac{-3.6}{-6} = \textbf{0.6}$

c. $0.9(-3) = \textbf{-2.7}$

d. $(+8)(+7) = \textbf{56}$

10. $\frac{\text{composite numbers}}{\text{total numbers}} = \frac{3}{8}$

11.

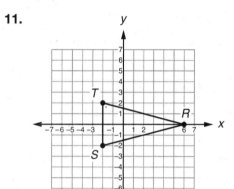

a. $(-2, 2)$

b. **Isosceles triangle**

c. $m\angle S = \frac{180° - 28°}{2} = \textbf{76°}$

12. If the signs of the two factors are the same—both positive or both negative—then the product is positive. If the signs of the two factors are different, the product is negative.

13. $(4 \text{ 1-ft cubes})(3 \text{ 1-ft cubes})$
$= 12 \text{ 1-ft cubes}$

$\frac{12 \text{ 1-ft cubes}}{1 \text{ layer}} \cdot 8 \text{ layers}$

$= \textbf{96 1-ft cubes}$

14. **a.** $C \approx 3.14(42 \text{ m})$
$C \approx \textbf{131.88 m}$

b. $C \approx \frac{22}{7}(42 \text{ m})$
$C \approx \textbf{132 m}$

Solutions

15. a. $2.5 = 2\dfrac{5}{10} = 2\dfrac{1}{2}$

b. $2.5 \times 100\% = \textbf{250\%}$

c. $0.2\% = \dfrac{0.2}{100} = \dfrac{1}{\textbf{500}}$

d. $0.2\% = \dfrac{0.2}{100} = \textbf{0.002}$

16. Right; scalene

$\text{Area} = \dfrac{(6\text{ cm})(8\text{ cm})}{2} = \textbf{24 cm}^2$

17. Obtuse; scalene

$\text{Area} = \dfrac{(4\text{ cm})(5\text{ cm})}{2} = \textbf{10 cm}^2$

18. Acute; isosceles

$\text{Area} = \dfrac{(6\text{ cm})(4\text{ cm})}{2} = \textbf{12 cm}^2$

19. a. Pyramid

b. Cylinder

c. Cone

20. $\dfrac{2}{3} \times 96 = 64$

$\dfrac{5}{6} \times 84 = 70$

$64 < 70$

$\dfrac{2}{3}$ of 96 $\bigotimes$ $\dfrac{5}{6}$ of 84

21. $\left(\dfrac{5}{6}\right)\left(\dfrac{3}{4}\right) - \left(\dfrac{5}{6} - \dfrac{3}{4}\right)$

$= \dfrac{5}{8} - \left(\dfrac{10}{12} - \dfrac{9}{12}\right) = \dfrac{5}{8} - \dfrac{1}{12}$

$= \dfrac{15}{24} - \dfrac{2}{24} = \dfrac{\textbf{13}}{\textbf{24}}$

22. $\dfrac{3}{5}w = 15$

$\left(\dfrac{\overset{1}{\cancel{5}}}{\cancel{3}}\right)\left(\dfrac{\overset{1}{\cancel{3}}}{\cancel{5}}\right)w = \left(\dfrac{5}{\cancel{3}}\right)\overset{5}{\cancel{15}}$

$w = 5(5)$

$w = \textbf{25}$

check: $\dfrac{3}{\cancel{5}}(\overset{5}{\cancel{25}}) = 15$

$3(5) = 15$

$15 = 15$

23. $b - 1.6 = (0.4)^2$

$b - 1.6 + 1.6 = (0.4)^2 + 1.6$

$b = 0.16 + 1.6$

$b = \textbf{1.76}$

check: $1.76 - 1.6 = (0.4)^2$

$0.16 = 0.16$

24. $20w = 5.6$

$\dfrac{\overset{1}{\cancel{20}}w}{\underset{1}{\cancel{20}}} = \dfrac{5.6}{20}$

$w = \textbf{0.28}$

check: $20(0.28) = 5.6$

$5.6 = 5.6$

25.

	2 yd	1 ft	7 in.
+	1 yd	2 ft	8 in.
	3 yd	3 ft	15 in.

15 in. = 1 ft   3 in.

$\begin{array}{r} 1\text{ ft} \quad 3\text{ in.} \\ +\ 3\text{ ft} \\ \hline 4\text{ ft} \quad 3\text{ in.} \end{array}$

4 ft = 1 yd 1 ft

$\begin{array}{r} 1\text{ yd} \quad 1\text{ ft} \quad 3\text{ in.} \\ +\ 3\text{ yd} \\ \hline \textbf{4 yd} \quad \textbf{1 ft} \quad \textbf{3 in.} \end{array}$

26. $0.5\ \cancel{m} \cdot \dfrac{100\ \cancel{cm}}{1\ \cancel{m}} \cdot \dfrac{10\ mm}{1\ \cancel{cm}} = \textbf{500 mm}$

27. $12\dfrac{1}{2} \cdot 4\dfrac{1}{5} \cdot 2\dfrac{2}{3} = \dfrac{\overset{5}{\cancel{25}}}{2} \cdot \dfrac{\overset{7}{\cancel{21}}}{\underset{1}{\cancel{5}}} \cdot \dfrac{\overset{4}{\cancel{8}}}{\underset{1}{\cancel{3}}} = \textbf{140}$

28. $6\dfrac{2}{3} \cdot 1\dfrac{1}{5} = \dfrac{\overset{4}{\cancel{20}}}{\cancel{3}} \cdot \dfrac{\overset{2}{\cancel{6}}}{\cancel{5}} = 8$

$7\dfrac{1}{2} \div 8 = \dfrac{15}{2} \div \dfrac{8}{1} = \dfrac{15}{2} \times \dfrac{1}{8}$

$= \dfrac{\textbf{15}}{\textbf{16}}$

29. a. $(-8) + (-7) - (-15)$

$(-8) + (-7) + [-(-15)]$

$(-8) + (-7) + [15]$

$\textbf{0}$

b. $(-15) + (+11) - |+24|$

$(-15) + (+11) + [-|+24|]$

$(-15) + (+11) + [-24]$

-28

c. $\left(-\dfrac{1}{3}\right) - \left(-\dfrac{2}{3}\right)$

$\left(-\dfrac{1}{3}\right) + \left[-\left(-\dfrac{2}{3}\right)\right]$

$\left(-\dfrac{1}{3}\right) + \left[\dfrac{2}{3}\right]$

$\dfrac{1}{3}$

30. $2.25 = 2\dfrac{1}{4}$

$2\dfrac{1}{4} \times 1\dfrac{1}{3} = \dfrac{\cancel{9}^{3}}{\cancel{4}_{1}} \times \dfrac{\cancel{4}^{1}}{\cancel{3}_{1}} = 3$

Early Finishers Solutions

a. Triangle, circle, triangle; see student work.

b. Square, rectangle, circle; see student work.

Practice Set 74

a. $W_F \times 130 = 80$

$\dfrac{W_F \times 130}{130} = \dfrac{80}{130}$

$W_F = \dfrac{8}{13}$

b. $75 = W_D \times 300$

$\dfrac{75}{300} = \dfrac{W_D \times 300}{300}$

$0.25 = W_D$

c. $80 = 0.4 \times W_N$

$\dfrac{80}{0.4} = \dfrac{0.4 \times W_N}{0.4}$

$200 = W_N$

d. $60 = \dfrac{5}{6} \times W_N$

$\dfrac{6}{5} \times 60 = \dfrac{6}{5} \times \dfrac{5}{6} \times W_N$

$6(12) = W_N$

$72 = W_N$

e. $60 = W_F \times 90$

$\dfrac{60}{90} = \dfrac{W_F \times 90}{90}$

$\dfrac{2}{3} = W_F$

f. $W_D \times 80 = 60$

$\dfrac{W_D \times 80}{80} = \dfrac{60}{80}$

$W_D = 0.75$

g. $40 = 0.08 \times W_N$

$\dfrac{40}{0.08} = \dfrac{0.08 \times W_N}{0.08}$

$500 = W_N$

h. $\dfrac{6}{5} \times W_N = 60$

$\dfrac{5}{6} \times \dfrac{6}{5} \times W_N = \dfrac{5}{6} \times 60$

$W_N = 5(10)$

$W_N = 50$

Written Practice 74

1. $3(28 \text{ pages}) + 4(42 \text{ pages})$

$= 84 \text{ pages} + 168 \text{ pages}$

$= 252 \text{ pages}$

$\dfrac{252 \text{ pages}}{7} = 36 \text{ pages}$

2. $\dfrac{\$1.14}{12 \text{ ounces}} = \dfrac{\$0.095}{1 \text{ ounce}}$

$\dfrac{\$1.28}{16 \text{ ounces}} = \dfrac{\$0.08}{1 \text{ ounce}}$

$\begin{array}{r} \$0.095 \\ - \$0.08 \\ \hline \$0.015 \end{array}$

1.5¢ per ounce

3. $4\dfrac{1}{2} \text{ \cancel{feet}} \cdot \dfrac{12 \text{ inches}}{1 \text{ \cancel{foot}}} = 54 \text{ inches}$

4.

	Ratio	Actual Count
Left-handed students	2	L
Right-handed students	3	18
Total	5	T

$\dfrac{3}{5} = \dfrac{18}{T}$

$3T = 90$

$T = 30 \text{ students}$

Solutions

5.

	Case 1	Case 2
Pounds	5	8
Cost	$1.40	C

$$\frac{5}{\$1.40} = \frac{8}{C}$$
$$5C = (\$1.40)(8)$$
$$C = \frac{\$11.20}{5}$$
$$C = \mathbf{\$2.24}$$

6.

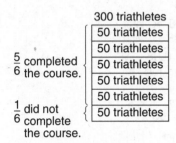

$\frac{5}{6}$ completed the course.

$\frac{1}{6}$ did not complete the course.

a. 250 triathletes

b. $\dfrac{\text{completed the course}}{\text{did not complete the course}} = \dfrac{\mathbf{5}}{\mathbf{1}}$

7.
$$15 = \frac{3}{8} \times W_N$$
$$\frac{8}{3} \times 15 = \frac{8}{3} \times \frac{3}{8} \times W_N$$
$$8(5) = W_N$$
$$\mathbf{40} = W_N$$

8.
$$70 = W_D \times 200$$
$$\frac{70}{200} = \frac{W_D \times 200}{200}$$
$$\mathbf{0.35} = W_D$$

9.
$$\frac{2}{5} \times W_N = 120$$
$$\frac{5}{2} \times \frac{2}{5} \times W_N = \frac{5}{2} \times 120$$
$$W_N = 5(60)$$
$$W_N = \mathbf{300}$$

10. $P = 0.6 \times \$180$
$P = \mathbf{\$108}$

11. $W_N = 0.2 \times \$35$
$W_N = \mathbf{\$7}$

12. a. $(3 \text{ in.})(3 \text{ in.}) = 9 \text{ in.}^2$
$$\frac{9 \text{ in.}^2}{1 \text{ layer}} \cdot (1 \text{ in.})(3 \text{ layers})$$
$$= \mathbf{27 \text{ in.}^3}$$

b. $6(9 \text{ in.}^2) = \mathbf{54 \text{ in.}^2}$

13. a. $C \approx \frac{22}{7}(14 \text{ m})$
$C \approx \mathbf{44 \text{ m}}$

b. $C = \pi(14 \text{ m})$
$C = \mathbf{14\pi \text{ m}}$

14. a. $3\frac{1}{2} = \mathbf{3.5}$

b. $3\frac{1}{2} = \frac{7}{2} \times 100\% = \frac{700\%}{2} = \mathbf{350\%}$

c. $35\% = \frac{35}{100} = \frac{\mathbf{7}}{\mathbf{20}}$

d. $35\% = \frac{35}{100} = \mathbf{0.35}$

15. To find *y*, multiply *x* by 3 and add 1.

$y = 3x + 1$

x	y
0	1
2	7
4	13
5	16
8	**25**

$y = 3(8) + 1$
$y = 24 + 1$
$y = 25$

16. 4.25×10^8

17. a. Parallelogram

b. Trapezoid

c. Isosceles triangle

18. a. $m\angle ABC = 180° - 100° = \mathbf{80°}$

b. $m\angle BCE = m\angle A = \mathbf{100°}$

c. $m\angle ECD = 180° - 100° = \mathbf{80°}$

d. $m\angle EDC = m\angle ECD = \mathbf{80°}$

e. $m\angle DEC = 180° - (80° + 80°)$
$$= 180° - 160° = \mathbf{20°}$$

f. $m\angle DEA = 20° + 80° = \mathbf{100°}$

19. 0.0103, 0.013, 0.021, 0.1023

20. $\left(1\frac{1}{2} + 2\frac{2}{3}\right) - \left(1\frac{1}{2}\right)\left(2\frac{2}{3}\right)$

$$= \left(\frac{3}{2} + \frac{8}{3}\right) - \left(\frac{3}{2}\right)\left(\frac{8}{3}\right)$$

$$= \left(\frac{3}{2} + \frac{8}{3}\right) - (4)$$

$$= \frac{9}{6} + \frac{16}{6} - \frac{24}{6}$$

$$= \frac{25}{6} - \frac{24}{6} = \mathbf{\frac{1}{6}}$$

21. $p + 3\frac{1}{5} = 7\frac{1}{2}$

$p + 3\frac{1}{5} - 3\frac{1}{5} = 7\frac{1}{2} - 3\frac{1}{5}$

$$p = \frac{15}{2} - \frac{16}{5}$$

$$p = \frac{75}{10} - \frac{32}{10}$$

$$p = \frac{43}{10} = \mathbf{4\frac{3}{10}}$$

check: $4\frac{3}{10} + 3\frac{1}{5} = 7\frac{1}{2}$

$4\frac{3}{10} + 3\frac{2}{10} = 7\frac{1}{2}$

$7\frac{5}{10} = 7\frac{1}{2}$

$7\frac{1}{2} = 7\frac{1}{2}$

22. $3n = 0.138$

$\frac{3n}{3} = \frac{0.138}{3}$

$n = \mathbf{0.046}$

check: $3(0.046) = 0.138$

$0.138 = 0.138$

23. $n - 0.36 = 4.8$

$n - 0.36 + 0.36 = 4.8 + 0.36$

$n = \mathbf{5.16}$

check: $5.16 - 0.36 = 4.8$

$4.8 = 4.8$

24. $\frac{2}{3}x = \frac{8}{9}$

$\left(\frac{\cancel{3}^{1}}{\cancel{2}_{1}}\right)\left(\frac{\cancel{2}^{1}}{\cancel{3}_{1}}x\right) = \left(\frac{\cancel{3}^{1}}{\cancel{2}_{1}}\right)\left(\frac{\cancel{8}^{4}}{\cancel{9}_{3}}\right)$

$$x = \mathbf{\frac{4}{3}}$$

check: $\left(\frac{2}{3}\right)\left(\frac{4}{3}\right) = \frac{8}{9}$

$\frac{8}{9} = \frac{8}{9}$

25. $\sqrt{49} + \{5[3^2 - (2^3 - \sqrt{25})] - 5^2\}$

$7 + \{5[9 - (8 - 5)] - 25\}$

$7 + \{5[9 - (3)] - 25\}$

$7 + \{5[6] - 25\}$

$7 + \{30 - 25\}$

$7 + \{5\}$

$\mathbf{12}$

26.

$\overset{\displaystyle\nearrow \text{(60 min)}}{}\ \overset{\displaystyle\nearrow\text{(60 s)}}{}$

$\overset{3}{\cancel{4}}\text{ hr }\ \overset{4}{\cancel{5}}\text{ min }15\text{ s} \longrightarrow$

$-\ 1\text{ hr }15\text{ min }30\text{ s}$

$\overset{3}{\cancel{4}}\text{ hr }\ \overset{64}{\cancel{5}}\text{ min }\overset{75}{\cancel{15}}\text{ s}$

$-\ 1\text{ hr }15\text{ min }30\text{ s}$

$\mathbf{2\text{ hr }\ 49\text{ min }\ 45\text{ s}}$

27. a. $(-9) + (-11) - (+14)$

$(-9) + (-11) + [-(+14)]$

$(-9) + (-11) + [-14]$

$\mathbf{-34}$

b. $(26) + (-43) - |-36|$

$(26) + (-43) + [-|-36|]$

$(26) + (-43) + [-36]$

$\mathbf{-53}$

28. a. $(-3)(1.2) = \mathbf{-3.6}$

b. $(-3)(-12) = \mathbf{36}$

c. $\dfrac{-12}{3} = \mathbf{-4}$

d. $\dfrac{-1.2}{-3} = \mathbf{0.4}$

29. $7.5 = 7\frac{1}{2}$

$8\frac{1}{3} + 7\frac{1}{2} = 8\frac{2}{6} + 7\frac{3}{6} = \mathbf{15\frac{5}{6}}$

30. South

Early Finishers Solutions

a. $\frac{4}{5} \cdot 15 = 12$; $12 \times \$35 = \$420$

b. $\$420 - \$366 = \$54$; $\$54 \div \$3 = \$18$

Solutions

a.

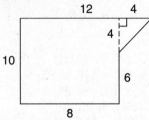

Area of rectangle = (8 cm)(10 cm)
= 80 cm²

$$\text{Area of triangle} = \frac{(4\text{ cm})(4\text{ cm})}{2}$$
= 8 cm²

Area of figure = 80 cm² + 8 cm²
= **88 cm²**

b.

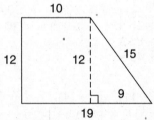

Area of rectangle = (10 cm)(12 cm)
= 120 cm²

$$\text{Area of triangle} = \frac{(9\text{ cm})(12\text{ cm})}{2}$$
= 54 cm²

Area of figure = 120 cm² + 54 cm²
= **174 cm²**

c.

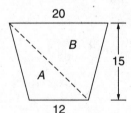

$$\text{Area of triangle } A = \frac{(12\text{ cm})(15\text{ cm})}{2}$$
= 90 cm²

$$\text{Area of triangle } B = \frac{(20\text{ cm})(15\text{ cm})}{2}$$
= 150 cm²

Area of figure = 90 cm² + 150 cm²
= **240 cm²**

d. $A = \frac{1}{2}(b_1 + b_2)h$

or

$A = \frac{(b_1 + b_2)h}{2}$

e. Round the bases to 3 inches and 5 inches. Find the average length of the base, which is 4 inches. Multiply the average base by the height.

$A \approx (4\text{ in.})(3\text{ in.})$
$A \approx$ **12 in.²**

1. 5(72 seconds) + 3(80 seconds)
= 360 seconds + 240 seconds

= 600 seconds $\frac{600\text{ seconds}}{8}$ = **75 seconds**

2. $\frac{\$2.49}{30\text{ ounces}} = \frac{\$0.083}{1\text{ ounce}}$
8.3¢ per ounce

3. 1500 m̶ $\times \frac{1\text{ km}}{1000\text{ m̶}}$ = **1.5 kilometers**

4. $\left(\frac{1}{2} + \frac{3}{5}\right) - \left(\frac{1}{2}\right)\left(\frac{3}{5}\right)$

$= \left(\frac{5}{10} + \frac{6}{10}\right) - \left(\frac{3}{10}\right)$

$= \frac{11}{10} - \frac{3}{10} = \frac{8}{10}$

$= \frac{4}{5}$

5. $\frac{3}{2} = \frac{60\text{ years}}{C}$
$3C = 2(60\text{ years})$
$C = 40\text{ years}$
60 years
− 40 years
20 years

6. 12.5×10^{-4} ⊜ 1.25×10^{-3}

7.

	Case 1	Case 2
Miles	40	100
Hours	3	h

$\frac{40}{3} = \frac{100}{h}$
$40h = 3(100)$
$h = \frac{300}{40}$
$h = \frac{15}{2} = 7\frac{1}{2}$ **hours**

Saxon Math Course 2 278 © Harcourt Achieve, Inc. and Stephen Hake. All rights reserved.

8.

	21,000 books
$\frac{2}{5}$ were checked out.	4200 books
	4200 books
$\frac{3}{5}$ were not checked out.	4200 books
	4200 books
	4200 books

a. **8400 books**

b. **12,600 books**

9. $60 = \dfrac{5}{12} \times W_N$

$\dfrac{12}{\underset{1}{\cancel{5}}}(\overset{12}{\cancel{60}}) = \dfrac{\overset{1}{\cancel{12}}}{\underset{1}{\cancel{5}}} \times \dfrac{\overset{1}{\cancel{5}}}{\underset{1}{\cancel{12}}} \times W_N$

$\quad\quad **144** = W_N$

10. $0.7 \times \$35.00 = M$
$\quad\quad\quad **\$24.50** = M$

11. $35 = W_F \times 80$

$\dfrac{35}{80} = \dfrac{W_F \times 80}{80}$

$\dfrac{\mathbf{7}}{\mathbf{16}} = W_F$

12. $56 = W_D \times 70$

$\dfrac{56}{70} = \dfrac{W_D \times 70}{70}$

$\mathbf{0.8} = W_D$

13. a. $\dfrac{-120}{4} = \mathbf{-30}$

b. $\left(-\dfrac{1}{2}\right)\left(\dfrac{2}{3}\right) = \mathbf{-\dfrac{1}{3}}$

c. $\dfrac{-120}{-5} = \mathbf{24}$

d. $\left(-\dfrac{1}{3}\right)\left(-\dfrac{3}{4}\right) = \mathbf{\dfrac{1}{4}}$

14. $(20\text{ cm})(15\text{ cm}) = 300\text{ cm}^2$

$\dfrac{300\text{ cm}^2}{1\text{ layer}} \cdot (1\text{ cm})(10\text{ layers})$

3000 cm³

15. $C \approx \dfrac{22}{7}(11\text{ inches})$

$C \approx \dfrac{242}{7}\text{ inches}$

$C \approx 34\dfrac{4}{7}\text{ inches} \approx \mathbf{34\dfrac{1}{2}\text{ inches}}$

16. $A = \dfrac{1}{2}(b_1 + b_2)h$

$A = \dfrac{1}{2}(10\text{ ft} + 14\text{ ft})8\text{ ft}$

$A = \dfrac{1}{2}(24\text{ ft})8\text{ ft}$

$A = \mathbf{96\text{ ft}^2}$

17.
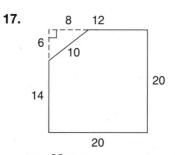

a. **20 cm**

b. Perimeter $= 12\text{ cm} + 20\text{ cm} + 20\text{ cm}$
$+ 14\text{ cm} + 10\text{ cm} = \mathbf{76\text{ cm}}$

c. Area of square $= (20\text{ cm})(20\text{ cm})$
$= 400\text{ cm}^2$

Area of triangle $= \dfrac{(8\text{ cm})(6\text{ cm})}{2}$
$= 24\text{ cm}^2$

Area of figure $= 400\text{ cm}^2 - 24\text{ cm}^2$
$= \mathbf{376\text{ cm}^2}$

18. a. $125\% = \dfrac{125}{100} = \mathbf{1\dfrac{1}{4}}$

b. $125\% = \dfrac{125}{100} = \mathbf{1.25}$

c. $8\overline{)1.000}$ with quotient **0.125**

d. $\dfrac{1}{8} \times 100\% = \dfrac{100\%}{8} = \mathbf{12\dfrac{1}{2}\%}$
$\text{or } \mathbf{12.5\%}$

19.
$$\begin{array}{r} \$12.50 \\ \times\quad 0.20 \\ \hline \$\;2.50 \end{array} \qquad \begin{array}{r} \$12.50 \\ +\;\$\;2.50 \\ \hline \mathbf{\$15.00} \end{array}$$

20. $(2)^3 - (2)(0.5) - \dfrac{2}{0.5}$

$= 8 - 1 - 4 = \mathbf{3}$

Solutions

21.

$$\frac{5}{8}x = 40$$

$$\left(\frac{\overset{1}{\cancel{8}}}{\cancel{5}}\right)\frac{\overset{1}{\cancel{5}}}{\cancel{8}}x = \left(\frac{8}{\cancel{5}}\right)\overset{8}{\cancel{40}}$$

$$x = \mathbf{64}$$

check: $\dfrac{5}{\cancel{8}}(\overset{8}{\cancel{64}}) = 40$

$$5(8) = 40$$
$$40 = 40$$

22.

$$1.2w = 26.4$$

$$\frac{1.2w}{1.2} = \frac{26.4}{1.2}$$

$$w = \mathbf{22}$$

check: $\quad 1.2(22) = 26.4$

$$26.4 = 26.4$$

23.

$$y + 3.6 = 8.47$$

$$y + 3.6 - 3.6 = 8.47 - 3.6$$

$$y = \mathbf{4.87}$$

check: $\quad 4.87 + 3.6 = 8.47$

$$8.47 = 8.47$$

24. $9^2 - [3^3 - (9 \cdot 3 - \sqrt{9})]$

$$81 - [27 - (27 - 3)]$$

$$81 - [27 - (24)]$$

$$81 - [3]$$

$$\mathbf{78}$$

25.

$$\begin{array}{l}
\overset{47}{} \longrightarrow (60\ s) \\
2\ \text{hr}\ \overset{47}{\cancel{48}}\ \text{min}\ 20\ s \\
-\ 1\ \text{hr}\ 23\ \text{min}\ 48\ s \longrightarrow \\
\hline
2\ \text{hr}\ \overset{47}{\cancel{48}}\ \text{min}\ \overset{80}{\cancel{20}}\ s \\
-\ 1\ \text{hr}\ 23\ \text{min}\ 48\ s \\
\hline
\mathbf{1\ hr\ 24\ min\ 32\ s}
\end{array}$$

26. $100\ \text{yd} \cdot \dfrac{3\ \text{ft}}{1\ \text{yd}} \cdot \dfrac{12\ \text{in.}}{1\ \text{ft}}$

$$= \mathbf{3600\ in.}$$

27. $3 \div 1\dfrac{1}{3} = \dfrac{3}{1} \div \dfrac{4}{3}$

$$= \frac{3}{1} \times \frac{3}{4} = \frac{9}{4}$$

$$5\frac{1}{3} \cdot \frac{9}{4} = \frac{\overset{4}{\cancel{16}}}{\cancel{3}} \cdot \frac{\overset{3}{\cancel{9}}}{\cancel{4}} = \mathbf{12}$$

28. $3\dfrac{1}{5} + 2\dfrac{1}{2} - 1\dfrac{1}{4}$

$$= 3\frac{4}{20} + 2\frac{10}{20} - 1\frac{5}{20}$$

$$= 5\frac{14}{20} - 1\frac{5}{20} = \mathbf{4\frac{9}{20}}$$

29. a. $(-26) + (-15) - (-40)$

$$(-26) + (-15) + [-(-40)]$$

$$(-26) + (-15) + [40]$$

$$\mathbf{-1}$$

b. $(-5) + (-4) - (-3) - (+2)$

$$(-5) + (-4) + [-(-3)] + [-(+2)]$$

$$(-5) + (-4) + [3] + [-2]$$

$$\mathbf{-8}$$

30. a. 5^7

b. 5^3

c. 5^0

d. 5^{-3}

EARLY FINISHERS SOLUTIONS

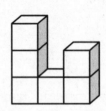

Practice Set 76

a. $\quad \dfrac{37\frac{1}{2}}{100} = \dfrac{\frac{75}{2}}{\frac{100}{1}}$

$$\frac{\frac{75}{2}}{\frac{100}{1}} \cdot \frac{\frac{1}{100}}{\frac{1}{100}} = \frac{\frac{75}{200}}{1} = \frac{75}{200}$$

$$= \frac{3}{8}$$

b. $\quad \dfrac{12}{\frac{5}{6}} = \dfrac{\frac{12}{1}}{\frac{5}{6}}$

$$\frac{\frac{12}{1}}{\frac{5}{6}} \cdot \frac{\frac{6}{5}}{\frac{6}{5}} = \frac{\frac{72}{5}}{1} = \frac{72}{5} = \mathbf{14\frac{2}{5}}$$

c. $\quad \dfrac{\frac{2}{5}}{\frac{2}{3}} \cdot \dfrac{\frac{3}{2}}{\frac{3}{2}} = \dfrac{\frac{6}{10}}{1} = \dfrac{6}{10} = \mathbf{\dfrac{3}{5}}$

d. $66\frac{2}{3}\% = \dfrac{66\frac{2}{3}}{100} = \dfrac{\frac{200}{3}}{\frac{100}{1}}$

$\dfrac{\frac{200}{3}}{\frac{100}{1}} \cdot \dfrac{\frac{1}{100}}{\frac{1}{100}} = \dfrac{\frac{200}{300}}{1} = \dfrac{200}{300} = \dfrac{2}{3}$

e. $8\frac{1}{3}\% = \dfrac{8\frac{1}{3}}{100} = \dfrac{\frac{25}{3}}{\frac{100}{1}}$

$\dfrac{\frac{25}{3}}{\frac{100}{1}} \cdot \dfrac{\frac{1}{100}}{\frac{1}{100}} = \dfrac{\frac{25}{300}}{1} = \dfrac{25}{300} = \dfrac{1}{12}$

f. $4\frac{1}{6}\% = \dfrac{4\frac{1}{6}}{100} = \dfrac{\frac{25}{6}}{\frac{100}{1}}$

$\dfrac{\frac{25}{6}}{\frac{100}{1}} \cdot \dfrac{\frac{1}{100}}{\frac{1}{100}} = \dfrac{\frac{25}{600}}{1} = \dfrac{25}{600} = \dfrac{1}{24}$

g. **Inverse property and identity property**

Written Practice **76**

1. $\dfrac{42 \text{ kilometers}}{1.75 \text{ hours}}$ = **24 kilometers per hour**

2.
$$\begin{array}{r} 7.9 \\ 8.3 \\ 8.1 \\ 8.1 \\ + \ 8.2 \\ \hline 40.6 \end{array} \qquad \begin{array}{r} 8.12 \\ 5\overline{)40.60} \end{array}$$

3.

	Ratio	Actual Count
Good guys	2	G
Bad guys	5	B
Total	7	35

$\dfrac{2}{7} = \dfrac{G}{35}$

$7G = 35(2)$

$G = \dfrac{70}{7}$

$G =$ **10 guys**

4. $3.5 \text{ grams} \cdot \dfrac{1000 \text{ milligrams}}{1 \text{ gram}}$

$=$ **3500 milligrams**

5. $16\frac{2}{3}\% = \dfrac{16\frac{2}{3}}{100} = \dfrac{\frac{50}{3}}{\frac{100}{1}}$

$\dfrac{\frac{50}{3}}{\frac{100}{1}} \cdot \dfrac{\frac{1}{100}}{\frac{1}{100}} = \dfrac{\frac{50}{300}}{1} = \dfrac{50}{300} = \dfrac{1}{6}$

6. **East**

7. $\dfrac{1}{\overset{}{\underset{1}{\cancel{6}}}} \times \overset{24}{\cancel{144}} \text{ grams} =$ **24 grams**

8. **a.** $\sqrt{2(2)^3} = \sqrt{2^4} = 2^2 =$ **4**

  b. $(2)^{-1} \cdot (2)^{-2} = \dfrac{1}{2} \cdot \dfrac{1}{4} = \dfrac{1}{8}$

9. **a.** $\dfrac{-60}{-12} =$ **5**

  b. $\left(-\dfrac{1}{2}\right)\left(\dfrac{1}{2}\right) = -\dfrac{1}{4}$

  c. $\dfrac{40}{-8} =$ **−5**

  d. $\left(-\dfrac{1}{4}\right)\left(-\dfrac{1}{4}\right) = \dfrac{1}{16}$

10. $C = \pi(30 \text{ cm})$
$C =$ **30π cm**

11.

  a. **5 faces**

  b. **8 edges**

  c. **5 vertices**

12. $W_N = 0.1 \times \$37.50$
$W_N =$ **\$3.75**

13. $W_N = \dfrac{5}{\underset{1}{\cancel{8}}} \times \overset{9}{\cancel{72}}$

$W_N =$ **45**

Solutions

14. $25 = W_F \times 60$

$\dfrac{25}{60} = \dfrac{W_F \times 60}{60}$

$\dfrac{5}{12} = W_F$

15. $60 = W_D \times 80$

$\dfrac{60}{80} = \dfrac{W_D \times 80}{80}$

$\mathbf{0.75} = W_D$

16. a. $m\angle ACB = 180° - 115° = \mathbf{65°}$

b. $m\angle ABC = m\angle ACB = \mathbf{65°}$

c. $m\angle CAB = 180° - (65° + 65°)$
$= 180° - 130° = \mathbf{50°}$

17. a. $6\overline{)5.00\ldots}\ \ \ \overset{0.83\ldots}{}$ $\mathbf{0.8\overline{3}}$

b. $\dfrac{5}{6} \times 100\% = \dfrac{500\%}{6} = \mathbf{83\dfrac{1}{3}\%}$

c. $0.1\% = \dfrac{0.1}{100} = \dfrac{1}{\mathbf{1000}}$

d. $0.1\% = \dfrac{0.1}{100} = \mathbf{0.001}$

18.

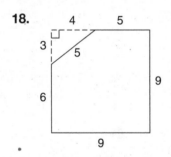

a. Perimeter $=$ 5 in. $+$ 9 in. $+$ 9 in.
$+$ 6 in. $+$ 5 in. $=$ **34 in.**

b. Area of square $=$ (9 in.)(9 in.)
$=$ 81 in.²
Area of triangle $= \dfrac{(4 \text{ in.})(3 \text{ in.})}{2}$
$=$ 6 in.²
Area of figure $=$ 81 in.² $-$ 6 in.²
$=$ **75 in.²**

19. Rectangle

20. $\begin{array}{r} 212°F \\ +\ 32\ F \\ \hline 244°F \end{array}$ $\dfrac{244°F}{2} = \mathbf{122°F}$

21. $x - 25 = 96$
$x - 25 + 25 = 96 + 25$
$x = \mathbf{121}$

check: $121 - 25 = 96$
$96 = 96$

22. $\dfrac{2}{3}m = 12$

$\left(\dfrac{\overset{1}{\cancel{3}}}{\underset{1}{\cancel{2}}}\right)\dfrac{\overset{1}{\cancel{2}}}{\underset{1}{\cancel{3}}}m = \left(\dfrac{3}{\cancel{2}}\right)\overset{6}{\cancel{12}}$

$m = \mathbf{18}$

check: $\dfrac{2}{\underset{1}{\cancel{3}}}(\overset{6}{\cancel{18}}) = 12$

$2(6) = 12$
$12 = 12$

23. $2.5p = 6.25$

$\dfrac{2.5p}{2.5} = \dfrac{6.25}{2.5}$

$p = \mathbf{2.5}$

check: $(2.5)(2.5) = 6.25$
$6.25 = 6.25$

24. $10 = f + 3\dfrac{1}{3}$

$10 - 3\dfrac{1}{3} = f + 3\dfrac{1}{3} - 3\dfrac{1}{3}$

$9\dfrac{3}{3} - 3\dfrac{1}{3} = f$

$\mathbf{6\dfrac{2}{3}} = f$

check: $10 = 6\dfrac{2}{3} + 3\dfrac{1}{3}$

$10 = 9\dfrac{3}{3}$

$10 = 10$

25. $\sqrt{13^2 - 5^2} = \sqrt{169 - 25}$
$= \sqrt{144} = \mathbf{12}$

26. 1 ton $=$ 2000 lb
2000 lb $-$ 400 lb $=$ **1600 lb**

282

27. $3\frac{3}{4} \times 4\frac{1}{6} \times (0.4)^2$

$= \frac{15}{4} \times \frac{25}{6} \times \left(\frac{4}{10}\right)^2$

$= \frac{\overset{5}{\cancel{15}}}{\underset{1}{\cancel{4}}} \times \frac{25}{\underset{2}{\cancel{6}}} \times \frac{\overset{1}{\cancel{16}}}{\underset{1}{\cancel{100}}}$

$= \frac{5}{2} = \mathbf{2\frac{1}{2}}$

28. $3\frac{1}{8} + 6.7 + 8\frac{1}{4}$

$= 3.125 + 6.7 + 8.25 = \mathbf{18.075}$

29. a. $(-3) + (-5) - (-3) - |+5|$
$(-3) + (-5) + [-(-3)] + [-|+5|]$
$(-3) + (-5) + [3] + [-5]$
$\mathbf{-10}$

b. $(-2.4) - (+1.2)$
$(-2.4) + [-(+1.2)]$
$(-2.4) + [-1.2]$
$\mathbf{-3.6}$

30. The quotient is a little more than 1 because the dividend is slightly greater than the divisor.

$\frac{\frac{5}{6}}{\frac{2}{3}} \cdot \frac{\frac{3}{2}}{\frac{3}{2}} = \frac{\frac{15}{12}}{1} = \frac{15}{12} = \frac{5}{4} = \mathbf{1\frac{1}{4}}$

Practice Set 77

a. $24 = W_P \times 40$

$\frac{\overset{3}{\cancel{24}}}{\underset{5}{\cancel{40}}} = \frac{W_P \times \overset{1}{\cancel{40}}}{\underset{1}{\cancel{40}}}$

$\frac{3}{5} = W_P$

$W_P = \frac{3}{5} \times 100\% = \mathbf{60\%}$

b. $W_P \times 6 = 2$

$\frac{W_P \times \overset{1}{\cancel{6}}}{\underset{1}{\cancel{6}}} = \frac{\overset{1}{\cancel{2}}}{\underset{3}{\cancel{6}}}$

$W_P = \frac{1}{3}$

$W_P = \frac{1}{3} \times 100\% = \mathbf{33\frac{1}{3}\%}$

c. $\frac{15}{100} \times W_N = 45$

$\frac{\overset{1}{\cancel{15}}}{\underset{1}{\cancel{100}}} \cdot \frac{\overset{1}{\cancel{100}}}{\underset{1}{\cancel{15}}} \times W_N = \overset{3}{\cancel{45}} \cdot \frac{100}{\underset{1}{\cancel{15}}}$

$W_N = \mathbf{300}$

d. $W_P \times 4 = 6$

$\frac{W_P \times 4}{4} = \frac{\overset{3}{\cancel{6}}}{\underset{2}{\cancel{4}}}$

$W_P = \frac{3}{2} \times 100\% = \mathbf{150\%}$

e. $24 = 120\% \times W_N$

$24 = \frac{120}{100} \times W_N$

$\frac{\overset{20}{\cancel{100}}}{\underset{\underset{1}{\cancel{10}}}{\cancel{120}}} \times \overset{\overset{1}{\cancel{2}}}{\cancel{24}} = \frac{\overset{1}{\cancel{100}}}{\underset{1}{\cancel{120}}} \times \frac{\overset{1}{\cancel{120}}}{\underset{1}{\cancel{100}}} \times W_N$

$\mathbf{20} = W_N$

f. $60 = \frac{\overset{3}{\cancel{150}}}{\underset{2}{\cancel{100}}} \times W_N$

$60 = \frac{3}{2} \times W_N$

$\frac{2}{3} \times \overset{20}{\cancel{60}} = \left(\frac{\overset{1}{\cancel{2}}}{\underset{1}{\cancel{3}}}\right)\left(\frac{\overset{1}{\cancel{3}}}{\underset{1}{\cancel{2}}}\right) \times W_N$

$\mathbf{40} = W_N$

g. $W_P \times \$5.00 = \$0.35$

$\frac{W_P \times \overset{1}{\cancel{\$5.00}}}{\underset{1}{\cancel{\$5.00}}} = \frac{\$0.35}{\$5.00}$

$W_P = 0.07$
$W_P = 0.07 \times 100\% = \mathbf{7\%}$

Written Practice 77

1.

	Ratio	Actual Count
Nickels	2	70
Pennies	5	P
Total	7	T

$\frac{2}{7} = \frac{70}{T}$

$2T = 7(70)$

$T = \frac{490}{2}$

$T = \mathbf{245\ coins}$

Solutions

2. 0.8(50 questions) = **40 questions**

3.
$$6\overline{)510\%} = 85\%$$

	80%
	75%
	80%
	95%
	80%
+	100%
	510%

4. **a.** **80%**

    b. 100% − 75% = **25%**

5. **a.** **Sphere**

    b. **Cylinder**

    c. **Rectangular prism**

6.

	Case 1	Case 2
Inches	100	250
Centimeters	254	C

$$\frac{100}{254} = \frac{250}{C}$$
$$100C = (254)(250)$$
$$C = \frac{63500}{100}$$
$$C = \textbf{635 centimeters}$$

7.

30 people

$\frac{3}{5}$ agreed.
$\left\{\begin{array}{l}\text{6 people}\\\text{6 people}\\\text{6 people}\end{array}\right.$

$\frac{2}{5}$ disagreed.
$\left\{\begin{array}{l}\text{6 people}\\\text{6 people}\end{array}\right.$

    a. $\frac{2}{5}$

    b. 12 ÷ 2 = 6, 6(5 people) = **30 people**

    c. 3(6 people) = **18 people**

    d. $\dfrac{\text{agreed}}{\text{disagreed}} = \dfrac{18}{12} = \dfrac{3}{2}$

8.
$$40 = \frac{4}{25} \times W_N$$
$$\frac{25}{4} \times 40 = \frac{25}{4} \times \frac{4}{25} \times W_N$$
$$250 = W_N$$

9. 0.24 × 10,000 = W_N

    2400 = W_N

10. 0.12 × W_N = 240
$$\frac{0.12 \times W_N}{0.12} = \frac{240}{0.12}$$
$$W_N = \textbf{2000}$$

11. 20 = W_P × 25
$$\frac{20}{25} = \frac{W_P \times 25}{25}$$
$$\frac{4}{5} = W_P$$
$$W_P = \frac{4}{5} \times 100\% = \textbf{80\%}$$

12. **a.** (2.5)(−5) = **−1.25**

    b. (−1.5)(−5) = **7.5**

    c. $\dfrac{-250}{-5} = \textbf{50}$

    d. $\dfrac{-225}{15} = \textbf{−15}$

13. **a.** $0.2 = \dfrac{2}{10} = \dfrac{1}{5}$

    b. $0.2 = \dfrac{2}{10} = \dfrac{20}{100} = \textbf{20\%}$

    c. $2\% = \dfrac{2}{100} = \dfrac{1}{50}$

    d. $2\% = \dfrac{2}{100} = \textbf{0.02}$

14.

	$21.00
×	0.075
	$1.575 ⟶ $1.58

	$21.00
+	$ 1.58
	$22.58

15. **a.**
$$\frac{14\frac{2}{7}}{100} = \frac{\frac{100}{7}}{\frac{100}{1}}$$

$$\frac{\frac{100}{7}}{\frac{100}{1}} \cdot \frac{\frac{1}{100}}{\frac{1}{100}} = \frac{\frac{100}{700}}{1} = \frac{100}{700} = \frac{1}{7}$$

    b.
$$\frac{60}{\frac{2}{3}} = \frac{\frac{60}{1}}{\frac{2}{3}}$$

$$\frac{\frac{60}{1}}{\frac{2}{3}} \cdot \frac{\frac{3}{2}}{\frac{3}{2}} = \frac{\frac{180}{2}}{1} = \frac{180}{2} = \textbf{90}$$

16.

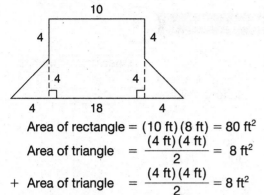

Area of rectangle = (10 ft)(8 ft) = 80 ft²

Area of triangle = $\dfrac{(4\text{ ft})(4\text{ ft})}{2}$ = 8 ft²

+ Area of triangle = $\dfrac{(4\text{ ft})(4\text{ ft})}{2}$ = 8 ft²

Area of figure = **96 ft²**

17.

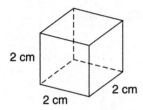

a. (2 cm)(2 cm) = 4 cm²

$\dfrac{4\text{ cm}^2}{1\text{ layer}}$ · 1 cm(2 layers) = **8 cm³**

b. One way to find the surface area of a cube is to find the area of one face of the cube and then multiply that area by 6.

18. **1.2 × 10¹⁰**

19. a. $C = \pi(20\text{ mm})$

$C = \textbf{20}\boldsymbol{\pi}$ **mm**

b. $C \approx 3.14(20\text{ mm})$

$C \approx \textbf{62.8 mm}$

20. $3x = 26.7$

$\dfrac{\cancel{3}x}{\cancel{3}} = \dfrac{\overset{8.9}{\cancel{26.7}}}{\cancel{3}}$

$x = \textbf{8.9}$

check: $3(8.9) = 26.7$

$26.7 = 26.7$

21. $y - 3\frac{1}{3} = 7$

$y - 3\frac{1}{3} + 3\frac{1}{3} = 7 + 3\frac{1}{3}$

$y = \mathbf{10\frac{1}{3}}$

check: $10\frac{1}{3} - 3\frac{1}{3} = 7$

$7 = 7$

22. $\dfrac{2}{3}x = 48$

$\left(\dfrac{\overset{1}{\cancel{3}}}{\cancel{2}}\right)\left(\dfrac{\overset{1}{\cancel{2}}}{\cancel{3}}\right)x = \left(\dfrac{3}{\cancel{2}}\right)\overset{24}{\cancel{48}}$

$x = \textbf{72}$

check: $\dfrac{2}{\cancel{3}}(\overset{24}{\cancel{72}}) = 48$

$2(24) = 48$

$48 = 48$

23. To find *y*, multiply *x* by 4 and add 1.

$y = 4x + 1$

x	y
3	13
1	5
2	9
4	17
0	**1**

$y = 4(0) + 1$

$y = 1$

24. $5^2 - \{2^3 + 3[4^2 - (4)(\sqrt{9})]\}$

$25 - \{8 + 3[16 - (4)(3)]\}$

$25 - \{8 + 3[16 - 12]\}$

$25 - \{8 + 3[4]\}$

$25 - \{8 + 12\}$

$25 - 20$

5

25.

```
      4 gal   3 qt   1 pt
    + 1 gal   2 qt   1 pt
      5 gal   5 qt   2 pt
```

2 pt = 1 qt, 5 qt + 1 qt = 6 qt

6 qt = 1 gal 2 qt

```
      1 gal   2 qt
    + 5 gal
      6 gal   2 qt
```

26. $1\text{ ft}^2 \cdot \dfrac{12\text{ in.}}{1\text{ ft}} \cdot \dfrac{12\text{ in.}}{1\text{ ft}}$

= **144 in.²**

27. $1\dfrac{1}{3} \div 3 = \dfrac{4}{3} \div \dfrac{3}{1} = \dfrac{4}{3} \times \dfrac{1}{3} = \dfrac{4}{9}$

$5\dfrac{1}{3} \div \dfrac{4}{9} = \dfrac{16}{3} \div \dfrac{4}{9} = \dfrac{\overset{4}{\cancel{16}}}{\cancel{3}} \times \dfrac{\overset{3}{\cancel{9}}}{\cancel{4}} = \textbf{12}$

28. $3\dfrac{1}{5} - 2\dfrac{1}{2} + 1\dfrac{1}{4} = \left(\dfrac{16}{5} - \dfrac{5}{2}\right) + \dfrac{5}{4}$

$= \left(\dfrac{64}{20} - \dfrac{50}{20}\right) + \dfrac{25}{20} = \dfrac{14}{20} + \dfrac{25}{20}$

$= \dfrac{39}{20} = \mathbf{1\dfrac{19}{20}}$

     285

Solutions

29.
$$2.5 = 2\frac{1}{2}$$

$$3\frac{1}{3} \div 2\frac{1}{2} = \frac{10}{3} \div \frac{5}{2}$$

$$= \frac{\overset{2}{\cancel{10}}}{3} \times \frac{2}{\cancel{5}} = \frac{4}{3} = 1\frac{1}{3}$$

30. a. $(-3) + (-4) - (+5)$
$(-3) + (-4) + [-(+5)]$
$(-3) + (-4) + [-5]$
−12

b. $(-6) - (-16) - (+30)$
$(-6) + [-(-16)] + [-(+30)]$
$(-6) + [16] + [-30]$
−20

Early Finishers Solutions

$$\underset{\text{mode}}{1, \overbrace{10, 10}}, 12, 16, \overset{\underset{\downarrow}{\text{median}}}{\boxed{31}}, 35, 40, 65, 75, 90$$

median = 31
mode = 10
mean
$$= \frac{1 + 10 + 10 + 12 + 16 + 31 + 35 + 40 + 65 + 75 + 90}{11}$$
$$= 35$$
range = 90 − 1 = 89
The range shows that the ages of the people at the dinner included young children, preteens, younger adults, middle-aged people, and senior citizens.

Practice Set 78

a. number line −1 0 1 2 3

b. number line 0 1 2 3 4

c. number line −4 −3 −2 −1 0

d. number line −2 −1 0 1 2

e. A dot means the number is included in the graph. An empty circle means the number is excluded.

Written Practice 78

1.

	Case 1	Case 2
Cartons	4	C
Hungry children	30	75

$$\frac{4}{30} = \frac{C}{75}$$
$$30C = 4(75)$$
$$C = \frac{300}{30}$$
$$C = \textbf{10 cartons}$$

2. $4(88) = 352, 6(90) = 540$

$$\begin{array}{r} 540 \\ -\ 352 \\ \hline 188 \end{array} \qquad \begin{array}{r} 94 \\ 2\overline{)188} \end{array}$$

3. $\left(\dfrac{2}{3} + \dfrac{3}{4}\right) \div \left(\dfrac{2}{3} \times \dfrac{3}{4}\right)$

$$= \left(\frac{8}{12} + \frac{9}{12}\right) \div \left(\frac{1}{2}\right)$$
$$= \frac{17}{12} \div \frac{1}{2}$$
$$= \frac{17}{\underset{6}{\cancel{12}}} \times \frac{\overset{1}{\cancel{2}}}{1} = \frac{17}{6} = 2\frac{5}{6}$$

4.

	Ratio	Actual Count
Monocotyledons	3	M
Dicotyledons	4	84

$$\frac{3}{4} = \frac{M}{84}$$
$$4M = 3(84)$$
$$M = \frac{252}{4}$$
$$M = \textbf{63 monocotyledons}$$

5. $C \approx 3.14(21 \text{ millimeters})$
$C \approx 65.94 \text{ millimeters}$
$C \approx \textbf{66 millimeters}$

6. a. number line 1 2 3 4 5

b. number line −2 −1 0 1 2

7. $1.5 \text{ k}\cancel{g} \cdot \dfrac{1000 \text{ g}}{1 \text{ k}\cancel{g}} = \textbf{1500 g}$

8. $\dfrac{5}{\cancel{6}^{1}} \times \cancel{30}^{5} = 25$ preferred Brand X

a. $25 - 5 = 20$
20 more people

b. $\dfrac{\text{preferred Brand } Y}{\text{preferred Brand } X} = \dfrac{5}{25} = \dfrac{1}{5}$

9. $42 = \dfrac{7}{10} \times W_N$

$\left(\dfrac{10}{7}\right)\cancel{42}^{6} = \left(\dfrac{\cancel{10}^{1}}{\cancel{7}^{1}}\right)\dfrac{\cancel{7}^{1}}{\cancel{10}^{1}} \times W_N$

$60 = W_N$

10. $1.5 \times W_N = 600$

$\dfrac{\cancel{1.5}^{1} \times W_N}{\cancel{1.5}^{1}} = \dfrac{600}{1.5}$

$W_N = 400$

11. $0.4 \times 50 = W_N$
$20 = W_N$

12. $40 = W_P \times 50$

$\dfrac{\cancel{40}^{4}}{\cancel{50}^{5}} = \dfrac{W_P \times \cancel{50}^{1}}{\cancel{50}^{1}}$

$\dfrac{4}{5} = W_P$

$W_P = \dfrac{4}{5} \times 100\% = \dfrac{400\%}{5} = \mathbf{80\%}$

13. a. 0.0015

b. 2.5×10^{7}

14. a. $\dfrac{-4.5}{9} = -0.5$

b. $\dfrac{-2.4}{-0.6} = 4$

c. $15(-20) = -300$

d. $(-15)(-12) = 180$

15. a. $50\% = \dfrac{50}{100} = \dfrac{1}{2}$

b. $50\% = \dfrac{50}{100} = 0.5$

c. $12\overline{)1.000\ldots}$ with quotient $0.08\overline{3}$

d. $\dfrac{1}{12} \times 100\% = \dfrac{100\%}{12} = 8\dfrac{1}{3}\%$

16. $\dfrac{83\frac{1}{3}}{100} = \dfrac{\frac{250}{3}}{\frac{100}{1}}$

$\dfrac{\frac{250}{3}}{\frac{100}{1}} \cdot \dfrac{\frac{1}{100}}{\frac{1}{100}} = \dfrac{\frac{250}{300}}{1}$

$= \dfrac{250}{300} = \dfrac{5}{6}$

17. $A = \dfrac{1}{2}(b_1 + b_2)h$

$A = \dfrac{1}{2}(20 \text{ in.} + 30 \text{ in.})(24 \text{ in.})$

$A = \dfrac{1}{2}(50 \text{ in.})(24 \text{ in.})$

$A = \mathbf{600 \text{ in.}^2}$

18.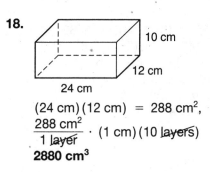

$(24 \text{ cm})(12 \text{ cm}) = 288 \text{ cm}^2,$
$\dfrac{288 \text{ cm}^2}{1 \text{ layer}} \cdot (1 \text{ cm})(10 \text{ layers})$
2880 cm^3

19. One possibility:

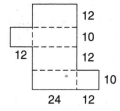

20. To find y, multiply x by 5 and subtract 1.

$y = 5x - 1$

x	y
2	9
3	14
4	**19**
5	24

$y = 5(4) - 1$
$y = 20 - 1$
$y = 19$

21. $\begin{array}{r} \$18.50 \\ \times \quad 0.30 \\ \hline \$5.5500 \end{array} = \mathbf{\$5.55}$

Solutions

22.
$$m + 8.7 = 10.25$$
$$m + 8.7 - 8.7 = 10.25 - 8.7$$
$$m = \mathbf{1.55}$$

check:
$$1.55 + 8.7 = 10.25$$
$$10.25 = 10.25$$

23.
$$\frac{4}{3}w = 36$$

$$\left(\frac{\overset{1}{\cancel{3}}}{\cancel{4}_1}\right)\frac{\overset{1}{\cancel{4}}}{\cancel{3}_1}w = \left(\frac{3}{4}\right)\overset{9}{\cancel{36}}$$

$$w = \mathbf{27}$$

check:
$$\left(\frac{4}{\cancel{3}}\right)\overset{9}{\cancel{27}} = 36$$

$$(4)9 = 36$$
$$36 = 36$$

24.
$$0.7y = 48.3$$
$$\frac{0.7y}{0.7} = \frac{48.3}{0.7}$$
$$y = \mathbf{69}$$

check:
$$0.7(69) = 48.3$$
$$48.3 = 48.3$$

25. $\{4^2 + 10[2^3 - (3)(\sqrt{4})]\} - \sqrt{36}$
$$\{16 + 10[8 - (3)(2)]\} - 6$$
$$\{16 + 10[8 - 6]\} - 6$$
$$\{16 + 10[2]\} - 6$$
$$\{16 + 20\} - 6$$
$$\{36\} - 6$$
$$\mathbf{30}$$

26. $|5 - 3| - |3 - 5|$
$$= |2| - |-2| = 2 - 2 = \mathbf{0}$$

27. $1\ \cancel{m^2} \cdot \dfrac{100\ cm}{1\ \cancel{m}} \cdot \dfrac{100\ cm}{1\ \cancel{m}} = \mathbf{10{,}000\ cm^2}$

28. $7\dfrac{1}{2} \cdot 3 \cdot \left(\dfrac{2}{3}\right)^2 =$

$$\frac{\overset{5}{\cancel{15}}}{\cancel{2}_1} \cdot \frac{\overset{1}{\cancel{3}}}{1} \cdot \frac{\overset{2}{\cancel{4}}}{\underset{\underset{1}{\cancel{3}}}{\cancel{9}}} = \mathbf{10}$$

29. $3\dfrac{1}{5} - \left(2\dfrac{1}{2} - 1\dfrac{1}{4}\right)$

$$= 3\frac{4}{20} - \left(2\frac{10}{20} - 1\frac{5}{20}\right)$$

$$= 3\frac{4}{20} - 1\frac{5}{20} = 2\frac{24}{20} - 1\frac{5}{20}$$

$$= 1\frac{19}{20}$$

30. a. $(-10) - (-8) - (+6)$
$$(-10) + [-(-8)] + [-(+6)]$$
$$(-10) + [8] + [-6]$$
$$\mathbf{-8}$$

b. $\left(-\dfrac{1}{5}\right) + \left(-\dfrac{2}{5}\right) - \left(-\dfrac{3}{5}\right)$

$$\left(-\frac{1}{5}\right) + \left(-\frac{2}{5}\right) + \left[-\left(-\frac{3}{5}\right)\right]$$

$$\left(-\frac{1}{5}\right) + \left(-\frac{2}{5}\right) + \left[\frac{3}{5}\right]$$

$$\mathbf{0}$$

Early Finishers Solutions

a. $(10\ ft)(23\ ft) + (4\ ft)(15\ ft) + \dfrac{1}{2}(3\ ft)(4\ ft)$
$$= \mathbf{296\ ft^2}$$

b. $296\ ft^2 \times \$2.95 = \mathbf{\$873.20}$

Practice Set 79

a. We count 12 whole or nearly whole squares and 4 "half squares" that we count as 2 whole squares. So we estimate the area of the lake as **14 sq. km.**

b. We count 12 whole or nearly whole squares and 4 "half squares" that we count as 2 whole squares. So we estimate the area of the circle as **14 sq. cm.**
The area of the square is 4 sq. cm; **the area of the circle is about 3 times the area of the square.**

Written Practice 79

1. $4(33.5\text{ students}) = 134\text{ students}$

$$5\overline{)134.0} \quad \mathbf{26.8\ students}$$

2. $\dfrac{315\text{ kilometers}}{35\text{ liters}} = \mathbf{9}\ \dfrac{\textbf{kilometers}}{\textbf{liter}}$

3.

	Ratio	Actual Count
Winners	7	W
Losers	5	L
Total	12	1260

$$\frac{7}{12} = \frac{W}{1260}$$

$$12W = 7(1260)$$

$$W = \frac{8820}{12}$$

$$W = 735 \text{ winners}$$

$$\frac{5}{12} = \frac{L}{1260}$$

$$12L = 5(1260)$$

$$L = \frac{6300}{12}$$

$$L = 525 \text{ losers}$$

$$\begin{array}{r} 735 \\ - 525 \\ \hline \mathbf{210} \text{ more winners} \end{array}$$

4. a. 3.75×10^{-5}

b. 3.75×10^{7}

5. About 3 in.²

6. a.

b.

7.

	Case 1	Case 2
Inches	4	12
Hours	3	h

$$\frac{4}{3} = \frac{12}{h}$$

$$4h = 3(12)$$

$$h = \frac{36}{4}$$

$$h = \mathbf{9 \text{ hours}}$$

8.

a. $\frac{12 \text{ students}}{3} = 4 \text{ students}$

$5(4 \text{ students}) = \mathbf{20 \text{ students}}$

b. $\frac{5}{8} \times 100\% = \frac{500\%}{8} = \mathbf{62\frac{1}{2}\%}$

9. $35 = 0.7 \times W_N$

$$\frac{35}{0.7} = \frac{0.7 \times W_N}{0.7}$$

$$\mathbf{50} = W_N$$

10. $W_P \times 20 = 17$

$$\frac{W_P \times 20}{20} = \frac{17}{20}$$

$$W_P = \frac{17}{20}$$

$$W_P = \frac{17}{20} \times 100\% = \frac{1700\%}{20} = \mathbf{85\%}$$

11. $W_P \times 20 = 25$

$$\frac{W_P \times 20}{20} = \frac{\overset{5}{\cancel{25}}}{\underset{4}{\cancel{20}}}$$

$$W_P = \frac{5}{4}$$

$$W_P = \frac{5}{4} \times 100\% = \frac{500\%}{4} = \mathbf{125\%}$$

12. $360 = \frac{3}{4} \times W_N$

$$\left(\frac{4}{\cancel{3}}\right)\overset{120}{\cancel{360}} = \left(\frac{\cancel{4}}{\cancel{3}}\right)\frac{\cancel{3}}{\cancel{4}} \times W_N$$

$$(4)120 = W_N$$

$$\mathbf{480} = W_N$$

13. a. $\frac{1.44}{-8} = \mathbf{-0.18}$

b. $\frac{-14.4}{+6} = \mathbf{-2.4}$

c. $-12(1.2) = \mathbf{-14.4}$

d. $-1.6(-9) = \mathbf{14.4}$

14. a. $25\overline{)1.00}$ $\overset{0.04}{}$

b. $\frac{1}{25} \times 100\% = \frac{100\%}{25} = \mathbf{4\%}$

c. $8\% = \frac{8}{100} = \mathbf{\frac{2}{25}}$

d. $8\% = \frac{8}{100} = \mathbf{0.08}$

15. $\begin{array}{r} \$4500 \\ \times 0.05 \\ \hline \$225.00 = \mathbf{\$225} \end{array}$

16. $\frac{62\frac{1}{2}}{100} = \frac{\frac{125}{2}}{\frac{100}{1}}$

$$\frac{\frac{125}{2}}{\frac{100}{1}} \cdot \frac{\frac{1}{100}}{\frac{1}{100}} = \frac{\frac{125}{200}}{1}$$

$$= \frac{125}{200} = \mathbf{\frac{5}{8}}$$

Solutions

17.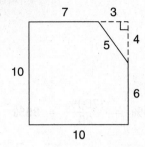

a. Perimeter = 10 in. + 7 in. + 5 in.
+ 6 in. + 10 in. = **38 in.**

b. Area of square = (10 in.)(10 in.)
= 100 in.^{2}

Area of triangle = $\dfrac{(3\text{ in.})(4\text{ in.})}{2}$

= 6 in.^{2}

Area of figure = 100 in.^{2} − 6 in.^{2}
= **94 in.^{2}**

18. a. (6 cubes)(3 cubes) = 18 cubes

$\dfrac{18\text{ cubes}}{1\text{ layer}} \cdot 4\text{ layers} = 72$ cubes

72 cm^3

b. (6 cm)(3 cm) = 18 cm^2
(4 cm)(3 cm) = 12 cm^2
(6 cm)(4 cm) = 24 cm^2
2(18 cm^2) + 2(12 cm^2) + 2(24 cm^2)
= 36 cm^2 + 24 cm^2 + 48 cm^2
= **108 cm^2**

19. a. $C \approx 3.14(1\text{ m})$
$C \approx$ **3.14 m**

b. $C = \pi(1\text{ m})$
$C = \pi$ **m**

20. a. Right; scalene

b. Obtuse; isosceles

c. Acute; equilateral

21. Equilateral triangle

22. $1.2x = 2.88$

$\dfrac{1.2x}{1.2} = \dfrac{2.88}{1.2}$

$x =$ **2.4**

check: $1.2(2.4) = 2.88$
$2.88 = 2.88$

23. $\dfrac{3}{2}w = \dfrac{9}{10}$

$\left(\dfrac{\overset{1}{\cancel{2}}}{\underset{1}{\cancel{3}}}\right)\dfrac{\overset{1}{\cancel{3}}}{\underset{1}{\cancel{2}}}w = \left(\dfrac{\overset{1}{\cancel{2}}}{\underset{1}{\cancel{3}}}\right)\dfrac{\overset{3}{\cancel{9}}}{\underset{5}{\cancel{10}}}$

$w = \dfrac{3}{5}$

check: $\left(\dfrac{3}{2}\right)\dfrac{3}{5} = \dfrac{9}{10}$

$\dfrac{9}{10} = \dfrac{9}{10}$

24. $\dfrac{\sqrt{100} + 5[3^3 - 2(3^2 + 3)]}{5}$

$\dfrac{10 + 5[27 - 2(9 + 3)]}{5}$

$\dfrac{10 + 5[27 - 2(12)]}{5}$

$\dfrac{10 + 5[27 - 24]}{5}$

$\dfrac{10 + 5[3]}{5}$

$\dfrac{10 + 15}{5}$

$\dfrac{25}{5}$

5

25.
$\overset{2}{\cancel{3}}$ hr $\overset{14}{\cancel{15}}$ min 24 s (60 min) (60 s)
− 2 hr 45 min 30 s

$\overset{2}{\cancel{3}}$ hr $\overset{\overset{74}{\cancel{14}}}{\cancel{15}}$ min $\overset{84}{\cancel{24}}$ s
− 2 hr 45 min 30 s
29 min 54 s

26. $1\text{ yd}^2 \cdot \dfrac{3\text{ ft}}{1\text{ yd}} \cdot \dfrac{3\text{ ft}}{1\text{ yd}} =$ **9 ft^2**

27. $7\dfrac{1}{2} \cdot \left(3 \div \dfrac{5}{9}\right) = \dfrac{15}{2} \cdot \left(\dfrac{3}{1} \div \dfrac{5}{9}\right)$

$= \dfrac{15}{2} \cdot \left(\dfrac{3}{1} \times \dfrac{9}{5}\right) = \dfrac{\overset{3}{\cancel{15}}}{2} \cdot \dfrac{27}{\underset{1}{\cancel{5}}}$

$= \dfrac{81}{2} =$ **40$\dfrac{1}{2}$**

28. $4\dfrac{5}{6} + 3\dfrac{1}{3} + 7\dfrac{1}{4}$

$= 4\dfrac{10}{12} + 3\dfrac{4}{12} + 7\dfrac{3}{12}$

$= 14\dfrac{17}{12} =$ **15$\dfrac{5}{12}$**

29. $3\dfrac{3}{4} = 3.75$, $3.75 \div 1.5 =$ **2.5**

30. a. $-0.1 - (-0.2) - (0.3)$
$-0.1 + [-(-0.2)] + [-(0.3)]$
$-0.1 + [0.2] + [-0.3]$
−0.2

Saxon Math Course 2   **290**   © Harcourt Achieve, Inc. and Stephen Hake. All rights reserved.

b.
$$(-10) - |(-20) - (+30)|$$
$$(-10) + [-|(-20) + [-(+30)]|]$$
$$(-10) + [-|(-20) + [-30]|]$$
$$(-10) + [-|-50|]$$
$$(-10) + [-(+50)]$$
$$(-10) + [-50]$$
$$\mathbf{-60}$$

Early Finishers Solutions

median = $140,000

mode = $130,000

mean = $\dfrac{120000 + 130000 + 130000 + 150000 + 160000 + 210000}{5}$

   = $150,000

range = $210,000 − $120,000 = $90,000

The median gives the best description because half the houses sell for more and half sell for less. The median is closer to the price of most of the houses.

Practice Set 80

a. See Lesson.

b. $W'(3, -4), X'(1, -4), Y'(1, -1), Z'(3, -1)$

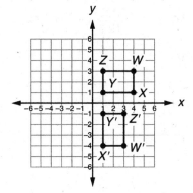

c. $J'(-1, -1), K'(-3, -2), L'(-1, -3)$

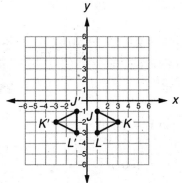

d. $P'(6, 0), Q'(5, -2), R'(2, -2), S'(3, 0)$

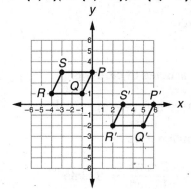

e.

(−2, 2) D' A' (2, 2)

         D A

         C B

(−2, −2) C' B' (2, −2)

Written Practice 80

1. 4($7.00) + 3($6.30)
   = $28.00 + $18.90 = $46.90
   $6.70 per hour
   $7\overline{)$46.90}$

2. $(4) + [(4)^2 - (4)(3)] - 3$
   $= 4 + [16 - 12] - 3$
   $= 4 + [4] - 3 = 8 - 3 = \mathbf{5}$

3. **a.** Sample space = {H1, H2, H3, H4, H5, H6, T1, T2, T3, T4, T5, T6}

   b. P(tails & odd) $= \dfrac{3}{12} = \dfrac{1}{4}$

4.

	Ratio	Actual Count
Clean clothes	2	C
Dirty clothes	3	D
Total	5	30

$$\frac{2}{5} = \frac{C}{30}$$
$$5C = 2(30)$$
$$C = \frac{60}{5}$$
$$C = \textbf{12 articles of clothing}$$

5. $C \approx 3.14(30 \text{ millimeters})$
$C \approx 94.2 \text{ millimeters}$
$C \approx \textbf{94 millimeters}$

6. $1\frac{1}{2} \text{ quarts} \cdot \dfrac{2 \text{ pints}}{1 \text{ quart}} = \textbf{3 pints}$

7. a.

b.

8.

	Case 1	Case 2
Minutes	25	60
Customers	400	c

$$\frac{25}{400} = \frac{60}{c}$$
$$25c = 400(60)$$
$$c = \frac{24{,}000}{25}$$
$$c = \textbf{960 customers}$$

9.

$\frac{1}{4}$ of total height
$\frac{3}{4}$ of total height

a. $4(18 \text{ inches}) = \textbf{72 inches}$

b. $\overset{6}{\cancel{72}} \text{ inches} \cdot \dfrac{1 \text{ foot}}{\underset{1}{\cancel{12}} \text{ inches}}$
$= \textbf{6 feet}$

10. $600 = \dfrac{5}{9} \times W_N$

$$\frac{9}{\cancel{5}}(\cancel{600}^{120}) = \left(\frac{\cancel{9}}{\cancel{5}}\right)\frac{\cancel{5}}{\cancel{9}} \times W_N$$
$$9(120) = W_N$$
$$\textbf{1080} = W_N$$

11. $280 = W_P \times 400$

$$\frac{\cancel{280}^{7}}{\cancel{400}_{10}} = \frac{W_P \times \cancel{400}^{1}}{\cancel{400}_{1}}$$
$$\frac{7}{10} = W_P$$
$$W_P = \frac{7}{10} \times 100\% = \frac{700\%}{10} = \textbf{70\%}$$

12. $W_N = 0.04 \times 400$
$W_N = \textbf{16}$

13. $60 = 0.6 \times W_N$

$$\frac{60}{0.6} = \frac{\overset{1}{\cancel{0.6}} \times W_N}{\underset{1}{\cancel{0.6}}}$$
$$\textbf{100} = W_N$$

14. a. $\dfrac{600}{-15} = \textbf{-40}$

b. $\dfrac{-600}{-12} = \textbf{50}$

c. $20(-30) = \textbf{-600}$

d. $+15(40) = \textbf{600}$

15.
$$\begin{array}{r} \$850 \\ \times\ 0.06 \\ \hline \$51.00 = \textbf{\$51} \end{array}$$

16. a. $0.3 = \dfrac{3}{10}$

b. $0.3 = \dfrac{3}{10} = \dfrac{30}{100} = \textbf{30\%}$

c. $12\overline{)5.000\ldots}\;^{0.41\overline{6}}$

d. $\dfrac{5}{12} \times 100\% = \dfrac{500\%}{12} = \textbf{41}\dfrac{\textbf{2}}{\textbf{3}}\textbf{\%}$

17. a. 3×10^7

b. 3×10^{-5}

18.

Area of rectangle $= (4 \text{ m})(5 \text{ m}) = 20 \text{ m}^2$
+ Area of triangle $= \dfrac{(2 \text{ m})(5 \text{ m})}{2} = 5 \text{ m}^2$

Area of figure $= \textbf{25 m}^2$

19. a. $(5 \text{ in.})(5 \text{ in.}) = 25 \text{ in.}^2$
$(5 \text{ in.})(25 \text{ in.}^2) = \textbf{125 in.}^3$

b. $6(25 \text{ in.}^2) = \textbf{150 in.}^2$

20. $\dfrac{\text{green marbles}}{\text{total marbles}} = \dfrac{40}{100} = \dfrac{2}{5}$

21. $17a = 408$

$$\dfrac{\overset{1}{\cancel{17}}a}{\underset{1}{\cancel{17}}} = \dfrac{\overset{24}{\cancel{408}}}{\underset{1}{\cancel{17}}}$$

$a = \textbf{24}$

check: $17(24) = 408$
$408 = 408$

22. $\dfrac{3}{8}m = 48$

$$\left(\dfrac{\overset{1}{\cancel{8}}}{\underset{1}{\cancel{3}}}\right)\dfrac{\overset{1}{\cancel{3}}}{\underset{1}{\cancel{8}}}m = \left(\dfrac{8}{3}\right)\overset{16}{\cancel{48}}$$

$m = (8)16$
$m = \textbf{128}$

check: $\dfrac{3}{\underset{1}{\cancel{8}}}(\overset{16}{\cancel{128}}) = 48$

$3(16) = 48$
$48 = 48$

23. $1.4 = x - 0.41$
$1.4 + 0.41 = x - 0.41 + 0.41$
$\textbf{1.81} = x$

check: $1.4 = 1.81 - 0.41$
$1.4 = 1.4$

24. $\dfrac{2^3 + 4 \cdot 5 - 2 \cdot 3^2}{\sqrt{25} \cdot \sqrt{4}}$

$$\dfrac{8 + 4 \cdot 5 - 2 \cdot 9}{5 \cdot 2}$$

$$\dfrac{8 + 20 - 2 \cdot 9}{10}$$

$$\dfrac{8 + 20 - 18}{10}$$

$$\dfrac{28 - 18}{10}$$

$$\dfrac{10}{10}$$

$$\textbf{1}$$

25. $7\dfrac{1}{7} \times 1.4 = 7\dfrac{1}{7} \times 1\dfrac{4}{10}$

$$= \dfrac{\overset{5}{\cancel{50}}}{\underset{1}{7}} \times \dfrac{\overset{2}{\cancel{14}}}{\underset{1}{\cancel{10}}} = \textbf{10}$$

26.

$\overset{9}{\cancel{10}}$ lb $\overset{\longrightarrow (16\ oz)}{6\ oz}$
$-\ \ 7$ lb 11 oz $\longrightarrow$

$\overset{9}{\cancel{10}}$ lb $\overset{22}{\cancel{6}}$ oz
$-\ \ 7$ lb 11 oz
$\quad \textbf{2 lb}\quad \textbf{11 oz}$

27. $1\ \cancel{cm}^2 \cdot \dfrac{10\ mm}{1\ \cancel{cm}} \cdot \dfrac{10\ mm}{1\ \cancel{cm}} = \textbf{100 mm}^2$

28. $\overset{1}{\cancel{3}} \cdot \dfrac{5}{\underset{3}{\cancel{9}}} = \dfrac{5}{3}$

$7\dfrac{1}{2} \div \dfrac{5}{3} = \dfrac{15}{2} \div \dfrac{5}{3}$

$$= \dfrac{\overset{3}{\cancel{15}}}{2} \times \dfrac{3}{\underset{1}{\cancel{5}}} = \dfrac{9}{2} = \textbf{4}\dfrac{1}{2}$$

29. $2^{-4} + 4^{-2} = \dfrac{1}{2^4} + \dfrac{1}{4^2}$

$$= \dfrac{1}{16} + \dfrac{1}{16} = \dfrac{2}{16} = \dfrac{1}{8}$$

30.

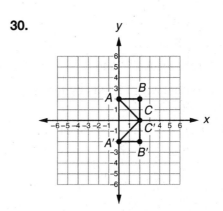

Investigation 〔 **8** 〕

1. 4 white marbles out of $3 + 4 + 5 = 12$ total; $\dfrac{4}{12} = \dfrac{1}{3}$

2. $3 + 5 = 8$ not-white marbles; $\dfrac{8}{12} = \dfrac{2}{3}$

3. 4 white to 8 not-white = **1 to 2**

4. 3 red marbles out of 12 total; $\dfrac{3}{12} = \dfrac{1}{4} = \textbf{0.25}$

5. $4 + 5 = 9$ not-red marbles; $\dfrac{9}{12} = \dfrac{3}{4} = \textbf{0.75}$

6. 3 red to 9 not-red = **1 to 3**

7. 5 blue to 7 not-blue = **5 to 7**

8. $100\% - 20\% = \textbf{80\%}$

9. 20% rain to 80% not-rain = **1 to 4**

Solutions

Example 1: Conclude

The probability of tails and 4, $P(T \text{ and } 4)$ is the probability of tails times the probability of 4.

$$P(T \text{ and } 4) = P(T) \times P(4)$$
$$= \frac{1}{2} \times \frac{1}{4}$$
$$= \frac{1}{8}$$

10. $\{H1, H2, H3, H4, T1, T2, T3, T4\}$

11. $P(H \text{ and } 2) = P(H) \times P(2)$
$$= \frac{1}{2} \times \frac{1}{4}$$
$$= \frac{1}{8}$$

12. One out of eight results = **1 to 8**

13. Multiply the probability of heads by the probability of not-2:

$$P(H \text{ and } not\ 2) = P(H) \times P(not\ 2)$$
$$= \frac{1}{2} \times \frac{3}{4}$$
$$= \frac{3}{8}$$

14. $P(H, H, H) = P(H) \times P(H) \times P(H)$
$$= \frac{1}{2} \times \frac{1}{2} \times \frac{1}{2}$$
$$= \frac{1}{8}$$

15. $P(6, 6) = P(6) \times P(6)$
$$= \frac{1}{6} \times \frac{1}{6}$$
$$= \frac{1}{36}$$

16. $P(6, H) = P(6) \times P(H)$
$$= \frac{1}{6} \times \frac{1}{2}$$
$$= \frac{1}{12}$$

17. $\dfrac{60 \text{ in A}}{360 \text{ total spins}} = \dfrac{1}{6}$

18. $\dfrac{90 \text{ in B}}{360 \text{ total spins}} = \dfrac{1}{4}$

19. $\dfrac{210 \text{ in C}}{360 \text{ total spins}} = \dfrac{7}{12}$

20. a. $\dfrac{7}{12}$

  b. $\dfrac{1}{4} = 25\%$

Activity

Students complete Investigation Activity 20; Check students' work.

Extension

Students extend Investigation Activity 20 by creating bar graphs representing the whole class' data. Results will vary. Check students' bar graphs.; The Extension activity should produce results closer to theoretical outcomes than were attained with 36 rolls.

Practice Set 81

a. Estimate: $\dfrac{21}{70} = \dfrac{3}{10} = 30\%$

$100\% - 30\% = \mathbf{70\%}$

	Percent	Actual Count
Planted with alfalfa	P_P	21
Not planted with alfalfa	P_N	49
Total	100	70

$$\frac{P_N}{100} = \frac{49}{70}$$
$$70P_N = 4900$$
$$P_N = \mathbf{70\%}$$

b. Estimate: $60 \times 3 = \mathbf{180 \text{ pages}}$

	Percent	Actual Count
Pages read	40	120
Pages left to read	60	P
Total	100	T

$$\frac{40}{60} = \frac{120}{P}$$
$$40P = 7200$$
$$P = \mathbf{180 \text{ pages}}$$

c. Estimate: $\frac{26}{30} = \frac{13}{15} \approx$ **87%**

	Percent	Actual Count
Missed	P_M	4
Correct	P_C	26
Total	100	30

$$\frac{P_C}{100} = \frac{26}{30}$$
$$30P_C = 2600$$
$$P_C = 86\frac{2}{3}\%$$

Written Practice 81

1.

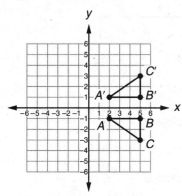

$$A'(2, 1),\ B'(5, 1),\ C'(5, 3)$$

2. a.

```
              86
       15)1290
   70
   85
   80
   85
   90
   80
   85
   80
   90
   95
   85
   90
  100
   85
 + 90
 ----
 1290
```

b. 70, 80, 80, 80, 85, 85, 85, <u>85</u>, 85, 90, 90, 90, 90, 95, 100
85

3. a. 85

b. $100 - 70 =$ **30**

4.
$$\begin{array}{r} \overset{5}{\cancel{6}}\ \text{ft} \xrightarrow{\ (12\ \text{in.})\ } 1\ \text{in.} \\ -\ 5\ \text{ft} \qquad 6\frac{1}{2}\ \text{in.} \\ \hline \end{array}$$
$$\begin{array}{r} \overset{5}{\cancel{6}}\ \text{ft} \quad \overset{13}{\cancel{1}}\ \text{in.} \\ -\ 5\ \text{ft} \quad 6\frac{1}{2}\ \text{in.} \\ \hline 6\frac{1}{2}\ \textbf{inches} \end{array}$$

5.

	Case 1	Case 2
Pencils	5	12
Price	75¢	p

$$\frac{5}{\$0.75} = \frac{12}{p}$$
$$5p = \$9.00$$
$$p = \textbf{\$1.80}$$

6. a. $x < 4$

```
———●————————○————————
    1   2   3   4   5
```

b. $x \geq -2$

```
————————●————————————
   -3  -2  -1   0   1
```

7.

```
                    60 questions
                   ┌─────────────┐
  4                │ 12 questions │
  — answered       │ 12 questions │
  5 correctly      │ 12 questions │
    (48).          │ 12 questions │
  1 answered       │ 12 questions │
  — incorrectly.   └─────────────┘
  5
```

a. $48 \div 4 = 12$
$5(12\ \text{questions}) = $ **60 questions**

b. $\dfrac{\text{correct answers}}{\text{incorrect answers}} = \dfrac{48}{12} = \dfrac{4}{1}$

8. $3\frac{3}{4} \div 2 = \frac{15}{4} \times \frac{1}{2}$
$$= \frac{15}{8} = 1\frac{7}{8}\ \textbf{inches}$$

9.

	Ratio	Actual Count
Gleeps	9	G
Bobbles	5	B
Total	14	2800

$$\frac{9}{14} = \frac{G}{2800}$$
$$14G = 25{,}200$$
$$G = \textbf{1800 gleeps}$$

Solutions

10. $(9)^2 + \sqrt{9} = 81 + 3 = \textbf{84}$

11. odds = favorable:unfavorable
1:5 or 1 to 5

12. a. $2\frac{1}{4} = 2\frac{25}{100} = \textbf{2.25}$

b. $2.25 \times 100\% = \textbf{225\%}$

c. $2\frac{1}{4}\% = \dfrac{2\frac{1}{4}}{100} = \dfrac{\frac{9}{4}}{\frac{100}{1}} \cdot \dfrac{\frac{1}{100}}{\frac{1}{100}} = \dfrac{\textbf{9}}{\textbf{400}}$

d. $2\frac{1}{4}\% = 2.25\% = \textbf{0.0225}$

13. $p = 0.4 \times \$12$
$p = \textbf{\$4.80}$

14. $0.5 \times W_N = 0.4$
$\dfrac{0.5 \times W_N}{0.5} = \dfrac{0.4}{0.5}$
$W_N = \textbf{0.8}$

15. $\dfrac{16\frac{2}{3}}{100} = \dfrac{\frac{50}{3}}{\frac{100}{1}}$

$\dfrac{\frac{50}{3}}{\frac{100}{1}} \cdot \dfrac{\frac{1}{100}}{\frac{1}{100}} = \dfrac{\frac{50}{300}}{1} = \dfrac{50}{300}$

$= \dfrac{\textbf{1}}{\textbf{6}}$

16.

	Percent	Actual Count
Correct	P_C	21
Incorrect	P_I	4
Total	100	25

$\dfrac{P_C}{100} = \dfrac{21}{25}$
$25P_C = 2100$
$P_C = \textbf{84\%}$

17.

	Percent	Actual Count
Left fallow	20	F
Not left fallow	80	N
Total	100	4000

$\dfrac{80}{100} = \dfrac{N}{4000}$
$100N = 320{,}000$
$N = \textbf{3200 acres}$

18. a. Angles *ABC* and *CBD* are supplementary (total 180°), so m∠*CBD* = **40°**.

b. Angles *CBD* and *DBE* are complementary (total 90°), so m∠*DBE* = **50°**.

c. Angles *DBE* and *EBA* are supplementary (total 180°), so m∠*EBA* = **130°**.

d. $140° + 40° + 50° + 130° = \textbf{360°}$

19. $\dfrac{3000}{6300} = \dfrac{\cancel{2} \cdot \cancel{2} \cdot 2 \cdot \cancel{3} \cdot \cancel{5} \cdot \cancel{5} \cdot 5}{\cancel{2} \cdot \cancel{2} \cdot \cancel{3} \cdot 3 \cdot \cancel{5} \cdot \cancel{5} \cdot 7}$
$= \dfrac{\textbf{10}}{\textbf{21}}$

20. a.

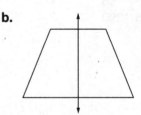

Area of triangle A $= \dfrac{(20 \text{ in.})(12 \text{ in.})}{2}$
$= 120 \text{ in.}^2$

Area of triangle B $= \dfrac{(10 \text{ in.})(12 \text{ in.})}{2}$
$= 60 \text{ in.}^2$

Area of figure $= 120 \text{ in.}^2 + 60 \text{ in.}^2$
$= \textbf{180 in.}^2$

b.

21. To find *y*, double *x* and subtract 1.

$y = 2x - 1$

x	y
−1	−3
3	5
4	7
6	11
0	**−1**

$y = 2(0) - 1$
$y = 0 - 1$
$y = -1$

22. a. 5.6×10^8

b. 5.6×10^{-6}

23. $5x = 16.5$

$\dfrac{5x}{5} = \dfrac{16.5}{5}$

$x = \textbf{3.3}$

check: $\quad 5(3.3) = 16.5$

$16.5 = 16.5$

24.

$3\dfrac{1}{2} + a = 5\dfrac{3}{8}$

$3\dfrac{1}{2} - 3\dfrac{1}{2} + a = 5\dfrac{3}{8} - 3\dfrac{1}{2}$

$a = 5\dfrac{3}{8} - 3\dfrac{4}{8}$

$a = 4\dfrac{11}{8} - 3\dfrac{4}{8}$

$a = \mathbf{1\dfrac{7}{8}}$

check: $\quad 3\dfrac{1}{2} + 1\dfrac{7}{8} = 5\dfrac{3}{8}$

$3\dfrac{4}{8} + 1\dfrac{7}{8} = 5\dfrac{3}{8}$

$4\dfrac{11}{8} = 5\dfrac{3}{8}$

$5\dfrac{3}{8} = 5\dfrac{3}{8}$

25. $3^2 + 5[6 - (10 - 2^3)]$

$9 + 5[6 - (10 - 8)]$

$9 + 5[6 - 2]$

$9 + 5[4]$

$9 + 20$

$\textbf{29}$

26. $\sqrt{2^2 \cdot 3^4 \cdot 5^2} = 2 \cdot 3^2 \cdot 5$

$= 2 \cdot 9 \cdot 5 = \textbf{90}$

27. $2\dfrac{2}{3} \times 4\dfrac{1}{2} \div 6$

$= \left(\dfrac{\overset{4}{\cancel{8}}}{\underset{1}{\cancel{3}}} \times \dfrac{\overset{3}{\cancel{9}}}{\underset{1}{\cancel{2}}}\right) \div 6 = 12 \div 6 = \textbf{2} \text{ or } \dfrac{\textbf{2}}{\textbf{1}}$

28. $(3.5)^2 - (5 - 3.4)$

$= (12.25) - (1.6) = \textbf{10.65}$

29. a. $(-1.2)(-9) = \textbf{10.8}$

b. $(-3)(2.5) = \textbf{-7.5}$

c. $\left(\dfrac{1}{2}\right)\left(-\dfrac{1}{2}\right) = -\dfrac{\textbf{1}}{\textbf{4}}$

d. $\left(-\dfrac{1}{2}\right)\left(-\dfrac{1}{2}\right) = \dfrac{\textbf{1}}{\textbf{4}}$

30. a. $(-3) + |-4| - (-5)$

$(-3) + (4) + [-(-5)]$

$(-3) + (4) + [5]$

$\textbf{6}$

b. $(-18) - (+20) + (-7)$

$(-18) + [-(+20)] + (-7)$

$(-18) + [-20] + [-7]$

$\textbf{-45}$

c. $\dfrac{1}{2} - \left(-\dfrac{1}{2}\right)$

$\dfrac{1}{2} + \left[-\left(-\dfrac{1}{2}\right)\right]$

$\dfrac{1}{2} + \left[\dfrac{1}{2}\right]$

$\textbf{1}$

Early Finishers Solutions

Line Graph; While a bar graph can be used to display comparisons, a line graph would be better because it clearly displays a change over time.

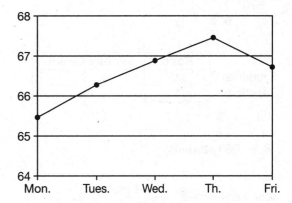

Practice Set 82

a. $A = \pi r^2$

$A \approx 3.14(36 \text{ ft}^2)$

$A \approx \textbf{113 ft}^2$

b. $A = \pi r^2$

$A \approx 3.14(16 \text{ cm}^2)$

$A \approx \textbf{50.24 cm}^2$

c. $A = \pi r^2$

$A = \pi(16 \text{ cm}^2)$

$A = \textbf{16}\pi \textbf{ cm}^2$

297

Solutions

d. $A = \pi r^2$

$A \approx \dfrac{22}{7}\,(16\text{ cm}^2)$

$A \approx \dfrac{352}{7}\text{ cm}^2$

$A \approx \mathbf{50\dfrac{2}{7}\text{ cm}^2}$

Written Practice ⬤ **82**

1. $(2\text{ ft})(4\text{ ft}) = 8\text{ ft}^2$

$\dfrac{8\text{ ft}^2}{1\text{ layer}}(1\text{ ft})(2.5\text{ layers})$

$= \mathbf{20\text{ ft}^3}$

2.
$\begin{aligned}
6'\,3'' &= 75'' \\
6'\,5'' &= 77'' \\
5'\,11'' &= 71'' \\
6'\,2'' &= 74'' \\
+\ 6'\,1'' &= 73'' \\
\hline
 &\ 370''
\end{aligned}$

$\begin{array}{r} 74'' \\ 5\overline{)370''} \end{array}$

$74'' = \mathbf{6'\,2''}$

3.

	Ratio	Actual Count
Students	20	S
Teachers	1	48

$\dfrac{20}{1} = \dfrac{S}{48}$

$S = \mathbf{960\text{ students}}$

4. $2.54\text{ centimeters} \cdot \dfrac{1\text{ meter}}{100\text{ centimeters}}$

$= \mathbf{0.0254\text{ meter}}$

5. a.
$\begin{array}{ccccc} -5 & -4 & -3 & -2 & -1 \end{array}$

b.
$\begin{array}{ccccc} -1 & 0 & 1 & 2 & 3 \end{array}$

6.

	Case 1	Case 2
Beats	225	b
Minutes	3	5

$\dfrac{225}{3} = \dfrac{b}{5}$

$3b = 1125$

$b = \mathbf{375\text{ times}}$

7.

25 students

$\dfrac{2}{5}$ were boys. $\left\{\begin{array}{l} \boxed{5\text{ students}} \\ \boxed{5\text{ students}} \end{array}\right.$

$\dfrac{3}{5}$ were girls (15). $\left\{\begin{array}{l} \boxed{5\text{ students}} \\ \boxed{5\text{ students}} \\ \boxed{5\text{ students}} \end{array}\right.$

a. $15 \div 3 = 5$

$5(5\text{ students}) = \mathbf{25\text{ students}}$

b. $\dfrac{\text{girls}}{\text{boys}} = \dfrac{15}{10} = \dfrac{\mathbf{3}}{\mathbf{2}}$

8. $x^2 - y^2 = 5^2 - 3^2 = 25 - 9 = 16$

$(x + y)(x - y) = (5 + 3)(5 - 3)$

$= (8)(2) = 16,\ 16 = 16$

$x^2 - y^2 \;\boxed{=}\; (x + y)(x - y)$

9. Percent unshaded: $25\% + 23\% = \mathbf{48\%}$

Percent shaded: $100\% - 48\% = \mathbf{52\%}$

10. **40%**

11. a. $C \approx 3.14\,(14\text{ cm})$

$C \approx \mathbf{43.96\text{ cm}}$

b. $C \approx \dfrac{22}{7}\overset{2}{(\cancel{1}4\text{ cm})}$

$C \approx \mathbf{44\text{ cm}}$

12. a. $A = \pi r^2$

$A \approx 3.14\,(49\text{ cm}^2)$

$A \approx \mathbf{153.86\text{ cm}^2}$

b. $A = \pi r^2$

$A \approx \dfrac{22}{7}\overset{7}{(\cancel{4}9\text{ cm}^2)}$

$A \approx \mathbf{154\text{ cm}^2}$

13. a. $1.6 = 1\dfrac{6}{10} = \mathbf{1\dfrac{3}{5}}$

b. $1.6 \times 100\% = \mathbf{160\%}$

c. $1.6\% = \dfrac{1.6}{100} \cdot \dfrac{10}{10} = \dfrac{16}{1000} = \dfrac{\mathbf{2}}{\mathbf{125}}$

d. $1.6\% = \mathbf{0.016}$

14. $M = 0.064 \times \$25$

$M = \mathbf{\$1.60}$

15. a. 1.2×10^6

b. 1.2×10^{-4}

16.

	Percent	Actual Count
Correctly described	64	C
Incorrectly described	36	63
Total	100	T

$\dfrac{64}{36} = \dfrac{C}{63}$

$36C = 4032$

$C = $ **112 students**

17.

	Percent	Actual Count
Pages read	60	180
Pages left to read	40	P
Total	100	T

$\dfrac{60}{40} = \dfrac{180}{P}$

$60P = 7200$

$P = $ **120 pages**

18.

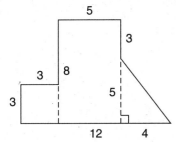

Area of rectangle $= (5\text{ in.})(8\text{ in.}) = 40\text{ in.}^2$

Area of square $= (3\text{ in.})(3\text{ in.}) = 9\text{ in.}^2$

$+$ Area of triangle $= \dfrac{(5\text{ in.})(4\text{ in.})}{2} = 10\text{ in.}^2$

Area of figure $= $ **59 in.^{2}**

19. a.

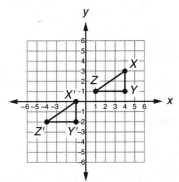

b. $X'(-1, 0)$, $Y'(-1, -2)$, $Z'(-4, -2)$

20. $\dfrac{240}{816} = \dfrac{\overset{1}{\cancel{2}} \cdot \overset{1}{\cancel{2}} \cdot \overset{1}{\cancel{2}} \cdot \overset{1}{\cancel{2}} \cdot \overset{1}{\cancel{3}} \cdot 5}{\underset{1}{\cancel{2}} \cdot \underset{1}{\cancel{2}} \cdot \underset{1}{\cancel{2}} \cdot \underset{1}{\cancel{2}} \cdot \underset{1}{\cancel{3}} \cdot 17}$

$= \dfrac{5}{17}$

21. a. **3 chords**

b. **6 chords**

c. **60°**

d. **120°**

22. 1×10^8

23. $\dfrac{3}{4}x = 36$

$\left(\dfrac{\overset{1}{\cancel{4}}}{\underset{1}{\cancel{3}}}\right)\dfrac{\overset{1}{\cancel{3}}}{\underset{1}{\cancel{4}}}x = \left(\dfrac{4}{\cancel{3}}\right)\overset{12}{\cancel{36}}$

$x = $ **48**

check: $\dfrac{3}{\underset{1}{\cancel{4}}}(\overset{12}{\cancel{48}}) = 36$

$3(12) = 36$

$36 = 36$

24. $3.2 + a = 3.46$

$3.2 - 3.2 + a = 3.46 - 3.2$

$a = $ **0.26**

check: $3.2 + 0.26 = 3.46$

$3.46 = 3.46$

25. $\dfrac{\sqrt{3^2 + 4^2}}{5} = \dfrac{\sqrt{9 + 16}}{5}$

$= \dfrac{\sqrt{25}}{5} = \dfrac{5}{5} = $ **1**

26. $(8 - 3)^2 - (3 - 8)^2$

$= (5)^2 - (-5)^2 = 25 - 25 = $ **0**

27. $3.5 \div (7 \div 0.2)$

$= 3.5 \div 35 = $ **0.1**

28. $4\dfrac{1}{2} + 2\dfrac{2}{3} - 3$

$= 4\dfrac{3}{6} + 2\dfrac{4}{6} - 2\dfrac{6}{6}$

$= 6\dfrac{7}{6} - 2\dfrac{6}{6} = $ **4$\dfrac{1}{6}$**

29. a. $\dfrac{(-3)(-4)}{(-2)} = \dfrac{12}{(-2)} = $ **−6**

b. $\left(-\dfrac{\overset{1}{\cancel{2}}}{\underset{1}{\cancel{3}}}\right)\left(-\dfrac{\overset{1}{\cancel{3}}}{\underset{2}{\cancel{4}}}\right) = \dfrac{1}{2}$

30. a. $(-0.3) + (-0.4) - (-0.2)$
$(-0.3) + (-0.4) + [-(-0.2)]$
$(-0.3) + (-0.4) + [0.2]$
$\mathbf{-0.5}$

b. $(-20) + (+30) - |-40|$
$(-20) + (+30) + [-|-40|]$
$(-20) + (+30) + [-40]$
$\mathbf{-30}$

Early Finishers Solutions

a. $\$172 \times 12 = \$2064$

b. $\$2064 - (\$127 \times 12) = \$540$

c. $\dfrac{540}{2064} = 0.2616 = 26\%$

Practice Set · 83

a. $(4.2 \times 1.4) \times (10^6 \times 10^3)$
$= \mathbf{5.88 \times 10^9}$

b. $(5 \times 3) \times (10^5 \times 10^7) = 15 \times 10^{12}$
$= \mathbf{1.5 \times 10^{13}}$

c. $(4 \times 2.1) \times (10^{-3} \times 10^{-7})$
$= \mathbf{8.4 \times 10^{-10}}$

d. $(6 \times 7) \times (10^{-2} \times 10^{-5}) = 42 \times 10^{-7}$
$= \mathbf{4.2 \times 10^{-6}}$

e.
$3 \times 10^3 \times 2 \times 10^4$	Given
$3 \times 2 \times 10^3 \times 10^4$	Commutative property
$(3 \times 2) \times (10^3 \times 10^4)$	Associative property
6×10^7	Simplified

Written Practice · 83

1. $\dfrac{\$1.12}{16 \text{ ounces}} = \dfrac{\$0.07}{1 \text{ ounce}}$

$\dfrac{\$1.32}{24 \text{ ounces}} = \dfrac{\$0.055}{1 \text{ ounce}}$

$\begin{array}{r} \$0.070 \\ - \ \$0.055 \\ \hline \mathbf{\$0.015} \textbf{ more per ounce} \end{array}$

2.

	Ratio	Actual Count
Good apples	5	G
Bad apples	2	B
Total	7	70

$\dfrac{5}{7} = \dfrac{G}{70}$
$7G = 350$
$G = \mathbf{50 \text{ apples}}$

3. $15(82) + 5(90) = 1230 + 450 = 1680$

$\begin{array}{r} 84 \\ 20\overline{)1680} \end{array}$

4. $\$6(2.5) = \mathbf{\$15}$

5. $24 \ \cancel{\text{shillings}} \cdot \dfrac{12 \text{ pence}}{1 \ \cancel{\text{shilling}}} = \mathbf{288 \text{ pence}}$

6.

-4 -3 -2 -1   0

7.

	Case 1	Case 2
First number	5	20
Second number	12	n

$\dfrac{5}{12} = \dfrac{20}{n}$
$5n = 240$
$n = \mathbf{48}$

8. $4(1.5) + 5 = 6 + 5 = \mathbf{11}$

9. $\dfrac{30 \text{ points}}{5} = 6 \text{ points}$

$4(6 \text{ points}) = \mathbf{24 \text{ points}}$

10. $(P \text{ heads and even}) = P(\text{heads}) \times P(\text{even})$

$\left(\dfrac{1}{2}\right)\left(\dfrac{1}{3}\right) = \dfrac{1}{6}$

11. a. $C = \pi(28 \text{ cm})$
$C = \mathbf{28\pi \text{ cm}}$

b. $C \approx \dfrac{22}{\underset{1}{\cancel{7}}} (\overset{4}{\cancel{28}} \text{ cm})$

$C \approx \mathbf{88 \text{ cm}}$

12. a. $A = \pi r^2$
$A = \pi(196\ \text{cm}^2)$
$A = \mathbf{196\pi\ cm^2}$

b. $A = \pi r^2$
$A \approx \dfrac{22}{7}\overset{28}{(196}\ \text{cm}^2)$
$\phantom{A \approx \dfrac{22}{7}}_{1}$
$A \approx \mathbf{616\ cm^2}$

13. a. $(10\ \text{cm})(10\ \text{cm}) = 100\ \text{cm}^2$
$(100\ \text{cm}^2)(10\ \text{cm}) = \mathbf{1000\ cm^3}$

b. $6(100\ \text{cm}^2) = \mathbf{600\ cm^2}$

14. a. $250\% = \dfrac{250}{100} = 2\dfrac{50}{100} = \mathbf{2\dfrac{1}{2}}$

b. $250\% = \dfrac{250}{100} = \mathbf{2.5}$

c.
$$\begin{array}{r}0.5833\ldots = \mathbf{0.58\overline{3}}\\[2pt]12\overline{)7.0000}\\6\,0\\\hline 1\,00\\96\\\hline 40\\36\\\hline 40\\36\\\hline 4\end{array}$$

d. $\dfrac{7}{12} \times 100\% = \dfrac{700\%}{12} = \mathbf{58\dfrac{1}{3}\%}$

$$\begin{array}{r}58\frac{4}{12} = 58\frac{1}{3}\%\\[2pt]12\overline{)700}\\60\\\hline 100\\96\\\hline 4\end{array}$$

15.
$$\begin{array}{r}\$8.50\\\times\ 0.065\\\hline \$0.5525 \longrightarrow \mathbf{\$0.55}\end{array}$$

16.

	Percent	Actual Count
Commercial time	P_C	12
Other	P_O	48
Total	100	60

$\dfrac{P_C}{100} = \dfrac{12}{60}$
$60P_C = 1200$
$P_C = \mathbf{20\%}$

17.

	Percent	Actual Count
Steam-powered	30	S
Not steam-powered	70	42
Total	100	T

$\dfrac{70}{100} = \dfrac{42}{T}$
$70T = 4200$
$T = \mathbf{60\ boats}$

18. $\dfrac{420}{630} = \dfrac{\overset{1}{2} \cdot \overset{1}{2} \cdot \overset{1}{3} \cdot \overset{1}{5} \cdot \overset{1}{7}}{\underset{1}{2} \cdot \overset{}{3} \cdot \underset{1}{3} \cdot \underset{1}{5} \cdot \underset{1}{7}}$
$= \mathbf{\dfrac{2}{3}}$

19.

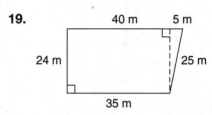

Area of rectangle $= (35\ \text{m})(24\ \text{m})$
$= 840\ \text{m}^2$
Area of triangle $= \dfrac{(24\ \text{m})(5\ \text{m})}{2}$
$= 60\ \text{m}^2$
Area of figure $= 840\ \text{m}^2 + 60\ \text{m}^2$
$= \mathbf{900\ m^2}$

20. a. $m\angle ECD = 180° - (90° + 54°)$
$= 180° - 144° = \mathbf{36°}$

b. $m\angle ECB = 180° - 36° = \mathbf{144°}$

c. $m\angle ACB = m\angle ECD = \mathbf{36°}$

d. $m\angle BAC = \dfrac{180° - 36°}{2} = \dfrac{144°}{2} = \mathbf{72°}$

21. To find y, multiply x by 2 and add 1.

$y = 2x + 1$

x	y
2	5
5	11
7	15
10	21
−5	**−9**

$y = 2(-5) + 1$
$y = -10 + 1$
$y = -9$

22. a. $(3 \times 6) \times (10^4 \times 10^5) = 18 \times 10^9$
$= \mathbf{1.8 \times 10^{10}}$

b. $(1.2 \times 4) \times (10^{-3} \times 10^{-6})$
$= \mathbf{4.8 \times 10^{-9}}$

301

Solutions

23.
$$b - 1\frac{2}{3} = 4\frac{1}{2}$$
$$b - 1\frac{2}{3} + 1\frac{2}{3} = 4\frac{1}{2} + 1\frac{2}{3}$$
$$b = 4\frac{3}{6} + 1\frac{4}{6}$$
$$b = 5\frac{7}{6}$$
$$b = \mathbf{6\frac{1}{6}}$$

check:
$$6\frac{1}{6} - 1\frac{2}{3} = 4\frac{1}{2}$$
$$6\frac{1}{6} - 1\frac{4}{6} = 4\frac{1}{2}$$
$$5\frac{7}{6} - 1\frac{4}{6} = 4\frac{1}{2}$$
$$4\frac{3}{6} = 4\frac{1}{2}$$
$$4\frac{1}{2} = 4\frac{1}{2}$$

24.
$$0.4y = 1.44$$
$$\frac{0.4y}{0.4} = \frac{1.44}{0.4}$$
$$y = \mathbf{3.6}$$

check:
$$0.4(3.6) = 1.44$$
$$1.44 = 1.44$$

25. $2^3 + 2^2 + 2^1 + 2^0 + 2^{-1}$
$$= 8 + 4 + 2 + 1 + \frac{1}{2} = \mathbf{15\frac{1}{2}}$$

26. $\frac{6}{10} \times 3\frac{1}{3} \div 2$
$$= \left(\frac{6}{10} \times \frac{10}{3}\right) \div 2 = 2 \div 2 = \mathbf{1}$$

27. a. 4

   b. −60

28.
$$\frac{5}{24} = \frac{25}{120}$$
$$-\frac{7}{60} = \frac{14}{120}$$
$$\frac{\mathbf{11}}{\mathbf{120}}$$

29. a. $(-3) + (-4) - (-5)$
   $(-3) + (-4) + [-(-5)]$
   $(-3) + (-4) + [5]$
   −2

b. $(-1.5) - (+1.4) + (+1.0)$
   $(-1.5) + [-(+1.4)] + (+1.0)$
   $(-1.5) + [-1.4] + (+1.0)$
   −1.9

30.

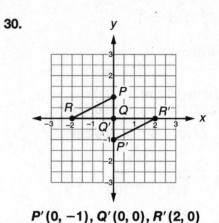

$P'(0, -1), Q'(0, 0), R'(2, 0)$

Practice Set 84

a. Binomial

b. Trinomial

c. Monomial

d. Binomial

e.

$2a^2 + a^2 + 3a - a$	Commutative property
$(2a^2 + a^2) + (3a - a)$	Associative property
$\mathbf{3a^2 + 2a}$	Simplified

f.

$5xy + xy - x - 2x$	Commutative property
$(5xy + xy) + (-x - 2x)$	Associative property
$\mathbf{6xy - 3x}$	Simplified

g.

$x^2 + 2x^2 + x + 3 - 5$	Commutative property
$(x^2 + 2x^2) + x + (+3 - 5)$	Associative property
$\mathbf{3x^2 + x - 2}$	Simplified

h.

$3\pi - \pi + 1.4 + 2.8$	Commutative property
$(3\pi - \pi) + (1.4 + 2.8)$	Associative property
$\mathbf{2\pi + 4.2}$	Simplified

Written Practice (84)

1. **18°F**

2. $2xy + xy - 3x + x$
   $3xy - 2x$

3. **a.** $79°F - 68°F =$ **11°F**

   b. Thursday

   c.
   $$
   \begin{array}{r}
   73°F \\
   68°F \quad 5\overline{)365°F} \\
   72°F \\
   70°F \\
   76°F \\
   + 79°F \\
   \hline
   365°F
   \end{array}
   $$
   $73°F - 70°F =$ **3°F**

4. **a.**
   $$
   \begin{array}{r}
   93.5 \\
   90 \quad 10\overline{)935.0} \\
   90 \\
   100 \\
   95 \\
   95 \\
   85 \\
   100 \\
   100 \\
   80 \\
   + 100 \\
   \hline
   935
   \end{array}
   $$

   b. 80, 85, 90, 90, 95, 95, 100, 100, 100, 100
   $$\frac{(95 + 95)}{2} = \frac{190}{2} = 95$$

   c. 100

   d. $100 - 80 =$ **20**

5.

	Ratio	Actual Count
Rowboats	3	R
Sailboats	7	S
Total	10	210

   $$\frac{7}{10} = \frac{S}{210}$$
   $$10S = 1470$$
   $$S = \textbf{147 sailboats}$$

6.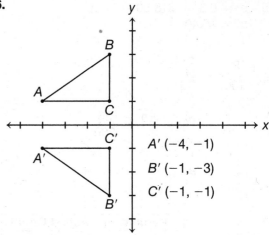

   $A'\ (-4, -1)$
   $B'\ (-1, -3)$
   $C'\ (-1, -1)$

7. $\dfrac{\$1.40}{4} = \dfrac{c}{10}$
   $4c = \$14$
   $c =$ **$3.50**

8. $36 \div 3 = 12$
   $5(12 \text{ members}) =$ **60 members**

9. **a.** $(5)^2 - 2(5) + 1 = 25 - 10 + 1$
   $= $ **16**

   b. $(5 - 1)^2 = (4)^2 =$ **16**

10. $f \ominus g$

11. **a.** $C \approx 3.14(6 \text{ in.})$
    $C \approx$ **18.84 in.**

    b. $A = \pi r^2$
    $A \approx 3.14\ (9 \text{ in.}^2)$
    $A \approx$ **28.26 in.²**

12. $4.8 \text{ meters} \cdot \dfrac{100 \text{ centimeters}}{1 \text{ meter}}$
    $= $ **480 centimeters**

13.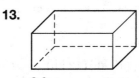

    6 faces

14. **a.** $1\frac{4}{5} = 1\frac{8}{10} =$ **1.8**

    b. $1.8 \times 100\% =$ **180%**

    c. $1.8\% = \dfrac{1.8}{100} \cdot \dfrac{10}{10} = \dfrac{18}{1000} = \dfrac{9}{500}$

    d. $1.8\% =$ **0.018**

Solutions

15. $p = 0.3 \times \$18.00$
$p = \mathbf{\$5.40}$

16. $\dfrac{12\frac{1}{2}}{100} = \dfrac{\frac{25}{2}}{\frac{100}{1}}$

$\dfrac{\frac{25}{2}}{\frac{100}{1}} \cdot \dfrac{\frac{1}{100}}{\frac{1}{100}} = \dfrac{\frac{25}{200}}{1} = \dfrac{25}{200}$

$= \dfrac{1}{8}$

17.

	Percent	Actual Count
Flew the coop	40	36
Stayed	60	S
Total	100	T

$\dfrac{40}{100} = \dfrac{36}{T}$
$40T = 3600$
$T = \mathbf{90\ pigeons}$

18.

	Percent	Actual Count
3 feet tall or less	60	L
More than 3 feet tall	40	M
Total	100	300

$\dfrac{40}{100} = \dfrac{M}{300}$
$100M = 12{,}000$
$M = \mathbf{120\ saplings}$

19.

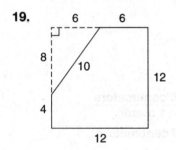

a. Perimeter $= 12\text{ in.} + 12\text{ in.} + 4\text{ in.}$
$+ 10\text{ in.} + 6\text{ in.}$
$= \mathbf{44\ in.}$

b. Area of square $= (12\text{ in.})(12\text{ in.})$
$= 144\text{ in.}^2$
Area of triangle $= \dfrac{(6\text{ in.})(8\text{ in.})}{2}$
$= 24\text{ in.}^2$
Area of figure $= 144\text{ in.}^2 - 24\text{ in.}^2$
$= \mathbf{120\ in.^2}$

20. **a.** $\dfrac{60°}{360°} = \dfrac{1}{6}$

b. $\dfrac{45°}{360°} = \dfrac{1}{8}$

c. $\dfrac{75°}{360°} = \dfrac{5}{24}$

21. To find a term in the sequence, double the preceding term and add 1.
Note: Other rule descriptions are possible, including "The value of the nth term is $2^n - 1$." Discuss various rules proposed by students.
$31 \times 2 + 1 = \mathbf{63}$
$63 \times 2 + 1 = \mathbf{127}$
$127 \times 2 + 1 = \mathbf{255}$

22. **a.** $(1.5 \times 3) \times (10^{-3} \times 10^{6})$
$= \mathbf{4.5 \times 10^3}$

b. $(3 \times 5) \times (10^4 \times 10^5) = 15 \times 10^9$
$= \mathbf{1.5 \times 10^{10}}$

23. **a.** 10^6

b. 10^{-4}

24. $b - 4.75 = 5.2$
$b - 4.75 + 4.75 = 5.2 + 4.75$
$b = \mathbf{9.95}$
check: $9.95 - 4.75 = 5.2$
$5.2 = 5.2$

25. $\dfrac{2}{3}y = 36$

$\left(\dfrac{\overset{1}{\cancel{3}}}{\cancel{2}}\right)\dfrac{\overset{1}{\cancel{2}}}{\cancel{3}}y = \left(\dfrac{3}{\cancel{2}}\right)\overset{18}{\cancel{36}}$

$y = \mathbf{54}$

check: $\dfrac{2}{\cancel{3}}\overset{18}{(\cancel{54})} = 36$

$2(18) = 36$
$36 = 36$

26. $\sqrt{5^2 - 4^2} + 2^3$
$= \sqrt{25 - 16} + 8 = \sqrt{9} + 8$
$= 3 + 8 = \mathbf{11}$

27. $1\text{ m} = 1000\text{ mm}$
$1000\text{ mm} - 45\text{ mm} = \mathbf{955\ mm}$

28. $0.9 \div 2.25 \times 24 = 0.4 \times 24 = \mathbf{9.6}$

29. a. $\dfrac{(-8)(+6)}{(-3)(+4)} = \dfrac{-48}{-12} = \mathbf{4}$

b. $\left(\dfrac{1}{2}\right)\left(-\dfrac{1}{3}\right)\left(\dfrac{1}{4}\right) = \mathbf{-\dfrac{1}{24}}$

30. a.
$$(+30) - (-50) - (+20)$$
$$(+30) + [-(-50)] + [-(+20)]$$
$$(+30) + [50] + [-20]$$
$$\mathbf{60}$$

b.
$$(-0.3) - (-0.4) - (0.5)$$
$$(-0.3) + [-(-0.4)] + [-(0.5)]$$
$$(-0.3) + [0.4] + [-0.5]$$
$$\mathbf{-0.4}$$

Early Finishers Solutions

stem-and-leaf plot; A stem-and-leaf plot is the most appropriate display because it can be used to display individual data points. A line graph usually displays a change over time.

15, 19, 20, 20, 21	22, 25, 25, 28, 28	30, 30, 32, 33, 36	37, 40, 42, 45, 50

Practice Set 85

a.
$$(-3)| + (-3)(-3)| - \dfrac{(-3)}{(+3)} \quad \text{Separated}$$

-3	$+9$	$+1$	Simplified

$$-3 + (+9 + 1) \quad \text{Associative property}$$
$$-3 + 10 \qquad +9 + 1 = +10$$
$$\mathbf{+7}$$

b.
$$(-3) - [(-4) - (-5)(-6)] \quad \text{Separated}$$
$$(-3) - [(-4) - (+30)] \quad (-5)(-6) = +30$$
$$(-3) - (-34) \qquad (-4) - (+30) = -34$$
$$(-3) + 34 \qquad -(-34) = +34$$
$$\mathbf{+31} \qquad -3 + 34 = +31$$

c.
$$(-2)[(-3) - (-4)(-5)] \quad \text{Separated}$$
$$(-2)[(-3) - (+20)] \qquad (-4)(-5) = +20$$
$$(-2)[(-3) + [-(+20)]] \; -(+20) = +[-(+20)]$$
$$(-2)[-23] \qquad -3 + -20 = -23$$
$$\mathbf{+46} \qquad -2 \times -23 = +46$$

d.
$$(-5) - (-5)(-5)| + |-5| \quad \text{Separated}$$
$$(-5) \quad -(+25) \quad +5 \qquad -5 \times -5 = +25$$
$$(-5) + [-(+25)] + 5 \quad -(+25) = +[-(+25)]$$
$$-5 + 5 + [-(+25)] \quad \text{Commutative property}$$
$$0 + [-25] \qquad -5 + 5 = 0$$
$$\mathbf{-25} \qquad \text{Identity property of addition}$$

e.
$$-3 + 4 - 5 - 2$$
$$+4 - 3 - 5 - 2 \quad \text{Commutative property}$$
$$+4 - 10 \qquad \text{Associative property}$$
$$\mathbf{-6} \qquad \text{Simplified}$$

f.
$$-2 + 3(-4) - 5(-2) \quad \text{Separated}$$
$$-2 + (-12) - (-10) \quad \text{Simplified}$$
$$-14 - (-10) \qquad \text{Associative property}$$
$$-14 + [-(-10)] \qquad -(-10) = +[-(-10)]$$
$$-14 + [10] \qquad -(-10) = +10$$
$$\mathbf{-4} \qquad \text{Simplified}$$

g.
$$-3(-2) - 5(2) + 3(-4) \quad \text{Separated}$$
$$(+6) - (+10) + (-12) \quad \text{Simplified}$$
$$(+6) + (-12) - (+10) \quad \text{Commutative property}$$
$$(-6) + [-(+10)] \qquad -(+10) = +[-(+10)]$$
$$(-6) + [-10] \qquad [-(+10)] = [-10]$$
$$\mathbf{-16} \qquad \text{Simplified}$$

h.
$$-4(-3)(-2) - 6(-4) \quad \text{Separated}$$
$$-4(+6) - (-24) \qquad \text{Simplified}$$
$$(-24) + [-(-24)] \quad \text{Simplified}, \; -(-24) = +[-(-24)]$$
$$(-24) + [24] \qquad [-(-24)] = [24]$$
$$\mathbf{0} \qquad \text{Simplified}$$

Written Practice 85

1. a.

$$10\overline{)840} = 84$$

70
80
90
80
70
90
75
95
100
$+\ 90$
840

b. 70, 70, 75, 80, **80, 90,** 90, 90, 95, 100
$$\dfrac{80 + 90}{2} = \dfrac{170}{2} = \mathbf{85}$$

Solutions

c. 90

d. $100 - 70 = \textbf{30}$

2.

	Ratio	Actual Count
Won	3	W
Lost	1	L
Total	4	24

$$\frac{1}{4} = \frac{L}{24}$$
$$4L = 24$$
$$L = \textbf{6 games}$$

3.

	Ratio	Actual Count
Dandelions	11	D
Marigolds	4	44

$$\frac{11}{4} = \frac{D}{44}$$
$$4D = 484$$
$$D = \textbf{121 dandelions}$$

4.

	Case 1	Case 2
Miles	2	m
Seconds	10	60

$$\frac{2}{10} = \frac{m}{60}$$
$$10m = 120$$
$$m = \textbf{12 miles}$$

5. $0.98 \text{ liter} \cdot \dfrac{1000 \text{ milliliters}}{1 \text{ liter}} = \textbf{980 milliliters}$

6.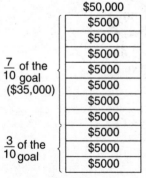

7.

$\frac{7}{10}$ of the goal ($35,000)

$50,000

$5000
$5000
$5000
$5000
$5000
$5000
$5000
$5000
$5000
$5000

$\frac{3}{10}$ of the goal

a. $\dfrac{\$35,000}{7} = \$5000$

$10 \times \$5000 = \textbf{\$50,000}$

b. **30%**

8. a. $C \approx 3.14\,(8\text{ m})$
$C \approx \textbf{25.12 m}$

b. $A = \pi r^2$
$A \approx 3.14\,(16\text{ m}^2)$
$A \approx \textbf{50.24 m}^2$

9. $\dfrac{2}{5} = \dfrac{8}{20}, \dfrac{1}{4} = \dfrac{5}{20}$

$$\frac{8}{20} + \frac{5}{20} = \frac{13}{20}$$

$$\frac{20}{20} - \frac{13}{20} = \frac{7}{20} \textbf{ shaded}$$

10. $\text{P(shaded)} \times \text{P(shaded)} = \dfrac{7}{20} \times \dfrac{7}{20} = \dfrac{\textbf{49}}{\textbf{400}}$

11.

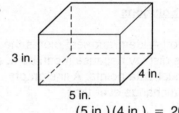

3 in.   4 in.   5 in.

$(5\text{ in.})(4\text{ in.}) = 20\text{ in.}^2$

$\dfrac{20\text{ in.}^2}{1\text{ layer}} \cdot 1\text{ in.}\,(3\text{ layers}) = \textbf{60 in.}^3$

12. One possibility:

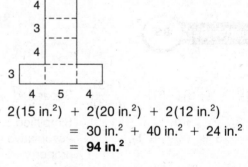

4   3   4   3   4   5   4

$2(15\text{ in.}^2) + 2(20\text{ in.}^2) + 2(12\text{ in.}^2)$
$= 30\text{ in.}^2 + 40\text{ in.}^2 + 24\text{ in.}^2$
$= \textbf{94 in.}^2$

13. a. $\dfrac{1}{40} \cdot \dfrac{25}{25} = \dfrac{25}{1000} = 0.025$

b. $\dfrac{1}{40} \times 100\% = \dfrac{100\%}{40} = \textbf{2}\dfrac{\textbf{1}}{\textbf{2}}\textbf{\%}$

$$40\overline{)100} \quad 2\tfrac{20}{40} = 2\tfrac{1}{2}\%$$
$$\underline{80}$$
$$20$$

c. $0.25\% = \dfrac{0.25}{100} \cdot \dfrac{100}{100} = \dfrac{25}{10,000} = \dfrac{\textbf{1}}{\textbf{400}}$

d. $0.25\% = \textbf{0.0025}$

14.
$$\begin{array}{r} \$180,000 \\ \times \quad 0.06 \\ \hline \$10,800 \end{array}$$

15.

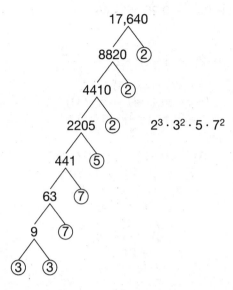

$2^3 \cdot 3^2 \cdot 5 \cdot 7^2$

a. $\mathbf{2^3 \cdot 3^2 \cdot 5 \cdot 7^2}$

b. **The exponents of the prime factors of 17,640 are not all even numbers.**

16.

$$\frac{8\frac{1}{3}}{100} = \frac{\frac{25}{3}}{\frac{100}{1}}$$

$$\frac{\frac{25}{3}}{\frac{100}{1}} \cdot \frac{\frac{1}{100}}{\frac{1}{100}} = \frac{\frac{25}{300}}{1} = \frac{25}{300}$$

$$= \mathbf{\frac{1}{12}}$$

17.

	Percent	Actual Count
Correct	P_C	38
Incorrect	P_I	2
Total	100	40

$$\frac{P_C}{100} = \frac{38}{40}$$
$$40P_C = 3800$$
$$P_C = \mathbf{95\%}$$

18.

	Percent	Actual Count
Happy faces	35	H
Not happy faces	65	91
Total	100	T

$$\frac{65}{100} = \frac{91}{T}$$
$$65T = 9100$$
$$T = \mathbf{140 \text{ children}}$$

19.

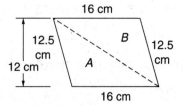

a. **Parallelogram**

b. Perimeter $= 12.5$ cm $+ 16$ cm
$+ 12.5$ cm $+ 16$ cm $= \mathbf{57\ cm}$

c. Area $= (12$ cm$)(16$ cm$)$
$= \mathbf{192\ cm^2}$

d.

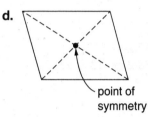

point of symmetry

20. a. $m\angle TOS = \mathbf{90°}$

b. $m\angle QOT = \mathbf{180°}$

c. $m\angle QOR = \dfrac{90°}{3} = \mathbf{30°}$

d. $m\angle TOR = 90° + 60° = \mathbf{150°}$

21.
$y = 2(5) - 1$
$y = 10 - 1$
$y = \mathbf{9};$
$y = 2(3) - 1$
$y = 6 - 1$
$y = \mathbf{5};$
$y = 2(1) - 1$
$y = 2 - 1$
$y = \mathbf{1}$

$y = 2x - 1$

x	y
5	9
3	5
1	1

22. $(5 \times 10^{-3})(6 \times 10^8) = (5 \times 6)(10^{-3} \times 10^8)$
$$= 30 \times 10^5$$
$$= 3.0 \times 10^6$$

$(5 \times 10^8)(6 \times 10^{-3}) = (5 \times 6)(10^8 \times 10^{-3})$
$$= 30 \times 10^5$$
$$= 3.0 \times 10^6$$

$(5 \times 10^{-3})(6 \times 10^8)$
$$= (5 \times 10^8)(6 \times 10^{-3})$$

23. $13.2 = 1.2w$
$$\frac{13.2}{1.2} = \frac{1.2w}{1.2}$$
$$\mathbf{11} = w$$

check: $\quad 13.2 = 1.2(11)$
$$13.2 = 13.2$$

24. $\quad c + \dfrac{5}{6} = 1\dfrac{1}{4}$

$c + \dfrac{5}{6} - \dfrac{5}{6} = 1\dfrac{1}{4} - \dfrac{5}{6}$

$\quad\quad\quad c = 1\dfrac{3}{12} - \dfrac{10}{12}$

$\quad\quad\quad c = \dfrac{15}{12} - \dfrac{10}{12}$

$\quad\quad\quad c = \mathbf{\dfrac{5}{12}}$

check: $\quad \dfrac{5}{12} + \dfrac{5}{6} = 1\dfrac{1}{4}$

$\quad\quad\quad \dfrac{5}{12} + \dfrac{10}{12} = 1\dfrac{1}{4}$

$\quad\quad\quad\quad \dfrac{15}{12} = 1\dfrac{1}{4}$

$\quad\quad\quad\quad 1\dfrac{3}{12} = 1\dfrac{1}{4}$

$\quad\quad\quad\quad 1\dfrac{1}{4} = 1\dfrac{1}{4}$

25. $3\{20 - [6^2 - 3(10 - 4)]\}$
$\quad 3\{20 - [36 - 3(6)]\}$
$\quad\quad 3\{20 - [36 - 18]\}$
$\quad\quad\quad 3\{20 - [18]\}$
$\quad\quad\quad\quad 3\{2\}$
$\quad\quad\quad\quad\quad \mathbf{6}$

26.

$\overset{(60\text{ min})}{\nearrow}$

$\overset{2}{\cancel{3}} \text{ hr } \overset{14}{\cancel{15}} \text{ min } 25 \text{ s} \quad\overset{(60\text{ s})}{\longrightarrow}$
$- \; 2 \text{ hr } 45 \text{ min } 30 \text{ s} \quad\longrightarrow$

$\overset{2}{\cancel{3}} \text{ hr } \overset{\overset{74}{14}}{\cancel{15}} \text{ min } \overset{85}{\cancel{25}} \text{ s}$
$- \; 2 \text{ hr } \quad 45 \text{ min } \quad 30 \text{ s}$
$\quad\quad\quad\quad \mathbf{29 \text{ min } 55 \text{ s}}$

27. $1 + 0.2 + 0.25 = \mathbf{1.45}$

28. a. $(-2) + (-2)(+2) - \dfrac{(-2)}{(-2)}$
$\quad\quad (-2) + (-4) - 1$
$\quad\quad (-2) + (-4) + [-(1)]$
$\quad\quad (-2) - (-4) + (-1)$
$\quad\quad\quad\quad \mathbf{-7}$

b. $(-3) - [(-2) - (+4)(-5)]$
$\quad (-3) - [(-2) - (-20)]$
$\quad\quad (-3) - [(-2) + 20]$
$\quad\quad\quad (-3) - [18]$
$\quad\quad\quad (-3) + [-(18)]$
$\quad\quad\quad (-3) + (-18)$
$\quad\quad\quad\quad \mathbf{-21}$

29. $x^2 + 6x - 2x - 12$
$\quad x^2 + 4x - 12$

30. a. $D(1, -1)$

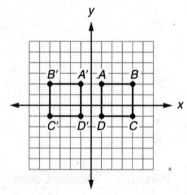

b. $A'(-1, 2), B'(-4, 2),$
$\quad C'(-4, -1), D'(-1, -1)$

Practice Set 86

a.

number line: dots at $-3, -2, -1, 0$; marks from -4 to 0

b.

number line: dots at $0, 1, 2, 3$; marks from -1 to 4

c. False

d. True

308

Written Practice 86

1.
$$\frac{\$28.50}{3 \text{ ounces}} = \frac{\$9.50}{1 \text{ ounce}}$$
$$\frac{\$4.96}{8 \text{ ounces}} = \frac{\$0.62}{1 \text{ ounce}}$$
$$\begin{array}{r} \$9.50 \\ -\ \$0.62 \\ \hline \end{array}$$
$8.88 more per ounce

2.

	Ratio	Actual Count
Rookies	2	R
Veterans	7	V
Total	9	252

$$\frac{2}{9} = \frac{R}{252}$$
$$9R = 504$$
$$R = \textbf{56 rookies}$$

3. a. 213 lb

   b. 197, 205, 207, <u>213</u>, 213, 238, 246
      213 lb

   c.
$$\begin{array}{r} \textbf{217 lb} \\ 7)\overline{1519} \end{array}$$

$$\begin{array}{r} 197 \\ 213 \\ 246 \\ 205 \\ 238 \\ 213 \\ +\ 207 \\ \hline 1519 \end{array}$$

   d. 246 lb − 197 lb = **49 lb**

4. 12 ~~bushels~~ · $\dfrac{4 \text{ pecks}}{1 \text{ ~~bushel~~}}$ = **48 pecks**

5. $\dfrac{468 \text{ miles}}{9 \text{ hours}}$ = **52 miles per hour**

6.

```
◄─●──●──●──●──●──┼─►
  -1  0  1  2  3  4
```

7.

	Case 1	Case 2
First number	9	n
Second number	6	30

$$\frac{9}{6} = \frac{n}{30}$$
$$6n = 270$$
$$n = \textbf{45}$$

8. a.
$$1800 \div 10 = 180$$
$$9(180 \text{ students}) = \textbf{1620 students}$$

   b. $\dfrac{1}{10} \times 100\% = \textbf{10\%}$

9. $\sqrt{(5)^2 - 4(1)(4)}$
$$= \sqrt{25 - 16} = \sqrt{9} = \textbf{3}$$

10. $\dfrac{\text{free throws made}}{\text{total free throws}} = \dfrac{40}{60} = \dfrac{\textbf{2}}{\textbf{3}}$

11. a. $C = \pi(24 \text{ in.})$
      $C = \textbf{24}\pi \textbf{ in.}$

   b. $A = \pi r^2$
      $A = \pi(144 \text{ in.}^2)$
      $A = \textbf{144}\pi \textbf{ in.}^2$

12. a. $\mathbf{10^5}$

   b. $\mathbf{10^{-3}}$

13.

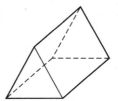

   a. 5 faces

   b. 9 edges

   c. 6 vertices

14. a. $0.9 = \dfrac{\textbf{9}}{\textbf{10}}$

   b. 0.9 = 90%

   c. $\dfrac{11}{12} = \mathbf{0.91\overline{6}}$

$$\begin{array}{r} 0.9166\ldots = \textbf{0.91}\overline{\textbf{6}} \\ 12)\overline{11.0000} \\ \underline{10\ 8} \\ 20 \\ \underline{12} \\ 80 \\ \underline{72} \\ 80 \\ \underline{72} \\ 8 \end{array}$$

d. $\frac{11}{12} \times 100\% = \frac{1100\%}{12} = 91\frac{2}{3}\%$

$$91\frac{8}{12} = 91\frac{2}{3}\%$$

$$
\begin{array}{r}
12)\overline{1100} \\
\underline{108} \\
20 \\
\underline{12} \\
8
\end{array}
$$

15. North

16.

	Percent	Actual Count
Sale price	60	$24
Regular price	100	R

$$\frac{60}{100} = \frac{\$24}{R}$$
$$60R = \$2400$$
$$R = \textbf{\$40}$$

17.

	Percent	Actual Count
Sprouted seeds	75	48
Unsprouted seeds	25	U
Total	100	T

$$\frac{75}{25} = \frac{48}{U}$$
$$75U = 1200$$
$$U = \textbf{16 seeds}$$

18. $30 = W_P \times 20$

$$\frac{30}{20} = \frac{W_P \times 20}{20}$$

$$\frac{3}{2} = W_P$$

$$W_P = \frac{3}{2} \times 100\% = \textbf{150\%}$$

19.

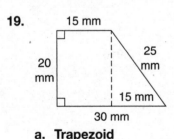

a. Trapezoid

b. Perimeter $= 15\text{ mm} + 25\text{ mm} + 30\text{ mm}$
$+ 20\text{ mm} = \textbf{90 mm}$

c. Area of rectangle $= (15\text{ mm})(20\text{ mm})$
$= 300\text{ mm}^2$
Area of triangle $= \dfrac{(15\text{ mm})(20\text{ mm})}{2}$
$= 150\text{ mm}^2$
Area of figure $= 300\text{ mm}^2 + 150\text{ mm}^2$
$= \textbf{450 mm}^2$

20. a. 120°

b. 165°

c. $165° - 30° = \textbf{135°}$

21.

$y = x + 1$			See student work for
			x, y pair:

x	y
3	4
5	6
1	2

$y = 3 + 1 = 4$ **Example:**
$y = 5 + 1 = 6$ $(0, 1)$
$y = 1 + 1 = 2$ $y = x + 1$
              $1 = 0 + 1$
              $1 = 1$

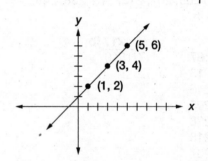

22. a. $(1.2 \times 1.2) \times (10^5 \times 10^{-8})$
$= \textbf{1.44} \times \textbf{10}^{-3}$

b. $(6 \times 7) \times (10^{-3} \times 10^{-4})$
$= 42 \times 10^{-7}$
$= \textbf{4.2} \times \textbf{10}^{-6}$

23. $56 = \dfrac{7}{8} w$

$$\left(\frac{8}{7}\right)^{1}\overset{8}{\cancel{56}} = \left(\frac{\cancel{8}}{\cancel{7}}\right)^{1}\frac{\cancel{7}}{\cancel{8}} w$$

$$\textbf{64} = w$$

check: $56 = \dfrac{7}{\cancel{8}}(\overset{8}{\cancel{64}})$

             $56 = 7(8)$

             $56 = 56$

24. $4.8 + c = 7.34$
$4.8 - 4.8 + c = 7.34 - 4.8$
$c = \mathbf{2.54}$

check: $\quad 4.8 + 2.54 = 7.34$
$7.34 = 7.34$

25. $\sqrt{10^2 - 6^2} - \sqrt{10^2 - 8^2}$
$\sqrt{100 - 36} - \sqrt{100 - 64}$
$\sqrt{64} - \sqrt{36}$
$8 - 6$
$\mathbf{2}$

26.
$$\begin{array}{r} 5\text{ lb} \quad 9\text{ oz} \\ + \ 4\text{ lb} \quad 7\text{ oz} \\ \hline 9\text{ lb} \quad 16\text{ oz} \end{array}$$
$16\text{ oz} = 1\text{ lb}$
$1\text{ lb} + 9\text{ lb} = \mathbf{10\ lb}$

27. $1.4 \div 3.5 \times 1000$
$= 0.4 \times 1000 = \mathbf{400}$

28. a. $(-4)(-5) - (-4)(+3)$
$+20 - (-12)$
$20 + [-(-12)]$
$+20 + 12$
$\mathbf{32}$

b. $(-2)[(-3) - (-4)(+5)]$
$(-2)[(-3) - (-20)]$
$(-2)[(-3) + (20)]$
$(-2)[+17]$
$\mathbf{-34}$

29. $x^2 + 3xy + 2x^2 - xy$
$x^2 + 2x^2 + 3xy - xy$
$\mathbf{3x^2 + 2xy}$

30. $3 \cdot 3 \cdot x \cdot y \cdot y$

Practice Set 87

a. $(-3x)(-2xy)$
$= (-3) \cdot x \cdot (-2) \cdot x \cdot y$ List factors
$= (-3)(-2) \cdot x \cdot x \cdot y$ Commutative property
$= \mathbf{6x^2y}$ Associative property

b. $3x^2(xy^3)$
$= (3) \cdot x \cdot x \cdot x \cdot y \cdot y \cdot y$ List factors
$= \mathbf{3x^3y^3}$ Associative property

c. $(2a^2)(-3ab^3)$
$= 2 \cdot a \cdot a \cdot (-3) \cdot a \cdot b \cdot b \cdot b$ List factors
$= (2)(-3) \cdot a \cdot a \cdot a \cdot b \cdot b \cdot b$ Commutative property
$= \mathbf{-6a^3b^3}$ Associative property

d. $(-4x)(-5x^2y)$
$= (-4) \cdot x \cdot (-5) \cdot x \cdot x \cdot y$ List factors
$= (-4)(-5) \cdot x \cdot x \cdot x \cdot y$ Commutative property
$= \mathbf{20x^3y}$ Associative property

e. $(-xy^2)(xy)(2y)$
$= (-1) \cdot x \cdot y \cdot y \cdot x \cdot y \cdot (2) \cdot y$
$= (-1)(2) \cdot x \cdot x \cdot y \cdot y \cdot y \cdot y$
$= \mathbf{-2x^2y^4}$

f. $(-3m)(-2mn)(m^2n)$
$= (-3) \cdot m \cdot (-2) \cdot m \cdot n \cdot m \cdot m \cdot n$
$= (-3)(-2) \cdot m \cdot m \cdot m \cdot m \cdot n \cdot n$
$= \mathbf{6m^4n^2}$

g. $(4wy)(3wx)(-w^2)(x^2y)$
$= (4) \cdot w \cdot y \cdot (3) \cdot w \cdot x \cdot (-1)$
$\quad \cdot w \cdot w \cdot x \cdot x \cdot y$
$= (4)(3)(-1) \cdot w \cdot w \cdot w \cdot w$
$\quad \cdot x \cdot x \cdot x \cdot y \cdot y$
$= \mathbf{-12w^4x^3y^2}$

h. $5d(-2df)(-3d^2fg)$
$= (5) \cdot d \cdot (-2) \cdot d \cdot f \cdot (-3) \cdot d \cdot d \cdot f \cdot g$
$= (5)(-2)(-3) \cdot d \cdot d \cdot d \cdot d \cdot f \cdot f \cdot g$
$= \mathbf{30d^4f^2g}$

i. Method 1—Show factors
$(3xy^3)^2$
$= (3xy^3)(3xy^3)$
$= (3) \cdot x \cdot y \cdot y \cdot y \cdot (3) \cdot x \cdot y \cdot y \cdot y$
$= (3) \cdot (3) \cdot x \cdot x \cdot y \cdot y \cdot y \cdot y \cdot y \cdot y$
$= \mathbf{9x^2y^6}$

Method 2—Exponent rules
$(3xy^3)^2$
$= (3)^2 (x)^2 (y^3)^2$
$= \mathbf{9x^2y^6}$

Written Practice 87

1. $2.5 \text{ hours} \cdot \dfrac{450 \text{ miles}}{1 \text{ hour}}$
$= \mathbf{1125\ miles}$

Solutions

2. $12.5 \text{ centimeters} \cdot \dfrac{1 \text{ meter}}{100 \text{ centimeters}}$

$= \textbf{0.125 meter}$

3.

	Ratio	Actual Count
Girls	4	240
Boys	3	180
Total	7	420

$\dfrac{\text{boys}}{\text{girls}} = \dfrac{3}{4}$

4.

$18'\,3'' = 219''$
$17'10'' = 214''$
$+\ 17'11'' = 215''$
$\underline{\hspace{3cm}}$
$648''$

$\dfrac{216''}{3\overline{)648''}}$

$216'' = \textbf{18}'$

5. $\dfrac{468 \text{ miles}}{18 \text{ gallons}} = \textbf{26 miles per gallon}$

6.

7.

	Case 1	Case 2
Yards	100	1500
Feet	36	f

$\dfrac{100}{36} = \dfrac{1500}{f}$
$100f = 54{,}000$
$f = \textbf{540 feet}$

8.
a. $m\angle a = 180° - 105° = \textbf{75°}$

b. $m\angle b = 180° - 75° = \textbf{105°}$

c. $m\angle c = 180° - 105° = \textbf{75°}$

d. $m\angle d = m\angle a = \textbf{75°}$

e. $m\angle e = m\angle b = \textbf{105°}$

9. $y = 3(-4) - 1$
$y = -12 - 1$
$y = \textbf{-13}$

10. a. $C \approx \dfrac{22}{7}(\overset{20}{\cancel{140}} \text{ mm})$

$ \underset{1}{}$

$C \approx \textbf{440 mm}$

b. $A = \pi r^2$

$A \approx \dfrac{22}{\underset{1}{7}}(\overset{700}{\cancel{4900}} \text{ mm}^2)$

$A \approx \textbf{15,400 mm}^2$

11.

a. Area $=$ (5 units)(5 units)
$\phantom{\text{Area}} = \textbf{25 units}^2$

b. $m\angle A = \textbf{135°}$
$m\angle B = \textbf{45°}$
$m\angle C = \textbf{135°}$
$m\angle D = \textbf{45°}$

12. Bottom Rectangular prism: (6 cubes)(3 cubes)
$ = 18 \text{ cubes}$

$\dfrac{18 \text{ cubes}}{1 \text{ layer}} \cdot 2 \text{ layers} = 36 \text{ cubes}$

36 in.^3

Top Rectangular prism: (2 cubes)(3 cubes)
$ = 6 \text{ cubes}$

$\dfrac{6 \text{ cubes}}{1 \text{ layer}} \cdot 2 \text{ layers} = 12 \text{ cubes}, 12 \text{ in.}^3$

$36 \text{ in.}^3 + 12 \text{ in.}^3 = \textbf{48 in.}^3$

13. a. $12\dfrac{1}{2}\% = \dfrac{12\frac{1}{2}}{100} = \dfrac{\frac{25}{2}}{100}$

$\dfrac{\frac{25}{2}}{\frac{100}{1}} \cdot \dfrac{\frac{1}{100}}{\frac{1}{100}} = \dfrac{\frac{25}{200}}{1} = \dfrac{25}{200} = \dfrac{1}{8}$

b. $12\dfrac{1}{2}\% = 12.5\% = \textbf{0.125}$

c. $\dfrac{7}{8} = \textbf{0.875}$

$\begin{array}{r} 0.875 \\ 8\overline{)7.000} \\ \underline{6\ 4} \\ 60 \\ \underline{56} \\ 40 \\ \underline{40} \\ 0 \end{array}$

d. $\frac{7}{8} \times 100\% = \frac{700\%}{8} = \mathbf{87\frac{1}{2}\%}$

$$87\frac{4}{8} = \mathbf{87\frac{1}{2}\%}$$

$$8\overline{)700}$$
$$\underline{64}$$
$$60$$
$$\underline{56}$$
$$4$$

14. $W_N = \frac{1}{4} \times 4$

$W_N = \mathbf{1}$

15.

	Percent	Actual Count
Sale price	80	$24
Regular price	100	P

$$\frac{80}{100} = \frac{\$24}{P}$$
$$80P = \$2400$$
$$P = \mathbf{\$30}$$

16.

	Percent	Actual Count
Meters ran	60	M
Meters left	40	2000
Total	100	T

$$\frac{40}{100} = \frac{2000}{T}$$
$$40T = 200{,}000$$
$$T = \mathbf{5000 \text{ meters}}$$

17. $100 = W_P \times 80$

$$\frac{100}{80} = \frac{W_P \times 80}{80}$$

$$\frac{5}{4} = W_P$$

$$W_P = \frac{5}{4} \times 100\% = \mathbf{125\%}$$

18.

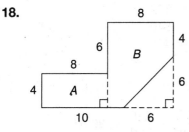

Area of rectangle A = (4 cm)(8 cm)
$\qquad$ = 32 cm²
Area of rectangle B = (8 cm)(10 cm)
$\qquad$ = 80 cm²
Area of A + B = 32 cm² + 80 cm²
$\qquad$ = 112 cm²
Area of triangle = $\dfrac{(6 \text{ cm})(6 \text{ cm})}{2}$

$\qquad\qquad\qquad$ = 18 cm²
112 cm² − 18 cm² = **94 cm²**

19. a. $m\angle AOB = \dfrac{90°}{3} = \mathbf{30°}$

b. $m\angle AOC = 30° + 30° = \mathbf{60°}$

c. $m\angle EOC = 90° + 30° = \mathbf{120°}$

d. $\angle \mathbf{COA}$ or $\angle \mathbf{AOC}$

20.
$$\frac{66\frac{2}{3}}{100} = \frac{\frac{200}{3}}{\frac{100}{1}}$$

$$\frac{\frac{200}{3}}{\frac{100}{1}} \cdot \frac{\frac{1}{100}}{\frac{1}{100}} = \frac{\frac{200}{300}}{1} = \frac{200}{300}$$

$$= \mathbf{\frac{2}{3}}$$

21. $y = 2x - 3$

x	y
1	−1
2	1
3	3

$y = 2(1) - 3 = 2 - 3 = -1$
$y = 2(2) - 3 = 4 - 3 = 1$
$y = 2(3) - 3 = 6 - 3 = 3$

See student work for x, y pair.
Example: (4, 5)
$$y = 2x - 3$$
$$(5) = 2(4) - 3$$
$$5 = 8 - 3$$
$$5 = 5$$

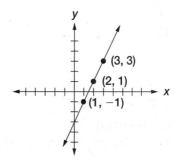

22. a. $(4 \times 2.1) \times (10^{-5} \times 10^{-7})$
$\qquad\qquad = \mathbf{8.4 \times 10^{-12}}$

b. $(4 \times 6) \times (10^5 \times 10^7) = 24 \times (10^{12})$
$\qquad\qquad\qquad\qquad = \mathbf{2.4 \times 10^{13}}$

23.
$$d - 8.47 = 9.1$$
$$d - 8.47 + 8.47 = 9.1 + 8.47$$
$$d = \mathbf{17.57}$$
check: $\qquad 17.57 - 8.47 = 9.1$
$$9.1 = 9.1$$

24. $0.25m = 3.6$

$$\frac{0.25m}{0.25} = \frac{3.6}{0.25}$$

$m = \mathbf{14.4}$

check: $0.25(14.4) = 3.6$

$3.6 = 3.6$

25. $\dfrac{3 + 5.2 - 1}{4 - 3 + 2}$

$\dfrac{8.2 - 1}{1 + 2}$

$\dfrac{7.2}{3}$

$\mathbf{2.4}$

26. $1 \text{ kg} = 1000 \text{ g}$, $1000 \text{ g} - 75 \text{ g} = \mathbf{925 \text{ g}}$

27. $3.7 + 2.625 + 15 = \mathbf{21.325}$

28. a. $(-5) - (-2)[(-3) - (+4)]$

$(-5) - (-2)[-7]$

$(-5) - (+14)$

$(-5) + [-(+14)]$

$(-5) + [-14]$

$\mathbf{-19}$

b. $\dfrac{(-3) + (-3)(+4)}{(+3) + (-4)}$

$\dfrac{(-3) + (-12)}{-1}$

$\dfrac{-15}{-1}$

$\mathbf{15}$

29. a. $(3x)(4y)$

$= (3) \cdot x \cdot (4) \cdot y$

$= (3)(4) \cdot x \cdot y = \mathbf{12xy}$

b. $(6m)(-4m^2n)(-mnp)$

$= (6) \cdot m \cdot (-4) \cdot m \cdot m \cdot n \cdot (-1)$

$\cdot m \cdot n \cdot p$

$= (6)(-4)(-1) \cdot m \cdot m \cdot m \cdot m$

$\cdot n \cdot n \cdot p$

$= \mathbf{24m^4n^2p}$

c. $(3x^3)^2 = (3)^2 \cdot (x^3)^2 = \mathbf{9x^6}$

30. $3ab + a - ab - 2ab + a$

$3ab - ab - 2ab + a + a$

$\mathbf{2a}$

Early Finishers Solutions

a. Beau's Bikes: $y = 10t$
Celine's Cycles: $y = 4t + 15$

b. Beau's Bikes; It costs $3 less per bike.

c. Celine's Cycles; It costs $9 less per bike.

Practice Set **88**

a. $5 \text{ yd} \cdot \dfrac{3 \text{ ft}}{1 \text{ yd}} \cdot \dfrac{12 \text{ in.}}{1 \text{ ft}} = \mathbf{180 \text{ in.}}$

b. $1\dfrac{1}{2} \text{ hr} \cdot \dfrac{60 \text{ min}}{1 \text{ hr}} \cdot \dfrac{60 \text{ s}}{1 \text{ min}}$

$= \mathbf{5400 \text{ s}}$

c. $15 \text{ yd}^2 \cdot \dfrac{3 \text{ ft}}{1 \text{ yd}} \cdot \dfrac{3 \text{ ft}}{1 \text{ yd}}$

$= \mathbf{135 \text{ ft}^2}$

d. $270 \text{ ft}^3 \times \dfrac{1 \text{ yd}}{3 \text{ ft}} \times \dfrac{1 \text{ yd}}{3 \text{ ft}} \times \dfrac{1 \text{ yd}}{3 \text{ ft}} = \mathbf{10 \text{ yd}^3}$

e. $\dfrac{800 \text{ m}}{2 \text{ min}} \times \dfrac{1 \text{ km}}{1000 \text{ m}} \times \dfrac{60 \text{ min}}{1 \text{ hr}} = \mathbf{24 \dfrac{\text{km}}{\text{hr}}}$

f. $1 \text{ in.}^3 \cdot \dfrac{2.54 \text{ cm}}{1 \text{ in.}} \cdot \dfrac{2.54 \text{ cm}}{1 \text{ in.}} \cdot \dfrac{2.54 \text{ cm}}{1 \text{ in.}}$

$= \mathbf{16.387064 \text{ cm}^3}$

One cubic inch is about 16 cubic cm.

Written Practice **88**

1. $\$6(3.25) = \mathbf{\$19.50}$

2. $4(93) = 372$

$10(84) = 840$

$840 - 372 = 468$

$6\overline{)468} = 78$

3. a. $4 \text{ yd}^2 \cdot \dfrac{3 \text{ ft}}{1 \text{ yd}} \cdot \dfrac{3 \text{ ft}}{1 \text{ yd}} = \mathbf{36 \text{ ft}^2}$

b. $4 \text{ yd}^3 \cdot \dfrac{3 \text{ ft}}{1 \text{ yd}} \cdot \dfrac{3 \text{ ft}}{1 \text{ yd}} \cdot \dfrac{3 \text{ ft}}{1 \text{ yd}} = \mathbf{108 \text{ ft}^3}$

4.

	Ratio	Actual Count
Woodwinds	3	15
Brass instruments	2	B

$$\frac{3}{2} = \frac{15}{B}$$
$$3B = 30$$
$$B = \textbf{10 brass instruments}$$

5.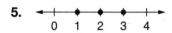

6.

	Case 1	Case 2
Artichokes	8	36
Price	\$2	p

$$\frac{8}{\$2} = \frac{36}{p}$$
$$8p = \$72$$
$$p = \textbf{\$9}$$

7.

$\frac{2}{3}$ were on (18). $\frac{1}{3}$ were off.

27 lights
| 9 lights |
| 9 lights |
| 9 lights |

a. $18 \div 2 = 9$, $1(9 \text{ lights}) = \textbf{9 lights}$

b. $\frac{2}{3} \times 100\% = \textbf{66}\frac{\textbf{2}}{\textbf{3}}\textbf{\%}$

8. $(5) - [(3) - (5 - 3)]$
$= 5 - [3 - 2] = 5 - [1] = \textbf{4}$

9. $60 - 42 = 18$ times stopped on A

$$P(A) = \frac{18}{60} = \textbf{0.3}$$

10. a. $C = \pi(60 \text{ ft})$
$C \approx 3.14(60 \text{ ft})$
$C \approx \textbf{188.4 ft}$

b. $A = \pi r^2$
$A \approx 3.14(900 \text{ ft}^2)$
$A \approx \textbf{2826 ft}^2$

11. $1 - \left(\frac{4}{12} + \frac{5}{12}\right) = \frac{3}{12} = \frac{1}{4}$

$$\frac{1}{4} \times 100\% = \textbf{25\%}$$

12.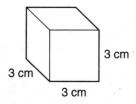

3 cm

3 cm

3 cm

a. $(3 \text{ cm})(3 \text{ cm}) = 9 \text{ cm}^2$
$$\frac{9 \text{ cm}^2}{1 \text{ layer}} \cdot (1 \text{ cm})(3 \text{ layers}) = \textbf{27 cm}^3$$

b. $6(9 \text{ cm}^2) = \textbf{54 cm}^2$

13. $2x + 3y - 5 + x - y - 1$
$2x + x + 3y - y - 5 - 1$
$\textbf{3x + 2y - 6}$

14. $x^2 + 2x - x - 2$
$\textbf{x}^2 + \textbf{x} - \textbf{2}$

15. a. $0.125 = \frac{125}{1000} = \frac{1}{8}$

b. $0.125 \times 100\% = 12.5\%$ or $\textbf{12}\frac{\textbf{1}}{\textbf{2}}\textbf{\%}$

c. $\frac{3}{8} = \textbf{0.375}$

$$
\begin{array}{r}
0.375 \\
8)\overline{3.000} \\
\underline{2\,4} \\
60 \\
\underline{56} \\
40 \\
\underline{40} \\
0
\end{array}
$$

d. $\frac{3}{8} \times 100\% = \frac{300\%}{8} = \textbf{37}\frac{\textbf{1}}{\textbf{2}}\textbf{\%}$

$$37\frac{4}{8} = 37\frac{1}{2}\%$$
$$
\begin{array}{r}
8)\overline{300} \\
\underline{24} \\
60 \\
\underline{56} \\
4
\end{array}
$$

16. $\dfrac{60}{1\frac{1}{4}} = \dfrac{\frac{60}{1}}{\frac{5}{4}}$

$$\frac{\frac{60}{1}}{\frac{5}{4}} \cdot \frac{\frac{4}{5}}{\frac{4}{5}} = \frac{\frac{240}{5}}{1} = \frac{240}{5}$$

$$= \textbf{48}$$

17.

	Percent	Actual Count
Sale price	P_S	\$18
Regular price	100	\$24

$$\frac{P_S}{100} = \frac{\$18}{\$24}$$
$$24P_S = 1800$$
$$P_S = \textbf{75\%}$$

315

18.

	Percent	Actual Count
With seats	30	375
Without seats	70	W
Total	100	T

$$\frac{30}{70} = \frac{375}{W}$$

$$30W = 26{,}250$$

$$W = \mathbf{875}$$

19.

$$24 = \frac{1}{4} \times W_N$$

$$\left(\frac{4}{1}\right)24 = \left(\frac{\cancel{4}^{\,1}}{\cancel{1}_{\,1}}\right)\left(\frac{\cancel{1}^{\,1}}{\cancel{4}_{\,1}}\right) \times W_N$$

$$\mathbf{96} = W_N$$

20.

10 mm
50 mm
30 mm
40 mm
50 mm

a. **Trapezoid**

b. Perimeter = 10 mm + 30 mm + 50 mm
         + 50 mm = **140 mm**

c. Area of rectangle = (10 mm)(30 mm)
                   = 300 mm²
    Area of triangle = $\dfrac{(40\ mm)(30\ mm)}{2}$
                   = 600 mm²
    Area of figure = 300 mm² + 600 mm²
                   = **900 mm²**

21. $y = x - 5$

x	y
3	**−2**
7	**2**
5	**0**

$y = 3 - 5 = -2$
$y = 7 - 5 = 2$
$y = 5 - 5 = 0$

Crosses the y-axis at −5:
$$y = x - 5$$
$$(-5) = (0) - 5$$
$$-5 = -5$$

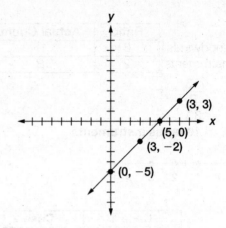

(3, 3)
(5, 0)
(3, −2)
(0, −5)

22. a. $(9 \times 4) \times (10^{-6} \times 10^{-8})$
         $= 36 \times (10^{-14})$
         $= \mathbf{3.6 \times 10^{-13}}$

b. $(9 \times 4) \times (10^{6} \times 10^{8})$
         $= 36 \times (10^{14})$
         $= \mathbf{3.6 \times 10^{15}}$

23.

$$8\frac{5}{6} = d - 5\frac{1}{2}$$

$$8\frac{5}{6} + 5\frac{1}{2} = d - 5\frac{1}{2} + 5\frac{1}{2}$$

$$8\frac{5}{6} + 5\frac{3}{6} = d$$

$$13\frac{8}{6} = d$$

$$14\frac{2}{6} = d$$

$$\mathbf{14\frac{1}{3}} = d$$

check:

$$8\frac{5}{6} = 14\frac{1}{3} - 5\frac{1}{2}$$

$$8\frac{5}{6} = 14\frac{2}{6} - 5\frac{3}{6}$$

$$8\frac{5}{6} = 13\frac{8}{6} - 5\frac{3}{6}$$

$$8\frac{5}{6} = 8\frac{5}{6}$$

24.

$$\frac{5}{6}m = 90$$

$$\left(\frac{\cancel{6}}{\cancel{5}}\right)\frac{\cancel{5}}{\cancel{6}}m = \left(\frac{6}{\cancel{5}}\right)\cancel{90}^{18}$$

$$m = \mathbf{108}$$

check:

$$\frac{5}{\cancel{6}}(\cancel{108}^{18}) = 90$$

$$90 = 90$$

25.

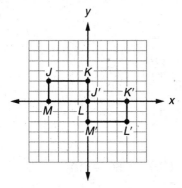

a. **M(−4, 0)**

b. **J′(0, 0), K′(4, 0),**
L′(4, −2), M′(0, −2)

26. D. $4^2 + 4$

27. $\frac{2}{3}(0.12) = 0.08$
$0.5(0.08) = \textbf{0.04}$

28. $6\{5 \cdot 4 - 3[6 - (3 - 1)]\}$
$6\{20 - 3[6 - 2]\}$
$6\{20 - 3[4]\}$
$6\{20 - 12\}$
$6\{8\}$
48

29. a. $\dfrac{(-3)(-4) - (-3)}{(-3) - (+4)(+3)}$
$\dfrac{12 - (-3)}{-3 - (12)}$
$\dfrac{12 + 3}{-3 - 12}$
$\dfrac{15}{-15}$
−1

b. $(+5) + (-2)[(+3) - (-4)]$
$(+5) + (-2)[+3 + (+4)]$
$(+5) + (-2)[7]$
$(+5) + (-14)$
−9

30. a. $(-2x)(-3x)$
$= (-2) \cdot x \cdot (-3) \cdot (x)$
$= (-2)(-3) \cdot x \cdot x = \textbf{6}\textbf{x}^2$

b. $(ab)(2a^2b)(-3a)$
$= a \cdot b \cdot (2) \cdot a \cdot a \cdot b \cdot (-3) \cdot a$
$= (2)(-3) \cdot a \cdot a \cdot a \cdot a \cdot b \cdot b$
$= \textbf{−6}\textbf{a}^4\textbf{b}^2$

c. $(-3x)^2$
$= (-3)^2 \cdot (x)^2$
$= \textbf{9}\textbf{x}^2$

Early Finishers Solutions

Circle graph; This data
represents parts of a
whole, which are well
displayed on a circle
graph. A histogram
is a type of bar
graph used to show
data displayed in
ranges of data.

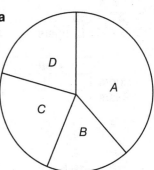

Practice Set 89

a. For answers, see solutions to examples
1–4.

b. One possibility:

2 diagonals

c. **3 triangles**

d. $5 \times 108° = \textbf{540°}$

e. $\dfrac{540°}{5} = \textbf{108°}$

f. $\dfrac{360°}{5} = \textbf{72°}$

g. $108° + 72° = \textbf{180°}$

Written Practice 89

1.

	Case 1	Case 2
Feet	440	5280
Seconds	10	s

$\dfrac{440}{10} = \dfrac{5280}{s}$
$440s = 52{,}800$
$s = \textbf{120 seconds}$ or **2 minutes**

2.

	Ratio	Actual Count
Lions	3	18
Tigers	2	T

Saxon Math Course 2   **317**

Solutions

$\dfrac{3}{2} = \dfrac{18}{T}$

$3T = 36$

$T = 12$ tigers

	Ratio	Actual Count
Tigers	3	12
Bears	4	B

$\dfrac{3}{4} = \dfrac{12}{B}$

$3B = 48$

$B = \textbf{16 bears}$

3. $(30 \text{ cm})(15 \text{ cm}) = 450 \text{ cm}^2$

$\dfrac{450 \text{ cm}^2}{1 \text{ layer}} \cdot (1 \text{ cm}) \cdot 12 \text{ layers} = \textbf{5400 cm}^3$

4. $\dfrac{24}{61} = 0.393442\ldots\ \textbf{0.393}$

5. $\dfrac{\overset{3}{\cancel{3000}}\ \cancel{m}}{\underset{1}{\cancel{10}}\ \cancel{min}} \times \dfrac{1 \text{ km}}{\underset{1}{\cancel{1000}}\ \cancel{m}} \times \dfrac{\overset{6}{\cancel{60}}\ \cancel{min}}{1 \text{ hr}} = \textbf{18}\ \dfrac{\textbf{km}}{\textbf{hr}}$

6.

$-4 \quad -3 \quad -2 \quad -1 \quad 0 \quad 1$

7.

```
            16 dollars
          ┌─────────────┐
 3        │  4 dollars  │
 ─ of regular ──────────┤
 4 price ($12) 4 dollars │
          ├─────────────┤
          │  4 dollars  │
          ├─────────────┤
 1 of regular 4 dollars │
 ─ price   └─────────────┘
 4
```

a. $\$12 \div 3 = \$4$

$(\$4)(4) = \textbf{\$16}$

b. $\dfrac{3}{4} \times 100\% = \textbf{75\%}$

8. **a.** $m\angle a = 180° - (90° + 35°) = \textbf{55°}$

b. $m\angle b = 180° - 55° = \textbf{125°}$

c. $m\angle c = m\angle a = \textbf{55°}$

d. $m\angle d = 180° - (55° + 70°) = \textbf{55°}$

9. **a.** $C \approx \dfrac{22}{\underset{1}{\cancel{7}}} (\overset{6}{\cancel{42}}\text{in.})$

$C \approx \textbf{132 in.}$

b. $A = \pi r^2$

$A \approx \dfrac{22}{\underset{1}{\cancel{7}}} (\overset{63}{\cancel{441}}\text{in.}^2)$

$A \approx \textbf{1386 in.}^2$

10. $\dfrac{91\frac{2}{3}}{100} = \dfrac{\frac{275}{3}}{\frac{100}{1}}$

$\dfrac{\frac{275}{3}}{\frac{100}{1}} \cdot \dfrac{\frac{1}{100}}{\frac{1}{100}} = \dfrac{\frac{275}{300}}{1} = \dfrac{275}{300}$

$= \dfrac{\textbf{11}}{\textbf{12}}$

11. $\dfrac{(10)(5) + (10)}{(10) + (5)} = \dfrac{50 + 10}{15}$

$= \dfrac{60}{15} = \textbf{4}$

12. $0.25\ \bigcirc\ 0.5$

$a^2\ \text{\small$\bigcirc$}\!<\ a$

13. **a.** $\dfrac{7}{8} = \textbf{0.875}$

```
        0.875
    8)7.000
      6 4
      ───
        60
        56
        ──
        40
        40
        ──
         0
```

b. $\dfrac{7}{8} \times 100\% = \dfrac{700\%}{8} = \textbf{87}\,\dfrac{\textbf{1}}{\textbf{2}}\,\%$

$87\frac{4}{8} = 87\frac{1}{2}\%$

```
    8)700
      64
      ──
      60
      56
      ──
       4
```

c. $875\% = \dfrac{875}{100} = 8\dfrac{75}{100} = \textbf{8}\dfrac{\textbf{3}}{\textbf{4}}$

d. $875\% = \textbf{8.75}$

14. **a.** **4:00, 8:00**

b. **120°**

15.

	Percent	Actual Count
Ordered a hamburger	45	H
Other customers	55	C
Total	100	3000

$\dfrac{45}{100} = \dfrac{H}{3000}$

$100H = 135{,}000$

$H = \textbf{1350 customers}$

16.

	Percent	Actual Count
Sale price	75	$24
Regular price	100	R

$$\frac{75}{100} = \frac{\$24}{R}$$

$$75R = \$2400$$

$$R = \$32$$

$$\$32 - \$24 = \textbf{\$8}$$

17. $20 = W_P \times 200$

$$\frac{20}{200} = \frac{W_P \times 200}{200}$$

$$\frac{1}{10} = W_P$$

$$W_P = \frac{1}{10} \times 100\% = \textbf{10\%}$$

18. a.

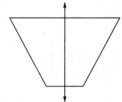

b.

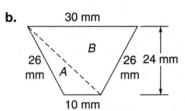

Area of triangle $A = \dfrac{(10 \text{ mm})(24 \text{ mm})}{2}$

$= 120 \text{ mm}^2$

Area of triangle $B = \dfrac{(30 \text{ mm})(24 \text{ mm})}{2}$

$= 360 \text{ mm}^2$

Area of figure $= 120 \text{ mm}^2 + 360 \text{ mm}^2$

$= \textbf{480 mm}^2$

19. $\dfrac{360°}{3} = \textbf{120°}$

20. $y = \dfrac{1}{2}x$

x	y
6	3
2	1
-2	-1

$y = \dfrac{1}{2}(6) = 3$

$y = \dfrac{1}{2}(2) = 1$

$y = \dfrac{1}{2}(-2) = -1$

The line intercepts the y-axis at $(0, 0)$.

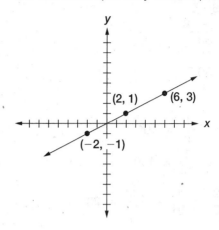

21. $(1.25 \times 8) \times (10^{-3} \times 10^{-5})$

$= 10 \times 10^{-8}$

$= \textbf{1} \times \textbf{10}^{-7}$

22. a.

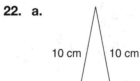

Perimeter $= 10 \text{ cm} + 10 \text{ cm} + 4 \text{ cm}$

$= \textbf{24 cm}$

b. There can only be one answer. A triangle with side lengths of 4 cm, 4 cm, and 10 cm cannot exist.

23. $\dfrac{4}{9}p = 72$

$$\left(\frac{\cancel{9}}{\cancel{4}}\right)\frac{\cancel{4}}{\cancel{9}}p = \left(\frac{9}{4}\right)\overset{18}{\cancel{72}}$$

$$p = \textbf{162}$$

check: $\dfrac{4}{\cancel{9}}(\overset{18}{\cancel{162}}) = 72$

$4(18) = 72$

$72 = 72$

24. $12.3 = 4.56 + f$

$12.3 - 4.56 = 4.56 - 4.56 + f$

$\textbf{7.74} = f$

check: $12.3 = 4.56 + 7.74$

$12.3 = 12.3$

25. $2x + 3y - 4 + x - 3y - 1$

$2x + x + 3y - 3y - 4 - 1$

$\textbf{3x} - \textbf{5}$

Solutions

26. $\dfrac{9 \cdot 8 - 7 \cdot 6}{6 \cdot 5}$

$\dfrac{72 - 42}{30}$

$\dfrac{30}{30}$

1

27. $3\dfrac{2}{10} \times \dfrac{1}{4^2} \times 10^2$

$3\dfrac{2}{10} \times \dfrac{1}{16} \times 100$

$= \dfrac{\overset{2}{\cancel{32}}}{\cancel{10}} \times \dfrac{1}{\cancel{16}} \times \dfrac{\overset{10}{\cancel{100}}}{1} = \mathbf{20}$

28. $4.75 + \dfrac{3}{4} = 4\dfrac{3}{4} + \dfrac{3}{4}$

$= 4\dfrac{6}{4} = 5\dfrac{2}{4} = 5\dfrac{1}{2}$

$13\dfrac{1}{3} - 5\dfrac{1}{2} = 13\dfrac{2}{6} - 5\dfrac{3}{6}$

$= 12\dfrac{8}{6} - 5\dfrac{3}{6} = \mathbf{7\dfrac{5}{6}}$

29. a. $\dfrac{(+3) + (-4)(-6)}{(-3) + (-4) - (-6)}$

$\dfrac{(+3) + (24)}{-7 - (-6)}$

$\dfrac{27}{-1}$

−27

b. $(-5) - (+6)(-2) + (-2)(-3)(-1)$

$(-5) - (-12) + (-6)$

$(-5) + (+12) + (-6)$

1

30. a. $(3x^2)(2x)$

$= (3) \cdot x \cdot x \cdot (2) \cdot x$

$= (3)(2) \cdot x \cdot x \cdot x$

$= \mathbf{6x^3}$

b. $(-2ab)(-3b^2)(-a)$

$= (-2) \cdot a \cdot b \cdot (-3) \cdot b \cdot b \cdot (-1) \cdot a$

$= (-2)(-3)(-1) \cdot a \cdot a \cdot b \cdot b \cdot b$

$= \mathbf{-6a^2b^3}$

c. $(-4ab^3)^2$

$= (-4)^2 \cdot (a)^2 \cdot (b^3)^2$

$= \mathbf{16a^2b^6}$

Early Finishers Solutions

F, T, T, F, T, F, T

---

a. $1\dfrac{1}{8}x = 36$

$\dfrac{9}{8}x = 36$

$\left(\dfrac{\overset{1}{\cancel{8}}}{\cancel{9}}\right)\left(\dfrac{\overset{1}{\cancel{9}}}{\cancel{8}}x\right) = \left(\dfrac{8}{\cancel{9}}\right) \cdot \overset{4}{\cancel{36}}$

$x = \mathbf{32}$

b. $3\dfrac{1}{2}a = 490$

$\dfrac{7}{2}a = 490$

$\left(\dfrac{\overset{1}{\cancel{2}}}{\cancel{7}}\right)\left(\dfrac{\overset{1}{\cancel{7}}}{\cancel{2}}a\right) = \left(\dfrac{2}{\cancel{7}}\right)\overset{70}{\cancel{490}}$

$a = \mathbf{140}$

c. $2\dfrac{3}{4}w = 6\dfrac{3}{5}$

$\dfrac{11}{4}w = \dfrac{33}{5}$

$\left(\dfrac{\overset{1}{\cancel{4}}}{\cancel{11}}\right)\left(\dfrac{\overset{1}{\cancel{11}}}{\cancel{4}}w\right) = \left(\dfrac{4}{\cancel{11}}\right)\left(\dfrac{\overset{3}{\cancel{33}}}{5}\right)$

$w = \dfrac{12}{5}$

d. $2\dfrac{2}{3}y = 1\dfrac{4}{5}$

$\dfrac{8}{3}y = \dfrac{9}{5}$

$\left(\dfrac{\overset{1}{\cancel{3}}}{\cancel{8}}\right)\left(\dfrac{\overset{1}{\cancel{8}}}{\cancel{3}}y\right) = \left(\dfrac{3}{8}\right)\left(\dfrac{9}{5}\right)$

$y = \dfrac{27}{40}$

e. $-3x = 0.45$

$\dfrac{-3x}{-3} = \dfrac{0.45}{-3}$

$x = \mathbf{-0.15}$

f. $-\dfrac{3}{4}m = \dfrac{2}{3}$

$\left(-\dfrac{\overset{1}{\cancel{4}}}{\cancel{3}}\right)\left(-\dfrac{\overset{1}{\cancel{3}}}{\cancel{4}}m\right) = \left(-\dfrac{4}{3}\right)\left(\dfrac{2}{3}\right)$

$m = -\dfrac{8}{9}$

g. $-10y = -1.6$

$\dfrac{-10y}{-10} = \dfrac{-1.6}{-10}$

$y = \mathbf{0.16}$

---

h.
$$-2\frac{1}{2}w = 3\frac{1}{3}$$
$$-\frac{5}{2}w = \frac{10}{3}$$
$$\left(-\frac{\cancel{2}^{1}}{\cancel{5}_{1}}\right)\left(-\frac{\cancel{5}^{1}}{\cancel{2}_{1}}w\right) = \left(-\frac{2}{\cancel{5}_{1}}\right)\left(\frac{\cancel{10}^{2}}{3}\right)$$
$$w = -\frac{4}{3}$$

Written Practice 90

1. $(0.8 + 0.9) - (0.8)(0.9)$
= 1.7 − 0.72 = 0.98
Ninety-eight hundredths

2. a.

```
              8.5
           12)102.0
```

8
6
9
10
8
7
9
10
8
10
9
+ 8
───
102

b. 6, 7, 8, 8, 8, <u>8, 9</u>, 9, 9, 10, 10, 10
$$\frac{8 + 9}{2} = \frac{17}{2} = \mathbf{8.5}$$

c. 8

d. 10 − 6 = **4**

3.
$$\frac{\$1.20}{24 \text{ ounces}} = \frac{\$0.05}{1 \text{ ounce}}$$
$$\frac{\$1.44}{32 \text{ ounces}} = \frac{\$0.045}{1 \text{ ounce}}$$

$$\begin{array}{r}\$0.050 \\ - \ \$0.045 \\ \hline \$0.005\end{array}$$

0.5¢ more per ounce

4. a. $\frac{360°}{10} = \mathbf{36°}$

b. $\frac{180°(10 - 2)}{10} = \frac{\overset{18}{\cancel{180°}} (8)}{\underset{1}{\cancel{10}}} = \mathbf{144°}$

5. $x^2 + 2xy + y^2 + x^2 - y^2$
$x^2 + x^2 + 2xy + y^2 - y^2$
$\mathbf{2x^2 + 2xy}$

6.

	Percent	Actual Count
Sale price	90	$36
Regular price	100	R

$$\frac{90}{100} = \frac{\$36}{R}$$
$$90R = \$3600$$
$$R = \mathbf{\$40}$$

7.

	Percent	Actual Count
Voted for Graham	75	V
Did not vote for Graham	25	D
Total	100	800

$$\frac{25}{100} = \frac{D}{800}$$
$$100D = 20,000$$
$$D = \mathbf{200 \text{ citizens}}$$

8. a. $24 = W_P \times 30$
$$\frac{24}{30} = \frac{W_P \times 30}{30}$$
$$\frac{4}{5} = W_P$$
$$W_P = \frac{4}{5} \times 100\% = \mathbf{80\%}$$

b. $30 = W_P \times 24$
$$\frac{30}{24} = \frac{W_P \times 24}{24}$$
$$\frac{5}{4} = W_P$$
$$W_P = \frac{5}{4} \times 100\% = \mathbf{125\%}$$

9. a. $2 \text{ ft}^2 \cdot \frac{12 \text{ in.}}{1 \text{ ft}} \cdot \frac{12 \text{ in.}}{1 \text{ ft}} = \mathbf{288 \text{ square inches}}$

b. $1 \text{ m}^3 \times \frac{100 \text{ cm}}{1 \text{ m}} \times \frac{100 \text{ cm}}{1 \text{ m}} \times \frac{100 \text{ cm}}{1 \text{ m}}$
$$= \mathbf{1,000,000 \text{ cm}^3}$$

10.

```
                750 doctors
 2/5 of doctors  ┌─ 150 doctors
 (300) did.     └─ 150 doctors
                 ┌─ 150 doctors
 3/5 of doctors  │  150 doctors
 did not.       └─ 150 doctors
```

a. 300 ÷ 2 = 150
5(150 doctors) = **750 doctors**

b. 3(150 doctors) = **450 doctors**

321

11. $y = 2(4.5) + 1$
$y = 9 + 1$
$y = \mathbf{10}$

12. a. **{HHH, HHT, HTH, HTT, THH, THT, TTH, TTT}**

b. P(heads at least twice) $= \dfrac{4}{8} = \mathbf{\dfrac{1}{2}}$

13. $\dfrac{12 \text{ inches}}{4} = 3 \text{ inches}$
(3 inches)(3 inches) = **9 square inches**

14. a. $1.75 = 1\dfrac{75}{100} = \mathbf{1\dfrac{3}{4}}$

b. $1.75 \times 100\% = \mathbf{175\%}$

15.
$$\begin{array}{r} \$325 \\ \times\ \ 0.06 \\ \hline \$19.50 \end{array}$$
$$\begin{array}{r} \$325 \\ +\ \$19.50 \\ \hline \mathbf{\$344.50} \end{array}$$

16. $(6 \times 8) \times (10^4 \times 10^{-7})$
$= (48 \times (10^{-3})$
$= \mathbf{4.8 \times 10^{-2}}$

17. a. Volume = (8 in.)(3 in.)(12 in.) = **288 in.³**

b. 2(8 in. $\times$ 12 in.) + 2(8 in. $\times$ 3 in.)
$\quad$ + 2(12 in. $\times$ 3 in.)
$\quad$ = 192 in.² + 48 in.² + 72 in.²
$\quad$ = **312 in.²**

18. a. $C \approx 3.14(100 \text{ mm})$
$C \approx \mathbf{314 \text{ mm}}$

b. $A = \pi r^2$
$A \approx 3.14(2500 \text{ mm}^2)$
$A \approx \mathbf{7850 \text{ mm}^2}$

19. 0

20.

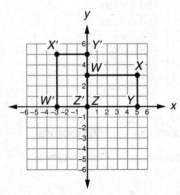

a. **Z (0, 0)**

b. **W′(−3, 0), X′(−3, 5), Y′(0, 5), Z′(0, 0)**

21. $\dfrac{2}{3} \times 20 = \dfrac{40}{3} = \mathbf{13\dfrac{1}{3}}$

22.

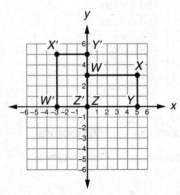

(number line from −1 to 5, point at 4)

23. $\quad x + 3.5 = 4.28$
$x + 3.5 - 3.5 = 4.28 - 3.5$
$\qquad x = \mathbf{0.78}$

24. $\quad 2\dfrac{2}{3}w = 24$

$\qquad \dfrac{8}{3}w = 24$

$\left(\dfrac{3}{8}\right)\dfrac{8}{3}w = \left(\dfrac{3}{8}\right)24$

$\qquad w = \mathbf{9}$

25. $\quad -4y = 1.4$
$\qquad \dfrac{-4y}{-4} = \dfrac{1.4}{-4}$
$\qquad\ y = \mathbf{-0.35}$

26. $10^1 + 10^0 + 10^{-1}$
$= 10 + 1 + \dfrac{1}{10} = 11 + 0.1$
$= \mathbf{11.1}$

27. a. $(-2x^2)(-3xy)(-y)$
$= (-2) \cdot x \cdot x \cdot (-3) \cdot x \cdot y \cdot (-1) \cdot y$
$= (-2)(-3)(-1) \cdot x \cdot x \cdot x \cdot y \cdot y$
$= \mathbf{-6x^3y^2}$

b. $(3x^2y^3)^2$
$= (3)^2 \cdot (x^2)^2 \cdot (y^3)^2$
$= \mathbf{9x^4y^6}$

28.
$$\begin{array}{r} \dfrac{8}{75} = \dfrac{32}{300} \\ - \dfrac{9}{100} = \dfrac{27}{300} \\ \hline \dfrac{5}{300} = \mathbf{\dfrac{1}{60}} \end{array}$$

29. a. $(-3) + (-4)(-5) - (-6)$

$\quad\quad (-3) + (20) + (+6)$

$\quad\quad\quad (-3) + (26)$

$\quad\quad\quad\quad\quad 23$

b. $\dfrac{(-2)(-4)}{(-4) - (-2)}$

$\quad\quad \dfrac{8}{-2}$

$\quad\quad -4$

30. $\quad\quad 10^2 - 5^2 = 100 - 25 = 75$

$(10 + 5)(10 - 5) = (15)(5) = 75$

$\quad\quad\quad\quad\quad 75 = 75$

$\quad\quad x^2 - y^2 \stackrel{=}{\ominus} (x + y)(x - y)$

Early Finishers Solutions

a. Area $= \dfrac{1}{2}(3.14)(16\text{ft})^2 - \dfrac{1}{2}(3.14)(8\text{ft})^2$

$\quad\quad = \dfrac{1}{2}(3.14)(256 \text{ ft}^2 - 64 \text{ ft}^2)$

$\quad\quad = 1.57 \times 192 \text{ ft}^2$

$\quad\quad = 301.44 \text{ ft}^2$

b. $\dfrac{301.44 \text{ ft}^2}{1} \cdot \dfrac{1 \text{ ton}}{22.5 \text{ ft}^2} \cong 13.4$ tons

c. $13.4 \times \$33 = \$442.20$

Investigation 9

Graphing Functions

1. One possible pair: (7, 8).

$y = x + 1$

$8 = 7 + 1$

$8 = 8$

2.

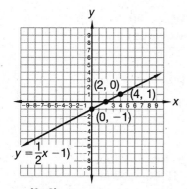

a. (8, 3)

b. No; The line doesn't pass through Quadrant II.

---

3. (0, 0); The graph is a ray extending from the origin (positive) because we can't have shapes defined by negative numbers.

4. Doubling the side length doubles the perimeter.

5. $p = 3s$;

p	s
3	1
6	2
9	3

{Students graph the equation using the data table. Their graph should be segment extending from the origin in the first quadrant.}

6. $d = 6h$; {Students graph the equation and then use the graph to answer questions 7–9.}

7. 4 miles; {The graph uses an interval of 10 minutes on the *x*–axis; The equation should be graphed to show a distance of 1 mile traveled for every 10 minutes.}

8. 90 minutes

9. The equation is graphed as a segment, not a ray, because Sam doesn't jog indefinitely.

10. Doubling the length of a side of a square quadruples the area (multiplies the area by 4).

11. {Students are asked to find the missing data in the table.}

$A = \frac{1}{2}s^2$

s	A
1	$\frac{1}{2}$
2	2
3	$4\frac{1}{2}$
4	8

12. {Students graph the coordinates from the table in 11.}

Solutions

Practice Set 91

a. $(3) + (3)(-2) - (-2)$
$(3) + (-6) - (-2)$
$(-3) - (-2)$
-1

b. $-(-2) + (-5) - (-2)(-5)$
$-(-2) + (-5) - (+10)$
$(-3) - (+10)$
-13

c. $4(-4) + 25 = 9$
$-16 + 25 = 9$
$9 = 9 ✓$

d. $3(-5) + 7 = 8$
$-15 + 7 = 8$
$-8 \neq 8$
-5 is not a solution.

e. $x = \dfrac{-20}{4}$
$x = \mathbf{-5}$
$4(-5) = -20$
$-20 = -20 ✓$

f. $x = \dfrac{16}{-2}$
$x = \mathbf{-8}$
$-2(-8) = 16$
$16 = 16 ✓$

Written Practice 91

1. $6(86) + 4(94) = 516 + 376$
$= 892$

$$\begin{array}{r} \mathbf{89.2} \\ 10\overline{)892.0} \end{array}$$

2. Median $= \dfrac{7 + 9}{2} = 8$ **$11 - 8 = 3$**
Median $= 88 \div 8 = 11$

3. $\dfrac{130 \text{ miles}}{2.5 \text{ hours}} = \mathbf{52}$ **miles per hour**

4.

	Ratio	Actual Count
Laborers	3	L
Supervisors	5	S
Total	8	120

$\dfrac{3}{8} = \dfrac{L}{120}$
$8L = 360$
$L = \mathbf{45}$ **laborers**

5.

	Case 1	Case 2
Notebooks	3	5
Price	$8.55	p

$\dfrac{3}{\$8.55} = \dfrac{5}{p}$
$3p = \$42.75$
$p = \mathbf{\$14.25}$

6.

	Percent	Actual Count
Sale price	90	S
Regular price	100	$36

$\dfrac{90}{100} = \dfrac{S}{\$36}$
$100S = \$3240$
$S = \mathbf{\$32.40}$

7.

	Percent	Actual Count
People who came	80	40
Invited people	100	I

$\dfrac{80}{100} = \dfrac{40}{I}$
$80I = 4000$
$I = \mathbf{50}$ **people**

8. a. $20 = 0.4 \times W_N$
$\dfrac{20}{0.4} = \dfrac{0.4 \times W_N}{0.4}$
$\mathbf{50} = W_N$

b. $20 = W_P \times 40$
$\dfrac{20}{40} = \dfrac{W_P \times 40}{40}$
$\dfrac{1}{2} = W_P$
$W_P = \dfrac{1}{2} \times 100\% = \mathbf{50\%}$

9. $\overset{25}{\cancel{3600}} \text{ in.}^2 \cdot \dfrac{1 \text{ foot}}{\cancel{12} \text{ in.}} \cdot \dfrac{1 \text{ foot}}{\cancel{12} \text{ in.}}$
$= \mathbf{25}$ **square feet**

10.

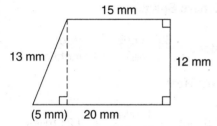

$\frac{3}{4}$ were multiple choice (60).

$\frac{1}{4}$ were not multiple choice.

80 questions
- 20 questions
- 20 questions
- 20 questions
- 20 questions

a. $60 \div 3 = 20$
$4(20 \text{ questions}) = \textbf{80 questions}$

b. **25%**

11. $(-3) - (-2) - (-3)(-2)$
$(-3) - (-2) - (+6)$
−7

12. $(3 \text{ people})(12 \text{ hours}) = (4 \text{ people})(h)$
$36 = 4h$
$h = \textbf{9 hours}$

13.

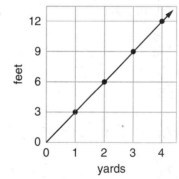

15 mm
13 mm
12 mm
(5 mm) 20 mm

a. **Trapezoid**

b. Perimeter = 15 mm + 12 mm + 20 mm
+ 13 mm = **60 mm**

c. Area of rectangle $= (15 \text{ mm})(12 \text{ mm})$
$= 180 \text{ mm}^2$

Area of triangle $= \dfrac{(5 \text{ mm})(12 \text{ mm})}{2}$

$= 30 \text{ mm}^2$
Area of figure $= 180 \text{ mm}^2 + 30 \text{ mm}^2$
$= \textbf{210 mm}^2$

d. $180° - 75° = \textbf{105°}$

14. **a.** **Associative property of addition**

b. **Commutative property of multiplication**

c. **Distributive property**

15.

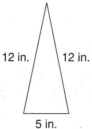

12 in.   12 in.

5 in.

Perimeter = 12 in. + 12 in. + 5 in.
= **29 in.**

16. $(2.4 \times 10^{-4})(5 \times 10^{-7})$
12×10^{-11}
$(1.2 \times 10^{1}) \times 10^{-11}$
$\textbf{1.2} \times \textbf{10}^{-10}$

17. **a.** **5 faces**

b. **8 edges**

c. **5 vertices**

18. **a.** $C \approx 3.14(8 \text{ cm})$
$C \approx \textbf{25.12 cm}$

b. $A \approx 3.14(16 \text{ cm}^2)$
$A \approx \textbf{50.24 cm}^2$

19.

feet

12
9
6
3
0

0 1 2 3 4
yards

Yes, the graph shows direct variation. The points are aligned. As one variable increases, the other increases. The pair (0, 0) is a solution, and solution pairs form proportions.

20. **a.** $m\angle x = 180° - (90° + 30°) = \textbf{60°}$

b. $m\angle y = m\angle x = \textbf{60°}$

c. $m\angle A = 180° - (60° + 65°) = \textbf{55°}$

d. **No. The triangles do not have the same shape, nor do they have matching angles.**

Solutions

21. a. $-3x - 3 - x - 1$
$-3x - x - 3 - 1$
$\mathbf{-4x - 4}$

b. $(-3x)(-3)(-x)(-1)$
$(-3) \cdot x \cdot (-3) \cdot (-1) \cdot x \cdot (-1)$
$(-3)(-3)(-1)(-1) \cdot x \cdot x$
$\mathbf{9x^2}$

22.

23. AB is 60 mm
BC is 40 mm
$60\text{ mm} - 40\text{ mm} = \mathbf{20\ mm}$

24.
$$5 = y - 4.75$$
$$5 + 4.75 = y - 4.75 + 4.75$$
$$\mathbf{9.75 = y}$$
$$5 = 9.75 - 4.75$$
$$5 = 5$$

25.
$$3\frac{1}{3}y = 7\frac{1}{2}$$
$$\frac{10}{3}y = \frac{15}{2}$$
$$\left(\frac{\overset{1}{\cancel{3}}}{\underset{1}{\cancel{10}}}\right)\frac{10}{3}y = \left(\frac{\overset{3}{\cancel{3}}}{\underset{2}{\cancel{10}}}\right)\frac{15}{2}$$
$$y = \mathbf{\frac{9}{4}}$$

$$3\frac{1}{3}\left(\frac{9}{4}\right) = 7\frac{1}{2}$$
$$\frac{\overset{5}{\cancel{10}}}{\underset{1}{\cancel{3}}}\left(\frac{\overset{3}{\cancel{9}}}{\underset{2}{\cancel{4}}}\right) = 7\frac{1}{2}$$
$$\frac{15}{2} = 7\frac{1}{2}$$
$$7\frac{1}{2} = 7\frac{1}{2}$$

26.
$$-9x = 414$$
$$\frac{-\cancel{9}x}{-\cancel{9}} = \frac{\overset{-46}{\cancel{414}}}{\underset{1}{-\cancel{9}}}$$
$$x = \mathbf{-46}$$
$$(-9)(-46) = 414$$
$$414 = 414$$

27. $\dfrac{32\text{ ft}}{1\ \cancel{s}} \cdot \dfrac{60\ \cancel{s}}{1\text{ min}} = \mathbf{1920\ \dfrac{ft}{min}}$

28. $5\frac{1}{3} + 2\frac{1}{2} + \frac{1}{6} = 5\frac{2}{6} + 2\frac{3}{6} + \frac{1}{6}$
$= 7\frac{6}{6} = \mathbf{8}$

29. $\dfrac{2.75 + 3.5}{2.5} = \dfrac{6.25}{2.5} = \mathbf{2.5}$

30. a. $\dfrac{(-3) - (-4)(+5)}{-2}$
$\dfrac{(-3) - (-20)}{-2}$
$\dfrac{17}{-2}$
$\mathbf{-8\frac{1}{2}}$

b. $-3(+4) - 5(+6) - 7$
$(-12) - (+30) - 7$
$\mathbf{-49}$

Early Finishers Solutions

a. $441\ \cancel{\text{steps}} \cdot \dfrac{30\ \cancel{\text{inches}}}{1\ \cancel{\text{step}}} \cdot \dfrac{1\text{ foot}}{12\ \cancel{\text{inches}}}$

$= 1102.5\text{ feet}$

b. $1102.5\ \cancel{\text{feet}} \cdot \dfrac{1\text{ mile}}{5280\ \cancel{\text{feet}}} \cong 0.21\text{ miles}$

c. If 0.21 miles is the typical distance Tobey travels during lunchtime, then in 5 days Tobey will walk about a mile. $5 \times 0.21\text{ mi} = 1.05\text{ mi}$

Practice Set 92

a.

	Percent	Actual Count
Original	100	$24.50
− Change	30	C
New	70	N

$$\frac{100}{70} = \frac{\$24.50}{N}$$
$$100N = \$1715$$
$$N = \mathbf{\$17.15}$$

b.

	Percent	Actual Count
Original	100	O
+ Change	20	C
New	120	60

$$\frac{100}{120} = \frac{O}{60}$$
$$120O = 6000$$
$$O = \mathbf{50\ students}$$

c.

	Percent	Actual Count
Original	100	O
− Change	20	C
New	80	$120

$$\frac{20}{80} = \frac{C}{\$120}$$
$$80C = \$2400$$
$$C = \mathbf{\$30}$$

d.

	Percent	Actual Count
Original	100	$15
+ Change	80	C
New	180	N

$$\frac{100}{180} = \frac{\$15}{N}$$
$$100N = 2700$$
$$N = \mathbf{\$27}$$

Written Practice 92

1. $(7 + 11 + 13) - (2 \times 3 \times 5)$
$$= 31 - 30$$
$$= \mathbf{1}$$

2.
$$5(88) = 440$$
$$7(90) = 630$$
$$630 - 440 = 190$$
$$190 \div 2 = \mathbf{95}$$

3. $\dfrac{2 \text{ miles}}{0.25 \text{ hour}} = \mathbf{8 \text{ miles per hour}}$

4.

	Ratio	Actual Count
Girls	9	45
Boys	7	35
Total	16	80

$$\frac{35}{45} = \frac{7}{9}$$

5.

	Case 1	Case 2
Sparklers	24	60
Price	$3.60	p

$$\frac{24}{\$3.60} = \frac{60}{p}$$
$$24p = \$216$$
$$p = \mathbf{\$9.00}$$

6.

	Percent	Actual Count
Original	100	340,000
+ Change	20	C
New	120	N

$$\frac{100}{120} = \frac{340,000}{N}$$
$$100N = 40,800,000$$
$$N = \mathbf{408,000}$$

7.

	Percent	Actual Count
Original	100	O
+ Change	50	C
New	150	96

$$\frac{100}{150} = \frac{O}{96}$$
$$150O = 9600$$
$$O = \mathbf{64¢ \text{ per pound}}$$

8. a. $60 = W_P \times 75$
$$\frac{60}{75} = \frac{W_P \times 75}{75}$$
$$\frac{12}{15} = W_P$$
$$W_P = \frac{12}{15} \times 100\% = \mathbf{80\%}$$

b. $75 = W_P \times 60$
$$\frac{75}{60} = \frac{W_P \times 60}{60}$$
$$\frac{15}{12} = W_P$$
$$W_P = \frac{15}{12} \times 100\% = \mathbf{125\%}$$

9. $\dfrac{1 \, \cancel{ft}}{\cancel{2 \, min}_{\,1}} \times \dfrac{1 \text{ yd}}{\cancel{3 \, ft}_{\,1}} \times \dfrac{\overset{10}{\cancel{\overset{30}{\cancel{60}}}} \text{ min}}{1 \text{ hr}} = \mathbf{10 \, \dfrac{yd}{hr}}$

10.

256 trees

32 trees
32 trees
32 trees
32 trees
32 trees
32 trees
32 trees
32 trees

$\frac{5}{8}$ were deciduous (160).

$\frac{3}{8}$ were not deciduous.

a. $160 \div 5 = 32$
$8(32 \text{ trees}) = \mathbf{256 \text{ trees}}$

b. $3(32 \text{ trees}) = \mathbf{96 \text{ trees}}$

11. $y = 3(-5) - 1$
$y = -15 - 1$
$y = \mathbf{-16}$

12. $30\% \times 20 = \dfrac{3}{10} \times 20 = 6$

$20\% \times 30 = \dfrac{2}{10} \times 30 = 6$

$6 = 6$

30% of 20 $\boxed{=}$ 20% of 30

13.

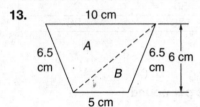

  a.   Area of triangle $A = \dfrac{(10\ \text{cm})(6\ \text{cm})}{2}$

                 $= 30\ \text{cm}^2$

     Area of triangle $B = \dfrac{(5\ \text{cm})(6\ \text{cm})}{2}$

                 $= 15\ \text{cm}^2$

     Area of figure $= 30\ \text{cm}^2 + 15\ \text{cm}^2$

                 $= \mathbf{45\ cm^2}$

  b.

14.

	Percent	Actual Count
Original	100	$90.00
+ Change	75	C
New	175	N

  a. $\dfrac{100}{175} = \dfrac{\$90}{N}$

     $100N = \$15{,}750$

        $N = \mathbf{\$157.50}$

  b. $\$157.50$ $\$157.50$
      $\underline{\times\quad 0.06}$ $\underline{+\quad \$9.45}$
        $\$9.45$ $\mathbf{\$166.95}$

15. $(8 \times 3)(10^{-5} \times 10^{12})$
     24×10^7
   $(2.4 \times 10^1) \times 10^7$
     $\mathbf{2.4 \times 10^8}$

16. a. $2\dfrac{1}{3} = \dfrac{7}{3} = \mathbf{2.\overline{3}}$

  b. $2\dfrac{1}{3} = \dfrac{7}{3} \times 100\% = \mathbf{233\dfrac{1}{3}\%}$

  c. $3\dfrac{1}{3}\% = \dfrac{\frac{10}{3}}{\frac{100}{1}} \times \dfrac{\frac{1}{100}}{\frac{1}{100}} = \dfrac{10}{300} = \dfrac{\mathbf{1}}{\mathbf{30}}$

  d. $3\dfrac{1}{3}\% = \dfrac{1}{30} = \mathbf{0.0\overline{3}}$

17. 3 aces, 51 cards

   $\dfrac{3}{51} = \dfrac{\mathbf{1}}{\mathbf{17}}$

18. $W_N = 2.5 \times 60$
    $W_N = \mathbf{150}$

19. a. 2

  b. 3

20. $C \approx 3.14(24\ \text{inches})$
   $C \approx 75.36\ \text{inches}$
   $C \approx \mathbf{75\ inches}$

21. $y = 2(0) + 1$
   $y = 0 + 1$
   $y = \mathbf{1};$
   $y = 2(3) + 1$
   $y = 6 + 1$
   $y = \mathbf{7};$
   $y = 2(-2) + 1$
   $y = -4 + 1$
   $y = \mathbf{-3}$

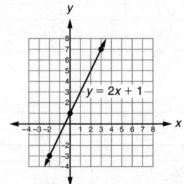

No, x and y are not directly proportional. Although the graph is a line and y increases as x increases, the (x, y) pair $(0, 0)$ is not a solution, so the other (x, y) pairs do not form proportions.

22.

	Ratio	Actual Measure
Smaller	4	s
Larger	5	l
Total	9	180°

$$\frac{4}{9} = \frac{s}{180°}$$
$$9s = 720°$$
$$s = \mathbf{80°}$$

23. a. $x + y + 3 + x - y - 1$
$x + x + y - y + 3 - 1$
$\mathbf{2x + 2}$

b. $(3x)(2x) + (3x)(2)$
$[(3) \cdot x \cdot (2) \cdot x] + [(3) \cdot x \cdot (2)]$
$[(3)(2) \cdot x \cdot x] + [(3)(2) \cdot x]$
$\mathbf{6x^2 + 6x}$

c. $(x^3y)^2$
$= (x^3)^2y^2$
$= \mathbf{x^6y^2}$

24. One possibility:

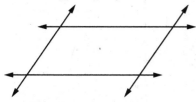

Parallelogram

25. $3\frac{1}{7}x = 66$

$$\frac{22}{7}x = 66$$

$$\left(\frac{\overset{1}{7}}{\overset{}{\underset{1}{22}}}\right)\frac{\overset{1}{22}}{\overset{}{\underset{1}{7}}}x = \left(\frac{7}{22}\right)\overset{3}{66}$$

$$x = \mathbf{21}$$

$$3\frac{1}{7}(21) = 66$$

$$\frac{22}{\underset{1}{7}}(\overset{3}{21}) = 66$$

$$66 = 66$$

26. $w - 0.15 = 4.9$
$w - 0.15 + 0.15 = 4.9 + 0.15$
$w = \mathbf{5.05}$
$5.05 - 0.15 = 4.9$
$4.9 = 4.9$

27. $-8y = 600$

$$\frac{-8y}{-8} = \frac{\overset{-75}{\cancel{600}}}{\underset{1}{\cancel{-8}}}$$

$$y = \mathbf{-75}$$

$$(-8)(-75) = 600$$
$$600 = 600$$

28. $(2 \cdot 3)^2 - 2(3^2)$
$= (6)^2 - 2(9) = 36 - 18 = \mathbf{18}$

29. $5 - \left(3\frac{1}{3} - 1\frac{1}{2}\right)$

$$= 4\frac{6}{6} - \left(3\frac{2}{6} - 1\frac{3}{6}\right)$$

$$= 4\frac{6}{6} - \left(2\frac{8}{6} - 1\frac{3}{6}\right)$$

$$= 4\frac{6}{6} - 1\frac{5}{6} = \mathbf{3\frac{1}{6}}$$

30. a. $\dfrac{(-8)(-6)(-5)}{(-4)(-3)(-2)}$

$$\frac{(48)(-5)}{(12)(-2)}$$

$$\frac{-240}{-24}$$

$$\mathbf{10}$$

b. $-6 - 5(-4) - 3(-2)(-1)$
$-6 - (-20) - 3(2)$
$-6 - (-20) - (6)$
$\mathbf{8}$

Early Finishers Solutions

a. $\dfrac{3600 \text{ dolls}}{45 \text{ workers}} = 80 \dfrac{\text{dolls}}{\text{workers}}$

b. $80 \times [45 + (0.70 \times 45)] = 6120$ dolls

Practice Set **93**

a.

$8x - 15 = 185$		equation
$8x - 15 + 15 = 185 + 15$		added 15 to both sides
$8x = 200$		simplified
$\dfrac{8x}{8} = \dfrac{200}{8}$		divided both sides by 8
$x = \mathbf{25}$		simplified

Check:
$8(25) - 15 = 185$
$200 - 15 = 185$
$185 = 185 \checkmark$

Solutions

b.

$$0.2y + 1.5 = 3.7 \quad \text{equation}$$

$$0.2y + 1.5 - 1.5 = 3.7 - 1.5 \quad \text{subtracted 1.5 from both sides}$$

$$0.2y = 2.2 \quad \text{simplified}$$

$$\frac{0.2y}{0.2} = \frac{2.2}{0.2} \quad \text{divided both sides by 2.2}$$

$$y = \mathbf{11} \quad \text{simplified}$$

Check:

$$0.2(11) + 1.5 = 3.7$$

$$2.2 + 1.5 = 3.7$$

$$3.7 = 3.7 \checkmark$$

c.

$$\frac{3}{4}m - \frac{1}{3} = \frac{1}{2} \quad \text{equation}$$

$$\frac{3}{4}m - \frac{1}{3} + \frac{1}{3} = \frac{1}{2} + \frac{1}{3} \quad \text{added } \frac{1}{3} \text{ to both sides}$$

$$\frac{3}{4}m = \frac{5}{6} \quad \text{simplified}$$

$$\left(\frac{4}{3}\right)\frac{3}{4}m = \left(\frac{4}{3}\right)\frac{5}{6} \quad \text{divided both sides by } \frac{3}{4} \text{ (multiplied both sides by } \frac{4}{3}\text{)}$$

$$m = \frac{20}{18} \quad \text{simplified}$$

$$m = \mathbf{\frac{10}{9}} \quad \text{simplified}$$

Check:

$$\overset{1}{\underset{2}{\cancel{\frac{3}{4}}}}\left(\overset{5}{\underset{3}{\cancel{\frac{10}{9}}}}\right) - \frac{1}{3} = \frac{1}{2}$$

$$\frac{5}{6} - \frac{2}{6} = \frac{1}{2}$$

$$\frac{3}{6} = \frac{1}{2}$$

$$\frac{1}{2} = \frac{1}{2} \checkmark$$

d.

$$1\frac{1}{2}n + 3\frac{1}{2} = 14 \quad \text{equation}$$

$$1\frac{1}{2}n + 3\frac{1}{2} - 3\frac{1}{2} = 14 - 3\frac{1}{2} \quad \text{subtracted } 3\frac{1}{2} \text{ from both sides}$$

$$1\frac{1}{2}n = 14 - 3\frac{1}{2} \quad \text{simplified}$$

$$1\frac{1}{2}n = 10\frac{1}{2} \quad \text{simplified}$$

$$\left(\frac{2}{3}\right)\frac{3}{2}n = \left(\frac{2}{3}\right)\frac{21}{2} \quad \text{divided both sides by } \frac{3}{2} \text{ (multiplied both sides by } \frac{2}{3}\text{)}$$

$$n = \frac{42}{6} \quad \text{simplified}$$

$$n = \mathbf{7} \quad \text{simplified}$$

Check:

$$1\frac{1}{2}(7) + 3\frac{1}{2} = 14$$

$$\frac{3}{2}(7) + \frac{7}{2} = 14$$

$$\frac{21}{2} + \frac{7}{2} = 14$$

$$\frac{28}{2} = 14$$

$$14 = 14 \checkmark$$

e.

$$-6p + 36 = 12 \quad \text{equation}$$

$$-6p + 36 - 36 = 12 - 36 \quad \text{subtracted 36 from both sides}$$

$$-6p = -24 \quad \text{simplified}$$

$$\frac{-6p}{-6} = \frac{-24}{-6} \quad \text{divided both sides by } -6$$

$$p = \mathbf{4} \quad \text{simplified}$$

Check:

$$-6(4) + 36 = 12$$

$$-24 + 36 = 12$$

$$12 = 12 \checkmark$$

f.

$$38 = 4w - 26 \quad \text{equation}$$

$$38 + 26 = 4w - 26 + 26 \quad \text{added 26 to both sides}$$

$$64 = 4w \quad \text{simplified}$$

$$\frac{64}{4} = \frac{4w}{4} \quad \text{divided both sides by 4}$$

$$\mathbf{16} = w \quad \text{simplified}$$

Check:
$38 = 4(16) - 26$
$38 = 64 - 26$
$38 = 38 \checkmark$

g.
$$2x + 5 \geq 1$$
$$2x + 5 - 5 \geq 1 - 5$$
$$2x \geq -4$$
$$\frac{2x}{2} \geq \frac{-4}{2}$$
$$\boldsymbol{x \geq -2}$$

$x \geq -2$

h.
$$2x - 5 < 1$$
$$2x - 5 + 5 < 1 + 5$$
$$2x < 6$$
$$\frac{2x}{2} < \frac{6}{2}$$
$$\boldsymbol{x < 3}$$

$x < 3$

Written Practice 93

1. $\dfrac{60 \text{ kilometers}}{2.5 \text{ hours}} = \textbf{24 kilometers per hour}$

2. a.

3	**9**
9	12)108
7	
5	
10	
4	
5	
8	
5	
4	
8	
+ 40	
108	

b. $40 - 3 = \textbf{37}$

3.

	Ratio	Actual Count
Red marbles	7	R
Blue marbles	5	B
Total	12	600

a. $\dfrac{5}{12} = \dfrac{B}{600}$
$12B = 3000$
$B = \textbf{250 marbles}$

b. $\dfrac{5}{12}$

4.

	Case 1	Case 2
Pterodactyls	500	p
Minutes	20	90

$\dfrac{500}{20} = \dfrac{p}{90}$
$20p = 45{,}000$
$p = \textbf{2250 plastic pterodactyls}$

5. a.

	Percent	Actual Count
Original	100	$24
− Change	25	C
New	75	N

$\dfrac{100}{75} = \dfrac{\$24}{N}$
$100N = \$1800$
$N = \textbf{\$18}$

b.

	Percent	Actual Count
Original	100	O
− Change	25	C
New	75	$24

$\dfrac{100}{75} = \dfrac{O}{\$24}$
$75O = \$2400$
$O = \textbf{\$32}$

6.
$$(-3x^2)(2xy)(-x)(3y^2)$$
$$(-3) \cdot x \cdot x \cdot (2) \cdot x \cdot y \cdot (-1) \cdot x \cdot (3) \cdot y \cdot y$$
$$(-3)(2)(-1)(3) \cdot x \cdot x \cdot x \cdot x \cdot y \cdot y \cdot y$$
$$\boldsymbol{18x^4y^3}$$

7. $\dfrac{2}{50} = \dfrac{1}{25}$

8. $7 \text{ days} \cdot \dfrac{24 \text{ hours}}{1 \text{ day}} \cdot \dfrac{60 \text{ minutes}}{1 \text{ hour}}$
$= \textbf{10,080 minutes}$

9.

45 cars

$\frac{5}{9}$ were not cattle cars.
$\frac{4}{9}$ were cattle cars.

a. $4 \times 5 \text{ cattle cars} = \textbf{20 cattle cars}$

b. $\dfrac{5}{9} \times 100\% = \dfrac{500}{9}\% = \textbf{55}\dfrac{\textbf{5}}{\textbf{9}}\textbf{\%}$

10. $\frac{1}{3}$ $\oslash$ 33%

11. $(-3)(-1) - (-3) - (-1)$
$(3) - (-3) - (-1)$
7

12.
$\begin{array}{r} \$7.95 \\ \$0.90 \\ \underline{\$2.35} \\ \$11.20 \end{array}$
$\begin{array}{r} \$11.20 \\ \times\quad 0.05 \\ \hline \$0.56 \end{array}$
$\begin{array}{r} \$11.20 \\ + \quad \$0.56 \\ \hline \mathbf{\$11.76} \end{array}$

13.

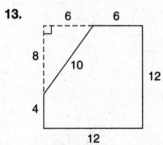

a. Perimeter = 6 in. + 12 in. + 12 in.
   + 4 in. + 10 in. = **44 in.**

b. Area of square = (12 in.)(12 in.)
   = 144 in.²
   Area of triangle = $\dfrac{(6\text{ in.})(8\text{ in.})}{2}$
   = 24 in.²
   Area of figure = 144 in.² − 24 in.²
   = **120 in.²**

14. a. $0.08 = \dfrac{8}{100} = \dfrac{2}{25}$

b. $0.08 = \dfrac{8}{100} = \mathbf{8\%}$

c. $8\frac{1}{3}\% = \dfrac{25}{3}\%$

$= \dfrac{\frac{25}{3}}{\frac{100}{1}} \times \dfrac{\frac{1}{100}}{\frac{1}{100}} = \dfrac{\overset{1}{25}}{\underset{12}{300}} = \dfrac{1}{12}$

d. $8\frac{1}{3}\% = \dfrac{1}{12} = \mathbf{0.08\overline{3}}$

15.

	Percent	Actual Count
Original	100	$3.60
+ Change	120	C
New	220	N

$\dfrac{100}{220} = \dfrac{\$3.60}{N}$
$100N = \$792$
$N = \mathbf{\$7.92}$

16. $(8 \times 10^{-3})(6 \times 10^{7})$
   48×10^{4}
   $(4.8 \times 10^{1})10^{4}$
   $\mathbf{4.8 \times 10^{5}}$

17. a. (10 cm)(10 cm)(10 cm)
   = **1000 cm³**

b. 6(100 cm²) = **600 cm²**

18. a. $A \approx 3.14(100\text{ cm}^2)$
   $A \approx \mathbf{314\text{ cm}^2}$

b. $C \approx 3.14(20\text{ cm})$
   $C \approx \mathbf{62.8\text{ cm}}$

19. $-x + 2x^2 - 1 + x - x^2$
   $2x^2 - x^2 - x + x - 1$
   $\mathbf{x^2 - 1}$

20. a. $y = 2(1) + 3$
   $y = 2 + 3$
   $y = \mathbf{5};$
   $y = 2(0) + 3$
   $y = 0 + 3$
   $y = \mathbf{3};$
   $y = 2(-2) + 3$
   $y = -4 + 3$
   $y = \mathbf{-1}$

b.

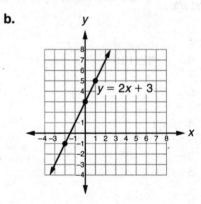

**c. No, x and y are not directly proportional.
   Although the graph is a line and y
   increases as x increases, the (x, y) pair
   (0, 0) is not a solution, so the (x, y)
   pairs do not form proportions.**

21. $60 = \dfrac{3}{8} \times W_N$

$\dfrac{8}{3} \cdot \overset{20}{60} = \left(\dfrac{\overset{1}{8}}{\underset{1}{3}}\right)\dfrac{\overset{1}{3}}{\underset{1}{8}} \times W_N$

$\mathbf{160} = W_N$

22.
$$2x - 5 > -1$$
$$2x - 5 + 5 > -1 + 5$$
$$2x > 4$$
$$\frac{2x}{2} > \frac{4}{2}$$
$$\mathbf{x > 2}$$

$x > 2$

23. a. $m\angle x = 180° - (90° + 50°)$
$$= \mathbf{40°}$$
$$m\angle y = m\angle x = \mathbf{40°}$$
$$m\angle z = 180° - (90° + 40°)$$
$$= \mathbf{50°}$$

b. Yes. The triangles have the same shape. Their corresponding angles are congruent.

24.
$$0.42$$
$$+ \ 0.45$$
$$\overline{\mathbf{0.87}}$$

25.
$$3x + 2 = 9$$
$$3x + 2 - 2 = 9 - 2$$
$$3x = 7$$
$$\frac{3x}{3} = \frac{7}{3}$$
$$x = \mathbf{\frac{7}{3}}$$

check: $\overset{1}{\cancel{3}}\left(\frac{7}{\cancel{3}}\right) + 2 = 9$

$$7 + 2 = 9$$
$$9 = 9 \checkmark$$

26.
$$\frac{2}{3}w + 4 = 14$$
$$\frac{2}{3}w + 4 - 4 = 14 - 4$$
$$\frac{2}{3}w = 10$$
$$\left(\frac{3}{2}\right)\frac{2}{3}w = \left(\frac{3}{2}\right)10$$
$$w = \mathbf{15}$$

check: $\underset{1}{\overset{}{\frac{2}{\cancel{3}}}}\left(\overset{5}{\cancel{15}}\right) + 4 = 14$

$$10 + 4 = 14$$
$$14 = 14 \checkmark$$

27.
$$0.2y - 1 = 7$$
$$0.2y - 1 + 1 = 7 + 1$$
$$0.2y = 8$$
$$\frac{0.2y}{0.2} = \frac{8}{0.2}$$
$$y = \mathbf{40}$$

check: $0.2(40) - 1 = 7$
$$8 - 1 = 7$$
$$7 = 7 \checkmark$$

28.
$$-\frac{2}{3}m = 6$$
$$\left(-\frac{3}{2}\right)\left(-\frac{2}{3}m\right) = \left(-\frac{3}{2}\right)6$$
$$m = \mathbf{-9}$$

check: $-\frac{2}{\underset{1}{\cancel{3}}}\left(-\overset{3}{\cancel{9}}\right) = 6$
$$6 = 6 \checkmark$$

29. $3(2^3 + \sqrt{16}) - 4^0 - 8 \cdot 2^{-3}$
$$3(8 + 4) - 1 - 8 \cdot \frac{1}{8}$$
$$3(12) - 1 - 1$$
$$36 - 2$$
$$\mathbf{34}$$

30. a. $\frac{(-9)(+6)(-5)}{(-4) - (-1)}$
$$\frac{(-54)(-5)}{-3}$$
$$\frac{270}{-3}$$
$$\mathbf{-90}$$

b. $-3(4) + 2(3) - 1$
$$(-12) + (6) - 1$$
$$\mathbf{-7}$$

Practice Set **94**

a. 1st Draw: $P(\text{Blue}) = \frac{4}{9}$

2nd Draw: $P(\text{Blue}) = \frac{3}{8}$

$$P(\text{Blue, Blue}) = \frac{\overset{1}{\cancel{4}}}{\underset{3}{\cancel{9}}} \cdot \frac{\overset{1}{\cancel{3}}}{\underset{2}{\cancel{8}}} = \mathbf{\frac{1}{6}}$$

333

Solutions

b. 1st Card: $P(\text{Diamond}) = \dfrac{13}{52} = \dfrac{1}{4}$

2nd Card: $P(\text{Diamond}) = \dfrac{12}{51} = \dfrac{4}{17}$

$P(\text{Diamond, Diamond}) = \dfrac{1}{\cancel{4}_{1}} \cdot \dfrac{\cancel{4}^{1}}{17} = \dfrac{1}{17}$

Written Practice 94

1.
$$\begin{array}{r} 21{,}000{,}000{,}000 \\ -\ 9{,}800{,}000{,}000 \\ \hline 11{,}200{,}000{,}000 \end{array} \qquad \mathbf{1.12 \times 10^{10}}$$

2. $\dfrac{96 \text{ miles} + 240 \text{ miles}}{2 \text{ hours} + 4 \text{ hours}}$

$= \dfrac{336 \text{ miles}}{6 \text{ hours}} = \textbf{56 miles per hour}$

3. $\dfrac{\$8.40}{10 \text{ pounds}} = \dfrac{\$0.84}{1 \text{ pound}}$

$\dfrac{\$10.50}{15 \text{ pounds}} = \dfrac{\$0.70}{1 \text{ pound}}$

$$\begin{array}{r} \$0.84 \\ -\ \$0.70 \\ \hline \end{array}$$

10-pound box; $0.14 per pound more

4. $\dfrac{6}{12} = \dfrac{1}{2}$

5.

	Ratio	Actual Count
Won	3	12
Lost	2	L
Total	5	T

$\dfrac{3}{5} = \dfrac{12}{T}$

$3T = 5(12)$

$3T = 60$

$T = \textbf{20 games}$

6.

	Case 1	Case 2
First number	24	42
Second number	36	n

$\dfrac{24}{36} = \dfrac{42}{n}$

$24n = 1512$

$n = \textbf{63}$

7.

	Percent	Actual Count
Original	100	360
− Change	20	C
New	80	N

$100\% - 20\% = \textbf{80\%}$

8.

	Percent	Actual Count
Original	100	O
− Change	20	C
New	80	$\$20$

$\dfrac{100}{80} = \dfrac{O}{\$20}$

$80O = \$2000$

$O = \textbf{\$25}$

9. a. $\overset{16}{\cancel{144}} \text{ ft}^2 \times \dfrac{1 \text{ yd}}{\cancel{3}_1 \text{ ft}} \times \dfrac{1 \text{ yd}}{\cancel{3}_1 \text{ ft}} = \textbf{16 yd}^2$

b. $1 \cancel{\text{km}} \cdot \dfrac{1000 \cancel{\text{m}}}{1 \cancel{\text{km}}} \cdot \dfrac{1000 \text{ mm}}{1 \cancel{\text{m}}}$

$= \textbf{1,000,000 millimeters}$

10.

$\dfrac{2}{5}$ were conscripted (120).

$\dfrac{3}{5}$ were not conscripted.

300 male serfs

60 male serfs
60 male serfs
60 male serfs
60 male serfs
60 male serfs

a. $120 \div 2 = 60$

$5(60 \text{ male serfs}) = \textbf{300 male serfs}$

b. $3(60 \text{ male serfs}) = \textbf{180 male serfs}$

11. a. 0

b. $P(1, 1) = \dfrac{1}{6} \cdot \dfrac{1}{6} = \dfrac{1}{36}$

c. $P(1, 2) = \dfrac{1}{6} \cdot \dfrac{1}{6} = \dfrac{1}{36}$

$P(2, 1) = \dfrac{1}{6} \cdot \dfrac{1}{6} = \dfrac{1}{36}$

$\dfrac{1}{36} + \dfrac{1}{36} = \dfrac{2}{36} = \dfrac{1}{18}$

12. $y = 4(-2) - 3$

$y = -8 - 3$

$y = \textbf{-11}$

13. $\dfrac{4 \text{ yards}}{4} = 1 \text{ yard} = 3 \text{ feet}$

$(3 \text{ feet})(3 \text{ feet})$

$= \textbf{9 square feet}$

    334

14. a.
$$\begin{array}{r} \$14{,}500 \\ \times\quad 0.065 \\ \hline \$942.50 \end{array}$$

b.
$$\begin{array}{r} \$14{,}500 \\ +\quad 942.50 \\ \hline \$15{,}442.50 \end{array}$$

c.
$$\begin{array}{r} \$14{,}500 \\ \times\quad 0.02 \\ \hline \$290 \end{array}$$

15. a. $66\frac{2}{3}\% = \dfrac{200}{3}\% = \dfrac{\frac{200}{3}}{\frac{100}{1}} \times \dfrac{\frac{1}{100}}{\frac{1}{100}}$

$= \dfrac{200}{300} = \dfrac{2}{3}$

b. $66\frac{2}{3}\% = \dfrac{2}{3} = \mathbf{0.\overline{6}}$

c. $1\frac{3}{4} = \mathbf{1.75}$

d. $1\frac{3}{4} = \dfrac{7}{4} \times 100\% = \dfrac{700}{4}\% = \mathbf{175\%}$

16. a. $2 \times \$7.50 = \mathbf{\$15.00}$

b. $\dfrac{100}{300} = \dfrac{\$7.50}{P}$

$P = \mathbf{\$22.50}$

17. $(2 \times 10^8)(8 \times 10^2)$
16×10^{10}
$(1.6 \times 10^1) \times 10^{10}$
$\mathbf{1.6 \times 10^{11}}$

18. (8 cubes)(6 cubes)(2 cubes)
$= \mathbf{96\ cubes}$

19. Area of square $=$ (14 in.)(14 in.)
$= 196\ \text{in.}^2$

Area of circle $\approx \dfrac{22}{7}(49\ \text{in.}^2)$

$\approx 154\ \text{in.}^2$

$$\begin{array}{r} 196\ \text{in.}^2 \\ -\ 154\ \text{in.}^2 \\ \hline \mathbf{42\ in.^2} \end{array}$$

20.

$$\begin{array}{r} 65.4545... \\ 0.11\overline{)7.200000} \\ 6\,6 \\ \hline 60 \\ 55 \\ \hline 50 \\ 44 \\ \hline 60 \\ 55 \\ \hline 50 \\ 44 \\ \hline 60 \\ 55 \\ \hline 5 \end{array}$$

$65.4545... = \mathbf{65.\overline{45}}$

21. $y = 3x$

x	y
3	9
0	0
−1	−3

$y = 3(3)$
$y = 9$
$y = 3(0)$
$y = 0$
$y = 3(-1)$
$y = -3$

Yes, x and y are directly proportional. The graph is a line, y increases as x increases, and (0, 0) is a solution, so the (x, y) pairs form proportions.

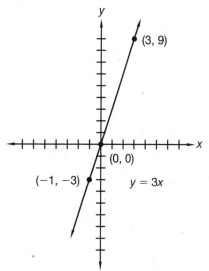

22.
$$\begin{aligned} 2x - 5 &< -1 \\ 2x - 5 + 5 &< -1 + 5 \\ 2x &< 4 \\ \dfrac{2x}{2} &< \dfrac{4}{2} \\ \mathbf{x} &\mathbf{< 2} \end{aligned}$$

$x < 2$

Solutions

23. a. $m\angle AOB = \dfrac{90°}{3} = \mathbf{30°}$

b. $m\angle EOC = 90° + 45° = \mathbf{135°}$

24. AB is $1\dfrac{3}{4}$ in.

BC is $1\dfrac{1}{2}$ in.

$$
\begin{array}{rcl}
1\dfrac{3}{4}\text{ in.} & \longrightarrow & 1\dfrac{3}{4}\text{ in.}\\[4pt]
-\,1\dfrac{1}{2}\text{ in.} & \longrightarrow & -\,1\dfrac{2}{4}\text{ in.}\\[4pt]
\hline
& & \dfrac{1}{4}\text{ in.}
\end{array}
$$

25.
$$1.2p + 4 = 28$$
$$1.2p + 4 - 4 = 28 - 4$$
$$1.2p = 24$$
$$\frac{1.2p}{1.2} = \frac{24}{1.2}$$
$$p = \mathbf{20}$$

26.
$$-6\frac{2}{3}m = 1\frac{1}{9}$$
$$-\frac{20}{3}m = \frac{10}{9}$$
$$\left(-\frac{3}{20}\right)\left(-\frac{20}{3}m\right) = \left(-\frac{3}{20}\right)\left(\frac{10}{9}\right)$$
$$m = \mathbf{-\frac{1}{6}}$$

27. a. $6x^2 + 3x - 2x - 1$
$$\mathbf{6x^2 + x - 1}$$

b.
$$(5x)(3x) - (5x)(-4)$$
$$[(5)\cdot x \cdot (3)\cdot x] - [(5)\cdot x \cdot (-4)]$$
$$[(5)(3)\cdot x \cdot x] - [(5)(-4)\cdot x]$$
$$15x^2 - (-20x)$$
$$\mathbf{15x^2 + 20x}$$

28. a.
$$\frac{-8 - (-6) - (4)}{-3}$$
$$\frac{-8 + 6 - 4}{-3}$$
$$\frac{-6}{-3}$$
$$\mathbf{2}$$

b. $-5(-4) - 3(-2) - 1$
$$20 - (-6) - 1$$
$$\mathbf{25}$$

29. $(-2)^2 - 4(-1)(3)$
$$4 - 4(-3)$$
$$4 - (-12)$$
$$\mathbf{16}$$

30. a. 1st Draw: $P(\text{White}) = \dfrac{3}{9} = \dfrac{1}{3}$

2nd Draw: $P(\text{White}) = \dfrac{3}{9} = \dfrac{1}{3}$

$P(\text{White, White}) = \dfrac{1}{3} \times \dfrac{1}{3} = \mathbf{\dfrac{1}{9}}$

The events are independent.

b. 1st Draw: $P(\text{White}) = \dfrac{3}{9} = \dfrac{1}{3}$

2nd Draw: $P(\text{White}) = \dfrac{2}{8} = \dfrac{1}{4}$

$P(\text{White, White}) = \dfrac{1}{3} \times \dfrac{1}{4} = \mathbf{\dfrac{1}{12}}$

The events are dependent.

Practice Set 95

a. Area of base $= \dfrac{(8\text{ cm})(6\text{ cm})}{2} = 24\text{ cm}^2$

Volume $= (24\text{ cm}^2)(12\text{ cm}) = \mathbf{288\text{ cm}^3}$

b. Area of base $= \dfrac{(10\text{ cm})(6\text{ cm})}{2}$
$$= 30\text{ cm}^2$$

Volume $= (30\text{ cm}^2)(12\text{ cm}) = \mathbf{360\text{ cm}^3}$

c. Area of base $= \pi(3\text{ cm})^2 = 9\pi\text{ cm}^2$

Volume $= (9\pi\text{ cm}^2)(10\text{ cm}) = \mathbf{90\pi\text{ cm}^3}$

d. Area of base $= (7\text{ cm})(2\text{ cm})$
$$+ (3\text{ cm})(3\text{ cm})$$
$$= 14\text{ cm}^2 + 9\text{ cm}^2 = 23\text{ cm}^3$$

Volume $= (23\text{ cm}^2)(10\text{ cm}) = \mathbf{230\text{ cm}^3}$

e. Area of base $= \pi(1\text{ cm})^2 = \pi\text{ cm}^2$

Volume $= (\pi\text{ cm}^2)(10\text{ cm}) = \mathbf{10\pi\text{ cm}^3}$

f. Area of base $= \dfrac{1}{2}(10\text{ ft} + 8\text{ ft})(10\text{ ft})$
$$= \dfrac{1}{2}(18\text{ ft})(10\text{ ft}) = 90\text{ ft}^2$$

Volume $= (90\text{ ft}^2)(20\text{ ft}) = \mathbf{1800\text{ ft}^3}$

Written Practice 95

1. $1.40 + 40($0.35)
   = $1.40 + $14.00 = $15.40

$$\frac{\$15.40}{4 \text{ miles}} = \textbf{\$3.85 per mile}$$

2.
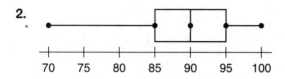

3.
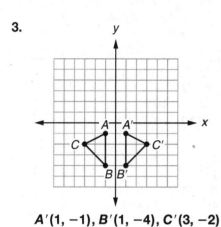

$A'(1, -1), B'(1, -4), C'(3, -2)$

4. $6\left(4\frac{1}{3}\right) = \$6\left(\frac{13}{3}\right) = \textbf{\$26}$

5. Area of rectangle $= (12)(8) = 96$

Area of triangle $= \dfrac{(6)(8)}{2} = 24$

$$\frac{24}{96} = \frac{1}{4} = \frac{\text{shaded area}}{\text{total area}}$$

$$\frac{\text{unshaded area}}{\text{total area}} = \frac{3}{4}$$

$$\frac{\text{shaded area}}{\text{unshaded area}} = \frac{1}{3}$$

6. 1 ton = 2000 pounds

$$\frac{600}{\$7.20} = \frac{2000}{p}$$

$600p = \$14,400$

$p = \textbf{\$24.00}$

7.

	Percent	Actual Count
Original	100	O
+ Change	30	C
New	130	$3.90

$$\frac{100}{130} = \frac{O}{\$3.90}$$

$130O = \$390$

$O = \textbf{\$3 per unit}$

8.

	Percent	Actual Count
Original	100	$3.90
+ Change	30	C
New	130	N

$$\frac{100}{130} = \frac{\$3.90}{N}$$

$100N = \$507$

$N = \textbf{\$5.07}$

9. $\overset{10}{\cancel{1000}} \text{ mm}^2 \cdot \dfrac{1 \text{ cm}}{\cancel{10} \text{ mm}} \cdot \dfrac{1 \text{ cm}}{\cancel{10} \text{ mm}}$

$= \textbf{10 cm}^2$

10.

150 Lilliputians

30 Lilliputians
30 Lilliputians
30 Lilliputians
30 Lilliputians
30 Lilliputians

$\frac{3}{5}$ believed.

$\frac{2}{5}$ did not believe (60).

a. $60 \div 2 = 30$

5(30 Lilliputians) = **150 Lilliputians**

b. 3(30 Lilliputians) = **90 Lilliputians**

11. (6 mph)(10 min) = (12 mph)(t)

$$\frac{(\overset{1}{\cancel{6 \text{ mph}}})(10 \text{ min})}{(\underset{2}{\cancel{12 \text{ mph}}})} = t$$

$t = \textbf{5 min}$

12. $(-2)[(-2) + (-3)]$

$-2[-5]$

10

13. a.
$$P(1, 6) = \frac{1}{6} \cdot \frac{1}{6} = \frac{1}{36}$$

$$P(3, 4) = \frac{1}{6} \cdot \frac{1}{6} = \frac{1}{36}$$

$$P(6, 1) = \frac{1}{6} \cdot \frac{1}{6} = \frac{1}{36}$$

$$P(4, 3) = \frac{1}{6} \cdot \frac{1}{6} = \frac{1}{36}$$

$$P(2, 5) = \frac{1}{6} \cdot \frac{1}{6} = \frac{1}{36}$$

$$P(5, 2) = \frac{1}{6} \cdot \frac{1}{6} = \frac{1}{36}$$

$$\frac{1}{36} + \frac{1}{36} + \frac{1}{36} + \frac{1}{36} + \frac{1}{36} + \frac{1}{36}$$

$$= \frac{6}{36} = \frac{1}{6}$$

b.
$$P(1, 1 \text{ or } 2 \text{ or } 3 \text{ or } 4 \text{ or } 5) = \frac{1}{6} \cdot \frac{5}{6} = \frac{5}{36}$$

$$P(2, 1 \text{ or } 2 \text{ or } 3 \text{ or } 4) = \frac{1}{6} \cdot \frac{4}{6} = \frac{4}{36}$$

$$P(3, 1 \text{ or } 2 \text{ or } 3) = \frac{1}{6} \cdot \frac{3}{6} = \frac{3}{36}$$

$$P(4, 1 \text{ or } 2) = \frac{1}{6} \cdot \frac{2}{6} = \frac{2}{36}$$

$$P(5, 1) = \frac{1}{6} \cdot \frac{1}{6} = \frac{1}{36}$$

$$\frac{5}{36} + \frac{4}{36} + \frac{3}{36} + \frac{2}{36} + \frac{1}{36}$$

$$= \frac{15}{36} = \frac{5}{12}$$

14. Volume of triangular prism $=$ Area of base

$$= \frac{(30 \text{ ft})(6 \text{ ft})}{2} = 90 \text{ ft}^2$$

Volume $= (90 \text{ ft}^2)(40 \text{ ft}) = 3600 \text{ ft}^3$

Volume of rectangular prism
$= (30 \text{ ft})(10 \text{ ft})(40 \text{ ft}) = 12{,}000 \text{ ft}^3$

Volume of building $= 3600 \text{ ft}^3$
$+ 12{,}000 \text{ ft}^3 = \mathbf{15{,}600 \text{ ft}^3}$

15. Area of base $\approx 3.14(9 \text{ cm}^2)$
$\approx 28.26 \text{ cm}^2$
Volume $\approx (28.26 \text{ cm}^2)(10 \text{ cm})$
$\approx \mathbf{282.6 \text{ cm}^3}$

16. $3(\$1.25) + 2(\$0.95) + \$1.30$
$= \$3.75 + \$1.90 + \$1.30 = \$6.95$

$$\begin{array}{r} \$6.95 \\ \times 0.06 \\ \hline \$0.417 \end{array} \rightarrow \$0.42$$

$$\begin{array}{r} \$6.95 \\ + \$0.42 \\ \hline \mathbf{\$7.37} \end{array}$$

17. 1st Draw: $P(\text{White}) = \frac{3}{9} = \frac{1}{3}$

2nd Draw: $P(\text{Blue}) = \frac{4}{8} = \frac{1}{2}$

$P(\text{White, Blue}) = \frac{1}{3} \times \frac{1}{2} = \mathbf{\frac{1}{6}}$

18. a. $\quad (-2xy)(-2x)(x^2 y)$
$(-2) \cdot x \cdot y \cdot (-2) \cdot x \cdot x \cdot x \cdot y$
$(-2)(-2) \cdot x \cdot x \cdot x \cdot x \cdot y \cdot y$
$\mathbf{4x^4 y^2}$

b. $6x - 4y + 3 - 6x - 5y - 8$
$6x - 6x - 4y - 5y + 3 - 8$
$\mathbf{-9y - 5}$

19. $(8 \times 10^{-6})(4 \times 10^4)$
32×10^{-2}
$(3.2 \times 10^1) \times 10^{-2}$
$\mathbf{3.2 \times 10^{-1}}$

20. a. $y = \frac{1}{2}(6) + 1$
$y = 3 + 1$
$y = \mathbf{4};$
$y = \frac{1}{2}(4) + 1$
$y = 2 + 1$
$y = \mathbf{3};$
$y = \frac{1}{2}(-2) + 1$
$y = -1 + 1$
$y = \mathbf{0}$

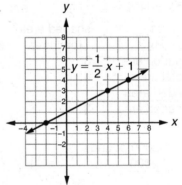

b. (0, 1)

21. a. $m\angle x = 180° - (90° + 55°) = \mathbf{35°}$

b. $m\angle y = 180° - (90° + 35°) = \mathbf{55°}$

c. $m\angle A = 180° - (110° + 55°)$
$= \mathbf{15°}$

22.

23. $(1.52 + 1.56) \div 2 = \textbf{1.54}$

24.
$$-5w + 11 = 51$$
$$-5w + 11 - 11 = 51 - 11$$
$$-5w = 40$$
$$\frac{-5w}{-5} = \frac{40}{-5}$$
$$w = \textbf{-8}$$

$$-5(-8) + 11 = 51$$
$$40 + 11 = 51$$
$$51 = 51 \checkmark$$

25.
$$\frac{4}{3}x - 2 = 14$$
$$\frac{4}{3}x - 2 + 2 = 14 + 2$$
$$\frac{4}{3}x = 16$$
$$\left(\frac{3}{4}\right)\frac{4}{3}x = \left(\frac{3}{4}\right)16$$
$$x = \textbf{12}$$

$$\frac{4}{\cancel{3}}(\cancel{12}) - 2 = 14$$
$$16 - 2 = 14$$
$$14 = 14 \checkmark$$

26.
$$0.9x + 1.2 \le 3$$
$$0.9x + 1.2 - 1.2 \le 3 - 1.2$$
$$0.9x \le 1.8$$
$$\frac{0.9x}{0.9} \le \frac{1.8}{0.9}$$
$$x \le \textbf{2}$$

$x \le 2$

27. $\dfrac{10^3 \cdot 10^2}{10^5} - 10^{-1}$

$= \dfrac{10^5}{10^5} - \dfrac{1}{10}$

$= 1 - \dfrac{1}{10} = \dfrac{10}{10} - \dfrac{1}{10} = \dfrac{\textbf{9}}{\textbf{10}}$ or **0.9**

28. $\sqrt{1^3 + 2^3} + (1 + 2)^3$

$= \sqrt{1 + 8} + (3)^3 = \sqrt{9} + 27$

$= 3 + 27 = \textbf{30}$

29. $5 - 2\dfrac{2}{3}\left(1\dfrac{3}{4}\right) = 5 - \dfrac{8}{3}\left(\dfrac{7}{4}\right)$

$= 5 - \dfrac{14}{3} = 4\dfrac{3}{3} - 4\dfrac{2}{3} = \dfrac{\textbf{1}}{\textbf{3}}$

30. a. $\dfrac{(-10) + (-8) - (-6)}{(-2)(+3)}$

$$\dfrac{-18 - (-6)}{-6}$$
$$\dfrac{-12}{-6}$$
$$\textbf{2}$$

b. $-8 + 3(-2) - 6$
$-8 + (-6) - 6$
-20

Early Finishers Solutions

a. There are 16; BBBB, BBBG, BBGB, BGBB, GBBB, BBGG, BGBG, GBBG, BGGB, GBGB, GGBB, BGGG, GBGG, GGBG, GGGB, GGGG

b. $\dfrac{6}{16} = \dfrac{3}{8}$

Practice Set 96

a. $4 \times 6° = \textbf{24°}$

b. $20 \times 6° = \textbf{120°}$

c. $7 \times 6° = \textbf{42°}$

d. See student work; **55°**

e. See student work; **15°**

f. See student work; **45°**

g. See student work; **145°**

h. $x(x - y)$
$\textbf{x}^2 - \textbf{xy}$

i. $-3(2x - 1)$
$\textbf{-6x + 3}$

j. $-x(x - 2)$
$\textbf{-x}^2 + \textbf{2x}$

k. $-2(4 - 3x)$
$\textbf{-8 + 6x}$

Solutions

l.

$x^2 + 2x - 3(x + 2)$	Given
$x^2 + 2x - 3x - 6$	Distributive property
$x^2 + (2x - 3x) - 6$	Associative property
$\mathbf{x^2 + x - 6}$	$2x - 3x = -x$

m.

$x^2 - 2x - 3(x - 2)$	Given
$x^2 - 2x - 3x + 6$	Distributive property
$x^2 + (-2x - 3x) + 6$	Associative property
$\mathbf{x^2 - 5x + 6}$	$-2x - 3x = -5x$

Written Practice 96

1. $3(\$280) + 5(\$240)$
$= \$840 + \$1200 = \$2040$

$\mathbf{\$255}$ **per ton**
$8)\overline{\$2040}$

2. $\dfrac{9^2}{\sqrt{9}} = \dfrac{81}{3} = \mathbf{27}$

3. $\dfrac{2000 \text{ miles}}{25 \text{ miles per gallon}} = 80 \text{ gallons}$

$\dfrac{80 \text{ gallons}}{16 \text{ gallons per tank}} = \mathbf{5 \text{ tanks}}$

4. $\dfrac{\text{vertices}}{\text{edges}} = \dfrac{6}{9} = \dfrac{\mathbf{2}}{\mathbf{3}}$

5.

	Case 1	Case 2
Dollars	12	d
Yuan	100	475

$\dfrac{12}{100} = \dfrac{d}{475}$
$100d = 5700$
$d = \mathbf{57 \text{ dollars}}$

6.

	Percent	Actual Count
Original	100	O
− Change	20	C
New	80	60

$\dfrac{100}{80} = \dfrac{O}{60}$
$80O = 6000$
$O = \mathbf{75}$

7.

	Percent	Actual Count
Original	100	120
+ Change	25	C
New	125	N

$\dfrac{100}{125} = \dfrac{120}{N}$
$100N = 15{,}000$
$N = \mathbf{150 \text{ customers per day}}$

8. a. $60 = W_P \times 50$

$\dfrac{60}{50} = \dfrac{W_P \times 50}{50}$

$\dfrac{6}{5} = W_P$

$W_P = \dfrac{6}{5} \times 100\% = \mathbf{120\%}$

b. $50 = W_P \times 60$

$\dfrac{50}{60} = \dfrac{W_P \times 60}{60}$

$\dfrac{5}{6} = W_P$

$W_P = \dfrac{5}{6} \times 100\% = \mathbf{83\dfrac{1}{3}\%}$

9. a. $\dfrac{\overset{1}{\cancel{12}} \text{ dollars}}{\cancel{\text{hour}}} \times \dfrac{100 \text{ cents}}{1 \cancel{\text{ dollar}}} \times \dfrac{1 \cancel{\text{ hour}}}{\underset{5}{\cancel{60}} \text{ minutes}}$

$= \mathbf{20 \text{ cents per minute}}$

b. Directly proportional

10. a. Angles: $\angle A$ and $\angle E$, $\angle B$ and $\angle D$, $\angle ACB$ and $\angle ECD$ (or $\angle BCA$ and $\angle DCE$)
Sides: $\overline{AB}$ and $\overline{ED}$ (or $\overline{BA}$ and $\overline{DE}$), $\overline{BC}$ and $\overline{DC}$ (or $\overline{CB}$ and $\overline{CD}$), $\overline{AC}$ and $\overline{EC}$ (or $\overline{CA}$ and $\overline{CE}$)

b. $m\angle ECD = 90° - 53° = \mathbf{37°}$

11.

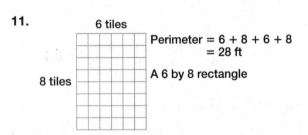

Perimeter = 6 + 8 + 6 + 8
= 28 ft

A 6 by 8 rectangle

12. $(-2)[(-4) + (-3)]$
$-2[-7]$
14

13. 1 yard = 36 inches ÷ 4 = 9 inches
Area = (9 inches)(9 inches)
= **81 square inches**

14. a. $P(3, 3) = \dfrac{1}{4} \cdot \dfrac{1}{4} = \dfrac{1}{16}$

b. $P(1, 1, 1, 1) = \dfrac{2}{4} \cdot \dfrac{2}{4} \cdot \dfrac{2}{4} \cdot \dfrac{2}{4}$
$= \dfrac{16}{256} = \dfrac{1}{16}$

15. a. Area of base = (3 cm)(3 cm)
= 9 cm^2
Volume = (9 cm^2)(3 cm) = **27 cm^3**

b. Area of base = $\dfrac{(4\ \text{cm})(6\ \text{cm})}{2}$
= 12 cm^2
Volume = (12 cm^2)(5 cm) = **60 cm^3**

16.

$14.50	$290	$290
× 20	× 0.07	+ $20.30
$290	$20.30	**$310.30**

17. a.
$3\dfrac{3}{4}\% = \dfrac{15}{4}\% = \dfrac{\frac{15}{4}}{\frac{100}{1}} \times \dfrac{\frac{1}{100}}{\frac{1}{100}} = \dfrac{15}{400} = \dfrac{3}{80}$

b. $3\dfrac{3}{4}\% = \dfrac{3}{80} = \mathbf{0.0375}$

18.

	Percent	Actual Count
Original	100	$24
− Change	$33\frac{1}{3}$	C
New	$66\frac{2}{3}$	N

a. $\dfrac{100}{33\frac{1}{3}} = \dfrac{\$24}{C}$

$100C = \$24\left(33\dfrac{1}{3}\right)$

$100C = \dfrac{\$2400}{3}$

$C = \mathbf{\$8}$

b.

$24
− $8
$16

19. $(3 \times 8)(10^3 \times 10^{-8})$
$24 \times 10^{-5} = \mathbf{2.4 \times 10^{-4}}$

20. a. $C = \pi(12\ \text{m})$
$C = \mathbf{12\pi\ m}$

b. $A = \pi(36\ \text{m}^2)$
$A = \mathbf{36\pi\ m^2}$

21. a. $15 \times 6° = \mathbf{90°}$

b. $25 \times 6° = \mathbf{150°}$

c. $8 \times 6° = \mathbf{48°}$

22. a. $\dfrac{360°}{8} = \mathbf{45°}$

b. $180° - 45° = \mathbf{135°}$

23. $Q'(8, -4), R'(4, 0), S'(0, -4), T'(4, -8)$

24.
$0.8x + 1.5 < 4.7$
$0.8x + 1.5 - 1.5 < 4.7 - 1.5$
$0.8x < 3.2$
$\dfrac{0.8x}{0.8} < \dfrac{3.2}{0.8}$
$\mathbf{x < 4}$

$x < 4$

25.
$2\dfrac{1}{2}x - 7 = 13$

$2\dfrac{1}{2}x - 7 + 7 = 13 + 7$

$2\dfrac{1}{2}x = 20$

$\left(\dfrac{2}{5}\right)\dfrac{5}{2}x = \left(\dfrac{2}{5}\right)20$

$x = \mathbf{8}$

check:

$2\dfrac{1}{2}(8) - 7 = 13$

$\dfrac{5}{\underset{1}{2}}\left(\overset{4}{8}\right) - 7 = 13$

$20 - 7 = 13$

$13 = 13$ ✓

341

26.

$$-3x + 8 = -10$$
$$-3x + 8 - 8 = -10 - 8$$
$$-3x = -18$$
$$\frac{-3x}{-3} = \frac{-18}{-3}$$
$$x = \textbf{6}$$

check:

$$-3(6) + 8 = -10$$
$$-18 + 8 = -10$$
$$-10 = -10 \checkmark$$

27. a. $-3(x - 4)$
$\quad\quad$ **$-3x + 12$**

b. $x(x + y)$
$\quad\quad$ **$x^2 + xy$**

28. a. $\dfrac{(-4) - (-8)(-3)(-2)}{-2}$

$\quad\quad\quad \dfrac{(-4) - (24)(-2)}{-2}$

$\quad\quad\quad \dfrac{(-4) - (-48)}{-2}$

$\quad\quad\quad \dfrac{44}{-2}$

$\quad\quad\quad$ **-22**

b. $(-3)^2 + 3^2 = 9 + 9 = \textbf{18}$

29. a. $(-4ab^2)(-3b^2c)(5a)$
$\quad\quad (-4) \cdot a \cdot b \cdot b \cdot (-3) \cdot b \cdot b \cdot c \cdot (5) \cdot a$
$\quad\quad (-4)(-3)(5) \cdot a \cdot a \cdot b \cdot b \cdot b \cdot b \cdot c$
$\quad\quad\quad\quad \textbf{60 } a^2b^4c$

b. $a^2 + ab - ab - b^2$
$\quad\quad \textbf{$a^2 - b^2$}$

30. 1st Draw: $P(\text{king}) = \dfrac{4}{52} = \dfrac{1}{13}$

$\quad\quad 2^{nd}$ Draw: $P(\text{king}) = \dfrac{3}{51} = \dfrac{1}{17}$

$\quad\quad 3^{rd}$ Draw: $P(\text{king}) = \dfrac{2}{50} = \dfrac{1}{25}$

$\quad P(\text{king, king, king}) = \dfrac{1}{13} \cdot \dfrac{1}{17} \cdot \dfrac{1}{25}$
$\quad\quad\quad\quad\quad\quad\quad = \dfrac{1}{\textbf{5525}}$

Practice Set 97

a. Corresponding angles: $\angle W$ and $\angle R$; $\angle Y$ and $\angle Q$; $\angle X$ and $\angle P$
Corresponding sides: $\overline{YW}$ and $\overline{QR}$; $\overline{WX}$ and $\overline{RP}$; $\overline{XY}$ and $\overline{PQ}$

b. See student work.

c. $\dfrac{6}{9} = \dfrac{x}{12}$
$\quad 9x = 72$
$\quad x = \textbf{8}$

d. See student work.

e. $\dfrac{6}{9} = \dfrac{12}{y}$
$\quad 6y = 108$
$\quad y = \textbf{18}$

f. $\dfrac{H_T}{6 \text{ ft}} = \dfrac{18 \text{ ft}}{9 \text{ ft}}$
$\quad 9 \text{ ft} \cdot H_T = 18 \text{ ft} \cdot 6 \text{ ft}$
$\quad H_T = \dfrac{\overset{6}{\cancel{18}} \text{ ft} \cdot \overset{2}{\cancel{6}} \text{ ft}}{\underset{1}{\underset{\cancel{3}}{\cancel{9}}} \text{ ft}}$
$\quad H_T = \textbf{12 ft}$

g. **About 11 ft**

Written Practice 97

1.

$$\begin{array}{r} \$8.95 \\ \times\ 0.06 \\ \hline \$0.537 \end{array} \longrightarrow \$0.54$$

$$\begin{array}{r} \$8.95 \\ +\ \$0.54 \\ \hline \$9.49 \end{array}$$

$$\begin{array}{r} \$10.00 \\ -\ \$9.49 \\ \hline \$0.51 \end{array}$$

2.

$$\begin{array}{r} \overset{1}{2,}000,000,000,000 \\ -\ 300,000,000,000 \\ \hline 1,700,000,000,000 \end{array} \quad 1.7 \times 10^{12}$$

3. a. 90

$\quad$ **b. 90**

$\quad$ **c. 20**

4.

	Case 1	Case 2
Miles	24	m
Minutes	60	5

$$\frac{24}{60} = \frac{m}{5}$$
$$60m = 120$$
$$m = \textbf{2 miles}$$

5.

	Case 1	Case 2
Yards	3520	y
Minutes	5	8

$$\frac{3520}{5} = \frac{y}{8}$$
$$5y = 28{,}160$$
$$y = \textbf{5632 yards}$$

6. **Translation of 5 units to the right**

7. 1 yard = 36 inches
$$\frac{3}{\overset{1}{\underset{}{4}}} \times \overset{9}{\cancel{36}} \text{ inches} = \textbf{27 inches}$$

8.

	Ratio	Actual Count
Leeks	5	L
Radishes	7	420

$$\frac{5}{7} = \frac{L}{420}$$
$$7L = 2100$$
$$L = \textbf{300 leeks}$$

9. $40 = 2.5 \times W_N$
$$\frac{40}{2.5} = \frac{2.5 \times W_N}{2.5}$$
$$\textbf{16} = W_N$$

10. $40 = W_P \times 60$
$$\frac{40}{60} = \frac{W_P \times 60}{60}$$
$$\frac{2}{3} = W_P$$
$$W_P = \frac{2}{3} \times 100\% = \textbf{66}\frac{\textbf{2}}{\textbf{3}}\textbf{\%}$$

11. $W_D = 0.4 \times 6$
$$W_D = \textbf{2.4}$$

12.

	Percent	Actual Count
Original	100	O
+ Change	10	C
New	110	$17,600

$$\frac{100}{110} = \frac{O}{\$17{,}600}$$
$$110O = \$1{,}760{,}000$$
$$O = \textbf{\$16,000}$$

13. $\dfrac{1.78 + 2.04}{2} = \textbf{1.91}$

14. a. $3\dfrac{1}{4}$

b. **325%**

c. **0.16̄**

d. $\textbf{16}\dfrac{\textbf{2}}{\textbf{3}}\textbf{\%}$

15. $(3 \text{ mph})(15 \text{ min}) = (5 \text{ mph})(m)$
$$45 = 5m$$
$$m = \textbf{9 min}$$

16. $(5.4 \times 6) \times (10^8 \times 10^{-4})$
$$= 32.4 \times 10^4 = \textbf{3.24} \times \textbf{10}^{\textbf{5}}$$

17. a. $C \approx 3.14(20 \text{ mm})$
$$C \approx \textbf{62.8 mm}$$

b. $A \approx 3.14(100 \text{ mm}^2)$
$$A \approx \textbf{314 mm}^{\textbf{2}}$$

18.

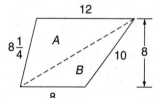

$$\text{Area of triangle } A = \frac{(12 \text{ ft})(8 \text{ ft})}{2} = 48 \text{ ft}^2$$
$$+ \text{ Area of triangle } B = \frac{(8 \text{ ft})(8 \text{ ft})}{2} = 32 \text{ ft}^2$$
$$\text{Area of figure} \qquad\qquad\qquad = \textbf{80 ft}^{\textbf{2}}$$

19. a. $\text{Area of base} = \dfrac{(1 \text{ m})(2 \text{ m})}{2} = 1 \text{ m}^2$
$$\text{Volume} = (1 \text{ m}^2)(2 \text{ m}) = \textbf{2 m}^{\textbf{3}}$$

b. $\text{Area of base} = \pi (1 \text{ m}^2) = \pi \text{ m}^2$
$$\text{Volume} = (\pi \text{ m}^2)(1 \text{ m}) = \boldsymbol{\pi}\textbf{m}^{\textbf{3}}$$

20. a. $m\angle X = 180° - (120° + 25°)$
   $= \mathbf{35°}$

b. $m\angle Y = 180° - (90° + 35°) = \mathbf{55°}$

c. $m\angle A = 180° - (60° + 55°)$
   $= \mathbf{65°}$

21. $\dfrac{x}{12\text{ cm}} = \dfrac{10\text{ cm}}{15\text{ cm}}$
   $15 \cdot x = 120\text{ cm}$
   $x = \mathbf{8\ cm}$

22. See student diagrams.
   $\dfrac{H_P}{3\text{ ft}} = \dfrac{72\text{ ft}}{4\text{ ft}}$
   $4\text{ ft} \times H_P = 3\text{ ft} \times 72\text{ ft}$
   $H_P = \dfrac{3\text{ ft} \times \overset{18}{\cancel{72}}\ \cancel{ft}}{\underset{1}{\cancel{4}\ \cancel{ft}}}$
   $H_P = \mathbf{54\ ft}$

23. $\dfrac{(40{,}000)(600)}{80} = \mathbf{300{,}000}$

24.
   $1.2m + 0.12 = 12$
   $1.2m + 0.12 - 0.12 = 12 - 0.12$
   $1.2m = 11.88$
   $\dfrac{1.2m}{1.2} = \dfrac{11.88}{1.2}$
   $m = \mathbf{9.9}$

   check:
   $1.2(9.9) + 0.12 = 12$
   $11.88 + 0.12 = 12$
   $12 = 12\ ✓$

25.
   $1\dfrac{3}{4}y - 2 = 12$
   $1\dfrac{3}{4}y - 2 + 2 = 12 + 2$
   $1\dfrac{3}{4}y = 14$
   $\left(\dfrac{\overset{1}{\cancel{4}}}{\underset{1}{\cancel{7}}}\right)\dfrac{\overset{1}{\cancel{7}}}{\underset{1}{\cancel{4}}}y = \left(\dfrac{4}{7}\right)\overset{2}{\cancel{14}}$
   $y = \mathbf{8}$

   check:
   $1\dfrac{3}{4}(8) - 2 = 12$
   $\dfrac{7}{\underset{1}{\cancel{4}}}\left(\overset{2}{\cancel{8}}\right) - 2 = 12$
   $14 - 2 = 12$
   $12 = 12\ ✓$

26. $3x - y + 8 + x + y - 2$
   $3x + x - y + y + 8 - 2$
   $\mathbf{4x + 6}$

27. a. $3(x - y)$
   $\mathbf{3x - 3y}$

b. $x(y - 3)$
   $\mathbf{xy - 3x}$

28. $4\dfrac{1}{2} \div 1\dfrac{1}{8} = \dfrac{\overset{1}{\cancel{9}}}{\underset{1}{\cancel{2}}} \times \dfrac{\overset{4}{\cancel{8}}}{\underset{1}{\cancel{9}}} = 4$

   $3\dfrac{1}{3} \div 4 = \dfrac{10}{3} \times \dfrac{1}{4} = \dfrac{10}{12} = \mathbf{\dfrac{5}{6}}$

29. $\dfrac{(-2) - (+3) + (-4)(-3)}{(-2) + (+3) - (+4)}$

   $\dfrac{(-2) - (+3) + (+12)}{(-2) + (+3) - (+4)}$

   $\dfrac{(-5) + (12)}{(1) - (+4)}$

   $\dfrac{7}{-3}$

   $\mathbf{-2\dfrac{1}{3}}$

30. a. 1ˢᵗ Draw: $P(\text{vowel}) = \dfrac{2}{5}$

   2ⁿᵈ Draw: $P(\text{vowel}) = \dfrac{1}{4}$

   $P(\text{vowel, vowel}) = \dfrac{2}{5} \cdot \dfrac{1}{4} = \dfrac{2}{20} = \mathbf{\dfrac{1}{10}}$

b. 1ˢᵗ Draw: $P(\text{consonant}) = \dfrac{3}{5}$

   2ⁿᵈ Draw: $P(\text{consonant}) = \dfrac{2}{4} = \dfrac{1}{2}$

   $P(\text{consonant, consonant}) = \dfrac{3}{5} \cdot \dfrac{1}{2} = \mathbf{\dfrac{3}{10}}$

Early Finishers Solutions

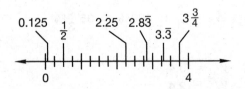

Practice Set 98

a. $\dfrac{6 \cdot \overset{2}{\cancel{24}}}{\underset{1}{\cancel{12}}} = $ **12 feet**

b. $\dfrac{54}{\underset{3}{\cancel{36}}} \cdot \overset{1}{\cancel{12}} = $ **18 inches**

c. $5 \times 3 = 15$
$7 \times 3 = $ **21**

d. $3 \times 7 = 21$
$42 \div 7 = $ **6**

e. $10f = 25$
$f = \dfrac{25}{10}$
$f = $ **2.5**

f. $(2.5)^2 = $ **6.25**

g.

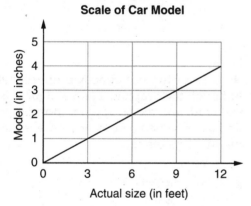

Scale of Car Model

h. C. **9 ft**

Written Practice 98

1. $P(\text{ace}) = \dfrac{3}{51} = \dfrac{1}{17}$

2.

	Percent	Actual Count
Original	100	$45
− Change	20	C
New	80	N

$\dfrac{100}{80} = \dfrac{\$45}{N}$
$100N = \$3600$
$N = \textbf{\$36}$

3.

	Case 1	Case 2
Dollars	5	d
Kroner	40	100

$\dfrac{5}{40} = \dfrac{d}{100}$
$40d = 500$
$d = \textbf{\$12.50}$

4.

	Percent	Actual Count
Original	100	O
+ Change	25	20
New	125	N

$\dfrac{25}{125} = \dfrac{20}{N}$
$25N = 2500$
$N = $ **100 students**

5. $(3x)(x) - (x)(2x)$
$[(3) \cdot x \cdot x] - [x \cdot (2) \cdot x]$
$[(3) \cdot x \cdot x] - [(2) \cdot x \cdot x]$
$3x^2 - 2x^2$
$\mathbf{x^2}$

6. $\dfrac{6(10) + 9(15)}{15}$
$= \dfrac{60 + 135}{15} = $ **13 points per game**

7. a. $\begin{array}{r} 44{,}010 \text{ miles} \\ - \ 43{,}764 \text{ miles} \\ \hline 246 \text{ miles} \end{array}$

$\dfrac{246 \text{ miles}}{12 \text{ gallons}} = $ **20.5 miles per gallon**

b. $\dfrac{246 \text{ miles}}{5 \text{ hours}} = $ **49.2 miles per hour**

8. $\dfrac{3}{5} \times W_N = 60$

$\left(\dfrac{\overset{1}{\cancel{5}}}{\underset{1}{\cancel{3}}}\right)\left(\dfrac{\overset{1}{\cancel{3}}}{\underset{1}{\cancel{5}}} \times W_N\right) = \left(\dfrac{5}{\underset{1}{\cancel{3}}}\right)\overset{20}{\cancel{60}}$

$W_N = $ **100**

9.

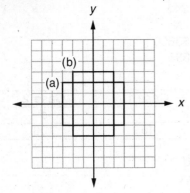

   a. (3, −2)
   b. (2, 3), (2, −3), (−2, −3), (−2, 3)

10. $\dfrac{2}{6} = \dfrac{1}{3}$

11. $a = 9$, $9^2 = $ **81**

12. $40 = W_P \times 250$

$$\dfrac{40}{250} = \dfrac{W_P \times 250}{250}$$

$$\dfrac{4}{25} = W_P$$

$$W_P = \dfrac{4}{25} \times 100\% = \mathbf{16\%}$$

13. $0.4 \times W_N = 60$

$$\dfrac{0.4 \times W_N}{0.4} = \dfrac{60}{0.4}$$

$$W_N = \mathbf{150}$$

14.

	Percent	Actual Count
Original	100	$40
+ Change	60	C
New	160	N

$$\dfrac{100}{160} = \dfrac{\$40}{N}$$

$$100N = \$6400$$

$$N = \mathbf{\$64}$$

15. **a.** $2\dfrac{1}{8} - 1\dfrac{3}{8} = \dfrac{17}{8} - \dfrac{11}{8} = \dfrac{6}{8} = \dfrac{3}{4}$ **inch**

   b. $AC = 3\dfrac{1}{2}$ in. $= \dfrac{7}{2}$ in.

$$\dfrac{7}{2} \text{ in.} \times \dfrac{2.54 \text{ cm}}{1 \text{ in.}} = \mathbf{8.89 \text{ cm}}$$

16.

```
  +---+---+--•--+---+
  0   1   2   3   4
```

17. **a.** $1.4\% = 1\dfrac{4}{10}\% = 1\dfrac{2}{5}\% = \dfrac{7}{5}\%$

$$= \dfrac{\frac{7}{5}}{100} = \dfrac{7}{500}$$

   b. **0.014**

18. $(1.4 \times 10^{-6})(5 \times 10^4)$
     $\mathbf{7.0 \times 10^{-2}}$

19. $y = -2(3)$
    $y = \mathbf{-6}$;
    $y = -2(0)$
    $y = \mathbf{0}$;
    $y = -2(-2)$
    $y = \mathbf{4}$

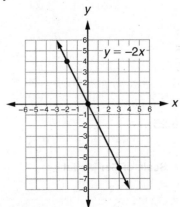

(0, 0)
No, x and y are not directly proportional. Although the graph is a line and (0, 0) is included, and the (x, y) pairs form proportions, one variable does not increase as the other increases.

20. **a.** $C \approx 3.14(2 \text{ ft})$
       $C \approx \mathbf{6.28 \text{ ft}}$

   b. $A \approx 3.14(1 \text{ ft}^2)$
       $A \approx \mathbf{3.14 \text{ ft}^2}$

21. **See student work; 40°.**

22. $\dfrac{x}{30} = \dfrac{20}{50}$
    $50x = 600$
    $x = \mathbf{12 \text{ in.}}$
    $\dfrac{y}{16} = \dfrac{50}{20}$
    $20y = 800$
    $y = \mathbf{40 \text{ in.}}$
    Area $= \dfrac{(16 \text{ in.})(12 \text{ in.})}{2} = \mathbf{96 \text{ in.}^2}$

23. $20f = 50$

$f = \dfrac{50}{20}$

$f = \textbf{2.5}$

24.

$-\dfrac{3}{5}m + 8 = 20$

$-\dfrac{3}{5}m + 8 - 8 = 20 - 8$

$-\dfrac{3}{5}m = 12$

$\left(-\dfrac{\overset{1}{5}}{\underset{1}{3}}\right)\left(-\dfrac{\overset{1}{3}}{\underset{1}{5}}m\right) = \left(-\dfrac{5}{3}\right)\overset{4}{\cancel{12}}$

$m = \textbf{-20}$

check:

$-\dfrac{3}{\underset{1}{5}}\left(-\overset{4}{\cancel{20}}\right) + 8 = 20$

$12 + 8 = 20$

$20 = 20\ \checkmark$

25.

$0.3x - 2.7 = 9$

$0.3x - 2.7 + 2.7 = 9 + 2.7$

$0.3x = 11.7$

$\dfrac{0.3x}{0.3} = \dfrac{11.7}{0.3}$

$x = \textbf{39}$

check:

$0.3(39) - 2.7 = 9$

$11.7 - 2.7 = 9$

$9 = 9\ \checkmark$

26. $\sqrt{5^3 - 5^2} = \sqrt{125 - 25} = \sqrt{100}$

$= \textbf{10}$

27.

$$\begin{array}{r}
\overset{0}{\cancel{1}}\text{ gal }\ \overset{0}{\cancel{1}}\text{ qt (2 pt)} \longrightarrow \\
-\qquad 1\text{ qt }\ 1\text{ pt} \\
\hline
\end{array}$$

(4 qt)

$$\begin{array}{r}
\overset{0}{\cancel{1}}\text{ gal }\ \overset{4}{\overset{0}{\cancel{1}}}\text{ qt }\ 2\text{ pt} \\
-\qquad 1\text{ qt }\ 1\text{ pt} \\
\hline
\textbf{3 qt }\ \textbf{1 pt}
\end{array}$$

28. $(0.25)(1.25 - 1.2)$

$= (0.25)(0.05) = \textbf{0.0125}$

29. $7\dfrac{1}{3} - \left(1\dfrac{3}{4} \div 3\dfrac{1}{2}\right)$

$= 7\dfrac{1}{3} - \left(\dfrac{7}{4} \div \dfrac{7}{2}\right) = 7\dfrac{1}{3} - \left(\dfrac{\overset{1}{7}}{\underset{2}{4}} \times \dfrac{\overset{1}{2}}{\underset{1}{7}}\right)$

$= 7\dfrac{1}{3} - \dfrac{1}{2} = 7\dfrac{2}{6} - \dfrac{3}{6} = 6\dfrac{8}{6} - \dfrac{3}{6}$

$= 6\dfrac{5}{6}$

30. $\dfrac{(-2)(3) - (3)(-4)}{(-2)(-3) - (4)}$

$\dfrac{(-6) - (-12)}{(6) - (4)}$

$\dfrac{6}{2}$

$\textbf{3}$

Early Finishers Solutions

a. $\dfrac{18}{15} = \dfrac{\overline{BC}}{900}; \overline{BC} = 1080$ ft

b. Area $= \dfrac{1}{2}(900\text{ ft})(1080\text{ ft})$

$= 486{,}000\text{ ft}^2$

Practice Set 99

a.

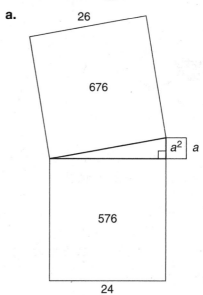

$a^2 + 576 = 676$

$a^2 = 100$

$a = \textbf{10}$

b.

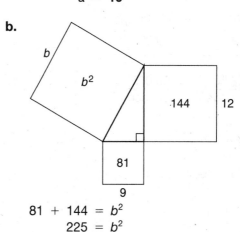

$81 + 144 = b^2$

$225 = b^2$

$\textbf{15} = b$

Solutions

c.

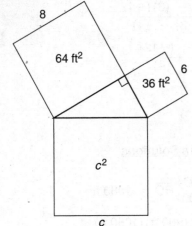

$$64 \text{ ft}^2 + 36 \text{ ft}^2 = c^2$$
$$100 = c^2$$
$$10 = c$$

Perimeter = 8 ft + 6 ft + 10 ft
= **24 ft**

d. B

Written Practice 99

1.
$15.00
$\times$ 0.15
$2.25

2.
$0.0 0 2 5^{4}5^{1}0 0$ **2.48 × 10⁻³**
$-0.0 0 0 0 2 0$
$\overline{0.0 0 2 4 8 0}$

3. **a.** $\dfrac{4(30) + 7(31) + 29}{12}$ = **30.5 days**

b. 31 days

c. 31 days

d. 2 days

4. 2 pounds = 32 ounces

$$\frac{\$2.72}{32 \text{ ounces}} = \frac{\$0.085}{1 \text{ ounce}}$$

$$\frac{\$3.60}{48 \text{ ounces}} = \frac{\$0.075}{1 \text{ ounce}}$$

$\$0.085
$-\$0.075$
$\overline{\$0.01}$

1¢ more per ounce

5.

	Case 1	Case 2
Pounds	80	300
Price	$96	p

$$\frac{80}{\$96} = \frac{300}{p}$$
$$80p = \$28{,}800$$
$$p = \textbf{\$360}$$

6.

	Ratio	Actual Count
Stalactites	9	C
Stalagmites	5	G
Total	14	1260

$$\frac{5}{14} = \frac{G}{1260}$$
$$14G = 6300$$
$$G = \textbf{450 stalagmites}$$

7. $\dfrac{5}{\underset{1}{\cancel{8}}}(\overset{2}{\cancel{16}} \text{ ounces})$ = **10 ounces**

8. **a.** $0.1 \times W_N = 20$
$$\frac{0.1 \times W_N}{0.1} = \frac{20}{0.1}$$
$$W_N = \textbf{200}$$

b. $20 = W_P \times 60$
$$\frac{20}{60} = \frac{W_P \times 60}{60}$$
$$\frac{1}{3} = W_P$$
$$W_P = \frac{1}{3} \times 100\% = \mathbf{33\tfrac{1}{3}\%}$$

9. **a. Right triangle**

b. Equilateral triangle

c. Isosceles triangle

10.

	Percent	Actual Count
Original	100	$3.40
− Change	20	C
New	80	N

$$\frac{100}{80} = \frac{\$3.40}{N}$$
$$100N = \$272$$
$$N = \textbf{\$2.72}$$

11. 100% − 20% = **80%**

12. Area = $\dfrac{(6 \text{ units})(3 \text{ units})}{2}$ = **9 units²**

13.

	Scale	Measure
Model	1	8
Object	60	m

$$\frac{1}{60} = \frac{8}{m}$$

$m = $ **480 inches**

$\overset{40}{\cancel{480 \text{ inches}}} \cdot \frac{1 \text{ foot}}{\cancel{12 \text{ inches}}} = $ **40 feet**

14. a. $\frac{1}{3} = 0.\overline{3}$

$1\frac{1}{3} = \mathbf{1.\overline{3}}$

b. $1\frac{1}{3} = 1.\overline{3} \times 100\% = \mathbf{133\frac{1}{3}\%}$

c. $1\frac{1}{3}\% = \frac{4}{3}\% = \frac{\frac{4}{3}}{\frac{100}{1}} = \frac{4}{3} \times \frac{\frac{1}{100}}{\frac{1}{100}} = \frac{4}{300} = \mathbf{\frac{1}{75}}$

d. $1\frac{1}{3}\% = \frac{1}{75} = \mathbf{0.01\overline{3}}$

15. a. $(ax^2)(-2ax)(-a^2)$
$a \cdot x \cdot x \cdot (-2) \cdot a \cdot x \cdot (-1) \cdot a \cdot a$
$(-2)(-1) \cdot a \cdot a \cdot a \cdot a \cdot x \cdot x \cdot x$
$\mathbf{2\,a^4x^3}$

b. $\frac{1}{2}\pi + \frac{2}{3}\pi - \pi = \frac{3}{6}\pi + \frac{4}{6}\pi - \frac{6}{6}\pi$
$= \frac{7}{6}\pi - \frac{6}{6}\pi = \mathbf{\frac{1}{6}\pi}$

16. $(8.1 \times 9) \times (10^{-6} \times 10^{10}) = 72.9 \times 10^4$
$= \mathbf{7.29 \times 10^5}$

17. $\sqrt{(15)^2 - (12)^2} = \sqrt{225 - 144}$
$= \sqrt{81} = \mathbf{9}$

18. $5^2 + c^2 = 13^2$
$25 + c^2 = 169$
$c^2 = 169 - 25$
$c^2 = 144$
$c = \mathbf{12}$

19. Area of base $\approx 3.14(100 \text{ cm}^2)$
$\approx 314 \text{ cm}^2$
Volume $\approx (314 \text{ cm}^2)(10 \text{ cm})$
$= \mathbf{3140 \text{ cm}^3}$

20. a. $m\angle X = 180° - 138° = \mathbf{42°}$

b. $m\angle Y = 180° - (100° + 42°) = \mathbf{38°}$

c. $m\angle Z = 180° - (90° + 38°) = \mathbf{52°}$

21. a. $\frac{x}{6} = \frac{12}{8}$
$8x = 72$
$x = \mathbf{9 \text{ inches}}$

b. $6f = 9$
$f = \frac{9}{6}$
$f = \mathbf{1.5}$

c. $(1.5)(1.5) = \mathbf{2.25 \text{ times}}$

22. $\frac{(40,000)(400)}{80} = \mathbf{200,000}$

23.
$4n + 1.64 = 2$
$4n + 1.64 - 1.64 = 2 - 1.64$
$4n = 0.36$
$\frac{4n}{4} = \frac{0.36}{4}$
$n = \mathbf{0.09}$

check:
$4(0.09) + 1.64 = 2$
$0.36 + 1.64 = 2$
$2 = 2 \checkmark$

24.
$3\frac{1}{3}x - 1 = 49$
$3\frac{1}{3}x - 1 + 1 = 49 + 1$
$3\frac{1}{3}x = 50$
$\left(\frac{3}{10}\right)\left(\frac{10}{3}x\right) = \left(\frac{3}{10}\right)50$
$x = \mathbf{15}$

check:
$3\frac{1}{3}(15) - 1 = 49$
$\frac{10}{\cancel{3}_{1}}\left(\cancel{15}^{5}\right) - 1 = 49$
$50 - 1 = 49$
$49 = 49 \checkmark$

25. $\frac{17}{25} = \frac{m}{75}$
$25m = 1275$
$m = \mathbf{51}$

26. $3^3 + 4^2 - \sqrt{225}$
$= 27 + 16 - 15 = \mathbf{28}$

27. $\sqrt{225} - 15^0 + 10^{-1} = 15 - 1 + \dfrac{1}{10}$

$= 14 + \dfrac{1}{10} = \mathbf{14\dfrac{1}{10}}$ or **14.1**

28. $\left(3\dfrac{1}{3}\right)\left(\dfrac{3}{4}\right)\left(\dfrac{40}{1}\right)$

$= \left(\dfrac{\overset{}{10}}{\underset{1}{\cancel{3}}}\right)\left(\dfrac{\overset{1}{\cancel{3}}}{\underset{1}{\cancel{4}}}\right)\left(\dfrac{\overset{10}{\cancel{40}}}{1}\right) = \mathbf{100}$

29. $\dfrac{-12 - (6)(-3)}{(-12) - (-6) + (3)}$

$\dfrac{-12 - (-18)}{(-6) + 3}$

$\dfrac{6}{-3}$

$\mathbf{-2}$

30. $3(x - 2) = 3(x) - 3(2) = \mathbf{3x - 6}$

Early Finishers Solutions

a. Venn Diagram; the data for the factors and common factors of the numbers 12 and 36 represents sets that overlap. A Venn diagram is a good choice for this type of data.

Factors of 12   Factors of 36

a. $\sqrt{4} < \sqrt{7} < \sqrt{9}$

$2 < \sqrt{7} < 3$

2 and 3

b. $\sqrt{64} < \sqrt{70} < \sqrt{81}$

$8 < \sqrt{70} < 9$

8 and 9

c. $\sqrt{676} < \sqrt{700} < \sqrt{729}$

$26 < \sqrt{700} < 27$

26 and 27

d. $x^2 = 1^2 + 1^2$

$x^2 = 1 + 1$

$x^2 = 2$

$x = \sqrt{2}$

e. $2^2 = 1^2 + y^2$

$4 = 1 + y^2$

$3 = y^2$

$\sqrt{3} = y$

f.

$\sqrt{3}, \pi$

1. $2.5(\$2.60) + 2(\$1.49)$
$= \$6.50 + \$2.98 = \$9.48$

$\$20.00$
$- \ \ \$9.48$
$\overline{\ \ \mathbf{\$10.52}}$

2. a. $P(6) = \dfrac{1}{5}$

$P(4) = \dfrac{1}{5}$

$\dfrac{1}{5} + \dfrac{1}{5} = \mathbf{\dfrac{2}{5}}$

b. $P(3, 3 \text{ or } 5 \text{ or } 7) = \dfrac{1}{5} \cdot \dfrac{3}{5} = \dfrac{3}{25}$

$P(5, 3 \text{ or } 5 \text{ or } 7) = \dfrac{1}{5} \cdot \dfrac{3}{5} = \dfrac{3}{25}$

$P(7, 3 \text{ or } 5 \text{ or } 7) = \dfrac{1}{5} \cdot \dfrac{3}{5} = \dfrac{3}{25}$

$\dfrac{3}{25} + \dfrac{3}{25} + \dfrac{3}{25} = \mathbf{\dfrac{9}{25}}$

3. Average $= (1 + 2 + 3 + 4 + 5 + 6$
$+ \ 7 + 8 + 9 + 10) \div 10$

$= \dfrac{55}{10} = \mathbf{5.5}$

4. $375 \text{ miles} \ \dfrac{1 \text{ hour}}{50 \text{ miles}} = \mathbf{7\dfrac{1}{2}} \text{ hours}$

5.

	Case 1	Case 2
Kilometers	300	500
Hours	4	h

$$\frac{300}{4} = \frac{500}{h}$$

$$300h = 2000$$

$$h = 6\frac{2}{3} \text{ hours}$$

$$6\frac{2}{3} \text{ hours} = \textbf{6 hours 40 minutes}$$

6.

	Ratio	Actual Count
Winners	1	W
Losers	15	L
Total	16	800

$$\frac{1}{16} = \frac{W}{800}$$

$$16W = 800$$

$$W = \textbf{50 winners}$$

7.

	Percent	Actual Count
Original	100	O
− Change	30	C
New	70	350

$$\frac{100}{70} = \frac{O}{350}$$

$$70O = 35{,}000$$

$$O = \textbf{500}$$

8.

$$\frac{3}{4} \cdot n = 36$$

$$\left(\overset{1}{\underset{1}{\frac{\cancel{4}}{\cancel{3}}}}\right)\left(\overset{1}{\underset{1}{\frac{\cancel{3}}{\cancel{4}}}}n\right) = \left(\frac{4}{\cancel{3}}\right)\overset{12}{\cancel{36}}$$

$$n = 48$$

$$\underset{1}{\frac{1}{\cancel{2}}} \cdot \overset{24}{\cancel{48}} = \textbf{24}$$

9. a. $\quad \textbf{300} = \textbf{0.06} \times \textbf{W}_\textbf{N}$

$$\frac{300}{0.06} = \frac{0.06 \times W_N}{0.06}$$

$$\textbf{5000} = \textbf{W}_\textbf{N}$$

b. $\quad \textbf{20} = \textbf{W}_\textbf{P} \times \textbf{10}$

$$\frac{20}{10} = \frac{W_P \times 10}{10}$$

$$2 = W_P$$

$$W_P = 2 \times 100\% = \textbf{200\%}$$

10.

$$\begin{array}{r} \$40.00 \\ \times\ 0.065 \\ \hline \$2.60 \end{array} \qquad \begin{array}{r} \$40.00 \\ +\ \$2.60 \\ \hline \mathbf{\$42.60} \end{array}$$

11. $x(x + 3) = x(x) + x(3)$
$$= \boldsymbol{x^2 + 3x}$$

12.

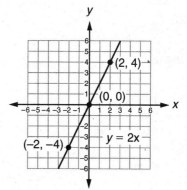

Another point from the 3rd quadrant could be **(−1, −2)** or **(−3, −6)**.

13. a. $2\frac{1}{2}$ inches

b. $120f = 5$

$$f = \frac{5}{120}$$

$$f = \frac{1}{24}$$

c. 14 feet

14. a. $2f = 6$

$$f = \frac{6}{2}$$

$$f = \textbf{3}$$

b. $(3)(3) = $ **9 times**

c. $3^3 = $ **27 times**

15. Sample space = **{A, A; A, B; A, C; B, A; B, B; B, C; C, A; C, B; C, C}**

16. a. $72\% = \frac{72}{100} = \frac{\textbf{18}}{\textbf{25}}$

b. $72\% = \frac{72}{100} = \textbf{0.72}$

17. $(4.5 \times 6) \times (10^6 \times 10^3) = 27 \times 10^9$
$$= \textbf{2.7} \times \textbf{10}^{\textbf{10}}$$

18. a. $6^2 = 36, 7^2 = 49$
6 and 7

b. $4^2 = 16, 5^2 = 25$
4 and 5

Solutions

19. a. $C \approx \dfrac{22}{\underset{1}{7}}(\overset{2}{14} \text{ in.})$

$\quad\quad C \approx \textbf{44 in.}$

b. $A \approx \dfrac{22}{\underset{1}{7}}(\overset{7}{49} \text{ in.}^2)$

$\quad\quad A \approx \textbf{154 in.}^2$

20. $15^2 + a^2 = 17^2$

$\quad\quad 225 + a^2 = 289$

$\quad\quad\quad\quad a^2 = 289 - 225$

$\quad\quad\quad\quad a^2 = 64$

$\quad\quad\quad\quad a = \textbf{8 cm}$

21. Area of base $= \dfrac{(3 \text{ cm})(4 \text{ cm})}{2}$

$\quad\quad\quad\quad\quad\quad = 6 \text{ cm}^2$

$\quad\quad$ Volume $= (6 \text{ cm}^2)(6 \text{ cm}) = \textbf{36 cm}^3$

22. Area of base $\approx 3.14(4 \text{ cm}^2)$

$\quad\quad\quad\quad\quad\quad \approx 12.56 \text{ cm}^2$

$\quad\quad$ Volume $\approx (12.56 \text{ cm}^2)(10 \text{ cm})$

$\quad\quad\quad\quad\quad\quad \approx \textbf{125.6 cm}^3$

23. $m\angle a = 180° - 48° = \textbf{132°}$

$\quad\quad m\angle b = 180° - 132° = \textbf{48°}$

$\quad\quad m\angle c = 180° - (90° + 48°) = \textbf{42°}$

24. $\quad\quad -4\dfrac{1}{2}x + 8^0 = 4^3$

$\quad -4\dfrac{1}{2}x + 1 - 1 = 64 - 1$

$\quad\quad\quad\quad -4\dfrac{1}{2}x = 63$

$\quad\left(-\dfrac{2}{9}\right)\left(-\dfrac{9}{2}x\right) = \left(-\dfrac{2}{9}\right)63$

$\quad\quad\quad\quad\quad\quad x = \textbf{-14}$

25. $\quad\dfrac{15}{w} = \dfrac{45}{3.3}$

$\quad (45)w = 15(3.3)$

$\quad \dfrac{45w}{45} = \dfrac{49.5}{45}$

$\quad\quad\quad w = \textbf{1.1}$

26. $\sqrt{6^2 + 8^2} = \sqrt{36 + 64} = \sqrt{100} = \textbf{10}$

27. $3\dfrac{1}{3}\left(7\dfrac{2}{10} \div \dfrac{3}{5}\right) = 3\dfrac{1}{3}\left(\dfrac{\overset{12}{\overset{24}{72}}}{\underset{1}{\underset{2}{10}}} \times \dfrac{\overset{1}{5}}{\underset{1}{3}}\right)$

$\quad\quad\quad\quad\quad = 3\dfrac{1}{3}(12) = \dfrac{10}{\underset{1}{3}}(\overset{4}{12}) = \textbf{40}$

28. $8\dfrac{5}{6} - 2\dfrac{1}{2} - 1\dfrac{1}{3}$

$\quad = 8\dfrac{5}{6} - 2\dfrac{3}{6} - 1\dfrac{2}{6} = 6\dfrac{2}{6} - 1\dfrac{2}{6}$

$\quad = \textbf{5}$

29. $\dfrac{|-18| - (2)(-3)}{(-3) + (-2) - (-4)}$

$\quad\quad \dfrac{18 - (-6)}{(-5) - (-4)}$

$\quad\quad\quad \dfrac{24}{-1}$

$\quad\quad\quad \textbf{-24}$

30.

Investigation 10

Probability, Chance and Odds

1. **.50**

2. **.03**

3. **The fraction is more precise because it isn't rounded.**

4. **60%**

5. **50%**

6. **75%**

7. $\dfrac{1}{3}$ **or .33**

8. $\dfrac{3}{4}$ **or .75**

9. **5:7**

10. $\dfrac{2}{3}$ **or .66**

11. **.02**

12. **Rates are higher for younger drivers.**

Practice Set 101

a. $3x + 6 = 30$
$3x = 24$
$x = \dfrac{24}{3}$
$x = \mathbf{8}$

b. $\dfrac{1}{2}x - 10 = 30$
$\dfrac{1}{2}x = 40$
$\left(\dfrac{2}{1}\right)\left(\dfrac{1}{2}x\right) = \left(\dfrac{2}{1}\right)40$
$x = \mathbf{80}$

c. $3x + 2x = 90°$
$5x = 90°$
$x = \dfrac{90°}{5}$
$x = \mathbf{18°}$
$2(18°) = \mathbf{36°}$

d. $x + 2x + 3x = 180°$
$6x = 180°$
$x = \dfrac{180°}{6}$
$x = \mathbf{30°}$
$2x = 2(30°) = \mathbf{60°}$
$3x = 3(30°) = \mathbf{90°}$

e. $p = \$8t + \$2$
$p = \$8(5) + \$2$
$p = \$40 + \$2$
$p = \mathbf{\$42}$

Written Practice 101

1. 11.6, 11.7, 11.8, 11.8, <u>11.9</u>, 11.9, 12.0, 12.1, 12.3

  a. **11.9**

  b. **11.8 and 11.9**

  c. $12.3 - 11.6 = \mathbf{0.7}$

2. $\$6(3.75) = \mathbf{\$22.50}$

3.

	Case 1	Case 2
Flour	3	15
Eggs	2	e

$\dfrac{3}{2} = \dfrac{15}{e}$
$3e = 30$
$e = \mathbf{10\ eggs}$

4.

	Case 1	Case 2
Words	48	w
Seconds	60	90

$\dfrac{48}{60} = \dfrac{w}{90}$
$60w = 4320$
$w = \mathbf{72\ words}$

5.

	Percent	Actual Count
Scored 100 percent	40	10
Did not score 100 percent	60	N
Total	100	T

$\dfrac{40}{100} = \dfrac{10}{T}$
$40T = 1000$
$T = \mathbf{25\ students}$

6.

	Percent	Actual Count
Original	100	$24
− Change	40	C
New	60	N

$\dfrac{100}{60} = \dfrac{\$24}{N}$
$100N = \$1440$
$N = \mathbf{\$14.40}$

7. $3(x - 4) - x$
$3x - 12 - x$
$3x - x - 12$
$\mathbf{2x - 12}$

8. $3\ \cancel{\text{gallons}} \cdot \dfrac{4\ \cancel{\text{quarts}}}{1\ \cancel{\text{gallon}}} \cdot \dfrac{2\ \text{pints}}{1\ \cancel{\text{quart}}} = \mathbf{24\ pints}$

Solutions

9.

24 games

$\frac{5}{6}$ won (20).
$\frac{1}{6}$ lost.

24 games
4 games
4 games
4 games
4 games
4 games
4 games

a. $20 \div 5 = 4,\ 6(4\ \text{games}) = $ **24 games**

b. $\dfrac{\text{won}}{\text{lost}} = \dfrac{20}{4} = \dfrac{5}{1}$

10. $\sqrt{196} < \sqrt{200} < \sqrt{225}$

$14 < \sqrt{200} < 15$

14 and 15

11. $w = 0.5$

$m = \dfrac{1}{0.5} = 2$

$0.5 < 2$

$w \ \textcircled{<}\ m$

12.

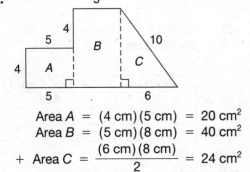

Area $A = (4\ \text{cm})(5\ \text{cm}) = 20\ \text{cm}^2$

Area $B = (5\ \text{cm})(8\ \text{cm}) = 40\ \text{cm}^2$

$+$ Area $C = \dfrac{(6\ \text{cm})(8\ \text{cm})}{2} = 24\ \text{cm}^2$

Area of figure $= $ **84 cm²**

13. $6n - 3 = 45$

$6n = 48$

$n = $ **8**

14. $(8 \times 4) \times (10^8 \times 10^{-2}) = 32 \times 10^6$

$= $ **3.2 × 10⁷**

15. a. $0.02 = \dfrac{2}{100} = \dfrac{1}{50}$

b. $0.02 = \dfrac{2}{100} = $ **2%**

c. $0.2\% = \dfrac{\frac{2}{10}}{100} = \dfrac{2}{1000} = \dfrac{1}{500}$

d. $0.2\% = \dfrac{2}{1000} = $ **0.002**

16. $y = 2(-1) + 1$

$y = -2 + 1$

$y = -\mathbf{1};$

$y = 2(0) + 1$

$y = 0 + 1$

$y = \mathbf{1};$

$y = 2(1) + 1$

$y = 2 + 1$

$y = \mathbf{3};$

$y = 2(2) + 1$

$y = 4 + 1$

$y = \mathbf{5}$

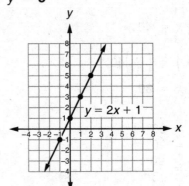

17. Volume of triangular prism

$= \dfrac{(2\ \text{in.})(4\ \text{in.})}{2} \times 4\ \text{in.}$

$= 16\ \text{in.}^3$

Volume of cube $= (4\ \text{in.})(4\ \text{in.})(4\ \text{in.})$

$= 64\ \text{in.}^3$

Volume of solid $= 16\ \text{in.}^3 + 64\ \text{in.}^3$

$= $ **80 in.³**

18. a. $C = \pi(18\ \text{cm})$

$C = $ **18π cm**

b. $A = \pi(81\ \text{cm}^2)$

$A = $ **81π cm²**

19. **5 to 1**

20. $2x + x = 90°$

$3x = 90°$

$x = \dfrac{90°}{3}$

$x = $ **30°**

$2x = 2(30°) = $ **60°**

21. a.

$$
\begin{array}{r}
0.1366\ldots \\
9)\overline{1.2300} \\
\underline{9} \\
33 \\
\underline{27} \\
60 \\
\underline{54} \\
60 \\
\underline{54} \\
6
\end{array}
$$

$0.1366\ldots = 0.13\overline{6}$

b. $0.1366\ldots$ rounded to three decimal places is **0.137**

22. $(AB)^2 = (9\text{ cm})^2 + (12\text{ cm})^2$
$(AB)^2 = 81\text{ cm}^2 + 144\text{ cm}^2$
$(AB)^2 = 225\text{ cm}^2$
$AB = \textbf{15 cm}$

23. a. Perimeter $= 2(9\text{ cm}) + 2(12\text{ cm})$
$\phantom{\text{Perimeter} =}+ 2(15\text{ cm})$
$\phantom{\text{Perimeter} }= 18\text{ cm} + 24\text{ cm} + 30\text{ cm}$
$\phantom{\text{Perimeter} }= \textbf{72 cm}$

b. Area $= \dfrac{(18\text{ cm})(24\text{ cm})}{2} = \textbf{216 cm}^2$

24. $P(B, B) = \dfrac{4}{10} \cdot \dfrac{3}{9} = \dfrac{12}{90} = \dfrac{\textbf{2}}{\textbf{15}}$

25.
$$3\frac{1}{7}d = 88$$
$$\left(\frac{7}{22}\right)\frac{22}{7}d = \left(\frac{7}{22}\right)88$$
$$d = \textbf{28}$$

26.
$$3x + 20 \geq 14$$
$$3x + 20 - 20 \geq 14 - 20$$
$$3x \geq -6$$
$$\frac{3x}{3} \geq \frac{-6}{3}$$
$$\textbf{x} \geq \textbf{-2}$$
$$x \geq -2$$

27. $5^2 + \left(3^3 - \sqrt{81}\right)$
$= 25 + (27 - 9) = 25 + 18 = \textbf{43}$

28. $3x + 2(x - 1)$
$3x + 2x - 2$
$\textbf{5x} - \textbf{2}$

29. $\left(4\frac{4}{9}\right)\left(2\frac{7}{10}\right)\left(1\frac{1}{3}\right) = \dfrac{\overset{4}{\cancel{40}}}{\underset{1}{\cancel{9}}} \cdot \dfrac{\overset{\overset{1}{\cancel{3}}}{\cancel{27}}}{\underset{1}{\cancel{10}}} \cdot \dfrac{4}{\underset{1}{\cancel{3}}} = \textbf{16}$

30. $(-2)(-3) - (-4)(-5)$
$(6) - (20)$
$-\textbf{14}$

Practice Set 102

a. $\angle s$ and $\angle u$, $\angle t$ and $\angle v$, $\angle w$ and $\angle y$, $\angle x$ and $\angle z$

b. $\angle t$ and $\angle y$, $\angle x$ and $\angle u$

c. $\angle s$ and $\angle z$, $\angle w$ and $\angle v$

d. $m\angle t = m\angle v = m\angle y = \textbf{80}°$
$m\angle s = m\angle u = m\angle x = m\angle z = \textbf{100}°$

e.
$3w - 10 + w = 90$	equation
$4w - 10 = 90$	$3w + w = 4w$
$4w - 10 + 10 = 90 + 10$	added 10 to both sides
$4w = 100$	$90 + 10 = 100$
$w = \dfrac{100}{4}$	divided both sides by 4
$w = \textbf{25}$	$\dfrac{100}{4} = 25$

f.
$x + x + 10 + 2x - 10 = 180$	equation
$4x + 10 - 10 = 180$	$x + x + 2x = 4x$
$4x = 180$	$10 - 10 = 0$
$x = \dfrac{180}{4}$	divided both sides by 4
$x = \textbf{45}$	$\dfrac{180}{4} = 45$

Solutions

g.

$3y + 5 = y - 25$	equation
$3y + 5 - y = y - 25 - y$	subtracted y from both sides
$2y + 5 = -25$	$3y - y = 2y$
$2y + 5 - 5 = -25 - 5$	subtracted 5 from both sides
$2y = -30$	$-25 - 5 = -30$
$y = \dfrac{-30}{2}$	divided both sides by 2
$y = -15$	$\dfrac{-30}{2} = -15$

h.

$4n - 5 = 2n + 3$	equation
$4n - 5 - 2n = 2n + 3 - 2n$	subtracted $2n$ from both sides
$2n - 5 = 3$	$4n - 2n = 2n$
$2n - 5 + 5 = 3 + 5$	added 5 to both sides
$2n = 8$	$3 + 5 = 8$
$n = \dfrac{8}{2}$	divided both sides by 2
$n = 4$	$\dfrac{8}{2} = 4$

i.

$3x - 2(x - 4) = 32$	equation
$3x - 2x + 8 = 32$	distributive property
$x + 8 = 32$	$3x - 2x = x$
$x + 8 - 8 = 32 - 8$	subtracted 8 from both sides
$x = 24$	$32 - 8 = 24$

j.

$3x = 2(x - 4)$	equation
$3x = 2x - 8$	distributive property
$3x - 2x = 2x - 8 - 2x$	subtracted $2x$ from both sides
$x = -8$	$3x - 2x = x$

Written Practice 102

1. a.

$$P(1, 4) = \frac{1}{6} \cdot \frac{1}{6} = \frac{1}{36}$$

$$P(4, 1) = \frac{1}{6} \cdot \frac{1}{6} = \frac{1}{36}$$

$$P(2, 3) = \frac{1}{6} \cdot \frac{1}{6} = \frac{1}{36}$$

$$P(3, 2) = \frac{1}{6} \cdot \frac{1}{6} = \frac{1}{36}$$

$$\frac{1}{36} + \frac{1}{36} + \frac{1}{36} + \frac{1}{36} = \frac{4}{36} = \frac{1}{9}$$

b. 8 to 1

2.

$$3x - 12 = 36$$
$$3x - 12 + 12 = 36 + 12$$
$$3x = 48$$
$$x = \frac{48}{3}$$
$$x = 16$$

3. a. $\dfrac{360°}{10} = 36°$

b. $180° - 36° = 144°$

4.

	Ratio	Actual Count
Youths	3	Y
Adults	7	A
Total	10	4500

$$\frac{7}{10} = \frac{A}{4500}$$
$$10A = 31{,}500$$
$$A = 3150 \text{ adults}$$

5.

	Case 1	Case 2
Over	2	8
Up	1	u

$$\frac{2}{1} = \frac{8}{u}$$
$$2u = 8$$
$$u = 4$$

6.

	Percent	Actual Count
People invited	100	40
People who came	80	P

$$\frac{100}{80} = \frac{40}{P}$$
$$100P = 3200$$
$$P = 32 \text{ people came}$$
$$40 - 32 = 8 \text{ people}$$

7.

	Percent	Actual Count
Sale price	60	$24
Regular price	100	R

$$\frac{60}{100} = \frac{\$24}{R}$$
$$60R = \$2400$$
$$R = \$40$$

8.
$$2n + 3 = -13$$
$$2n + 3 - 3 = -13 - 3$$
$$2n = -16$$
$$n = \frac{-16}{2}$$
$$n = \mathbf{-8}$$

9.
$$(3x - 25) + (x + 5) = 180°$$
$$4x - 20 = 180°$$
$$4x - 20 + 20 = 180° + 20$$
$$4x = 200°$$
$$x = \frac{200°}{4}$$
$$x = 50°$$
$$\mathbf{x + 5} = 50° + 5 = \mathbf{55°}$$
$$\mathbf{3x - 25} = 3(50°) - 25 = \mathbf{125°}$$

10.

2000 voters

200 voters
200 voters
200 voters
200 voters
200 voters
200 voters
200 voters
200 voters
200 voters
200 voters

$\frac{7}{10}$ voted for incumbent (1400).

$\frac{3}{10}$ did not vote for incumbent.

a. $1400 ÷ 7 = 200$
$10(200 \text{ voters}) = \mathbf{2000 \text{ voters}}$

b. **30%**

11. $(3) + (3)(-2) - (3)(-2)$
$3 + (-6) - (-6)$
3

12. No, the triangle is not a right triangle because the sum of the squares of the two shorter sides does not equal the square of the longest side.

13. $\frac{1 \text{ meter}}{4} = \frac{100 \text{ cm}}{4} = 25 \text{ cm}$
$(25 \text{ cm})(25 \text{ cm}) = \mathbf{625 \text{ cm}^2}$

14.

$12.95	$70.30
$7.85	× 0.07
+ $49.50	$4.921 ⟶ $4.92
$70.30	
$70.30	
+ $4.92	
$75.22	

15. $(3.5 \times 3) \times (10^5 \times 10^6) = 10.5 \times 10^{11}$
$= \mathbf{1.05 \times 10^{12}}$

16. a. $\angle g$

  b. $\angle d$

  c. $\angle a$

  d. **70°**

17. a. $1.25 \times 84 = W_N$
$\mathbf{105} = W_N$

  b. $1.25 \times 84 = \mathbf{105}$

18. 3 to 2

19. Area of base $= (6 \text{ ft})(4 \text{ ft}) = 24 \text{ ft}^2$
Volume $= (24 \text{ ft}^2)(3 \text{ ft}) = \mathbf{72 \text{ ft}^3}$

20. a. $C \approx \frac{22}{7}(14 \text{ m})$
$C \approx \mathbf{44 \text{ m}}$

  b. $A \approx \frac{22}{7}(49 \text{ m}^2)$
$A \approx \mathbf{154 \text{ m}^2}$

21. $y = 3x$

x	y
−1	−3
0	0
2	6

$y = 3(-1) = -3$
$y = 3(0) = 0$
$y = 3(2) = 6$

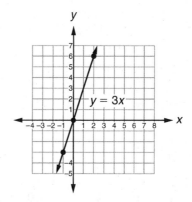

22. a. $m\angle a = m\angle c = 180° - (90° + 34°)$
$= \mathbf{56°}$

  b. $m\angle b = 90° - 56° = \mathbf{34°}$

  c. $m\angle c = 90° - 34° = \mathbf{56°}$

357

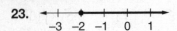

23.

$$-3 \quad -2 \quad -1 \quad 0 \quad 1$$

24.

$$\frac{1}{4} \quad 0.4 \qquad \sqrt{4}$$

$$0 \qquad 1 \qquad 2$$

All three numbers are rational.

25. $3x + x + 3^0 = 49$

$$4x + 1 = 49$$

$$4x + 1 - 1 = 49 - 1$$

$$4x = 48$$

$$x = \frac{48}{4}$$

$$x = \mathbf{12}$$

26. $3y + 2 = y + 32$

$$3y + 2 - y = y + 32 - y$$

$$2y + 2 = 32$$

$$2y + 2 - 2 = 32 - 2$$

$$2y = 30$$

$$\frac{2y}{2} = \frac{30}{2}$$

$$y = \mathbf{15}$$

27. $x + 2(x + 3) = 36$

$$x + 2x + 6 = 36$$

$$3x + 6 - 6 = 36 - 6$$

$$3x = 30$$

$$\frac{3x}{3} = \frac{30}{3}$$

$$x = \mathbf{10}$$

28. a. $(3x^2y)(-2x)(xy^2)$

$$(3) \cdot x \cdot x \cdot y \cdot (-2) \cdot x \cdot x \cdot y \cdot y$$

$$\mathbf{-6x^4y^3}$$

b. $-3x + 2y - x - y$

$$-3x - x + 2y - y$$

$$\mathbf{-4x + y}$$

c. $(-2xy^3)^2$

$$(-2)^2(x)^2(y^3)^2$$

$$\mathbf{4x^2y^6}$$

29. $\left(4\frac{1}{2}\right)\left(\frac{2}{10}\right)\left(\frac{100}{1}\right) = \frac{9}{2} \cdot \frac{\overset{1}{\cancel{2}}}{\underset{1}{\cancel{10}}} \cdot \frac{\overset{10}{\cancel{100}}}{1} = \mathbf{90}$

30. $\dfrac{\dfrac{(-4)(+3)}{(-2)}}{} - (-1)$

$$\dfrac{(-12)}{(-2)} + 1$$

$$6 + 1$$

$$\mathbf{7}$$

Early Finishers Solutions

Since the height of each triangle is equal to the distance from the center of its base to the center of the octagon, you could fold the friangles over to cover the octagon. Since the area of the octagon is equal to the area of the 8 triangles, the area of the octagon is $\frac{1}{2}$ the area of the figure and the area of the 8 triangles is $\frac{1}{2}$ the area of the figure. $\frac{1}{2} \div 8 = \frac{1}{16}$, so one triangle is $\frac{1}{16}$ the area of the entire figure.

Practice Set 103

a. $(-5)(-4)(-3)(-2)(-1) = \mathbf{-120}$

b. $(+5)(-4)(+3)(-2)(+1) = \mathbf{120}$

c. $(-2)^3 = (-2)(-2)(-2) = \mathbf{-8}$

d. $(-3)^4 = (-3)(-3)(-3)(-3) = \mathbf{81}$

e. $(-9)^2 = (-9)(-9) = \mathbf{81}$

f. $(-1)^5 = (-1)(-1)(-1)(-1)(-1) = \mathbf{-1}$

g. $\dfrac{6a^2b^3c}{3ab} = \dfrac{2 \cdot \overset{1}{\cancel{3}} \cdot \overset{1}{\cancel{a}} \cdot a \cdot \overset{1}{\cancel{b}} \cdot b \cdot b \cdot c}{\underset{1}{\cancel{3}} \cdot \underset{1}{\cancel{a}} \cdot \underset{1}{\cancel{b}}}$

$$= \mathbf{2ab^2c}$$

h. $\dfrac{8xy^3z^2}{6x^2y} = \dfrac{\overset{1}{\cancel{2}} \cdot 2 \cdot 2 \cdot \overset{1}{\cancel{x}} \cdot \overset{1}{\cancel{y}} \cdot y \cdot y \cdot z \cdot z}{\underset{1}{\cancel{2}} \cdot 3 \cdot \underset{1}{\cancel{x}} \cdot x \cdot \underset{1}{\cancel{y}}}$

$$= \mathbf{\dfrac{4y^2z^2}{3x}}$$

Saxon Math Course 2   **358**

i. $\dfrac{15mn^2p}{25m^2n^2} = \dfrac{3 \cdot \overset{1}{\cancel{5}} \cdot \overset{1}{\cancel{m}} \cdot \overset{1}{\cancel{n}} \cdot \overset{1}{\cancel{n}} \cdot p}{\underset{1}{\cancel{5}} \cdot 5 \cdot \underset{1}{\cancel{m}} \cdot m \cdot \underset{1}{\cancel{n}} \cdot \underset{1}{\cancel{n}}} = \dfrac{3p}{5m}$

j. **Not a perfect square**

k. **Perfect square;** $\sqrt{49a^2b^6c^4} = \mathbf{7ab^3c^2}$

l. **Perfect square;** $\sqrt{x^6y^2} = \mathbf{x^3y}$

m. **Not a perfect square**

Written Practice 103

1. $\begin{array}{r} \$25.00 \\ \times \quad 0.15 \\ \hline \mathbf{\$3.75} \end{array}$

2. a. **85**

   b. **90**

3.
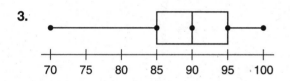

4. $\dfrac{1280 \text{ kilometers}}{2.5 \text{ hours}} = \mathbf{512 \text{ kilometers per hour}}$

5.

	Case 1	Case 2
Dollars	$25	d
Hours	4	7

$\dfrac{\$25}{4} = \dfrac{d}{7}$

$4d = \$175$

$d = \mathbf{\$43.75}$

6.

	Percent	Ratio
Lights on	40	2
Lights off	60	3

$\dfrac{40}{60} = \dfrac{\mathbf{2}}{\mathbf{3}}$

7.

	Percent	Actual Count
Original	100	O
− Change	20	$25
New	80	N

$\dfrac{100}{20} = \dfrac{O}{\$25}$

$20O = \$2500$

$O = \mathbf{\$125}$

8.

	Percent	Actual Count
Original	100	$30
+ Change	60	C
New	160	N

$\dfrac{100}{60} = \dfrac{\$30}{C}$

$100C = \$1800$

$C = \mathbf{\$18}$

9. a. $20 (54 \text{ inches}) = \mathbf{1080 \text{ inches}}$

   b. $\overset{90}{\cancel{1080 \text{ inches}}} \cdot \dfrac{1 \text{ foot}}{\underset{1}{\cancel{12 \text{ inches}}}} = \mathbf{90 \text{ feet}}$

10. $20^3 = \mathbf{8000 \text{ times}}$

11. $\dfrac{8}{\underset{1}{\cancel{5}}} \text{ km} \times \dfrac{\overset{200}{\cancel{1000}} \text{ m}}{1 \text{ km}} = \mathbf{1600 \text{ meters}}$

12.
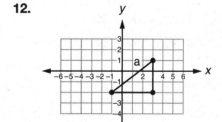

$a^2 = (4 \text{ units})^2 + (3 \text{ units})^2$

$a^2 = 16 \text{ units}^2 + 9 \text{ units}^2$

$a^2 = 25 \text{ units}^2$

$a = \mathbf{5 \text{ units}}$

13. $\dfrac{35}{50} = \mathbf{70\%}$

14. $W_P \times 25 = 20$

$\dfrac{W_P \times 25}{25} = \dfrac{20}{25}$

$W_P = \dfrac{4}{5}$

$W_P = \dfrac{4}{5} \times 100\% = \mathbf{80\%}$

Solutions

15. a. $\dfrac{120°}{360°} = \dfrac{1}{3}$

b. $\dfrac{2}{3} \times 100\% = \mathbf{66\dfrac{2}{3}\%}$

16. $y = -2;$
$y = -0$
$y = \mathbf{0};$
$y = -(-1)$
$y = \mathbf{1}$

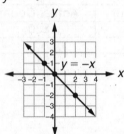

No, x and y are not directly proportional because y does not increase when x increases.

17. $2x - 3 = -7$
$2x - 3 + 3 = -7 + 3$
$2x = -4$
$\dfrac{2x}{2} = \dfrac{-4}{2}$
$x = \mathbf{-2}$

18. a. $m\angle CAB = 90° - 36° = \mathbf{54°}$

b. $m\angle CAD = m\angle ACB = \mathbf{36°}$

c. $m\angle ACD = m\angle CAB = \mathbf{54°}$

19. a. **See student work;**
$\dfrac{x}{12} = \dfrac{12}{16}$
$16x = 144$
$x = \mathbf{9}$

b. $12f = 9$
$\dfrac{12f}{12} = \dfrac{9}{12}$
$f = \dfrac{3}{4} = \mathbf{0.75}$

20. See student work; 50°

21. a. $C \approx 3.14\,(2\ \text{ft})$
$C \approx \mathbf{6.28\ ft}$

b. $A \approx 3.14(1\ \text{ft}^2)$
$A \approx \mathbf{3.14\ ft^2}$

22. $\sqrt{144} = 12$ and $\sqrt{169} = 13$
C. $\sqrt{150}$ **is between** $\sqrt{144}$ **and** $\sqrt{169}$

23. a. Area of base $= \dfrac{(6\ \text{ft})(3\ \text{ft})}{2} = 9\ \text{ft}^2$
Volume $= (9\ \text{ft}^2)(6\ \text{ft}) = \mathbf{54\ ft^3}$

b. $54\ \text{ft}^3 \times \dfrac{1\ \text{yd}}{3\ \text{ft}} \times \dfrac{1\ \text{yd}}{3\ \text{ft}} \times \dfrac{1\ \text{yd}}{3\ \text{ft}} = \mathbf{2\ yd^3}$

24. Area of base $\approx 3.14(9\ \text{units}^2)$
$\approx 28.26\ \text{units}^2$
Volume $\approx (28.26\ \text{units}^2)(3\ \text{units})$
$\approx \mathbf{84.78\ units^3}$

25. $3x + x - 5 = 2(x - 2)$
$4x - 5 = 2x - 4$
$4x - 5 - 2x = 2x - 4 - 2x$
$2x - 5 = -4$
$2x - 5 + 5 = -4 + 5$
$2x = 1$
$\dfrac{2x}{2} = \dfrac{1}{2}$
$x = \mathbf{\dfrac{1}{2}}$

26. $6\dfrac{2}{3}f - 5 = 5$
$6\dfrac{2}{3}f - 5 + 5 = 5 + 5$
$6\dfrac{2}{3}f = 10$
$\left(\dfrac{3}{20}\right)\left(\dfrac{20}{3}f\right) = \left(\dfrac{3}{20}\right)10$
$f = \mathbf{\dfrac{3}{2}}$

27. $10\dfrac{1}{2} \cdot 1\dfrac{3}{7} \cdot 5^{-2} = \dfrac{21}{2} \cdot \dfrac{10}{7} \cdot \dfrac{1}{25} = \mathbf{\dfrac{3}{5}}$

28. $12\dfrac{1}{2} - 8\dfrac{1}{3} + 1\dfrac{1}{6}$
$= 12\dfrac{3}{6} - 8\dfrac{2}{6} + 1\dfrac{1}{6} = 5\dfrac{2}{6} = \mathbf{5\dfrac{1}{3}}$

360

29. a.
$$\frac{(-3)(-2)(-1)}{-|(-3)(+2)|}$$
$$\frac{(6)(-1)}{-|(-6)|}$$
$$\frac{-6}{-(+6)}$$
$$\mathbf{1}$$

b. $3^2 - (-3)^2 = 9 - (9) = \mathbf{0}$

30. a.
$$\frac{6a^3b^2c}{2abc} = \frac{\overset{1}{\cancel{2}} \cdot 3 \cdot \overset{1}{\cancel{a}} \cdot a \cdot a \cdot \overset{1}{\cancel{b}} \cdot b \cdot \overset{1}{\cancel{c}}}{\underset{1}{\cancel{2}} \cdot \underset{1}{\cancel{a}} \cdot \underset{1}{\cancel{b}} \cdot \underset{1}{\cancel{c}}}$$
$$= \mathbf{3a^2b}$$

b. $\sqrt{9x^2y^4} = \mathbf{3xy^2}$

Early Finishers Solutions

a. about 10 cm

b. Yes, $6^2 + 8^2 = c^2$
$$36 + 64 = c^2$$
$$\sqrt{100} = c$$
$$10 = c$$

c. $\dfrac{1\ cm}{0.6\ miles} = \dfrac{14\ cm}{x\ miles}$; $x = 8.4$ miles

Practice Set 104

a. $C \approx \dfrac{3.14(6\ cm)}{2}$
$C \approx 9.42$ cm
Perimeter ≈ 3 cm $+ 4$ cm $+ 9.42$ cm
$+ 3$ cm $+ 10$ cm $\approx$ **29.42 cm**

b.

$A_1 = (3\ cm)(10\ cm) = 30\ cm^2$
$A_2 \approx \dfrac{3.14(9\ cm^2)}{2} \approx 14.13\ cm^2$
$A_1 + A_2 \approx \mathbf{44.13\ cm^2}$

c. $\dfrac{45°}{360°} = \dfrac{1}{8}$
$A = \dfrac{\pi(16\ cm^2)}{8}$
$A = \dfrac{16\pi\ cm^2}{8}$
$A = \mathbf{2\pi\ cm^2}$

d. $C \approx \dfrac{3.14(8\ cm)}{8}$
$C \approx 3.14$ cm
Perimeter ≈ 3.14 cm $+ 4$ cm $+ 4$ cm
$\approx$ **11.14 cm**

Written Practice 104

1.
$$\begin{array}{r} \$12.50 \\ \times\quad 0.4 \\ \hline \mathbf{\$5.00} \end{array}$$

2. 1st Draw: P(green) $= \dfrac{7}{21} = \dfrac{1}{3}$

2nd Draw: P(green) $= \dfrac{6}{20} = \dfrac{3}{10}$

P(green, green) $= \dfrac{1}{\underset{1}{\cancel{3}}} \times \dfrac{\overset{1}{\cancel{3}}}{10} = \dfrac{1}{10} = \mathbf{0.1}$

3. $10(88) = 880$
$880 - 70 = 810$
$\dfrac{810}{9} = \mathbf{90}$

4. $\dfrac{\$3.42}{36\ ounces} = \dfrac{\$0.095}{1\ ounce}$
$\dfrac{\$3.84}{48\ ounces} = \dfrac{\$0.08}{1\ ounce}$
$$\begin{array}{r} \$0.095 \\ -\ \$0.08 \\ \hline \$0.015 \end{array}$$
1.5¢ more per ounce

5. $308 - 128 = 180$ pages left to read

	Case 1	Case 2
Pages	18	180
Minutes	30	m

$$\frac{18}{30} = \frac{180}{m}$$
$$18m = 5400$$
$$m = 300 \text{ minutes}$$

$\overset{5}{\cancel{300 \text{ minutes}}} \cdot \dfrac{1 \text{ hour}}{\underset{1}{\cancel{60 \text{ minutes}}}} = \textbf{5 hours}$

6. $\dfrac{5}{6} \times W_N = 75$

$$\frac{6}{5}\left(\frac{5}{6} \times W_N\right) = \left(\frac{6}{5}\right)75$$
$$W_N = 90$$

$$\frac{3}{5}(90) = \textbf{54}$$

7.

	Ratio	Actual Count
Crawfish	2	C
Tadpoles	21	1932

$$\frac{2}{21} = \frac{C}{1932}$$
$$21C = 3864$$
$$C = \textbf{184 crawfish}$$

8. a.
$$W_P \times \$60 = \$45$$
$$\frac{W_P \times \$60}{\$60} = \frac{\$45}{\$60}$$
$$W_P = \frac{3}{4}$$

$$W_P = \frac{3}{4} \times 100\% = \textbf{75\%}$$

b. $M = 0.45 \times \$60$
$M = \textbf{\$27}$

9. a. $A = \pi(144 \text{ units}^2)$
$A = \textbf{144}\boldsymbol{\pi}\textbf{ units}^2$

b. $C = \pi(24 \text{ units})$
$C = \textbf{24}\boldsymbol{\pi}\textbf{ units}$

10. $360° - (60° + 180°) = 120°$
$$\frac{120°}{360°} = \frac{1}{3}$$
$$A = \frac{144\pi \text{ units}^2}{3}$$
$$A = \textbf{48}\boldsymbol{\pi}\textbf{ units}^2$$

11. a. $360° - 120° = \textbf{240°}$

b. $\dfrac{240°}{360°} = \dfrac{2}{3}$

$$C = \frac{2(24\pi \text{ units})}{3}$$
$$C = \textbf{16}\boldsymbol{\pi}\textbf{ units}$$

12. $y = 2x - 1$

x	y
-1	-3
0	-1
1	1

$y = 2(-1) - 1 = -2 - 1$
$\quad = \textbf{-3}$
$y = 2(0) - 1 = 0 - 1 = \textbf{-1}$
$y = 2(1) - 1 = 2 - 1 = \textbf{1}$

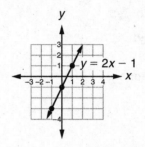

13. a. $2.2\% = 2\dfrac{2}{10}\% = \dfrac{22}{10}\%$

$$= \frac{\frac{22}{10}}{\frac{100}{1}} \times \frac{\frac{1}{100}}{\frac{1}{100}} = \frac{22}{1000} = \frac{\textbf{11}}{\textbf{500}}$$

b. $2.2\% = \dfrac{11}{500} = \textbf{0.022}$

14. a. **75 miles**

b. **The car traveled about 60 miles in 1 hour, so its speed was about 60 miles per hour.**

15. $ab \; \textcircled{<} \; a - b$

16. $(3.6 \times 10^{-4})(9 \times 10^{8})$
$\quad 32.4 \times 10^{4}$
$\quad (3.24 \times 10^{1}) \times 10^{4}$
$\quad \textbf{3.24} \times \textbf{10}^{\textbf{5}}$

17.

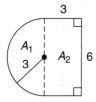

$A_1 \approx \dfrac{3.14(9 \text{ cm}^2)}{2}$

$A_1 \approx 14.13 \text{ cm}^2$

$A_2 = (3 \text{ cm})(6 \text{ cm}) = 18 \text{ cm}^2$

$A_1 + A_2 \approx \mathbf{32.13 \text{ cm}^2}$

18. $C \approx \dfrac{3.14(6 \text{ cm})}{2}$

$C \approx 9.42 \text{ cm}$

Perimeter $\approx 3 \text{ cm} + 9.42 \text{ cm} + 3 \text{ cm}$
$+ 6 \text{ cm} \approx \mathbf{21.42 \text{ cm}}$

19. a. Area of base $= (1 \text{ ft})(1 \text{ ft}) = 1 \text{ ft}^2$

Volume $= (1 \text{ ft}^2)(1 \text{ ft}) = 1 \text{ ft}^3$

$1 \text{ ft}^3 \cdot \dfrac{12 \text{ in.}}{1 \text{ ft}} \cdot \dfrac{12 \text{ in.}}{1 \text{ ft}} \cdot \dfrac{12 \text{ in.}}{1 \text{ ft}} = \mathbf{1728 \text{ in.}^3}$

b. $6(1 \text{ ft}^2) = \mathbf{6 \text{ ft}^2}$

20. $25(6°) = \mathbf{150°}$

21.
$180° - 139° = 41°$
$m\angle x = 180° - (90° + 41°) = \mathbf{49°}$

22. a. $\dfrac{x}{13} = \dfrac{6}{12}$

$12x = 78$

$x = \dfrac{78}{12}$

$x = \mathbf{6\dfrac{1}{2}}$

b. $6f = 12$

$\dfrac{6f}{6} = \dfrac{12}{6}$

$f = \mathbf{2}$

c. $(2)(2) = \mathbf{4 \text{ times}}$

23.
$12^2 + y^2 = 13^2$
$144 + y^2 = 169$
$144 + y^2 - 144 = 169 - 144$
$y^2 = 25$
$y = \mathbf{5}$

24. $2\dfrac{3}{4}w + 4 = 48$

$2\dfrac{3}{4}w + 4 - 4 = 48 - 4$

$2\dfrac{3}{4}w = 44$

$\left(\dfrac{4}{11}\right)\left(\dfrac{11}{4}w\right) = \left(\dfrac{4}{11}\right)44$

$w = \mathbf{16}$

check: $2\dfrac{3}{4}(16) + 4 = 48$

$\dfrac{11}{\overset{1}{\cancel{4}}}\left(\overset{4}{\cancel{16}}\right) + 4 = 48$

$44 + 4 = 48$

$48 = 48 \checkmark$

25. $2.4n + 1.2n - 0.12 = 7.08$

$3.6n - 0.12 + 0.12 = 7.08 + 0.12$

$3.6n = 7.2$

$\dfrac{3.6n}{3.6} = \dfrac{7.2}{3.6}$

$n = \mathbf{2}$

check: $2.4(2) + 1.2(2) - 0.12 = 7.08$

$4.8 + 2.4 - 0.12 = 7.08$

$7.2 - 0.12 = 7.08$

$7.08 = 7.08 \checkmark$

26. $\sqrt{(3^2)(10^2)} = \sqrt{(9)(100)} = \sqrt{900} = \mathbf{30}$

27. a. $\dfrac{24x^2y}{8x^3y^2} = \dfrac{\overset{1}{\cancel{2}} \cdot \overset{1}{\cancel{2}} \cdot \overset{1}{\cancel{2}} \cdot 3 \cdot \overset{1}{\cancel{x}} \cdot \overset{1}{\cancel{x}} \cdot \overset{1}{\cancel{y}}}{\underset{1}{\cancel{2}} \cdot \underset{1}{\cancel{2}} \cdot \underset{1}{\cancel{2}} \cdot \underset{1}{\cancel{x}} \cdot \underset{1}{\cancel{x}} \cdot x \cdot \underset{1}{\cancel{y}} \cdot y} = \dfrac{3}{xy}$

b. $2x(x - 1) - \sqrt{4x^4}$

$2x^2 - 2x - 2x^2$

$\mathbf{-2x}$

28. $12\dfrac{1}{2} - \left(8\dfrac{1}{3} + 1\dfrac{1}{6}\right)$

$= 12\dfrac{3}{6} - \left(8\dfrac{2}{6} + 1\dfrac{1}{6}\right)$

$= 12\dfrac{3}{6} - 9\dfrac{3}{6} = \mathbf{3}$

29. $\left(4\dfrac{1}{6} \div 3\dfrac{3}{4}\right) \div 2.5$

$= \left(\dfrac{\overset{5}{\cancel{25}}}{\underset{3}{\cancel{6}}} \times \dfrac{\overset{2}{\cancel{4}}}{\underset{3}{\cancel{15}}}\right) \div 2\dfrac{1}{2} = \dfrac{10}{9} \div \dfrac{5}{2}$

$= \dfrac{\overset{2}{\cancel{10}}}{9} \times \dfrac{2}{\underset{1}{\cancel{5}}} = \dfrac{\mathbf{4}}{\mathbf{9}}$

30. a. $\dfrac{(-3)(4)}{-2} - \dfrac{(-3)(-4)}{-2}$

$$\dfrac{(-12)}{-2} - \dfrac{(12)}{-2}$$
$$6 - (-6)$$
$$\mathbf{12}$$

b. $\dfrac{(-2)^3}{(-2)^2} = \dfrac{\cancel{(-2)}^1\cancel{(-2)}^1(-2)}{\cancel{(-2)}_1\cancel{(-2)}_1} = \mathbf{-2}$

Early Finishers Solutions

a. $c = \sqrt{9^2 + 5^2} = \sqrt{106} \cong 10.3 \text{ yards}$

b. $(10.3 \text{ yds} + 9 \text{ yds} + 5 \text{ yds}) \times 3 \frac{\text{feet}}{\text{yard}} = 72.9 \text{ ft}$

c. $72.9 \text{ ft} \cdot \dfrac{12 \text{ in.}}{1 \text{ ft}} = 874.8 \text{ in.};$

$\dfrac{874.8 \text{ in.}}{7 \text{ in.}} = 125 \text{ bricks}$

Practice Set 105

a. $A_s = 2lw + 2lh + 2wh$
$A_s = 2(10 \text{ in.})(6 \text{ in.}) + 2(10 \text{ in.})(4 \text{ in.})$
$\qquad + 2(6 \text{ in.})(4 \text{ in.})$
$A_s = 2(60 \text{ in.}^2) + 2(40 \text{ in.}^2) + 2(24 \text{ in.}^2)$
$A_s = 120 \text{ in.}^2 + 80 \text{ in.}^2 + 48 \text{ in.}^2$
$A_s = \mathbf{248 \text{ in.}^2}$

b.

Area of triangle	$= \dfrac{(6 \text{ in.})(8 \text{ in.})}{2}$
	$= 24 \text{ in.}^2$
Area of triangle	$= \dfrac{(6 \text{ in.})(8 \text{ in.})}{2}$
	$= 24 \text{ in.}^2$
Area of rectangle	$= (10 \text{ in.})(10 \text{ in.})$
	$= 100 \text{ in.}^2$
Area of rectangle	$= (10 \text{ in.})(8 \text{ in.})$
	$= 80 \text{ in.}^2$
$+$ Area of rectangle	$= (10 \text{ in.})(6 \text{ in.})$
	$= 60 \text{ in.}^2$

Total surface area $= 24 \text{ in.}^2 + 24 \text{ in.}^2$
$\qquad + 100 \text{ in.}^2 + 80 \text{ in.}^2$
$\qquad + 60 \text{ in.}^2$
$\qquad = \mathbf{288 \text{ in.}^2}$

c. $\text{Area} = \pi d \cdot \text{height}$
$\text{Area} \approx (3.14)(10 \text{ cm})(4 \text{ cm})$
$\text{Area} \approx \mathbf{125.6 \text{ cm}^2}$

d. $A \approx 3.14(25 \text{ cm}^2) \approx 78.5 \text{ cm}^2$

Area of top	$= 78.5 \text{ cm}^2$
Area of bottom	$= 78.5 \text{ cm}^2$
$+$ Area of lateral surface	$= 125.6 \text{ cm}^2$
Total surface area	$= \mathbf{282.6 \text{ cm}^2}$

e. $A = 4\pi r^2$
$A \approx 4(3.14)(4 \text{ cm}^2)$
$A \approx 50.24 \text{ cm}^2$
$A \approx \mathbf{50 \text{ cm}^2}$

f.

Area of trapezoid	$= \dfrac{(4 \text{ in.} + 12 \text{ in.})6 \text{ in.}}{2} = 48 \text{ in.}^2$
Area of trapezoid	$= \dfrac{(4 \text{ in.} + 12 \text{ in.})6 \text{ in.}}{2} = 48 \text{ in.}^2$
Area of rectangle	$= (12 \text{ in.})(10 \text{ in.}) = 120 \text{ in.}^2$
Area of rectangle	$= (6 \text{ in.})(10 \text{ in.}) = 60 \text{ in.}^2$
Area of rectangle	$= (10 \text{ in.})(4 \text{ in.}) = 40 \text{ in.}^2$
$+$ Area of rectangle	$= (10 \text{ in.})(10 \text{ in.}) = 100 \text{ in.}^2$

Total surface area $= 48 \text{ in.}^2 + 48 \text{ in.}^2$
$\qquad + 120 \text{ in.}^2 + 60 \text{ in.}^2 + 40 \text{ in.}^2 + 100 \text{ in.}^2$
$= \mathbf{416 \text{ in.}^2}$

g. **The top of the rectangular prism and the bottom of the triangular prism are not part of the surface area of the combined shape.**

Written Practice 105

1. $\overset{1\ \ 9}{2\ \cancel{0},\overset{1}{0}\ 0\ 0,0\ 0\ 0,0\ 0\ 0} \qquad \mathbf{1.91 \times 10^{10}}$
$\quad -\qquad 9\ 0\ 0,0\ 0\ 0,0\ 0\ 0$
$\quad\ \ \ 1\ 9,1\ 0\ 0,0\ 0\ 0,0\ 0\ 0$

2. $\text{Mean} = 12.95 \div 5 = 2.59$
$\text{Median} - \text{mean} = 3.1 - 2.59 = \mathbf{0.51}$

3. $\sqrt{(10)^2 - (8)^2} = \sqrt{100 - 64} = \sqrt{36} = \mathbf{6}$

4. $6.5(\$8.50) = \mathbf{\$55.25}$

5.

	Case 1	Case 2
Cost	$2.48	c
Kilograms	6	45

$$\frac{\$2.48}{6} = \frac{c}{45}$$
$$6c = \$111.60$$
$$c = \mathbf{\$18.60}$$

6.

	Percent	Actual Count
Regular price	100	$30
Sale price	75	S

a. $$\frac{100}{75} = \frac{\$30}{S}$$
$$100S = \$2250$$
$$S = \mathbf{\$22.50}$$

b. **75%**

7.

	Ratio	Actual Count
Whigs	7	W
Tories	3	T
Total	10	210

$$\frac{3}{10} = \frac{T}{210}$$
$$10T = 630$$
$$T = \mathbf{63\ Tories}$$

8.

	Percent	Actual Count
Original	100	$60
− Change	30	C
New	70	N

$$\frac{100}{70} = \frac{\$60}{N}$$
$$100N = \$4200$$
$$N = \mathbf{\$42}$$

9. $60 \text{ feet} \cdot \dfrac{12 \text{ inches}}{1 \text{ foot}} = 720 \text{ inches}$

	Scale	Actual Count
Model	1	m
Airplane	36	720

$$\frac{1}{36} = \frac{m}{720}$$
$$36m = 720$$
$$m = \mathbf{20\ inches}$$

10. $4x + 5x = 180°$
$$9x = 180°$$
$$\frac{9x}{9} = \frac{180°}{9}$$
$$x = \mathbf{20°}$$

11.
$$W_P \times \$60 = \$3$$
$$\frac{W_P \times \$60}{\$60} = \frac{\$3}{\$60}$$
$$W_P = \frac{1}{20}$$
$$W_P = \frac{1}{20} \times 100\% = \mathbf{5\%}$$

12. $W_F = \dfrac{1}{10} \times 4$
$$W_F = \mathbf{\frac{2}{5}}$$

13.
$$2x - 12 = 86$$
$$2x - 12 + 12 = 86 + 12$$
$$2x = 98$$
$$\frac{2x}{2} = \frac{98}{2}$$
$$x = \mathbf{49}$$

14.

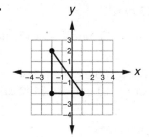

$$a^2 = (4 \text{ units})^2 + (3 \text{ units})^2$$
$$a^2 = 16 \text{ units}^2 + 9 \text{ units}^2$$
$$a^2 = 25 \text{ units}^2$$
$$a = \mathbf{5\ units}$$

15. $a^3 \; \boxed{<} \; a^2$

16. $\dfrac{13}{52} \cdot \dfrac{12}{51} = \dfrac{156}{2652} = \mathbf{\dfrac{1}{17}}$

17. $A = 4\pi r^2$
$$A \approx 4(3.14)(100 \text{ in.}^2)$$
$$A \approx \mathbf{1256\ in.^2}$$

18. $(8 \times 3.2) \times (10^{-4} \times 10^{-10})$
$$= 25.6 \times 10^{-14} = \mathbf{2.56 \times 10^{-13}}$$

19.
$$C \approx \frac{3.14(20 \text{ m})}{2}$$
$$C \approx 31.4 \text{ m}$$
Perimeter $\approx 31.4 \text{ m} + 5 \text{ m} + 30 \text{ m} + 5 \text{ m}$
$$+ 10 \text{ m} \approx \mathbf{81.4\ m}$$

Solutions

20. $y = -2(3) - 1$
$y = \textbf{-7};$
$y = -2(-2) - 1$
$y = 4 - 1$
$y = \textbf{3};$
$y = -2(0) - 1$
$y = \textbf{-1}$

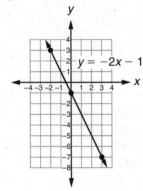

$y = -2x - 1$

21. **a.** Volume $= (5\,\text{mm})(5\,\text{mm})(5\,\text{mm})$
$= \textbf{125 mm}^3$

b. Surface area $= 6(25\,\text{mm}^2) = \textbf{150 mm}^2$

22. Area of base $\approx 3.14(100\,\text{cm}^2) \approx 314\,\text{cm}^2$
Volume $\approx (314\,\text{cm}^2)(10\,\text{cm}) \approx \textbf{3140 cm}^3$

23. Lateral surface area $\approx$
$(3.14)(20\,\text{cm})(10\,\text{cm}) \approx 628\,\text{cm}^2$

Area of top	$= 314\,\text{cm}^2$
Area of bottom	$= 314\,\text{cm}^2$
$+$ Lateral surface area	$= 628\,\text{cm}^2$
Total surface area	$= \textbf{1256 cm}^2$

24. $m\angle a = 180° - (90° + 30°) = 60°$
$m\angle y = m\angle a = 60°$
$m\angle b = 180° - (90° + 60°) = \textbf{30°}$

25. **a.** **See student work;**
$\dfrac{x}{6} = \dfrac{8}{12}$
$12x = 48$
$x = \textbf{4}$

b. $8f = 12$
$f = \dfrac{12}{8}$
$f = \dfrac{3}{2}$
$f = 1\dfrac{1}{2} = \textbf{1.5}$

c. $(1.5)^2 = \textbf{2.25 times}$

26.
$4\dfrac{1}{2}x + 4 = 48 - x$
$4\dfrac{1}{2}x + 4 + x = 48 - x + x$
$5\dfrac{1}{2}x + 4 = 48$
$5\dfrac{1}{2}x + 4 - 4 = 48 - 4$
$5\dfrac{1}{2}x = 44$
$\left(\dfrac{2}{11}\right)\left(\dfrac{11}{2}x\right) = \left(\dfrac{2}{11}\right)44$
$x = \textbf{8}$

27. $\dfrac{3.9}{75} = \dfrac{c}{25}$
$75c = 97.5$
$\dfrac{75c}{75} = \dfrac{97.5}{75}$
$c = \textbf{1.3}$

28. $3.2 \div \left(2\dfrac{1}{2} \div \dfrac{5}{8}\right)$
$= 3\dfrac{2}{10} \div \left(\dfrac{5}{2} \times \dfrac{8}{5}\right) = \dfrac{32}{10} \div \dfrac{4}{1}$
$= \dfrac{32}{10} \times \dfrac{1}{4} = \dfrac{\textbf{4}}{\textbf{5}}$ or **0.8**

29. **a.** $\dfrac{(2xy)(4x^2y)}{8x^2y}$

$= \dfrac{\overset{1}{\cancel{2}} \cdot \overset{1}{\cancel{x}} \cdot \overset{1}{\cancel{y}} \cdot \overset{1}{\cancel{2}} \cdot \overset{1}{\cancel{2}} \cdot \overset{1}{\cancel{x}} \cdot x \cdot y}{\underset{1}{\cancel{2}} \cdot \underset{1}{\cancel{2}} \cdot \underset{1}{\cancel{2}} \cdot \underset{1}{\cancel{x}} \cdot \underset{1}{\cancel{x}} \cdot \underset{1}{\cancel{y}}} = \textbf{xy}$

b. $3(x + 3) - \sqrt{9x^2}$
$3x + 9 - 3x$
$\textbf{9}$

30. **a.** $\dfrac{(-10)(-4) - (3)(-2)(-1)}{(-4) - (-2)}$
$\dfrac{(40) - (6)}{-2}$
$\dfrac{34}{-2}$
$\textbf{-17}$

b. $(-2)^4 - (-2)^2 + 2^0$
$16 - 4 + 1$
$\textbf{13}$

Early Finishers Solutions

a. $21 \times 45 = 945; 4000 - 945 = 3055;$
$3055 \div 65 = 47$ large boxes

b. $\dfrac{4000}{\$1800} = \dfrac{3055}{x}$; $x = \$1374.75$

Acceptable answers range from $1300 to $1400.

Practice Set 106

a.
$$a + b = c$$
$$a + b - b = c - b$$
$$\boldsymbol{a = c - b}$$

b.
$$wx = y$$
$$\dfrac{wx}{x} = \dfrac{y}{x}$$
$$\boldsymbol{w = \dfrac{y}{x}}$$

c.
$$y - b = mx$$
$$y - b + b = mx + b$$
$$\boldsymbol{y = mx + b}$$

d.
$$A = bh$$
$$\dfrac{A}{h} = \dfrac{bh}{h}$$
$$\boldsymbol{\dfrac{A}{h} = b}$$

e. **4, −4**

f. $\sqrt[3]{125} = \sqrt[3]{5 \cdot 5 \cdot 5} = \boldsymbol{5}$

g. $\sqrt[3]{-8} = \sqrt[3]{(-2) \cdot (-2) \cdot (-2)} = \boldsymbol{-2}$

Written Practice 106

1.

$1.85	$14.50	$14.50
$1.85	× 0.06	+ $0.87
$1.85	$0.87	$15.37
+ $8.95		
$14.50		

$20.00
− $15.37
$4.63

---

2. a. 4 to 8 = **1 to 2**

b. 1st Spin: $P(\text{even}) = \dfrac{6}{12} = \dfrac{1}{2}$

2nd Spin: $P(\text{even}) = \dfrac{6}{12} = \dfrac{1}{2}$

$P(\text{even, even}) = \dfrac{1}{2} \times \dfrac{1}{2} = \dfrac{1}{4} = \boldsymbol{25\%}$

3. $\dfrac{\$2.80}{16 \text{ ounces}} = \boldsymbol{17.5\text{¢ per ounce}}$

4. $6(90) = 540, \quad 540 - 75 = 465$

$\dfrac{465}{5} = \boldsymbol{93}$

5.

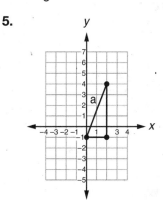

$$a^2 = (2 \text{ units})^2 + (5 \text{ units})^2$$
$$a^2 = 4 \text{ units}^2 + 25 \text{ units}^2$$
$$a^2 = 29 \text{ units}^2$$
$$a = \sqrt{29} \textbf{ units}$$

6.

	Case 1	Case 2
Problems	3	27
Minutes	4	m

$$\dfrac{3}{4} = \dfrac{27}{m}$$
$$3m = 108$$
$$m = \boldsymbol{36 \text{ minutes}}$$

7.

	Ratio	Actual Count
Residents	2	R
Visitors	3	V
Total	5	60

$$\dfrac{3}{5} = \dfrac{V}{60}$$
$$5V = 180$$
$$V = \boldsymbol{36 \text{ visitors}}$$

8.

	Percent	Actual Count
Original	100	O
+ Change	25	C
New	125	80

$$\frac{100}{125} = \frac{O}{80}$$
$$125O = 8000$$
$$O = \textbf{64 students}$$

9. a. **8 and −8**

b. $3\sqrt{-64} = \sqrt[3]{(-4)(-4)(-4)} = \textbf{−4}$

10. $W_N = 2.25 \times 40$
$W_N = \textbf{90}$

11. a.

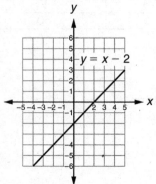

b. $|-2|, \dfrac{2}{2}, 2^2$

12.
$$66 = \frac{2}{3} \times W_N$$
$$\left(\frac{3}{2}\right)66 = \left(\frac{3}{2}\right)\frac{2}{3} \times W_N$$
$$\textbf{99} = W_N$$

13. $0.75 \times W_N = 2.4$
$$\frac{0.75 \times W_N}{0.75} = \frac{2.4}{0.75}$$
$$W_N = \textbf{3.2}$$

14. a. $105\% = \dfrac{105}{100} = 1\dfrac{5}{100} = 1\dfrac{1}{20}$

b. $105\% = 1\dfrac{5}{100} = \textbf{1.05}$

15. **See student work;**

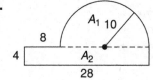

16.

$$81\overline{)6.7500} \quad \frac{0.0833\ldots}{} \rightarrow \textbf{0.083}$$

```
        0.0833... →  0.083
81)6.7500
   6 48
   ____
    270
    243
    ____
     270
     243
     ____
      27
```

17. $(4.8 \times 6) \times (10^{-10} \times 10^{-6})$
$= 28.8 \times 10^{-16}$
$= \textbf{2.88} \times \textbf{10}^{-15}$

18. $(-3)^2 + (-5)(-3) + (6)$
$9 + (15) + 6$
30

19.

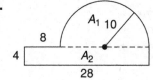

$$A_1 \approx \frac{(3.14)(100\ mm^2)}{2}$$
$$A_1 \approx 157\ mm^2$$
$$A_2 = (4\ mm)(28\ mm) = 112\ mm^2$$
$$A_1 + A_2 \approx 157\ mm^2 + 112\ mm^2 \approx \textbf{269 mm}^2$$

20. a.

$$\text{Area of triangle} = \frac{(4\ cm)(3\ cm)}{2} = 6\ cm^2$$
$$\text{Area of triangle} = \frac{(4\ cm)(3\ cm)}{2} = 6\ cm^2$$
$$\text{Area of rectangle} = (10\ cm)(5\ cm) = 50\ cm^2$$
$$\text{Area of rectangle} = (10\ cm)(4\ cm) = 40\ cm^2$$
$$+\ \text{Area of rectangle} = (10\ cm)(3\ cm) = 30\ cm^2$$
$$\text{Total surface area} = \textbf{132 cm}^2$$

b.
$$132\ cm^2 \times \frac{10\ mm}{1\ cm} \times \frac{10\ mm}{1\ cm} = \textbf{13,200 mm}^2$$

21. Area of base $\approx 3.14(1\ \text{in.})^2 \approx 3.14\ \text{in.}^2$
Volume $\approx (3.14\ \text{in.}^2)(10\ \text{in.})$
$\approx \textbf{31.4 in.}^3$

22.
$$180° - 140° = 40°$$
$$180° - (90° + 40°) = 50°$$
$$m\angle b = 180° - (90° + 50°) = \textbf{40°}$$

23. a. $x + c = d$
$x + c - c = d - c$
$\mathbf{x = d - c}$

b. $an = b$
$\dfrac{an}{a} = \dfrac{b}{a}$
$\mathbf{n = \dfrac{b}{a}}$

24. $6w - 2(4 + w) = w + 7$
$6w - 8 - 2w = w + 7$
$4w - 8 = w + 7$
$4w - 8 - w = w + 7 - w$
$3w - 8 = 7$
$3w - 8 + 8 = 7 + 8$
$3w = 15$
$\dfrac{3w}{3} = \dfrac{15}{3}$
$\mathbf{w = 5}$

25. $6x + 8 < 14$
$6x + 8 - 8 < 14 - 8$
$6x < 6$
$\dfrac{6x}{6} < \dfrac{6}{6}$
$\mathbf{x < 1}$

$x < 1$

26. $37 = 3x - 5$
$37 + 5 = 3x - 5 + 5$
$\dfrac{42}{3} = \dfrac{3x}{3}$
$\mathbf{14 = x}$

27. $25 - [3^2 + 2(5 - 3)] = 25 - [9 + 4]$
$= 25 - 13 = \mathbf{12}$

28. $\dfrac{6x^2 + (5x)(2x)}{4x}$
$\dfrac{6x^2 + 10x^2}{4x}$
$\dfrac{16x^2}{4x}$
$\dfrac{\overset{1}{\cancel{4}} \cdot 4 \cdot \overset{1}{\cancel{x}} \cdot x}{\underset{1}{\cancel{4}} \cdot \underset{1}{\cancel{x}}} = \mathbf{4x}$

29. $4^0 + 3^{-1} + 2^{-2}$
$1 + \dfrac{1}{3} + \dfrac{1}{4} = \dfrac{12}{12} + \dfrac{4}{12} + \dfrac{3}{12} = \dfrac{19}{12}$
$= \mathbf{1\dfrac{7}{12}}$

30.
$(-3)(-2)(+4)(-1) + (-3)^2$
$+ \sqrt[3]{-64} - (-2)^3$
$(6)(+4)(-1) + (-3)(-3)$
$+ \sqrt[3]{(-4)(-4)(-4)} - (-2)(-2)(-2)$
$-24 + (9) + (-4) - (-8)$
$\mathbf{-11}$

Early Finishers Solutions

a. Area $= \dfrac{1}{2}(3.14)(4\text{ ft})^2$
$= 25.12\text{ ft}^2$

b. Area $= (3.14)(2\text{ ft})^2$
$= 12.56\text{ ft}^2$

c. $25.12\text{ ft}^2 - 12.56\text{ ft}^2 = 12.56\text{ ft}^2$

d. $\dfrac{12.56\text{ ft}^2}{25.12\text{ ft}^2} = \dfrac{1}{2}$;
The stained glass is half the size of the semicircle.

Practice Set 107

a. "Yards to feet": $\dfrac{\text{rise}}{\text{run}} = \dfrac{3}{1} = \mathbf{3}$
"Feet to Yards": $\dfrac{\text{rise}}{\text{run}} = \dfrac{1}{3}$

b. Graph (a): $\dfrac{\text{rise}}{\text{run}} = \dfrac{1}{1} = \mathbf{1}$
Graph (c): $\dfrac{\text{rise}}{\text{run}} = \dfrac{1}{-2} = \mathbf{-\dfrac{1}{2}}$

c. $\dfrac{\text{rise}}{\text{run}} = \mathbf{\dfrac{1}{3}}$
$\dfrac{\text{rise}}{\text{run}} = \dfrac{2}{-3} = \mathbf{-\dfrac{2}{3}}$
$\dfrac{\text{rise}}{\text{run}} = \mathbf{0}$
$\dfrac{\text{rise}}{\text{run}} = \dfrac{2}{-1} = \mathbf{-2}$

d. $\dfrac{1}{3}; -\dfrac{2}{3}; 0; -2$

Solutions

1. $\frac{2}{3} \times \$21 = \$14$

2.
$$\overset{0\ 9\ 9}{\cancel{1},\ \cancel{0}\ \cancel{0}^1 0,000,000,000}$$
$$-\ \ 9\ 7\ 5,000,000,000$$
$$\overline{\ \ \ \ 2\ 5,000,000,000}$$
2.5 $\times$ 10^{10}

3. a. $17 - 6 = 11$

   b. **16**

4.

	Case 1	Case 2
Miles	18	m
Minutes	60	40

$$\frac{18}{60} = \frac{m}{40}$$
$$60m = 720$$
$$m = \textbf{12 miles}$$

5.

	Ratio	Actual Count
Earthworms	5	E
Cutworms	2	C
Total	7	140

$$\frac{5}{7} = \frac{E}{140}$$
$$7E = 700$$
$$E = \textbf{100 earthworms}$$

6.

	Percent	Actual Count
Original	100	$16,550
+ Change	8	C
New	108	N

$$\frac{100}{108} = \frac{\$16,550}{N}$$
$$100N = \$1,787,400$$
$$N = \textbf{\$17,874}$$

7.

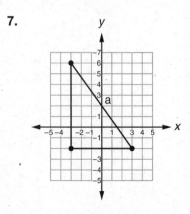

8. a. m$\angle ABD = 180° - (90° + 50°) = \textbf{40°}$

   b. m$\angle DBC = 90° - 40° = \textbf{50°}$

   c. m$\angle BCD = 180° - (90° + 50°) = \textbf{40°}$

   d. **All three triangles are similar.**

$$a^2 = (6 \text{ units})^2 + (8 \text{ units}^2)$$
$$a^2 = 36 \text{ units}^2 + 64 \text{ units}^2$$
$$a^2 = 100 \text{ units}^2$$
$$a = 10 \text{ units}$$
$$\text{Perimeter} = 6 \text{ units} + 8 \text{ units}$$
$$+ 10 \text{ units} = \textbf{24 units}$$

9.
$$60 = 1.25 \times W_N$$
$$\frac{60}{1.25} = \frac{1.25 \times W_N}{1.25}$$
$$48 = W_N$$

10.
$$60 = W_P \times 25$$
$$\frac{60}{25} = \frac{W_P \times 25}{25}$$
$$\frac{12}{5} = W_P$$
$$W_P = \frac{12}{5} \times 100\% = \textbf{240\%}$$

11.
$$60 = 2n + 4$$
$$60 - 4 = 2n + 4 - 4$$
$$56 = 2n$$
$$\frac{56}{2} = \frac{2n}{2}$$
$$\textbf{28} = n$$

12. a. $\dfrac{\text{not red marbles}}{\text{total marbles}} = \dfrac{80}{100} = \textbf{80\%}$

   b. $P(y, y) = \dfrac{10}{100} \cdot \dfrac{9}{99} = \dfrac{90}{9900} = \dfrac{1}{110}$

13. a. $\textbf{0.8}\overline{\textbf{3}}$

   b. $\textbf{83}\dfrac{\textbf{1}}{\textbf{3}}\textbf{\%}$

14. 60 minutes = 1 hour
$$d = rt$$
$$12 \text{ miles} = r(1 \text{ hour})$$
$$\textbf{12 mph} = r$$

15. $(1.8 \times 9) \times (10^{10} \times 10^{-6})$
$$= 16.2 \times 10^4$$
$$= \textbf{1.62} \times \textbf{10}^5$$

16. a. $\sqrt{576} < \sqrt{600} < \sqrt{625}$

$24 < \sqrt{600} < 25$

24 and 25

b. $\sqrt{10}$ **and** $-\sqrt{10}$

17. See student work;

a.

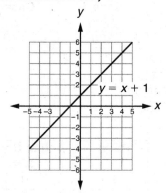

$y = x + 1$

b. $\dfrac{\text{rise}}{\text{run}} = \dfrac{1}{1} = \mathbf{1}$

18. $360° - 120° = 240°$, $\dfrac{240°}{360°} = \dfrac{2}{3}$

$A = \dfrac{2\pi(36\text{ cm}^2)}{3}$

$A = \mathbf{24\pi \text{ cm}^2}$

19.
Area of square	=	(4 in.)(4 in.)	=	16 in.²
Area of square	=	(4 in.)(4 in.)	=	16 in.²
Area of rectangle	=	(4 in.)(8 in.)	=	32 in.²
Area of rectangle	=	(4 in.)(8 in.)	=	32 in.²
Area of rectangle	=	(4 in.)(8 in.)	=	32 in.²
+ Area of rectangle	=	(4 in.)(8 in.)	=	32 in.²
Total surface area			=	**160 in.²**

20. Area of base $\approx 3.14(16\text{ cm}^2)$

$\approx 50.24\text{ cm}^2$

Volume $\approx (50.24\text{ cm}^2)(10\text{ cm})$

$\approx \mathbf{502.4 \text{ cm}^3}$

21. $C \approx 3.14(8\text{ cm})$

$C \approx 25.12\text{ cm}$

Area of lateral surface = (25.12 cm)(10 cm)

= 251.2 cm²

Area of base = 50.24 cm²

+ Area of top = 50.24 cm²

Total surface area = **351.68 cm²**

22. $180° - (90° + 60°) = 30°$

$90° - 30° = 60°$

$180° - (90° + 60°) = \mathbf{30°} = m\angle X$

23. $\dfrac{\text{rise}}{\text{run}} = \dfrac{2}{1} = \mathbf{2}$

24. a.
$$x - y = z$$
$$x - y + y = z + y$$
$$\mathbf{x = z + y}$$

b.
$$w = xy$$
$$\dfrac{w}{y} = \dfrac{xy}{y}$$
$$\dfrac{\mathbf{w}}{\mathbf{y}} = \mathbf{x}$$

25.
$$\dfrac{a}{21} = \dfrac{1.5}{7}$$
$$7a = 31.5$$
$$\dfrac{7a}{7} = \dfrac{31.5}{7}$$
$$a = \mathbf{4.5}$$

26.
$$6x + 5 = 7 + 2x$$
$$6x + 5 - 2x = 7 + 2x - 2x$$
$$4x + 5 = 7$$
$$4x + 5 - 5 = 7 - 5$$
$$4x = 2$$
$$\dfrac{4x}{4} = \dfrac{2}{4}$$
$$x = \dfrac{\mathbf{1}}{\mathbf{2}}$$

27. $62 + 5\{20 - [4^2 + 3(2 - 1)]\}$

$62 + 5\{20 - [16 + 3(1)]\}$

$62 + 5\{20 - [19]\}$

$62 + 5\{1\}$

$62 + (5)$

67

28. $\dfrac{(6x^2y)(2xy)}{4xy^2} = \dfrac{\overset{1}{\cancel{2}} \cdot 3 \cdot \overset{1}{\cancel{x}} \cdot x \cdot \overset{1}{\cancel{y}} \cdot \overset{1}{\cancel{2}} \cdot x \cdot \overset{1}{\cancel{y}}}{\underset{1}{\cancel{2}} \cdot \underset{1}{\cancel{2}} \cdot \underset{1}{\cancel{x}} \cdot \underset{1}{\cancel{y}} \cdot \underset{1}{\cancel{y}}}$

$= \mathbf{3x^2}$

29. $5\dfrac{1}{6} + 3\dfrac{1}{2} - \dfrac{1}{3} = 5\dfrac{1}{6} + 3\dfrac{3}{6} - \dfrac{2}{6}$

$= 8\dfrac{4}{6} - \dfrac{2}{6} = 8\dfrac{2}{6} = \mathbf{8\dfrac{1}{3}}$

371

Solutions

30. $\dfrac{(5)(-3)(2)(-4) + (-2)(-3)}{|-6|}$

$\dfrac{(-30)(-4) + (6)}{6}$

$\dfrac{120 + 6}{6}$

21

Early Finishers Solutions

a. This data shows frequency so use a line plot.

b. Mean: 9.5
Median: 8.5
Mode: 8
Range: 10
Outliers: 17

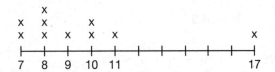

c. See student work.

Practice Set 108

a. $20 = b(4)$
$\dfrac{20}{4} = b$
5 $= b$

b. $20 = \dfrac{1}{2}(b)(4)$
$20 = 2b$
$\dfrac{20}{2} = b$
10 $= b$

c. $F = 1.8(-40) + 32$
$F = $ **−40**

Written Practice 108

1.
$\begin{array}{r} \$8.35 \\ \$1.25 \\ +\ \$2.40 \\ \hline \$12.00 \end{array}$ $\begin{array}{r} \$12.00 \\ \times\quad 0.15 \\ \hline \mathbf{\$1.80} \end{array}$

2.
$\begin{array}{r} 0.000120 \\ -\ 0.000020 \\ \hline 0.000100 \end{array}$ 1×10^{-4}

3. 4, 7, 8, 8, 8, 9, 9, 10, 12, 15
Median = 8.5
Mode = 8

4. $P(5, 5) = \dfrac{4}{52} \cdot \dfrac{3}{51} = \dfrac{1}{221}$

5.

	Case 1	Case 2
Dollars	$200	d
Francs	300	240

$\dfrac{\$200}{300} = \dfrac{d}{240}$
$300d = \$48,000$
$d = $ **$160**

6.

	Ratio	Actual Count
Red beans	5	175
Brown beans	7	B
Total	12	T

$\dfrac{5}{12} = \dfrac{175}{T}$
$5T = 2100$
$T = $ **420 beans**

7.

	Percent	Actual Count
Original	100	$90
− Change	35	C
New	65	N

$\dfrac{100}{65} = \dfrac{\$90}{N}$
$100N = \$5850$
$N = \$58.50$
$2(\$58.50) = $ **$117**

8. $\qquad$ 1 ton = 2000 pounds
$\dfrac{3}{8}$ (2000 pounds) = **750 pounds**

9. $W_N = 0.025 \times 800$
$W_N = $ **20**

10. $0.1 \times W_N = \$2500$
$\dfrac{0.1 \times W_N}{0.1} = \dfrac{\$2500}{0.1}$
$W_N = $ **$25,000**

11. $\quad 56 = 2x - 8$
$56 + 8 = 2x - 8 + 8$
$64 = 2x$
$\dfrac{64}{2} = \dfrac{2x}{2}$
32 $= x$

12. $\dfrac{\text{rise}}{\text{run}} = \dfrac{2}{-3} = \mathbf{-\dfrac{2}{3}}$

13. a.

	Scale	Measure
Model	1	$6/7\frac{1}{2}$
Object	24	O_1/O_2

$\dfrac{1}{24} = \dfrac{6}{O_1}$ $\dfrac{1}{24} = \dfrac{7.5}{O_2}$

$O_1 = 144$ $O_2 = 180$

$O_1 = 12\ \text{ft}$ $O_2 = 15\ \text{ft}$

$12\ \text{ft} \times 15\ \text{ft} = \mathbf{180\ ft^2}$

b. 9 in.; We round 17 ft $9\frac{1}{2}$ in. to 18 ft. Since every 2 ft is 1 in. in the floor plan, we estimate by dividing 18 by 2.

14. $4x = \mathbf{180°}$

$\dfrac{4x}{4} = \dfrac{180°}{4}$

$x = \mathbf{45°}$

$2x = 2(45°) = \mathbf{90°}$

15. $(2.8 \times 8) \times (10^5 \times 10^{-8})$

$= 22.4 \times 10^{-3}$

$= \mathbf{2.24 \times 10^{-2}}$

16. $c = 2.54(12)$

$c = \mathbf{30.48\ cm}$

17. See student work;

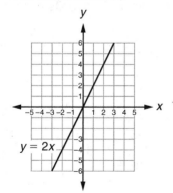

$y = 2x$

18.

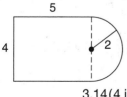

$C \approx \dfrac{3.14(4\ \text{in.})}{2}$

$C \approx 6.28\ \text{in.}$

Perimeter $\approx 4\ \text{in.} + 5\ \text{in.} + 6.28\ \text{in.}$

$+ 5\ \text{in.} \approx \mathbf{20.28\ in.}$

19. $6(100\ \text{in.}^2) = \mathbf{600\ in.^2}$

20. Area of base $\approx 3.14(25\ \text{cm}^2)$

$\approx 78.5\ \text{cm}^2$

Volume $\approx (78.5\ \text{cm}^2)(5\ \text{cm})$

$\approx \mathbf{392.5\ cm^3}$

21. $m\angle x = 180° - 150° = \mathbf{30°}$

22. a. $\dfrac{y}{10} = \dfrac{9}{6}$

$6y = 90$

$y = \mathbf{15\ cm}$

b. $6f = 9$

$f = \dfrac{9}{6}$

$f = 1\frac{1}{2} = \mathbf{1.5}$

c. $(1.5)(1.5) = \mathbf{2.25\ times}$

23. $x^2 + (6\ \text{cm})^2 = (10\ \text{cm})^2$

$x^2 + 36\ \text{cm}^2 = 100\ \text{cm}^2$

$x^2 + 36\ \text{cm}^2 - 36\ \text{cm}^2 = 100\ \text{cm}^2 - 36\ \text{cm}^2$

$x^2 = 64\ \text{cm}^2$

$x = \mathbf{8\ cm}$

24. Surface area $= 4\pi r^2$

$\approx 4(3.14)(25\ \text{in.}^2)$

$\approx \mathbf{314\ in.^2}$

25. $1\frac{2}{3}x = 32 - x$

$1\frac{2}{3}x + x = 32 - x + x$

$2\frac{2}{3}x = 32$

$\left(\dfrac{3}{8}\right)\left(\dfrac{8}{3}x\right) = \left(\dfrac{3}{8}\right)32$

$x = \mathbf{12}$

26. $2x(2y + 1) - \sqrt{16x^2y^2}$

$4xy + 2x - 4xy$

$\mathbf{2x}$

27. $\dfrac{\overset{1}{\cancel{(2)}} \cdot 2 \cdot a \cdot \overset{1}{\cancel{x}} \cdot \overset{1}{\cancel{3}} \cdot \overset{1}{\cancel{x}} \cdot y}{\underset{1}{\cancel{(2)}} \cdot \underset{1}{\cancel{3}} \cdot \underset{1}{\cancel{x}} \cdot \underset{1}{\cancel{x}}}$

$= \mathbf{2ay}$

Solutions

28. $1.1\{1.1[1.1(1000)]\}$
$\quad\quad 1.1\{1.1[1100]\}$
$\quad\quad 1.1\{1210\}$
$\quad\quad\quad \mathbf{1331}$

29. $3\dfrac{3}{4} \cdot 2\dfrac{2}{3} \div 10$

$= \dfrac{\overset{5}{\cancel{15}}}{\underset{1}{\cancel{4}}} \cdot \dfrac{\overset{2}{\cancel{8}}}{\underset{1}{\cancel{3}}} \div \dfrac{10}{1} = \overset{1}{\cancel{10}} \times \dfrac{1}{\underset{1}{\cancel{10}}} = \mathbf{1}$

30. a. $(-6) - (7)(-4) + \sqrt[3]{125} + \dfrac{(-8)(-9)}{(-3)(-2)}$

$(-6) - (-28) + (5) + \dfrac{72}{6}$

$\quad\quad 22 + (5) + 12$
$\quad\quad\quad \mathbf{39}$

b. $(-1) + (-1)^2 + (-1)^3 + (-1)^4$
$\quad (-1) + (1) + (-1) + (1)$
$\quad\quad\quad\quad \mathbf{0}$

Early Finishers Solutions

a. $SA = \pi dh$
$\quad\quad = (3.14)(43\text{ m})(43\text{ m})$
$\quad\quad = 5805.86\text{ m}^2$

b. $SA = \dfrac{1}{2}(4\pi r^2)$
$\quad\quad = (6.28)(21.5\text{ m}^2)$
$\quad\quad = 2902.93\text{ m}^2$

c. $SA = \pi r^2$
$\quad\quad = (3.14)(\tfrac{1}{2} \cdot 43\text{ m})^2$
$\quad\quad = (3.14)(462.25\text{ m}^2)$
$\quad\quad \approx 1451.46\text{ m}^2$

d. $2902.93\text{ m}^2 + 5805.86\text{ m}^2 + 1451.46\text{ m}^2$
$\quad = 10{,}160.25\text{ m}^2$

Practice Set 109

a. $\quad 3x^2 - 8 = 100$
$3x^2 - 8 + 8 = 100 + 8$
$\quad\quad\quad 3x^2 = 108$
$\quad\quad\quad\quad x^2 = 36$
$\quad\quad\quad\quad x = \mathbf{6, -6}$

Check:

$3(6)^2 - 8 = 100 \quad\quad 3(-6)^2 - 8 = 100$
$3(36) - 8 = 100 \quad\quad 3(36) - 8 = 100$
$\quad 108 - 8 = 100 \quad\quad\quad 108 - 8 = 100$
$\quad\quad 100 = 100 \checkmark \quad\quad\quad 100 = 100 \checkmark$

b. $\quad x^2 + x^2 = 12$
$\quad\quad\quad 2x^2 = 12$
$\quad\quad\quad\quad x^2 = 6$
$\quad\quad\quad\quad x = \mathbf{\sqrt{6}, -\sqrt{6}}$

Check: $\left(\sqrt{6}\right)^2 + \left(\sqrt{6}\right)^2 = 12$
$\quad\quad\quad\quad 6 + 6 = 12$
$\quad\quad\quad\quad\quad 12 = 12 \checkmark$

$\left(-\sqrt{6}\right)^2 + \left(-\sqrt{6}\right)^2 = 12$
$\quad\quad\quad\quad 6 + 6 = 12$
$\quad\quad\quad\quad\quad 12 = 12 \checkmark$

c. $\quad\quad 157 = 2(-x)^2 - 5$
$\quad\quad\quad 157 = 2x^2 - 5$
$\quad 157 + 5 = 2x^2 - 5 + 5$
$\quad\quad\quad 162 = 2x^2$
$\quad\quad\quad\quad 81 = x^2$
$\quad\quad 9, -9 = x$
$\quad\quad\quad\quad \mathbf{-9}$

Check: $157 = 2(-9)^2 - 5$
$\quad\quad\quad 157 = 2(81) - 5$
$\quad\quad\quad 157 = 162 - 5$
$\quad\quad\quad 157 = 157 \checkmark$

d. $\text{Area}_{\text{square}} = s^2$
$\quad\quad\quad s^2 = 3\text{ sq. units}$
$\quad\quad\quad s = \sqrt{3}\text{ units}, -\sqrt{3}\text{ units}$
$\quad\quad\quad\quad \mathbf{\sqrt{3}\text{ units}}$

Check: $\left(\sqrt{3}\text{ units}\right)^2 = 3\text{ sq. units}$
$\quad\quad\quad 3\text{ sq. units} = 3\text{ sq. units} \checkmark$

e. $\dfrac{w}{4} = \dfrac{9}{w}$
$w^2 = 36$
$w = \mathbf{6, -6}$

Check:

$\dfrac{6}{4} = \dfrac{9}{6} \quad\quad\quad \dfrac{-6}{4} = \dfrac{9}{-6}$
$36 = 36 \checkmark \quad\quad\quad 36 = 36 \checkmark$

Written Practice 109

1. $\dfrac{(0.2)(0.05)}{0.2 + 0.05} = \dfrac{0.01}{0.25} = \mathbf{0.04}$

2. a. $\angle z$

b. $\angle w$

c. $\angle y$

d. $3m + m = 180°$

$4m = 180°$

$m = 45°$

$3m = 3(45°) = \mathbf{135°}$

3. $20 = 5 + (10 \times W_D)$

$20 - 5 = 5 + (10 \times W_D) - 5$

$15 = 10 \times W_D$

$\dfrac{15}{10} = \dfrac{10 \times W_D}{10}$

$\mathbf{1.5} = W_D$

4. $4(5) = 20$

$10(5) = 50$

$\dfrac{\text{quarters}}{\text{dimes}} = \dfrac{20}{50} = \mathbf{\dfrac{2}{5}}$

5.

	Percent	Actual Count
Original	100	O
+ Change	20	C
New	120	60

$\dfrac{100}{120} = \dfrac{O}{60}$

$120O = 6000$

$O = \mathbf{50}$

6.

	Percent	Actual Count
Original	100	$36
− Change	25	C
New	75	N

$\dfrac{100}{75} = \dfrac{\$36}{N}$

$100N = \$2700$

$N = \mathbf{\$27}$

7.

	Case 1	Case 2
Meters	3000	5000
Minutes	9	m

$\dfrac{3000}{9} = \dfrac{5000}{m}$

$3000m = 45{,}000$

$m = \mathbf{15 \text{ minutes}}$

8. $\dfrac{\overset{1}{\cancel{\overset{\scriptstyle 1}{3000}}}\ \cancel{m}}{\underset{\underset{1}{\cancel{3}}}{\cancel{9}}\ \cancel{min}} \times \dfrac{1 \text{ km}}{\underset{1}{\cancel{1000}}\ \cancel{m}} \times \dfrac{\overset{20}{\cancel{60}}\ \cancel{min}}{1 \text{ hr}} = \mathbf{\dfrac{20 \text{ km}}{\text{per hour}}}$

9. $\mathbf{60 = 1.5 \times W_N}$

$\dfrac{60}{1.5} = \dfrac{1.5 \times W_N}{1.5}$

$\mathbf{40} = W_N$

10.

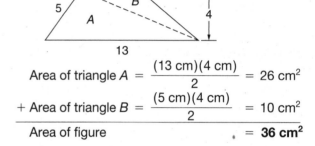

$\left.\begin{array}{l}\dfrac{2}{3}\text{ kept}\\[4pt]\dfrac{1}{3}\text{ given}\\ \text{away}\\ (234)\end{array}\right.$

702 cards
234 cards
234 cards
234 cards

a. $3(234 \text{ cards}) = \mathbf{702 \text{ cards}}$

b. $2(234 \text{ cards}) = \mathbf{468 \text{ cards}}$

11. **Directly proportional**

12. $P(c, c, c, c, c) = \dfrac{1}{2} \cdot \dfrac{1}{2} \cdot \dfrac{1}{2} \cdot \dfrac{1}{2} \cdot \dfrac{1}{2}$

$= \left(\dfrac{1}{2}\right)^5 = \mathbf{\dfrac{1}{32}}$

13.

Area of triangle $A = \dfrac{(13 \text{ cm})(4 \text{ cm})}{2} = 26 \text{ cm}^2$

+ Area of triangle $B = \dfrac{(5 \text{ cm})(4 \text{ cm})}{2} = 10 \text{ cm}^2$

Area of figure $= \mathbf{36 \text{ cm}^2}$

14. Volume of triangular prism $= \dfrac{(3 \text{ in.})(6 \text{ in.})}{2} \times 6 \text{ in.} = 54 \text{ in.}^3$

Volume of rectangular prism $= (6 \text{ in.})(6 \text{ in.})(3 \text{ in.}) = 108 \text{ in.}^3$

Volume of solid $= 54 \text{ in.}^3 + 108 \text{ in.}^3 = \mathbf{162 \text{ in.}^3}$

15. $C \approx 3.14(6 \text{ in.})$

$C \approx 18.84 \text{ in.}$

Area $\approx (18.84 \text{ in.})(3 \text{ in.}) \approx \mathbf{56.52 \text{ in.}^2}$

16. a. $\begin{array}{r} \$36.00 \\ \times\ \ 0.065 \\ \hline \mathbf{\$2.34} \end{array}$

b. $\begin{array}{r} \$36.00 \\ +\ \ \$2.34 \\ \hline \mathbf{\$38.34} \end{array}$

Solutions

17. a. $\frac{1}{2}\% = \dfrac{\frac{1}{2}}{\frac{100}{1}} \times \dfrac{\frac{1}{100}}{\frac{1}{100}} = \dfrac{1}{\mathbf{200}}$

b. $\frac{1}{2}\% = \dfrac{1}{200} = \mathbf{0.005}$

18. $\dfrac{100}{166\frac{2}{3}} = \dfrac{\frac{100}{1}}{\frac{500}{3}} \cdot \dfrac{\frac{3}{500}}{\frac{3}{500}} = \dfrac{\frac{300}{500}}{\frac{500}{1}} = \dfrac{3}{5}$

$\dfrac{3}{5} = \dfrac{48}{n}$

$3n = 240$

$n = \mathbf{80}$

19. $(6 \times 10^{-8})(8 \times 10^{4})$

48×10^{-4}

$(4.8 \times 10^{1}) \times 10^{-4}$

$\mathbf{4.8 \times 10^{-3}}$

20. $y = \dfrac{2}{3}(6) - 1$

$y = 2(2) - 1$

$y = 4 - 1$

$y = \mathbf{3};$

$y = \dfrac{2}{3}(0) - 1$

$y = 0 - 1$

$y = \mathbf{-1};$

$y = \dfrac{2}{3}(-3) - 1$

$y = 2(-1) - 1$

$y = -2 - 1$

$y = \mathbf{-3}$

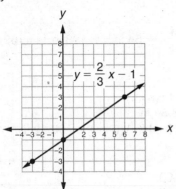

$\dfrac{\text{rise}}{\text{run}} = \dfrac{\mathbf{2}}{\mathbf{3}}$

21.

	Ratio	Actual Count
Angle 1	7	A_1
Angle 2	8	A_2
Total	15	90°

$\dfrac{7}{15} = \dfrac{A_1}{90°}$

$15\,A_1 = 630°$

$A_1 = \mathbf{42°}$

22. $4x + 3x + 2x + x = 360°$

$10x = 360°$

$x = \mathbf{36°}$

23. $d^2 = (2 \text{ units})^2 + (5 \text{ units})^2$

$d^2 = 4 \text{ units}^2 + 25 \text{ units}^2$

$d^2 = 29 \text{ units}^2$

$d = \sqrt{\mathbf{29}} \text{ units}$

24. $3m^2 + 2 = 50$

$3m^2 + 2 - 2 = 50 - 2$

$3m^2 = 48$

$m^2 = 16$

$m = \mathbf{4, -4}$

Check:

$3(4)^2 + 2 = 50$ $3(-4)^2 + 2 = 50$

$3(16) + 2 = 50$ $3(16) + 2 = 50$

$48 + 2 = 50$ $48 + 2 = 50$

$50 = 50 \checkmark$ $50 = 50 \checkmark$

25. $7(y - 2) = 4 - 2y$

$7y - 14 = 4 - 2y$

$7y - 14 + 2y = 4 - 2y + 2y$

$9y - 14 = 4$

$9y - 14 + 14 = 4 + 14$

$9y = 18$

$\dfrac{9y}{9} = \dfrac{18}{9}$

$y = \mathbf{2}$

Check: $7(2 - 2) = 4 - 2(2)$

$7(0) = 4 - 4$

$0 = 0 \checkmark$

26. $\sqrt{144} - \left(\sqrt{36}\right)\left(\sqrt{4}\right)$
  $= 12 - (6)(2) = 12 - 12 = \mathbf{0}$

27. $x^2y + xy^2 + x(xy - y^2)$
  $= x^2y + xy^2 + x^2y - xy^2$
  $= \mathbf{2x^2y}$

28. $\left(1\frac{5}{9}\right)\left(1\frac{1}{2}\right) \div 2\frac{2}{3}$
  $= \left(\frac{14}{9}\right)\left(\frac{3}{2}\right) \div \frac{8}{3} = \frac{7}{3} \div \frac{8}{3}$
  $= \frac{7}{3} \times \frac{3}{8} = \mathbf{\frac{7}{8}}$

29. $9.5 - (4.2 - 3.4)$
  $= 9.5 - 0.8 = \mathbf{8.7}$

30. a. $\dfrac{(-18) + (-12) - (-6)(3)}{-3}$
  $\dfrac{(-30) - (-18)}{-3}$
  $\dfrac{-12}{-3}$
  4

  b. $\sqrt[3]{1000} - \sqrt[3]{125} = 10 - 5 = \mathbf{5}$

  c. $2^2 + 2^1 + 2^0 + 2^{-1}$
    $= 4 + 2 + 1 + \frac{1}{2} = \mathbf{7\frac{1}{2}}$ or **7.5**

Practice Set 110

a. **$132,528.15**

b. $6000 × 0.04 = $240
  $\frac{8}{12} × $240 = 160
  $6000 + $160 = **$6160**
  $\frac{8}{12}$ or $\frac{2}{3}$

c. 80% of 80% of $300
  $= 0.8 × 0.8 × 300
  $= 0.64 × $300 = **$192**

Solutions

Written Practice 110

1. $3($5.95) = 17.85

  $\begin{array}{r} $17.85 \\ \times\ \ 0.06 \\ \hline $1.071 \end{array}$ $\longrightarrow$ 1.07 $\begin{array}{r} $17.85 \\ +\ \ $1.07 \\ \hline $18.92 \end{array}$

  $\begin{array}{r} $20.00 \\ -\ $18.92 \\ \hline \mathbf{$1.08} \end{array}$

2. $\begin{array}{r} $\ 24 \\ \times\ 0.25 \\ \hline 6.00 \end{array}$ $\begin{array}{r} $24.00 \\ -\ \ 6.00 \\ \hline $18.00 \end{array}$ sale price

  $\begin{array}{r} $18.10 \\ \times\ \ 0.10 \\ \hline $1.80 \end{array}$ $\begin{array}{r} $18.00 \\ -\ 1.80 \\ \hline \mathbf{$16.20} \end{array}$

3.

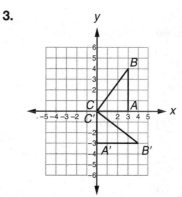

  $\mathbf{A'(0, -3), B'(4, -3), C'(0, 0)}$

4. a.

	Case 1	Case 2
Hours	1	2.5
Calories	370	C

  $\dfrac{1}{370} = \dfrac{2.5}{C}$
  $C = (2.5)(370)$
  $C = 925$
  925 calories

  b.

	Case 1	Case 2
Hours	1	h
Calories	370	685

  $\dfrac{1}{370} = \dfrac{h}{685}$
  $370h = 685$
  $h = 1.85$
  1.85 hours 5 111 minutes
  = 1 hour, 51 minutes

Saxon Math Course 2   **377**

5.

	Case 1	Case 2
Roses	12	30
Dollars	$20.90	d

$$\frac{12}{\$20.90} = \frac{30}{d}$$
$$12d = \$627$$
$$d = \mathbf{\$52.25}$$

6.
$$C \approx \frac{\frac{22}{7}(7 \text{ in.})}{2}$$
$$C \approx \frac{22 \text{ in.}}{2}$$
$$C \approx 11 \text{ in.}$$
Perimeter $\approx$ 11 in. + 7 in. + 7 in. + 7 in. $\approx$ **32 in.**

7.
$$8(4) = 32$$
$$32 - (2 + 4 + 6) = \mathbf{20}$$

8. $\mathbf{150 = W_P \times 60}$
$$\frac{150}{60} = \frac{W_P \times 60}{60}$$
$$\frac{5}{2} = W_P$$
$$W_P = \frac{5}{2} \times 100\% = \mathbf{250\%}$$

9. $\mathbf{0.6 \times W_N = 150}$
$$\frac{0.6 \times W_N}{0.6} = \frac{150}{0.6}$$
$$W_N = \mathbf{250}$$

10. $\mathbf{(-x)^2 + 6 = 150}$
$$x^2 + 6 = 150$$
$$x^2 + 6 - 6 = 150 - 6$$
$$x^2 = 144$$
$$x = 12, -12$$
$$\mathbf{-12}$$

11.

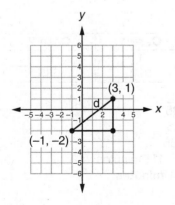

$$d^2 = (4 \text{ units})^2 + (3 \text{ units})^2$$
$$d^2 = 16 \text{ units}^2 + 9 \text{ units}^2$$
$$d^2 = 25 \text{ units}^2$$
$$d = \mathbf{5 \text{ units}}$$

12.

	Percent	Actual Count
Original	100	O
− Change	40	C
New	60	$48

$$\frac{100}{60} = \frac{O}{\$48}$$
$$60O = \$4800$$
$$O = \mathbf{\$80}$$

13.

	Scale	Actual Size
Model	1	m
Car	36	180

$$\frac{1}{36} = \frac{m}{180}$$
$$36m = 180$$
$$m = \mathbf{5 \text{ inches}}$$

14. 8 and 9

15. See student work;

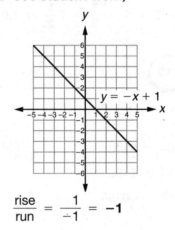

$y = -x + 1$

$$\frac{\text{rise}}{\text{run}} = \frac{1}{-1} = \mathbf{-1}$$

16.
$$5x + 12 \geq 2$$
$$5x + 12 - 12 \geq 2 - 12$$
$$5x \geq -10$$
$$\frac{5x}{5} \geq \frac{-10}{5}$$
$$\mathbf{x \geq -2}$$

$x \geq -2$

17. $(6.3 \times 9) \times (10^7 \times 10^{-3})$
$= 56.7 \times 10^4$
$= \mathbf{5.67 \times 10^5}$

18. $\frac{1}{2}y = x + 2$
$\left(\frac{2}{1}\right)\frac{1}{2}y = \frac{2}{1}(x + 2)$
$\mathbf{y = 2x + 4}$

19.
$$
\begin{array}{r}
\$4000 \\
\times \ 1.09 \\
\hline
\$4360 \\
\times \ 1.09 \\
\hline
\$4752.40 \\
\times \ 1.09 \\
\hline
\$5180.116 \longrightarrow \ \mathbf{\$5180.12}
\end{array}
$$

20. **a.** **See student work;**
$\frac{x}{8} = \frac{3}{4}$
$4x = 24$
$x = \mathbf{6 \ in.}$

b. $4f = 3$
$f = \frac{3}{4} = \mathbf{0.75}$

21. Area of base $= \dfrac{(16 \text{ in.})(12 \text{ in.})}{2}$
$= 96 \text{ in.}^2$
Volume $= (96 \text{ in.}^2)(10 \text{ in.}) = \mathbf{960 \ in.^3}$

22.
Area of triangle	$= 96 \text{ in.}^2$
Area of triangle	$= 96 \text{ in.}^2$
Area of rectangle $= (10 \text{ in.})(20 \text{ in.})$	$= 200 \text{ in.}^2$
Area of rectangle $= (10 \text{ in.})(16 \text{ in.})$	$= 160 \text{ in.}^2$
$+$ Area of rectangle $= (10 \text{ in.})(12 \text{ in.})$	$= 120 \text{ in.}^2$
Total surface area	$= \mathbf{672 \ in.^2}$

23. $m\angle x = 180° - (80° + 30°) = 70°$
$180° - 70° = \mathbf{110°}$

24. $\frac{w}{2} = \frac{18}{w}$
$w^2 = 36$
$w = \mathbf{6, -6}$

25. $3\frac{1}{3}w^2 - 4 = 26$
$3\frac{1}{3}w^2 - 4 + 4 = 26 + 4$
$\frac{10}{3}w^2 = 30$
$\left(\frac{3}{10}\right)\frac{10}{3}w^2 = \left(\frac{3}{10}\right)30$
$w^2 = 9$
$w = \mathbf{3, -3}$

26. $16 - \{27 - 3[8 - (3^2 - 2^3)]\}$
$16 - \{27 - 3[8 - (9 - 8)]\}$
$16 - \{27 - 3[8 - (1)]\}$
$16 - \{27 - 3[7]\}$
$16 - \{27 - 21\}$
$16 - \{6\}$
$\mathbf{10}$

27. $\dfrac{(6ab^2)(8ab)}{12a^2b^2}$
$= \dfrac{\overset{1}{\cancel{2}} \cdot \overset{1}{\cancel{3}} \cdot \overset{1}{\cancel{a}} \cdot \overset{1}{\cancel{b}} \cdot \overset{1}{\cancel{b}} \cdot \overset{1}{\cancel{2}} \cdot 2 \cdot 2 \cdot \overset{1}{\cancel{a}} \cdot b}{\underset{1}{\cancel{2}} \cdot \underset{1}{\cancel{2}} \cdot \underset{1}{\cancel{3}} \cdot \underset{1}{\cancel{a}} \cdot \underset{1}{\cancel{a}} \cdot \underset{1}{\cancel{b}} \cdot \underset{1}{\cancel{b}}}$
$= \mathbf{4b}$

28. $3\frac{1}{3} + 1\frac{1}{2} + 4\frac{5}{6}$
$= 3\frac{2}{6} + 1\frac{3}{6} + 4\frac{5}{6} = 8\frac{10}{6} = 9\frac{4}{6}$
$= \mathbf{9\frac{2}{3}}$

29. $20 \div \left(3\frac{1}{3} \div 1\frac{1}{5}\right) = 20 \div \left(\frac{10}{3} \times \frac{5}{\underset{3}{\cancel{6}}}\right)$
$= 20 \div \frac{25}{9} = \frac{\overset{4}{\cancel{20}}}{1} \times \frac{9}{\underset{5}{\cancel{25}}} = \frac{36}{5} = \mathbf{7\frac{1}{5}}$

30. $(-3)^2 + (-2)^3 = 9 + (-8) = \mathbf{1}$

Early Finishers Solutions

a. $\text{SA} = 2[(3.14)(15 \text{ ft})^2]$
$+ [(3.14)(30 \text{ ft})(20 \text{ ft})]$
$= 1413 \text{ ft}^2 + 1884 \text{ ft}^2$
$= 3297 \text{ ft}^2$

b. $3297 \div 250 = 13.188$; The town needs to purchase 14 gallons of paint.

Scale Factor In Surface Area And Volume

{Students complete a table. Their tables should match the information here.}

Measures of Four Cubes

	1-cm	2-cm	3-cm	4-cm
Edge length	1	2	3	4
Surface area	6	24	54	96
Volume	1	8	27	64

1. 2 times

2. 4 times

3. 8 times

4. 2 times

5. 4 times

6. 8 times

7. 3 times

8. 9 times

9. 27 times

10. 3 times

11. 9 times

12. 27 times

13. a. 216 cm²

   b. 216 cm³

14. 9 times

15. 27 times

16. a. 4

   b. 16

   c. 64

17. a. 8

   b. 9

18. a. 2

   b. 4

19. $15.00

20. a. 100

   b. 10,000

   c. 1,000,000

21. 96 cm²

22. 192 cm²

23. 384 cm²

24. The smaller blocks of ice will melt sooner because more surface area is exposed to the air and warmer temperature.

25. Assuming the sparrow is smaller and has the same body temperature as the hawk, the sparrow must consume more food, relative to its body weight.

Practice Set 111

a. $2\overline{)3.6}$ → 1.8 **1.8 × 10⁶**

b. $25\overline{)75}$ → 3 **3 × 10⁻⁶**

c. $3\overline{)4.5}$ → 1.5 **1.5 × 10⁻⁴**

d. $15\overline{)60}$ → 4 **4 × 10⁴**

e. $8\overline{)4.0}$ → 0.5
$0.5 × 10^8 \longrightarrow$ **5 × 10⁷**

f. $3\overline{)1.5}$ → 0.5
$0.5 × 10^{-8} \longrightarrow$ **5 × 10⁻⁹**

g. $6\overline{)3.6}$ → 0.6
$0.6 × 10^{-6} \longrightarrow$ **6 × 10⁻⁷**

h. $9\overline{)1.8}$ → 0.2
$0.2 × 10^6 \longrightarrow$ **2 × 10⁵**

Written Practice 111

1.
$$\begin{array}{r} 1909 \\ -\ 1859 \\ \hline 50 \end{array}$$
50 years + 1 year = **51 years (The year 1859 should be counted.)**

2.
$$15y = 600$$
$$\frac{15y}{15} = \frac{600}{15}$$
$$y = 40$$
$$40 + 15 = \textbf{55}$$

3. a. $70\% = \frac{70}{100} = \frac{7}{10}$

b. $\dfrac{\text{agreed}}{\text{disagreed}} = \dfrac{3}{7}$

4.

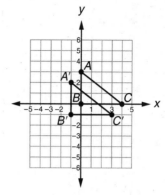

A′(−1, 2), B′(−1, −1), C′(3, −1)

5. a.

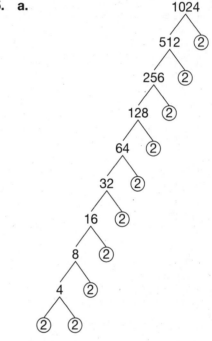

2¹⁰

b. 32

6. a. $180° − 150° = \textbf{30°}$

b. $\dfrac{360°}{30°} = 12,$ **12 sides**

c. Dodecagon

7. $\dfrac{100}{60} = \dfrac{p}{\$48}$
$60p = \$4800$
$p = \textbf{\$80}$

8. a. $P(R, W, B) = \dfrac{3}{12} \cdot \dfrac{4}{11} \cdot \dfrac{5}{10} = \dfrac{1}{22}$

b. $P(B, W, R) = \dfrac{5}{12} \cdot \dfrac{4}{11} \cdot \dfrac{3}{10} = \dfrac{1}{22}$

381

Solutions

9.
$$2x + 6 = 36$$
$$2x + 6 - 6 = 36 - 6$$
$$2x = 30$$
$$\frac{2x}{2} = \frac{30}{2}$$
$$x = \textbf{15}$$

10.
$$2x + x + x = 180°$$
$$4x = 180°$$
$$\frac{4x}{4} = \frac{180°}{4}$$
$$x = \textbf{45°}$$

11.
$$c^2 - b^2 = a^2$$
$$c^2 - b^2 + b^2 = a^2 + b^2$$
$$\boldsymbol{c^2 = a^2 + b^2}$$

12. **a.** $m\angle a = m\angle h = \textbf{105°}$

b. $m\angle b = 180° - 105° = \textbf{75°}$

c. $m\angle c = m\angle b = \textbf{75°}$

d. $m\angle d = m\angle a = \textbf{105°}$

13. $F = 1.8C + 32$
$F = 1.8(17) + 32$
$F = 62.6°$
63°F

14. $\dfrac{45°}{360°} = \dfrac{1}{8}$

$$A \approx \frac{3.14(144 \text{ in.}^2)}{8}$$
$$A \approx 56.52 \text{ in.}^2 \approx \textbf{57 in.}^2$$

15. See student work;

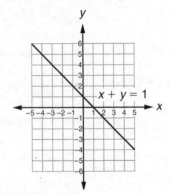

$x + y = 1$

16. a. $\dfrac{\text{rise}}{\text{run}} = \dfrac{1}{-1} = \textbf{-1}$

b. (0, 1)

17. 24 in. = 2 ft; 36 in. = 3 ft
$C \approx 3.14(2 \text{ ft})$
$C \approx 6.28 \text{ ft}$
$A \approx (6.28 \text{ ft})(3 \text{ ft})$
$A \approx \textbf{18.84 ft}^2$

18. Area of base $\approx 3.14(1 \text{ ft}^2)$
$\approx 3.14 \text{ ft}^2$
Volume $\approx (3.14 \text{ ft}^2)(3 \text{ ft})$
$\approx \textbf{9.42 ft}^3$

19. a.
$$2x^2 + 1 = 19$$
$$2x^2 + 1 - 1 = 19 - 1$$
$$2x^2 = 18$$
$$\frac{2x^2}{2} = \frac{18}{2}$$
$$x^2 = 9$$
$$x = \textbf{3, -3}$$

b.
$$2x^2 - 1 = 19$$
$$2x^2 - 1 + 1 = 19 + 1$$
$$2x^2 = 20$$
$$\frac{2x^2}{2} = \frac{20}{2}$$
$$x^2 = 10$$
$$x = \boldsymbol{\sqrt{10}, -\sqrt{10}}$$

20.

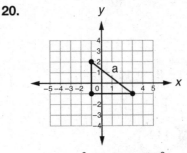

$a^2 = (3 \text{ units})^2 + (4 \text{ units})^2$
$a^2 = 9 \text{ units}^2 + 16 \text{ units}^2$
$a^2 = 25 \text{ units}^2$
$a = 5 \text{ units}$
Perimeter = 5 units + 3 units
$+ 4 \text{ units} = \textbf{12 units}$

21.
$$\begin{array}{r} \$5000 \\ \times \quad 1.05 \\ \hline \$5250 \\ \times \quad 1.05 \\ \hline \$5512.50 \\ \times \quad 1.05 \\ \hline \$5788.125 \\ \times \quad 1.05 \\ \hline \$6077.53125 \\ \times \quad 1.05 \\ \hline \$6381.407813 \end{array} \longrightarrow \textbf{\$6381.41}$$

22. a. $AB^2 = (15 \text{ cm})^2 + (20 \text{ cm})^2$
$AB^2 = 225 \text{ cm}^2 + 400 \text{ cm}^2$
$AB^2 = 625 \text{ cm}^2$
$AB = \textbf{25 cm}$

b. $\dfrac{20 \text{ cm}}{25 \text{ cm}} = \dfrac{CD}{15 \text{ cm}}$
$(25 \text{ cm})CD = 300 \text{ cm}^2$
$CD = \textbf{12 cm}$

23. a. $6\overline{)3.6}$ with 0.6 on top $\quad 0.6 \times 10^2 \longrightarrow \textbf{6} \times \textbf{10}^1$

b. $12\overline{)36}$ with 3 on top $\quad \textbf{3} \times \textbf{10}^{-2}$

24. $180° - 140° = 40°$
$180° - (90° + 40°) = 50°$
$m\angle y = 180° - 50° = \textbf{130°}$

25. $5x + 3x = 18 + 2x$
$8x - 2x = 18 + 2x - 2x$
$6x = 18$
$\dfrac{6x}{6} = \dfrac{18}{6}$
$x = \textbf{3}$

26. $\dfrac{3.6}{x} = \dfrac{4.5}{0.06}$
$4.5x = 0.216$
$\dfrac{4.5x}{4.5} = \dfrac{0.216}{4.5}$
$x = \textbf{0.048}$

27. a. $(-1)^6 + (-1)^5 = 1 + (-1) = \textbf{0}$

b. $(-10)^6 \div (-10)^5 = (-10)^1 = \textbf{-10}$

28. a. $\dfrac{(4a^2b)(9ab^2c)}{6abc}$

$= \dfrac{2 \cdot 2 \cdot 3 \cdot 3 \cdot a \cdot a \cdot a \cdot b \cdot b \cdot b \cdot c}{2 \cdot 3 \cdot a \cdot b \cdot c}$

$= \textbf{6} \, \boldsymbol{a^2 b^2}$

b. $x(x - c) + \sqrt{c^2 x^2}$
$x^2 - cx + cx$
$\boldsymbol{x^2}$

29. $(-3) + (+2)(-4) - (-6)(-2) - (-8)$
$(-3) + (-8) - (12) - (-8)$
$\textbf{-15}$

30. $3\dfrac{1}{3} \cdot 1\dfrac{4}{5} = \dfrac{\overset{2}{\cancel{10}}}{\underset{1}{\cancel{3}}} \cdot \dfrac{\overset{3}{\cancel{9}}}{\underset{1}{\cancel{5}}} = 6$
$6 + 1.5 = 7.5$
$\dfrac{7.5}{0.03} = \textbf{250}$

Early Finishers Solutions

a. $(\$1500 \times 1.04) \times 1.04 = \$1622.40$

b. $\$2000 - (\$1622.40 \times 1.04) = \$312.70$

Practice Set 112

a.

$(5 \text{ ft})^2 + c^2 = (12 \text{ ft})^2$
$25 \text{ ft}^2 + c^2 = 144 \text{ ft}^2$
$25 \text{ ft}^2 + c^2 - 25 \text{ ft}^2 = 144 \text{ ft}^2 - 25 \text{ ft}^2$
$c^2 = 119 \text{ ft}^2$
$c = \sqrt{119 \text{ ft}^2} \approx 10.9 \text{ ft}$
$c \approx \textbf{10 feet 11 inches}$

b. $(AC)^2 = (400 \text{ ft})^2 + (300 \text{ ft})^2$
$(AC)^2 = 160{,}000 \text{ ft}^2 + 90{,}000 \text{ ft}^2$
$(AC)^2 = 250{,}000 \text{ ft}^2$
$AC = 500 \text{ feet}$
$(300 \text{ feet} + 400 \text{ feet}) - 500 \text{ feet} = \textbf{200 feet}$

c. The corner is not a right angle. If the corner were a right angle, then the distance between the marks would be 10 feet even, because 6-8-10 is a Pythagorean triplet. (Since the distance is a little more than 10 feet, the angle is a little more than 90°.)

Written Practice 112

1.
```
      $3000
    ×  1.08
     $3240
    ×  1.08
   $3499.20
    ×    1.08
   $3779.1360  ⟶  $3779.14
```

Solutions

2. $\sqrt{(3)^2 + (4)^2} = \sqrt{9 + 16} = \sqrt{25} = $ **5**

3. a. **90**

b. **95**

4. $\dfrac{840 \text{ kilometers}}{10.5 \text{ hours}} = $ **80 kilometers per hour**

5.

	Case 1	Case 2
Hours	6	9
Earnings	$28	e

$\dfrac{6}{\$28} = \dfrac{9}{e}$

$6e = \$252$

$e = $ **$42**

6.

	Percent	Actual Count
Original	100	O
− Change	25	C
New	75	$48

$\dfrac{100}{75} = \dfrac{O}{\$48}$

$75O = \$4800$

$O = $ **$64**

7.

	Percent	Actual Count
Original	100	$6
+ Change	25	C
New	125	N

$\dfrac{100}{25} = \dfrac{\$6}{C}$

$100C = \$150$

$C = $ **$1.50**

8. 50% of 50% of $1.00

$= (0.5)(0.5) \times \$1.00 = 0.25 \times \$1.00$

$= $ **$0.25**

9. $60\% = \dfrac{60}{100} = \dfrac{6}{10} = \dfrac{3}{5} = \dfrac{\text{boys}}{\text{total}}$

$\dfrac{\text{boys}}{\text{girls}} = \dfrac{3}{2}$

10.

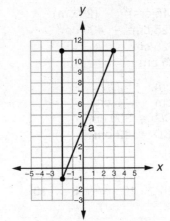

$a^2 = (12 \text{ units})^2 + (5 \text{ units})^2$
$a^2 = 144 \text{ units}^2 + 25 \text{ units}^2$
$a^2 = 169 \text{ units}^2$
$a = $ **13 units**

11.

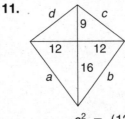

$a^2 = (12 \text{ in.})^2 + (16 \text{ in.})^2$
$a^2 = 144 \text{ in.}^2 + 256 \text{ in.}^2$
$a^2 = 400 \text{ in.}^2$
$a = 20 \text{ in.}$
$b = a = 20 \text{ in.}$
$c^2 = (9 \text{ in.})^2 + (12 \text{ in.})^2$
$c^2 = 81 \text{ in.}^2 + 144 \text{ in.}^2$
$c^2 = 225 \text{ in.}^2$
$c = 15 \text{ in.}$
$d = c = 15 \text{ in.}$
Perimeter $= 2(20 \text{ in.}) + 2(15 \text{ in.})$
$= 40 \text{ in.} + 30 \text{ in.} = $ **70 inches**

12. $W_P \times 2.5 = 2$

$\dfrac{W_P \times 2.5}{2.5} = \dfrac{2}{2.5}$

$W_P = 0.8$

$W_P = 0.8 \times 100\% = $ **80%**

13. $2 \times 2 \times 2 \times 2 = 16$ possible outcomes
1 favorable outcome
15 unfavorable outcomes
Odds = favorable to unfavorable
$= $ **1 to 15**

14.
$$
\begin{array}{r}
\$4000 \\
\times\ \ 0.09 \\
\hline
\$360
\end{array}
\qquad \frac{6}{12} = \frac{1}{2}
$$

$$\left(\frac{1}{2}\right)\$360 = \mathbf{\$180}$$

15. a. 0.625

    b. 62.5%

16. a.
$$
\begin{array}{r}
2.5 \\
2\overline{)5.0}
\end{array}
\qquad \mathbf{2.5 \times 10^4}
$$

    b.
$$
\begin{array}{r}
0.3 \\
4\overline{)1.2}
\end{array}
\qquad 0.3 \times 10^{-4} \longrightarrow \mathbf{3 \times 10^{-5}}
$$

17. $\dfrac{10\ \cancel{km}}{\underset{\underset{1}{2}}{24\ \cancel{min}}} \times \dfrac{\overset{0.3}{\cancel{0.6}}\ mi}{1\ \cancel{km}} \times \dfrac{\overset{5}{\cancel{60}}\ \cancel{min}}{1\ hr} = \mathbf{15\ mi\ per\ hr}$

18. $d = rt$

    $\dfrac{d}{r} = \dfrac{rt}{r}$

    $\dfrac{\boldsymbol{d}}{\boldsymbol{r}} = \boldsymbol{t}$

19. See student work;

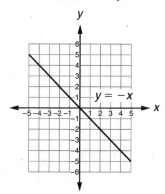

20. $C \approx \dfrac{3.14(20\ cm)}{2}$

    $C \approx 31.4\ cm$

    Perimeter $\approx 31.4\ cm + 20\ cm$
$$+ 20\ cm + 20\ cm \approx \mathbf{91.4\ cm}$$

21. Area of triangle $= \dfrac{(9\ ft)(12\ ft)}{2} = 54\ ft^2$

    Area of triangle $= \dfrac{(9\ ft)(12\ ft)}{2} = 54\ ft^2$

    Area of rectangle $= (10\ ft)(12\ ft) = 120\ ft^2$

    Area of rectangle $= (10\ ft)(15\ ft) = 150\ ft^2$

 + Area of rectangle $= (10\ ft)(9\ ft) = 90\ ft^2$
$$\overline{}$$
    Total surface area $= \mathbf{468\ ft^2}$

22. a. $\mathbf{2^{12} \cdot 5^{12}}$

    b. 1,000,000

23. a. $\dfrac{x}{9} = \dfrac{8}{12}$

      $12x = 72$

      $x = \mathbf{6\ cm}$

    b. $8f = 12$

      $f = \dfrac{12}{8}$

      $f = \dfrac{3}{2} = \mathbf{1.5}$

24. $\dfrac{16}{2.5} = \dfrac{48}{f}$

    $16f = 120$

    $f = \mathbf{7.5}$

25. $2\dfrac{2}{3}x - 3 = 21$

    $2\dfrac{2}{3}x - 3 + 3 = 21 + 3$

        $2\dfrac{2}{3}x = 24$

    $\left(\dfrac{3}{8}\right)\dfrac{8}{3}x = \left(\dfrac{3}{8}\right)24$

        $x = \mathbf{9}$

26. $10^2 - [10 - 10(10^0 - 10^{-1})]$

    $100 - \left[10 - 10\left(1 - \dfrac{1}{10}\right)\right]$

      $100 - \left[10 - 10\left(\dfrac{9}{10}\right)\right]$

        $100 - [10 - 9]$

          $100 - [1]$

           99

27. $2\dfrac{3}{4} - \left(1\dfrac{1}{2} - \dfrac{1}{6}\right)$

    $= \dfrac{11}{4} - \left(\dfrac{9}{6} - \dfrac{1}{6}\right) = \dfrac{11}{4} - \dfrac{8}{6}$

    $= \dfrac{33}{12} - \dfrac{16}{12} = \dfrac{17}{12} = \mathbf{1\dfrac{5}{12}}$

28. $3\dfrac{1}{2} \div 1\dfrac{2}{5} \div 3$

    $= \left(\dfrac{7}{2} \times \dfrac{5}{7}\right) \div 3 = \dfrac{5}{2} \times \dfrac{1}{3} = \dfrac{\mathbf{5}}{\mathbf{6}}$

Solutions

29. $|-4| - (-3)(-2)(-1) + \dfrac{(-5)(4)(-3)(2)}{-1}$

$4 - (-6) + \dfrac{(-20)(-6)}{-1}$

$4 - (-6) + \dfrac{120}{-1}$

$4 - (-6) - 120$

$10 + (-120)$

-110

30. Surface area $= 4\pi r^2$

$\approx 4\left(\dfrac{22}{7}\right)(49 \text{ cm}^2)$

$\approx 4(22)(7 \text{ cm}^2)$

$\approx 616 \text{ cm}^2$

$\approx \mathbf{600 \text{ cm}^2}$

Early Finishers Solutions

a. A Venn diagram shows all the pets and all the people who have them. A line plot could only show one kind of pet.

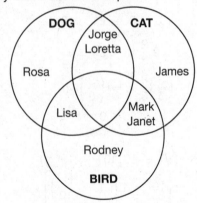

b. See student work.

Practice Set 113

a. $\dfrac{1}{3}$

b. $\dfrac{2}{3}$

c. $\dfrac{2}{3}$

d. $\dfrac{1}{3}$

---

e. **All of the box would be filled.**

$\left(\dfrac{1}{3} + \dfrac{2}{3} = 1\right)$

f. Volume of box $=$ (12 in.)(12 in.)(12 in.)

$= \mathbf{1728 \text{ in.}^3}$

Volume of pyramid $= \dfrac{1}{3}(1728 \text{ in.}^3)$

$= \mathbf{576 \text{ in.}^3}$

g. Area of base $= \pi(9 \text{ in.}^2)$

$= 9\pi \text{ in.}^2$

Volume $= \dfrac{1}{3}(9\pi \text{ in.}^2)(6 \text{ in.})$

$= \mathbf{18\pi \text{ in.}^3}$

h. Volume $= \dfrac{4}{3}\pi(3 \text{ in.})^3$

$= \dfrac{4}{3}\pi(27 \text{ in.}^3) = \mathbf{36\pi \text{ in.}^3}$

Written Practice 113

1. 75% of 75% of $24

$= (0.75)(0.75) \times \$24 = \mathbf{\$13.50}$

2.
```
   0 9 91
  1̸0̸,0̸ 0 0,0 0 0,0 0 0
 −   9 8 0,0 0 0,0 0 0
    9,0 2 0,0 0 0,0 0 0
```
$\mathbf{9.02 \times 10^9}$

3. Mean $= 8.45 \div 5 = 1.69$

Mean $-$ median $= 1.69 - 0.75$

$= \mathbf{0.94}$

4. a. $\dfrac{\$24}{5 \text{ hours}} = \mathbf{\$4.80 \text{ per hour}}$

b. $\dfrac{\$33}{6 \text{ hours}} = \mathbf{\$5.50 \text{ per hour}}$

c.
```
   $5.50
 − $4.80
```
$0.70 more per hour

5.

	Case 1	Case 2
Kilograms	24	42
Cost	$31	c

$\dfrac{24}{\$31} = \dfrac{42}{c}$

$24c = \$1302$

$c = \mathbf{\$54.25}$

6. $\frac{5}{8}$ (1760 yards) = **about 1100 yards**

7. **a.** $P(H, H) = \frac{13}{52} \cdot \frac{13}{52} = \frac{1}{4} \cdot \frac{1}{4} = \frac{1}{16}$

   b. $P(H, H) = \frac{13}{52} \cdot \frac{12}{51} = \frac{1}{4} \cdot \frac{4}{17} = \frac{1}{17}$

8. $W_P \times \$30 = \$1.50$
$$\frac{W_P \times \$30}{\$30} = \frac{\$1.50}{\$30}$$
$$W_P = 0.05$$
$$W_P = 0.05 \times 100\% = 5\%$$

9. $\frac{1}{2} \times W_N = 2\frac{1}{2}$
$$\frac{2}{1}\left(\frac{1}{2} \times W_N\right) = \left(\frac{2}{1}\right)\frac{5}{2}$$
$$W_N = 5$$

10.
$$\begin{array}{r} \$5000 \\ \times\ \ 1.08 \\ \hline \$5400 \\ \times\ \ 1.08 \\ \hline \$5832 \\ \times\ \ 1.08 \\ \hline \$6298.56 \\ -\ \$5000.00 \\ \hline \mathbf{\$1298.56} \end{array}$$

11.

	Percent	Actual Count
Original	100	$12
− Change	20	C
New	80	N

$$\frac{100}{80} = \frac{\$12}{N}$$
$$100N = \$960$$
$$N = \mathbf{\$9.60}$$

12.

	Scale	Actual Size
Model	24	6 ft = 72 in.
Figurine	1	F

$$\frac{24}{1} = \frac{72 \text{ in.}}{F}$$
$$24F = 72 \text{ in.}$$
$$F = \mathbf{3 \text{ inches}}$$

13.

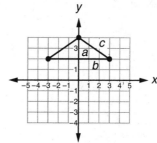

$$A = \frac{(6 \text{ units})(2 \text{ units})}{2} = \mathbf{6 \text{ units}^2}$$

14. $(2 \text{ units})^2 + (3 \text{ units})^2 = c^2$
$$4 \text{ units}^2 + 9 \text{ units}^2 = c^2$$
$$13 \text{ units}^2 = c^2$$
$$\sqrt{13} \textbf{ units} = c$$

15. Volume $\approx \frac{4}{3}(3)(3 \text{ cm})^3$

$$\approx \frac{4}{3}(3)(27 \text{ cm}^3)$$
$$\approx 4(27 \text{ cm}^3)$$
$$\approx 108 \text{ cm}^3$$
$$\approx \mathbf{110 \text{ cm}^3}$$

16. $(6.3 \times 7) \times (10^6 \times 10^{-3})$
$$= 44.1 \times 10^3$$
$$= \mathbf{4.41 \times 10^4}$$

17. $s^2 = (40 \text{ yd})^2 + (30 \text{ yd})^2$
$$s^2 = 1600 \text{ yd}^2 + 900 \text{ yd}^2$$
$$s^2 = 2500 \text{ yd}^2$$
$$s = 50 \text{ yd}$$
$$(40 \text{ yd} + 30 \text{ yd}) - 50 \text{ yd} = \mathbf{20 \text{ yards}}$$

18. **a.** $A = \frac{1}{2}bh$
$$\left(\frac{2}{1}\right)A = \frac{2}{1}\left(\frac{1}{2}bh\right)$$
$$2A = bh$$
$$\frac{2A}{b} = \frac{bh}{b}$$
$$\frac{2A}{b} = \mathbf{h}$$

   b. $h = \frac{2(16)}{8}$
$$h = 2(2)$$
$$h = \mathbf{4}$$

19. See student work;

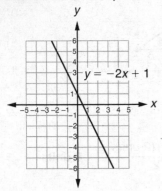

$y = -2x + 1$

$$\frac{\text{rise}}{\text{run}} = \frac{2}{-1} = \textbf{-2}$$

20. Area of base = $(40 \text{ m})(40 \text{ m}) = 1600 \text{ m}^2$

Volume = $\frac{1}{3}(1600 \text{ m}^2)(30 \text{ m})$

$= \textbf{16,000 m}^3$

21. Area of base ≈ $3.14(100 \text{ cm}^2) \approx 314 \text{ cm}^2$

Volume ≈ $\frac{1}{3}(314 \text{ cm}^2)(60 \text{ cm})$

$\approx \textbf{6280 cm}^3$

22. a. $m\angle D = 180° - (90° + 30°) = \textbf{60°}$

b. $m\angle E = m\angle D = \textbf{60°}$

c. $m\angle A = m\angle C = \textbf{30°}$

23. $\dfrac{4 \text{ cm}}{6 \text{ cm}} = \dfrac{8 \text{ cm}}{CD}$

$(4 \text{ cm})CD = 48 \text{ cm}^2$

$CD = \textbf{12 cm}$

24. $\dfrac{7.5}{d} = \dfrac{25}{16}$

$25d = 120$

$d = \textbf{4.8}$

25. $1\frac{3}{5}w + 17 = 49$

$1\frac{3}{5}w + 17 - 17 = 49 - 17$

$1\frac{3}{5}w = 32$

$\left(\frac{5}{8}\right)\frac{8}{5}w = \left(\frac{5}{8}\right)32$

$w = \textbf{20}$

26. $5^2 - \{4^2 - [3^2 - (2^2 - 1^2)]\}$

$25 - \{16 - [9 - (4 - 1)]\}$

$25 - \{16 - [9 - (3)]\}$

$25 - \{16 - [6]\}$

$25 - \{10\}$

$\textbf{15}$

27. $\dfrac{\overset{22}{\cancel{440}} \text{ yd}}{1 \text{ min}} \cdot \dfrac{1 \text{ min}}{\underset{20}{\underset{1}{\cancel{60}}} \text{ s}} \cdot \dfrac{\overset{1}{\cancel{3}}\text{ft}}{1 \text{ yd}} = \textbf{22}\dfrac{\textbf{ft}}{\textbf{s}}$

28. $1\frac{3}{4} + 2\frac{2}{3} - 3\frac{5}{6}$

$= 1\frac{9}{12} + 2\frac{8}{12} - 3\frac{10}{12} = \dfrac{\textbf{7}}{\textbf{12}}$

29. $\left(1\frac{3}{4}\right)\left(2\frac{2}{3}\right) \div 3\frac{5}{6}$

$= \left(\frac{7}{4} \cdot \frac{8}{3}\right) \div \frac{23}{6} = \frac{14}{3} \times \frac{6}{23}$

$= \dfrac{28}{23} = \textbf{1}\dfrac{\textbf{5}}{\textbf{23}}$

30. $(-7) + |-3| - (2)(-3) + (-4)$
$\quad - (-3)(-2)(-1)$

$(-7) + 3 - (-6) + (-4) - (-6)$

$-4 - (-6) + (-4) - (-6)$

$2 + (-4) - (-6)$

$-2 - (-6)$

$\textbf{4}$

Early Finishers Solutions

a.

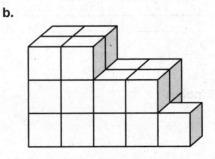

b.

Practice Set (114)

a. **2 kg or 2000 g**

b. **3000 cm³**

c. **1000 milliliters**

d. Volume = (25 cm)(10 cm)(8 cm)
   = 2000 cm³ = 2000 mL
   = **2 liters**

Written Practice (114)

1.

	Percent	Actual Count
Original	100	$72.50
− Change	20	C
New	80	N

$$\frac{100}{80} = \frac{\$72.50}{N}$$
$$100N = \$5800$$
$$N = \$58$$

$58.00	$58.00
× 0.07	+ $4.06
$4.06	**$62.06**

2. 4(87) = 348, 6(90) = 540
   540 − 348 = 192, $\frac{192}{2}$ = **96**

3. a. $P(B) = \frac{12}{27} = \frac{4}{9}$

b. $\frac{9}{27} = 0.333\overline{3} = 33\frac{1}{3}\%$

c. favorable to
   unfavorable = 21 to 6 = **7 to 2**

4. $\frac{\$10.80}{144 \text{ pencils}} = \frac{\$0.075}{1 \text{ pencil}}$
   $7\frac{1}{2}$¢ per pencil

5.
   $5000
   × 0.08
   $400

   $\frac{6}{12} = \frac{1}{2}$, $\frac{\$400}{2}$ = **$200**

6. a. **Class Test Scores**

b. 6(4 students) = 24 students
   $\frac{24 \text{ students}}{3}$ = 8 students
   24 students − (8 students + 6 students)
   = **10 students**

7.

	Ratio	Actual Count
Cars	5	C
Trucks	2	T
Total	7	3500

$$\frac{5}{7} = \frac{C}{3500}$$
$$7C = 17,500$$
$$C = \textbf{2500 cars}$$

8. Volume $\approx \frac{4}{3}(3)(2 \text{ ft})^3$
   $\approx 4(8 \text{ ft}^3)$
   $\approx$ **32 ft³**

9. $W_N = 1.2 \times \$240$
   $W_N = \textbf{\$288}$

10. $60 = W_P \times 150$
   $\frac{60}{150} = \frac{W_P \times 150}{150}$
   $\frac{2}{5} = W_P$
   $W_P = \frac{2}{5} \times 100\% = \textbf{40\%}$

11.

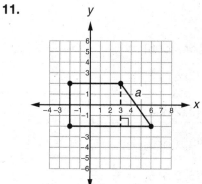

a. Area of triangle = $\frac{(3 \text{ units})(4 \text{ units})}{2}$
   = 6 units²
   Area of rectangle = (5 units)(4 units)
   = 20 units²
   Area of figure = 6 units² + 20 units²
   = **26 units²**

389

Solutions

b.
$$a^2 = (4 \text{ units})^2 + (3 \text{ units})^2$$
$$a^2 = 16 \text{ units}^2 + 9 \text{ units}^2$$
$$a^2 = 25 \text{ units}^2$$
$$a = 5 \text{ units}$$
$$\text{Perimeter} = 5 \text{ units} + 8 \text{ units}$$
$$+ 4 \text{ units} + 5 \text{ units}$$
$$= \textbf{22 units}$$

12. a. $-6, 0.6, \sqrt{6}, 6^2$

b. $6^2, -6, 0.6$

13. a. 1.8

b. 180%

14. a. $2\overline{)5.0}$ quotient 2.5 $\textbf{2.5} \times \textbf{10}^{-3}$

b. $5\overline{)2.0}$ quotient 0.4 $0.4 \times 10^3 \longrightarrow \textbf{4} \times \textbf{10}^2$

15.
$$(2.5 \times 10^{-3})(4 \times 10^2)$$
$$(2.5 \times 4)(10^{-3} \times 10^2)$$
$$10 \times 10^{-1} \to 1 \times 10^0 \to \textbf{1}$$

16. $1 \ \cancel{km^2} \times \dfrac{1000 \text{ m}}{1 \ \cancel{km}} \times \dfrac{1000 \text{ m}}{1 \ \cancel{km}} = \textbf{1,000,000 m}^2$

17. a.
$$C = \pi d$$
$$\frac{C}{\pi} = \frac{\pi d}{\pi}$$
$$\frac{C}{\pi} = d$$

b. $\dfrac{62.8}{3.14} \approx d$
$$\textbf{20} \approx d$$

18. $P(1, 1 \text{ or } 2 \text{ or } 4 \text{ or } 6) = \dfrac{1}{6} \cdot \dfrac{4}{6} = \dfrac{4}{36}$

$P(2, 1 \text{ or } 3 \text{ or } 5) = \dfrac{1}{6} \cdot \dfrac{3}{6} = \dfrac{3}{36}$

$P(3, 2 \text{ or } 4) = \dfrac{1}{6} \cdot \dfrac{2}{6} = \dfrac{2}{36}$

$P(4, 1 \text{ or } 3) = \dfrac{1}{6} \cdot \dfrac{2}{6} = \dfrac{2}{36}$

$P(5, 2 \text{ or } 6) = \dfrac{1}{6} \cdot \dfrac{2}{6} = \dfrac{2}{36}$

$P(6, 1 \text{ or } 5) = \dfrac{1}{6} \cdot \dfrac{2}{6} = \dfrac{2}{36}$

$\dfrac{4}{36} + \dfrac{3}{36} + \dfrac{2}{36} + \dfrac{2}{36} + \dfrac{2}{36} + \dfrac{2}{36}$

$= \dfrac{15}{36} = \dfrac{5}{12}$

19. $C \approx \dfrac{3.14(6 \text{ cm})}{2}$

$C \approx 9.42 \text{ cm}$

$$a^2 = (6 \text{ cm})^2 + (8 \text{ cm})^2$$
$$a^2 = 36 \text{ cm}^2 + 64 \text{ cm}^2$$
$$a^2 = 100 \text{ cm}^2$$
$$a = 10 \text{ cm}$$
$$\text{Perimeter} \approx 9.42 \text{ cm} + 10 \text{ cm} + 8 \text{ cm}$$
$$\approx \textbf{27.42 cm}$$

20. a. Surface area $= 6(3 \text{ ft} \times 3 \text{ ft})$
$$= 6(9 \text{ ft}^2) = \textbf{54 ft}^2$$

b. Volume $= \dfrac{1}{3}(9 \text{ ft}^2)(3 \text{ ft}) = \textbf{9 ft}^3$

21. Area of base $\approx 3.14(25 \text{ m}^2)$
$$\approx 78.5 \text{ m}^2$$
Volume $\approx (78.5 \text{ m}^2)(3 \text{ m})$
$$\approx \textbf{235.5 m}^3$$

22. a. $m\angle ACB = 180° - 130° = \textbf{50°}$

b. $m\angle CAB = 180° - (90° + 50°) = \textbf{40°}$

c. $m\angle CED = m\angle ECD$
$$= 180° - 130° = 50°$$
$$m\angle CDE = 180° - (50° + 50°) = \textbf{80°}$$

23. Volume $= (40 \text{ cm})(10 \text{ cm})(20 \text{ cm})$
$$= \textbf{8000 cm}^3$$

24.
$$0.8m - 1.2 = 6$$
$$0.8m - 1.2 + 1.2 = 6 + 1.2$$
$$0.8m = 7.2$$
$$\frac{0.8m}{0.8} = \frac{7.2}{0.8}$$
$$m = \textbf{9}$$

25.
$$3(x - 4) < x - 8$$
$$3x - 12 < x - 8$$
$$3x - 12 + 12 < x - 8 + 12$$
$$3x < x + 4$$
$$3x - x < x + 4 - x$$
$$2x < 4$$
$$\frac{2x}{2} < \frac{4}{2}$$
$$\mathbf{x < 2}$$

$x < 2$

-2 –1 0 1 2 3

26. $4^2 \cdot 2^{-3} \cdot 2^{-1} = \overset{1}{\cancel{16}} \cdot \dfrac{1}{\underset{1}{\cancel{8}}} \cdot \dfrac{1}{\underset{1}{\cancel{2}}} = \mathbf{1}$

27. 1 kilogram = 1000 grams
1000 grams − 50 grams = **950 grams**

28. $1\dfrac{2}{10}\left(3\dfrac{3}{4}\right) \div 4\dfrac{1}{2} = \left(\dfrac{\overset{3}{\cancel{12}}}{\underset{2}{\cancel{10}}} \cdot \dfrac{\overset{3}{\cancel{15}}}{\underset{1}{\cancel{4}}}\right) \div \dfrac{9}{2}$

$= \dfrac{\overset{1}{\cancel{9}}}{2} \cdot \dfrac{2}{\underset{1}{\cancel{9}}} = \mathbf{1}$

29. $2\dfrac{3}{4} - 1\dfrac{1}{2} - \dfrac{1}{6} = 2\dfrac{9}{12} - 1\dfrac{6}{12} - \dfrac{2}{12}$

$= \mathbf{1\dfrac{1}{12}}$

30.
$$(-3)(-2) - (2)(-3) - (-8) + (-2)(-3) + |-5|$$
$$(6) - (-6) - (-8) + (6) + (5)$$
$$12 - (-8) + 6 + (5)$$
$$20 + 6 + 5$$
$$\mathbf{31}$$

Early Finishers Solutions

a. $A'(1, -4), B'(4, -4), C'(1, -1)$

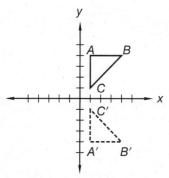

b. $(-1, 4), (-4, 4), (-1, 1)$

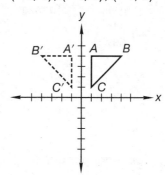

Practice Set 115

a. $8m^2n = \mathbf{(2)(2)(2)mmn}$

b. $12mn^2 = \mathbf{(2)(2)(3)mnn}$

c. $18x^3y^2 = \mathbf{(2)(3)(3)xxxyy}$

d. $\dfrac{8m^2n}{4mn} + \dfrac{12mn^2}{4mn}$
$2m + 3n$
$\mathbf{4\,mn(2m + 3n)}$

e. $\dfrac{8xy^2}{4xy} - \dfrac{4xy}{4xy}$
$2y - 1$
$\mathbf{4xy(2y - 1)}$

f. $\dfrac{6a^2b^3}{3a^2b^2} + \dfrac{9a^3b^2}{3a^2b^2} + \dfrac{3a^2b^2}{3a^2b^2}$
$2b + 3a + 1$
$\mathbf{3a^2b^2(2b + 3a + 1)}$

Written Practice 115

1.
$$\begin{array}{r} \$7000 \\ \times\ \ 0.08 \\ \hline \$560 \end{array}$$

$\dfrac{9}{12} = \dfrac{3}{4}, \ \dfrac{3}{4}(\$560) = \mathbf{\$420}$

2. a. $P(H, H) = \dfrac{1}{2} \cdot \dfrac{1}{2} = \dfrac{1}{4}$

b. 25%

c. 1 to 3

Solutions

3. $4(410) = 1640$

1640 miles + 600 miles = 2240 miles

$$\frac{2240 \text{ miles}}{5 \text{ days}} = \textbf{448 } \frac{\textbf{mi}}{\textbf{day}}$$

4. $\dfrac{\$2.16}{18 \text{ ounces}} = \dfrac{\$0.12}{1 \text{ ounce}}$

$\dfrac{\$3.36}{32 \text{ ounces}} = \dfrac{\$0.105}{1 \text{ ounce}}$

$\begin{array}{r} \$0.120 \\ -\ \$0.105 \\ \hline \$0.015 \end{array}$ $\quad 1\frac{1}{2}$¢ **more per ounce**

5.

	Case 1	Case 2
Words	160	800
Minutes	5	m

$$\frac{160}{5} = \frac{800}{m}$$

$160m = 4000$

$m = \textbf{25 minutes}$

6.

	Ratio	Actual Count
Guinea pigs	7	G
Rats	5	R
Total	12	120

$$\frac{7}{12} = \frac{G}{120}$$

$12G = 840$

$G = \textbf{70 guinea pigs}$

7. $\dfrac{3}{4}x = 48$

$\left(\dfrac{4}{3}\right)\dfrac{3}{4}x = \left(\dfrac{4}{3}\right)48$

$x = 64$

$\dfrac{5}{8}(64) = \textbf{40}$

8.

	Percent	Actual Count
Original	100	$\$1500$
+ Change	40	C
New	140	N

$$\frac{100}{140} = \frac{\$1500}{N}$$

$100N = \$210,000$

$N = \$2100$

$\begin{array}{r} \$2100 \\ \times\ \ 0.08 \\ \hline \$168 \end{array}$ $\qquad \begin{array}{r} \$2100 \\ +\ \$168 \\ \hline \textbf{\$2268} \end{array}$

9. 80% of 75% of $80 = (0.8)(0.75) \times \$80$
$$= \textbf{\$48}$$

10.

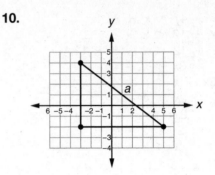

a. Area $= \dfrac{(8 \text{ units})(6 \text{ units})}{2} = \textbf{24 units}^2$

b. $\qquad a^2 = 64 \text{ units}^2 + 36 \text{ units}^2$

$\qquad a^2 = 100 \text{ units}^2$

$\qquad a = 10 \text{ units}$

Perimeter $= 10 \text{ units} + 8 \text{ units}$
$+ 6 \text{ units} = \textbf{24 units}$

11. Volume $= (25 \text{ cm})(20 \text{ cm})(10 \text{ cm})$
$= 5000 \text{ cm}^3 = 5000 \text{ g} = 5 \text{ kg}$

$5 \text{ kg} + 5 \text{ kg} = \textbf{10 kg}$

12. a. $\dfrac{7}{8}$

b. $87\dfrac{1}{2}\%$

13.

Seconds	Beats
15	17
60	b

$$\frac{17}{b} = \frac{15}{60}$$

$15b = 17 \cdot 60$

$15b = 1020$

$b = \textbf{68}$

60 seconds = 1 min.

68 beats per minute

14. a. $(6.4 \times 10^6)(8 \times 10^{-8})$

$\qquad 51.2 \times 10^{-2}$

$\quad (5.12 \times 10^1) \times 10^{-2}$

$\qquad \textbf{5.12} \times \textbf{10}^{-1}$

b. $\dfrac{6.4 \times 10^6}{8 \times 10^{-8}}$

$\qquad 8\overline{)6.4}^{\,0.8}$

$10^6 \div 10^{-8} = 10^{14} \longleftarrow [6 - (-8) = 14]$

0.8×10^{14}

$(8 \times 10^{-1}) \times 10^{14}$

8×10^{13}

15. $3 \text{ ft} \times \dfrac{36 \text{ in.}}{1 \text{ ft.}} \times \dfrac{2.54 \text{ cm}}{1 \text{ in.}}$

$= \textbf{91.44 centimeters}$

16. a. $\qquad A = \dfrac{1}{2} bh$

$\left(\dfrac{2}{1}\right) A = \left(\dfrac{2}{1}\right) \dfrac{1}{2} bh$

$2A = bh$

$\dfrac{2A}{h} = \dfrac{bh}{h}$

$\dfrac{2A}{h} = b$

b. $\dfrac{2(24)}{6} = b$

$8 = b$

17. See student work;

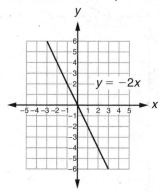

$y = -2x$

$\dfrac{\text{rise}}{\text{run}} = \dfrac{2}{-1} = \textbf{-2}$

18. $A \approx \dfrac{3.14(4 \text{ mm}^2)}{2}$

$A \approx 6.28 \text{ mm}^2$

Area of square $= (6 \text{ mm})(6 \text{ mm})$
$\qquad\qquad\qquad = 36 \text{ mm}^2$
$-$ Area of semicircle $\approx 6.28 \text{ mm}^2$
$\overline{\text{Area of figure} \qquad \approx \textbf{29.72 mm}^2}$

19. a. $6(100 \text{ cm} \times 100 \text{ cm})$

$= 6(10{,}000 \text{ cm}^2) = \textbf{60,000 cm}^2$

b. Volume $= (100 \text{ cm})(100 \text{ cm})(100 \text{ cm})$

$= \textbf{1,000,000 cm}^3$

c. 1 m

20. a. Area of base $= \pi(15 \text{ in.})^2$
$\qquad\qquad\qquad = 225\pi \text{ in.}^2$
$\qquad$ Volume $= (225\pi \text{ in.}^2)(30 \text{ in.})$
$\qquad\qquad\qquad = \textbf{6750}\boldsymbol{\pi} \textbf{ in.}^3$

b. Volume $= \dfrac{4}{3}\pi(15 \text{ in.})^3$

$= \textbf{4500}\boldsymbol{\pi} \textbf{ in.}^3$

21. a. $\text{m}\angle YXZ = 180° - (90° + 35°) = \textbf{55°}$

b. $\text{m}\angle WXV = 180° - (90° + 55°) = \textbf{35°}$

c. $\text{m}\angle WVX = 180° - (90° + 35°) = \textbf{55°}$

22. $\qquad \dfrac{21}{14} = \dfrac{12}{WV}$

$21(WV) = 168$

$WV = \textbf{8 cm}$

23. Volume $= \dfrac{1}{3}(6 \text{ in.} \times 6 \text{ in.} \times 6 \text{ in.})$

$= \textbf{72 in.}^3$

24. $\qquad\quad 0.4n + 5.2 = 12$

$0.4n + 5.2 - 5.2 = 12 - 5.2$

$0.4n = 6.8$

$\dfrac{0.4n}{0.4} = \dfrac{6.8}{0.4}$

$n = \textbf{17}$

25. $\qquad \dfrac{18}{y} = \dfrac{36}{28}$

$36y = 504$

$\dfrac{36y}{36} = \dfrac{504}{36}$

$y = \textbf{14}$

26. $\sqrt{5^2 - 3^2} + \sqrt{5^2 - 4^2}$
$= \sqrt{25 - 9} + \sqrt{25 - 16} = \sqrt{16} + \sqrt{9}$
$= 4 + 3 = \textbf{7}$

27.

$\overset{2}{3} \text{ yd} \; (\overset{2}{3} \text{ ft}) \; (12 \text{ in.}) \longrightarrow$
$- \qquad\qquad 2 \text{ ft} \qquad 1 \text{ in.}$

$\overset{2}{3} \text{ yd} \qquad \overset{2}{3} \text{ ft} \qquad 12 \text{ in.}$
$- \qquad\qquad\quad 2 \text{ ft} \qquad 1 \text{ in.}$
$\overline{\textbf{2 yd} \qquad\qquad\qquad \textbf{11 in.}}$

28. $3\dfrac{1}{2} \div \left(1\dfrac{2}{5} \div 3\right)$

$= \dfrac{7}{2} \div \left(\dfrac{7}{5} \times \dfrac{1}{3}\right) = \dfrac{7}{2} \div \dfrac{7}{15}$

$= \dfrac{\overset{1}{7}}{2} \times \dfrac{15}{\underset{1}{7}} = \dfrac{15}{2} = \textbf{7}\dfrac{1}{2} \text{ or } \textbf{7.5}$

Solutions

29. $3.5 + 2^{-2} - 2^{-3} = 3\frac{1}{2} + \frac{1}{4} - \frac{1}{8}$

$= 3\frac{4}{8} + \frac{2}{8} - \frac{1}{8} = \mathbf{3\frac{5}{8}}$ or **3.625**

30.

$\dfrac{(3)(-2)(4)}{(-6)(2)} + (-8) + (-4)(+5) - (2)(-3)$

$\dfrac{(-6)(4)}{-12} + (-8) + (-20) - (-6)$

$\dfrac{-24}{-12} + (-8) + (-20) - (-6)$

$2 + (-8) + (-20) - (-6)$

$-6 + (-20) - (-6)$

$\mathbf{-20}$

Practice Set 116

a.
$2x + y = 3$
$2x + y - 2x = 3 - 2x$
$y = 3 - 2x$
$\mathbf{y = -2x + 3}$

b.
$y - 3 = x$
$y - 3 + 3 = x + 3$
$\mathbf{y = x + 3}$

c.
$2x + y - 3 = 0$
$2x + y - 3 + 3 = 0 + 3$
$2x + y = 3$
$2x + y - 2x = 3 - 2x$
$y = 3 - 2x$
$\mathbf{y = -2x + 3}$

d.
$x + y = 4 - x$
$x + y - x = 4 - x - x$
$y = 4 - 2x$
$\mathbf{y = -2x + 4}$

e.

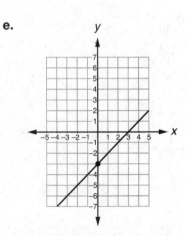

f.

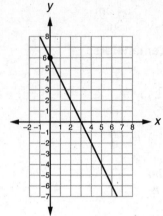

g.

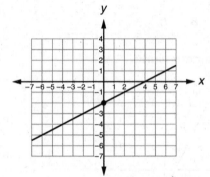

h.

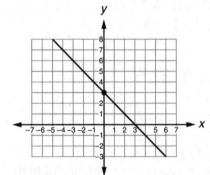

Written Practice 116

1. a. $P(1, 4) = \dfrac{1}{6} \cdot \dfrac{1}{6} = \dfrac{1}{36}$

$P(4, 1) = \dfrac{1}{6} \cdot \dfrac{1}{6} = \dfrac{1}{36}$

$P(2, 3) = \dfrac{1}{6} \cdot \dfrac{1}{6} = \dfrac{1}{36}$

$P(3, 2) = \dfrac{1}{6} \cdot \dfrac{1}{6} = \dfrac{1}{36}$

$4\left(\dfrac{1}{36}\right) = \dfrac{1}{9} = 0.\overline{11},\ \mathbf{0.11}$

394

b. $P(4) = \dfrac{1}{12}$

   $P(7) = \dfrac{1}{6}$

   $P(4 \text{ or } 7) = \dfrac{1}{12} + \dfrac{1}{6} = \dfrac{1}{12} + \dfrac{2}{12}$

   $= \dfrac{3}{12} = \dfrac{1}{4} = \mathbf{25\%}$

c. 1 to 35

2. 2^{10} bytes = **1024 bytes**

3. The better sale seems to be the "40% of" sale, which is 60% off the regular price. Sixty percent off is better than forty percent off.

4. a. $1\dfrac{3}{4}$

   b. 1.75

   c. $0.08\overline{3}$

   d. $8\dfrac{1}{3}\%$

5.

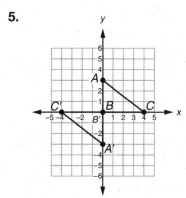

$A'(0, -3), B'(0, 0), C'(-4, 0)$

6. Exterior angle: $\dfrac{360°}{20} = \mathbf{18°}$

   Interior angle: $180° - 18° = \mathbf{162°}$

7.

	Percent	Actual Count
Original	100	O
− Change	30	C
New	70	$42

$\dfrac{30}{70} = \dfrac{C}{\$42}$

$70C = \$1260$

$C = \mathbf{\$18}$

8. a. Volume $= (40 \text{ cm})(20 \text{ cm})(30 \text{ cm})$
   $= 24{,}000 \text{ cm}^3 = 24{,}000 \text{ mL}$
   $24{,}000 \text{ mL} = \mathbf{24 \text{ liters}}$

   b. 24 kg

9. $24 \text{ kg} \cdot \dfrac{2.2 \text{ lb}}{1 \text{ kg}} = \mathbf{52.8 \text{ lb}}$

10. $2x - 6 = 48$
   $2x - 6 + 6 = 48 + 6$
   $2x = 54$
   $\dfrac{2x}{2} = \dfrac{54}{2}$
   $x = \mathbf{27}$

11. $(8x - 8) + (7x + 8) + (6x + 12) = 180$
   $21x + 12 = 180$
   $21x + 12 - 12 = 180 - 12$
   $21x = 168$
   $\dfrac{21x}{21} = \dfrac{168}{21}$
   $x = 8°$
   $7(8°) + 8 = \mathbf{64°}$

12. $F = 1.8C + 32$
   $F - 32 = 1.8C + 32 - 32$
   $F - 32 = 1.8C$
   $\dfrac{F - 32}{1.8} = \dfrac{1.8C}{1.8}$
   $\dfrac{F - 32}{1.8} = C$

13. $C \approx \dfrac{3.14(40 \text{ in.})}{2}$
   $C \approx 62.8 \text{ in.}$
   Perimeter $\approx 62.8 \text{ in.} + 66 \text{ in.} + 66 \text{ in.}$
   $\approx 194.8 \text{ in.} \approx \mathbf{195 \text{ in.}}$

Solutions

14. $a^2 = (15 \text{ cm})^2 + (20 \text{ cm})^2$
$a^2 = 225 \text{ cm}^2 + 400 \text{ cm}^2$
$a^2 = 625 \text{ cm}^2$
$a = 25 \text{ cm}$

$$\text{Area of triangle} = \frac{(20 \text{ cm})(15 \text{ cm})}{2}$$
$$= 150 \text{ cm}^2$$
$$\text{Area of triangle} = \frac{(20 \text{ cm})(15 \text{ cm})}{2}$$
$$= 150 \text{ cm}^2$$
$$\text{Area of square} = (20 \text{ cm})(20 \text{ cm})$$
$$= 400 \text{ cm}^2$$
$$\text{Area of rectangle} = (15 \text{ cm})(20 \text{ cm})$$
$$= 300 \text{ cm}^2$$
$$+ \text{ Area of rectangle} = (20 \text{ cm})(25 \text{ cm})$$
$$= 500 \text{ cm}^2$$
$$\overline{\text{Total surface area} = \textbf{1500 cm}^2}$$

15. Volume $= (150 \text{ cm}^2)(20 \text{ cm})$
$= \textbf{3000 cm}^3$

16. a. $\dfrac{\text{rise}}{\text{run}} = \dfrac{1}{1} = \textbf{1};$
(0, −2)

b. $\dfrac{\text{rise}}{\text{run}} = \dfrac{2}{-1} = \textbf{−2};$
(0, 4)

17. $A = \dfrac{1}{2}(12 \text{ cm} + 18 \text{ cm})8 \text{ cm}$
$= \dfrac{1}{2}(30 \text{ cm})8 \text{ cm}$
$= (15 \text{ cm})\,8 \text{ cm}$
$= \textbf{120 cm}^2$

18. $3x^2 - 5 = 40$
$3x^2 - 5 + 5 = 40 + 5$
$3x^2 = 45$
$\dfrac{3x^2}{3} = \dfrac{45}{3}$
$x^2 = 15$
$x = \sqrt{15}, -\sqrt{15}$

19. a. $4\overline{)8}^{\;2}$ $\textbf{2} \times \textbf{10}^{-12}$

b. $8\overline{)4.0}^{\;0.5}$ $0.5 \times 10^{12} \longrightarrow \textbf{5} \times \textbf{10}^{11}$

20. The product is 1 because the numbers are reciprocals.

21. a. $9x^2y = (3)(3)xxy$

b. $\dfrac{10a^2b}{5ab} + \dfrac{15a^2b^2}{5ab} + \dfrac{20abc}{5ab}$
$2a + 3ab + 4c$
$\textbf{5ab(2a + 3ab + 4c)}$

22. Volume $\approx \dfrac{4}{3}(3.14)(6 \text{ in.})^3$
$\approx \dfrac{4}{3}(3.14)(216 \text{ in.}^3)$
$\approx 904.32 \text{ in.}^3$
$\approx \textbf{904 in.}^3$

23. a. $m\angle BCD = 180° - (90° + 25°)$
$= 180° - 115° = \textbf{65°}$

b. $m\angle BAC = 180° - (25° + 90°) = \textbf{65°}$

c. $m\angle ACD = 180° - (90° + 65°) = \textbf{25°}$

d. The three triangles are similar.

24. $\dfrac{BD}{BC} = \dfrac{\textbf{CD}}{\textbf{CA}}$

25.
$x - 15 = x + 2x + 1$
$x - 15 = 3x + 1$
$x - 15 - x = 3x + 1 - x$
$-15 = 2x + 1$
$-15 - 1 = 2x + 1 - 1$
$-16 = 2x$
$\dfrac{-16}{2} = \dfrac{2x}{2}$
$\textbf{−8} = x$

26.
$0.12(m - 5) = 0.96$
$0.12m - 0.6 = 0.96$
$0.12m - 0.6 + 0.6 = 0.96 + 0.6$
$0.12m = 1.56$
$\dfrac{0.12m}{0.12} = \dfrac{1.56}{0.12}$
$m = \textbf{13}$

27. $a(b - c) + b(c - a)$
$ab - ac + bc - ba$
$\textbf{−ac + bc}$ or $\textbf{bc − ac}$

Solutions

28. $\sqrt{\dfrac{(8x^2y)(12x^3y^2)}{(4xy)(6y^2)}}$

$\sqrt{\dfrac{\overset{1}{\cancel{2}}\cdot\overset{1}{\cancel{2}}\cdot\overset{1}{\cancel{2}}\cdot 2\cdot 2\cdot\overset{1}{\cancel{3}}\cdot\overset{1}{\cancel{x}}\cdot x\cdot x\cdot x\cdot x\cdot\overset{1}{\cancel{y}}\cdot\overset{1}{\cancel{y}}\cdot\overset{1}{\cancel{y}}}{\underset{1}{\cancel{2}}\cdot\underset{1}{\cancel{2}}\cdot\underset{1}{\cancel{2}}\cdot\underset{1}{\cancel{3}}\cdot\underset{1}{\cancel{x}}\cdot\underset{1}{\cancel{y}}\cdot\underset{1}{\cancel{y}}\cdot\underset{1}{\cancel{y}}}}$

$\sqrt{4x^4}$

$2x^2$

29. a. $(-3)^2 + (-2)(-3) - (-2)^3$
$9 + (6) - (-8)$
$15 - (-8)$
23

b. $\sqrt[3]{-8} + \sqrt[3]{8} = -2 + 2 = \textbf{0}$

30. $AD = 1.2$ units $- 0.75$ unit
$= \textbf{0.45 unit}$

Early Finishers Solutions

a. $b^2 = c^2 - a^2; b = \sqrt{260^2 - 100^2}$
$= \sqrt{57600} = 240$ yd

b. $c = \sqrt{(120 + 240)^2 + 100^2} \cong 374$ yd

c. $\$8\,[(100\text{ yd} + 360\text{ yd} + 374\text{ yd})$
$\times 3\frac{\text{feet}}{\text{yd}}] = \$20,016$

Practice Set 117

a. Answers may vary. See student work.

b. Answers may vary. See student work.

Written Practice 117

1.
$\begin{array}{r} \$10,000 \\ \times\ \ \ \ 1.07 \\ \hline \$10,700 \\ \times\ \ \ \ 1.07 \\ \hline \$11,449 \\ \times\ \ \ \ 1.07 \\ \hline \$12,250.43 \\ \times\ \ \ \ 1.07 \\ \hline \$13,107.9601 \end{array}$

$\begin{array}{r} \$13,107.96 \\ -\ \$10,000.00 \\ \hline \textbf{\$3107.96} \end{array}$

2. a. $\dfrac{1}{4}$

b. 1 to 3

3. $4(75\%) + 6(85\%) = 810\%$
$\dfrac{810\%}{10} = \textbf{81\%}$

4. a. $1\dfrac{2}{5}$

b. 140%

c. $0.91\overline{6}$

d. $91\dfrac{2}{3}\%$

5.

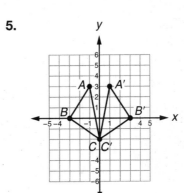

$A'(1, 3),\ B'(3, 0),\ C'(0, -2)$

6. a. $\dfrac{360°}{8} = \textbf{45°}$

b. $180° - 45° = \textbf{135°}$

c. 5 diagonals

7. $\dfrac{100}{N} = \dfrac{1.2}{0.3}$
$1.2N = 30$
$N = \textbf{25\%}$

8. a. 500 cubic centimeters

b. $500\text{ mL} = 500\text{ g} = \textbf{0.5 kilogram}$

9. $\overset{60}{\underset{\cancel{180}}{\cancel{540}}}\text{ ft}^2 \cdot \dfrac{1\text{ yd}}{\underset{1}{\cancel{3}}\ \cancel{\text{ft}}} \cdot \dfrac{1\text{ yd}}{\underset{1}{\cancel{3}}\ \cancel{\text{ft}}} = \textbf{60 yd}^2$

Saxon Math Course 2

397

10.
$$3x^2 + 6 = 81$$
$$3x^2 + 6 - 6 = 81 - 6$$
$$3x^2 = 75$$
$$\frac{3x^2}{3} = \frac{75}{3}$$
$$x^2 = 25$$
$$x = \mathbf{5, -5}$$

11.
$$(3x + 5) + (x - 5) = 180°$$
$$4x = 180°$$
$$\frac{4x}{4} = \frac{180°}{4}$$
$$x = 45°$$
$$2x + (x - 5) = 2(45°) + (45° - 5)$$
$$= 90° + 40° = 130°$$
$$m\angle y = 180 - 130° = \mathbf{50°}$$

12.
$$c^2 - a^2 = b^2$$
$$c^2 - a^2 + a^2 = b^2 + a^2$$
$$\mathbf{c^2 = b^2 + a^2} \quad \text{or} \quad \mathbf{c^2 = a^2 + b^2}$$

13. a. 0.25

b. $33\frac{1}{3}\%$

c. 1 to 5

14.

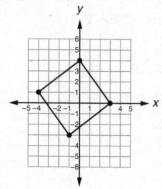

a. 5 units

b. Perimeter = 4(5 units) = **20 units**

c. Area = (5 units)(5 units) = **25 units²**

15. a. Area of base = $\pi(3 \text{ in.})^2$
$$= 9\pi \text{ in.}^2$$
$$\text{Volume} = (9\pi \text{ in.}^2)(8 \text{ in.})$$
$$= \mathbf{72\pi \text{ in.}^3}$$

b. Volume = $\frac{1}{3}(72\pi \text{ in.}^3) = \mathbf{24\pi \text{ in.}^3}$

16. a.
$$V = lwh$$
$$\frac{V}{lw} = \frac{lwh}{lw}$$
$$\frac{V}{lw} = h$$

b. $h = \dfrac{\overset{10}{\cancel{6000} \text{ cm}^3}}{(\underset{1}{\cancel{20} \text{ cm}})(\underset{1}{\cancel{30} \text{ cm}})} = \mathbf{10 \text{ cm}}$

17. a. $\dfrac{\text{rise}}{\text{run}} = \dfrac{2}{1} = \mathbf{2}$

b. **(0, 4)**

c. $y = 2x + 4$

18. a.
$$y + 5 = x$$
$$y + 5 - 5 = x - 5$$
$$\mathbf{y = x - 5}$$

b.
$$2x + y = 4$$
$$2x + y - 2x = 4 - 2x$$
$$\mathbf{y = -2x + 4}$$

19. a. $24xy^2 = \mathbf{(2)(2)(2)(3)xyy}$

b. $\dfrac{3x^2}{3x} + \dfrac{6xy}{3x} - \dfrac{9x}{3x}$
$$x + 2y - 3$$
$$\mathbf{3x(x + 2y - 3)}$$

20. a. $(5 \times 10^3 \text{ mm})(5 \times 10^3 \text{ mm})$
$$= 25 \times 10^6 \text{ mm}^2$$
$$= \mathbf{2.5 \times 10^7 \text{ mm}^2}$$

b. **25,000,000 mm²**

21. $\overset{25}{\cancel{25,000,000} \text{ mm}^2} \cdot \dfrac{1 \text{ m}}{\underset{1}{\cancel{1000} \text{ mm}}} \cdot \dfrac{1 \text{ m}}{\underset{1}{\cancel{1000} \text{ mm}}}$
$$= \mathbf{25 \text{ m}^2}$$

22. a. **Side BD**

b. **Side AD**

23. $\dfrac{5}{3} \text{ in.} - \dfrac{5}{4} \text{ in.} = \dfrac{20}{12} \text{ in.} - \dfrac{15}{12} \text{ in.} = \dfrac{\mathbf{5}}{\mathbf{12}} \text{ in.}$

24.
$$\frac{3}{4}x + 12 < 15$$
$$\frac{3}{4}x + 12 - 12 < 15 - 12$$
$$\frac{3}{4}x < 3$$
$$\left(\frac{4}{3}\right)\frac{3}{4}x < \left(\frac{4}{3}\right)3$$
$$\mathbf{x < 4}$$

$x < 4$

25.
$$6w - 3w + 18 = 9(w - 4)$$
$$3w + 18 = 9w - 36$$
$$3w + 18 - 18 = 9w - 36 - 18$$
$$3w = 9w - 54$$
$$3w - 9w = 9w - 54 - 9w$$
$$-6w = -54$$
$$\frac{-6w}{-6} = \frac{-54}{-6}$$
$$w = \mathbf{9}$$

26.
$$3x(x - 2y) + 2xy(x + 3)$$
$$3x^2 - 6xy + 2x^2y + 6xy$$
$$\mathbf{3x^2 + 2x^2y}$$

27.
$$2^{-2} + 4^{-1} + \sqrt[3]{27} + (-1)^3$$
$$= \frac{1}{4} + \frac{1}{4} + 3 + (-1) = \frac{2}{4} + 2$$
$$= \mathbf{2\frac{1}{2}}$$

28.
$$(-3) + (-2)[(-3)(-2) - (+4)] - (-3)(-4)$$
$$(-3) + (-2)[(6) - (+4)] - (12)$$
$$(-3) + (-2)[2] - (12)$$
$$(-3) + (-4) - (12)$$
$$\mathbf{-19}$$

29. $4\overline{)1.2}^{\,0.3}$ $0.3 \times 10^{-9} \longrightarrow \mathbf{3 \times 10^{-10}}$

30.
$$\frac{36a^2b^3c}{12ab^2c}$$
$$\frac{\overset{1}{\cancel{2}}\cdot\overset{1}{\cancel{2}}\cdot\overset{1}{\cancel{3}}\cdot 3\cdot\overset{1}{\cancel{a}}\cdot a\cdot\overset{1}{\cancel{b}}\cdot\overset{1}{\cancel{b}}\cdot b\cdot\overset{1}{\cancel{c}}}{\underset{1}{\cancel{2}}\cdot\underset{1}{\cancel{2}}\cdot\underset{1}{\cancel{3}}\cdot\underset{1}{\cancel{a}}\cdot\underset{1}{\cancel{b}}\cdot\underset{1}{\cancel{b}}\cdot\underset{1}{\cancel{c}}}$$
$$\mathbf{3ab}$$

Early Finishers Solutions

a. 756 ft $\times$ 4 = 3024 ft

b. Volume $= \frac{1}{3}lwh$
$$= \frac{1}{3}(756\text{ ft})(756\text{ ft})(480\text{ ft})$$
$$= 91{,}445{,}760\text{ ft}^3$$

c. SA $= (756\text{ ft})^2 + 4\left[\frac{1}{2}(756\text{ ft})\right.$
$$\left. \times \left(\sqrt{(480\text{ ft})^2 + (378\text{ ft})^2}\right)\right]$$
$$= 1{,}495{,}368\text{ ft}^2$$

Practice Set 118

a. A typical error message display is [E   0].
Error messages vary.

b. $0 \div 0 = 7$ is not a fact, because division by zero is not possible.

c. $w \neq 0$

d. $x \neq 1$

e. $w \neq 0$

f. $y \neq 3$

g. $x \neq 2, -2$

h. $c \neq 0$

Written Practice 118

1.
$$\frac{100}{C} = \frac{\$180{,}000}{\$9000}$$
$$\$180{,}000C = \$900{,}000$$
$$C = \mathbf{5\%}$$

2.
$$\frac{40\text{ cm}}{100\text{ cm}} = \frac{600\text{ cm}}{l}$$
$$(40\text{ cm})l = 60{,}000\text{ cm}^2$$
$$l = 1500\text{ cm}$$
About 15 meters

Solutions

3. Armando can select a Pythagorean triplet like 3-4-5 to verify that he has formed a right angle. For example, he can measure and mark from a corner 3 meters along one line and 4 meters along a proposed perpendicular line. Then he can check to see whether it is 5 meters between the marks.

4. $15 \text{ meters} \cdot \dfrac{3.28 \text{ feet}}{1 \text{ meter}} \approx 49.2 \text{ feet}$
$\approx \textbf{49 feet}$

5. $\dfrac{1}{120} = \dfrac{1.5}{x}$
$(1)x = (1.5)(120)$
$x = (1.5)(120)$
$x = 180 \text{ in.} = 15 \text{ ft}$
$A = (15 \text{ ft})(15 \text{ ft}) = \textbf{225 ft}^2$

6. **a.** $P(9) = 4\left(\dfrac{1}{36}\right) = \dfrac{4}{36} = \dfrac{\textbf{1}}{\textbf{9}}$

  b. $P(10) = 3\left(\dfrac{1}{36}\right) = \dfrac{3}{36} = \dfrac{1}{12} = \textbf{8}\dfrac{\textbf{1}}{\textbf{3}}\textbf{\%}$

  c. $2 \text{ to } 34 = \textbf{1 to 17}$

7.

$d^2 = (12 \text{ units})^2 + (5 \text{ units})^2$
$d^2 = 144 \text{ units}^2 + 25 \text{ units}^2$
$d^2 = 169 \text{ units}^2$
$d = \textbf{13 units}$

8. **a.** $2 \text{ L} = 2000 \text{ mL}$
  $= \textbf{2000 cubic centimeters}$

  b. 2 kilograms

9. $\dfrac{1}{2}x - \dfrac{2}{3} = \dfrac{5}{6}$
$\dfrac{1}{2}x - \dfrac{2}{3} + \dfrac{2}{3} = \dfrac{5}{6} + \dfrac{2}{3}$
$\dfrac{1}{2}x = \dfrac{5}{6} + \dfrac{4}{6}$
$\dfrac{1}{2}x = \dfrac{9}{6}$
$\left(\dfrac{2}{1}\right)\dfrac{1}{2}x = \left(\dfrac{2}{1}\right)\left(\dfrac{9}{6}\right)$
$x = \dfrac{9}{3} = \textbf{3}$

10. $\dfrac{200°}{2} = 100°$
$m\angle g = 180° - 100° = \textbf{80°}$

11. $3x + y = 6$
$3x + y - 3x = 6 - 3x$
$y = 6 - 3x$
$\textbf{y = -3x + 6}$

$y = -3x + 6$

12. $(x + 30) + 3x + 2x = 180°$
$6x + 30 = 180°$
$6x + 30 - 30 = 180° - 30$
$6x = 150°$
$\dfrac{6x}{6} = \dfrac{150°}{6}$
$x = 25°$
$2x = 2(25°) = \textbf{50°}$

13. $\text{Area of base} = (12 \text{ in.})(12 \text{ in.})$
$= 144 \text{ in.}^2$
$\text{Volume of pyramid} = \dfrac{1}{3}(144 \text{ in.}^2)(8 \text{ in.})$
$= 384 \text{ in.}^3$
$\text{Volume of cube} = (12 \text{ in.})(12 \text{ in.})(12 \text{ in.})$
$= 1728 \text{ in.}^3$
$384 \text{ in.}^3 + 1728 \text{ in.}^3 = \textbf{2112 cubic inches}$

14. $AD = c - 12$

15. $\dfrac{x}{20} = \dfrac{20}{25}$

$25x = 400$

$x = \mathbf{16}$

$y = 25 - 16$

$y = \mathbf{9}$

16. $A \approx 4(3)(4 \text{ cm})^2$

$\approx (12)(16 \text{ cm}^2)$

$\approx \mathbf{192 \text{ cm}^2}$

17. $y - 2x + 5 = 1$

$y - 2x + 2x + 5 = 1 + 2x$

$y + 5 = 1 + 2x$

$y + 5 - 5 = 1 + 2x - 5$

$\mathbf{y = 2x - 4}$

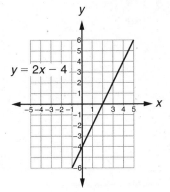

$y = 2x - 4$

18. a. $\dfrac{\text{rise}}{\text{run}} = \dfrac{\mathbf{1}}{\mathbf{2}}$

b. $\mathbf{-1}$

c. $y = \dfrac{\mathbf{1}}{\mathbf{2}}\mathbf{x - 1}$

19. **See student work.**

20. $C \approx \dfrac{\frac{22}{7}(7 \text{ in.})}{2}$

$C \approx \dfrac{22 \text{ in.}}{2}$

$C \approx 11 \text{ in.}$

Perimeter $\approx 11 \text{ in.} + 4\dfrac{1}{4} \text{ in.} + 4\dfrac{1}{4} \text{ in.}$

$+ 11 \text{ in.} + 2 \text{ in.} + 2 \text{ in.}$

$\approx 26 \text{ in.} + 8\dfrac{2}{4} \text{ in.} \approx \mathbf{34\dfrac{1}{2} \text{ in.}}$

21. $\dfrac{1 \times 10^3}{1 \times 10^{-3}} = \mathbf{1 \times 10^6 \text{ dimes}}$

22. a. $\dfrac{x^2}{x} + \dfrac{x}{x}$

$x + 1$

$\mathbf{x(x + 1)}$

b. $\dfrac{12m^2n^3}{6mn^2} + \dfrac{18mn^2}{6mn^2} - \dfrac{24m^2n^2}{6mn^2}$

$2mn + 3 - 4m$

$\mathbf{6mn^2(2mn + 3 - 4m)}$

23. $-2\dfrac{2}{3}w - 1\dfrac{1}{3} = 4$

$-2\dfrac{2}{3}w - 1\dfrac{1}{3} + 1\dfrac{1}{3} = 4 + 1\dfrac{1}{3}$

$-2\dfrac{2}{3}w = 5\dfrac{1}{3}$

$\left(-\dfrac{3}{8}\right)\left(-\dfrac{8}{3}w\right) = \left(-\dfrac{3}{8}\right)\left(\dfrac{16}{3}\right)$

$\mathbf{w = -2}$

24. $5x^2 + 1 = 81$

$5x^2 + 1 - 1 = 81 - 1$

$5x^2 = 80$

$\dfrac{5x^2}{5} = \dfrac{80}{5}$

$x^2 = 16$

$x = \mathbf{4, -4}$

25. $\left(\dfrac{1}{2}\right)^2 - 2^{-2} = \dfrac{1}{4} - \dfrac{1}{4} = \mathbf{0}$

26. $66\dfrac{2}{3}\%$ of $\dfrac{5}{6}$ of 0.144

$= 66\dfrac{2}{3}\%$ of 0.12

$= (0.66\overline{6})(0.12) = \mathbf{0.08}$ or $\dfrac{\mathbf{2}}{\mathbf{25}}$

27. $[-3 + (-4)(-5)] - [-4 - (-5)(-2)]$

$[-3 + (20)] - [-4 - (10)]$

$[17] - [-14]$

$\mathbf{31}$

28. $\dfrac{(5x^2yz)(6xy^2z)}{10 \, xyz}$

$\dfrac{\overset{1}{\cancel{2}} \cdot 3 \cdot \overset{1}{\cancel{5}} \cdot \overset{1}{\cancel{x}} \cdot x \cdot x \cdot \overset{1}{\cancel{y}} \cdot y \cdot y \cdot \overset{1}{\cancel{z}} \cdot z}{\underset{1}{\cancel{2}} \cdot \underset{1}{\cancel{5}} \cdot \underset{1}{\cancel{x}} \cdot \underset{1}{\cancel{y}} \cdot \underset{1}{\cancel{z}}}$

$\mathbf{3x^2y^2z}$

29. $x(x + 2) + 2(x + 2)$

$x^2 + 2x + 2x + 4$

$\mathbf{x^2 + 4x + 4}$

Solutions

30. $a^2 = (20 \text{ mm})^2 + (10 \text{ mm})^2$
$a^2 = 500 \text{ mm}^2$
$a = \sqrt{500} \text{ mm}$
22 mm and 23 mm

Early Finishers Solutions

a. 1. translation, the P was moved to the right.
2. reflection; the P is flipped over the vertical line
3. rotation; the P is turned to the right.

b. Figure 2. A line of symmetry divides a figure into mirror images. The Ps in Figure 2 are mirror images of each other.

a. $A = \dfrac{1}{2}s^2$

s	A
1	$\frac{1}{2}$
2	2
3	$4\frac{1}{2}$
4	8

$A = \dfrac{1}{2}(3)^2 = \dfrac{1}{2}(9) = 4\dfrac{1}{2}$

$A = \dfrac{1}{2}(4)^2 = \dfrac{1}{2}(16) = 8$

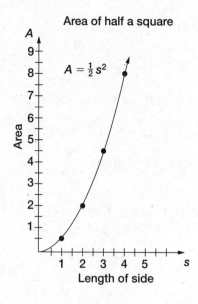

Area of half a square

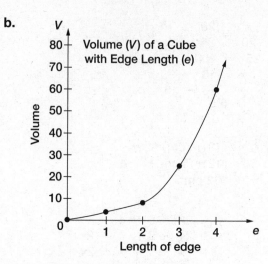

Volume (V) of a Cube with Edge Length (e)

1. $\dfrac{2}{50} = \dfrac{1}{25} = \mathbf{4\%}$

2. $\dfrac{100}{C} = \dfrac{\$20}{\$5}$
$\$20C = \$500$
$C = \mathbf{25\%}$

3.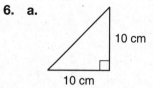

4. **360°**

5. **a.** $\dfrac{1}{200}$

b. **0.005**

c. $0.\overline{8}$

d. $88\dfrac{8}{9}\%$

6. **a.**

```
        |
        | 10 cm
_____|
 10 cm
```

b. **45%**

c. **14 cm**

7. $\dfrac{(6 \times 10^5)(2 \times 10^6)}{(3 \times 10^4)} = \dfrac{12 \times 10^{11}}{3 \times 10^4}$

$3\overline{)12}^{\,4}$ **4×10^7**

8. a. $\dfrac{2x^2}{x} + \dfrac{x}{x}$

$2x + 1$

$x(2x + 1)$

b. $\dfrac{3a^2b}{3a} - \dfrac{12a^2}{3a} + \dfrac{9ab^2}{3a}$

$ab - 4a + 3b^2$

$3a(ab - 4a + 3b^2)$

9. Volume $= (3 \text{ cm}^3) + 6(1 \text{ cm}^3) + 9(1 \text{ cm}^3)$

$= $ **18 cm^3**

10. Surface area $= 2(6 \text{ cm}^2) + 6(3 \text{ cm}^2)$

$+ 2(9 \text{ cm}^2) = $ **48 cm^2**

11. $A = \dfrac{1}{2}bh$

$\left(\dfrac{2}{1}\right)A = \left(\dfrac{2}{1}\right)\dfrac{1}{2}bh$

$2A = bh$

$\dfrac{2A}{b} = \dfrac{bh}{b}$

$\dfrac{2A}{b} = h$

$\dfrac{2(1.44 \text{ m}^2)}{1.6 \text{ m}} = h$

$\dfrac{2.88 \text{ m}^2}{1.6 \text{ m}} = h$

1.8 m $= h$

12. $\dfrac{\text{boys}}{\text{total}} = \dfrac{3}{8} \times 100\% = $ **$37\dfrac{1}{2}\%$**

13. $(6 \text{ ft})^2 + h^2 = (10 \text{ ft})^2$

$36 \text{ ft}^2 + h^2 = 100 \text{ ft}^2$

$36 \text{ ft}^2 + h^2 - 36 \text{ ft}^2 = 100 \text{ ft}^2 - 36 \text{ ft}^2$

$h^2 = 64 \text{ ft}^2$

$h = $ **8 ft**

14. a. **$y = 2x - 4$**

b. **$y = -\dfrac{1}{2}x + 1$**

15. The product of the slopes is -1. The slopes are negative reciprocals.

16.
$$
\begin{array}{r}
\$8000 \\
\times \quad 1.06 \\
\hline
\$8480 \\
\times \quad 1.06 \\
\hline
\$8988.80 \\
\times \quad 1.06 \\
\hline
\$9528.1280 \\
\times \quad 1.06 \\
\hline
\$10,099.81568 \longrightarrow \mathbf{\$10,099.82}
\end{array}
$$

17. $1250 \text{ sq. ft} \cdot \dfrac{1 \text{ yd}}{3 \text{ ft}} \cdot \dfrac{1 \text{ yd}}{3 \text{ ft}} = 138.8\overline{8}$

$\approx$ **139 square yards**

18. a. **$w \neq 0$**

b. **$m \neq -3$**

19. **$DA = c - x$**

20. $\dfrac{y}{20} = \dfrac{15}{25}$

$25y = 300$

$y = 12 \text{ in.}$

$(12 \text{ in.})^2 + z^2 = (15 \text{ in.})^2$

$144 \text{ in.}^2 + z^2 = 225 \text{ in.}^2$

$144 \text{ in.}^2 + z^2 - 144 \text{ in.}^2$

$= 225 \text{ in.}^2 - 144 \text{ in.}^2$

$z^2 = 81 \text{ in.}^2$

$z = 9 \text{ in.}$

Area $= \dfrac{(12 \text{ in.})(9 \text{ in.})}{2} = $ **54 in.^2**

21. Volume $\approx \dfrac{4}{3}(3.14)(15 \text{ cm})^3$

$\approx \dfrac{4}{3}(3.14)(3375 \text{ cm}^3)$

$\approx$ **$14,130 \text{ cm}^3$**

22. **See student work.**

Solutions

23.
$$\frac{2}{3}m + \frac{1}{4} = \frac{7}{12}$$

$$\frac{2}{3}m + \frac{1}{4} - \frac{1}{4} = \frac{7}{12} - \frac{1}{4}$$

$$\frac{2}{3}m = \frac{7}{12} - \frac{3}{12}$$

$$\frac{2}{3}m = \frac{4}{12}$$

$$\left(\frac{\overset{1}{\cancel{3}}}{\underset{1}{\cancel{2}}}\right)\left(\frac{\overset{1}{\cancel{2}}}{\underset{1}{\cancel{3}}}m\right) = \left(\frac{\overset{1}{\cancel{3}}}{\underset{1}{\cancel{2}}}\right)\frac{\overset{1}{\cancel{4}}}{\underset{\cancel{2}}{\cancel{12}}}$$

$$m = \frac{1}{2}$$

24.
$$5(3 - x) = 55$$
$$15 - 5x = 55$$
$$15 - 5x - 15 = 55 - 15$$
$$-5x = 40$$
$$\frac{-5x}{-5} = \frac{40}{-5}$$
$$x = -8$$

25.
$$x + x + 12 = 5x$$
$$2x + 12 = 5x$$
$$2x + 12 - 12 = 5x - 12$$
$$2x = 5x - 12$$
$$2x - 5x = 5x - 12 - 5x$$
$$-3x = -12$$
$$\frac{-3x}{-3} = \frac{-12}{-3}$$
$$x = 4$$

26.
$$10x^2 = 100$$
$$\frac{10x^2}{10} = \frac{100}{10}$$
$$x^2 = 10$$
$$x = \sqrt{10}, -\sqrt{10}$$

27. **300**

28.
$$x(x + 5) - 2(x + 5)$$
$$x^2 + 5x - 2x - 10$$
$$x^2 + 3x - 10$$

29.
$$\frac{(12xy^2z)(9x^2y^2z)}{36xyz^2}$$

$$\frac{\overset{1}{\cancel{2}} \cdot \overset{1}{\cancel{2}} \cdot \overset{1}{\cancel{3}} \cdot \overset{1}{\cancel{3}} \cdot 3 \cdot \cancel{x} \cdot x \cdot x \cdot \cancel{y} \cdot y \cdot y \cdot y \cdot \overset{1}{\cancel{z}} \cdot \overset{1}{\cancel{z}}}{\underset{1}{\cancel{2}} \cdot \underset{1}{\cancel{2}} \cdot \underset{1}{\cancel{3}} \cdot \underset{1}{\cancel{3}} \cdot \underset{1}{\cancel{x}} \cdot \underset{1}{\cancel{y}} \cdot \underset{1}{\cancel{z}} \cdot \underset{1}{\cancel{z}}}$$

$$3x^2y^3$$

30. $33\frac{1}{3}\%$ of 0.12 of $3\frac{1}{3}$

$$= \left(\frac{1}{3}\right) \times \left(\frac{\overset{4}{\cancel{12}}}{\underset{10}{\cancel{100}}} \cdot \frac{\overset{1}{\cancel{10}}}{\underset{1}{\cancel{3}}}\right)$$

$$= \frac{1}{3} \times \frac{4}{10} = \frac{2}{15} \text{ or } \mathbf{0.1\overline{3}}$$

---

a. See student work.

b. See student work.

c. See student work.

d. See student work.

1. $P(\text{sum of 7}) = \frac{1}{6}$; **1 to 5**

2. $\frac{\$2.70}{1.08} = \mathbf{\$2.50}$

3. $\frac{105}{280}$ Reduce

$\frac{21}{56}$ divided by 5

$\frac{3}{8}$ divided by 7

$$\begin{array}{r} 0.375 \\ 8\overline{)3000} \\ \underline{24}\downarrow \\ 60 \\ \underline{56}\downarrow \\ 40 \\ \underline{40} \\ 0 \end{array}$$

0.375×100

37.5% or $37\frac{1}{2}$%

4. **100°; 80°; 80°**

5. a. $\frac{1}{1000}$

    b. **0.001**

    c. **1.6**

    d. **160%**

---

6. a.
$$a^2 + (1 \text{ cm})^2 = (2 \text{ cm})^2$$
$$a^2 + 1 \text{ cm}^2 = 4 \text{ cm}^2$$
$$a^2 + 1 \text{ cm}^2 - 1 \text{ cm}^2 = 4 \text{ cm}^2 - 1 \text{ cm}^2$$
$$a^2 = 3 \text{ cm}^2$$
$$a = \sqrt{3} \text{ cm}$$

b. 1.7 cm

7. $\dfrac{(4 \times 10^{-5})(6 \times 10^{-4})}{8 \times 10^3} = \dfrac{24 \times 10^{-9}}{8 \times 10^3}$

$8\overline{)24}^{\,3} \quad \mathbf{3 \times 10^{-12}}$

8. a. $\dfrac{3y^2}{y} - \dfrac{y}{y}$

$3y - 1$

$\mathbf{y(3y - 1)}$

b. $\dfrac{6w^2}{3w} + \dfrac{9wx}{3w} - \dfrac{12w}{3w}$

$2w + 3x - 4$

$\mathbf{3w(2w + 3x - 4)}$

9. $\dfrac{\mathbf{1}}{\mathbf{3}}$

10. $C \approx (3.14)(6 \text{ cm})$
$C \approx 18.84 \text{ cm}$
$A \approx (18.84 \text{ cm})(6 \text{ cm})$
$\approx 113.04 \text{ cm}^2 \approx \mathbf{113 \text{ cm}^2}$

11. $E = mc^2$
$\dfrac{E}{c^2} = \dfrac{mc^2}{c^2}$
$\dfrac{\mathbf{E}}{\mathbf{c^2}} = \mathbf{m}$

12. $\dfrac{60}{100} = \dfrac{3}{5} = \dfrac{\text{girls}}{\text{total}}$

$\dfrac{\text{boys}}{\text{girls}} \quad \dfrac{2}{3}$

13. line m: $\mathbf{y = -\dfrac{2}{3}x + 2}$

line n: $\mathbf{y = \dfrac{3}{2}x - 2}$

14. The product of the slopes is −1. The slopes are negative reciprocals.

15.
$$\left.\begin{array}{r} \$1000 \\ \times \quad 1.2 \\ \hline \$1200 \end{array}\right\} \text{Year 1}$$

$$\left.\begin{array}{r} \times \quad 1.2 \\ \hline \$1440 \end{array}\right\} \text{Year 2}$$

$$\left.\begin{array}{r} \times \quad 1.2 \\ \hline \$1728 \end{array}\right\} \text{Year 3}$$

$$\left.\begin{array}{r} \times \quad 1.2 \\ \hline \$2073.60 \end{array}\right\} \text{Year 4}$$

About 4 years

16. $d^2 = (17 \text{ in.})^2 + (12 \text{ in.})^2$
$d^2 = 289 \text{ in.}^2 + 144 \text{ in.}^2$
$d^2 = 433 \text{ in.}^2$
$d = \sqrt{433} \text{ in.}^2$
$d \approx \mathbf{21 \text{ in.}}$

17. a. Volume $= (36 \text{ feet})(21 \text{ feet})\left(\dfrac{1}{2} \text{ feet}\right)$

$= \mathbf{378 \text{ cubic feet}}$

b. $\overset{14}{\cancel{378}} \text{ ft}^3 \cdot \dfrac{1 \text{ yd}}{\underset{1}{\cancel{3 \text{ ft}}}} \cdot \dfrac{1 \text{ yd}}{\underset{1}{\cancel{3 \text{ ft}}}} \cdot \dfrac{1 \text{ yd}}{\underset{1}{\cancel{3 \text{ ft}}}}$

$= \mathbf{14 \text{ cubic yards}}$

18. a. $\mathbf{m \neq 2}$

b. $\mathbf{y \neq -5}$

19.

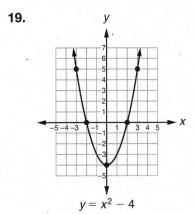

$y = x^2 - 4$

20. $\dfrac{c}{a} = \dfrac{a}{y}$

21. Surface area $\approx 4(3.14)(3 \text{ in.})^2$
$\approx 4(3.14)(9 \text{ in.}^2)$
$\approx 113.04 \text{ in.}^2$
$\approx \mathbf{113 \text{ in.}^2}$

22. 250 cubic centimeters = 250 mL = **0.25 liter**

23.
$$15 + x = 3x - 17$$
$$15 + x - 3x = 3x - 17 - 3x$$
$$15 - 2x = -17$$
$$15 - 2x - 15 = -17 - 15$$
$$-2x = -32$$
$$\frac{-2x}{-2} = \frac{-32}{-2}$$
$$x = \mathbf{16}$$

24.
$$3\frac{1}{3}x - 16 = 74$$
$$3\frac{1}{3}x - 16 + 16 = 74 + 16$$
$$3\frac{1}{3}x = 90$$
$$\left(\frac{\overset{1}{\cancel{3}}}{\cancel{10}}\right)\left(\frac{\overset{1}{\cancel{10}}}{\cancel{3}}x\right) = \left(\frac{3}{\cancel{10}}\right)\overset{9}{\cancel{90}}$$
$$x = \mathbf{27}$$

25.
$$\frac{m^2}{4} = 9$$
$$m^2 = 36$$
$$m = \mathbf{6, -6}$$

26.
$$\frac{1.2}{m} = \frac{0.04}{8}$$
$$0.04m = 9.6$$
$$\frac{0.04m}{0.04} = \frac{9.6}{0.04}$$
$$m = \mathbf{240}$$

27. $x(x - 5) - 2(x - 5)$
$x^2 - 5x - 2x + 10$
$\mathbf{x^2 - 7x + 10}$

28. $\dfrac{(3xy)(4x^2y)(5x^2y^2)}{10x^3y^3}$

$$\frac{\overset{1}{\cancel{2}} \cdot 2 \cdot 3 \cdot \overset{1}{\cancel{5}} \cdot \overset{1}{\cancel{x}} \cdot \overset{1}{\cancel{x}} \cdot \overset{1}{\cancel{x}} \cdot x \cdot x \cdot \overset{1}{\cancel{y}} \cdot \overset{1}{\cancel{y}} \cdot \overset{1}{\cancel{y}} \cdot y}{\underset{1}{\cancel{2}} \cdot \underset{1}{\cancel{5}} \cdot \underset{1}{\cancel{x}} \cdot \underset{1}{\cancel{x}} \cdot \underset{1}{\cancel{x}} \cdot \underset{1}{\cancel{y}} \cdot \underset{1}{\cancel{y}} \cdot \underset{1}{\cancel{y}}}$$

$\mathbf{6x^2y}$

29. $|-8| + 3(-7) - [(-4)(-5) - 3(-2)]$
$8 + (-21) - [(20) - (-6)]$
$8 + (-21) - [26]$
$\mathbf{-39}$

30. $\dfrac{7\frac{1}{2} - \frac{2}{3}(0.9)}{0.03} = \dfrac{7\frac{1}{2} - \frac{\overset{1}{\cancel{2}}}{\cancel{3}}\left(\frac{\overset{3}{\cancel{9}}}{\underset{5}{\cancel{10}}}\right)}{0.03}$

$= \dfrac{7\frac{1}{2} - \frac{3}{5}}{0.03} = \dfrac{7\frac{5}{10} - \frac{6}{10}}{0.03}$

$= \dfrac{6\frac{15}{10} - \frac{6}{10}}{0.03} \qquad 6\frac{9}{10}}{0.03}$

$= \dfrac{6.9}{0.03} = \mathbf{230}$

Investigation 12

Proof of the Pythagorean Theorem

1. {Students sketch a right triangle. The vertices should be labeled *A*, *B* and *C*, and $\angle C$ is the right angle.}

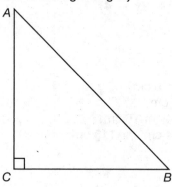

2. {Students identify the sides of the triangle as *a*, *b* and *c*.}

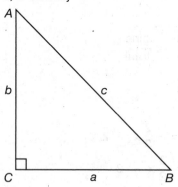

3. {Students draw a segment from vertex C to side AB, perpendicular to AB and label the point of intersection D.}

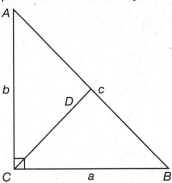

4. {Students label segments BD and AD.}

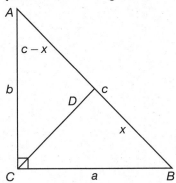

5. 90°; The sum of all three angles must equal 180° and the right angle is 90°.

6. $\angle A = 90 - m$

7. $\angle BCD = 90°$; $\angle ACD = 90°$

8. Yes; All three triangles are right triangles.

9. Leg a of $\triangle ABC$: Leg x of $\triangle BCD$, or $a:x$

10. Leg b of $\triangle ABC$: Leg $c - x$ of $\triangle ACD$, or $b:c - x$

11. $a^2 = cx$ and $b^2 = c(c - x)$
$$b^2 = c^2 - cx$$

12. $b^2 = c^2 - a^2$

13. $a^2 + b^2 = c^2$; the Pythagorean Theorem

Solutions

1. $\dfrac{15 \cdot 40}{15 + 45} = \dfrac{600}{60} = 10$

2. $4 + 5 = 5 + 4$

3. a. commutative property

   b. associative property

4. twenty-one million, six hundred thousand, fifty

5. 25, 36, 49

6. $(7 \times 10{,}000) + (5 \times 1000)$

7. $-8 > -11$

8. $ab = 15 \cdot 3 = \mathbf{45}$

9. 8,100,060

10.
$$
\begin{array}{r}
\$15.00 \\
- \quad \$4.30 \\
\hline
\$10.70
\end{array}
$$

11.
$$
\begin{array}{r}
6{,}300 \\
+ \; 8{,}860 \\
\hline
15{,}160
\end{array}
$$

12.
$$
\begin{array}{r}
\$9.25 \\
8)\overline{\$74.00} \\
72 \\
\hline
2\,0 \\
1\,6 \\
\hline
40 \\
40 \\
\hline
0
\end{array}
$$

13.
$$
\begin{array}{r}
1426 \\
- \quad 78 \\
\hline
1348
\end{array}
$$

14.
$$
\begin{array}{r}
35 \\
45)\overline{1575} \\
135 \\
\hline
225 \\
225 \\
\hline
0
\end{array}
$$

15.
$$
\begin{array}{r}
32{,}800 \\
- \quad 9{,}360 \\
\hline
23{,}440
\end{array}
$$

16.
$$
\begin{array}{r}
18 \\
\times \; 12 \\
\hline
36 \\
18 \\
\hline
216
\end{array}
\qquad
\begin{array}{r}
216 \\
\times \; 11 \\
\hline
216 \\
216 \\
\hline
2376
\end{array}
$$

17.
$$
\begin{array}{r}
560 \\
- \quad 79 \\
\hline
481
\end{array}
\qquad
\begin{array}{r}
1000 \\
- \quad 481 \\
\hline
519
\end{array}
$$

18.
$$
\begin{array}{r}
5{,}799 \\
8)\overline{46{,}392} \\
40 \\
\hline
6\,3 \\
5\,6 \\
\hline
79 \\
72 \\
\hline
72 \\
72 \\
\hline
0
\end{array}
$$

19.
$$
\begin{array}{r}
160 \\
\times \quad 17 \\
\hline
1120 \\
160 \\
\hline
2720
\end{array}
$$

20.
$$
\begin{array}{r}
\$2.95 \\
10)\overline{\$29.50} \\
20 \\
\hline
9\,5 \\
9\,0 \\
\hline
50 \\
50 \\
\hline
0
\end{array}
$$

1. $\dfrac{20 \cdot 30}{20 + 30} = \dfrac{600}{50} = 12$

2. $5 \cdot 6 = 6 \cdot 5$

3. a. commutative property (of multiplication)

   b. associative property (of multiplication)

4. thirty-one million, twenty thousand, thirty

5. 36, 49, 64

6. $(2 \times 100{,}000) + (5 \times 1000)$

7. $-9 > -10$

8. $ab = 12 \cdot 4 = \mathbf{48}$

9. 12,300,040

10.
$$\begin{array}{r} \$15.00 \\ -\ \$3.40 \\ \hline \$11.60 \end{array}$$

11.
$$\begin{array}{r} 7{,}240 \\ +\ 5{,}630 \\ \hline 12{,}870 \end{array}$$

12.
$$\begin{array}{r} \$7.10 \\ 6\overline{)\$42.60} \\ 42 \\ \hline 0\,6 \\ 6 \\ \hline 00 \\ 0 \\ \hline 0 \end{array}$$

13.
$$\begin{array}{r} 5860 \\ -\ 3714 \\ \hline 2146 \end{array}$$

14.
$$\begin{array}{r} 22 \\ 35\overline{)770} \\ 70 \\ \hline 70 \\ 70 \\ \hline 0 \end{array}$$

15.
$$\begin{array}{r} 3400 \\ -\ 986 \\ \hline 2414 \end{array}$$

16.
$$\begin{array}{r} 12 \\ \times\ 6 \\ \hline 72 \end{array} \qquad \begin{array}{r} 72 \\ \times\ 15 \\ \hline 360 \\ 72 \\ \hline 1080 \end{array}$$

17.
$$\begin{array}{r} 650 \\ -\ 97 \\ \hline 553 \end{array} \qquad \begin{array}{r} 1000 \\ -\ 553 \\ \hline 447 \end{array}$$

18.
$$\begin{array}{r} 5{,}145\ \text{R}\ 1 \\ 9\overline{)46{,}306} \\ 45 \\ \hline 1\,3 \\ 9 \\ \hline 40 \\ 36 \\ \hline 46 \\ 45 \\ \hline 1 \end{array}$$

19.
$$\begin{array}{r} 150 \\ \times\ 16 \\ \hline 900 \\ 150 \\ \hline 2400 \end{array}$$

20.
$$\begin{array}{r} \$7.65 \\ 10\overline{)\$76.50} \\ 70 \\ \hline 6\,5 \\ 6\,0 \\ \hline 50 \\ 50 \\ \hline 0 \end{array}$$

Cumulative Test 2A

1. a. $\dfrac{3\ \text{dimes}}{10\ \text{dimes}} = \dfrac{3}{10}$

b. $\dfrac{30¢}{100¢} = 30\%$

2. $\overline{CB}$ (or $\overline{BC}$)

3. $\dfrac{4}{3}$

4. $3\dfrac{1}{8} = \dfrac{(8 \times 3) + 1}{8} = \dfrac{25}{8}$

5. a. $-3, 0, \dfrac{1}{3}, 3$ b. $\dfrac{1}{3}$

6. $(2 + 3) + 5 = 2 + (3 + 5)$

7. a. $\dfrac{7}{12}$ b. $\dfrac{5}{12}$

8.
$$\begin{array}{r} 100{,}000{,}000 \\ -\ 58{,}000{,}000 \\ \hline 42{,}000{,}000 \end{array}$$
forty-two million

9. a. 1, 3, 7, 21

b. 1, 2, 3, 4, 6, 8, 12, 16, 24, 48

c. 1, 3

d. 3

10. inverse property (of multiplication)

11.
$$\begin{array}{r} 4760 \\ -\ 2320 \\ \hline 2440 \end{array}$$

12.
$$\begin{array}{r} \$9.55 \\ +\ \$8.75 \\ \hline \$18.30 \end{array}$$

Solutions

13.
$$
\begin{array}{r}
26 \\
35\overline{)910} \\
\underline{70} \\
210 \\
\underline{210} \\
0
\end{array}
$$

14. $\dfrac{3}{5} + \dfrac{1}{5} = \dfrac{4}{5}$

15. $\dfrac{9}{11} - \dfrac{3}{11} = \dfrac{6}{11}$

16. $\dfrac{3}{5} \times \dfrac{4}{7} = \dfrac{12}{35}$

17.
$$
\begin{array}{r}
8{,}256 \text{ R } 5 \\
9\overline{)74{,}309} \\
\underline{72} \\
2\,3 \\
\underline{1\,8} \\
50 \\
\underline{45} \\
59 \\
\underline{54} \\
5
\end{array}
$$

18.
$$
\begin{array}{r}
\$1.63 \\
\times \quad 40 \\
\hline
\$65.20
\end{array}
$$

19. $\dfrac{2}{5} \cdot \dfrac{2}{5} \cdot \dfrac{2}{5} = \dfrac{8}{125}$

20. a. ray; $\overrightarrow{MC}$

   b. line; $\overleftrightarrow{PM}$ (or $\overleftrightarrow{MP}$)

   c. segment; $\overline{FH}$ (or $\overline{HF}$)

Cumulative Test 2B

1. a. $\dfrac{7 \text{ dimes}}{10 \text{ dimes}} = \dfrac{7}{10}$

   b. $\dfrac{70¢}{100¢} = 70\%$

2. $\angle C$ (or $\angle ACB$ or $\angle BCA$)

3. $\dfrac{3}{2}$

4. $6\dfrac{2}{3} = \dfrac{(3 \times 6) + 2}{3} = \dfrac{20}{3}$

5. a. $-2, 0, \dfrac{1}{2}, 2$ **b.** $\dfrac{1}{2}$

6. $(2 \cdot 3) \cdot 6 = 2 \cdot (3 \cdot 6)$

7. a. $\dfrac{5}{9}$ **b.** $\dfrac{4}{9}$

8.
$$
\begin{array}{r}
100{,}000{,}000 \\
- \;\; 47{,}000{,}000 \\
\hline
53{,}000{,}000
\end{array}
$$
fifty-three million

9. a. 1, 3, 9, 27

   b. 1, 3, 5, 9, 15, 45

   c. 1, 3, 9

   d. 9

10. inverse property (of multiplication)

11.
$$
\begin{array}{r}
6184 \\
- \; 5370 \\
\hline
814
\end{array}
$$

12.
$$
\begin{array}{r}
\$9.50 \\
+ \; \$7.85 \\
\hline
\$17.35
\end{array}
$$

13.
$$
\begin{array}{r}
24 \\
35\overline{)840} \\
\underline{70} \\
140 \\
\underline{140} \\
0
\end{array}
$$

14. $\dfrac{3}{7} + \dfrac{2}{7} = \dfrac{5}{7}$

15. $\dfrac{8}{9} - \dfrac{4}{9} = \dfrac{4}{9}$

16. $\dfrac{2}{5} \times \dfrac{3}{7} = \dfrac{6}{35}$

17.
$$
\begin{array}{r}
9{,}250 \\
8\overline{)74{,}000} \\
\underline{72} \\
2\,0 \\
\underline{1\,6} \\
40 \\
\underline{40} \\
00 \\
\underline{0} \\
0
\end{array}
$$

18.
$$
\begin{array}{r}
\$1.75 \\
\times \quad 40 \\
\hline
\$70.00
\end{array}
$$

19. $\dfrac{3}{4} \cdot \dfrac{1}{2} \cdot \dfrac{3}{5} = \dfrac{9}{40}$

20. a. Segment; $\overline{AB}$ (or $\overline{BA}$)

   b. line; $\overleftrightarrow{CD}$ (or $\overleftrightarrow{DC}$)

   c. ray; $\overrightarrow{GH}$

Cumulative Test 3A

1. 100,219
   $-$ 96,212
   4,007

2.   15
   $\times$ 80
   1200 beach balls

3. $(7 \cdot 9) - (7 + 9) = 63 - 16 =$ **47**

4. $8.75
   $3.50
   $+$ $0.90
   $13.15

5.   1699
   $-$ 1673
   26 years

6.   100%
   $-$ 28%
   72%

7.
$3\frac{1}{3} = \frac{10}{3}$

8. a. $\frac{3}{4} \cdot \frac{3}{3} = \frac{9}{12}$ b. $\frac{2}{3} \cdot \frac{4}{4} = \frac{8}{12}$

9. $\frac{2}{3} \cdot \frac{2}{2} = \frac{4}{6}, \frac{5}{6} - \frac{4}{6} = \frac{1}{6}$

10. a. **1, 3, 7, 21**

   b. **1, 2, 3, 6, 7, 14, 21, 42**

   c. **21**

11. $\overline{BC}$ (or $\overline{CB}$), $\overline{AB}$ (or $\overline{BA}$), $\overline{AC}$ (or $\overline{CA}$)

12. $1\frac{6}{7}$

13. $\frac{7}{11} + \frac{5}{11} = \frac{12}{11} = 1\frac{1}{11}$

14. $\frac{2}{3} \cdot \frac{7}{4} = \frac{14}{12} = \frac{7}{6} = 1\frac{1}{6}$

15.
   2,201 R 2
   7)15,409
    14
    ‾‾
    1 4
    1 4
    ‾‾
    00
     0
    ‾‾
    09
     7
    ‾‾
     2

16.
    221
   40)8840
    80
    ‾‾
    84
    80
    ‾‾
    40
    40
    ‾‾
     0

17.   735
   $\times$ 14
   2940
   735
   10,290

18. $(9 + 4)(3) = (13)(3) =$ **39**

19.
    300
   15)4500

20. $20.00
   $-$ $8.43
   $11.57

Cumulative Test 3B

1.   31,080
   $-$ 27,312
   3,768

2.   18
   $\times$ 50
   900 beach balls

3. $(7 \cdot 6) - (7 + 6) = 42 - 13 =$ **29**

4. $8.50
   $2.75
   $+$ $0.90
   $12.15

5.   1789
   $-$ 1776
   13 years

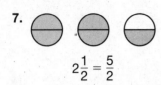

6.
$$\begin{array}{r} 100\% \\ -\ 26\% \\ \hline 74\% \end{array}$$

7.

$$2\frac{1}{2} = \frac{5}{2}$$

8. a. $\frac{5}{6} \cdot \frac{2}{2} = \frac{\mathbf{10}}{\mathbf{12}}$ **b.** $\frac{1}{2} \cdot \frac{6}{6} = \frac{\mathbf{6}}{\mathbf{12}}$

9. $\frac{1}{2} \cdot \frac{4}{4} = \frac{4}{8}; \frac{7}{8} - \frac{4}{8} = \frac{\mathbf{3}}{\mathbf{8}}$

10. a. **1, 3, 5, 15**

   b. **1, 2, 3, 5, 6, 10, 15, 30**

   c. 15

11. $\overline{XY}$ (or $\overline{YX}$), $\overline{YZ}$ (or $\overline{ZY}$), $\overline{XZ}$ (or $\overline{ZX}$)

12. $4\frac{4}{5}$

13. $\frac{5}{7} + \frac{3}{7} = \frac{8}{7} = 1\frac{1}{7}$

14. $\frac{3}{4} \cdot \frac{11}{6} = \frac{33}{24} = \frac{11}{8} = 1\frac{3}{8}$

15.
$$\begin{array}{r} 2{,}004\ \text{R } 3 \\ 9)\overline{18{,}039} \\ \underline{18}\phantom{{,}039} \\ 0\ 0 \\ \underline{0} \\ 03 \\ \underline{0} \\ 39 \\ \underline{36} \\ 3 \end{array}$$

16.
$$\begin{array}{r} 296 \\ 30)\overline{8880} \\ \underline{60} \\ 288 \\ \underline{270} \\ 180 \\ \underline{180} \\ 0 \end{array}$$

17.
$$\begin{array}{r} 635 \\ \times\quad 14 \\ \hline 2540 \\ 635 \\ \hline 8890 \end{array}$$

18. $(6 + 5)(4) = (11)(4) = \mathbf{44}$

19.
$$\begin{array}{r} 375 \\ 12)\overline{4500} \end{array}$$

20.
$$\begin{array}{r} \$20.00 \\ -\ \$4.83 \\ \hline \$15.17 \end{array}$$

Cumulative Test   **4A**

1.
$$\begin{array}{r} 2006 \\ -\quad 75 \\ \hline 1931 \end{array}$$

2.
$$\begin{array}{r} 160 \text{ bushels} \\ 50)\overline{8000} \end{array}$$

3. $\dfrac{1 \text{ quart}}{4 \text{ quarts}} = \dfrac{1}{4} = \mathbf{25\%}$

4. $\dfrac{2}{8} = \dfrac{\mathbf{1}}{\mathbf{4}}$

5.
$$\begin{array}{r} 1{,}000{,}000{,}000 \\ -\quad 47{,}000{,}000 \\ \hline 953{,}000{,}000 \end{array}$$

nine hundred fifty-three million

6. a. $\left(\dfrac{1}{8} + \dfrac{3}{8}\right) + \dfrac{4}{8} = \dfrac{1}{8} + \left(\dfrac{3}{8} + \dfrac{4}{8}\right)$

   b. associative property of addition

7. $7 - 9 = -2$

8. a. Perimeter = 9 cm + 5 cm + 9 cm + 5 cm
$$= \mathbf{28\ cm}$$

   b. Area = (9 cm)(5 cm) = **45 cm²**

9. a. $3\dfrac{24}{36} = 3\dfrac{\mathbf{2}}{\mathbf{3}}$ **b.** $\dfrac{9}{21} = \dfrac{\mathbf{3}}{\mathbf{7}}$

10. $2\dfrac{1}{2} = \dfrac{5}{2}; \dfrac{5}{2} \times \dfrac{1}{3} = \dfrac{\mathbf{5}}{\mathbf{6}}$

11. a. $\dfrac{3}{4} \cdot \dfrac{9}{9} = \dfrac{\mathbf{27}}{\mathbf{36}}$ **b.** $\dfrac{4}{9} \cdot \dfrac{4}{4} = \dfrac{\mathbf{16}}{\mathbf{36}}$

12.

13.
$$\begin{array}{r} 7937 \\ -1169 \\ \hline 6768 \end{array}$$

14. $30\overline{)\$41.10}$ → **$1.37**

15. $\dfrac{11}{3} = 3\dfrac{2}{3}$

    A. $\dfrac{11}{3}$

16. $\dfrac{3}{4} + \dfrac{3}{4} + \dfrac{3}{4} = \dfrac{9}{4} = \mathbf{2\dfrac{1}{4}}$

17. $\dfrac{9}{11} - \dfrac{7}{11} = \mathbf{\dfrac{2}{11}}$

18. $\left(\dfrac{3}{4}\right)^2 = \dfrac{3}{4} \cdot \dfrac{3}{4} = \mathbf{\dfrac{9}{16}}$

19. $\sqrt{121} = \mathbf{11}$

20. $13(11 + 13) = 13(24) = \mathbf{312}$

Cumulative Test 4B

1.
$$\begin{array}{r} 2007 \\ -\ \ 75 \\ \hline \mathbf{1932} \end{array}$$

2. $50\overline{)7000}$ → **140 bushels**

3. $\dfrac{1\ \text{foot}}{3\ \text{feet}} = \dfrac{1}{3} = \mathbf{33\dfrac{1}{3}\%}$

4. $\dfrac{2}{6} = \mathbf{\dfrac{1}{3}}$

5.
$$\begin{array}{r} 1,000,000,000 \\ -\ \ \ \ 74,000,000 \\ \hline 926,000,000 \end{array}$$
nine hundred twenty-six million

6. a. $\left(\dfrac{1}{6} + \dfrac{2}{6}\right) + \dfrac{3}{6} = \dfrac{1}{6} + \left(\dfrac{2}{6} + \dfrac{3}{6}\right)$

    b. associative property of addition

7. $7 - 10 = \mathbf{-3}$

8. a. Perimeter = 8 cm + 4 cm + 8 cm + 4 cm
                = **24 cm**

    b. Area = (8 cm)(4 cm) = **32 cm²**

9. a. $5\dfrac{18}{24} = \mathbf{5\dfrac{3}{4}}$ **b.** $\dfrac{12}{21} = \mathbf{\dfrac{4}{7}}$

10. $1\dfrac{2}{3} = \dfrac{5}{3};\ \dfrac{5}{3} \times \dfrac{1}{2} = \mathbf{\dfrac{5}{6}}$

11. a. $\dfrac{5}{6} \cdot \dfrac{6}{6} = \mathbf{\dfrac{30}{36}}$ **b.** $\dfrac{5}{9} \cdot \dfrac{4}{4} = \mathbf{\dfrac{20}{26}}$

12.

13.
$$\begin{array}{r} 3797 \\ -\ 1169 \\ \hline \mathbf{2628} \end{array}$$

14. $30\overline{)\$40.20}$ → **$1.34**

15. $\dfrac{7}{4} = 1\dfrac{3}{4}$

    C. $\dfrac{7}{4}$

16. $\dfrac{3}{5} + \dfrac{3}{5} + \dfrac{3}{5} = \dfrac{9}{5} = \mathbf{1\dfrac{4}{5}}$

17. $\dfrac{9}{10} - \dfrac{7}{10} = \dfrac{2}{10} = \mathbf{\dfrac{1}{5}}$

18. $\left(\dfrac{2}{3}\right)^2 = \dfrac{2}{3} \cdot \dfrac{2}{3} = \mathbf{\dfrac{4}{9}}$

19. $\sqrt{144} = \mathbf{12}$

20. $12(11 + 13) = 12(24) = \mathbf{288}$

Cumulative Test 5A

1. $26\overline{)624}$ → **24 books**

2.
$$\begin{array}{r} 1806 \\ -\ \ 800 \\ \hline \mathbf{1006}\ \text{years} \end{array}$$

3.
$$\begin{array}{r} \$20.00 \\ -\ \$9.30 \\ \hline \mathbf{\$10.70} \end{array}$$

4.
$$\begin{array}{r} 253 \\ -\ 127 \\ \hline \mathbf{126}\ \text{pages} \end{array}$$

5.

64 marbles

$\frac{3}{8}$ were blue.
| 8 marbles |
| 8 marbles |
| 8 marbles |

$\frac{5}{8}$ were not blue.
| 8 marbles |
| 8 marbles |
| 8 marbles |
| 8 marbles |
| 8 marbles |

a. 3×8 marbles = **24 marbles**

b. 5×8 marbles = **40 marbles**

c. $\frac{24}{64} = \frac{3}{8}$

6.

7.

$480 = \mathbf{2 \cdot 2 \cdot 2 \cdot 2 \cdot 2 \cdot 3 \cdot 5}$

8. a. $\frac{108}{8} = 13\frac{4}{8} = \mathbf{13\frac{1}{2}}$

b. $8\frac{8}{6} = 9\frac{2}{6} = \mathbf{9\frac{1}{3}}$

c. $\frac{120}{900} \div \frac{60}{60} = \mathbf{\frac{2}{15}}$

9. B.

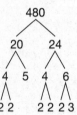

10. a. $\frac{5}{8} \cdot \frac{6}{6} = \mathbf{\frac{30}{48}}$ **b.** $\frac{7}{16} \cdot \frac{3}{3} = \mathbf{\frac{21}{48}}$

11.
```
  700
- 350
  350
```

12.
```
  25
+ 48
  73
```

13. $12\overline{)264}$ → **22**

14. $7 - 1\frac{5}{6} = 6\frac{6}{6} - 1\frac{5}{6} = \mathbf{5\frac{1}{6}}$

15. $5\frac{4}{5} + 6\frac{3}{5} = 11\frac{7}{5} = \mathbf{12\frac{2}{5}}$

16. $5\frac{1}{8} - 1\frac{7}{8} = 4\frac{9}{8} - 1\frac{7}{8} = 3\frac{2}{8} = \mathbf{3\frac{1}{4}}$

17. $\frac{2}{3} \cdot \frac{\overset{1}{\cancel{3}}}{\cancel{4}} \cdot \frac{\overset{1}{\cancel{4}}}{5} = \mathbf{\frac{2}{5}}$

18. $\frac{2}{3} \div \frac{1}{2} = \frac{2}{3} \cdot \frac{2}{1} = \frac{4}{3} = \mathbf{1\frac{1}{3}}$

19. $10^2 - \sqrt{25} = 100 - 5 = \mathbf{95}$

20. a. side **AD** (or **DA**)

 b. Area = (25 mm)(15 mm) = **375 mm²**

Cumulative Test 5B

1. $24\overline{)624}$ → **26 books**

2.
```
  1509
-  864
   645 years
```

3.
```
  $20.00
-  $7.30
  $12.70
```

4.
```
  223
- 137
   86 pages
```

5.

64 marbles

$\frac{3}{4}$ were not red.
| 16 marbles |
| 16 marbles |
| 16 marbles |

$\frac{1}{4}$ were red.
| 16 marbles |

a. 1×16 marbles = **16 marbles**

b. 3×16 marbles = **48 marbles**

c. $\frac{16}{64} = \mathbf{\frac{1}{4}}$

6.

7.

```
        490
       /   \
      7     70
           /  \
          7    10
              /  \
             2    5
```

$490 = \mathbf{2 \cdot 5 \cdot 7 \cdot 7}$

8. a. $\dfrac{66}{9} = 7\dfrac{3}{9} = \mathbf{7\dfrac{1}{3}}$

   b. $6\dfrac{6}{9} = \mathbf{6\dfrac{2}{3}}$

   c. $\dfrac{660}{900} \div \dfrac{60}{60} = \mathbf{\dfrac{11}{15}}$

9. D. ◯

10. a. $\dfrac{5}{8} \cdot \dfrac{3}{3} = \mathbf{\dfrac{15}{24}}$ **b.** $\dfrac{5}{12} \cdot \dfrac{2}{2} = \mathbf{\dfrac{10}{24}}$

11.
$$\begin{array}{r} 600 \\ -\ 250 \\ \hline \mathbf{350} \end{array}$$

12.
$$\begin{array}{r} 46 \\ +\ 25 \\ \hline \mathbf{71} \end{array}$$

13. $12\overline{)276}$ quotient $\mathbf{23}$

14. $6 - 1\dfrac{1}{6} = 5\dfrac{6}{6} - 1\dfrac{1}{6} = \mathbf{4\dfrac{5}{6}}$

15. $5\dfrac{4}{5} + 3\dfrac{4}{5} = 8\dfrac{8}{5} = \mathbf{9\dfrac{3}{5}}$

16. $3\dfrac{1}{8} - 1\dfrac{3}{8} = 2\dfrac{9}{8} - 1\dfrac{3}{8} = 1\dfrac{6}{8} = \mathbf{1\dfrac{3}{4}}$

17. $\dfrac{2}{\cancel{3}} \cdot \dfrac{\overset{1}{\cancel{3}}}{\cancel{6}} \cdot \dfrac{\overset{1}{\cancel{6}}}{7} = \mathbf{\dfrac{2}{7}}$

18. $\dfrac{2}{3} \div \dfrac{1}{4} = \dfrac{2}{3} \cdot \dfrac{4}{1} = \dfrac{8}{3} = \mathbf{2\dfrac{2}{3}}$

19. $10^2 - \sqrt{100} = 100 - 10 = \mathbf{90}$

20. a. **side BA (or AB)**

   b. Area = (20 mm)(15 mm) = **300 mm²**

Cumulative Test 6A

1. $\dfrac{70 \text{ in.} + 71 \text{ in.} + 72 \text{ in.} + 73 \text{ in.} + 84 \text{ in.}}{5}$

$= \dfrac{370 \text{ in.}}{5} = \mathbf{74 \text{ in.}}$

2.
$$\begin{array}{r} \$0.82 \\ \times\quad 8 \\ \hline \$6.56 \end{array} \qquad \begin{array}{r} \$10.00 \\ -\ \$6.56 \\ \hline \mathbf{\$3.44} \end{array}$$

3.
$$\begin{array}{r} 2598 \text{ miles} \\ -\ 683 \text{ miles} \\ \hline \mathbf{1915 \text{ miles}} \end{array}$$

4. a.

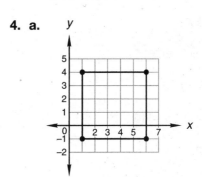

The fourth vertex is at **(1, 4)**.

   b. Area = (5 units)(5 units) = **25 units²**

5.

2170 miles	
$\frac{1}{5}$ (or 20%) completed	434 miles
$\frac{4}{5}$ (or 80%) left to drive	434 miles
	434 miles
	434 miles
	434 miles

   a. **434 mi**

   b. 4×434 mi = **1736 mi**

6. 3 ft = 3 × 12 in. = 36 in.
36 in. ÷ 4 = **9 in.**

7.
$$\begin{array}{r} \dfrac{2}{5} \cdot \dfrac{4}{4} = \dfrac{8}{20} \\ +\ \dfrac{3}{4} \cdot \dfrac{5}{5} = \dfrac{15}{20} \\ \hline \dfrac{23}{20} = \mathbf{1\dfrac{3}{20}} \end{array}$$

8. **To find the output, multiply the input by 4.**

9. $30{,}000 \div 30 = \mathbf{1000}$

Solutions

10. $\dfrac{120}{540} = \dfrac{\cancel{2} \cdot \cancel{2} \cdot 2 \cdot \cancel{3} \cdot \cancel{5}}{\cancel{2} \cdot \cancel{2} \cdot \cancel{3} \cdot 3 \cdot 3 \cdot \cancel{5}} = \dfrac{2}{9}$

11. $\dfrac{3}{5} \cdot \dfrac{3}{3} = \dfrac{9}{15}$

$\dfrac{5}{3} \cdot \dfrac{5}{5} = \dfrac{25}{15}$

$\dfrac{9}{15} < \dfrac{25}{15}$

$\dfrac{3}{5} < \dfrac{5}{3}$

12. Multiples of 8: 8, 16, 24, ...
Multiples of 12: 12, 24, 36, ...
The LCM of 8 and 12 is **24.**

13. a. $\overline{AB}$ (or $\overline{BA}$)

b. $\angle BCA$ (or $\angle ACB$)

14. a. $225 = 3 \cdot 3 \cdot 5 \cdot 5$

b. $\sqrt{225} = 3 \cdot 5 = 15$

15. $\dfrac{4 \cdot 21}{7} = 12$

16.
$$\begin{array}{r} 653 \\ - \ 417 \\ \hline \mathbf{236} \end{array}$$

17.
$$\begin{array}{r} 91 \\ - \ 42 \\ \hline \mathbf{49} \end{array}$$

18.
$$\begin{array}{r} \dfrac{1}{4} \cdot \dfrac{3}{3} = \dfrac{3}{12} \\ + \ \dfrac{1}{3} \cdot \dfrac{4}{4} = \dfrac{4}{12} \\ \hline \dfrac{7}{12} \end{array}$$

19. $\left(\dfrac{3}{4} \cdot \dfrac{1}{3} \right) - \dfrac{1}{6} = \dfrac{1}{4} - \dfrac{1}{6} = \dfrac{3}{12} - \dfrac{2}{12} = \dfrac{1}{12}$

20. $1\dfrac{3}{5} \div 2\dfrac{1}{2} = \dfrac{8}{5} \div \dfrac{5}{2} = \dfrac{8}{5} \cdot \dfrac{2}{5} = \dfrac{16}{25}$

Cumulative Test 6B

1. $\dfrac{71 \text{ in.} + 72 \text{ in.} + 73 \text{ in.} + 75 \text{ in.} + 84 \text{ in.}}{5}$

$= \dfrac{375 \text{ in.}}{5} = \mathbf{75 \text{ in.}}$

2.
$$\begin{array}{r} \$0.78 \\ \times \quad 7 \\ \hline \$5.46 \end{array} \qquad \begin{array}{r} \$10.00 \\ - \ \$5.46 \\ \hline \mathbf{\$4.54} \end{array}$$

3.
$$\begin{array}{r} 2058 \text{ miles} \\ - \quad 586 \text{ miles} \\ \hline \mathbf{1472 \text{ miles}} \end{array}$$

4. a.

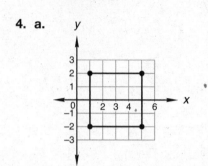

The fourth vertex is at **(1, 2).**

b. Area = (4 units)(4 units) = **16 units²**

5.
2030 miles

$\dfrac{1}{5}$ (or 20%) completed	406 miles
	406 miles
$\dfrac{4}{5}$ (or 80%) left to drive	406 miles
	406 miles
	406 miles

a. **406 mi**

b. $4 \times 406 \text{ mi} = \mathbf{1624 \text{ mi}}$

6. 5 ft = 5 × 12 in. = 60 in.
60 in. ÷ 4 = **15 in.**

7.
$$\begin{array}{r} \dfrac{3}{5} \cdot \dfrac{4}{4} = \dfrac{12}{20} \\ + \ \dfrac{3}{4} \cdot \dfrac{5}{5} = \dfrac{15}{20} \\ \hline \dfrac{27}{20} = 1\dfrac{7}{20} \end{array}$$

8. To find the output, multiply the input by 5.

9. $20{,}000 \div 20 = \mathbf{1000}$

10. $\dfrac{120}{270} = \dfrac{\cancel{2} \cdot 2 \cdot 2 \cdot \cancel{3} \cdot \cancel{5}}{\cancel{2} \cdot \cancel{3} \cdot 3 \cdot 3 \cdot \cancel{5}} = \dfrac{4}{9}$

11. $\dfrac{3}{4} \cdot \dfrac{3}{3} = \dfrac{9}{12}$

$\dfrac{4}{3} \cdot \dfrac{4}{4} = \dfrac{16}{12}$

$\dfrac{9}{12} < \dfrac{16}{12}$

$\dfrac{3}{4} < \dfrac{4}{3}$

12. Multiples of 10: 10, 20, 30, 40, 50, 60, ...
Multiples of 12: 12, 24, 36, 48, 60, ...
The LCM of 10 and 12 is **60.**

13. a. $\overline{PR}$ (or $\overline{RP}$)

    b. $\angle QMP$ (or $\angle PMQ$)

14. a. $441 = 3 \cdot 3 \cdot 7 \cdot 7$

    b. $\sqrt{441} = 3 \cdot 7 = \textbf{21}$

15. $\dfrac{5 \cdot 14}{7} = \textbf{10}$

16.
$$\begin{array}{r} 653 \\ - 516 \\ \hline \textbf{137} \end{array}$$

17.
$$\begin{array}{r} 81 \\ - 42 \\ \hline \textbf{39} \end{array}$$

18.
$$\begin{array}{r} \dfrac{3}{4} \cdot \dfrac{3}{3} = \dfrac{9}{12} \\ - \dfrac{1}{3} \cdot \dfrac{4}{4} = \dfrac{4}{12} \\ \hline \dfrac{\textbf{5}}{\textbf{12}} \end{array}$$

19. $\left(\dfrac{3}{4} \cdot \dfrac{2}{3}\right) - \dfrac{1}{6} = \dfrac{1}{2} - \dfrac{1}{6} = \dfrac{3}{6} - \dfrac{1}{6} = \dfrac{2}{6}$
$= \dfrac{\textbf{1}}{\textbf{3}}$

20. $2\dfrac{1}{2} \div 1\dfrac{3}{5} = \dfrac{5}{2} \div \dfrac{8}{5} = \dfrac{5}{2} \cdot \dfrac{5}{8} = \dfrac{25}{16}$
$= \textbf{1}\dfrac{\textbf{9}}{\textbf{16}}$

Cumulative Test   **7A**

1.
$$\begin{array}{r} \$120.46 \\ \$134.59 \\ \$118.38 \\ + \quad \$96.29 \\ \hline \$469.72 \end{array}$$

$$\begin{array}{r} \$117.43 \\ 4\overline{)\$469.72} \end{array}$$

2.
$$\begin{array}{r} \$4496 \\ + \$1893 \\ \hline \$2603 \end{array}$$

3. $\dfrac{\$15.60}{12} = \$1.30$
$\$1.95 - \$1.30 = \textbf{\$0.65}$

4.
$$\begin{array}{r} 65.2 \text{ sec} \\ - \; 62.7 \text{ sec} \\ \hline \textbf{2.5 sec} \end{array}$$

5. Perimeter of pentagon: 5×16 cm $= 80$ cm
Side of square: 80 cm $\div 4 = \textbf{20 cm}$

6.

63 fish

$\dfrac{4}{9}$ were guppies.
| 7 fish |
| 7 fish |
| 7 fish |
| 7 fish |

$\dfrac{5}{9}$ were not guppies.
| 7 fish |
| 7 fish |
| 7 fish |
| 7 fish |
| 7 fish |

    a. 4×7 fish $= \textbf{28 fish}$

    b. 5×7 fish $= \textbf{35 fish}$

7. 7, 14, 21, 28, 35, 42, 49, 56, 63, ...
9, 18, 27, 36, 45, 54, 63, ...
21, 42, 63, ...
The LCM of 7, 9, and 21 is **63.**

8. 3.14 rounds to 3.
5.125 rounds to 5.
$3 \times 5 = \textbf{15}$

9. a. $\dfrac{25}{100} = \dfrac{\textbf{1}}{\textbf{4}}$

    b. $\dfrac{25}{100} = \textbf{25\%}$

10. 14.5

11. a.

The fourth vertex is at **(−1, 2).**

    b. Area $= (5 \text{ units})(4 \text{ units}) = \textbf{20 units}^2$

Solutions

12. **0.34**

13. $\dfrac{9 \cdot 10}{18} = 5$

14. one hundred and one hundred thirteen thousandths

15.
$$\begin{array}{r} 1.5 \\ \times\ 1.5 \\ \hline 75 \\ 15 \\ \hline \mathbf{2.25} \end{array}$$

16.
$$\begin{array}{r} 1.25 \\ 5\overline{)6.25} \\ 5 \\ \hline 1\,2 \\ 1\,0 \\ \hline 25 \\ 25 \\ \hline 0 \end{array}$$

17.
$$\begin{array}{r} 4.3 \\ 1.79 \\ +\ 11. \\ \hline \mathbf{17.09} \end{array}$$

18.
$$\begin{array}{r} 42.610 \\ -\ 3.095 \\ \hline \mathbf{39.515} \end{array}$$

19. $1\dfrac{1}{5} - \left(\dfrac{1}{4} \cdot \dfrac{2}{5}\right) = 1\dfrac{1}{5} - \dfrac{1}{10} = 1\dfrac{2}{10} - \dfrac{1}{10}$

$= \mathbf{1\dfrac{1}{10}}$

20. $\left(2\dfrac{1}{4} + 1\dfrac{1}{3}\right) \div \left(2 - 1\dfrac{1}{6}\right)$

$= \left(2\dfrac{3}{12} + 1\dfrac{4}{12}\right) \div \left(1\dfrac{6}{6} - 1\dfrac{1}{6}\right) = 3\dfrac{7}{12} \div \dfrac{5}{6}$

$= \dfrac{43}{12} \cdot \dfrac{6}{5} = \dfrac{43}{10} = \mathbf{4\dfrac{3}{10}}$

Cumulative Test 7B

1.
$$\begin{array}{r} \$115.46 \\ \$129.59 \\ \$113.38 \\ +\ \$91.29 \\ \hline \$449.72 \end{array}$$

$$\begin{array}{r} \$112.43 \\ 4\overline{)\$449.72} \end{array}$$

2.
$$\begin{array}{r} \$1296 \\ -\ \$998 \\ \hline \mathbf{\$298} \end{array}$$

3. $\dfrac{\$14.88}{12} = \mathbf{\$1.24}$

$\$1.95 - \$1.24 = \mathbf{\$0.71}$

4.
$$\begin{array}{r} 64.4 \text{ sec} \\ -\ 62.8 \text{ sec} \\ \hline \mathbf{1.6 \text{ sec}} \end{array}$$

5. Perimeter of square: 4×15 cm $= 60$ cm
Side of regular pentagon: 60 cm $\div$ 5 = **12 cm**

6.

63 fish

9 fish
9 fish
9 fish
9 fish
9 fish
9 fish
9 fish

$\dfrac{4}{7}$ were guppies.

$\dfrac{3}{7}$ were not guppies.

a. 4×9 fish = **36 fish**

b. 3×9 fish = **27 fish**

7. 10, 20, 30, 40, 50, 60, ...
12, 24, 36, 48, 60, ...
15, 30, 45, 60, ...
The LCM of 10, 12, and 15 is **60**.

8. 3.14 rounds to 3
6.25 rounds to 6
$3 \times 6 = \mathbf{18}$

9. a. $\dfrac{75}{100} = \dfrac{3}{4}$

b. $\dfrac{75}{100} = \mathbf{75\%}$

10. **16.5**

11. a.

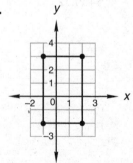

The fourth vertex is at **(−1, −2)**.

b. Area = (5 units)(3 units) = **15 units^2**

12. **0.57**

13. $\dfrac{8 \cdot 10}{16} = 5$

14. **one hundred and thirteen hundredths**

15.
$$\begin{array}{r} 1.2 \\ \times\ 1.2 \\ \hline 24 \\ 12 \\ \hline \mathbf{1.44} \end{array}$$

16.
$$\begin{array}{r} \mathbf{0.75} \\ 5\overline{)3.75} \\ \underline{3\ 5} \\ 25 \\ \underline{25} \\ 0 \end{array}$$

17.
$$\begin{array}{r} 3.4 \\ 1.78 \\ +\ 12. \\ \hline \mathbf{17.18} \end{array}$$

18.
$$\begin{array}{r} 21.620 \\ -\ 3.083 \\ \hline \mathbf{18.537} \end{array}$$

19. $1\dfrac{2}{5} - \left(\dfrac{3}{4} \cdot \dfrac{1}{5}\right) = 1\dfrac{2}{5} - \dfrac{3}{20} = 1\dfrac{8}{20} - \dfrac{3}{20}$

$= 1\dfrac{5}{20} = \mathbf{1\dfrac{1}{4}}$

20. $\left(2\dfrac{1}{4} - 1\dfrac{1}{3}\right) \div \left(2 + 1\dfrac{1}{16}\right)$

$= \left(2\dfrac{3}{12} - 1\dfrac{4}{12}\right) \div 3\dfrac{1}{6} = \left(1\dfrac{15}{12} - 1\dfrac{4}{12}\right) \div \dfrac{19}{6}$

$= \dfrac{11}{12} \cdot \dfrac{6}{19} = \mathbf{\dfrac{11}{38}}$

Cumulative Test 8A

1.
$$\begin{array}{r} 5\ \text{red} \\ +\ 4\ \text{white} \\ \hline 9\ \text{total} \end{array} \qquad \dfrac{\text{white}}{\text{total}} = \dfrac{\mathbf{4}}{\mathbf{9}}$$

2. a. 5 minutes 40 seconds = **340 seconds**

b. 340 seconds ÷ 4 = **85 seconds**

3. $21\dfrac{\text{miles}}{\text{gallon}} \times 21\ \cancel{\text{gallons}} = \mathbf{441\ miles}$

4.

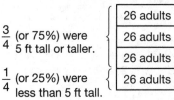

104 adults

$\dfrac{3}{4}$ (or 75%) were 5 ft tall or taller.

$\dfrac{1}{4}$ (or 25%) were less than 5 ft tall.

26 adults
26 adults
26 adults
26 adults

a. 26 adults

b. 3 × 26 adults = **78 adults**

5. Perimeter = 0.6 m + 0.3 m + 0.6 m + 0.3 m
$= \mathbf{1.8\ m}$

6. Area = 0.6 m × 0.3 m = **0.18 m²**

7. $AB + BC + CD = AD$
35 mm + BC = 45 mm = 110 mm
BC = **30 mm**

8. 45 mm = **4.5 cm**

9.

$$H \begin{cases} 1 \\ 2 \\ 3 \end{cases}$$
$$T \begin{cases} 1 \\ 2 \\ 3 \end{cases}$$

Sample space = {H_1, H_2, H_3, T_1, T_2, T_3}

10. $50° + 50° + a = 180°$
The third angle measures **80°**.

11. 0.83

12. a. 65.03   **b.** $65\dfrac{3}{100}$

13. Area $= \dfrac{(12\ \text{cm})(5\ \text{cm})}{2} = \mathbf{30\ cm^2}$

14.
$$\begin{array}{r} 0.12 \\ \times\ 0.06 \\ \hline \mathbf{0.0072} \end{array}$$

15.
$$\begin{array}{r} \mathbf{0.024} \\ 6\overline{)0.144} \\ \underline{12} \\ 24 \\ \underline{24} \\ 0 \end{array}$$

16. $5\dfrac{1}{3} - 3\dfrac{5}{6} = 5\dfrac{2}{6} - 3\dfrac{5}{6} = 4\dfrac{8}{6} - 3\dfrac{5}{6} = 1\dfrac{3}{6}$

$= \mathbf{1\dfrac{1}{2}}$

Solutions

17. $8\frac{1}{4} - 1\frac{7}{11} = \frac{\overset{3}{\cancel{33}}}{\underset{2}{\cancel{4}}} \cdot \frac{\overset{9}{\cancel{18}}}{\underset{1}{\cancel{11}}} = \frac{27}{2} = 13\frac{1}{2}$

18. $5\frac{4}{9} \div 7 = \frac{\overset{7}{\cancel{49}}}{9} \cdot \frac{1}{\underset{1}{\cancel{7}}} = \frac{7}{9}$

19. $\frac{8}{10} = \frac{w}{15}$

$10w = 8 \cdot 15$

$w = \frac{120}{10}$

$w = \mathbf{12}$

20.
$$\begin{array}{r} 1.54 \\ -\ 0.72 \\ \hline \mathbf{0.82} \end{array}$$

Cumulative Test 8B

1.
$$\begin{array}{r} 5 \text{ red} \\ +\ 3 \text{ blue} \\ \hline 8 \text{ total} \end{array} \qquad \frac{\text{blue}}{\text{total}} = \frac{3}{8}$$

2. a. 6 minutes 20 seconds = **380 seconds**

    b. 380 seconds ÷ 4 = **95 seconds**

3. $24\frac{\text{miles}}{\text{gallon}} \times 18 \text{ gallons} = \mathbf{432\ miles}$

4.

105 adults

| 21 adults |
| 21 adults |
| 21 adults |
| 21 adults |
| 21 adults |

$\frac{4}{5}$ (or 80%) were 5 ft tall or taller.

$\frac{1}{5}$ (or 20%) were less than 5 ft tall.

    a. 21 adults

    b. 4 × 21 adults = **84 adults**

5. Perimeter = 0.8 m + 0.4 m + 0.8 m + 0.4 m
$$= \mathbf{2.4\ m}$$

6. Area = 0.8 m × 0.4 m = **0.32 m²**

7.
$$AB + BC + CD = AD$$
$$25 \text{ mm} + BC = 45 \text{ mm} = 110 \text{ mm}$$
$$BC = \mathbf{40\ mm}$$

8. 25 mm = **2.5 cm**

9.

$$H \begin{cases} 1 \\ 2 \\ 3 \\ 4 \end{cases}$$

Sample space =
{H₁, H₂, H₃, H₄
T₁, T₂, T₃, T₄}

$$T \begin{cases} 1 \\ 2 \\ 3 \\ 4 \end{cases}$$

10. $70° + 70° + a = 180°$
The third angle measures **40°**.

11. 0.57

12. a. 34.07   **b.** $34\frac{7}{100}$

13. Area $= \frac{(12 \text{ cm})(9 \text{ cm})}{2} = \mathbf{54\ cm^2}$

14.
$$\begin{array}{r} 0.15 \\ \times\ 0.05 \\ \hline \mathbf{0.0075} \end{array}$$

15.
$$\begin{array}{r} 0.018 \\ 8\overline{)0.144} \\ \underline{8} \\ 64 \\ \underline{64} \\ 0 \end{array}$$

16. $5\frac{2}{3} - 2\frac{5}{6} = 5\frac{4}{6} - 2\frac{5}{6} = 4\frac{10}{6} - 2\frac{5}{6} = \mathbf{2\frac{5}{6}}$

17. $6\frac{1}{4} \cdot 1\frac{3}{5} = \frac{\overset{5}{\cancel{25}}}{\underset{1}{\cancel{4}}} \cdot \frac{\overset{2}{\cancel{8}}}{\underset{1}{\cancel{5}}} = \mathbf{10}$

18. $7 \div 5\frac{4}{9} = \frac{7}{1} \div \frac{49}{9} = \frac{7}{1} \cdot \frac{9}{\underset{7}{\cancel{49}}} = \frac{9}{7} = \mathbf{1\frac{2}{7}}$

19. $\frac{6}{10} = \frac{w}{15}$

$10w = 6 \cdot 15$

$w = \frac{90}{10}$

$w = \mathbf{9}$

20.
$$\begin{array}{r} 1.54 \\ -\ 0.27 \\ \hline \mathbf{1.27} \end{array}$$

Cumulative Test 9A

1. Primes: 2, 3, 5   Probability: $\frac{3}{6} = \frac{1}{2}$

2. a. $(80 + 87 + 88 + 89 + 90 + 90 + 91 + 95 + 100 + 100) \div 10 = \mathbf{91}$

b. $\dfrac{90 + 90}{2} = \mathbf{90}$

3. $a(b + c) = 0.4(2.1 + 0.4) = 0.4(2.5) = \mathbf{1}$

4. a. $18 - 16 = \mathbf{2\ votes}$

b. $\dfrac{22}{70} = \dfrac{\mathbf{11}}{\mathbf{35}}$

5.

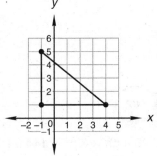

$\text{Area} = \dfrac{5 \cdot 4}{2} = \mathbf{10\ units^2}$

6. a. $\dfrac{5}{8}$ **were vertiginous.**

b. $\dfrac{\text{euphoric}}{\text{vertiginous}} = \dfrac{\mathbf{3}}{\mathbf{5}}$

7. $l + 12\ \text{cm} = \text{half of the perimeter} = 34\ \text{cm}$
$l = 34\ \text{cm} - 12\ \text{cm} = \mathbf{22\ cm}$

8. $m\angle a = 180° - (90° + 55°) = \mathbf{35°}$
$m\angle b = 180° - m\angle a = 180° - 35° = \mathbf{145°}$
$m\angle c = m\angle a = \mathbf{35°}$

9. 2.25

10. $5)\overline{9.0}$ $\mathbf{1.8}$

11. $52.\overline{23} = 52.23\,\textcircled{2}\,3\ldots$
52.232

12. $9)\overline{4.300\ldots}$ $0.477\ldots \doteq \mathbf{0.4\overline{7}}$
$\dfrac{36}{70}$
$\dfrac{63}{70}$
$\dfrac{63}{7}$

13. $\dfrac{12}{8} = \dfrac{0.3}{m}$
$12m = (0.3)(8)$
$m = \dfrac{(0.3)(8)}{12} = \mathbf{0.2}$

14.
$\begin{array}{r} 7.00 \\ -\ 3.14 \\ \hline \mathbf{3.86} \end{array}$

15.
$\begin{array}{r} 1.000 \\ -\ 0.091 \\ \hline \mathbf{0.909} \end{array}$

16. $5\dfrac{3}{5} + \dfrac{3}{4} + 2\dfrac{1}{2} = 5\dfrac{12}{20} + \dfrac{15}{20} + 2\dfrac{10}{20}$
$= 7\dfrac{37}{20} = 8\dfrac{\mathbf{17}}{\mathbf{20}}$

17. $3\dfrac{1}{4} - \left(3 - 1\dfrac{5}{6}\right) = 3\dfrac{1}{4} - \left(2\dfrac{6}{6} - 1\dfrac{5}{6}\right)$
$= 3\dfrac{1}{4} - 1\dfrac{1}{6} = 3\dfrac{3}{12} - 1\dfrac{2}{12} = 2\dfrac{\mathbf{1}}{\mathbf{12}}$

18. $3\dfrac{3}{4} \cdot 3\dfrac{1}{5} \cdot 6 = \dfrac{\overset{3}{\cancel{15}}}{\underset{1}{\cancel{4}}} \cdot \dfrac{\overset{4}{\cancel{16}}}{\underset{1}{\cancel{5}}} \cdot \dfrac{6}{1} = \mathbf{72}$

19. $4 \div 10\dfrac{2}{3} = \dfrac{4}{1} \div \dfrac{32}{3} = \dfrac{\overset{1}{\cancel{4}}}{1} \cdot \dfrac{3}{\underset{8}{\cancel{32}}} = \dfrac{\mathbf{3}}{\mathbf{8}}$

20. $06.)\overline{14.4}$ $\mathbf{2.4}$
$\dfrac{12}{2\ 4}$
$\dfrac{2\ 4}{0}$

Cumulative Test 9B

1. Composite numbers: 4,6   Probability: $\dfrac{2}{6} = \dfrac{\mathbf{1}}{\mathbf{3}}$

2. a. $(80 + 84 + 87 + 88 + 88 + 90 + 90$
$+\ 95 + 98 + 100) \div 10 = \mathbf{90}$

b. $\dfrac{88 + 90}{2} = \mathbf{89}$

3. $a(b + c) = 0.2(1.5 + 1) = 0.2(2.5) = \mathbf{0.5}$

4. a. $22 - 16 = \mathbf{6\ votes}$

b. $\dfrac{14}{70} = \dfrac{\mathbf{1}}{\mathbf{5}}$

5.

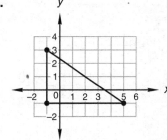

Area $= \dfrac{4 \cdot 6}{2} =$ **12 units²**

6. a. $\dfrac{5}{9}$ were vertiginous.

b. $\dfrac{\text{euphoric}}{\text{vertiginous}} = \dfrac{4}{5}$

7. $l + 12$ cm $=$ half of the perimeter $= 30$ cm
$l = 30$ cm $- 12$ cm $=$ **18 cm**

8. $m\angle a = 180° - (90° + 40°) =$ **50°**
$m\angle b = 180° - m\angle a = 180° - 50° =$ **130°**
$m\angle c = m\angle a =$ **50°**

9. **1.25**

10. $5\overline{)8.0}$ → **1.6**

11. $15.\overline{54} = 15.54\boxed{5}4 \ldots$
15.545

12. $9\overline{)3.400\ldots}$ → $0.377\ldots = \mathbf{0.3\overline{7}}$
$\dfrac{27}{70}$
$\dfrac{63}{70}$
$\dfrac{63}{7}$

13. $\dfrac{12}{9} = \dfrac{0.8}{m}$
$12m = (0.8)(9)$
$m = \dfrac{(0.8)(9)}{12} = \mathbf{0.6}$

14. $\begin{array}{r} 6.00 \\ -\ 3.14 \\ \hline \mathbf{2.86} \end{array}$

15. $\begin{array}{r} 1.00 \\ -\ .0.91 \\ \hline \mathbf{0.09} \end{array}$

16. $5\dfrac{2}{5} + \dfrac{3}{4} + 3\dfrac{1}{2} = 5\dfrac{8}{20} + \dfrac{15}{20} + 3\dfrac{10}{20}$
$= 8\dfrac{33}{20} = \mathbf{9\dfrac{13}{20}}$

17. $5\dfrac{1}{4} - \left(3 - 1\dfrac{1}{6}\right) = 5\dfrac{1}{4} - \left(2\dfrac{6}{6} - 1\dfrac{1}{6}\right)$
$= 5\dfrac{1}{4} - 1\dfrac{5}{6} = 5\dfrac{3}{12} - 1\dfrac{10}{12} = 4\dfrac{15}{12} - 1\dfrac{10}{12}$
$= \mathbf{3\dfrac{5}{12}}$

18. $3\dfrac{3}{4} \cdot 3\dfrac{3}{5} \cdot 6 = \dfrac{\overset{3}{\cancel{15}}}{\underset{\underset{1}{2}}{\cancel{4}}} \cdot \dfrac{\overset{9}{\cancel{18}}}{\underset{1}{\cancel{5}}} \cdot \dfrac{\overset{3}{\cancel{6}}}{1} = \mathbf{81}$

19. $10\dfrac{2}{3} \div 4 = \dfrac{32}{3} \div \dfrac{4}{1} = \dfrac{\overset{8}{\cancel{32}}}{3} \cdot \dfrac{1}{\underset{1}{\cancel{4}}} = \dfrac{8}{3} = \mathbf{2\dfrac{2}{3}}$

20. $0.8\overline{)14.4}$ → **1.8**
$\dfrac{8}{6\ 4}$
$\dfrac{6\ 4}{0}$

Cumulative Test 10A

1. $d = rt \qquad d = 48$ mph $\times$ 3 hr $=$ **144 mi**

2. $12\overline{)\$1.56}$ → $\$0.13$
$\begin{array}{r} \$0.13 \\ +\ \$0.02 \\ \hline \$0.15 \end{array}$
$\begin{array}{r} \$0.15 \\ \times \qquad 15 \\ \hline \$2.25 \end{array}$

3. **5 to 12** or $\dfrac{\mathbf{5}}{\mathbf{12}}$

4. $\begin{array}{r} \$109.60 \\ \$114.56 \\ \$85.90 \\ +\ \$122.14 \\ \hline \$432.20 \end{array}$ $\dfrac{\$432.20}{4} = \$108.05 = \mathbf{\$108.00}$

5. $\dfrac{4}{8} = \dfrac{1}{2} = \mathbf{0.5}$

6.

70 buttons

$\dfrac{2}{5}$ (40%) had 5 holes. $\left\{\begin{array}{|c|} \hline \text{14 buttons} \\ \hline \text{14 buttons} \\ \hline \end{array}\right.$

$\dfrac{3}{5}$ (60%) did not have 5 holes. $\left\{\begin{array}{|c|} \hline \text{14 buttons} \\ \hline \text{14 buttons} \\ \hline \text{14 buttons} \\ \hline \end{array}\right.$

a. $\dfrac{\mathbf{3}}{\mathbf{5}}$

b. 3×14 buttons $=$ **42 buttons**

7. Area $= (8 \text{ cm} \cdot 8 \text{ cm}) + \left(\dfrac{6 \text{ cm} \cdot 8 \text{ cm}}{2}\right)$
$= 64 \text{ cm}^2 + 24 \text{ cm}^2 = \mathbf{88 \text{ cm}^2}$

8. $24\% = \dfrac{24}{100} = \dfrac{\mathbf{6}}{\mathbf{25}}$

Saxon Math Course 2

422

9.
$$0.43636... = \mathbf{0.4\overline{36}}$$
$$11\overline{)4.80000...}$$
$$\underline{4\,4}$$
$$40$$
$$\underline{33}$$
$$70$$
$$\underline{66}$$
$$40$$
$$\underline{33}$$
$$70$$
$$\underline{40}$$
$$4$$

10. $\dfrac{490}{560} = \dfrac{2 \cdot \cancel{5} \cdot 7 \cdot 7}{2 \cdot 2 \cdot 2 \cdot 2 \cdot \cancel{5} \cdot 7} = \mathbf{\dfrac{7}{8}}$

11. Length of side = 32 in. ÷ 4 = 8 in.
    Area = 8 in. × 8 in. = **64 in.²**

12. $\dfrac{49}{56} = \dfrac{21}{f}$
$$49f = 21 \cdot 56$$
$$f = \dfrac{\overset{3}{\cancel{21}} \cdot \overset{8}{\cancel{56}}}{\underset{\underset{1}{\cancel{7}}}{\cancel{49}}} = \mathbf{24}$$

13. $\begin{array}{r} \mathbf{2.8} \\ 3\overline{)8.4} \end{array}$

14. $\begin{array}{r} 5.00 \\ -\ 1.36 \\ \hline \mathbf{3.64} \end{array}$

15. $8^2 - 3^3 = 64 - 27 = \mathbf{37}$

16.
$$\begin{array}{r} 1\,\text{yd} \quad 1\,\text{ft} \phantom{7\,\text{in.}} \\ 1\ \text{yd} \quad 2\ \text{ft} \quad 7\ \text{in.} \\ +\ 2\ \text{yd} \quad 1\ \text{ft} \quad 8\ \text{in.} \\ \hline \mathbf{4\ \text{yd}} \quad \mathbf{1\ \text{ft}} \quad \mathbf{3\ \text{in.}} \end{array}$$

17. $14\dfrac{11}{12} - 8\dfrac{3}{8} = 14\dfrac{22}{24} - 8\dfrac{9}{24} = \mathbf{6\dfrac{13}{24}}$

18. $5\dfrac{3}{7} \div 3\dfrac{4}{5} = \dfrac{38}{7} \div \dfrac{19}{5} = \dfrac{\overset{2}{\cancel{38}}}{7} \cdot \dfrac{5}{\underset{1}{\cancel{19}}} = \dfrac{10}{7} = \mathbf{1\dfrac{3}{7}}$

19. $0.245 \times 10^3 = \mathbf{245}$

20.
$$\begin{array}{r} \mathbf{1.255} \\ 008.\overline{)010.040} \end{array}$$
$$\underline{8}$$
$$2\,0$$
$$\underline{1\,6}$$
$$44$$
$$\underline{40}$$
$$40$$
$$\underline{40}$$
$$0$$

---

1. $d = rt \qquad d = 54\ \text{mph} \times 3\ \text{hr} = \mathbf{162\ mi}$

2. $\begin{array}{r} \$0.15 \\ 11\overline{)\$1.65} \end{array}$

$\begin{array}{r} \$0.15 \\ +\ \$0.02 \\ \hline \$0.17 \end{array}$ $\qquad$ $\begin{array}{r} \$0.17 \\ \times15 \\ \hline \mathbf{\$2.55} \end{array}$

3. **2 to 5** or $\mathbf{\dfrac{2}{5}}$

4. $\begin{array}{r} \$107.60 \\ \$112.56 \\ \$83.90 \\ +\ \$120.14 \\ \hline \$424.20 \end{array}$ $\qquad \dfrac{\$424.20}{4} = \$106.05 \approx \mathbf{\$106.00}$

5. $\dfrac{4}{8} = \dfrac{1}{2} = \mathbf{0.5}$

6.

70 buttons

$\dfrac{3}{10}$ (30%) had 4 holes.
7 buttons
7 buttons
7 buttons

$\dfrac{7}{10}$ (70%) did not have 4 holes.
7 buttons
7 buttons
7 buttons
7 buttons
7 buttons
7 buttons
7 buttons

a. $\mathbf{\dfrac{7}{10}}$

b. 7×7 buttons = **49 buttons**

7. Area = $(6\ \text{cm} \cdot 8\ \text{cm}) + \left(\dfrac{6\ \text{cm} \cdot 8\ \text{cm}}{2}\right)$
$$= 48\ \text{cm}^2 + 24\ \text{cm}^2 = \mathbf{72\ cm^2}$$

8. $28\% = \dfrac{28}{100} = \mathbf{\dfrac{7}{25}}$

9.
$$0.44545... = \mathbf{0.4\overline{45}}$$
$$11\overline{)4.90000...}$$
$$\underline{4\,4}$$
$$50$$
$$\underline{44}$$
$$60$$
$$\underline{55}$$
$$50$$
$$\underline{44}$$
$$60$$
$$\underline{55}$$
$$5$$

Solutions

10. $\dfrac{560}{720} = \dfrac{\cancel{2} \cdot \cancel{2} \cdot \cancel{2} \cdot \cancel{2} \cdot \cancel{5} \cdot 7}{\cancel{2} \cdot \cancel{2} \cdot \cancel{2} \cdot \cancel{2} \cdot 3 \cdot 3 \cdot \cancel{5}} = \dfrac{7}{9}$

11. Length of side = 28 in. ÷ 4 = 7 in.
Area = 7 in. × 7 in. = **49 in.²**

12. $\dfrac{35}{55} = \dfrac{21}{f}$
$35f = 55 \cdot 21$
$f = \dfrac{\overset{11}{\cancel{55}} \cdot \overset{3}{\cancel{21}}}{\underset{\underset{1}{7}}{\cancel{35}}} = \mathbf{33}$

13. $3\overline{)8.7}$ → **2.9**

14.
```
   5.00
 − 1.42
   3.58
```

15. $8^2 - 4^3 = 64 - 64 = \mathbf{0}$

16.
```
       1 yd   1 ft
     2 yd  1 ft  9 in.
   + 1 yd  2 ft  7 in.
   ────────────────────
     4 yd  1 ft  4 in.
```

17. $12\dfrac{5}{8} - 8\dfrac{7}{12} = 12\dfrac{15}{24} - 8\dfrac{14}{24} = \mathbf{4\dfrac{1}{24}}$

18. $5\dfrac{1}{5} \div 2\dfrac{1}{6} = \dfrac{26}{5} \div \dfrac{13}{6} = \dfrac{\overset{2}{\cancel{26}}}{5} \cdot \dfrac{6}{\underset{1}{\cancel{13}}} = \dfrac{12}{5}$
$= \mathbf{2\dfrac{2}{5}}$

19. $0.425 \times 10^3 = \mathbf{425}$

20.
```
           12.6
  008.)100.8
        8
       ──
       20
       16
       ──
        4 8
        4 8
        ───
          0
```

Cumulative Test 11A

1. $\dfrac{7}{5} = \dfrac{63}{k}$
$7k = 5 \cdot 63$
$k = \dfrac{5 \cdot \overset{9}{\cancel{63}}}{\underset{1}{\cancel{7}}} = \mathbf{45\ skiffs}$

2.
```
    98
  × 4
  ───
  392
```
$86 + 87 + 91 + f = 392$
The fourth number is **128.**

3. $12\overline{)\$7.68}$ → $0.64

```
  73¢ per quart
− 64¢ per quart
  9¢ per quart
```

4. $1\dfrac{1}{4}$ in. $- \dfrac{3}{4}$ in. $= \mathbf{\dfrac{1}{2}}$ **in.**

5. a. $40 \div 10 = 4$
3×4 trucks = **12 trucks**

b. $\dfrac{3}{10} \times 100\% = \mathbf{30\%}$

6. a. $40{,}000{,}000{,}000 = \mathbf{4 \times 10^{10}}$

b. $1.86 \times 10^7 = \mathbf{18{,}600{,}000}$

7. $1.42 + 0.5 = 1.92$
$5 - 3.09 = 1.91$
$1.92 > 1.91$

8. $800\ \cancel{mm} \cdot \dfrac{1\ cm}{10\ \cancel{mm}} = \mathbf{80\ cm}$

9. a. $250\% = \dfrac{250}{100} = \mathbf{2\dfrac{1}{2}}$

b. $250\% = \dfrac{250}{100} = \mathbf{2.5}$

c. $10\overline{)9.0}$ → **0.9**

d. $\dfrac{9}{10} = \dfrac{90}{100} = \mathbf{90\%}$

10. $ab - bc = (4)(3) - (3)(2) = 12 - 6 = \mathbf{6}$

11.

Area = (5 in. × 4 in.) + (12 in. × 4 in.)
= 20 in.² + 48 in.²
= **68 in.²**

12. Perimeter = 5 in. + 4 in. + 7 in. + 4 in.
+ 12 in. + 8 in. = **40 in.**

13.
```
   10.00
 − 5.64
   4.36
```

14. $\dfrac{a}{8} = \dfrac{45}{10}$

$10a = 8 \cdot 45$

$a = \dfrac{\overset{4}{8} \cdot \overset{9}{45}}{\underset{\underset{1}{5}}{10}} = \textbf{36}$

15. $13^2 - 2^5 - 3^3 - \sqrt{169} = 169 - 32 - 27$
$- 13 = \textbf{97}$

16. $4 + 4 \cdot 4 - 4 \div 4 = 4 + 16 - 1 = \textbf{19}$

17. $2\dfrac{1}{4} + 2\dfrac{5}{6} + 3\dfrac{5}{8} = 2\dfrac{6}{24} + 2\dfrac{20}{24} + 3\dfrac{15}{24}$

$= 7\dfrac{41}{24} = \mathbf{8\dfrac{17}{24}}$

18. $6\dfrac{2}{3} \cdot 5\dfrac{1}{4} \cdot 2\dfrac{1}{10} = \dfrac{\overset{5}{20}}{\underset{1}{3}} \cdot \dfrac{\overset{7}{21}}{\underset{1}{4}} \cdot \dfrac{21}{\underset{2}{10}} = \dfrac{147}{2}$

$= \mathbf{73\dfrac{1}{2}}$

19. $0.4(0.25)(0.01) = (0.1)(0.01) = \textbf{0.001}$

20.
$$
\begin{array}{r}
300 \\
0016.\overline{)4800.} \\
48 \\
\overline{00} \\
0 \\
\overline{00} \\
0 \\
\overline{0}
\end{array}
$$

Cumulative Test (**11B**)

1. $\dfrac{5}{7} = \dfrac{70}{d}$

$5d = 7 \cdot 70$

$d = \dfrac{7 \cdot \overset{14}{70}}{\underset{1}{5}} = \textbf{98 dinghies}$

2.
$$
\begin{array}{r}
97 \\
\times 4 \\
\hline
388
\end{array}
$$
$87 + 91 + 99 + f = 388$
The fourth number is **111.**

3.
$$
\begin{array}{r}
\$0.63 \\
12\overline{)\$7.56}
\end{array}
$$
$\begin{array}{r} 68¢ \text{ per liter} \\ - 63¢ \text{ per liter} \\ \hline 5¢ \text{ per liter} \end{array}$

4. $2\dfrac{1}{4}$ in. $- 1\dfrac{1}{4}$ in. $= \textbf{1 in.}$

5. a. $40 \div 5 = 8$

2×8 trucks $= \textbf{16 trucks}$

b. $\dfrac{2}{5} \times 100\% = \textbf{40\%}$

6. a. $14{,}000{,}000{,}000 = \mathbf{1.4 \times 10^{10}}$

b. $1.5 \times 10^6 = \textbf{1,500,000}$

7. $3 - 1.08 = 1.92$
$1.32 + 0.5 = 1.82$
$1.92 > 1.82$

8. $600 \text{ mm} \cdot \dfrac{1 \text{ cm}}{10 \text{ mm}} = \textbf{60 cm}$

9. a. $350\% = \dfrac{350}{100} = \mathbf{3\dfrac{1}{2}}$

b. $350\% = \dfrac{350}{100} = \textbf{3.5}$

c. $\begin{array}{r} 0.7 \\ 10\overline{)7.0} \end{array}$

d. $\dfrac{7}{10} = \dfrac{70}{100} = \textbf{70\%}$

10. $ab - bc = (5)(4) - (4)(2) = 20 - 8 = \textbf{12}$

11.

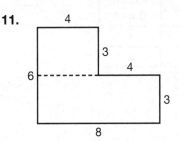

Area $= (4 \text{ cm} \cdot 3 \text{ cm}) + (8 \text{ cm} \cdot 3 \text{ cm})$
$= 12 \text{ cm}^2 + 24 \text{ cm}^2$
$= \textbf{36 cm}^2$

12. Perimeter $= 4 \text{ cm} + 3 \text{ cm} + 4 \text{ cm} + 3 \text{ cm}$
$+ 8 \text{ cm} + 6 \text{ cm} = \textbf{28 cm}$

13.
$$
\begin{array}{r}
10.00 \\
- 6.54 \\
\hline
3.46
\end{array}
$$

14. $\dfrac{9}{a} = \dfrac{45}{10}$

$45a = 9 \cdot 10$

$a = \dfrac{\overset{1}{9} \cdot \overset{2}{10}}{\underset{\underset{1}{5}}{45}} = \textbf{2}$

15. $12^2 - 3^4 - 2^3 - \sqrt{144} = 144 - 81 - 8$
$- 12 = \textbf{43}$

16. $3 + 3 \cdot 3 - 3 \div 3 = 3 + 9 - 1 = \textbf{11}$

17. $2\dfrac{3}{4} + 2\dfrac{1}{6} + 3\dfrac{7}{8} = 2\dfrac{18}{24} + 2\dfrac{4}{24} + 3\dfrac{21}{24}$

$= 7\dfrac{43}{24} = \mathbf{8\dfrac{19}{24}}$

Solutions

18. $5\frac{1}{3} \cdot 5\frac{1}{4} \cdot 1\frac{3}{4} = \frac{\overset{4}{\cancel{16}}}{\underset{1}{\cancel{3}}} \cdot \frac{\overset{7}{\cancel{21}}}{\underset{1}{\cancel{4}}} \cdot \frac{7}{\underset{1}{\cancel{4}}} = \mathbf{49}$

19. $0.8(0.25)(0.05) = (0.2)(0.05) = \mathbf{0.01}$

20.
$$
\begin{array}{r}
300 \\
00\underline{15,}\overline{)4500,} \\
45 \\
\hline
00 \\
0 \\
\hline
00 \\
0 \\
\hline
0
\end{array}
$$

Cumulative Test 12A

1. A half gallon is 4 pints.
$\$1.24 \div 4 = \mathbf{\$0.31}$ **per pint**

2.

	Ratio	Actual Count
Oatmeal	3	4
Raisins	1	c

$\frac{3}{1} = \frac{4}{c}$
$3c = 4$
$c = \frac{4}{3} = \mathbf{1\frac{1}{3}}$ **cups**

3.
$$
\begin{array}{r}
54.0 \text{ s} \\
\times 3 \\
\hline
162.0 \text{ s}
\end{array}
$$
$52.3 \text{ s} + 56.3 \text{ s} + t = 162.0 \text{ s}$
$t = \mathbf{53.4 \text{ s}}$

4. $y = 2x + 1$

x	y
0	1
1	3
2	5
3	7

5. Tax:
$$
\begin{array}{r}
\$12.50 \\
\times 0.06 \\
\hline
\$0.7500 = \$0.75
\end{array}
$$
Total:
$$
\begin{array}{r}
\$12.50 \\
+ \$ 0.75 \\
\hline
\mathbf{\$13.25}
\end{array}
$$

6. a. $\frac{6}{10} \times 100\% = \mathbf{60\%}$

b. $\dfrac{\text{news area}}{\text{advertisement area}} = \frac{4}{6} = \mathbf{\frac{2}{3}}$

---

7. a. $0.00205 = \mathbf{2.05 \times 10^{-3}}$

b. $5.62 \times 10^{-5} = \mathbf{0.0000562}$

8. 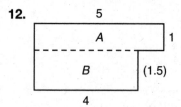 (sketches will vary)

trapezoid

9. $1760 \text{ y\!d} \cdot \frac{3 \text{ ft}}{1 \text{ y\!d}} = \mathbf{5280 \text{ ft}}$

10. a. $12\% = \frac{12}{100} = \mathbf{\frac{3}{25}}$

b. $12\% = \frac{12}{100} = \mathbf{0.12}$

c.
$$
\begin{array}{r}
0.04 \\
25\overline{)1.00}
\end{array}
$$

d. $\frac{1}{25} = \frac{4}{100} = \mathbf{4\%}$

11. Perimeter $= 5 \text{ cm} + 2.5 \text{ cm} + 4 \text{ cm} + 1.5 \text{ cm}$
$\phantom{\text{Perimeter} = } + 1 \text{ cm} + 1 \text{ cm}$
$\phantom{\text{Perimeter}} = \mathbf{15 \text{ cm}}$

12.

Area $=$ area A + area B
$\phantom{\text{Area}} = (5 \text{ cm} \cdot 1 \text{ cm}) + (4 \text{ cm} \cdot 1.5 \text{ cm})$
$\phantom{\text{Area}} = 5 \text{ cm}^2 + 6 \text{ cm}^2 = \mathbf{11 \text{ cm}^2}$

13. $\frac{4}{18} = \frac{n}{27}$
$18n = 4 \cdot 27$
$n = \dfrac{\overset{2}{\cancel{4}} \cdot \overset{3}{\cancel{27}}}{\underset{1}{\underset{9}{\cancel{18}}}}$
$n = \mathbf{6}$

14.
$$
\begin{array}{r}
5.0 \\
- 4.2 \\
\hline
\mathbf{0.8}
\end{array}
$$

15. $10 + 10 \times 10 - 10 \div 10 = 10 + 100 - 1$
$= \mathbf{109}$

16. $10^4 - \sqrt{121} + 3^3 + 4^0 =$
$10,000 - 11 + 27 + 1 = \mathbf{10,017}$

17. $|-12| = \mathbf{12}$

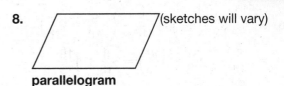

18. $5\dfrac{7}{9} + \left(2\dfrac{1}{3} - 1\dfrac{1}{2}\right) = 5\dfrac{14}{18} + \left(2\dfrac{6}{8} - 1\dfrac{9}{18}\right)$

$= 5\dfrac{14}{18} + \left(1\dfrac{24}{18} - 1\dfrac{9}{18}\right) = 5\dfrac{14}{18} + \dfrac{15}{18} = 5\dfrac{29}{18}$

$= \mathbf{6\dfrac{11}{18}}$

19. $7\dfrac{1}{2} \div \left(2\dfrac{2}{5} \div 4\right) = 7\dfrac{1}{2} \div \left(\dfrac{12}{5} \cdot \dfrac{1}{4}\right)$

$= 7\dfrac{1}{2} \div \dfrac{3}{5} = \dfrac{\overset{5}{\cancel{15}}}{2} \cdot \dfrac{5}{\underset{1}{\cancel{3}}} = \dfrac{25}{2} = \mathbf{12\dfrac{1}{2}}$

20. $4.3(0.05)(0.005) = (0.215)(0.005) = \mathbf{0.001075}$

Cumulative Test 12B

1. A half gallon is 4 pints.
$\$1.28 \div 4 = \mathbf{\$0.32 \text{ per pint}}$

2.

	Ratio	Actual Count
Raisins	3	c
Nuts	2	1

$\dfrac{3}{2} = \dfrac{c}{1}$

$2c = 3$

$c = \dfrac{3}{2} = \mathbf{1\dfrac{1}{2} \text{ cups}}$

3.

$\begin{array}{r} 28.0 \text{ s} \\ \times \quad 3 \\ \hline 84.0 \text{ s} \end{array}$

$26.3 \text{ s} + 30.3 \text{ s} + t = 84.0 \text{ s}$
$t = \mathbf{27.4 \text{ s}}$

4. $\mathbf{y + 3x + 1}$

x	y
0	1
1	4
2	7
3	10

5. Tax: $\begin{array}{r} \$12.50 \\ \times \quad 0.08 \\ \hline \$1.0000 = \$1.00 \end{array}$ Total: $\begin{array}{r} \$12.50 \\ + \$ \ 1.00 \\ \hline \mathbf{\$13.50} \end{array}$

6. a. $\dfrac{7}{10} \times 100\% = \mathbf{70\%}$

b. $\dfrac{\text{news area}}{\text{advertisement area}} = \dfrac{3}{7}$

7. a. $0.00405 = \mathbf{4.05 \times 10^{-3}}$

b. $6.25 \times 10^{-5} = \mathbf{0.0000625}$

8.

parallelogram

(sketches will vary)

9. $1320 \ \cancel{\text{yd}} \cdot \dfrac{3 \text{ ft}}{1 \ \cancel{\text{yd}}} = \mathbf{3960 \text{ ft}}$

10. a. $16\% = \dfrac{16}{100} = \dfrac{\mathbf{4}}{\mathbf{25}}$

b. $16\% = \dfrac{16}{100} = \mathbf{0.16}$

c. $20\overline{)1.00}^{\,0.05}$

d. $\dfrac{1}{20} = \dfrac{5}{100} = \mathbf{5\%}$

11. Perimeter $= 3\dfrac{1}{2} + 3 \text{ in.} + 1 \text{ in.} + 1 \text{ in.}$

$+ 2\dfrac{1}{2} \text{ in.} + 2 \text{ in.} = \mathbf{13 \text{ in.}}$

12.

Area $=$ area A $+$ area B

$= (3 \text{ in.} \cdot 1 \text{ in.}) + \left(2\dfrac{1}{2} \text{ in.} \cdot 2 \text{ in.}\right)$

$= 3 \text{ in.}^2 + 5 \text{ in.}^2 = \mathbf{8 \text{ in.}^2}$

13. $\dfrac{10}{18} = \dfrac{n}{27}$

$18n = 10 \cdot 27$

$n = \dfrac{\overset{5}{\cancel{10}} \cdot \overset{3}{\cancel{27}}}{\underset{\underset{1}{9}}{\cancel{18}}}$

$n = \mathbf{15}$

14. $\begin{array}{r} 6.0 \\ - 4.1 \\ \hline \mathbf{1.9} \end{array}$

15. $5 + 5 \times 5 - 5 \div 5 = 5 + 25 - 1 = \mathbf{29}$

16. $10^3 - \sqrt{169} + 2^4 + 3^0 = 1000 - 13 + 16 + 1 = \mathbf{1004}$

17. $|-8| = \mathbf{8}$

Solutions

18. $5\frac{4}{9} + \left(3\frac{1}{2} - 1\frac{2}{3}\right) = 5\frac{8}{18} + \left(3\frac{9}{18} - 1\frac{12}{18}\right)$

$= 5\frac{8}{18} + \left(2\frac{27}{18} - 1\frac{12}{18}\right) = 5\frac{8}{18} + 1\frac{15}{18}$

$= 6\frac{23}{18} = \mathbf{7\frac{5}{18}}$

19. $3\frac{3}{4} \div \left(4 \div 2\frac{2}{5}\right) = 3\frac{3}{4} \div \left(\frac{4}{1} \cdot \frac{5}{12}\right)$

$= 3\frac{3}{4} \div \frac{5}{3} = \frac{\overset{3}{\cancel{15}}}{4} \cdot \frac{3}{\underset{1}{\cancel{5}}} = \frac{9}{4} = \mathbf{2\frac{1}{4}}$

20. $2.2(0.05)(0.005) = (0.11)(0.005) = \mathbf{0.00055}$

Cumulative Test 13A

1. Tax: $\begin{array}{r} \$10,000 \\ \times\quad 0.075 \\ \hline \$750.000 = \$750 \end{array}$ Total: $\begin{array}{r} \$10,000 \\ \times\quad \$750 \\ \hline \mathbf{\$10,750} \end{array}$

2. $\frac{\$38.50}{7 \text{ hr}} = \mathbf{\$5.50 \text{ per hour}}$

3.

	Ratio	Actual Count
Boys	5	80
Girls	4	g

$\frac{5}{4} = \frac{80}{g}$

$5g = 320$

$g = \mathbf{64 \text{ girls}}$

4. $\dfrac{4\frac{1}{2} + 3\frac{1}{3} + 2 + 2\frac{1}{6}}{6} = \frac{12}{4} = \mathbf{3}$

5. $W_N = 25\% \cdot 96$

$W_N = \frac{1}{4} \cdot 96$

$W_N = \mathbf{24}$

6.

236 stamps

$\frac{1}{4}$ given to his sister $\left\{\begin{array}{|c|} \hline 59 \text{ stamps} \\ \hline \end{array}\right.$

$\frac{3}{4}$ left $\left\{\begin{array}{|c|} \hline 59 \text{ stamps} \\ \hline 59 \text{ stamps} \\ \hline 59 \text{ stamps} \\ \hline \end{array}\right.$

a. $\frac{1}{4} = \mathbf{25\%}$

b. $3 \cdot 59 \text{ stamps} = \mathbf{177 \text{ stamps}}$

7. a. $0.00008 = \mathbf{8 \times 10^{-5}}$

b. $2.4 \times 10^{-4} = \mathbf{0.00024}$

8. $m\angle B = 180° - m\angle A = 180° - 70° = \mathbf{110°}$

9. $4.5 \cancel{\text{ km}} \cdot \dfrac{1000 \text{ m}}{1 \cancel{\text{ km}}} = 4500 \text{ m}$

$4.5 \text{ km} = \mathbf{4500 \text{ m}}$

10. $027. \overline{)700.0}$ $\overset{25.9}{}$ 25.9 rounds to **26**

11. $(+6) + (-11) + (+5) + (-7)$

$= (-5) + (+5) + (-7) = 0 + (-7) = \mathbf{-7}$

12. a. $5\overline{)1.0}$ $\overset{0.2}{}$

b. $\frac{1}{5} = \frac{20}{100} = \mathbf{20\%}$

c. $0.12 = \frac{12}{100} = \mathbf{\frac{3}{25}}$

d. $0.12 = \mathbf{12\%}$

13. Area $= 18 \text{ cm} \times 10 \text{ cm} = \mathbf{180 \text{ cm}^2}$

14. $ab + a + b = \frac{1}{2} \cdot \frac{1}{4} + \frac{1}{2} + \frac{1}{4}$

$= \frac{1}{8} + \frac{4}{8} + \frac{2}{8} = \mathbf{\frac{7}{8}}$

15. $\frac{w}{45} = \frac{8}{20}$

$20w = 8 \cdot 45$

$w = \frac{360}{20}$

$w = \mathbf{18}$

16. $25.\overline{)01.25}$ $\overset{0.05}{}$

17. $100 - 3[2(7-2)] = 100 - 3[2(5)]$

$= 100 - 3(10) = 100 - 30 = \mathbf{70}$

18. $4\frac{1}{4} \div \left(2\frac{1}{6} - 1\frac{1}{3}\right) = 4\frac{3}{12} + \left(2\frac{2}{12} - 1\frac{4}{12}\right)$

$= 4\frac{3}{12} + \left(1\frac{14}{12} - 1\frac{4}{12}\right) = 4\frac{3}{12} + \frac{10}{12} = 4\frac{13}{12}$

$= \mathbf{5\frac{1}{12}}$

19. $5\frac{1}{4}\left(4 \div 1\frac{1}{2}\right) = 5\frac{1}{4}\left(\frac{4}{1} \cdot \frac{2}{3}\right) = \frac{21}{4}\left(\frac{8}{3}\right) = \mathbf{14}$

20. $0.5(0.1)(1.2) = (0.05)(1.2) = \mathbf{0.06}$

Cumulative Test 13B

1. Tax: $10,000
$\quad\quad \times\quad 0.065$
$\quad\quad \overline{\$650.000} = \$650$

Total: $10,000
$\quad\quad + \quad \$650$
$\quad\quad \mathbf{\$10,650}$

2. $\dfrac{\$39.00}{6\ hr} = $ **$6.50 per hour**

3.

	Ratio	Actual Count
Girls	5	g
Boys	3	60

$\dfrac{5}{3} = \dfrac{g}{60}$
$3g = 300$
$g = $ **100 girls**

4. $\dfrac{5\frac{1}{2} + 3 + 4\frac{1}{3} + 3\frac{1}{6}}{4} = \dfrac{16}{4} = 4$

5. $W_N = 6\% \cdot 850$
$W_N = 0.06 \cdot 850$
$W_N = $ **51**

6. 235 cards

$\frac{1}{5}$ given to his sister { 47 cards / 47 cards
$\frac{4}{5}$ left { 47 cards / 47 cards / 47 cards

a. $\dfrac{1}{5} = $ **20%**

b. $4 \cdot 47$ cards = **188 cards**

7. a. $0.0006 = \mathbf{6 \times 10^{-4}}$

b. $7.5 \times 10^{-3} = \mathbf{0.0075}$

8. $m\angle B = 180° - m\angle A = 180° - 120° = \mathbf{60°}$

9. $1.5\ kg \cdot \dfrac{1000\ g}{1 kg} = 1500\ g$
$1.5\ kg > 150\ g$

10. $015.\overline{)800.0}$ 53.3   53.3 rounds to **53**

11. $(-3) + (+3) + (-8) + (+12)$
$= 0 + (-8) + (+12) = (-8) + (+12) = \mathbf{4}$

12. a. $5\overline{)4.0}$ 0.8

b. $\dfrac{4}{5} = \dfrac{80}{100} = \mathbf{80\%}$

c. $0.15 = \dfrac{15}{100} = \dfrac{3}{20}$

d. $0.15 = \mathbf{15\%}$

13. Area $= 14\ cm \times 10\ cm = \mathbf{140\ cm^2}$

14. $ab + a + b = \dfrac{1}{4} \cdot \dfrac{1}{2} + \dfrac{1}{4} + \dfrac{1}{2}$
$= \dfrac{1}{8} + \dfrac{2}{8} + \dfrac{4}{8} = \dfrac{7}{8}$

15. $\dfrac{w}{45} = \dfrac{12}{20}$
$20w = 12 \cdot 45$
$w = \dfrac{540}{20}$
$w = \mathbf{27}$

16. $15.\overline{)22.5}$ 1.5

17. $100 - 4[2(6-2)] = 100 - 4[2(4)]$
$= 100 - 4(8) = 100 - 32 = \mathbf{68}$

18. $3\frac{3}{4} + \left(2\frac{1}{6} - 1\frac{1}{3}\right) = 3\frac{9}{12} + \left(2\frac{2}{12} - 1\frac{4}{12}\right)$
$= 3\frac{9}{12} + \left(1\frac{14}{12} - 1\frac{4}{12}\right) = 3\frac{9}{12} + \frac{10}{12} = 3\frac{19}{12}$
$= \mathbf{4\frac{7}{12}}$

19. $7\frac{7}{8} + \left(6 \div 2\frac{1}{4}\right) = 7\frac{7}{8} + \left(\frac{6}{1} \cdot \frac{4}{9}\right) = \frac{63}{8}\left(\frac{8}{3}\right) = \mathbf{21}$

20. $0.05(0.1)(2.4) = 0.005(2.4) = \mathbf{0.012}$

Cumulative Test 14A

1. $96\ km + 96\ km = 192\ km$
$\dfrac{192\ km}{8\ hr} = \mathbf{24\dfrac{km}{hr}}$

2.

	Ratio	Actual Count
Dogs	3	d
Cats	7	c
Total	10	210

$\dfrac{7}{10} = \dfrac{c}{210}$
$10c = 1470$
$c = $ **147 cats**

3. Becky Jo's estimate was a **little too large, because $\pi > 3$.**

4. a. $\dfrac{\$6.99}{3} = \textbf{\$2.33}$

   b. $\$2.33 \times 10 = \textbf{\$23.30}$

5. $(0.2 + 0.4) - (0.6 \times 0.3) = 0.6 - 0.18 = \textbf{0.42}$

6.

60 cookies

$\dfrac{3}{5}$ were chocolate.
| 12 cookies |
| 12 cookies |
| 12 cookies |

$\dfrac{2}{5}$ were not chocolate.
| 12 cookies |
| 12 cookies |

   a. 3(12 cookies) = **36 cookies**

   b. $\dfrac{2}{5} \times 100\% = \textbf{40\%}$

7. a. 8 vertices

   b. Volume = 3 ft · 3 ft · 3 ft = **27 ft³**

8. a. Circumference = πd
                   = $\pi \cdot 2(11 \text{ cm})$
                   = **22π cm**

   b. Circumference = πd
                   $\approx \dfrac{22}{7} \cdot \overset{40}{\cancel{280}}$ mm
                   $\approx$ **880 mm**

9. a. $11 \times 10^{-7} = \textbf{1.1} \times \textbf{10}^{-6}$

   b. $11 \times 10^{7} = \textbf{1.1} \times \textbf{10}^{8}$

10. Area = $\dfrac{40 \text{ mm} \cdot 30 \text{ mm}}{2} = \textbf{600 mm}^2$

11. Area = $\dfrac{50 \text{ mm} \cdot 30 \text{ mm}}{2} = \textbf{750 mm}^2$

12. $ab - (a - b) = (0.5)(0.4) - (0.5 - 0.4)$
                 = $0.2 - 0.1 = \textbf{0.1}$

13. $W_N = 25\% \cdot 1200$
    $W_N = \dfrac{1}{4} \cdot 1200$
    $W_N = \textbf{300}$

14. a. $8)\overline{1.000}$ → 0.125

   b. $\dfrac{1}{8} = 0.125 = \textbf{12.5\%}$

c. $18\% = \dfrac{18}{100} = \dfrac{9}{50}$

d. $18\% = \textbf{0.18}$

15. $8000 \text{ g} \cdot \dfrac{1 \text{ kg}}{1000 \text{ g}} = \textbf{8 kg}$

16.
$$\begin{array}{r} 42.6 \\ \times\ 36. \\ \hline 6.6 \end{array}$$

17. $\dfrac{32}{5} = \textbf{6}\dfrac{\textbf{2}}{\textbf{5}}$ or **6.4**

18. $8.6 \times 5\dfrac{1}{4} = 8.6 \times 5.25 = \textbf{45.15}$

19. $(-6) + (-3) - (-1) - (+4)$
    $= (-6) + (-3) + (+1) + (-4) = \textbf{-12}$

20. $1\dfrac{1}{3} \div \left(3\dfrac{1}{2} \cdot 2 \right) = 1\dfrac{1}{3} \cdot \left(\dfrac{7}{2} \cdot \dfrac{2}{1} \right) = 1\dfrac{1}{3} \div 7$
    $= \dfrac{4}{3} \cdot \dfrac{1}{7} = \dfrac{\textbf{4}}{\textbf{21}}$

Cumulative Test   14B

1. 32 mi + 32 mi = 64 mi
$$\dfrac{64 \text{ mi}}{4 \text{ hr}} = \textbf{16}\dfrac{\textbf{mi}}{\textbf{hr}}$$

2.

	Ratio	Actual Count
Dogs	2	d
Cats	3	c
Total	5	30

$\dfrac{3}{5} = \dfrac{c}{30}$
$5c = 90$
  $c = \textbf{18 cats}$

3. Melanie's estimate was a **little too large, because $\pi > 3$.**

4. a. $\dfrac{\$1.23}{3} = \textbf{\$0.41}$

   b. $\$0.41 \times 10 = \textbf{\$4.10}$

5. $(0.4 + 0.6) - (0.4 \times 0.6) = 1 - 0.24 = \textbf{0.76}$

6.

60 cookies

$\frac{2}{5}$ were oatmeal. $\left\{\begin{array}{l}\boxed{12 \text{ cookies}}\\\boxed{12 \text{ cookies}}\end{array}\right.$

$\frac{3}{5}$ were not oatmeal. $\left\{\begin{array}{l}\boxed{12 \text{ cookies}}\\\boxed{12 \text{ cookies}}\\\boxed{12 \text{ cookies}}\end{array}\right.$

a. 2(12 cookies) = **24 cookies**

b. $\frac{3}{5} \times 100\% = $ **60%**

7. a. 12 edges

b. Volume = 5 in. · 5 in. · 5 in. = **125 in.³**

8. a. Circumference = πd
$= \pi \cdot 2(8 \text{ in.})$
$= $ **16π in.**

b. Circumference = πd
$\approx 3.14(2 \cdot 0.5 \text{ cm})$
$\approx $ **3.14 cm**

9. a. $12 \times 10^{-6} = $ **1.2×10^{-5}**

b. $12 \times 10^{6} = $ **1.2×10^{7}**

10. Area $= \dfrac{8 \text{ mm} \cdot 6 \text{ mm}}{2} = $ **24 mm²**

11. Area $= \dfrac{10 \text{ mm} \cdot 6 \text{ mm}}{2} = $ **30 mm²**

12. $ab - (a - b) = (0.6)(0.4) - (0.6 - 0.4)$
$= 0.24 - 0.2 = $ **0.04**

13. $W_N = 15\% \cdot 1200$
$W_N = 0.15 \cdot 1200$
$W_N = $ **180**

14. a. $\begin{array}{r} 0.375 \\ 8\overline{)3.000} \end{array}$

b. $\frac{3}{8} = 0.375 = $ **37.5%**

c. $14\% = \dfrac{14}{100} = $ **$\dfrac{7}{50}$**

d. $14\% = $ **0.14**

15. $9000 \text{ g} \cdot \dfrac{1 \text{ kg}}{1000 \text{ g}} = $ **9 kg**

16. $\begin{array}{r} 42.6 \\ -\ 26. \\ \hline 16.6 \end{array}$

17. $\dfrac{33}{6} = 5\dfrac{1}{2}$ or **5.5**

18. $4.6 \times 3\dfrac{1}{4} = 4.6 \times 3.25 = $ **14.95**

19. $(-6) + (+3) - (-2) - (+5)$
$= (-6) + (+3) + (+2) + (-5) = $ **−6**

20. $2\dfrac{2}{3} \div \left(3\dfrac{1}{3} \cdot 2\right) = 2\dfrac{2}{3} \div \left(\dfrac{10}{3} \cdot \dfrac{2}{1}\right)$
$= 2\dfrac{2}{3} \div \dfrac{20}{3} = \dfrac{8}{3} \cdot \dfrac{3}{20} = $ **$\dfrac{2}{5}$**

Cumulative Test 15A

1.

	Case 1	Case 2
Books	12	21
Pounds	40	p

$\dfrac{12}{40} = \dfrac{21}{p}$
$12p = 840$
$p = $ **70 pounds**

2. $\dfrac{3.8 + 5.8}{2} = $ **4.8**

3. Perimeter = 10 in. + 12 in. + 19 in. + 15 in.
$= $ **56 in.**

4.

Area = area A + area B
$= \dfrac{10 \text{ in.} \cdot 12 \text{ in.}}{2} + \dfrac{19 \text{ in.} \cdot 12 \text{ in.}}{2}$
$= 60 \text{ in.}^2 + 114 \text{ in.}^2 = $ **174 in.²**

5. $4^2 - \sqrt{4} = 16 - 2 = $ **14**

6.

	Ratio	Actual Count
Boys	6	b
Girls	5	g
Students	11	550

$\dfrac{5}{11} = \dfrac{g}{550}$
$11g = 2750$
$g = $ **250 girls**

Solutions

7. $6.4 \cancel{g} \cdot \dfrac{1000 \text{ mg}}{1 \cancel{g}} = \textbf{6400 mg}$

8. 60 games

| 12 games |
| 12 games |
| 12 games |
| 12 games |
| 12 games |

$\dfrac{1}{5} \Big\{$ at the 12 games rows

a. total = 5(12 games) = **60 games**

b. $w = 60\% \cdot 60$
$w = 0.6 \cdot 60$
$w = \textbf{36 games}$

9. $72 = \dfrac{4}{5} \times W_N$

$\dfrac{5}{4} \times 72 = \dfrac{5}{4} \times \dfrac{4}{5} \times W_N$

$\textbf{90} = W_N$

10. $\dfrac{1}{10} \times W_N = 201$

$10 \times \dfrac{1}{10} \times W_N = 10 \times 201$

$W_N = \textbf{2010}$

11. a. $-9(-2) = \textbf{18}$

b. $-9(+6) = \textbf{-54}$

c. $\dfrac{-9}{-3} = \textbf{3}$

d. $\dfrac{9}{-1} = \textbf{-9}$

12. Volume $= (5 \text{ cm})^3 = \textbf{125 cm}^3$

13. a. Circumference $= \pi d$
$\approx \dfrac{22}{7} \cdot 2(21 \text{ m})$
$\approx \textbf{132 m}$

b. Circumference $= \pi d$
$= \pi \cdot 2(20 \text{ mm})$
$= \textbf{40}\pi \textbf{ mm}$

14. a. $6 \overline{)1.0000...} = 0.1666...$ $0.1666... = \textbf{0.1}\overline{\textbf{6}}$

b. $\dfrac{1}{6} \times 100\% = \textbf{16}\dfrac{\textbf{2}}{\textbf{3}}\textbf{\%}$

c. $0.45 = \dfrac{45}{100} = \dfrac{\textbf{9}}{\textbf{20}}$

d. $0.45 \times 100\% = \textbf{45\%}$

15. $10m - (my - y^2) = 10 \cdot 10 - (10 \cdot 6 - 6^2) =$
$100 - (60 - 36) = \textbf{76}$

16. $\dfrac{2}{3}m = 18$

$\dfrac{3}{2} \cdot \dfrac{2}{3}m = \overset{9}{\cancel{18}} \cdot \dfrac{3}{\underset{1}{\cancel{2}}}$

$m = \textbf{27}$

17. $n + 3.4 = 7$
$n + 3.4 - 3.4 = 7 - 3.4$
$n = \textbf{3.6}$

18. $3\dfrac{3}{4} \div \left(1\dfrac{2}{3} + 2\dfrac{1}{2}\right) = 3\dfrac{3}{4} \div \left(1\dfrac{4}{6} + 2\dfrac{3}{6}\right) =$

$3\dfrac{3}{4} \div 4\dfrac{1}{6} = \dfrac{15}{4} \cdot \dfrac{6}{25} = \dfrac{90}{100} = \dfrac{\textbf{9}}{\textbf{10}}$

19. $(-7) - (-4) + (-3) = (-7) + (+4) + (-3)$
$= \textbf{-6}$

20. **C. cylinder**

Cumulative Test 15B

1.

	Case 1	Case 2
Books	12	40
Pounds	18	p

$\dfrac{12}{18} = \dfrac{40}{p}$
$12p = 720$
$p = \textbf{60 pounds}$

2. $\dfrac{2.6 + 4.8}{2} = \textbf{3.7}$

3. Perimeter $= 13 \text{ in.} + 10 \text{ in.} + 7 \text{ in.} + 8 \text{ in.}$
$= \textbf{38 in.}$

4.

Area $=$ area A + area B
$= \dfrac{13 \text{ in.} \cdot 8 \text{ in.}}{2} + \dfrac{7 \text{ in.} \cdot 8 \text{ in.}}{2}$
$= 52 \text{ in.}^2 + 28 \text{ in.}^2 = \textbf{80 in.}^2$

5. $9^2 - \sqrt{9} = 81 - 3 = \mathbf{78}$

6.

	Ratio	Actual Count
Boys	7	b
Girls	4	g
Students	11	550

$$\frac{4}{11} = \frac{g}{550}$$
$$11g = 2200$$
$$g = \mathbf{200 \ girls}$$

7. $4.6 \ \cancel{g} \cdot \dfrac{1000 \ mg}{1 \ \cancel{g}} = \mathbf{4600 \ mg}$

8. 48 games

12 games
12 games
12 games
12 games

$\frac{1}{4}\{$ 12 games

  a. total = 4(12 games) = **48 games**

  b. $w = 75\% \cdot 48$
  $$w = \frac{3}{4} \cdot 48$$
  $$w = \mathbf{36 \ games}$$

9. $72 = \dfrac{3}{4} \times W_N$
$$\frac{4}{3} \times 72 = \frac{4}{3} \times \frac{3}{4} \times W_N$$
$$\mathbf{96} = W_N$$

10. $\dfrac{1}{10} \times W_N = 120$
$$10 \times \frac{1}{10} \times W_N = 10 \times 120$$
$$W_N = \mathbf{1200}$$

11. a. $-8(-3) = \mathbf{24}$

  b. $-6(+3) = \mathbf{-18}$

  c. $\dfrac{-8}{-2} = \mathbf{4}$

  d. $\dfrac{9}{-3} = \mathbf{-3}$

12. Volume $= (3 \ cm)^3 = \mathbf{27 \ cm^3}$

13. a. Circumference $= \pi d$
$$\approx 3.14 \cdot 20 \ cm$$
$$\approx \mathbf{62.8 \ cm}$$

b. Circumference $= \pi d$
$$= \pi \cdot 2(15 \ in.)$$
$$= \mathbf{30\pi \ in.}$$

14. a. $12\overline{)1.00000...}^{\ 0.08333...}$ $0.08333... = \mathbf{0.0\overline{3}}$

  b. $\dfrac{1}{12} \times 100\% = \mathbf{8\dfrac{1}{3}\%}$

  c. $0.35 = \dfrac{35}{100} = \mathbf{\dfrac{7}{20}}$

  d. $0.35 \times 100\% = \mathbf{35\%}$

15. $10m - (my - y^2) = 10 \cdot 6 - (6 \cdot 3 - 3^2)$
$$= 60 - (18 - 9) = \mathbf{51}$$

16. $\dfrac{3}{4}y = 12$
$$\frac{4}{3} \cdot \frac{3}{4}y = \frac{4}{\cancel{3}_1} \cdot \cancel{12}^{\,4}$$
$$y = \mathbf{16}$$

17. $x + 2.6 = 5$
$$x + 2.6 - 2.6 = 5 - 2.6$$
$$x = \mathbf{2.4}$$

18. $1\dfrac{7}{8} \div \left(4\dfrac{1}{6} - 2\dfrac{1}{2}\right) = 1\dfrac{7}{8} \div \left(3\dfrac{7}{6} - 2\dfrac{3}{6}\right)$
$$= 1\frac{7}{8} \div 1\frac{2}{3} = \frac{15}{8} \cdot \frac{3}{5} = \frac{9}{8} = \mathbf{1\dfrac{1}{8}}$$

19. $(-6) - (-5) + (-4) = (-6) + (+5) + (-4)$
$$= \mathbf{-5}$$

20. **B. cone**

Cumulative Test 16A

1. $\dfrac{(2 \times \$7.50) + (4 \times \$6.30)}{6 \ hr}$
$$= \frac{\$15.00 + \$25.20}{6 \ hr} = \mathbf{\dfrac{\$6.70}{hr}}$$

2. $x + (x^2 - xy) - y = 5 + (5^2 - 5 \cdot 4) - 4$
$$= 5 + 5 - 4 = \mathbf{6}$$

3.

4.

	Ratio	Actual Count
Clean	3	c
Dirty	4	d
Total	7	35

$\frac{3}{7} = \frac{c}{35}$

$7c = 105$

$c = $ **15 articles of clothing**

5.

	Case 1	Case 2
Customers	400	c
Minutes	25	60

$\frac{400}{25} = \frac{c}{60}$

$25c = 24{,}000$

$c = $ **960 customers**

6. Circumference $= \pi d$

$\approx 3.14 \cdot 15 \text{ m}$

$\approx 47.1 \text{ m}$

$\approx$ **47 m**

7.

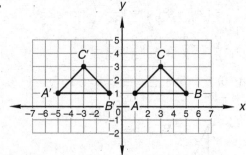

A' **(−5, 1)**

B' **(−1, 1)**

C' **(−3, 3)**

8.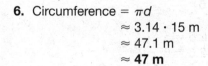

9. $14 \text{ in.} \times 4 = $ **56 in.**

10. a. $\frac{400}{-5} = $ **−80**

b. $\frac{-7.2}{-6} = $ **1.2**

c. $15(-20) = $ **−300**

d. $\left(\frac{1}{2}\right)\left(-\frac{1}{3}\right) = $ **−$\frac{1}{6}$**

11. a. $6\overline{)5.0000...}$ gives $0.8333...$ $0.8333... = $ **$0.8\overline{3}$**

b. $\frac{5}{6} \times 100\% = $ **$83\frac{1}{3}\%$**

c. $0.6 = \frac{6}{10} = $ **$\frac{3}{5}$**

d. $0.6 = \frac{60}{100} = $ **60%**

12.

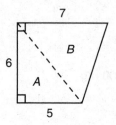

Area $= $ area $A + $ area B

$= \frac{5\text{ m} \cdot 6\text{ m}}{2} + \frac{7\text{ m} \cdot 6\text{ m}}{2}$

$= 15 \text{ m}^2 + 21 \text{ m}^2 = $ **36 m²**

13. $600 = \frac{4}{9} \times W_N$

$\frac{9}{4} \times \overset{150}{600} = \frac{9}{4} \times \frac{4}{9} \times W_N$

$1350 = W_N$

14. $W_P \times 40 = 30$

$\frac{W_P \times 40}{40} = \frac{30}{40}$

$W_P = \frac{3}{4}$

$W_P = $ **75%**

15. $\frac{3}{5}m = 48$

$\frac{5}{3} \cdot \frac{3}{5}m = \frac{5}{3} \times \overset{16}{48}$

$m = $ **80**

16. $1.5 = x - 0.08$

$1.5 + 0.08 = x - 0.08 + 0.08$

$1.58 = x$

17. $\frac{5\frac{1}{3}}{100} = \frac{16}{3} \cdot \frac{1}{100} = \frac{16}{300} = $ **$\frac{4}{75}$**

18. $\frac{3^3 + 2 \cdot 5 - 3 \cdot 2^2}{\sqrt{3^2 + 4^2}} = \frac{27 + 10 - 12}{\sqrt{25}} = \frac{25}{5}$

$= $ **5**

19. $4\frac{2}{3} \div 1.4 = 4\frac{2}{3} \div 1\frac{2}{5} = \frac{\overset{2}{14}}{3} \cdot \frac{5}{\underset{1}{7}} = \frac{10}{3}$

$= 3\frac{1}{3}$

20. $-2.6 - (-4.2) + (+3.5)$
$-2.6 + 4.2 + 3.5$
$-2.6 + 7.7 = \textbf{5.1}$

Cumulative Test 16B

1. $\dfrac{(2 \times \$7.50) + (3 \times \$6.25)}{5\ hr}$

$= \dfrac{\$15.00 + \$18.75}{5\ hr} = \dfrac{\textbf{\$6.75}}{\textbf{hr}}$

2. $x + (x^2 - xy) - y = 5 + (5^2 - 5 \cdot 3) - 3$
$= 5 + 10 - 3 = \textbf{12}$

3.

(triangle figure)

4.

	Ratio	Actual Count
Clean	2	c
Dirty	5	d
Total	7	35

$\frac{2}{7} = \frac{c}{35}$
$7c = 70$
$c = \textbf{10 articles of clothing}$

5.

	Case 1	Case 2
Customers	300	c
Minutes	25	60

$\frac{300}{25} = \frac{c}{60}$
$25c = 18{,}000$
$c = \textbf{720 customers}$

6. Circumference $= \pi d$
$\approx 3.14 \cdot 14\ m$
$\approx 43.96\ m$
$\approx \textbf{44 m}$

7.

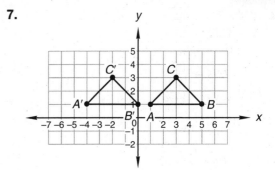

$A'\ (-4, 1)$
$B'\ (0, 1)$
$C'\ (-2, 3)$

8.

(number line with point at -5, marks from -6 to 1)

9. $16\ in. \times 4 = \textbf{64 in.}$

10. a. $\dfrac{300}{-5} = \textbf{-60}$

b. $\dfrac{-7.2}{6} = \textbf{-1.2}$

c. $15(-30) = \textbf{-450}$

d. $\left(-\frac{1}{2}\right)\left(-\frac{1}{3}\right) = \dfrac{\textbf{1}}{\textbf{6}}$

11. a. $9\overline{)1.000...}$ $\;\;$ $0.111... $ $\;\;$ $0.111 = \textbf{0.}\overline{\textbf{1}}$

b. $\frac{1}{9} \times 100\% = \textbf{11}\frac{\textbf{1}}{\textbf{9}}\textbf{\%}$

c. $0.8 = \frac{8}{10} = \dfrac{\textbf{4}}{\textbf{5}}$

d. $0.8 = \frac{80}{100} = \textbf{80\%}$

12.

(quadrilateral figure with dimensions 6, 4, 5, regions A and B)

Area $=$ area A + area B
$= \dfrac{5\ m \cdot 4\ m}{2} + \dfrac{6\ m \cdot 4\ m}{2}$
$= 10\ m^2 + 12\ m^2 = \textbf{22 m}^2$

13. $\;\;600 = \frac{5}{9} \times W_N$

$\frac{9}{\underset{1}{5}} \times \overset{120}{600} = \frac{9}{5} \times \frac{5}{9} \times W_N$

$\textbf{1080} = W_N$

14. $W_P \times 50 = 40$

$$\frac{W_P \times 50}{50} = \frac{40}{50}$$

$$W_P = \frac{80}{100}$$

$$W_P = \textbf{80\%}$$

15. $\frac{3}{5}m = 45$

$$\frac{5}{3} \cdot \frac{3}{5}m = \frac{5}{\cancel{3}} \times \cancel{45}^{15}$$

$$m = \textbf{75}$$

16. $2.5 = x = 0.07$

$2.5 + 0.07 = x - 0.07 + 0.07$

$\textbf{2.57} = x$

17. $\frac{6\frac{2}{3}}{100} = \frac{20}{3} \cdot \frac{1}{100} = \frac{20}{300} = \frac{1}{\textbf{15}}$

18. $\frac{2^3 + 3 \cdot 5 - 2 \cdot 3^2}{\sqrt{3^2 + 4^2}} = \frac{8 + 15 - 18}{\sqrt{25}} = \frac{5}{5} = \textbf{1}$

19. $1.4 \div 4\frac{2}{3} = 1\frac{2}{5} \div 4\frac{2}{3} = \frac{7}{5} \cdot \frac{3}{\cancel{14}_2}^{1} = \frac{3}{\textbf{10}}$

20. $-2.3 - (-3.6) + (-1.5)$

$-2.3 + 3.6 - 1.5$

$-2.3 - 1.5 + 3.6$

$-3.8 + 3.6$

$\textbf{-0.2}$

Cumulative Test 17A

1.

	Ratio	Actual Count
Won	5	w
Failed to win	1	f
Played	6	36

$$\frac{1}{6} = \frac{f}{36}$$

$6f = 36$

$f = \textbf{6 games}$

2. a. $(60 + 60 + 65 + 70 + 70 + 80 + 80 + 90 + 95 + 100) \div 10 = \textbf{77}$

b. $\frac{70 + 80}{2} = \textbf{75}$

c. 60, 70, 80

d. $100 - 60 = \textbf{40}$

3.

	Ratio	Actual Count
Dandelions	11	d
Peonies	4	36

$$\frac{11}{4} = \frac{d}{36}$$

$4d = 11 \cdot 36$

$$d = \frac{11 \cdot \cancel{36}^9}{\cancel{4}_1}$$

$d = \textbf{99 dandelions}$

4. $0.47 \, \cancel{L} \cdot \frac{1000 \text{ mL}}{1 \, \cancel{L}} = \textbf{470mL}$

5.

6. $3xy + xy - 4x + x = \textbf{4xy - 3x}$

7.

	Case 1	Case 2
Distance	2 mi	d
Time	10 s	120 s

$$\frac{2}{10} = \frac{d}{120}$$

$10d = 240$

$d = \textbf{24 miles}$

8.

	Ratio	Actual Count
Happy	35	h
Unhappy	65	117
Total	100	t

$$\frac{65}{100} = \frac{117}{t}$$

$65t = 11,700$

$t = \textbf{180 children}$

9.

(continued on page 437)

a. goal = $10 \times \$5000 = \mathbf{\$50{,}000}$

b. The drive fell short by $\frac{1}{10}$, which is **10%**.

10.

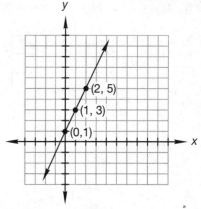

2 in.

3 in.

4 in.

Volume = 4 in. $\times$ 2 in. $\times$ 3 in. = **24 in.^{3}**

11. Area = πr^2
$\approx 3.14(6 \text{ in.})^2$
$\approx \mathbf{113.04 \text{ in.}^2}$

12. a. $20\overline{)7.00}$ (quotient **0.35**)

b. $\frac{7}{20} = \frac{35}{100} = \mathbf{35\%}$

c. $6\% = \frac{6}{100} = \mathbf{\frac{3}{50}}$

d. $6\% = \mathbf{0.06}$

13. $(2.5 \times 10^6)(1.3 \times 10^9) = \mathbf{3.25 \times 10^{15}}$

14. parallelogram
Perimeter
= 14 cm + 10.5 cm + 14 cm + 10.5 cm
= **49 cm**

15. Area = 14 cm $\cdot$ 10 cm = **140 cm^2**

16. $15.4 = 1.4p$
$\frac{15.4}{1.4} = \frac{1.4p}{1.4}$
$\mathbf{11} = p$

17. $z + \frac{4}{9} = 1\frac{1}{3}$
$z + \frac{4}{9} - \frac{4}{9} = 1\frac{1}{3} - \frac{4}{9}$
$z = \mathbf{\frac{8}{9}}$

18. $3\{25 - [7^2 - 4(11 - 4)]\}$
$= 3\{25 - [49 - 4(7)]\} = 3[25 - (49 - 28)]$
$= 3(25 - 21) = 3(4) = \mathbf{12}$

19. $(-3) + (-4) - (-7) + (-8)$
$= (-3) + (-4) + (+7) + (-8)$
$= (-7) + (+7) + (-8) = 0 + (-8) = \mathbf{-8}$

20. $y = 2x + 1$

x	y
0	1
1	3
2	5

(2, 5)
(1, 3)
(0,1)

Cumulative Test 17B

1.

	Ratio	Actual Count
Won	4	w
Failed to win	3	f
Played	7	35

$\frac{3}{7} = \frac{f}{35}$
$7f = 105$
$f = \mathbf{15 \text{ games}}$

2. a. $(50 + 50 + 55 + 60 + 60 + 70 + 70 + 80 + 85 + 90) \div 10 = \mathbf{67}$

b. $\frac{60 + 70}{2} = \mathbf{65}$

c. 50, 60, 70

d. $90 - 50 = \mathbf{40}$

3.

	Ratio	Actual Count
Dandelions	9	d
Daisies	4	36

$\frac{9}{4} = \frac{d}{36}$
$4d = 9 \cdot 36$
$d = \frac{9 \cdot \overset{9}{\cancel{36}}}{\underset{1}{\cancel{4}}}$
$d = \mathbf{81 \text{ dandelions}}$

4. $0.84 \cancel{L} \cdot \frac{1000 \text{ mL}}{1 \cancel{L}} = \mathbf{840 \text{ mL}}$

5.

$\begin{array}{ccccccccc} & & & \bullet & & & & & \\ \hline -4 & -3 & -2 & -1 & 0 & 1 & 2 & 3 \end{array}$

Solutions

6. $4xy + xy - 3x + x =$ **$5xy - 2x$**

7.

	Case 1	Case 2
Distance	2 mi	d
Time	10 s	180 s

$$\frac{2}{10} = \frac{d}{180}$$
$$10d = 360$$
$$d = \textbf{36 miles}$$

8.

	Ratio	Actual Count
Happy	45	h
Unhappy	55	110
Total	100	t

$$\frac{55}{100} = \frac{110}{t}$$
$$55t = 11{,}000$$
$$t = \textbf{200 children}$$

9.

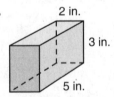

$60,000

$6000
$6000
$6000
$6000
$6000
$6000
$6000
$6000
$6000
$6000

$\frac{7}{10}$ of goal

a. goal $= 10 \times \$6000 =$ **$60,000**

b. The drive fell short by $\frac{3}{10}$, which is **30%.**

10.

2 in.

3 in.

5 in.

Volume $= 5$ in. $\times 2$ in. $\times 3$ in. $=$ **30 in.^{3}**

11. Area $= \pi r^2$
$$\approx \frac{22}{7}(7 \text{ in.})^2$$
$$\approx \textbf{154 in.}^2$$

12. a. $20\overline{)3.00}$ quotient 0.15

b. $\frac{3}{20} = \frac{15}{100} =$ **15%**

c. $8\% = \frac{8}{100} = \frac{2}{25}$

d. $8\% =$ **0.08**

13. $(2.4 \times 10^6)(1.5 \times 10^7) =$ **3.6×10^{13}**

14. parallelogram
Perimeter
$= 28$ mm $+ 21$ mm $+ 28$ mm $+ 21$ mm
$=$ **98 mm**

15. Area $= 28$ mm $\cdot 20$ mm $=$ **560 mm^2**

16. $16.8 = 1.4p$
$$\frac{16.8}{1.4} = \frac{1.4p}{1.4}$$
$$\textbf{12} = p$$

17. $y + \frac{5}{6} = 1\frac{4}{5}$
$$y + \frac{5}{6} - \frac{5}{6} = 1\frac{4}{5} - \frac{5}{6}$$
$$y = \frac{\textbf{29}}{\textbf{30}}$$

18. $2\{25 - [7^2 - 4(11 - 5)]\}$
$= 2[25 - (49 - 24)] = 2(25 - 25)$
$= 2 \cdot 0 =$ **0**

19. $(-4) + (-5) - (-8) + (-7)$
$= (-4) + (-5) + (+8) + (-7)$
$= (-9) + (+8) + (-7) = (-1) + (-7) =$ **-8**

20. **$y = 2x - 1$**

x	y
0	-1
2	3
3	5

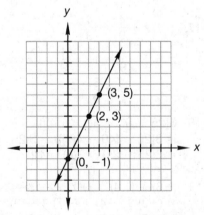

1.

	Ratio	Actual Count
Lions	3	9
Tigers	2	t

$\dfrac{3}{2} = \dfrac{9}{t}$

$3t = 18$

$t = \textbf{6 tigers}$

	Ratio	Actual Count
Tigers	3	6
Bears	4	b

$\dfrac{3}{4} = \dfrac{6}{b}$

$3b = 24$

$b = \textbf{8 bears}$

2. Volume $= 25$ cm $\cdot$ 15 cm $\cdot$ 8 cm $= \textbf{3000 cm}^3$

3. $P(H, 6) = \dfrac{1}{2} \cdot \dfrac{1}{6} = \dfrac{\textbf{1}}{\textbf{12}}$

4. $81 \ \cancel{ft}^2 \cdot \dfrac{1 \text{ yd}}{3 \ \cancel{ft}} \cdot \dfrac{1 \text{ yd}}{3 \ \cancel{ft}} = \textbf{9 yd}^2$

5.

```
 ←──┼──┼──◆──┼──◆──┼──┼──┼──┼──→
   -4  -3  -2  -1   0   1   2   3
```

6. $\dfrac{1}{6} \cdot 360° = \textbf{60}°$

7. $48

```
        ┌─────┐
        │ $12 │
        ├─────┤
        │ $12 │
  3  ┤  ├─────┤
  ─     │ $12 │
  4  ┤  ├─────┤
        │ $12 │
        └─────┘
```

a. regular price $= 4 \times \$12 = \textbf{\$48}$

b. $\dfrac{3}{4} \cdot 100\% = \textbf{75\%}$

8. a. $90° + 35° + m\angle w = 180°$
$\qquad\qquad\qquad\quad m\angle w = \textbf{55}°$

b. $m\angle y = m\angle w$
$\quad 70° + m\angle y + m\angle z = 180°$
$\quad 70° + 55° + m\angle z = 180°$
$\qquad\qquad\qquad m\angle z = \textbf{55}°$

9.

3 diagonals

10. Circumference $= \pi d$
$\qquad\qquad\qquad \approx \dfrac{22}{7} \cdot 28$ in.
$\qquad\qquad\qquad \approx \textbf{88 in.}$

11.

30 mm
(20 mm)
10 mm

Area $=$ area A $+$ area B
$\quad = \dfrac{30 \text{ mm} \cdot 20 \text{ mm}}{2} + \dfrac{10 \text{ mm} \cdot 20 \text{ mm}}{2}$
$\quad = 300 \text{ mm}^2 + 100 \text{ mm}^2 = \textbf{400 mm}^2$

12. $(10^3)(10^4) = 10^\square$
$(10 \cdot 10 \cdot 10)(10 \cdot 10 \cdot 10 \cdot 10) = \textbf{10}^7$

13. a. $0.02 = \dfrac{2}{100} = \dfrac{\textbf{1}}{\textbf{50}}$

b. $0.02 = 0.02 \cdot 100\% = \textbf{2\%}$

14. $W_P \times 200 = 40$

$\dfrac{W_P \times 200}{200} = \dfrac{40}{200}$

$\qquad\quad W_P = \textbf{20\%}$

15.

	Ratio	Actual Count
Ordered hamburgers	45	h
Did not order hamburgers	55	n
Total	100	5000

$\dfrac{55}{100} = \dfrac{n}{5000}$

$100n = 275,000$

$\qquad n = \textbf{2750 customers}$

16. $(1.25 \times 10^{-3})(8 \times 10^{-5}) = 10.00 \times 10^{-8}$
$\qquad\qquad\qquad\qquad\qquad\quad = \textbf{1} \times \textbf{10}^{-7}$

17. $2\frac{1}{2}y = 75$

$$\frac{2}{5} \cdot \frac{5}{2}y = \frac{2}{\cancel{5}_1} \cdot \cancel{75}^{15}$$

$$y = \mathbf{30}$$

18. $\quad 12.3 = 5.73 + f$

$12.3 - 5.73 = 5.73 + f - 5.73$

$\qquad \mathbf{6.57} = f$

19. $(-4x)(-2xy) = \mathbf{8x^2y}$

20. $(-5) - (+6)(-2) - (-3)(-4) = -5 + 12 - 12$
$= \mathbf{-5}$

1.

	Ratio	Actual Count
Lions	2	16
Tigers	3	t

$$\frac{2}{3} = \frac{16}{t}$$
$$2t = 48$$
$$t = 24 \text{ tigers}$$

	Ratio	Actual Count
Tigers	4	24
Bears	3	b

$$\frac{4}{3} = \frac{24}{b}$$
$$4b = 72$$
$$b = \mathbf{18 \text{ bears}}$$

2. Volume $= 30 \text{ cm} \cdot 15 \text{ cm} \cdot 10 \text{ cm}$
$= \mathbf{4500 \text{ cm}^3}$

3. $P(T, 1) = \frac{1}{2} \cdot \frac{1}{6} = \frac{1}{12}$

4. $54 \text{ ft}^2 \cdot \frac{1 \text{ yd}}{3 \text{ ft}} \cdot \frac{1 \text{ yd}}{3 \text{ ft}} = \mathbf{6 \text{ yd}^2}$

5.
```
  ←――+――+――●――●――●――+――+――+――→
    -5  -4  -3  -2  -1   0   1   2
```

6. $\frac{1}{8} \cdot 360° = \mathbf{45°}$

7. a.

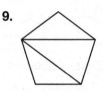

$\$40$
$\$8$
$\$8$
$\$8$
$\$8$
$\$8$
$\frac{4}{5}$

regular price $= 5 \times \$8 = \mathbf{\$40}$

b. $\frac{4}{5} \cdot 100\% = \mathbf{80\%}$

8. a. $90° + 40° + m\angle a = 180°$
$\qquad\qquad m\angle a = \mathbf{50°}$

b. $m\angle c = m\angle a$
$70° + m\angle c + m\angle d = 180°$
$70° + 50° + m\angle d = 180°$
$\qquad\qquad m\angle d = \mathbf{60°}$

9.

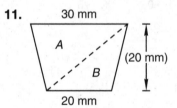

2 diagonals

10. Circumference $= \pi d$
$\approx 3.14(30 \text{ in.})$
$\approx \mathbf{94.2 \text{ in.}}$

11.

30 mm

A

(20 mm)

B

20 mm

Area $= $ area $A + $ area B
$= \frac{30 \text{ mm} \cdot 20 \text{ mm}}{2} + \frac{20 \text{ mm} \cdot 20 \text{ mm}}{2}$
$= 300 \text{ mm}^2 + 200 \text{ mm}^2 = \mathbf{500 \text{ mm}^2}$

12. $2^3 \cdot 2^4 = 2^\square$
$(2 \cdot 2 \cdot 2)(2 \cdot 2 \cdot 2 \cdot 2) = \mathbf{2^7}$

13. a. $0.04 = \frac{4}{100} = \frac{1}{25}$

b. $0.04 = 0.04 \cdot 100\% = \mathbf{4\%}$

14. $W_P \times 200 = 80$

$$\frac{W_P \times 200}{200} = \frac{80}{200}$$
$$W_P = \mathbf{40\%}$$

15.

	Ratio	Actual Count
Ordered hamburgers	45	h
Did not order hamburgers	55	n
Total	100	3000

$$\frac{55}{100} = \frac{n}{3000}$$
$$100n = 165{,}000$$
$$n = \textbf{1650 customers}$$

16. $(2.5 \times 10^{-3})(4 \times 10^{-6}) = 10.0 \times 10^{-9}$
$$= \mathbf{1 \times 10^{-8}}$$

17. $1\frac{2}{3}y = 75$
$$\frac{3}{5} \cdot \frac{5}{3}y = \frac{3}{\cancel{5}} \cdot \cancel{75}^{15}$$
$$y = \textbf{45}$$

18.
$$12.5 = 1.25 + f$$
$$12.5 - 1.25 = 1.25 + f - 1.25$$
$$\mathbf{11.25} = f$$

19. $(2ab)(-3a^2b) = \mathbf{-6a^3b^2}$

20. $(-3) - (+4)(-2) - (-2)(-6) = -3 + 8 - 12$
$$= \mathbf{-7}$$

Cumulative Test 19A

1.
$$\begin{array}{r} 83 \\ \times\ 3 \\ \hline 264 \end{array} \qquad \begin{array}{r} 90 \\ \times\ 4 \\ \hline 360 \end{array} \qquad \begin{array}{r} 360 \\ -\ 264 \\ \hline \mathbf{96} \end{array}$$

2.
$$\begin{array}{r} 45 \text{ girls} \\ +\ ? \text{ boys} \\ \hline 80 \text{ total} \end{array} \rightarrow \begin{array}{r} 45 \text{ girls} \\ +\ 35 \text{ boys} \\ \hline 80 \text{ total} \end{array}$$

The ratio of boys to girls is $\frac{35}{45}$, which reduces to $\mathbf{\frac{7}{9}}$.

3. $60 \text{ juice bars} \times \dfrac{\$4.80}{36 \text{ juice bars}} = \dfrac{\$288.00}{36}$
$$= \mathbf{\$8.00}$$

4. $P(R, R) = \dfrac{3}{9} \cdot \dfrac{2}{8} = \mathbf{\dfrac{1}{12}}$

5.

	%	Cost
Original	100	b
Increase	50	c
New	150	60¢

$$\frac{100}{150} = \frac{b}{60}$$
$$150b = 6000$$
$$b = \textbf{40¢ per pound}$$

6. $60 = W_P \times 80$
$$\frac{60}{80} = \frac{W_P \times 80}{80}$$
$$\frac{3}{4} = W_P$$
$$\mathbf{75\%} = W_P$$

7. $1000 \text{ cm}^2 \cdot \dfrac{10 \text{ mm}}{1 \text{ cm}} \cdot \dfrac{10 \text{ mm}}{1 \text{ cm}} = \mathbf{100{,}000 \text{ mm}^2}$

8. $y = 4x - 1$
$$y = 4(-3) - 1$$
$$y = -12 - 1$$
$$y = \mathbf{-13}$$

9. Volume = area of base $\times$ height
$$= \left(\frac{6 \text{ cm} \cdot 8 \text{ cm}}{2}\right)(10 \text{ cm}) = \mathbf{240 \text{ cm}^3}$$

10. a. $2\frac{1}{2} = 2\frac{5}{10} = \mathbf{2.5}$

b. $2\frac{1}{2} \times 100\% = 2.5 \times 100\% = \mathbf{250\%}$

c. $2\frac{1}{2}\% = \dfrac{2\frac{1}{2}}{100} = \dfrac{5}{2} \cdot \dfrac{1}{100} = \dfrac{5}{200} = \mathbf{\dfrac{1}{40}}$

d. $2\frac{1}{2}\% = \dfrac{2.5}{100} = \mathbf{0.025}$

11. a. Tax:
$$\begin{array}{r} \$96.00 \\ \times\ \ 0.06 \\ \hline \mathbf{\$5.76} \end{array}$$

b. Total:
$$\begin{array}{r} \$96.00 \\ +\ \ 5.76 \\ \hline \mathbf{\$101.76} \end{array}$$

12. $(7 \times 10^{-4})(4 \times 10^8) = 28 \times 10^4 = \mathbf{2.8 \times 10^5}$

13.

14. $1\frac{2}{3}x = 60$
$$\frac{3}{5} \cdot \frac{5}{3}x = \frac{3}{\cancel{5}} \cdot \cancel{60}^{12}$$
$$x = \mathbf{36}$$

Solutions

15.
$$3m - 45 = 54$$
$$3m - 45 + 45 = 54 + 45$$
$$3m = 99$$
$$\frac{3m}{3} = \frac{99}{3}$$
$$m = \mathbf{33}$$

16. $(2 \cdot 5)^2 - 2(5)^2 = 10^2 - 2(25) = 100 - 50$
$= \mathbf{50}$

17. $(-3x)(2xy)(-xy^2) = \mathbf{6x^3y^3}$

18. $4 - \left(2\frac{2}{3} - 1.5\right) = 4 - \left(2\frac{2}{3} - 1\frac{1}{2}\right)$

$= 4 - \left(2\frac{4}{6} - 1\frac{3}{6}\right) = 4 - 1\frac{1}{6} = 3\frac{6}{6} - 1\frac{1}{6}$

$= \mathbf{2\frac{5}{6}}$

19. $3x + y - x + y = 3x - x + y + y = \mathbf{2x + 2y}$

20. $\dfrac{6 - 9 + 4 - 15 + 3(-4)}{2} = \dfrac{-26}{2} = \mathbf{-13}$

Cumulative Test 19B

1.
88	90	450
× 4	× 5	− 352
352	450	**98**

2.
50 girls		50 girls
+ ? boys	→	+ 30 boys
80 total		80 total

The ratio of boys to girls is $\dfrac{30}{50}$, which reduces to $\mathbf{\dfrac{3}{5}}$.

3. 60 j̶u̶i̶c̶e̶ ̶b̶a̶r̶s̶ $\times \dfrac{\$4.80}{24 \text{ j̶u̶i̶c̶e̶ ̶b̶a̶r̶s̶}} = \dfrac{\$288.00}{24}$

$= \mathbf{\$12.00}$

4. $P(B, R) = \dfrac{4}{10} \cdot \dfrac{3}{9} = \mathbf{\dfrac{2}{15}}$

5.

	%	Cost
Original	100	b
Increase	50	c
New	150	90¢

$$\frac{100}{150} = \frac{b}{90}$$
$$150b = 9000$$
$$b = \mathbf{60¢ \text{ per pound}}$$

6.
$$64 = W_P \times 80$$
$$\frac{64}{80} = \frac{W_P \times 80}{80}$$
$$\frac{4}{5} = W_P$$
$$\mathbf{80\%} = W_P$$

7. $10 \text{ c̶m̶}^2 \cdot \dfrac{10 \text{ mm}}{1 \text{ c̶m̶}} \cdot \dfrac{10 \text{ mm}}{1 \text{ c̶m̶}} = \mathbf{1000 \text{ mm}^2}$

8.
$$y = 2x - 1$$
$$y = 2(-4) - 1$$
$$y = -8 - 1$$
$$y = \mathbf{-9}$$

9. Volume = area of base × height
$$= \left(\frac{4 \text{ cm} \cdot 4 \text{ cm}}{2}\right)(8 \text{ cm}) = \mathbf{64 \text{ cm}^3}$$

10. a. $1\frac{1}{2} = 1\frac{5}{10} = \mathbf{1.5}$

b. $1\frac{1}{2} \times 100\% = 1.5 \times 100\% = \mathbf{150\%}$

c. $7\frac{1}{2}\% = \dfrac{7\frac{1}{2}}{100} = \dfrac{15}{2} \cdot \dfrac{1}{100} = \dfrac{15}{200} = \mathbf{\dfrac{3}{40}}$

d. $7\frac{1}{2}\% = \dfrac{7.5}{100} = \mathbf{0.075}$

11. a. Tax:
$124.00
× 0.06
$7.44

b. Total:
$124.00
+ 7.44
$131.44

12. $(8 \times 10^{-3})(2 \times 10^{10}) = 16 \times 10^7 = \mathbf{1.6 \times 10^8}$

13.

14.
$$3\frac{1}{3}x = 60$$
$$\frac{3}{10} \cdot \frac{10}{3}x = \frac{3}{\cancel{10}} \cdot \overset{6}{\cancel{60}}$$
$$x = \mathbf{18}$$

15.
$$3w - 45 = 42$$
$$3w - 45 + 45 = 42 + 45$$
$$3w = 87$$
$$\frac{3w}{3} = \frac{87}{3}$$
$$w = \mathbf{29}$$

16. $(2 \cdot 4)^2 - 3(4)^2 = 8^2 - 3(16) = 64 - 48 = \mathbf{16}$

17. $(-5xy)(x^2y)(3y) = \mathbf{-15x^3y^3}$

18. $6 - \left(2\frac{1}{3} - 1.5\right) = 6 - \left(2\frac{1}{3} - 1\frac{1}{2}\right)$

$= 6 - \left(2\frac{2}{6} - 1\frac{3}{6}\right) = 6 - \left(1\frac{8}{6} - 1\frac{3}{6}\right)$

$= 6 - \frac{5}{6} = 5\frac{6}{6} - \frac{5}{6} = \mathbf{5\frac{1}{6}}$

19. $3x - y - x - y = 3x - x - y - y = \mathbf{2x - 2y}$

20. $\dfrac{7 - 10 + 6 - 12 + 4(-3)}{3} = \dfrac{-21}{3} = \mathbf{-7}$

Cumulative Test 20A

1. $\dfrac{(3 \cdot 88) + (5 \cdot 84)}{8} = \mathbf{85.5}$

2.

	%	Pay
Original	100	$7.20
Increase	25	c
New	125	n

$\dfrac{100}{125} = \dfrac{7.20}{n}$

$100n = 900$

$n = \mathbf{\$9.00 \text{ per hour}}$

3. $70 = W_P \times 50$

$\dfrac{70}{50} = \dfrac{W_P \times 50}{50}$

$\dfrac{140}{100} = W_P$

$\mathbf{140\%} = W_P$

4. $2 \text{ m}^3 \cdot \dfrac{100 \text{ cm}}{1 \text{ m}} \cdot \dfrac{100 \text{ cm}}{1 \text{ m}} \cdot \dfrac{100 \text{ cm}}{1 \text{ m}}$

$= \mathbf{2{,}000{,}000 \text{ cm}^3}$

5.

```
              30 eggs
            ┌─────────┐
            │ 5 eggs  │
            │ 5 eggs  │
5/6 were not│ 5 eggs  │
cracked.    │ 5 eggs  │
            │ 5 eggs  │
1/6 were    │ 5 eggs  │
cracked.    └─────────┘
```

a. total $= 6(5 \text{ eggs}) = \mathbf{30 \text{ eggs}}$

b. If $\frac{1}{6}$ of the eggs were cracked, then $\frac{5}{6}$ of the eggs were not cracked.

$\dfrac{5}{6} \times 100\% = \dfrac{500\%}{6} = \mathbf{83\frac{1}{3}\%}$

6. $\dfrac{a + b}{c} = \dfrac{(-6) + (-4)}{(-2)} = \dfrac{-10}{-2} = \mathbf{5}$

7. Side length: 12 in. ÷ 4 = 3 in.
Area $= (3 \text{ in.})^2 = \mathbf{9 \text{ in.}^2}$

8. $P(V, V) = \dfrac{2}{6} \cdot \dfrac{2}{6} = \dfrac{4}{36} = \mathbf{\dfrac{1}{9}}$

9. Volume = area of base × height

$= \left(\dfrac{8 \text{ cm} \cdot 3 \text{ cm}}{2}\right)(6 \text{ cm}) = \mathbf{72 \text{ cm}^3}$

10. Area $= \pi r^2$

$\approx 3.14(10 \text{ cm})^2$

$\approx \mathbf{314 \text{ cm}^2}$

11.

Price: $18.00
× 20
$360.00

Tax: $360
× 0.06
$21.60

Total: $360.00
+ 21.60
$381.60

12. $W_N = 33\frac{1}{3}\% \times \$42.00$

$W_N = \dfrac{1}{3}\% \times \$42.00$

$W_N = \mathbf{\$14.00}$

13. $\dfrac{2}{12} \cdot 360° = \mathbf{60°}$

14. $(4 \times 10^3)(8 \times 10^{-8}) = 32 \times 10^{-5}$

$= \mathbf{3.2 \times 10^{-4}}$

15. $0.6\,m + 1.5 = 4.8$

$0.6\,m + 1.5 - 1.5 = 4.8 - 1.5$

$0.6\,m = 3.3$

$\dfrac{0.6m}{0.6} = \dfrac{3.3}{0.6}$

$m = \mathbf{5.5}$

16. $\dfrac{2}{3}x - 6 = 18$

$\dfrac{2}{3}x - 6 + 6 = 18 + 6$

$\dfrac{2}{3}x = 24$

$\dfrac{3}{2} \cdot \dfrac{2}{3}x = \dfrac{2}{3} \cdot 24$

$x = \mathbf{36}$

17. $3^3 - \sqrt{49} + 5 \cdot 2^4 = 27 - 7 + 80 = \mathbf{100}$

18.

```
      1 yd   1ft
   3 yd  2 ft  9 in.
 +             8 in.
 ─────────────────────
   4 yd        5 in.
```

19. $2x + 3(x + 2) = 2x + 3x + 6 = \mathbf{5x + 6}$

20. $\dfrac{-5(-4) - 3(-2)(-1)}{(-2)} = \dfrac{20 - 6}{-2} = \mathbf{-7}$

Cumulative Test 20B

1. $\dfrac{(3 \cdot 84) + (5 \cdot 88)}{8} = \mathbf{86.5}$

2.

	%	Pay
Original	100	$6.40
Increase	25	c
New	125	n

$\dfrac{100}{125} = \dfrac{6.40}{n}$

$100n = 800$

$n = \mathbf{\$8.00 \text{ per hour}}$

3. $65 = W_P \times 50$

$\dfrac{65}{50} = \dfrac{W_P \times 50}{50}$

$\dfrac{130}{100} = W_P$

$\mathbf{130\%} = W_P$

4. $3 \text{ m}^3 \cdot \dfrac{100 \text{ cm}}{1 \text{ m}} \cdot \dfrac{100 \text{ cm}}{1 \text{ m}} \cdot \dfrac{100 \text{ cm}}{1 \text{ m}}$

$= \mathbf{3{,}000{,}000 \text{ cm}^3}$

5.

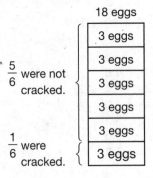

18 eggs

$\frac{5}{6}$ were not cracked.

$\frac{1}{6}$ were cracked.

(6 boxes of "3 eggs")

a. total = 6(3 eggs) = **18 eggs**

b. If $\frac{1}{6}$ of the eggs were cracked, then $\frac{5}{6}$ of the eggs were not cracked.

$\dfrac{5}{6} \times 100\% = \dfrac{500\%}{6} = \mathbf{83\frac{1}{3}\%}$

6. $\dfrac{a+b}{c} = \dfrac{(-8) + (-6)}{(-2)} = \dfrac{-14}{-2} = \mathbf{7}$

7. Side length: 24 in. ÷ 4 = 6 in.

Area = $(6 \text{ in.})^2 = \mathbf{36 \text{ in.}^2}$

8. $P(O, O) = \dfrac{2}{6} \cdot \dfrac{2}{6} = \dfrac{4}{36} = \mathbf{\dfrac{1}{9}}$

9. Volume = area of base × height

$= \dfrac{6 \text{ cm} \cdot 4 \text{ cm}}{2} (8 \text{ cm}) = \mathbf{96 \text{ cm}^2}$

10. Area = πr^2

$\approx \dfrac{22}{7} (14 \text{ in.})^2$

$\approx \mathbf{616 \text{ in.}^2}$

11. Price: $16.00   Tax: $320
$\times$ 20 $\times$ 0.07
$320.00 $22.40

Total: $320.00
+   22.40
$342.40

12. $W_N = 33\frac{1}{3}\% \times \$48.00$

$W_N = \dfrac{1}{3} \times \$48.00$

$W_N = \mathbf{\$16.00}$

13. $\dfrac{4}{12} \times 360° = \mathbf{120°}$

14. $(3 \times 10^4)(7 \times 10^{-9}) = 21 \times 10^{-5}$

$= \mathbf{2.1 \times 10^{-4}}$

15. $0.6m - 1.5 = 4.8$

$0.6m - 1.5 + 1.5 = 4.8 + 1.5$

$0.6m = 6.3$

$\dfrac{0.6m}{0.6} = \dfrac{6.3}{0.6}$

$m = \mathbf{10.5}$

16. $\dfrac{2}{3}x + 6 = 18$

$\dfrac{2}{3}x + 6 - 6 = 18 - 6$

$\dfrac{2}{3}x = 12$

$\dfrac{3}{2} \cdot \dfrac{2}{3}x = \dfrac{3}{2} \cdot 12$

$x = \mathbf{18}$

17. $3^3 - \sqrt{64} + 4 \cdot 2^4 = 27 - 8 + 64 = \mathbf{83}$

18.
$\overset{1 \text{ yd}}{} \overset{1 \text{ ft}}{}$
2 yd 2 ft 7 in.
+   8 in.
3 yd   3 in.

19. $4x + 2(x + 3) = 4x + 2x + 6 = \mathbf{6x + 6}$

20. $\dfrac{-5(-4) + 3(-2)(-1)}{(-2)} = \dfrac{20 + 6}{-2} = \mathbf{-13}$

Cumulative Test 21A

1. 15% of $24.00 = 0.15 \times \$24.00 = \mathbf{\$3.60}$

2. $\dfrac{200 \text{ km}}{2.5 \text{ hr}} = \dfrac{\mathbf{80 \text{ km}}}{\mathbf{hr}}$

Solutions

3.

	Scale	Measure
Model	1	48
Object	12	h

$$\frac{1}{12} = \frac{48}{h}$$
$$h = \textbf{576 in. or 48 ft}$$

4.

	%	Cost
Original	100	r
Discount	20	35
New	80	s

$$\frac{100}{20} = \frac{r}{35}$$
$$20r = 3500$$
$$r = \textbf{\$175}$$

5.

	%	Cost
Original	100	30
Increase	50	c
New	150	p

$$\frac{100}{150} = \frac{30}{p}$$
$$100p = 4500$$
$$p = \textbf{\$45}$$

6.

Tax	Total
\$48.00	\$48.00
$\times$ 0.065	$+$ \$ 3.12
\$3.12	**\$51.12**

7. Perimeter of semicircle $= \dfrac{\pi d}{2}$
$$\approx \frac{(3.14)(10 \text{ cm})}{2}$$
$$\approx 15.7 \text{ cm}$$
Perimeter $\approx 10 \text{ cm} + 3 \text{ cm} + 15.7 \text{ cm} + 3 \text{ cm}$
$$\approx \textbf{31.7 cm}$$

8.
$$a^2 + b^2 = c^2$$
$$a^2 + (24 \text{ in.})^2 = (26 \text{ in.})^2$$
$$a^2 + 576 \text{ in.}^2 = 676 \text{ in.}^2$$
$$a^2 = 100 \text{ in.}^2$$
$$a = \textbf{10 in.}$$

9. Area of triangle $= \dfrac{3 \text{ in.} \cdot 4 \text{ in.}}{2} = 6 \text{ in.}^2$

Area of triangle $= \dfrac{3 \text{ in.} \cdot 4 \text{ in.}}{2} = 6 \text{ in.}^2$

Area of rectangle $= 3 \text{ in.} \cdot 2 \text{ in.} = 6 \text{ in.}^2$
Area of rectangle $= 4 \text{ in.} \cdot 2 \text{ in.} = 8 \text{ in.}^2$
$+$ Area of rectangle $= 5 \text{ in.} \cdot 2 \text{ in.} = 10 \text{ in.}^2$

Total surface area $= \textbf{36 in.}^2$

10. Volume $=$ area of base $\times$ height
Area of base $= \pi r^2$
$$\approx (3.14)(3 \text{ cm})^2$$
$$\approx 28.26 \text{ cm}^2$$
Volume $\approx (28.26 \text{ cm}^2)(10 \text{ cm})$
$$\approx \textbf{282.6 cm}^3$$

11. $\dfrac{12}{8} = \dfrac{x}{6}$
$$8x = 72$$
$$x = \textbf{9}$$

12.
$$2x + 3x + 90° = 180°$$
$$5x + 90° = 180°$$
$$5x + 90° - 90° = 180° - 90°$$
$$5x = 90°$$
$$\frac{5x}{5} = \frac{90°}{5}$$
$$x = 18°$$
$$m\angle BOC = 2x = 2(18°) = \textbf{36°}$$

13. a. $-3, \sqrt{3}, 3, 3^2$

b. $\sqrt{3}$

14. $P(H, H) = \dfrac{1}{2} \cdot \dfrac{1}{2} = \dfrac{1}{4}$

The chance that the coin will land heads up twice is **1 to 4.**

15. Since $\sqrt{8} < 3$, the answer is not A. Since $\sqrt[3]{64} = 4$, the answer is not C. Since $\sqrt{49} = 7$ and $\sqrt{81} = 9$, the number between 7 and 9 is **B.** $\sqrt{79}$.

16.
$$3x - 12 + x = 24$$
$$4x - 12 = 24$$
$$4x - 12 + 12 = 24 + 12$$
$$4x = 36$$
$$\frac{4x}{4} = \frac{36}{4}$$
$$x = \textbf{9}$$

Solutions

17. $\dfrac{20}{w} = \dfrac{45}{3.6}$

$45w = 20 \cdot 3.6$

$w = \dfrac{72}{45}$

$w = \mathbf{1.6}$

18. $\dfrac{(2xy)(6x^2)}{3x^2y} = \dfrac{12x^3y}{3x^2y} = \mathbf{4x}$

19. $3^2 + (-2)^3 = 9 + (-8) = \mathbf{1}$

20. $\dfrac{(-18) - (-2)(-3)}{(-2) + (-2) - (+4)} = \dfrac{(-18) + (-6)}{(-2) + (-2) + (-4)}$

$= \dfrac{-24}{-8} = \mathbf{3}$

Cumulative Test 21B

1. 15% of $18.00 = 0.15 \times \$18.00 = \mathbf{\$2.70}$

2. $\dfrac{2100 \text{ mi}}{3.5 \text{ hr}} = \dfrac{\mathbf{600 \text{ mi}}}{\mathbf{hr}}$

3.

	Scale	Measure
Model	1	30
Object	12	h

$\dfrac{1}{12} = \dfrac{30}{h}$

$h = \mathbf{360 \text{ in. or } 30 \text{ ft}}$

4.

	%	Cost
Original	100	r
Discount	20	15
New	80	s

$\dfrac{100}{20} = \dfrac{r}{15}$

$20r = 1500$

$r = \mathbf{\$75}$

5.

	%	Cost
Original	100	50
Increase	30	c
New	130	p

$\dfrac{100}{130} = \dfrac{50}{p}$

$100p = 6500$

$p = \mathbf{\$65}$

6.

Tax	Total
$84.00	$84.00
× 0.065	+ $ 5.46
$5.46	**$89.46**

7. Perimeter of semicircle $= \dfrac{\pi d}{2}$

$\approx \dfrac{(3.14)(10 \text{ cm})}{2}$

$\approx 15.7 \text{ cm}$

Perimeter $\approx 10 \text{ cm} + 2 \text{ cm} + 15.7 \text{ cm} + 2 \text{ cm}$

$\approx \mathbf{29.7 \text{ cm}}$

8. $a^2 + b^2 = c^2$

$a^2 + (15 \text{ in.})^2 = (17 \text{ in.})^2$

$a^2 + 225 \text{ in.}^2 = 289 \text{ in.}^2$

$a^2 = 64 \text{ in.}^2$

$a = \mathbf{8 \text{ in.}}$

9.

Area of triangle $= \dfrac{6 \text{ in.} \cdot 8 \text{ in.}}{2} = 24 \text{ in.}^2$

Area of triangle $= \dfrac{6 \text{ in.} \cdot 8 \text{ in.}}{2} = 24 \text{ in.}^2$

Area of rectangle $= 6 \text{ in.} \cdot 4 \text{ in.} = 24 \text{ in.}^2$

Area of rectangle $= 8 \text{ in.} \cdot 4 \text{ in.} = 32 \text{ in.}^2$

+ Area of rectangle $= 10 \text{ in.} \cdot 4 \text{ in.} = 40 \text{ in.}^2$

Total surface area $= \mathbf{144 \text{ in.}^2}$

10. Volume = area of base × height

Area of base $= \pi r^2$

$\approx (3.14)(4 \text{ cm})^2$

$\approx 50.24 \text{ cm}^2$

Volume $\approx (50.24 \text{ cm}^2)(5 \text{ cm})$

$\approx \mathbf{251.2 \text{ cm}^3}$

11. $\dfrac{6}{x} = \dfrac{8}{20}$

$8x = 120$

$x = \mathbf{15}$

12. $5x + 4x + 90° = 180°$

$9x + 90° = 180°$

$9x + 90° - 90° = 180° - 90°$

$9x = 90°$

$\dfrac{9x}{9} = \dfrac{90°}{9}$

$x = 10°$

$m\angle BOC = 5x = 5(10°) = \mathbf{50°}$

13. a. $-5, \sqrt{5}, 5, 5^2$

b. $\sqrt{5}$

Saxon Math Course 2   **446**

© Harcourt Achieve Inc. and Stephen Hake. All rights reserved.

14. $P(T, T) = \frac{1}{2} \cdot \frac{1}{2} = \frac{1}{4}$

Probability of favorable outcome: $\frac{1}{4}$

Probability of unfavorable outcome: $\frac{3}{4}$

Odds: **1 to 3**

15. Since $\sqrt{6} < 3$, the answer is not A. Since $\sqrt[3]{27} = 3$, the answer is not C. Since $\sqrt{25} = 5$ and $\sqrt{49} = 7$, the number between 5 and 7 is **B. $\sqrt{35}$.**

16.
$$2x - 12 + x = 24$$
$$3x - 12 = 24$$
$$3x - 12 + 12 = 24 + 12$$
$$3x = 36$$
$$\frac{3x}{3} = \frac{36}{3}$$
$$x = \mathbf{12}$$

17.
$$\frac{30}{w} = \frac{45}{3.6}$$
$$45w = 30(3.6)$$
$$w = \frac{108}{45}$$
$$w = \mathbf{2.4}$$

18. $\dfrac{(6x^2 y)(4x^2)}{3xy} = \dfrac{24x^4 y}{3xy} = \mathbf{8x^3}$

19. $2^3 + (-2)^2 = 8 + 4 = \mathbf{12}$

20. $\dfrac{(-16) + (-2)(-3)}{(-3) + (-2)} = \dfrac{(-16) + (+6)}{-5}$

$= \dfrac{-10}{-5} = \mathbf{2}$

Cumulative Test 22A

1. a. $(84 + 87 + 88 + 88 + 88 + 89 + 89 + 90 + 92 + 95) \div 10 = \mathbf{89}$

b. $\dfrac{88 + 89}{2} = \mathbf{88.5}$

c. 88

d. $95 - 84 = \mathbf{11}$

2. $P(H, H) = \dfrac{\cancel{13}^{1}}{\cancel{52}_{4}} \cdot \dfrac{\cancel{12}^{4}}{\cancel{51}_{17}} = \dfrac{\mathbf{1}}{\mathbf{17}}$

3.

	Case 1	Case 2
Dollars	200	d
Francs	300	210

$$\frac{200}{300} = \frac{d}{210}$$
$$300d = 42{,}000$$
$$d = \mathbf{\$140}$$

4.

	Ratio	Actual Count
Red	5	r
Blue	7	b
Total	12	180

$$\frac{100}{65} = \frac{120}{n}$$
$$12r = 900$$
$$r = \mathbf{75\ marbles}$$

5.

	%	$
Original	100	120
Decrease	35	d
New	65	n

$$\frac{100}{65} = \frac{120}{n}$$
$$100n = 7800$$
$$n = \mathbf{\$78\ per\ day}$$

6. Volume = area of base × height

Area of base = πr^2
$$\approx (3.14)(10\ \text{cm})^2$$
$$\approx 314\ \text{cm}^2$$

Volume $\approx (314\ \text{cm}^2)(50\ \text{cm})$
$$\approx \mathbf{15{,}700\ cm^3}$$

7. $t = 1.06p$
$t = 1.06(8.5)$
$t = \mathbf{9.01}$

8. $y = 2x - 2$

x	y
0	−2
1	0
2	2

Check student work. Number pairs will vary.

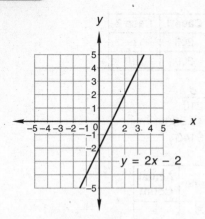

$$\text{Slope} = \frac{\text{rise}}{\text{run}} = \frac{+2}{1} = \textbf{2}$$

9.

Tax	Total
$80.00	$80.00
× 0.075	+ $ 6.00
$6.00	**$86.00**

10. $0.1 \times W_N = 350$

$$W_N = \frac{350}{0.1}$$

$$W_N = \textbf{3500}$$

11.

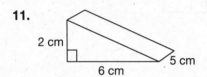

$$\text{Volume} = \frac{1}{2} \cdot 2 \text{ cm} \cdot 6 \text{ cm} \cdot 5 \text{ cm} = 30 \text{ cm}^3$$

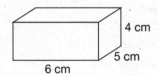

$$\text{Volume} = 6 \text{ cm} \times 5 \text{ cm} \times 4 \text{ cm} = 120 \text{ cm}^3$$
$$\text{Total Valume} = \textbf{150 cm}^3$$

12. In the figure the acute angles are supplementary to the obtuse angles.

$$m\angle h = 180° - m\angle a$$
$$m\angle h = 180° - 105°$$
$$m\angle h = \textbf{75°}$$

13. $d = rt$

$$\frac{d}{r} = \frac{rt}{r}$$

$$\frac{d}{r} = t$$

14. Since the triangles are similar,
$$m\angle x = 180° - 160°$$
$$m\angle x = 20°$$

15. a. $\dfrac{8}{y} = \dfrac{6}{9}$

$$6y = 72$$
$$y = \textbf{12}$$

b. $6f = 9$

$$f = \frac{9}{6}$$

$$f = \frac{3}{2} \text{ or } \textbf{1.5}$$

16. $1\frac{2}{3}x - 15 = 45$

$$1\frac{2}{3}x - 15 + 15 = 45 + 15$$

$$1\frac{2}{3}x = 60$$

$$\frac{3}{5} \cdot \frac{5}{3}x = \frac{3}{5} \cdot 60$$

$$x = \textbf{36}$$

17.
$$3x - 12 = x + 24$$
$$3x - 12 - x = x + 24 - x$$
$$2x - 12 = 24$$
$$2x - 12 + 12 = 24 + 12$$
$$2x = 36$$
$$\frac{2x}{2} = \frac{36}{2}$$
$$x = \textbf{18}$$

18. $\dfrac{(-6) - (7)(-4) - (-1)^2}{(-1) + (-2)}$

$$= \frac{-6 + 28 - 1}{-3} = \frac{21}{-3} = \textbf{-7}$$

19. $100 - \{80 - 3[2 + 2(3^2)]\}$
$$= 100 - [80 - 3(2 + 18)] = 100 - (80 - 60)$$
$$= 100 - 20 = \textbf{80}$$

20. $\dfrac{(-3ax)(4x^2)}{6ax^3} = \dfrac{-12ax^3}{6ax^3} = \textbf{-2}$

Cumulative Test **22B**

1. a. $(90 + 92 + 93 + 93 + 93 + 94 + 97 + 100) \div 8 = \textbf{94}$

b. $\dfrac{93 + 93}{2} = 93$

c. **93**

d. $100 - 90 = \textbf{10}$

2. One quarter of the 52 cards, or 13 cards, are diamonds. After the first diamond is drawn, 12 of the 51 remaining cards are diamonds.

$$P(D \text{ and } D) = \frac{1}{4} \times \frac{12}{51} = \frac{12}{204} = \mathbf{\frac{1}{17}}$$

3.

	Case 1	Case 2
Dollars	200	d
Francs	300	960

$$\frac{200}{300} = \frac{d}{210}$$
$$300d = 192{,}000$$
$$d = \mathbf{\$640}$$

4.

	Ratio	Actual Count
Peanuts	11	p
Cashews	4	c
Total	15	630

$$\frac{11}{15} = \frac{p}{630}$$
$$15p = 6930$$
$$p = \mathbf{462 \text{ peanuts}}$$

5.

	%	$
Original	100	140
Decrease	35	d
New	65	n

$$\frac{100}{65} = \frac{140}{n}$$
$$100n = 9100$$
$$n = \mathbf{\$91 \text{ per day}}$$

6. Volume = area of base × height

Area of base = πr^2
$$\approx (3.14)(1 \text{ cm})^2$$
$$\approx 3.14 \text{ cm}^2$$

Volume $\approx (3.14 \text{ cm}^2)(6 \text{ cm})$
$$\approx \mathbf{18.84 \text{ cm}^3}$$

7. $c = 2.54n$
$c = 2.54(4)$
$c = \mathbf{10.16}$

8. $y = 2x + 2$

x	y
−1	0
0	2
1	4

Check student work. Number pairs will vary.

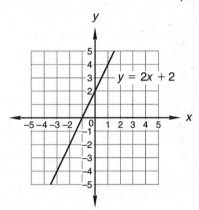

$$\text{Slope} = \frac{\text{rise}}{\text{run}} = \frac{+2}{1} = \mathbf{2}$$

9.

Tax	Total
$40.00	$40.00
× 0.075	+ $ 3.00
$ 3.00	**$43.00**

10. $0.1 \times W_N = 175$
$$W_N = \frac{175}{0.1}$$
$$W_N = \mathbf{1750}$$

11.

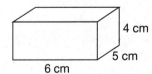

$$\text{Volume} = \frac{1}{2} \cdot 6 \text{ cm} \cdot 6 \text{ cm} \cdot 5 \text{ cm} = 90 \text{ cm}^3$$

$$\text{Volume} = 6 \text{ cm} \cdot 5 \text{ cm} \cdot 4 \text{ cm} = 120 \text{ cm}^3$$
$$\text{Total Volume} = \mathbf{210 \text{ cm}^3}$$

12. In the figure the acute angles are supplementary to the obtuse angles.

$$m\angle f = 180° - m\angle a$$
$$m\angle f = 180° - 115°$$
$$m\angle f = \mathbf{65°}$$

Solutions

13. $d = rt$

$\dfrac{d}{t} = \dfrac{rt}{t}$

$\dfrac{d}{r} = r$

14. Since the triangles are similar,
$m\angle x = 180° - 140°$
$m\angle x = \mathbf{40°}$

15. a. $\dfrac{y}{12} = \dfrac{6}{18}$

$18y = 72$

$y = \mathbf{4}$

b. $6f = 18$

$f = \dfrac{18}{6}$

$f = \mathbf{3}$

16. $1\dfrac{2}{3}x + 15 = 45$

$1\dfrac{2}{3}x + 15 - 15 = 45 - 15$

$1\dfrac{2}{3}x = 30$

$\dfrac{3}{5} \cdot \dfrac{5}{3}x = \dfrac{3}{5} \cdot 30$

$x = \mathbf{18}$

17. $3x - 24 = x + 12$
$3x - 24 - x = x + 12 - x$
$2x - 24 = 12$
$2x - 24 + 24 = 12 + 24$
$2x = 36$
$\dfrac{2x}{2} = \dfrac{36}{2}$
$x = \mathbf{18}$

18. $\dfrac{(-6) + (7)(-4) - (-1)^2}{(-1) - (-2)}$

$= \dfrac{-6 - 28 - 1}{-1 + 2} = \dfrac{-35}{1} = \mathbf{-35}$

19. $100 - \{90 - 3[4 + 3(2^3)]\}$
$= 100 - [90 - 3(4 + 24)] = 100 - (90 - 84)$
$= 100 - 6 = \mathbf{94}$

20. $\dfrac{(-4xy)(6x)}{12x^2} = \dfrac{-24x^2y}{12x^2} = \mathbf{-2y}$

Cumulative Test 23A

1.

	%	$
Original	100	21
Discount	30	d
New	70	n

$\dfrac{100}{70} = \dfrac{21}{n}$

$100n = 1470$

$n = \mathbf{\$14.70}$

2.

	Case 1	Case 2
Amount	24 kg	42 kg
Cost	$37	d

$\dfrac{24}{37} = \dfrac{42}{d}$

$24d = 1554$

$d = \mathbf{\$64.75}$

3.

	%	$
Original	100	r
Discount	30	d
New	70	21

$\dfrac{100}{70} = \dfrac{r}{21}$

$70r = 2100$

$r = \mathbf{\$30}$

4. $\dfrac{6 \times 10^6}{3 \times 10^3} = \mathbf{2 \times 10^3}$

5. Mean: $\dfrac{0.6 + 0.7 + 0.85 + 1.5 + 5.3}{5} = 1.79$

Median: 0.85
Mean − median = 1.79 − 0.85 = **0.94**

6. Sample space = {AB, AC, BA, BC, CA, CB}

$P(A \text{ or } A) = \dfrac{4}{6} = \dfrac{\mathbf{2}}{\mathbf{3}}$

7. $3000
$\underline{\times\ \ \ 1.08}$
   $3240 1st year total
$\underline{\times\ \ \ 1.08}$
$3499.20 2nd year total

Interest earned: **$499.20**

8. $W_P \times 30 = 4.50$

$$\frac{W_P \times 30}{30} = \frac{4.50}{30}$$

$$W_P = 0.15$$

$$W_P = \mathbf{15\%}$$

9. a. Volume $= (20 \text{ cm})(10 \text{ cm})(15 \text{ cm})$
$= 3000 \text{ cm}^3$

$= 3000 \text{ cm}^3 \cdot \dfrac{1 \text{ L}}{1000 \text{ cm}^3}$

$= \mathbf{3\ L}$

b. $3 \text{ L} \cdot \dfrac{1 \text{ kg}}{1 \text{ L}} = \mathbf{3\ kg}$

10. $4 \text{ ft}^2 \cdot \dfrac{12 \text{ in.}}{1 \text{ ft}} \cdot \dfrac{12 \text{ in.}}{1 \text{ ft}} = \mathbf{576 \text{ in.}^2}$

11. $a = 60$ yd, $b = 80$ yd, $c = $ length of shortcut
$$a^2 + b^2 = c^2$$
$$(60 \text{ yd})^2 + (80 \text{ yd})^2 = c^2$$
$$3600 \text{ yd}^2 + 6400 \text{ yd}^2 = c^2$$
$$10{,}000 \text{ yd}^2 = c^2$$
$$100 \text{ yd} = c$$
Yards saved $= 140 \text{ yd} - 100 \text{ yd} = \mathbf{40\ yd}$

12. Volume of pyramid $= \dfrac{1}{3} \cdot$ area of base $\cdot$ height

$= \dfrac{1}{3} \cdot (30 \text{ m})(30 \text{ m}) \cdot 20 \text{ m}$

$= \mathbf{6000 \text{ m}^3}$

13. $y = -x + 2$

x	y
0	2
1	1
2	0

Check student work. Number pairs will vary.

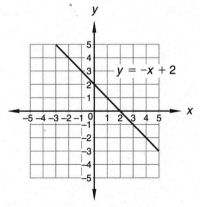

Slope $= \dfrac{\text{rise}}{\text{run}} = \dfrac{-2}{2} = \mathbf{-1}$

14. $A = \dfrac{1}{2}bh$

$20 = \dfrac{1}{2}(10)h$

$20 = 5h$

$\mathbf{4} = h$

15.

[figure of triangles with angles 80°, x, 40°, 50°, 100°, 30°, 150°]

$$\text{m}\angle x + 40° + 80° = 180°$$
$$\text{m}\angle x + 120° = 180°$$
$$\text{m}\angle x + 120° - 120° = 180° - 120°$$
$$\text{m}\angle x = \mathbf{60°}$$

16. $1\dfrac{3}{5}w - 17 = 23$

$1\dfrac{3}{5}w - 17 + 17 = 23 + 17$

$1\dfrac{3}{5}w = 40$

$\dfrac{5}{8} \cdot \dfrac{8}{5}w = \dfrac{5}{8} \cdot 40$

$w = \mathbf{25}$

17. $2x + 3 < 5$

$2x + 3 - 3 < 5 - 3$

$2x < 2$

$\dfrac{2x}{2} < \dfrac{2}{2}$

$x < \mathbf{1}$

[number line from -3 to 4 with open circle at 1]

18. $(-2)^2 \cdot 2^{-2} = 4 \cdot \dfrac{1}{2^2}$

$= 4 \cdot \dfrac{1}{4}$

$= \mathbf{1}$

19. $\dfrac{3x \cdot 3x}{3x + 3x} = \dfrac{9x^2}{6x} = \dfrac{\mathbf{3x}}{\mathbf{2}}$

20. $\dfrac{(-7) - (-3) + (2)(-3)}{(-3) - (2)} = \dfrac{-7 + 3 - 6}{-5}$

$= \dfrac{-10}{-5} = \mathbf{2}$

1.

	%	$
Original	100	21
Discount	25	d
New	75	n

$$\frac{100}{75} = \frac{21}{n}$$
$$100n = 1575$$
$$n = \mathbf{\$15.75}$$

2.

	Case 1	Case 2
Amount	24 lb	42 lb
Cost	$41	d

$$\frac{24}{41} = \frac{42}{d}$$
$$24d = 1722$$
$$d = \mathbf{\$71.75}$$

3.

	%	$
Original	100	r
Discount	25	d
New	75	21

$$\frac{100}{75} = \frac{r}{21}$$
$$75r = 2100$$
$$r = \mathbf{\$28}$$

4. $\dfrac{8 \times 10^8}{2 \times 10^2} = 4 \times 10^6$

5. Mean: $\dfrac{0.6 + 0.7 + 0.85 + 2.0 + 5.3}{5} = 1.89$

Median: 0.85
Mean − median = 1.89 − 0.85 = **1.04**

6. {AB, AC, BA, BC, CA, CB}

$P(C, C) = \dfrac{4}{6} = \mathbf{\dfrac{2}{3}}$

7.
```
    $4000
  ×   1.07
    $4280   1st year total
  ×   1.07
  $4579.60  2nd year total
```
Interest earned: **$579.60**

8. $W_P \times 30 = 7.50$

$$\frac{W_P \times 30}{30} = \frac{7.50}{30}$$
$$W_P = 0.25$$
$$W_P = \mathbf{25\%}$$

9. a. Volume = (30 cm)(15 cm)(20 cm)
$$= 9000 \text{ cm}^3$$
$$= 9000 \text{ cm}^3 \cdot \frac{1 \text{ L}}{1000 \text{ cm}^3}$$
$$= \mathbf{9 \text{ L}}$$

b. $9 \text{ L} \cdot \dfrac{1 \text{ kg}}{1 \text{ L}} = \mathbf{9 \text{ kg}}$

10. $6 \text{ yd}^2 \cdot \dfrac{3 \text{ ft}}{1 \text{ yd}} \cdot \dfrac{3 \text{ ft}}{1 \text{ yd}} = \mathbf{54 \text{ ft}^2}$

11. $a = 20$ yd, $b = 15$ yd, $c =$ length of shortcut
$$a^2 + b^2 = c^2$$
$$(20 \text{ yd})^2 + (15 \text{ yd})^2 = c^2$$
$$400 \text{ yd}^2 + 225 \text{ yd}^2 = c^2$$
$$625 \text{ yd}^2 = c^2$$
$$25 \text{ yd} = c$$
Yards saved = 35 yd − 25 yd = **10 yd**

12. Volume of a cone = $\dfrac{1}{3} \cdot$ area of base $\cdot$ height
$$\approx \frac{1}{3} \cdot (3.14)(10 \text{ in.})^2 \cdot 15 \text{ in.}$$
$$\approx \mathbf{1570 \text{ in.}^3}$$

13. $y = -x - 1$

x	y
0	−1
1	−2
2	−3

Check student work. Number pairs will vary.

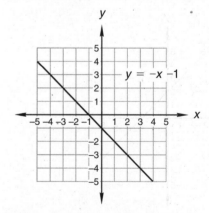

Slope = $\dfrac{\text{rise}}{\text{run}} = \dfrac{-2}{2} = \mathbf{-1}$

14. $A = \frac{1}{2}bh$

$20 = \frac{1}{2}(5)h$

$20 = \frac{5}{2}h$

8 $= h$

15.

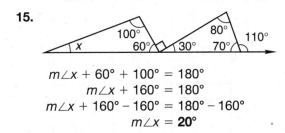

$m\angle x + 60° + 100° = 180°$
$m\angle x + 160° = 180°$
$m\angle x + 160° - 160° = 180° - 160°$
$m\angle x = \textbf{20°}$

16. $2\frac{3}{5}y + 13 = 39$

$2\frac{3}{5}y + 13 - 13 = 39 - 13$

$2\frac{3}{5}y = 26$

$\frac{5}{13} \cdot \frac{13}{5}y = \frac{5}{13} \cdot 26$

$y = \textbf{10}$

17. $2x + 3 \geq 5$
$2x + 3 - 3 \geq 5 - 3$
$2x \geq 2$
$\frac{2x}{2} \geq \frac{2}{2}$
$x \geq \textbf{1}$

```
  ←——+——+——+——●——+——+——+——→
    -2  -1   0   1   2   3   4   5
```

18. $(-3)^2 \cdot 3^{-2} = 9 \cdot \frac{1}{3^2} = 9 \cdot \frac{1}{9} = \textbf{1}$

19. $\frac{2x \cdot 2x}{2x + 2x} = \frac{4x^2}{4x} = \textbf{x}$

20. $\frac{(-7) + (-3) + (-2)(-3)}{(-3) - (-2)} = \frac{-7 - 3 + 6}{-3 + 2}$

$= \frac{-4}{-1} = \textbf{4}$

Name _____ Time _____

Facts	Multiply.								
9 × 8 72	8 × 2 16	10 × 10 100	6 × 3 18	4 × 2 8	5 × 5 25	9 × 9 81	6 × 4 24	9 × 6 54	7 × 3 21
9 × 3 27	6 × 5 30	0 × 0 0	7 × 6 42	8 × 8 64	7 × 4 28	5 × 3 15	9 × 7 63	2 × 2 4	8 × 6 48
7 × 7 49	6 × 2 12	4 × 3 12	8 × 5 40	4 × 4 16	3 × 2 6	n × 0 0	8 × 4 32	6 × 6 36	9 × 2 18
8 × 3 24	5 × 4 20	n × 1 n	7 × 2 14	9 × 5 45	8 × 7 56	3 × 3 9	9 × 4 36	5 × 2 10	7 × 5 35

Problem Solving	Answer the question below.

Problem: Kids on a field trip to a dairy farm are gathered in the barn with cows. If there are 11 heads and 28 legs in the barn, how many kids and how many cows are in the barn?

Understand

I know there are 11 heads, 28 legs and that the only occupants are kids and cows.

I can use the known quantities to draw a picture to find the number of kids and cows in the barn.

Plan

Strategy: Use logical reasoning and draw a picture.

Solve

Draw eleven small circles to represent the heads. Each head has at least one pair of legs, so draw 22 of the 28 legs onto the 11 heads. The remaining 6 legs must be viewed as 3 additional pairs of legs that can be drawn onto 3 of the heads.

```
   3 cows   3 heads   12 legs
+  8 kids   8 heads   16 legs
  11 total  11 heads  28 legs
```

Answer: There are 8 kids and 3 cows in the barn.

Check

Did I use the correct information?
Did I do what was asked?
Is my answer reasonable?

Name _____ Time _____

Facts   Solve each equation.

$a + 12 = 20$	$b - 8 = 10$	$5c = 40$	$\dfrac{d}{4} = 12$	$11 + e = 24$
$a = 8$	$b = 18$	$c = 8$	$d = 48$	$e = 13$
$25 - f = 10$	$10g = 60$	$\dfrac{24}{h} = 6$	$15 = j + 8$	$20 = k - 5$
$f = 15$	$g = 6$	$h = 4$	$j = 7$	$k = 25$
$30 = 6m$	$9 = \dfrac{n}{3}$	$18 = 6 + p$	$5 = 15 - q$	$36 = 4r$
$m = 5$	$n = 27$	$p = 12$	$q = 10$	$r = 9$
$2 = \dfrac{16}{s}$	$t + 8 = 12$	$u - 15 = 30$	$8v = 48$	$\dfrac{w}{3} = 6$
$s = 8$	$t = 4$	$u = 45$	$v = 6$	$w = 18$

Problem Solving   Answer the question below.

Problem: An art teacher makes earrings from silver nuggets. Each nugget makes 1 earring. The shavings left over from 6 nuggets are then melted and recast to form one more nugget. The teacher ordered 36 nuggets for her class. How many earrings can be made from 36 nuggets?

Understand

I know each nugget makes at least one earring, but there are shavings left over.
Shavings from 6 nuggets can be used to make 1 additional earring.

I need to create and use an equation to solve a problem. I need to find the number of earrings the teacher can make with 36 nuggets.

- -

Plan

Strategy: Write a number sentence or equation.

I can use the total number of nuggets to determine how many shavings are left over.

I can use the amount of shavings to calculate how many additional nuggets can be made. Then I can calculate how many earrings can be produced with 36 nuggets.

- -

Solve

The original 36 nuggets will make 36 earrings. The shavings from six nuggets provide enough silver to make another earring. So $36 \div 6 = 6$ more nuggets and earrings. Those six nuggets will produce enough shavings to make one final nugget and earring. $36 + 6 + 1 = 43$
Answer: 43 earrings

- -

Check

Name _____ Time _____

Facts   Write each improper fraction as a whole number or mixed number.

$\dfrac{5}{2} = 2\dfrac{1}{2}$	$\dfrac{7}{4} = 1\dfrac{3}{4}$	$\dfrac{12}{5} = 2\dfrac{2}{5}$	$\dfrac{10}{3} = 3\dfrac{1}{3}$	$\dfrac{15}{2} = 7\dfrac{1}{2}$
$\dfrac{15}{5} = 3$	$\dfrac{11}{8} = 1\dfrac{3}{8}$	$2\dfrac{3}{2} = 3\dfrac{1}{2}$	$4\dfrac{5}{4} = 5\dfrac{1}{4}$	$3\dfrac{7}{4} = 4\dfrac{3}{4}$

Write each mixed number as an improper fraction.

$1\dfrac{1}{2} = \dfrac{3}{2}$	$2\dfrac{2}{3} = \dfrac{8}{3}$	$3\dfrac{3}{4} = \dfrac{15}{4}$	$2\dfrac{1}{2} = \dfrac{5}{2}$	$6\dfrac{2}{3} = \dfrac{20}{3}$
$2\dfrac{3}{4} = \dfrac{11}{4}$	$3\dfrac{1}{3} = \dfrac{10}{3}$	$4\dfrac{1}{2} = \dfrac{9}{2}$	$1\dfrac{7}{8} = \dfrac{15}{8}$	$12\dfrac{1}{2} = \dfrac{25}{2}$

Problem Solving   Answer the question below.

Problem: Sarah remembered that the three numbers she used to open her combination lock were 32, 16, and 8, but she could not remember the order. List all the permutations (arrangements) of the three numbers Sarah could try.

Understand

I know there are only three numbers—32, 16 and 8—and that each number can only be used once.

I need to make a list of all possible permutations.

Plan

Strategy: Make an organized list.

I can arrange the numbers in a list of possible outcomes.

Solve

32, 16, 8
32, 8, 16
16, 32, 8
16, 8, 32
8, 32, 16
8, 16, 32
There are 6 possible permutations of the 3 numbers.

Check

Facts   Reduce each fraction to lowest terms.

$\frac{50}{100} = \frac{1}{2}$	$\frac{4}{16} = \frac{1}{4}$	$\frac{6}{8} = \frac{3}{4}$	$\frac{8}{12} = \frac{2}{3}$	$\frac{10}{100} = \frac{1}{10}$
$\frac{8}{16} = \frac{1}{2}$	$\frac{20}{100} = \frac{1}{5}$	$\frac{3}{12} = \frac{1}{4}$	$\frac{60}{100} = \frac{3}{5}$	$\frac{9}{12} = \frac{3}{4}$
$\frac{6}{9} = \frac{2}{3}$	$\frac{90}{100} = \frac{9}{10}$	$\frac{5}{10} = \frac{1}{2}$	$\frac{12}{16} = \frac{3}{4}$	$\frac{25}{100} = \frac{1}{4}$
$\frac{4}{10} = \frac{2}{5}$	$\frac{4}{6} = \frac{2}{3}$	$\frac{75}{100} = \frac{3}{4}$	$\frac{4}{12} = \frac{1}{3}$	$\frac{6}{10} = \frac{3}{5}$

Problem Solving   Answer the question below.

Problem: A bookworm finds itself on page 1 of volume 1, and begins eating straight through to the last page of volume 5. The volumes are in order on the shelf, and each book is 6 cm thick, including the front and back covers, which are each $\frac{1}{2}$ cm thick. How far will the bookworm travel?

Understand

I know there are 5 books on the shelf, in order from volume 1 to volume 5. Each book is 6 cm thick and each cover is $\frac{1}{2}$ cm thick. The bookworm does not eat through the front cover of volume 1 or through the back cover of volume 5. It eats through all of volumes 2, 3, and 4, and it eats through all but $\frac{1}{2}$ cm of volumes 1 and 5, or $5\frac{1}{2}$ cm per volume.

I need to calculate the total distance that the worm traveled.

- -

Plan

Strategy: Write a number sentence.

I can use the information given to calculate the distance.

- -

Solve

Add the distances traveled through each volume to find the total distance:

$d = 5\frac{1}{2}$ cm $+$ 6cm $+$ 6cm $+$ 6cm $+$ $5\frac{1}{2}$ cm

$d = 29$ cm

Answer: 29 cm

- -

Check

Facts Write the word or words to complete each definition.

The distance around a circle is its ___circumference___.	Every point on a circle is the same distance from its ___center___.	The distance across a circle through its center is its ___diameter___.	The distance from a circle to its center is its ___radius___.
Two or more circles with the same center are ___concentric circles___.	A segment between two points on a circle is a ___chord___.	Part of a circumference is an ___arc___.	Part of a circle bounded by an arc and two radii is a ___sector___.
Half of a circle is a ___semicircle___.	An angle whose vertex is the center of a circle is a ___central angle___.	An angle whose vertex is on the circle whose sides include chords is an ___inscribed angle___.	A polygon whose vertices are on the circle and whose edges are within the circle is an ___inscribed polygon___.

Problem Solving Answer the question below.

Problem: Fiona has 8 coins totaling 50¢. What combinations of coins could Fiona have?

Understand

I know there are 8 coins of any value less than 50¢ (1¢, 5¢, 10¢, 25¢), and the total value of the coins is 50¢.

I need to find a combination using unknown quantities of known values. The number of coins (8) limits the number of variables. The total given (50¢) limits the sum of variables.

Plan

Strategy: Use logical reasoning, and guess-and-check different combinations to find the correct sum.

Solve

6 nickels (30¢) + 2 dimes (20¢) = 50¢
1 quarter (25¢) + 2 dimes (20¢) + 5 pennies (5¢) = 50¢

Check

Name _____ Time _____

Facts   Name each figure illustrated.

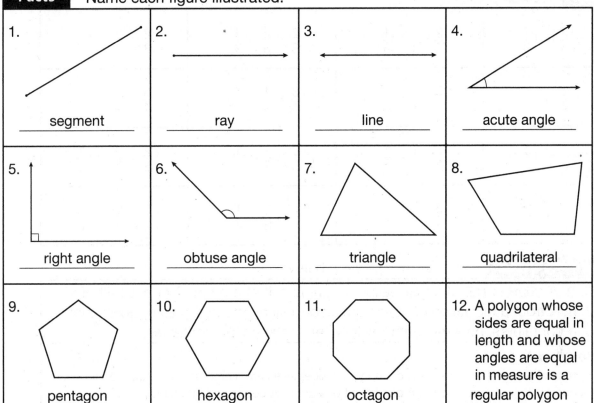

1.	2.	3.	4.
segment	ray	line	acute angle
5.	6.	7.	8.
right angle	obtuse angle	triangle	quadrilateral
9.	10.	11.	12. A polygon whose sides are equal in length and whose angles are equal in measure is a regular polygon.
pentagon	hexagon	octagon	

Problem Solving   Answer the question below.

Problem: Copy this problem and find the missing digits.
No two digits may be alike.

$$\begin{array}{r} \_\;\_\;\_ \\ \times \quad 7 \\ \hline 9\;\_\;\_ \end{array}$$

Understand

I know that an unknown 3-digit number is multiplied by 7. The product is an unknown 3-digit number. The first digit of the product is 9, so the number is greater than 900 but less than 1000.

I need to find the missing digits without repeating any digits.

- -

Plan

Strategy: Use logical reasoning, work backwards, and guess and check.

Divide the unknown answer by the multiplier, 7.

- -

Solve   Divide 999 and 901 by 7 to identify the range of factors to try.

$999 \div 7$ is about 143; and $901 \div 7$ is about 129. I can guess-and-check to find the missing 3-digit factor between 129 and 143.

$7 \times 140 = 980$ (0 repeats)   Answer: $\underline{1\ 3\ 6}$
$7 \times 135 = 945$ (5 repeats) $\times \quad \underline{7}$
$7 \times 130 = 910$ (1 repeats) $9\ \underline{5}\ 2$
$7 \times 136 = 952$

- -

Check

Name _____ Time _____

Facts Simplify.			
$\frac{2}{3} + \frac{2}{3} = 1\frac{1}{3}$	$\frac{2}{3} - \frac{1}{3} = \frac{1}{3}$	$\frac{2}{3} \times \frac{2}{3} = \frac{4}{9}$	$\frac{2}{3} \div \frac{2}{3} = 1$
$\frac{3}{4} + \frac{1}{4} = 1$	$\frac{3}{4} - \frac{1}{4} = \frac{1}{2}$	$\frac{3}{4} \times \frac{1}{4} = \frac{3}{16}$	$\frac{3}{4} \div \frac{1}{4} = 3$
$\frac{2}{3} + \frac{1}{2} = 1\frac{1}{6}$	$\frac{2}{3} - \frac{1}{2} = \frac{1}{6}$	$\frac{2}{3} \times \frac{1}{2} = \frac{1}{3}$	$\frac{2}{3} \div \frac{1}{2} = 1\frac{1}{3}$
$\frac{3}{4} + \frac{2}{3} = 1\frac{5}{12}$	$\frac{3}{4} - \frac{2}{3} = \frac{1}{12}$	$\frac{3}{4} \times \frac{2}{3} = \frac{1}{2}$	$\frac{3}{4} \div \frac{2}{3} = 1\frac{1}{8}$

Problem Solving   Answer the question below.

Problem: A quart is half of a half-gallon. A pint is half of a quart. A cup is half of a pint. If milk from a full gallon container is used to fill empty half-gallon, quart, pint and cup containers, how much milk will be left in the gallon container?

Understand

The volume at the start is 1 gallon. The empty container sizes are a half-gallon, a quart, a pint and a cup. A quart is half of a half-gallon. A pint is half of a quart. A cup is half of a pint.

I am asked to calculate an unknown quantity given related known quantities. I need to determine how much milk is left in the gallon container when it is used to fill all the other containers.

Plan

Strategy: Make a table, write a number sentence, and work backwards.

Starting with a gallon, I can subtract each of the smaller quantities to find the remaining milk.

Solve

Equivalence of Customary Units of Capacity

gallon	$\frac{1}{2}$ gallon	quart	pint	cup
1	2	4	8	16
	1	2	4	8
		1	2	4
			1	2

1 gallon $- \frac{1}{2}$ gallon $= \frac{1}{2}$ gallon
$\frac{1}{2}$ gallon $-$ quart $= 1$ quart
1 quart $-$ 1 pint $= 1$ pint
1 pint $-$ 1 cup $= 1$ cup of milk left in the gallon container

Check

Name _____ Time _____

Facts   Write the number that completes each equivalent measure.

1. 1 foot	= __12__ inches	15. 1 kilogram	≈ __2.2__ pounds
2. 1 yard	= __36__ inches	16. 1 pint	= __16__ ounces
3. 1 yard	= __3__ feet	17. 1 pint	= __2__ cups
4. 1 mile	= __5280__ feet	18. 1 quart	= __2__ pints
5. 1 centimeter	= __10__ millimeters	19. 1 gallon	= __4__ quarts
6. 1 meter	= __1000__ millimeters	20. 1 liter	= __1000__ milliliters
7. 1 meter	= __100__ centimeters		
8. 1 kilometer	= __1000__ meters		
9. 1 inch	= __2.54__ centimeters		

21–24. 1 milliliter of water has a volume of __1 cm³__ and a mass of __1 gram__.
One liter of water has a volume of __1000__ cm³ and a mass of __1__ kg.

10. 1 pound	= __16__ ounces
11. 1 ton	= __2000__ pounds
12. 1 gram	= __1000__ milligrams
13. 1 kilogram	= __1000__ grams
14. 1 metric ton	= __1000__ kilograms

25–26. Water freezes at __32__ °F and __0__ °C.

27–28. Water boils at __212__ °F and __100__ °C.

29–30. Normal body temperature is __98.6__ °F and __37__ °C.

Problem Solving   Answer the question below.

Problem: If 2 chickens can lay a total of 2 eggs in 2 days, how many eggs can 4 chickens lay in 4 days?

Understand
I am told that 2 chickens can lay 2 eggs in 2 days.
I need to find the number of eggs 4 chickens can lay in 4 days.

Plan   Strategy: Use logical reasoning and write an equation.
Use the information to find out how long it takes 1 chicken to lay 1 egg. Then use this information to find the number of eggs that 4 chickens can lay in 4 days.

Solve   Each chicken lays an egg independently of the other chickens. So if two chickens can lay 2 eggs in two days, 1 chicken can lay 1 egg in 2 days. Divide the number of days by the number of days needed to lay an egg to find the number of eggs 1 chicken can lay. Multiply this number by the number of chickens to find the number of eggs laid.
4 days ÷ 2 days = 2 (eggs 1 chicken can lay in 4 days)
2 eggs × 4 chickens = 8 eggs (number of eggs 4 chickens can lay in 4 days)
Answer: 8 eggs

Check

Facts	Find the number that completes each proportion.			
$\frac{3}{4} = \frac{a}{12}$ $a = 9$	$\frac{3}{4} = \frac{12}{b}$ $b = 16$	$\frac{c}{5} = \frac{12}{20}$ $c = 3$	$\frac{2}{d} = \frac{12}{24}$ $d = 4$	$\frac{8}{12} = \frac{4}{e}$ $e = 6$
$\frac{f}{10} = \frac{10}{5}$ $f = 20$	$\frac{5}{g} = \frac{25}{100}$ $g = 20$	$\frac{10}{100} = \frac{5}{h}$ $h = 50$	$\frac{8}{4} = \frac{j}{16}$ $j = 32$	$\frac{24}{k} = \frac{8}{6}$ $k = 18$
$\frac{9}{12} = \frac{36}{m}$ $m = 48$	$\frac{50}{100} = \frac{w}{30}$ $w = 15$	$\frac{3}{9} = \frac{5}{p}$ $p = 15$	$\frac{q}{60} = \frac{15}{20}$ $q = 45$	$\frac{2}{5} = \frac{r}{100}$ $r = 40$

Problem Solving	Answer the question below.

Problem: Two children want to build a triangular dog pen in a corner of their backyard for their dog. They have 100 feet of fencing. They stretch 55 feet of fencing diagonally across the corner of the yard. What can you predict about the rest of the fencing project?

Understand

I know there is a total of 100 feet of fencing available. 55 feet of fencing is used to fence the side of the dog pen that is opposite from the corner, which is the hypotenuse of the triangular area.

I need to predict whether the dimensions of the dog pen are reasonable, given the length of fencing available.

Plan

Strategy: Use logical reasoning and write an equation.

Specifically, I can use the measurement of the diagonal section of fencing as the hypotenuse of a triangle. Then I can apply knowledge of the properties of triangles to determine whether there is enough fencing to complete the dog pen.

Solve

The sum of the lengths of any two sides of a triangle will always be greater than the length of the third side.

total length − side = remaining fencing for 2 sides
100 ft − 55 ft = 45 ft
55 ft > 45 ft

Answer: The children do not have enough fencing to enclose the dog pen if one side is 55 ft. They either need more fencing or they need to change the dimensions of the pen.

Check

Facts   Simplify.

$0.8 + 0.4 = 1.2$	$0.8 - 0.4 = 0.4$	$0.8 \times 0.4 = 0.32$	$0.8 \div 0.4 = 2$
$1.2 + 0.4 = 1.6$	$1.2 - 0.4 = 0.8$	$1.2 \times 0.4 = 0.48$	$1.2 \div 0.4 = 3$
$6 + 0.3 = 6.3$	$6 - 0.3 = 5.7$	$6 \times 0.3 = 1.8$	$6 \div 0.3 = 20$
$1.2 + 4 = 5.2$	$0.01 - 0.01 = 0$	$0.3 \times 0.3 = 0.09$	$0.12 \div 4 = 0.03$

Problem Solving   Answer the question below.

Problem: Mariabella was $\frac{1}{4}$ of the way through her book. Twenty pages later she was $\frac{1}{3}$ of the way through her book. When she is $\frac{3}{4}$ of the way through the book, how many pages will she have to read to finish the book?

Understand

I know that $\frac{1}{4}$ of book + 20 pages = $\frac{1}{3}$ of book

I need to find how many pages Mariabella has to read when she is $\frac{3}{4}$ finished.

Plan

Strategy: Use logical reasoning and set up an equation.

Use the information given to understand the relationship between the number of pages read and fraction of the book those pages represent.

Solve

$\frac{1}{3}$ of the pages of the book $= \frac{1}{4}$ of the pages of the book $+$ 20 pages.

Since $\frac{1}{3} - \frac{1}{4} = \frac{1}{12}$, 20 pages is $\frac{1}{12}$ of the number of pages in the book

Therefore, the total number of pages in the book is $20 \times 12 = 240$ pages.

To find the number of pages Mariabella has read when she is $\frac{3}{4}$ finished, multiple 240 by $\frac{3}{4}$ or 0.75.

$240 \times 0.75 = 180$ pages.

Subtract to find the number of pages Mariabella has to read to finish the book: $240 - 180 = 60$ pages.

Answer: 60 pages

Check

Facts	Simplify each power or root.			
$\sqrt{100} = 10$	$\sqrt{16} = 4$	$\sqrt{81} = 9$	$\sqrt{4} = 2$	$\sqrt{144} = 12$
$\sqrt{64} = 8$	$\sqrt{49} = 7$	$\sqrt{25} = 5$	$\sqrt{9} = 3$	$\sqrt{36} = 6$
$8^2 = 64$	$5^2 = 25$	$3^2 = 9$	$12^2 = 144$	$10^2 = 100$
$7^2 = 49$	$2^3 = 8$	$3^3 = 27$	$10^3 = 1000$	$5^3 = 125$

Problem Solving   Answer the question below.

Problem: The captain told Alexa that a lobster's age in years is approximately its weight multiplied by 4, plus three years. Write the captain's statement as an equation. About how much will a 13-year-old lobster weigh? What is the approximate age of a lobster that weighs 6 pounds?

Understand

I am given an algorithm to calculate a lobster's age or weight.

I need to calculate a lobster's weight given its age and its age given its weight. I can use the information given to write an equation and then use the equation to solve for unknown variables.

Plan

Strategy: Write an equation.

Use the equation to estimate the weight of a lobster, given its age.

Use the equation to estimate the age of a lobster, given its weight.

Solve

$age = 4(weight) + 3$, or $a = 4w + 3$

If a lobster is 13 years old, $a = 13$
$a = 4w + 3$
$13 = 4w + 3$
$10 = 4w$
$w = 2.5$ pounds
The lobster weighs about 2 and a half pounds.

If a lobster weighs 6 lbs, $w = 6$
$a = 4w + 3$
$a = 4(6) + 3$
$a = 24 + 3$
$a = 27$ years
The lobster is about 27 years old.

Check

Facts   Write the equivalent decimal and percent for each fraction.

Fraction	Decimal	Percent	Fraction	Decimal	Percent
$\frac{1}{2}$	0.5	50%	$\frac{1}{8}$	0.125	$12\frac{1}{2}$%
$\frac{1}{3}$	$0.\overline{3}$	$33\frac{1}{3}$%	$\frac{1}{10}$	0.1	10%
$\frac{2}{3}$	$0.\overline{6}$	$66\frac{2}{3}$%	$\frac{3}{10}$	0.3	30%
$\frac{1}{4}$	0.25	25%	$\frac{9}{10}$	0.9	90%
$\frac{3}{4}$	0.75	75%	$\frac{1}{100}$	0.01	1%
$\frac{1}{5}$	0.2	20%	$1\frac{1}{2}$	1.5	150%

Problem Solving   Answer the question below.

Problem: Marsha started a 1024-meter race, ran half the distance to the finish line, and then handed the baton to Greg. Greg ran half the remaining distance and handed off to Alice, who ran half the remaining distance. How far from the finish line did Alice stop? If the team continues this pattern, how many more runners will they need in order to cross the finish line?

Understand

I know the length of the race is 1024 m. Marsha ran 512 m, Greg ran 256 m and Alice ran 128 m.

I need to find where Alice stopped and how many more runners the team needs to cross the finish line.

Plan

Strategy: Write a number sentence.

I can subtract the distances that the runners ran from the race length to find how far from the finish Alice stopped. I can divide this by 2 to find the next runner's distance, and so on, until the total distance ran equals 1024 m.

Solve

$1024 - 512 - 256 - 128 = 128$. Alice stopped 128 m from the finish.
Terms in the sequence: 512, 256, 128, 64, 32, 16, 8, 4, 2, 1, 0.5, ...

This sequence will approach zero (the finish line) but never equal zero. If each runner runs half the remaining distance, runner 11 will be within an arm's reach of the finish line, and will be able to pass the baton over the line, ending the race without a runner stepping over the line.

Check

Facts	Write the number for each conversion or factor.

1. 2 m = __200__ cm

2. 1.5 km = __1500__ m

3. 2.54 cm = __25.4__ mm

4. 125 cm = __1.25__ m

5. 10 km = __10,000__ m

6. 5000 m = __5__ km

7. 50 cm = __0.5__ m

8. 50 cm = __500__ mm

9. 2 L = __2000__ mL

10. 250 mL = __0.25__ L

11. 4 kg = __4000__ g

12. 2.5 g = __2500__ mg

13. 500 mg = __0.5__ g

14. 0.5 kg = __500__ g

15–16. Two liters of water have a volume of __2000__ cm^3 and a mass of __2__ kg.

	Prefix	Factor
17.	kilo-	1000
18.	hecto-	100
19.	deka-	10
	(unit)	1
20.	deci-	0.1
21.	centi-	0.01
22.	milli-	0.001

Problem Solving	Answer the question below.

Problem: Two sisters, Gaby and Natalia, decide to buy a computer together. Natalia earns money helping the girls' grandparents. Gaby is older and has a full-time job for the summer. Because Gaby will be earning three times as much as her sister, she says that Natalia should pay for $\frac{1}{4}$ of the computer. Natalia thinks she should pay for $\frac{1}{3}$ of the computer. Who is correct?

Understand

I know Gaby earns 3 times as much money as Natalia. Both Gaby's and Natalia's money will be used together to buy the computer.

I need to determine which sister's calculation is correct.

- -

Plan

Strategy: Use logical reasoning

Set up a ratio.

- -

Solve

Earning "three times more" means that for every $1 that Natalia earns, Gaby earns $3, and together the girls have earned $4. Natalia has earned 1 of the 4 dollars, or $\frac{1}{4}$ of the money, and Gaby has earned 3 of the 4 dollars, or $\frac{3}{4}$ of the money.

Answer: Gaby is correct.

- -

Check

Facts	Simplify. Reduce the answers if possible.		
$3 + 1\frac{2}{3} = 4\frac{2}{3}$	$3 - 1\frac{2}{3} = 1\frac{1}{3}$	$3 \times 1\frac{2}{3} = 5$	$3 \div 1\frac{2}{3} = 1\frac{4}{5}$
$1\frac{2}{3} + 1\frac{1}{2} = 3\frac{1}{6}$	$1\frac{2}{3} - 1\frac{1}{2} = \frac{1}{6}$	$1\frac{2}{3} \times 1\frac{1}{2} = 2\frac{1}{2}$	$1\frac{2}{3} \div 1\frac{1}{2} = 1\frac{1}{9}$
$2\frac{1}{2} + 1\frac{2}{3} = 4\frac{1}{6}$	$2\frac{1}{2} - 1\frac{2}{3} = \frac{5}{6}$	$2\frac{1}{2} \times 1\frac{2}{3} = 4\frac{1}{6}$	$2\frac{1}{2} \div 1\frac{2}{3} = 1\frac{1}{2}$
$4\frac{1}{2} + 2\frac{1}{4} = 6\frac{3}{4}$	$4\frac{1}{2} - 2\frac{1}{4} = 2\frac{1}{4}$	$4\frac{1}{2} \times 2\frac{1}{4} = 10\frac{1}{8}$	$4\frac{1}{2} \div 2\frac{1}{4} = 2$

Problem Solving	Answer the question below.

Problem: One-foot-square tiles, packed 20 per box, will be used to cover the floor of a rectangular room. The room is 20 ft 6 in. long and 14 ft 6 in. wide. If all cut-off portions of tiles can be used, how many boxes of tile are needed? If only one portion from each cut tile may be used, how many boxes are needed?

Understand

I know each tile is 1 sq. ft. There are 20 tiles in a box. The floor measures 20 ft. 6 in. by 14 ft. 6 in.

I need to find the number of boxes of tile it would take to tile the floor.

- -

Plan

Strategy: Draw a picture or diagram and write an equation.

Calculate the total square footage needed to tile the floor and divide that by the square footage covered per box.

- -

Solve

$20.5 \times 14.5 = 297.25$ square feet, or about 300 square feet
$300 \div 20 = 15$ boxes of tiles (if all cut-off pieces are used)

The long side of the room requires 20 half-tiles and the short side requires 14 half-tiles (plus $\frac{1}{4}$ of a tile for the final corner). If only one portion from each cut tile may be used, a full box will only provide 20 cut halves when 34 are needed, meaning one more box of tiles will be required (total of 16).

- -

Check

Facts   Select from the words below to describe each figure.

1.

equilateral triangle

acute triangle

isosceles triangle

2.

isosceles triangle

right triangle

3.

scalene triangle

obtuse triangle

4.

parallelogram

rectangle

rhombus

square

5.

parallelogram

rectangle

6.

parallelogram

trapezoid

7.

parallelogram

rhombus

8.

parallelogram

kite	rectangle	isosceles triangle	right triangle
trapezoid	rhombus	scalene triangle	acute triangle
parallelogram	square	equilateral triangle	obtuse triangle

Problem Solving   Answer the question below.

Problem: Telephone poles, spaced 100 feet apart, line the road on which Jesse lives. If Jesse runs from the first pole to the seventh pole, how many feet does he run? Draw a picture that illustrates the problem.

Understand

I know the distance between poles is 100 ft. Jesse starts running at the 1st pole and stops running when he reaches the 7th pole.

I need to find the distance Jesse ran to the seventh pole.

Plan

Strategy: Draw a picture.

I can use the information to draw and label an accurate representation of the problem.

Solve

Answer: Jesse runs 600 ft

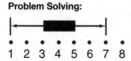

Problem Solving:

1 2 3 4 5 6 7 8

Check

468

Name _____ Time _____

Facts Simplify.			
$(-8) + (-2) = -10$	$(-8) - (-2) = -6$	$(-8)(-2) = 16$	$\dfrac{-8}{-2} = 4$
$(-9) + (+3) = -6$	$(-9) - (+3) = -12$	$(-9)(+3) = -27$	$\dfrac{-9}{+3} = -3$
$12 + (-2) = 10$	$12 - (-2) = 14$	$(12)(-2) = -24$	$\dfrac{12}{-2} = -6$
$(-4) + (-3) + (-2) = -9$	$(-4) - (-3) - (-2) = 1$	$(-4)(-3)(-2) = -24$	$\dfrac{(-4)(-3)}{(-2)} = -6$

Problem Solving   Answer the question below.

Problem: How many cubic yards of concrete must be ordered to pour the section below?

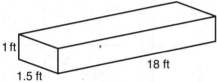

1 ft

18 ft

1.5 ft

Understand

The dimensions of a rectangular prism are given as: 18 ft long × 1.5 ft wide × 1 ft high.

I need to calculate the volume of a rectangular prism given the linear dimensions.

Plan

Strategy: Write an equation or create a model.

Calculate the volume in cubic feet and convert to cubic yards.

Solve

$18 \times 1.5 \times 1 = 27$ cubic feet
1 cubic yard $= 3$ ft $\times 3$ ft $\times 3$ ft $= 27$ cubic feet
So 18 ft $\times$ 1.5 ft $\times$ 1 ft $= 1$ cubic yard

Or

Convert dimensions to yards before multiplying

1 ft $= \dfrac{1}{3}$ yd, 1.5 ft $= \dfrac{1}{2}$ yd, 18 ft $= 6$ yd

$\dfrac{1}{3}$ yd $\times \dfrac{1}{2}$ yd $\times$ 6 yd $= 1$ cubic yd

Check

Facts Write the equivalent decimal and fraction for each percent.

Percent	Decimal	Fraction	Percent	Decimal	Fraction
10%	0.1	$\frac{1}{10}$	$33\frac{1}{3}\%$	$0.\overline{3}$	$\frac{1}{3}$
90%	0.9	$\frac{9}{10}$	20%	0.2	$\frac{1}{5}$
5%	0.05	$\frac{1}{20}$	75%	0.75	$\frac{3}{4}$
$12\frac{1}{2}\%$	0.125	$\frac{1}{8}$	$66\frac{2}{3}\%$	$0.\overline{6}$	$\frac{2}{3}$
50%	0.5	$\frac{1}{2}$	1%	0.01	$\frac{1}{100}$
25%	0.25	$\frac{1}{4}$	250%	2.5	$2\frac{1}{2}$

Problem Solving Answer the question below.

Problem: A goat is kept on a 4-meter chain connected to a metal hook in the ground. Approximately what area of grass can she eat? If she is chained at the center of the 8-m side of the garage what area of grass can she eat?

Understand

I'm given the length of the chain, 4 meters and the length of the garage, 8 meters.
I know a goat is chained to the center of the side of the garage.

I need find the area of a circle to determine how much of the lawn the goat can reach and eat.

Plan

Strategy: Write an equation.

Use the equation to calculate the area of the circle and half-circle.

Solve

The chain length equals the radius of a circle surrounding the goat.
The wall length equals the diameter of a circle.
The wall bisects the circle and limits the goat to half a circle.
When chained to a metal hook in the ground, the goat can eat grass in an area described by
$A = \pi(r)^2$
$A = 3.14(4)^2$
$A = 50.24$ square meters.

When chained to the center of the garage, the goat can only eat $\frac{1}{2}$ of the area of the circle, or approximately 25 square meters.

Check

Name _____ Time _____

Find the area of each figure. Angles that look like
Facts right angles are right angles.

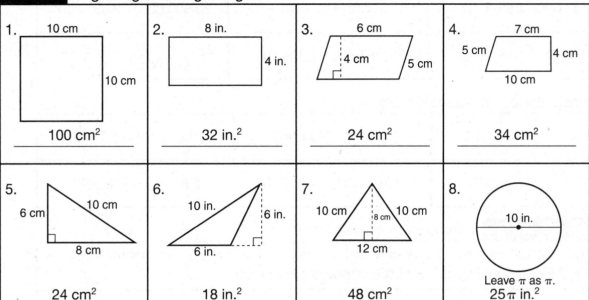

1. 10 cm
   10 cm
   100 cm²

2. 8 in.
   4 in.
   32 in.²

3. 6 cm
   4 cm
   5 cm
   24 cm²

4. 7 cm
   5 cm   4 cm
   10 cm
   34 cm²

5. 10 cm
   6 cm
   8 cm
   24 cm²

6. 10 in.
   6 in.
   6 in.
   18 in.²

7. 10 cm 10 cm
   8 cm
   12 cm
   48 cm²

8. 10 in.
   Leave π as π.
   25π in.²

Problem Solving   Answer the question below.

Problem: A summer baseball league is made up of four teams. If each team will play each other three times, how many games must be scheduled?

Understand

I know there are 4 teams in the league and each team plays each other 3 times.

I need to find the total number of games scheduled for the season.

- -

Plan

Strategy: Draw a diagram or write a number sentence or equation.

Use a model to diagram or calculate the number of games that need to be played.

- -

Solve

For each of the four teams to play each other ONCE, $3 + 2 + 1 = 6$ games must be played. If we call the teams A, B, C, and D, then this diagram shows the six game pairings.

For each team to play each other team three times, $6 \times 3 = 18$ games must be scheduled.

- -

Check

Facts	Write each number in scientific notation.	
$186{,}000 = 1.86 \times 10^5$	$0.0005 = 5 \times 10^{-4}$	$30{,}500{,}000 = 3.05 \times 10^7$
2.5 billion $= 2.5 \times 10^9$	12 million $= 1.2 \times 10^7$	$\dfrac{1}{1{,}000{,}000} = 1 \times 10^{-6}$

Write each number in standard form.

$1 \times 10^6 = 1{,}000{,}000$	$1 \times 10^{-6} = 0.000001$	$2.4 \times 10^4 = 24{,}000$
$5 \times 10^{-4} = 0.0005$	$4.75 \times 10^5 = 475{,}000$	$2.5 \times 10^{-3} = 0.0025$

Problem Solving   Answer the question below.

Problem: Candis has an 11-liter can and a 5-liter can. How can she measure out exactly 7 liters of water into a third unmarked container?

Understand

Given one can has a capacity of 11 liters and another can has a capacity of 5 liters, while a third can is unmarked.

I need to describe a method to pour an exact quantity of water into a container of unknown volume.

Plan

Strategy: Use logical reasoning and write a number sentence or equation.

I can add and subtract known volumes of water to measure out 7 liters.

Solve

Fill the 11-liter container, and then use it to fill the 5-liter container. Pour the 6 liters that remain in the 11-liter container into the unmarked container.

Refill the 11-liter container. This time empty and fill the 5-liter container TWICE from the 11-liter container. Pour the one liter of water that remains in the 11-liter container into the unmarked container for a total of 7 liters.

$11 - 5 = 6$
$11 - 5 - 5 = 1$
$6 + 1 = 7$

Check

Facts	Simplify.

$6 + 6 \times 6 - 6 \div 6 = 41$	$3^2 + \sqrt{4} + 5(6) - 7 + 8 = 42$
$4 + 2(3 + 5) - 6 \div 2 = 17$	$2 + 2[3 + 4(7 - 5)] = 24$
$\sqrt{1^3 + 2^3 + 3^3} = 6$	$\dfrac{4 + 3(7 - 5)}{6 - (5 - 4)} = 2$
$(-3)(-3) + (-3) - (-3) = 9$	$\dfrac{3(-3) - (-3)(-3)}{(-3) - (3)(-3)} = -3$

Problem Solving	Answer the question below.

Problem: Some tiled floors use regular hexagonal tiles because the tiles can be arranged side-to-side and end-to-end without gaps or overlaps. What geometric properties determine whether a regular polygon can tile a floor the same way? Identify two other regular polygons with these properties. Can regular pentagons or octagons be used to tile a floor as described?

Understand

Given that regular hexagonal tiles can be arranged in a continuous pattern without gaps or overlaps, I need to identify geometric properties that allow this. Then, I need to identify other regular polygons with the same properties, and determine whether regular pentagons and octagons share those properties.

Plan

Strategy: Make a table or chart; Use logical reasoning.

Apply knowledge of the properties of regular polygons and their interior angles to answer the questions.

Solve

If the interior angle of a regular polygon is a factor of 360°, it can tile a floor without gaps or overlaps. Other regular polygons that can tile a floor include equilateral triangles and squares. As the table shows, neither regular pentagons or octagons will work.

Regular Polygon	Vertex Angle	Factor of 360°
triangle	60°	$360 \div 60 = 6$
square	90°	$360 \div 90 = 4$
pentagon	108°	no
hexagon	120°	$360 \div 120 = 3$
octagon	135°	no

Check

Facts   Complete each step to solve each equation.

$2x + 5 = 45$	$3y + 4 = 22$	$5n - 3 = 12$	$3m - 7 = 14$
$2x = 40$	$3y = 18$	$5n = 15$	$3m = 21$
$x = 20$	$y = 6$	$n = 3$	$m = 7$
$15 = 3a - 6$	$24 = 2w + 6$	$-2x + 9 = 23$	$20 - 3y = 2$
$21 = 3a$	$18 = 2w$	$-2x = 14$	$-3y = -18$
$7 = a$	$9 = w$	$x = -7$	$y = 6$
$\frac{1}{2}m + 6 = 18$	$\frac{3}{4}n - 12 = 12$	$3y + 1.5 = 6$	$0.5w - 1.5 = 4.5$
$\frac{1}{2}m = 12$	$\frac{3}{4}n = 24$	$3y = 4.5$	$0.5w = 6$
$m = 24$	$n = 32$	$y = 1.5$	$w = 12$

Problem Solving   Answer the question below.

Problem: Sharon took her daughter Susan to a playground. Use the graph to write a brief story about what Susan was doing on the playground.

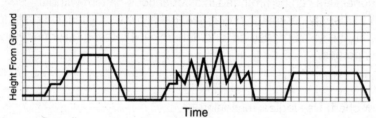

Understand

The graphed data indicates unknown activity on a playground over a period of time.

I need to interpret and describe graphed data to write a story about what Susan was doing on the playground.

- -

Plan

Strategy: Use logical reasoning.

Read the graph to make a reasonable guess about the kinds of activities Susan was doing and the order in which she did them.

- -

Solve

One possible interpretation:
Susan is carefully climbing the rungs to the top of a slide. She pauses at the top of the slide, then slides quickly down. She walks over to the swings where she gets on a swing and begins to swing higher and higher. She slows down and walks over to a set of monkey bars that she climbs onto and then crosses, hand-over-hand, before climbing down.

- -

Check

Facts	Solve each equation.		
$6x + 2x = 8x$	$6x - 2x = 4x$	$(6x)(2x) = 12x^2$	$\dfrac{6x}{2x} = 3$
$9xy + 3xy = 12xy$	$9xy - 3xy = 6xy$	$(9xy)(3xy) = 27x^2y^2$	$\dfrac{9xy}{3xy} = 3$
$x + y + x = 2x + y$	$x + y - x = y$	$(x)(y)(-x) = -x^2y$	$\dfrac{xy}{x} = y$
$3x + x + 3 = 4x + 3$	$3x - x - 3 = 2x - 3$	$(3x)(-x)(-3) = 9x^2$	$\dfrac{(2x)(8xy)}{4y} = 4x^2$

Problem Solving   Answer the question below.

Problem: 40 scouts went on a camping trip. During 3-days, 14 scouts cleaned-up the lakeshore, 13 cut down overgrown brush, and 16 blazed a hiking trail. Three of these scouts cut brush AND cleaned the shore. Five scouts cleaned the shore AND blazed the trail. Eight cut brush AND blazed the trail. Two of them helped with all three projects. How many worked on projects other than the shore, the brush, or the trail?

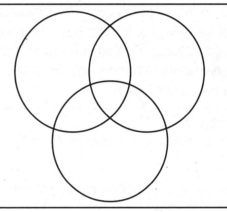

Understand

Given: Total scouts, 40; Scouts at the lakeshore, 14; Scouts cutting brush, 13; Scouts blazing trail, 16; Scouts that cut brush and cleaned the lakeshore, 3; Scouts that cleaned the shore and blazed the trail, 5; Scouts that cut brush and blazed the trail, 8; Scouts that worked on all three projects: 2

I need to find the data excluded from the sets charted in a Venn diagram.

- -

Plan

Strategy: Use a table, chart or graph; draw a picture or diagram.

Read the graph and count the numbers of scouts in each activity area.

- -

Solve

According to the completed Venn diagram,
$2 + 3 + 5 + 8 + 4 + 0 + 1 = 23$ scouts
worked on the shore, brush, and trail projects.
$40 - 23 = 17$ scouts who worked on other projects.

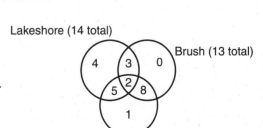

Lakeshore (14 total)

Brush (13 total)

Hiking Trail (16 total)

- -

Check

Facts   Simplify. Write each answer in scientific notation.

$(1 \times 10^6)(1 \times 10^6) =$ 1×10^{12}	$(3 \times 10^3)(3 \times 10^3) =$ 9×10^6	$(4 \times 10^{-5})(2 \times 10^{-6}) =$ 8×10^{-11}
$(5 \times 10^5)(5 \times 10^5) =$ 2.5×10^{11}	$(6 \times 10^{-3})(7 \times 10^{-4}) =$ 4.2×10^{-6}	$(3 \times 10^6)(2 \times 10^{-4}) =$ 6×10^2
$\dfrac{8 \times 10^8}{2 \times 10^2} = 4 \times 10^6$	$\dfrac{5 \times 10^6}{2 \times 10^3} = 2.5 \times 10^3$	$\dfrac{9 \times 10^3}{3 \times 10^8} = 3 \times 10^{-5}$
$\dfrac{2 \times 10^6}{4 \times 10^2} = 5 \times 10^3$	$\dfrac{1 \times 10^{-3}}{4 \times 10^8} = 2.5 \times 10^{-12}$	$\dfrac{8 \times 10^{-8}}{2 \times 10^{-2}} = 4 \times 10^{-6}$

Problem Solving   Answer the question below.

Problem: A friend tells you, "The probability of 3 tossed coins turning up all heads or tails is $\frac{1}{2}$, because anytime you toss 3 coins, at least 2 must match (2 heads or 2 tails), so that means that the third coin determines the probability." Is your friend right? What do you think the probability is that 3 tossed coins will turn up all heads or all tails?

Understand

Given the prediction that the probability of 3 independently tossed coins turning up all heads or all tails is $\frac{1}{2}$.

I need to calculate the probability of a specific coin-toss outcome to determine whether my friend's prediction is correct.

Plan

Strategy: Make an organized list.

List the possible outcomes of the coin toss to determine the odds.

Solve

There are 8 possible outcomes for tossing three coins (HHH, HHT, HTH, THH, HTT, THT, TTH, TTT). By counting all heads (HHH) or all tails (TTT), the probability can be calculated:

$\frac{2}{8} = \frac{1}{4}$. The probability of three heads or three tails is $\frac{1}{4}$ not $\frac{1}{2}$. The friend's prediction is incorrect.

Check

Performance Task 1A

1. **a.** True. The difference between 20,320 feet and 16,023 feet is 4297 feet.

   b. True. Twice the greatest depth of Mammoth Caves is 900 feet. 1014 feet is a little more than 900 feet.

   c. False. The measurement for Carlsbad and Mammoth Caves are given in miles. The measurement for Ellison's Cave and Neff Canyon are given in feet. Since there are 5280 feet in a mile, Ellison's Cave is about 12 miles long. Neff Canyon is less than 1 mile long. The caves in order from shortest length to longest is: Neff Canyon, Ellison's Cave, Carlsbad Caverns, Mammoth Caves.

Performance Task 1B

2. Sample: about $\frac{1}{2}$; Ellisons' cave is about 12 miles long and Carlsbad Caverns is 23 miles long. Ellison's cave is $\frac{12}{23}$ of the length of Carlsbad Caverns. That's very close to $\frac{12}{24}$ which is $\frac{1}{2}$.

3. Sample 1: At 29,029 ft., the tallest mountain, Mt. Everest, is less than half as tall as Ellison's cave is long.

   Sample 2: The difference in the heights of Mt. Denali and Mt. Kilamanjaro is about equal in feet to the deepest point in Carlsbad Caverns. $20,320 - 19,339 = 981$ ft. 987 ft. is close to 1014 ft.

4. **a.** $1685

   b. Sample: Music: $420
      Invitations: $285
      Food: $560
      Decorations: $420
      TOTAL: $1685

Performance Activity 2

1. Sample: Statement 1 goes with Diagram 3. I chose Diagram 3 to go with Statement 1 because it is the only diagram that shows an area divided into fifths and we need to have a diagram that shows the area of the garden.

2. Statement 2 goes with Diagram 2. I chose Diagram 2 to go with Statement 2 because we need a model that shows $\frac{3}{5}$ of a length.

3. Statement 3 goes with Diagram 1. I chose Diagram 1 to go with Statement 3 because we need a model that shows individuals.

Performance Task 3A

1.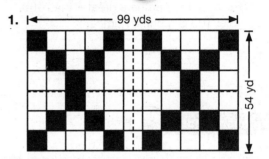

2. Sample: 918 ft

3. Sample: There are vertical and horizontal lines of symmetry at the center of the flag. If the flag were folded in half horizontally or vertically, the black tiles would overlay each other.

4. Sample: 11 tiles $\times$ 6 tiles = 66 tiles. And 66 tiles $\times$ 81 square yards = 5,346 square yards.

Performance Task 3B

5. Sample: (81 sq. yd)((20 black tiles $\times$ $1.38) + (46 white tiles $\times$ $0.57)) = $4,359.42; And (81 sq. yd)(66 tiles $\times$ $0.81) = $4,330.26; $4,359.42 > $4,330.26, so the discount retailer is more expensive.

6. Sample: I would order from the discount vinyl retailer. Vinyl for 10 white tiles from the sign and banner company would cost $656.10, but only $461.70 from the discount retailer because of the lower per unit cost.

Performance Activity 4

1. You cannot apply the Commutative Property to subtraction.
   Sample: $7 - 2 = 5$ but $2 - 7 \neq 5$

Solutions

2. You cannot apply the Associative Property to subtraction.
Sample: $(9 - 6) - 1 = 2$ but $9 - (6 - 1) = 4$

3. The fraction can be reduced; Sample: In the fraction $\frac{15}{36}$ the numerator is divisible by 5 and the denominator is divisible by 6, but both 15 and 36 are divisible by 3, so the fraction can be reduced to $\frac{5}{12}$.

4. There are prime numbers greater than 100. Sample: 109 is a prime number.

5. a. $5 - 3 = 2; 2 < 5$

   b. $-3 - (-5) = 2; 2 > -3$

Performance Task 5A

1.

Number of Loaves of Rye Bread	3	6	9	12	15	18	21
Number of Cups of Flour	$5\frac{1}{4}$	$10\frac{1}{2}$	$15\frac{3}{4}$	21	26	$31\frac{1}{2}$	$36\frac{3}{4}$

2. 2 bags of flour; the baker needs $36\frac{3}{4}$ cups of flour to make 21 loaves. 1 bag of flour is not enough because it just holds 34 cups. But 2 bags of flour hold 68 cups so 2 bags will be enough flour.

3. a. $y = 1\frac{3}{4} x$

   b. $y = 1\frac{3}{4} (30)$

   $y = 52\frac{1}{2}$

   $52\frac{1}{2}$ cups of flour

Performance Task 5B

4.

Number of Loaves of Bread	4	8	12	16	20	24	28
Number of Cups of Whole Wheat Flour	$8\frac{1}{3}$	$16\frac{2}{3}$	25	$33\frac{1}{3}$	$41\frac{2}{3}$	50	$58\frac{1}{3}$

5. 2 bags of whole wheat flour; Sample: I need $41\frac{2}{3}$ cups of flour to make 20 loaves. 1 bag of flour is not enough because it just holds 34 cups. But 2 bags of flour hold 68 cups so 2 bags will give me enough flour.

6. $62\frac{1}{2}$ cups; Sample: It takes $8\frac{1}{3}$ cups of flour to make 4 loaves, so it takes half that amount or $4\frac{1}{6}$ cups to make 2 loaves. Since 30 is 2×15; one way to get the answer is to multiply $4\frac{1}{6}$ cups by 15 to find out how much flour is needed for 30 loaves. $4\frac{1}{6} \times 15 = 62\frac{1}{2}$ cups. Another way is to add $4\frac{1}{6}$ cups to the number of cups needed to make 28 loaves. $58\frac{1}{3} + 4\frac{1}{6} = 62\frac{1}{2}$ cups.

Performance Activity 6

1. Line plot; Sample: Line plots are good for showing the spread of data.

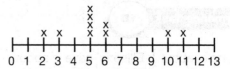

2. Venn diagram; Sample: With one Venn diagram, I can show all of the necessary data.

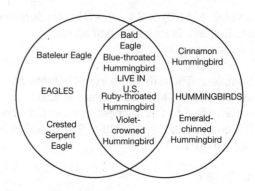

Performance Task 7A

1. Sample: They would conclude (or predict) that everyone in the town wanted a swimming pool.

2. Sample: about 2310 people wanted a swimming pool, about 4960 people wanted a baseball field, and about 2730 people wanted a tennis court. $\frac{1}{10}$ of the people answered the survey question. So I multiplied each category of survey response by 10. The numbers are in proportion and add to 10,000.

3. A baseball field

4. Sample of 1000; Sample: If you ask only a few people, by chance you might get responses that are not typical. But if you ask more people so that you are asking a greater percent of the population, you have a much better chance of getting a result that is close to what a count of the entire population would be.

Performance Task 7B

5. a. Sample: 2 people said baseball, 1 said football, and 1 said basketball.

   b. Sample: baseball

   c. Sample: 5 people said football, 3 people said baseball, and 2 people said basketball.

   d. Sample: basketball

   e. Sample: 16 people liked football the best, 8 people liked baseball the best, and 5 people liked basketball the best.

   f. Sample: I got the best idea of the results for the class with the sample size of 10. I think this is because it was closer to the actual number of people in the class. A sample size of 4 isn't very big.

Performance Activity 8

1. If you double the side of a square you do **not** double the area. You quadruple the area. Sample: The area of a square with a side that is 3 inches long is 9 square inches. The area of a square with a side that is 6 inches long is 36 square inches.

2. If two different rectangles have the same area, they will **not** always have the same perimeter. Sample: A 4 in. by 3 in. rectangle has an area of 12 square inches and a 6 in. by 2 in. rectangles has an area of 12 square inches. However, the perimeter of the 4 in. by 3 in. rectangle is 14 in. and the perimeter of the 6 in. by 2 in. rectangle is 16 in.

3. If one angle of a triangle measures 100°, the other two angles in the triangle must have a sum that is equal to 80°. Sample: For the triangle with angles 100°, 30°, and 50°, the sum of 30° and 50°, is 80°.

4. The sum of two angles in a triangle is 90°. For right triangles, the sum of two of the angles is equal to 90°. Sample: In a right triangle with angles 90°, 60°, and 30°, the sum of 60° and 30° is 90°. For triangles that are not right, the sum of two of the angles is not equal to 90°. In a triangle with angles 40°, 60°, and 80°, there are no two angles that have a sum of 90°.

Performance Task 9A

1.

Frequency Table	
Time Range	**Number of Finishers**
2:20 − 2:29	3
2:30 − 2:39	7
2:40 − 2:49	6
2:50 − 2:59	22

2.

2005 Boston Marathon
Women Finishers Under 3 Hours

Performance Activity 10

1. $\frac{4}{10}$ or $\frac{2}{5}$

2.

Number of Red Marbles	4	20	40	100	200
Total Number of Marbles	10	50	100	250	500

3. 400; Sample: Double the number of red marbles in 500; Multiply the number of red marbles in 100 by 10.

Solutions

4. Answers will vary. Sample: The ratio of blue marbles to the total number of marbles in the package is 2 to 10. In a package of 10 marbles there will be 2 blue marbles. Decide what to multiply 10 by to get the total number of blue marbles in the package. For example, if you want 50 marbles in a package multiply 10 by 5. Then multiply 2 by 5 to get the total number of blue marbles in a package of 50 marbles. For each package size in the table, find a ratio equivalent to $\frac{2}{10}$, in which the denominator is the number of marbles in the package.

Performance Task 11A

1.

C (Number of Chirps in 15 Seconds)	T (Temperature in Degrees Fahrenheit)
20	60°F
25	65°F
30	70°F
35	75°F
40	80°F

Performance Task 11B

3. 90°F

4. Answers will vary. Sample: Crickets chirp faster as the temperature goes up.

5.

N (Number of Chirps in a minute)	T (Temperature in Degrees Fahrenheit)
50	70°F
55	72°F
60	74°F
65	75°F
70	77°F

6. a. Answers will vary but should be between 78°F and 79°F.

b. about 79°F

Performance Activity 12

1.

Number of Sheets in Album	1	2	3	4	5	6	7
Number of Photos Album Can Hold	4	8	12	16	20	24	28

2. Multiply the number of sheets in the album by 4 to find the number of photos the album can hold.

3. a. Sample: Since a sheet holds 4 photographs, three sheets are needed. However, the sheets will not all be full because three full sheets would hold 12 photos.

b. Sample: No. 203 is not divisible by 4.

Performance Task 13A

1. a. Mean; Sample: Even though all of the readings are close, two temperatures (71°F and 72°F) appear three times in the data, so we can't find a mode for the data.

b. 27° {Error Alert: Students should identify the range as the difference between the low and high temperature readings, not the first and last.}

c. Mean for all 9 readings $\cong$ 70.89°F; Mean without first reading = 71.00°F; Sample: Eliminating the starting temperature reading increased the mean.

2. a. Experiment B; Sample: By looking at the graphs, the readings in Experiment A and C alternate about equally up and down, while readings in Experiment B increase more than decrease.

b. Sample: I would predict that the median is higher than the mean temperature in Experiment B.

c. Experiment A: mean $\cong$ 71°, median = 71°; Experiment B: mean = 77°, median = 76°; Experiment C: mean $\cong$ 71°, media = 71°; Sample: No. The mean is greater than the median

Performance Task 13B

3. a. Sample: The blinds are open so sunlight begins to warm the room, but the air-conditioner is also on, attempting to cool the room. Sample: If I changed when the air-conditioning was on the room temperature might vary less, and the mean would be higher.

b. Sample: With the window facing south, instead of east, the morning temperatures might not be as high, so the mean temperature of the day would be lower.

c. Sample: The range of temperatures in Experiment B is greatest because the temperatures in the other experiments were regulated by air-conditioning.

4. a. Sample: I could arrange the temperature readings of each experiment from least to greatest and find the middle temperature among each data set. For example, the median of the temperatures in Experiment B is 76°F; Or, I could arrange the readings at each reading time and select the middle value. For example, the median temperature at Reading 2 is 71°F from the set {60°, 71°, 74°}.

b. Reading 4; Range = 26°

Performance Activity 14

1. Answers will vary. Sample answers in table.

Diameter	Circumference
2 inches	About $6\frac{1}{4}$ inches
3 inches	About $9\frac{1}{2}$ inches
5 inches	About $15\frac{3}{4}$ inches
6 inches	About 19 inches

3. The circumference is about 3 times the diameter.

Performance Task 15A

1.

2. Sample: Color red: Red rise is 4×5 or 20 square feet. Red tread is 8 square feet. Total for red: 28 square feet. Color blue: Blue rise is 4×1 or 4 square feet. Blue tread is 16 square feet. Total for Blue: 20 square feet. Color yellow: Yellow rise is 4×3 or 12 square feet. yellow tread is 1 square foot. Total for yellow is 13 square feet.

Performance Task 15B

3. Sample: Red: $9.80   Blue: $4.00
Yellow: $1.95
TOTAL: $15.75

4. b. Check students' work.

Performance Activity 16

1. $6 \div (-4 + 1) = -2$

2. $-2 - (12 \div 4) = -5$

3. $-3 + (5 \times -2) = -13$

4. $-4 + (10 \div -2) = -9$

5. $(-4 \times -5) + (3 \times -6) = 2$

6. $(4 + 8) \div (1 - -2) = 4$

7. $40 - 12 - 9 = x;$ $28 - 9 = x;$ $19 = x$
Sample: You don't need to follow orders of operations but you must pay attention to grouping of terms. All of the people swimming *and* water skiing are subtracted from the total to find the number of people on the beach.

Solutions

8. $3 \times 7 - 5 = n;$ $21 - 5 = n;$ $16 - n$
   Sample: If you don't follow the order of operations you will end up multiplying 3 by 2 and have an answer of 6 hats not being sold. That is not correct so you need to use the order of operations and multiply 3 by 7 first and then subtract 5.

9. Check students' work.

Performance Task 17A

1. Answers will vary. Possible Answer:

Discount	New Price
10% off	$1.80 per pound
30% off	$2.10 per foot
$\frac{1}{4}$ off	$9 apiece
$\frac{1}{3}$ off	$50 apiece

2. Answers will vary. Answer for the plan shown as an answer in Exercise 1:
   Sale of nails: $100 \times \$1.80 = \$180$
   Sale of fencing: $400 \times \$2.10 = \$840$
   Sale of hammers: $20 \times \$9 = \$180$
   Sale of lawn mowers: $8 \times \$50 = \$400$
   $\$180 + \$840 + \$180 + \$400 = \$1600$
   $\$1600 > \$1500$

Performance Task 17B

3. Answers will vary. Answer for the plan shown as an answer in Exercise 1: $y = \$1.80x$

4. a. Answers will vary. Answer for the plan shown as an answer in Exercise 1: $\frac{180}{1600}$ or $\frac{9}{80}$

   b. Answers will vary. Sample answer for the plan shown as an answer in Exercise 1: You can't just take half of each number in the ratio to get the new ratio. If you start with the ratio $\frac{180}{1600}$, you can take half of 180 for the top number in the ratio. But you can't take half of 1600 because that number is made up of sales of other items that didn't get reduced by a half. You have to find out what the new total sales is.

5. No. 10% of $90 is $9. 20% of $40 is $8. $9 is greater than $8.

Performance Activity 18

1. Sample: I would use mental math because I can easily multiply 300 by $5 in my head.

2. Sample: I would use estimation since I only need to find out about how much I will spend.

3. Sample: I would use the calculator because I want the exact amount and I have to do a lot of addition and subtraction with numbers that aren't rounded.

4. Sample: I would use the calculator or paper and pencil since I want an exact answer and the numbers aren't rounded. I already chose the calculator for Exercise 3, so I would choose paper and pencil for this problem because it has fewer computations than Exercise 3.

Performance Task 19A

1. Sample:

11	21	31	41	51	61
12	22	32	42	52	62
13	23	33	43	53	63
14	24	34	44	54	64
15	25	35	45	55	65
16	26	36	46	56	66

I made a 6 by 6 table since I knew there were 6 possibilities for the tens place and 6 possibilities for the ones place. I put all of the possible numbers with 1 in the tens place in the first column, all of the possible numbers with 2 in the tens place in the second column, etc. In each column I listed all of the possibilities with that number in the tens place.

2. Sample: There are 8 possible outcomes that are prime numbers: 11, 13, 23, 31, 41, 43, 53, 61. There are a total of 36 possible outcomes. So the probability of the outcome being a prime number is $\frac{8}{36}$ or $\frac{2}{9}$.

Performance Task **19B**

3. Sample: I can subtract the possible outcomes that are prime, 8, from the total number of possible outcomes, 36, to find the number of possible outcomes that are composite numbers. 36 − 8 is 28. $\frac{28}{36}$ or $\frac{7}{9}$ is the probability that an outcome is a composite number.

4. Sample: All of the possible outcomes are either prime or composite so the probability of having a prime or composite number as an outcome is 1.

5. Sample: All whole numbers are factors of themselves so the probability that the outcome is a factor of itself is 1.

6. Sample: None of the possible outcomes is a number that is a factor of 10 so the probability that the outcome is a factor of 10 is 0.

7. Sample: The only possible outcome that is a factor of 100 is 25 so the probability that the outcome is a factor of 100 is $\frac{1}{36}$.

Performance Activity **20**

1. $y = 30x$; Sample: Since 1 cm = 30 km, you have to multiply the number of centimeters on the map by 30 to find the number of kilometers.

2. $y = 315 − 150$;   165 km

3. $y = 330 + 60$;   390 km

4. Sample: What is the difference between the distance from Town A to Town D and the distance from Town B to Town C?

5. Sample: If you travel from Town A to Town D and back again, how far will you have traveled? $y = 330 \times 2$;   660 km

Performance Task **21A**

1. Sample: The graph shows that the population in the United States in 1990 was about 250,000,000. The graph also shows that the population grew by about 30,000,000 between 1990 and 2000. It is reasonable to suppose that since 1995 is about half way between 1990 and 2000 the population grew by 15,000,000 to 265,000,000.

2. Sample: The population in the United States in 2010 will be 310,000,000. The graph shows that the population is growing by about 30,000,000 each decade. In 2000 the population was about 280,000,000 so in 2010, I estimate the population would be about 310,000,000.

Performance Task **21B**

3. Sample: The graph shows that about 29% of the population was between the ages of 20 and 39 and about 26% of the population was between the ages of 40 and 59. 29% + 26% = 55%

4. Sample: A randomly selected person in the population of the United States in 2000 would more likely be under 40 than over 40. From looking at the graph it looks like about 58% of the population was under 40 and about 42% of the population was over 40. 58% is greater than 42% so it would be more likely that a random person would be under 40.

Performance Activity **22A**

1. Sample: All four triangular faces are both similar and congruent. They are congruent because there is just one unique triangle that will have sides of those lengths. If triangles are congruent, they are also similar.

2. Yes. Sample: I can set up a proportion to show that the sides of the two triangular faces are proportional to each other.
$\frac{5}{7.5} = \frac{5}{7.5} \cdot \frac{6}{9}$

Solutions

3. Yes. Sample: All of the lengths of the edges in one pyramid are proportional to the length of the edges in the other pyramid. If you multiply the length of each edge in the smaller pyramid by 2 you will get the length of the corresponding edge in the larger pyramid.

Performance Task 23A

1. Sample:

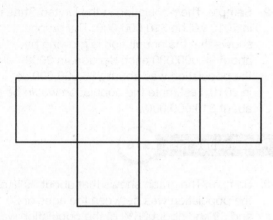

The length of each edge of the cube is 2 inches.

2. The volume of the cube is 8 cubic inches. Sample: The volume of a cube is the area of the base multiplied by the height. The area of the base is 4 square inches and the height is 2 inches so the volume is 8 cubic inches.

Performance Task 23B

3.

Figure	Dimensions	Volume
pyramid	Base that is 2 in. square, height is 2 in.	2.67 cubic inches
cylinder	Base is circle with diameter of 2 in., height is 2 in.	6.28 cubic inches
sphere	Diameter is 2 in.	4.19 cubic inches
cone	Base is circle with diameter of 2 in., height is 2 in.	2.09 cubic inches

4. Sample: The formula for the volume of a cone is $\frac{1}{3}\pi r^2 h$. The radius of the base is 1 inch. The height is 2 inches. $\frac{1}{3} \times 3.14 \times 1 \times 2 \approx$ 2.09 in.^{3}

5. Sample: Since each dimension is 2 times 2 in. and there are three dimensions (length, width, and height), you can multiply $2 \times 2 \times 2$ to find that the volume would be 8 times as much.

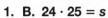

Solutions

1. B. $24 \cdot 25 = s$
24 students in each of 25 classrooms
= total number of students

2. A. 156
$$\begin{array}{r} 1776 \\ -\ 1620 \\ \hline 156 \end{array}$$

3. C. \$12.65
$$\begin{array}{r} \overset{1}{\cancel{2}}\overset{9}{\cancel{0}}.\overset{9}{\cancel{0}}\overset{10}{\cancel{0}} \\ -\ \$\ 7.35 \\ \hline \$12.65 \end{array}$$

4. A. $\frac{1}{2}$
$P(<4) = \dfrac{\text{favorable outcomes}}{\text{total possibilities}}$
$= \dfrac{1 \text{ or } 2 \text{ or } 3}{6} = \dfrac{3}{6} = \dfrac{1}{2}$

5. C. 8
$2 \times 4 = 8$

6. C. 21
$\dfrac{3}{\cancel{4}_1}\left(\overset{7}{\cancel{28}}\right) = 21$

7. C. $2 \cdot 2 \cdot 2 \cdot 3 \cdot 5 \cdot 5$

8. B. $\frac{4}{5}$
$\dfrac{480}{600} \div \dfrac{120}{120} = \dfrac{4}{5}$

9. B.

The pentagon is the only figure that is
closed, flat, and has straight lines.

10. C. $\frac{63}{72}$
$\dfrac{7}{8} \times \dfrac{9}{9} = \dfrac{63}{72}$

11. B. $\frac{360}{15}$
$\dfrac{15x}{15} = \dfrac{360}{15}$
$x = \dfrac{360}{15}$

12. A. 24 + 36
$n - 36 = 24$
$n - 36 + 36 = 24 + 36$
$n = 24 + 36$

13. D. $\frac{1}{16}, \frac{1}{8}, \frac{1}{4}, \frac{1}{2}$
The denominators decrease which means
the fractions increase in size.

14. C. $1\frac{3}{4}$ $6\frac{4}{4}$ in. $-\ 5\frac{1}{4}$ in. $= 1\frac{3}{4}$ in.

15. D. $3\frac{1}{10}$ miles $1\frac{3}{10} + 1\frac{8}{10} = 2\frac{11}{10}$
$= 3\frac{1}{10}$

16. C. $2\frac{1}{3}$ $4\frac{1}{6} - 1\frac{5}{6} = 3\frac{7}{6} - 1\frac{5}{6}$
$= 2\frac{2}{6} = 2\frac{1}{3}$

17. B. $\frac{1}{2}$ $\dfrac{\overset{1}{\cancel{4}}}{\cancel{3}} \cdot \dfrac{\overset{1}{\cancel{5}}}{\cancel{6}_2} \cdot \dfrac{\overset{1}{\cancel{3}}}{\cancel{4}_1} = \dfrac{1}{2}$

18. C. $\frac{3}{5}$ $\dfrac{2}{5} \div \dfrac{2}{3} = \dfrac{\overset{1}{\cancel{2}}}{5} \times \dfrac{3}{\cancel{2}_1} = \dfrac{3}{5}$

19. D. 90 $10^2 - \sqrt{100} = 100 - 10$
$= 90$

20. B. $\overline{DC}$
Parallel lines are in the same plane but do
not intersect.

21. D. 875 mm² $A = lw = 35\text{ mm} \times 25\text{ mm}$
$= 875 \text{ mm}^2$

22. A. Commutative Property
Changing the order of factors does not
change their product.

23. D. Inverse Property
The product of a fraction and its
reciprocal is 1.

24. C. 36 $6^2 = 36$

25. D. 36 · 2 = 72
6×6 square does not equal 72.

1. C. 40

$$\frac{2}{3} = \frac{f}{60}$$
$$3f = 120$$
$$f = 40$$

2. B. 7 years

$11 \times 3 = 33$
$14 + 12 = 26$
$33 - 26 = 7$ years old

3. D. 26

$$\frac{78 \text{ miles}}{3 \text{ hours}} = 26 \text{ mph}$$

4. B.

$$H \Big\langle \begin{matrix} A \\ B \\ C \end{matrix}$$

{HA, HB, HC, TA, TB, TC}

$$T \Big\langle \begin{matrix} A \\ B \\ C \end{matrix}$$

5. D. 36

$$\frac{3}{\cancel{5}} \left(\overset{12}{\cancel{60}} \right) = 36 \text{ trucks}$$

6. B. 9.3×10^7

$93{,}000{,}000 \rightarrow 9.3 \times 10^7$

7. B. $0.6, 0.65, 0.\overline{6}$

$0.600, 0.650, 0.666...$

8. A. $12 \text{ yd} \times \dfrac{3 \text{ ft}}{1 \text{ yd}} = 36 \text{ ft}$

There are 3 ft in 1 yd. $12 \times 6 = 36$.

9. C. 0.4, 40%

$$\frac{2}{5} = 5 \overline{)2.0}$$
$$\underline{2\,0}$$
$$0$$
$$0.4 = \frac{40}{100} = 40\%$$

10. C. 8

$ab - bc = (5)(4) - (4)(3)$
$ = 20 - 12 = 8$

11. C. 36 cm

Missing lengths: $10 \text{ cm} - 4 \text{ cm} = 6 \text{ cm}$,
$ 8 \text{ cm} - 4 \text{ cm} = 4 \text{ cm}$

Perimeter $= 4 \text{ cm} + 10 \text{ cm} + 8 \text{ cm}$
$ + 4 \text{ cm} + 4 \text{ cm} + 6 \text{ cm}$
$ = 36 \text{ cm}$

12. A. $A \approx 4 \text{ in.} \times 2 \text{ in.}$

$3\frac{7}{8} \text{ in.} \rightarrow 4 \text{ in.}, \ 2\frac{1}{4} \text{ in.} \rightarrow 2 \text{ in.}$

$A = lw$
$A \approx 4 \text{ in.} \times 2 \text{ in.}$

13. D. 4.4

$5.6 + w - 5.6 = 10 - 5.6$
$ w = 4.4$

14. B. 8

$$\frac{n}{6} = \frac{24}{18}$$
$$18n = 144$$
$$n = 8$$

15. C. 23

$3^2 + 2^3 + \sqrt{36} = 9 + 8 + 6$
$\phantom{3^2 + 2^3 + \sqrt{36}} = 23$

16. D. 5

$2 + 2 \times 2 - 2 \div 2$
$ 2 + 4 - 1$
$ 6 - 1$
$ 5$

17. B. $5\frac{1}{12}$

$2\frac{1}{4} + 2\frac{5}{6} = 2\frac{3}{12} + 2\frac{10}{12}$
$\phantom{2\frac{1}{4} + 2\frac{5}{6}} = 4\frac{13}{12} = 5\frac{1}{12}$

18. C. $2\frac{1}{4}$

One whole square, two half squares, and a quarter square equal $2\frac{1}{4}$.

19. B. 0.1 m^2

$A = lw$
$A = (0.4 \text{ m})(0.25 \text{ m})$
$A = 0.1 \text{ m}^2$

20. A. 30

$$\begin{array}{r} 30 \\ 8\overline{)240} \\ \underline{24} \\ 00 \end{array}$$

21. D. 0.4

$P(\text{red}) = \dfrac{8}{20} = 0.4$

22. C. 6

$2 + 4 = 6$

23. D. 54 cm^2

Area $= \dfrac{(9 \text{ cm})(12 \text{ cm})}{2}$
$ = 54 \text{ cm}^2$

24. A. $d = 4 \text{ hr} \cdot 55 \text{ mi per hour}$

distance $=$ rate $\times$ time

25. B. Point B   (over 3, down 2)

Solutions

1. C. 12 days $\frac{2}{\underset{1}{\cancel{5}}}\left(\overset{6}{\cancel{30}}\right) = 12$ days

2. B. $305,000
$275,000, $275,000, $305,000, $320,000, $425,000

3. B. 56 mph
$$\frac{120 \text{ miles } + 48 \text{ miles}}{3 \text{ hours}} = \frac{168 \text{ miles}}{3 \text{ hours}}$$
$$= 56 \text{ mph}$$

4. D. 15.24 cm $6 \text{ in.} \times \frac{2.54 \text{ cm}}{1 \text{ in.}} = 15.24 \text{ cm}$

5. B. $x < 1$
x represents all numbers less than, but not including, one.

6. A. $5xy + 3x$
$3xy + 2xy + 4x - x = 5xy + 3x$

7. D. 6 miles $\frac{2}{10} = \frac{m}{30}$
$$10m = 60$$
$$m = 6 \text{ miles}$$

8. B. 300 $\frac{70}{100} = \frac{210}{p}$
$$70p = 21000$$
$$p = 300$$

9. A. 240 $\frac{3}{4}x = 180$
$$\left(\frac{4}{3}\right)\frac{3}{4}x = 180\left(\frac{4}{3}\right)$$
$$x = 240$$

10. C. 360 in.^{3} $V = lwh$
$$V = (12 \text{ in.})(6 \text{ in.})(5 \text{ in.})$$
$$V = 360 \text{ in.}^3$$

11. C. 36π cm^2 $A = \pi r^2$
$$A = \pi(6 \text{ cm})^2$$
$$A = 36\pi \text{ cm}^2$$

12. C. $\frac{4}{5}$, 80% $0.8 = \frac{8}{10} = \frac{4}{5}$
$$0.8 = 80\%$$

13. B. 7.5×10^{11} $(3.0 \times 2.5)(10^6 \times 10^5)$
$$7.5 \times 10^{11}$$

14. B.

A parallelogram has two sets of parallel lines.

15. A. 96 cm^2 $A = bh$
$$A = (12 \text{ cm})(8 \text{ cm}) = 96 \text{ cm}^2$$

16. B. 12 $1.2x = 14.4$
$$x = \frac{14.4}{1.2} = 12$$

17. C. $\frac{1}{2}$ $y + \frac{3}{5} = 1\frac{1}{10}$
$$y + \frac{3}{5} - \frac{3}{5} = 1\frac{1}{10} - \frac{3}{5}$$
$$y = 1\frac{1}{10} - \frac{6}{10}$$
$$y = \frac{11}{10} - \frac{6}{10}$$
$$y = \frac{5}{10} = \frac{1}{2}$$

18. C. 8 $2\{16 - [6^2 - 4(8 - 2)]\}$
$$2\{16 - [36 - 4(6)]\}$$
$$2\{16 - [36 - (24)]\}$$
$$2\{16 - [12]\}$$
$$2\{4\}$$
$$8$$

19. A. 0 $(-2) + (-4) - (-6)$
$$-6 + [-(-6)]$$
$$-6 + 6$$
$$0$$

20. B. $y = 2x$
y values are twice x values; the slope of the line is 2.

21. B. 75 inches $C = \pi d$
$$C = 3.14 \times 24 \text{ inches}$$
$$C \approx 75 \text{ inches}$$

22. C. $\frac{1}{9}$ $P(3, 3) = \frac{1}{3} \times \frac{1}{3} = \frac{1}{9}$

23. B. 55° $m\angle A = 180° - (90° + 35°)$
$$= 55°$$

24. D. -4 $xy - x^2 = (4)(3) - 4^2$
$$= 12 - 16 = -4$$

25. C. 88 ft^2 $A = \frac{1}{2}(b_1 + b_2)h$
$$A = \frac{1}{2}(14 \text{ ft} + 8 \text{ ft})8 \text{ ft}$$
$$= \frac{1}{2}(22 \text{ ft})8 \text{ ft} = 88 \text{ ft}^2$$

1.
$$
\begin{array}{r}
20.8 \\
25\overline{)520.0} \\
\underline{50} \\
20 \\
\underline{0} \\
20\ 0 \\
\underline{20\ 0} \\
0
\end{array}
$$

A. 20.8

2.
$$
\begin{array}{r}
40.6 \\
27.84 \\
+\ 12. \\
\hline
80.44
\end{array}
$$

C. 80.44

3.
$$
\begin{array}{r}
2.00 \\
-\ 0.18 \\
\hline
1.82
\end{array}
\qquad
\begin{array}{r}
3.80 \\
-\ 1.82 \\
\hline
1.98
\end{array}
$$

B. 1.98

4.
$$
\begin{array}{r}
0.14 \\
\times\ 0.15 \\
\hline
70 \\
14 \\
\hline
0.0210
\end{array}
$$

B. 0.021

5.
$$
\begin{array}{r}
0.002 \\
70\overline{)0.140} \\
\underline{140} \\
0
\end{array}
$$

D. 0.002

6. $2\frac{1}{2} + 3\frac{1}{6} + 2\frac{1}{3} =$

$2\frac{3}{6} + 3\frac{1}{6} + 2\frac{2}{6} = 7\frac{6}{6} = 8$

A. 8

7. $5\frac{1}{6} - 3\frac{3}{4} = 5\frac{2}{12} - 3\frac{9}{12} =$

$4\frac{14}{12} - 3\frac{9}{12} = 1\frac{5}{12}$

B. $1\frac{5}{12}$

8. $3\frac{3}{4} \cdot 3\frac{1}{3} = \dfrac{\overset{5}{\cancel{15}}}{\underset{2}{\cancel{4}}} \cdot \dfrac{\overset{5}{\cancel{10}}}{\underset{1}{\cancel{3}}} = \dfrac{25}{2} = 12\frac{1}{2}$

C. $12\frac{1}{2}$

9. $5\frac{5}{6} \div 2\frac{1}{2} = \dfrac{35}{6} \div \dfrac{5}{2} = \dfrac{\overset{7}{\cancel{35}}}{\underset{3}{\cancel{6}}} \cdot \dfrac{\overset{1}{\cancel{2}}}{\underset{1}{\cancel{5}}} = \dfrac{7}{3} = 2\frac{1}{3}$

A. $2\frac{1}{3}$

10. $\dfrac{24\ x^2 y}{40\ xy^2} = \dfrac{\cancel{2} \cdot \cancel{2} \cdot 2 \cdot 3 \cdot \cancel{x} \cdot x \cdot \cancel{y}}{\cancel{2} \cdot \cancel{2} \cdot 2 \cdot 5 \cdot \cancel{x} \cdot y \cdot \cancel{y}} = \dfrac{3x}{5y}$

C. $\dfrac{3x}{5y}$

11. The 7 is in the hundredths place in 6.8792. In 50.143, the hundredths place contains the digit 4.

B. 4

12. $(8 \times 10^3)(4 \times 10^4) = 32 \times 10^7 = 3.2 \times 10^8$

D. 3.2×10^8

13. $1\ \cancel{ft} \cdot \dfrac{12\ \cancel{in.}}{1\ \cancel{ft}} \cdot \dfrac{2.54\ cm}{1\ \cancel{in.}} = 30.48\ cm$

A. 30.48 cm

14. $F = 1.8(30) + 32$
$F = 54.0 + 32$
$F = 86$

C. 86°F

15. $0.04 \times 100\% = 4\%$

$\dfrac{4}{100} \times 100\% = \dfrac{400\%}{100} = 4\%$

$\dfrac{1}{25} \times \dfrac{4}{4} = \dfrac{4}{100} = 4\%$

$\dfrac{2}{50} \times \dfrac{2}{2} = \dfrac{4}{100} = 4\%$

E. None correct

16. $\dfrac{2^4 \cdot 2^6}{2^2} = \dfrac{2^{10}}{2^2} = 2^8$

B. 2^8

17. $\sqrt{5^2 - 3^2} = \sqrt{25 - 9} = \sqrt{16} = 4$

C. 4

18. B. 10.02

19. $9\frac{5}{8} \times 11\frac{2}{5}$
$\downarrow \qquad \downarrow$
$10 \times 11 = 110$

C. 110

20. A. −1, 0, 0.1, 1

21. $\dfrac{2.4}{m} = \dfrac{3}{4.5}$

$3m = 2.4(4.5)$

$3m = 10.8$

$m = \dfrac{10.8}{3}$

$m = 3.6$

B. 3.6

22.

	Ratio	Actual Count
Wins	5	w
Losses	3	l
Total	8	120

$\dfrac{5}{8} = \dfrac{w}{120}$

$8w = 600$

$w = 75$

A. 75

23. $\dfrac{(3 \cdot 90) + (2 \cdot 95)}{5} = \dfrac{460}{5} = 92$

A. 92

24. The scores, when ordered, are 80, 80, 80, 90, 90, and 100. There is an even number of scores, so we average the middle two scores:

Median $\dfrac{80 + 90}{2} = \dfrac{170}{2} = 85$

B. 85

25. For each draw:

$P(W) = \dfrac{\text{Favorable}}{\text{Possible}} = \dfrac{1}{6}$

For both draws:

$P(W, W) = \dfrac{1}{6} \cdot \dfrac{1}{6} = \dfrac{1}{36}$

D. $\dfrac{1}{36}$

26. First year:

$\$2000 + (\$2000 \cdot 0.05) = \$2100$

Second year:

$\$2100 + (\$2100 \cdot 0.05) = \$2205$

Interest earned in 2 years $= \$2205 - \$2000$
$= \$205$

C. $205

27. $\dfrac{386 \text{ miles}}{20 \text{ gallons}} = 19.3 \dfrac{\text{miles}}{\text{gallon}}$

B. 19.3 mpg

28.

	%	$
Original	100	r
Discount	25	d
New	75	36

$\dfrac{100}{75} = \dfrac{r}{36}$

$75r = 3600$

$r = \$48$

C. $48.00

29. $W_P \times 24 = 21$

$\dfrac{W_P \times 24}{24} = \dfrac{21}{24}$

$W_P = \dfrac{7}{8}$

$\dfrac{7}{8} \times 100\% = 87.5\%$

A. $87\dfrac{1}{2}\%$

30. $5000 \text{ m} \times \dfrac{6 \text{ min}}{2000 \text{ m}} = 15 \text{ min}$

C. 15 min

31. A trapezoid has just one pair of parallel sides.

C.

32.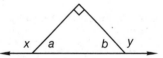

$\angle x$ and $\angle a$ are supplementary, so
$m\angle a = 180° - m\angle x = 180° - 140° = 40°$

sum of angles in a triangle is 180°, so
$m\angle b = 180° - 90° - m\angle a$
$= 180° - 90° - 40° = 50°$

$\angle y$ and $\angle b$ are supplementary, so
$m\angle y = 180° - m\angle b = 180° - 50° = 130°$

D. 130°

33. Perimeter $= 3 \text{ m} + 1.5 \text{ m} + 1.3 \text{ m} + 2.1 \text{ m}$
$+ 1.7 \text{ m} + 3.6 \text{ m} = 13.2 \text{ m}$

A. 13.2 m

34. Perimeter of semicircle $= \dfrac{\pi d}{2}$

$\approx \dfrac{3.14(40 \text{ in.})}{2}$

$\approx 62.8 \text{ in.}$

C. 63 in.

35. Surface area $= 6 \cdot (3 \text{ in.} \cdot 3 \text{ in.})$
$= 6 \cdot 9 \text{ in.}^2$
$= 54 \text{ in.}^2$

C. 54 in.²

36. Area of 90° sector $= \dfrac{\pi r^2}{4}$

$\approx \dfrac{(3.14)(6 \text{ in.})^2}{4}$

$\approx 28.26 \text{ in.}^2$

B. 28.26 in.²

37. Volume of prism = area of base · height
$= \left(\dfrac{1}{2} \cdot 8 \text{ cm} \cdot 6 \text{ cm}\right) \cdot 10 \text{ cm} = 240 \text{ cm}^3$

B. 240 cm³

38. $\dfrac{8}{12} = \dfrac{10}{x}$
$8x = 120$
$x = 15$

A. 15

39. The numbers 30, 40, and 50 form a Pythagorean triplet. Thus, QS is 50 mm.

C. 50 mm

40. Because $\angle a$ and $\angle c$ are supplementary,
$m\angle c = 180° - m\angle a = 180° - 105° = 75°$

Because $\angle c$ and $\angle g$ are corresponding,
$m\angle g = m\angle c = 75°$
$m\angle g = 75°$

C. 75°

41. $(-6) - (-7)(-4) = (-6) - 28 = -34$

B. −34

42. $b^2 - 4ac = 4^2 - 4(3)(-2)$
$= 16 - (-24) = 16 + 24 = 40$

A. 40

43. $(-2)^3 - (-2)^2 = (-8) - (4) = -12$

D. −12

44.

```
        500
       /   \
      25    20
     / \   / \
    5  5  5   4
             / \
            2   2
```

$500 = 2^2 \cdot 5^3$

C. $2^2 \cdot 5^3$

45. $3(x - 3) = 3x - 9$

A. 3x − 9

46. $3.6n - 0.18 = 7.02$
$3.6n = 7.02 + 0.18$
$3.6n = 7.20$
$n = \dfrac{7.20}{3.6}$
$n = 2$

B. 2

47. C. 2x − 6

48. $\dfrac{(2xy)(4x^2y)}{8x^2y} = \dfrac{2 \cdot 2 \cdot 2 \cdot x \cdot x \cdot x \cdot y \cdot y}{2 \cdot 2 \cdot 2 \cdot x \cdot x \cdot x \cdot y}$
$= xy$

D. xy

49. $2x - 1 < 5$
$2x < 6$
$x < 3$

A.

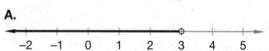

50.

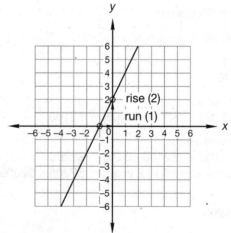

slope $= \dfrac{\text{rise}}{\text{run}} = \dfrac{2}{1} = 2$
y-intercept $= +2$

C. $y = 2x + 2$